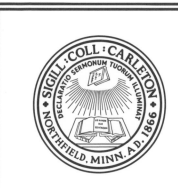

RELIGIOUS PROCESS

RELIGIOUS PROCESS

The *Purāṇas* and the Making of a Regional Tradition

Kunal Chakrabarti

OXFORD
UNIVERSITY PRESS

OXFORD
UNIVERSITY PRESS

YMCA Library Building, Jai Singh Road, New Delhi 110001

Oxford University Press is a department of the University of Oxford. It furthers the University's objective of excellence in research, scholarship, and education by publishing worldwide in

Oxford New York

Athens Auckland Bangkok Bogota Buenos Aires Calcutta
Cape Town Chennai Dar es Salaam Delhi Florence Hong Kong Istanbul
Karachi Kuala Lumpur Madrid Melbourne Mexico City Mumbai
Nairobi Paris Sao Paolo Shanghai Singapore Taipei Tokyo Toronto Warsaw

with associated companies in Berlin Ibadan

Published in India
By Oxford University Press, New Delhi

First Published 2001

ISBN 019 564989 3

Typeset by Urvashi Press, Meerut 250001
Printed in India at Saurabh Print-o-Pack, Noida, U.P.
and published by Manzar Khan, Oxford University Press
YMCA Library Building, Jai Singh Road, New Delhi 110001

For my teacher

Ashin Das Gupta

now a cherished memory

Acknowledgements

This book took shape over a long period of time, with the help of many teachers, friends, and colleagues. Professor Ashin Das Gupta initiated me into the study of history, and sustained me with his unfailing intellectual and emotional support. This book is dedicated to his memory in the words in which he dedicated his work to his teacher, Professor N.K. Sinha. This is my tribute to a tradition to which I have the honour to belong.

I am indebted to my teachers at the Presidency College, Calcutta, and the Jawaharlal Nehru University, New Delhi, for their contribution to my academic development. I especially thank Shri Kamal Kumar Ghatak and Shri Sunil Kumar Chattopadhyaya for their interest, patience, and rigour. My advisor, Professor B.D. Chattopadhyaya, had set a standard of scholarship both daunting and stimulating. He helped me to explore with his suggestions and reflect by his silence. His remarks on the first draft have been invaluable. Professor Romila Thapar inspired, enriched, and provided support in ways too numerous to mention. I gratefully acknowledge the encouragement and assistance I received from Professor R. Champakalakshmi, Professor Satish Saberwal, Professor Majid Siddiqi, Professor Rajan Gurukkal, Professor Sabyasachi Bhattacharya, Professor Dilbagh Singh, Dr K. Meenakshi, Dr Kirti Trivedi and Dr Yogesh Sharma. Professor Muzaffar Alam and Professor Neeladri Bhattacharya have been incredibly generous with their time, spurring me on with their friendly criticism and advice. They helped me to sustain my faith in my work. I am indebted to Professor Shereen Ratnagar for her precise critical comments and editorial suggestions. I have also greatly benefited from the comments of Professor Ludo Rocher, Professor N.N. Bhattacharyya, and Professor K.M. Shrimali.

This book would have been inconceivable without the contribution of scholars who wrote on various aspects of the subject before me. They are acknowledged in the notes, but I would particularly like to mention the seminal works of Professor R.C. Hazra, Professor Niharranjan Ray,

Professor Shashibhushan Dasgupta, and Dr Hitesranjan Sanyal. I have had the privilege of knowing Professor Hazra, and I remember with gratitude how tolerantly he entertained and helped to clarify the many queries of a young researcher. Dr Sanyal was an extraordinary man, who had everything to give and little to gain from our many hours of conversation.

I am indebted to the staff of the National Library, Asiatic Society, and Bangiya Sahitya Parishat libraries at Calcutta, and the libraries of Jawaharlal Nehru University, Archaeological Survey of India, National Museum, and Nehru Memorial Museum and Library, New Delhi, for their co-operation. I especially thank Mr L.N. Malik of the Jawaharlal Nehru University; I have seldom come across a more quietly helpful person. A British Council visiting fellowship to the Cambridge University enabled me to make use of the libraries in the UK, and gave me the opportunity to interact with Professor F.R. Allchin. I am grateful to *Studies in History* and the editors of *Tradition, Dissent and Ideology* (Oxford University Press, 1996), who published early versions of parts of this work. Shri Om Prakash typed a difficult manuscript with exemplary competence.

My father, Shri Bhabes Chandra Chakrabarti, and my uncle, Professor Satyes Chakrabarti, are two of the best teachers I have ever had. I thank my mother, Ms Manjusri Chakrabarti for her concern. My friends, Professor Sudip Chaudhuri, Professor Biswajit Dhar, Dr Pinaki Chakrabarti, Dr Roshen Dalal, and Shri Amit Banerji helped me tide over difficult circumstances and make them appear meaningful. Ms Indrani Guha and Professor Ashok Sanjay Guha have been always reassuring with their deep understanding. Ms Jayasri Sen and Shri Paritosh Sen have remained more than a source of support. Shri Sen willingly accedes to the frequent demands I make on his generosity. The cover of this book is an example. My student Shri Agni Kumar Hota helped me with the proofs and Ms Naina Dayal prepared the index. Baishakh has been a source of delight.

I take this opportunity of expressing my deep sense of gratitude to all of them.

Contents

Acknowledgements vii

Abbreviations x

I. Introduction 1

II. Texts and Traditions: The Bengal *Purāṇas* 44

III. Cultural Interaction and Religious Process 81

IV. The Diffusion of Brahmanism and the Transformation of Buddhism 109

V. Appropriation as a Historical Process: The Cult of the Goddess 165

VI. *Vratas:* The Transmission of Brahmanical Culture 234

VII. The Making of the Regional Tradition of Bengal 288

Bibliography 338

Index 362

Abbreviations

BP	*Bṛhaddharma Purāṇa*
BnP	*Bṛhannāradīya Purāṇa*
BvP	*Brahmavaivarta Purāṇa*
DP	*Devī Purāṇa*
DbP	*Devībhāgavata Purāṇa*
KP	*Kālikā Purāṇa*
Ks	*Kriyāyogasāra*
MbP	*Mahābhāgavata Purāṇa*

I

Introduction

When Bhabani, the protagonist of the novel *Ichāmatī*, returns to Bengal after his religious apprenticeship in the 'West' studying the *Vedas* and *Upaniṣads*, he finds to his dismay that the Vedic tradition forms no part of Bengali religious culture. There are only the songs of Maṅgalacaṇḍī, the *bhāsān* of Manasā and the marriage of Śiva. At best, the Bengalis are familiar with the epics.[1] How accurate is this depiction of the state of religion in Bengal? Is it correct to say that the Vedic tradition never sufficiently penetrated there, so that a Bengali seeking 'the wisdom of Hinduism' had to travel to the proverbial 'West' (the Gangetic valley mainland) even in the nineteenth century? In other words, did Bengal create and preserve a distinct socio-religious tradition, one distinguishable from the dominant high culture of Vedic Hinduism? In this study of the Bengal *Purāṇas*, I propose to investigate this problem. In particular, I intend to examine the process by which the religious tradition of Bengal came into being.

While Indologists have tended to focus on the overarching Sanskritic tradition, social anthropologists have remained concerned with the study of Indian village societies. Thus both disciplines have tended to ignore the regional traditions of South Asia which, in my opinion, embody the cultural continuum of Indian civilization. It has been suggested that this neglect is primarily due to an uneasy feeling that the regional traditions represent neither the unspoilt Sanskritic tradition nor popular culture in its pure form, but a distorted provincial variant of both.[2] But it is the making of regional traditions and the formation of regional identities which reveal the pattern of socio-cultural interaction between the pan-Indian and the local levels, so crucial for an understanding of the long-term historical processes in India.

To date the only significant work on a regional tradition in India, which is based on the crystallization of a religious complex, has been a volume on Jagannātha.[3] However, while Orissa developed a central cult focus and the factors that contributed to the construction of its regional tradition revolved around the temple of Jagannātha, Bengal singularly lacked a dominant symbol supported by the regional state, and its many local traditions, although they converged on a number of autonomous goddesses, were fragmented. It was only when brahmanism established its social order in Bengal by the early medieval period that a semblance of homogeneity appeared in this variegated cultural landscape. The account of this process of cultural interaction is contained in a set of texts called the *Upapurāṇas*, many of which were composed in Bengal roughly between the eighth and the thirteenth centuries AD. Thus Bengal, like other regions, charted its distinct course. There is nevertheless an essential similarity in the process of formation of regional traditions in India and therefore my conclusions may also apply to areas beyond Bengal.

I

Despite the abundance of material, the Bengal *Purāṇas* have been persistently ignored as evidence for the reconstruction of the early history of Bengal. The date, provenance and negotiations involved in the process of codification of the Bengal *Purāṇas* are discussed in the next chapter. Here I deal with historiography in an attempt to explain why historians have remained so reluctant to accept the *Purāṇas* in general and the Bengal *Purāṇas* in particular as a valid and reliable source of historical information.

In a recent article Gregory Schopen has argued that the early European historians of Indian Buddhism had relied more or less exclusively on literary evidence, although archaeological and epigraphical materials, reflecting the actual beliefs and practices of the lay Buddhists, were available in plenty. He suggests that this curious preference may have been due to an assumption that 'real religion' is located in the 'Word of God' and not in the material objects of its practitioners. Schopen concludes that this assumption derives from the sixteenth-century Protestant polemic on 'true' religion that was thoroughly absorbed by the Western intellectual tradition.[4]

Although the Western intellectual tradition exhibited the same attitude to Vedic religion, it was the reverse in the case of the *Purāṇas*. For one thing, in brahmanism 'direct' divine revelation ended with the

Vedas. The later Vedic literature, through association, also acquired a high degree of sacredness. Yet, even as the gods continued to speak through the mouths of the *brāhmaṇas*, the later texts were too numerous to constitute an authentic corpus of scripture of a status acceptable to all votaries of brahmanism. Thus while the brahmanical law codes acquired the status of remembered truth, the *Purāṇas* came to occupy a curious position with neither the unquestioned sanctity of the *Vedas* nor the decisive normative significance of the *Smṛtis*. European scholars who began to write about the *Purāṇas* from the mid-nineteenth century to some extent treated these texts as repositories of fantastic tales about gods and demons which contaminated the high seriousness and idealism of the Vedic religion. H.H. Wilson's translation of the *Viṣṇu Purāṇa*[5] contains a long preface which may be considered the first systematic and scholarly statement in English on Puranic literature (although incidental observations on the *Purāṇas* had already been published by Colebrook and Ellis in the *Asiatic Researches*). In his preface Wilson remarked that the *Purāṇas* were sectarian in character, which indeed is true, but the conclusion he drew from this was that these texts were composed by 'pious frauds for temporary purposes', 'in subservience to . . . sectarian imposture',[6] and therefore not authoritative about Hindu beliefs as a whole. This seems to be a little baffling in view of the fact that two decades later Wilson, in his major study of Hindu beliefs and practices,[7] had classified practising Hindus into three major Puranic sects, the Śaivas, the Vaiṣṇavas and the Śāktas. Perhaps his suspicion about the authenticity of the *Purāṇas* is symptomatic of the approach of early scholars to the stages in the evolution of Hinduism.

In 1855 E.W. Hopkins published his study on the religions of India[8] with detailed studies of the *Ṛg Veda*, brahmanic pantheism and the *Upaniṣads*. The section on 'Hinduism' contains an account of Viṣṇu and Śiva, primarily based on the epics. Significantly, Wilson considered the two epics as 'the safest sources for the ancient legends of the Hindus',[9] after the *Vedas*. Clearly, the unwieldy corpus of *Purāṇas* with conflicting claims about their names and numbers and uncertainty about their dates, had made the *Purāṇas* less acceptable to these scholars than the epics. Hopkins had devoted a short, indifferent chapter to the *Purāṇas*. It dealt with the early sects, the religious festivals, and the formation of the Trinity. His preference for Vedism as the true religion of the Hindus, compared to the later debasement, is inescapable.

A number of important monographs were published on the subject in the late 1870s and early 1880s. M. Monier-Williams' study of

Hinduism[10] makes a distinction between Vedic religion, brahmanical law and domestic usages on the one hand, and Hinduism on the other, which

> best expresses Brahmanism after it had degenerated—to wit, that complicated system of polytheistic doctrines and caste usages which has gradually resulted out of the mixture of Brahmanism and Buddhism, with the non-Aryan creeds of Dravidians and aborigines. Hence Hindūism [sic] is something very different from Brahmanism, though the one is derived from the other.[11]

We see that the Vedic origin of later Hinduism is recognized, but as a reluctant concession. The book contains a separate chapter on the *Purāṇas* and the *Tantras* in connection with the development of *bhakti,* 'the doctrine of faith'. In an expanded version of the work,[12] Monier-Williams makes a similar distinction between Vedism/brahmanism which now includes the six systems of Hindu philosophy, and Hinduism which is characterized by the subordination of 'the purely spiritual Brahman' to the personal deities Śiva and Viṣṇu, though he admits that these are not 'mutually antagonistic'.[13] The book however carries detailed discussions on aspects of popular worship such as village deities, festivals and centres of pilgrimage, and the rites of passage, based on the *Purāṇas*, the *Smṛtis*, and personal observations. Grudging acknowledgement of the fact that the living beliefs and practices of the Hindus had substantially moved away from pristine origins is, once again, perceptible. A. Barth's study of the religions of India[14] also distinguishes between brahmanism and Hinduism, but he takes the Puranic evidence into account in his reconstruction of the sectarian religions of the Vaiṣṇavas and the Śaivas. W.J. Wilkins' study of Hindu mythology,[15] published a year after Barth's, implicitly accepts the division of Hinduism into Vedic and Puranic, but the Puranic deities receive far greater coverage.

At the turn of the century, the most important trait discernible for historiography is a gradual recognition of the Puranic religion. Consequently, the three landmark volumes published in 1913 contain strong emphasis on the *Purāṇas* as a valid source of early Indian history from different points of view. F.E. Pargiter[16] argued that several *Purāṇas* contain resonances of the actual political events of the so-called Kali age, supposedly ushered in by the Mahābhārata war, and the account was brought 'up to date' through continuous redactions. A number of Pargiter's assumptions and conclusions are wrong, or at least doubtful, but he treated the Puranic material with a respect previously unheard of. A volume of Hindu and Buddhist myths retold by Ananda Coomaraswamy and Sister Nivedita with illustrations by Abanindranath

Tagore,[17] came as a covert nationalist defence against the colonial critique of the current state of the beliefs and practices of the Hindus. The apparent disorganization in the arrangement of the book, both chronological and thematic, seems to have been deliberate, for the Vedic and the Puranic myths, which follow those from the epics, were purposely clubbed together to both emphasize and justify the existence of a continuous tradition. The most significant contribution to Puranic studies, however, came from the historian R.G. Bhandarkar.[18] Here was the first rigorous account of religious sects based on texts from the Vedic through the Puranic to the later *bhakti* literature. Bhandarkar pointed out that the prevalent 'mental attitude' of distinguishing between Vedantism and theism did not always work in the Hindu context. Nicol Macnicol on the other hand, in his study of Indian theism[19] published only a couple of years later, ignored the Puranic evidence altogether. Despite Macnicol's erudition in the current theological issues, he misjudged the nature of brahmanical religion, for the *Purāṇas*, though outwardly polytheistic, being sectarian are essentially theistic in character.[20] Thus while the *Purāṇas* were being steadily subsumed into the mainstream of historiography on Indian religions, uncertainty about their status continued to persist.

In the early 1920s another set of important monographs appeared which further strengthened the prevalent trend. H.C. Raychaudhuri, in putting together materials for the study of the early history of the Vaiṣṇava sect, had utilized Puranic texts without undue scepticism, and treated them on a par with the *Vedas*, *Brāhmaṇas, Āraṇyakas, Upaniṣads*, epics, Buddhist *Jātakas*, Jaina *Sūtras*, and the vernacular *bhakti* literature of the Tamils.[21]

It may be said that with Bhandarkar and Raychaudhuri, Puranic studies came into their own. Even so their studies did not completely dispel doubts that still lingered on the authenticity of the *Purāṇas*. J.N. Farquhar,[22] for example, in an otherwise comprehensive study of the religious literature of India, placed disproportionate emphasis on the six systems of Hindu philosophy. The *Purāṇas* are only occasionally and briefly mentioned, even as it is acknowledged that these 'are the real Bible of the common people'.[23] It is also interesting that in a discussion devoted to the religious literature of India, the *Purāṇas* occupy much less space than the specialized texts of even comparatively obscure sub-sects. However, with the publication of Charles Eliot's authoritative study of Hinduism and Buddhism in three volumes,[24] the framework for subsequent studies was securely laid. Puranic religion received due attention and neither the phallic emblem of Śiva nor the butter-thief motif in the Kṛṣṇa cycle of myths was treated with condescension.

Yet scholars were only beginning to recognize the worth of the *Purāṇas*. In the popular introductions of Western authors[25] that began to appear, the *Purāṇas* continued to be disregarded. It is not surprising therefore that even in the late 1920s and the early 1930s eminent scholars like Haraprasad Shastri[26] and V.R. Ramachandra Dikshitar[27] were making a plea for the *Purāṇas*, outlining their dates and corpus, and projecting them as the repository of an overwhelmingly important segment of Hindu beliefs. It was only after the publication of R.C. Hazra's study of the Puranic records on Hindu rites and customs in 1940,[28] in which he delineated with meticulous care the period of composition of the *Purāṇas*—both the approximate time bracket of individual texts as well as the several layers of redactions in each of these—on the basis of a close comparison between the contents of the *Purāṇas*, the *Smṛtis* and other contemporary texts, that historians began to feel comfortable with these texts as important and authentic.

If this has been the checkered history of the *Mahāpurāṇas*, it is not difficult to imagine that the *Upapurāṇas*, disadvantaged by designation at the outset and relegated to a secondary position even within the Puranic corpus, took much longer to be noticed as a valuable source of history. Once again, it was primarily due to the efforts of R.C. Hazra that the dates and provenance of the *Upapurāṇas* were fixed.[29] Although Hazra pointed out that these texts are regionally identifiable and, due to fewer interpolations, often better preserved than the *Mahāpurāṇas*, historians by and large remained indifferent to them. Hazra argued convincingly that the majority of the extant *Upapurāṇas* were composed in Bengal, but standard histories of ancient Bengal persistently refused to take these into cognizance. It is not that these texts were unknown: the Vaṅgavāsī editions of most of the Bengal *Purāṇas* were published by the early twentieth century. But historians have remained exceptionally wary of using them, presumably because these were not considered sufficiently dependable, at least as compared with archaeological and inscriptional evidence. Unlike the early historiography on Vedism and Buddhism, material objects were preferred to written texts for the reconstruction of the history of brahmanical religion of early Bengal.

The first definitive history of ancient Bengal, edited by R.C. Majumdar, was published in 1943.[30] The chapter on religion, a substantial part of which is devoted to the development of Puranic mythology and sects, was written by Prabodh Chandra Bagchi, who more or less entirely relied on epigraphic evidence in his essay. Even the *Tantras*, for some unstated reasons, are more frequently mentioned than the Bengal *Purāṇas*, one of which is cited, rather casually, just once.[31] S.K. De, on Sanskrit literature, discussed the Bengal *Smṛtis* in some detail, but not the *Purāṇas*.[32] Scholarly scepticism towards the Bengal *Purāṇas* has remained with us since then. Niharranjan Ray's history of the Bengalis, an outstanding example of regional history, was published just a few years later.[33] Ray gives a little more space to the *Purāṇas*, but only marginally. He refers to two *arvācina*' (literally young) *Purāṇas*, the *Brahmavaivarta* and *Bṛhaddharma*, in connection with the *jāti* structure of early medieval Bengal,[34] but for religion he stays with the epigraphic and iconographic evidence.[35] Despite his strong emphasis on the compelling presence of indigenous elements in the religious culture of Bengal, Ray chooses to ignore the voluminous data in the *Purāṇas* that supports this contention, and only cursorily mentions the *Bṛhaddharma* and the *Kālikā* for *Śabarotsava*[36] to affirm the non-brahmanical antecedents of goddess worship in Bengal.

These two books were published before Hazra's seminal volumes on the *Upapurāṇas*, and we can understand the historian's caution about the Puranic evidence. However, it is somewhat surprising that in 1971, when R.C. Majumdar published his fully revised version of the volume on the history of ancient Bengal, the Bengal *Purāṇas* continued to remain out of reckoning, except for a brief mention in the sub-section on the non-*brāhmaṇa* castes[37] and a short appendix on the date and provenance of the *Brahmavaivarta* and the *Bṛhaddharma Purāṇas*, based entirely on Hazra.[38] Resistance to the Bengal *Purāṇas* as a source of information persists, as is evident from Rama Chatterjee's comparatively recent monograph on the religion of ancient Bengal.[39] Chatterjee refers to a few of the Bengal *Purāṇas* in her bibliography, but rarely, if ever, in the text.

There exists another genre of literature, thematic summaries of the contents of one or the other *Purāṇa*. Several of the *Mahāpurāṇas* have had the dubious distinction of having been thus studied; so do two of the Bengal *Purāṇas*. Of these, P.G. Lalye has at least made an attempt to correlate the contents of the *Devībhāgavata* with those of the other *Purāṇas*, place the ideas contained in the text in the perspective of relevant philosophical doctrines, and assess its literary qualities.[40] But A.J. Rawal's study of the *Brahmavaivarta* is practically an annotated index of the text, arranged under such uninspiring chapter-heads as society, economy, religion and mythology, with appendices thrown in on flora and fauna.[41] Pushpendra Kumar's work on the Śakti cult in ancient India has a chapter on the *Upapurāṇas* which also follows the same dreary format.[42]

The *Purāṇas* now enjoy undisputed sway over the field of early Indian religion. Anglo-American scholarship in particular has taken to the *Purāṇas* with a vengeance. Competent and imaginative as most of these studies are, the historian's problem is their general disregard for context. A good example is Mackenzie Brown's dense textual study of the *Brahmavaivartā Purāṇa*.[43] Brown has conceived and articulated the problematic of 'a feminine theology' with analytical sophistication and empirical rigour, but appears oblivious of the fact that the *Purāṇa* in its present form was composed in early medieval Bengal. Thus it appears as if the centrality of Rādhā in Bengal Vaiṣṇavism developed in a vacuum, without the support of a congenial religious milieu, and implicitly therefore that the process is generalizable at the pan-Indian level.

The emphasis on assumed elements of continuity in a number of such studies has discouraged strict adherence to chronology and consequently the anonymous *Purāṇas* have been rendered even more impersonal. The long and learned introduction of van Kooij to his translation of parts of the *Kālikā Purāṇa*, on the other hand, is much more meaningful, because he placed it in the context of eastern India and particularly Assam, where it belongs.[44] This helped him appreciate the tension inherent in the process of the introduction of brahmanism into a region where indigenous religious traditions were fairly well developed. But such instances are rare. The indications are that the currently dominant trend in Puranic studies has come to stay for a considerable period of time and studies such as Brown's will continue to proliferate in the contextual vacuity of structuralism. The historian will have to be careful in assimilating their many attractive and provocative insights.

II

I argue that through the codification of these *Purāṇas*, the *brāhmaṇas* attempted to construct an ideological system which eventually became coextensive with the regional tradition of Bengal. Hence, a brief discussion on the sense in which I have used the term ideology is called for.

It is generally agreed that all societies require one or more ideology to function. This suggests that ideology fulfils a vitally important social requirement. The stability of social organization is threatened when class interests clash, or by non-conforming individuals or groups, or in the face of contradictions between the forces of continuity and change, liberty and political order. Ideology helps contain potentially disruptive elements either by justifying the established social order to the oppressed who are somehow persuaded to be reconciled to their lot, in which case it is an 'exploitative value-system' imposed on the people, or by providing remedial support through explanation, obfuscation or amelioration of social discrepancies by non-rational means such as religion, in which case it is a 'patterned response to patterned strains' allowing symbolic outlet to emotional disturbances.[45]

In these understandings ideology has been conceived primarily in the prejorative sense. Ideology performs necessary social functions, but it does so by distorting objective realities and obscuring real contradictions, even though it may satisfy some very genuine and deep-seated human needs, such as freedom from a sense of alienation, impotence or guilt. Raymond Geuss argues that traditional religions owe their persistence to their ability to meet some of these basic needs by providing human beings with approved models of action, goals, ideals and values and by furnishing interpretations of such existential features of life as birth and death, suffering and evil.[46] But the explanatory and didactic framework is an assumption of the existence of some empirically unverifiable transcendental power which never intervenes directly to alter the human condition. Thus ideology does not solve actual problems, it only diffuses them and in the process may even justify, reinforce, and perpetuate human suffering. It offers the imaginary resolution of real contradictions. In this sense ideology is a form of consciousness which is sustained by false beliefs.

This Marxist characterization of ideology as false consciousness[47] has been one of the most influential understandings of the concept. However, it is now being argued that so complex and pervasive a concept as ideology can hardly be pushed into one or the other of the black and white compartments of true or false, because an ideological formulation often contains elements of both. What is important for us is to recognize that, true or false, ideologies are conditioned by the objective situation in any society. As Eagleton puts it,

> in order to be truly effective, ideologies must make at least some minimal sense of people's experience, must conform to some degree with what they know of social reality from their practical interaction with it. . . . They must be 'real' enough to provide the basis on which individuals can fashion a coherent identity, must furnish some solid motivations for effective action, and must make at least some feeble attempt to explain away their own more flagrant contradictions and

incoherences. In short, successful ideologies must be more than imposed illusions, and for all their inconsistencies must communicate to their subjects a version of social reality which is real and recognizable enough not to be simply rejected out of hand.[48]

Clifford Geertz has remarked with even greater emphasis, 'Whatever else ideologies may be . . . they are, most distinctively, maps of problematic social reality and matrices for the creation of collective conscience.'[49]

As a result, a number of Marxist scholars are now rejecting the notion that normative conceptions of what is good or bad, possible or impossible are accessible only through 'true knowledge' of the reality of existence, which ideologies suppress and mask.[50] Instead, it is necessary to remember that if ideologies are lived beliefs, then they are internal to social practice and thus constitutive of those practices. Therefore they can hardly be false in the sense of unreal. Ideologies are much more than mere states of mind, for they continuously constitute and reconstitute social subjects. Hence it is possible to move a step further and argue that ideologies are not only shaped by existential reality but are a part of it, an active material force which must have enough cognitive content to help organize the practical lives of human beings. This is not to deny that ideologies often contain beliefs which are empirically untrue, or at least undemonstrable. But what kind of falsehood this involves also depends on the availability of social options, since an ideology must appear plausible for it to succeed.

Ideology is more than a neutral set of beliefs, articulated through a pattern of interlocking symbols. The function of ideology in a society cannot be understood without reference to the question of power. Power may be exercised through coercion, or legitimation, or more frequently, through a combination of both. It has been the cumulative experience of complex societies that power cannot be sustained over a large and diverse group of people for a long period of time by means of coercion alone. It requires ideological support to legitimize the authority of the dominant social group.

David Beetham characterizes legitimate power as power 'that provides grounds for obedience on the part of those subordinate to it, because of the normative force that derives from rules, from justificatory principles, and from actions expressing consent'.[51] He adds that the maintenance and reproduction of legitimacy do not take place independently of the structures of power that they legitimate. The ongoing power structures legitimate themselves through their preferential access to the means of cultural development and the dissemination of ideas within society. Beetham reminds us that the processes of developing and transmitting ideas require independence from the powerful in order to secure authenticity, for the power of ideas, unlike other forms of power, can be measured only in terms of credibility. However, even this credibility is indirectly created by that same system of power, for it shapes the expectations and interests of subordinate groups through a variety of social processes, so that justifications for the rules of power become credible because they are confirmed by their own experience. Thus legitimation is a self-confirming circle which makes the socially constructed appear as natural, although this fact is obscured by the complexity of the process.[52] Beetham sums up the functions of a system of power thus:

> to confirm the differentiation between dominant and subordinate which justifies their respective positions; to structure the common interest so that it can only be met through satisfying the purposes of the powerful; to help shape the desires of the subordinate in directions that the system is capable of meeting; to limit the choices available so that consent to a position of subordination, although constrained, is also at the same time voluntary.[53]

Legitimation therefore can be effective in maintaining unequal relations of power on a long-term basis, because it depresses rather than excites opposing forces.

III

The question of domination and consent brings us to the related concept of hegemony, formulated by the Italian political philosopher Antonio Gramsci. Most of Gramsci's thoughts, contained in his *Prison Notebooks*,[54] are polemical, deliberately abstruse to baffle prison censors, and fragmented and provisional, for they were never intended for publication, at least in their extant form. As a result some of the most important concepts which Gramsci developed are not defined with precision, leading to the production of a large exegetical literature containing conflicting interpretations. Gramsci's most interesting ideas cluster around the concept of cultural hegemony[55] which I have used as the theoretical premise for my understanding of the phenomenon of brahmanism in Bengal.

Gramsci made a distinction between domination, which is realized through the coercive organs of the state, and intellectual and moral leadership, which is objectified in and exercised through the institutions of civil society. It is the latter which is far more pervasive and durable than that achieved through coercion. Gwyn Williams has summed up the nature and extent of hegemonic control thus: hegemony consists of

> an order in which a certain way of life and thought is dominant, in which one concept of reality is diffused throughout society, in all its institutional and private manifestations, informing with its spirit all tastes, morality, customs, religions and political principles, and all social relations, particularly in their intellectual and moral connotations.[56]

In other words, hegemony is a relation of domination, not by means of force but through ideological legitimation. It is the organization of consent.

Is the consent, thus achieved, an active one? Gramsci himself seems to have been unclear on this question. At times he suggests that consent in a hegemonic situation takes the form of active commitment which derives from complete internalization of dominant values and definitions. On other occasions he implies that consent is only passive, because of partial assimilation of dominant values, and is conditioned by an uneasy feeling that the status quo, while shamefully iniquitous, is nevertheless the only viable form of society.[57] Thus consent for Gramsci is never one-dimensional; it is a complex mental state where approval and indifference, resistance and resignation coexist. Therefore hegemonic situations differ in intensity and the degree of variation depends on the dynamics of historical development. That is why 'hegemony maintenance' has to be an active unfolding process, 'a process of continuous creation'.[58]

The most important contribution of the concept of hegemony to intellectual and cultural history is that it offers historians 'an opportunity to connect ideas with the "social matrix" that they are being constantly urged to locate, without reducing the ideas to mere epiphenomena'.[59] However, this flexibility in Gramsci has raised doubts about his credentials as a Marxist thinker. Gramsci undeniably departed in important ways from classical Marxism. In his scheme of things mental life is more than a pale reflection of more basic developments in material life and the relationship between the two realms is one of circular interaction rather than of linear causality. Therefore Gramsci broadened and deepened Marxist notions of ideology in significant ways. His emphasis on the role of consciousness in maintaining social equilibrium as well as in accelerating social change has led many critics to discover idealist tendencies in his writings. However, Gramsci did not reject the crucial centrality of the material basis in shaping this consciousness. Gramsci never made a complete theoretical statement on this issue, but in several passages in his notebooks either explicitly stated or obviously implied that 'the economic base not only sets limits but also determines . . . the form and content of the superstructure.'[60] He merely suggests that the base does not automatically determine consciousness; it indicates the forms of consciousness possible.[61] Therefore hegemonic situations must be understood with reference to the total historical context.

The strongest criticism of Gramsci, best expressed by Perry Anderson in his famous critique, has been that he has overemphasized ideology and underplayed coercion. Gramsci is said to have neglected the fact that culture and power are too pervasive and intertwined to be conceived of as separable categories and that the state in the capitalist system combines within itself both the mechanism of coercion and the ideological apparatus. This is why, Anderson says, Gramsci is mistaken in locating hegemony exclusively in civil society rather than the state.[62]

While it is undeniable that Gramsci's major concern is legitimation obtained through ideological discourse, he has neither relegated coercion to the background nor conceived of culture and ideology independently of power. Indeed, he has pointed out how consciousness itself is shaped by power relations and has drawn attention to the advantages of invisibility of power which is disseminated throughout the texture of social life and thus naturalized as custom, habit, and spontaneous practice. It is the power of the dominant in all senses of the term—politically through control of the state, economically through control of relations of production, and socially through control of culture and mass media—that ideology legitimates. But coercion need not be exercised through violence alone; the threat of retrenchment or of divine retribution may be as effective. Power is such a constant in determining social relations as also in the Marxist understanding of social formations that Gramsci, in his attempt to create greater space for the role of consciousness, tends to give the impression that beliefs, values, and norms, and not power, are the key variables for explaining social order. In fact Gramsci never said so, although by his insistence on the importance of shared values he does seem to suggest relative autonomy of spheres.

James Scott accuses Gramsci, and more particularly his followers Miliband and Althusser, of substituting a kind of ideological determinism for the material determinism they sought to avoid. He argues that the notion of hegemony fails to differentiate between submission offered under economic compulsion and consent willingly offered due to ideological conversion. Thus theories of hegemony frequently confound what is inevitable with what is just, an error that the subordinate classes rarely, if ever, make. As a result, in power-laden situations, the subordinate classes only routinely submit to the dominant group out of pragmatic considerations, although they are perfectly capable of penetrating and demystifying the prevailing ideology on the basis of their daily material experience.[63] However, it has been argued that Scott's critique is based on a rather limited conception of Gramsci which insists that hegemony can exist only when the ruling ideology determines all consciousness.[64] Recent interpretations of Gramsci, notably from Femia, Adamson and Lears, are increasingly emphasizing that Gramsci recognized the possibility of conflict and coexistence of contradictory consciousness in the outlook of single individuals as well as groups within any given hegemony.[65]

The problems of utilizing the insights of Gramsci for an understanding of how brahmanism organized consent are obvious. Gramsci was attempting to understand how capitalist society functions. He also assumed that the dominant group or ruling class necessarily controls the production process. Finally, his was a pre-eminently political agenda: he was seeking ways to subvert the passive consent the working class offers its capitalist masters.

None of these conditions facilitates an understanding of the creation and maintenance of brahmanical hegemony in early medieval Bengal. To begin with, the nature of both the social organization and the state was vastly different in the two cases. Obviously, the typical institutions of civil society that Gramsci had in mind did not exist in early medieval Bengal. Second, and this is crucial, the *brāhmaṇas* cannot be said to have been the leaders in the production sector, even though it is difficult to decide who were. Independent petty peasant producers seem to have formed the backbone of the economy of early medieval Bengal. A sizeable section of the peasantry must have been under varying degrees of subordination to the dominant socio-economic groups. There would have been intermediaries and landlords, some of whom were *brāhmaṇas,* under the general surveillance of the state. Even if the interest of the *brāhmaṇa* donee/landlord was closely tied to that of the ruling class/state in economic management, *brāhmaṇas* themselves hardly controlled production.[66]

And yet there is an essential similarity in the manner in which hegemony operates anywhere. The context-specific variables determine the nature and intensity of hegemonic control, but the need for ideological support for a stable socio-political order, irrespective of its form, cannot be denied. Georges Duby's description of the process of diffusion of cultural patterns in eleventh-century France may serve as an illustrative parallel. He noticed that the centres of cultural creation were located in the upper levels of the social structure, among the members of the ecclesiastical *avante-garde*.

> But since they were consciously working towards a popular audience, they readily accepted some of the diffuse tendencies, general ideas and mental images which were widely spread in lower cultural levels. The intention was to harness these tendencies, so that the propaganda, couched in familiar terms, could more easily reach the masses.[67]

Barring a few specifics, such as the absence of the knight as the other and competing cultural model, this could easily have been a description of the Puranic process in early medieval Bengal. The efforts of the clerics to reshape a popular culture and transmit it through carnivals finds an unmistakable resonance in the *brāhmaṇa* adoption of indigenous goddesses as a symbol of *apparently* shared myths, rituals and beliefs and the dissemination of these through the *vratas*, involving the entire village community. Moreover, the role of the *brāhmaṇas*, performing the function of 'traditional intellectuals', their attempts to manipulate popular themes, the location of ideological domination in non-coercive organs of society, and the mutually supportive function of the state and civil institutions in terms of division of power[68] are all conditions that fit into the Gramscian conception of hegemony.

However, this phenomenon was not unique to Bengal. Ainslie Embree has described brahmanical ideology as one of the two most important unifying linkages in Indian civilization. By brahmanical he does not imply an ideology that is confined to one group, 'but rather a set of values, ideas, concepts, practices and myths that are identifiable in the literary tradition and social institutions'.[69] Embree argues that Hinduism comprises divergent strands which vary in time and space, while brahmanism consists of much more coherent and consistent intellectual statements about a cosmic order that links all its elements in a continuous and understandable pattern. The *brāhmaṇa*, who possesses the knowledge of the *Brahman* and therefore has the right to decide the rules of conduct (*dharma*), maintains this order in which each entity occupies a necessary and logical place in a hierarchical structure. It is this remarkable continuity of the core of brahmanism with the flexibility to adjust to radically different political and social situations without yielding ground, that gave the *brāhmaṇas* an awareness of sharing a common heritage of language and values with others of their *varṇa* throughout the subcontinent, despite fluctuating patronage under different political authorities.

Embree thus suggests that the *brāhmaṇas* were not an aristocracy in the European sense, which combines blood lineages with economic and political power, but a group which identified itself with the ideology that provided rationality and coherence to society. Individual kings could have been ignorant or impious, large segments of the population might have been unfamiliar with brahmanical ideology in its articulated form, but the deference paid to it over the ages shows its extraordinary dominance as ideology.[70] I agree with Embree's reading of the basic contents and the essentially unchanging nature of the core of brahmanical ideology, except that he tends to underscore the textual basis of brahmanism and view *brāhmaṇas* as a homogeneous community, ignoring the enormous regional variations and complex internal differentiations. However, it should also be noted that when it came to assertions of *brāhmaṇa* superiority, particularly in such peripheral areas as Bengal where the intermediate *varṇas* were conspicuous by their absence, they did succeed in projecting a collective identity.

This conception of the structure and function of the *brāhmaṇa varṇa* helps us understand not only the process of construction and propagation of brahmanical ideology in early medieval Bengal, but also the creative and symbolic dimension of the social world defined in the Puranic texts that contributed to the cultural tradition and regional identity of Bengal. As mentioned above, the goddesses and the *vratas* were two important elements adopted by the *brāhmaṇas* from religious practices of the local population, and these were invested with a significance that transcended local boundaries. The *brāhmaṇas* did not disturb most of the prevailing normative goals, such as those sought through the performance of indigenous *vratas*, but they made it appear as if these goals would be best realized if the *vratas* were performed in the brahmanical way. Such measures facilitated the acceptance of the *brāhmaṇas* by the local people and at the same time demonstrated that they possessed a superior knowledge and had access to supra-local resources. Thus the diverse local traditions were brought under the overarching canopy of brahmanism which paved the way for a larger social identity. The institutionalization of the brahmanical principle of social organization—the caste hierarchy—strengthened this bond. While this ensured *brāhmaṇa* dominance beyond question, it also allowed the fragmented indigenous social groups entry into wider social networks, a point noted by Nirmal Kumar Basu in passing,[71] although its significance and multiple ramifications have not yet been fully explored. Implicit in this complex relationship was the asymmetrical organization of power, sustained by the persuasive potential of brahmanical ideology. With the gradual acceptance of this ideology, what was once the world-view of a privileged social group became coextensive with almost the entire cultural sphere of Bengal.[72]

I have found the concept of hegemony useful in understanding the socio-religious processes initiated by the *brāhmaṇas* in Bengal from the post-Gupta period, the effects of which began to crystallize in the early medieval period. Ever since the discovery of Gramsci by the English-speaking world in the early 1970s, his insights have been widely used to explain a variety of historical situations, but rarely by the Marxist historians of ancient India. They have by and large remained indifferent to or wary of him.[73] Their objections are, however, misconceived. Gramsci does not advocate ideological determinism; he firmly locates ideology within the power relations which the ruling class controls by virtue of ownership of the means of production. Therefore the disjunction he posits between the state and the civil society is a theoretical one for the sake of analytical convenience. Despite his notorious inconsistency, Gramsci clearly accords primacy to the base in determining what forms of consciousness are possible. Gramsci's insistence on the role of ideology in shaping consciousness only helps to bring into relief what already existed,[74] but remained dormant, in classical Marxism.

The question of autonomy of the religious sphere is a complex one and Gramsci never directly addressed this question. Religious speculation, at a certain stage of its evolution, may acquire relative autonomy from its immediate determinants, but religion in isolation of the larger social needs can survive only as an esoteric faith. In any case the religious process of this study is actually a social process expressed through religious idiom. The most significant aspect of the concept of hegemony is its comprehensiveness and its ability to understand and explain the multiple ramifications of the dynamics of social existence. Brahmanism succeeded in establishing an order in early medieval Bengal in which the brahmanical conception of reality pervaded political principles and social relations, particularly in their ideological connotations. It is of no consequence if this domination does not qualify as hegemonic. The nomenclature is not important.

IV

An unavoidable word about the method of analysis, particularly when my sources are, quite literally, 'texts'. I have dwelt at length on the method of reading the Puranic texts primarily for two reasons. In recent years the pervasive influence of literary critical theory on the social sciences has so undermined some of their fundamental assumptions that it has become necessary to acknowledge its presence and assess its applicability to the historical study of texts, especially the didactic *Purāṇas*, instead of simply dismissing it or making eclectic use of the terminology. This requires enunciation of the relevant issues. The question of how a qualified acceptance of some aspects of critical theory for an understanding of the narrative strategy of the *Purāṇas* is compatible with the larger conceptual framework of brahmanical hegemony also calls for explanation. I feel that a starting statement of my position will save repetition later in the argument.

For long historians have understood the text as displaying the intention of the author, which in turn is shaped by the socio-economic and politico-cultural context in which the author is located. It was believed that the two reinforce each other and together provide the clues to the explanation of historical processes of continuity and change. Historians took every possible precaution to check the authenticity of their text and safeguard the neutrality of the information, always assuming that the information thus derived would 'reflect' the 'reality' of the situation in which it was composed or to which it refers. Once the veracity of the information was proved beyond reasonable doubt and the biases neutralized, the text was considered to be a storehouse of historical 'truths' from which the historian was supposed to select and arrange relevant material for the reconstruction of past events.

The greater the sophistication in method, the more discriminating has been the approach to the text. But very few historians have discarded as a matter of principle context-dependent causality as the fundamental factor in historical explanation. Those practising historians who have written on the historian's craft,[75] and those philosophers of history who have speculated on its nature and function,[76] have usually upheld the centrality of a hierarchy of causes and the human agency which dictates them as two of the most important constituents of history.

As late as 1969 Quentin Skinner insisted that the study of intellectual history presupposes an understanding of what authors of texts meant to say in different historical contexts and communicative situations.

Skinner argued that our ideas constitute a response to more immediate circumstances and therefore we should study not the texts in themselves but the context of other happenings which explains them. If this is accepted then it seems clear that at least a part of such understanding must lie in grasping what sort of society the given author was writing for and trying to persuade.[77] This context, he said, gets mistakenly treated as the determinant of what is said in a text. 'It needs rather to be treated as an ultimate framework for helping to decide what conventionally recognizable meanings, in a society of that kind, it might in principle have been possible for someone to have intended to communicate.'[78] Thus the context consists of both what the texts were intended to mean and how this meaning was supposed to be understood.[79] For the sacred texts in particular, Joseph Kitagawa has emphasized the need to take into consideration the 'total context', or the culture as a whole in order to comprehend the meaning of specific symbols, myths or rituals contained in such texts.[80]

Yet what has been termed postmodernist critical debate has radically questioned these assumptions in the last twenty years and has threatened to alter the foundation of the historian's traditional understanding of the text. The most easily discernible consequence of this debate from the historian's point of view has been the shift from material reality to language as the constitutive agent of human consciousness and the social production of meaning. Language is no longer construed as simply a transparent medium for the representation of a reality outside of itself, but a self-contained system of signs whose meanings are determined by their relations to each other rather than some extralinguistic object or subject. Thus postmodernism tends to posit that far from being a part of the social world, language precedes the world and makes it intelligible by constructing it according to its own rules of signification. It denies the idea of an objective universe existing independently of speech or universally comprehensible despite one's membership in any particular language system.[81]

The first casualty of this understanding was the individuality of the author. Roland Barthes declared the author dead, because 'writing is that neutral, composite, oblique space where our subject slips away, the negative where all identity is lost, starting with the very identity of the body writing'.[82] Barthes drew upon linguistics to show that the whole of the enunciation is an empty process, functioning perfectly without any need for it to be filled with the person of the interlocutors. He argued that a text is not a sequence of words releasing a single theological meaning (which he dismissively called 'the message of the Author-God') but a multidimensional space in which a variety of writings blend and clash. None of these writings are, however, 'original', because the author is born into an already existing language which governs him. Thus, 'once the author is removed the claim to decipher a text becomes quite futile. To give a text an Author is to impose a limit on that text, to furnish it with a final signified, to close the writing.'[83] Such a view transforms the traditional notion of the author as a centred subject, in conscious control of and responsible for his own utterances.

The second major categorical opposition questioned by this semiologically oriented history of meanings is that between representation and reality. If meanings do not simply represent but actually constitute the reality experienced by human beings, then there can be no extratextual reality. When the author ceases to exist, the variables which situate an author, which Barthes called his 'hypostases'[84]—society, history, psyche—also become redundant. It therefore follows that context must itself be conceived as

> a compound world of constituted meanings, as a text requiring interpretation. Both text and context are complex relations of 'signifying practices'. The connections between them must thus be construed as 'intertextual'. The context never 'explains' the text in the sense of providing the essence of its appearance or the cause of its effect or the reality of its representation.[85]

Thus text and society are homologous and the focus of interpretation is directed not to their content but to the linguistic codes which constitute social and discursive formations.

An inevitable consequence of this understanding is the dismantling of the hierarchy of causes in historical explanation, because it is impossible to establish the priority of society over text or claim that society determines or causes the cultural production of meaning. Mental structures no longer depend on their material determinants. The representations of the social world themselves constitute social reality. In other words, as Gabrielle Spiegel points out, what is real is the semiotic codes that govern the representation of life both in writing and in incorporated social structures. 'If the imaginary is real and the real imaginary and there are no epistemological grounds for distinguishing between them, then it is impossible to create an explanatory hierarchy that establishes a causal relationship between history and literature, life and thought, matter and meaning.'[86] When society is emptied of its normal significance and reinscribed as social text, text and context are collapsed into one big discursive production.

This conception of text and context so fundamentally militates against the traditional notions of the construction of the past that one would have thought it to be unacceptable to historians. However, many seem to share this understanding.[87] Dominick LaCapra, for example, suggests that to believe that authorial intentions fully control the meaning or functioning of texts is to assume a proprietary relation between the author and the text as well as a unitary meaning for an utterance, while this relationship may involve multiple forms of tension, including self-contestation.[88] He similarly discounts a straight correlation between author's life and text, and society and text.[89] Instead, LaCapra advocates that the text should be seen as 'the "place" where long tradition and specific time intersect, and it effects variations on both. But the text is not immobilized or presented as an autonomous node; it is situated in a fully relational network.'[90] Thus put, it may superficially appear that he is neither completely denying authorial intention nor materiality of the text, but is merely attempting to correct the social historian's supposedly one-dimensional reading of texts as documentary representations of reality. Yet implicit in his formulation is the negation of the context as the source of the realities traditionally believed to have been reflected in the text and, by extension, of causality, stability of meaning, human agency and social determination.

Recently there appears to have occurred a slight shift from this disregard for extralinguistic context and the 'authorial intention fallacy' to a more circumspect appraisal of the discipline of history. For instance, J.R. Jackson makes a distinction between historical criticism and literary criticism in unearthing the meaning of texts. 'Historical criticism,' according to Jackson, 'is criticism that tries to read past works of literature in the way in which they were read when they were new.'[91] This view does not gloss over the text–context relationship by treating culture, institution, ideology, and power as merely interworked systems of symbolic codes, but recognizes an intention that was contemporaneously understood. Cultural materialism, advocated by Raymond Williams, addresses this problem through its insistence on the materiality of thought and writing as 'actions-in-the-world' with real consequences comparable to what historians call events.[92] Another variation of the relationship between the 'real' and the literary text within Marxist categories has been suggested by Fredric Jameson. He views literary texts as an allegory of history in which 'the literary text . . . may . . . be seen as the rewriting or restructuration of a prior historical or ideological *subtext* . . . .'[93] He also seems to accord priority to history as the 'interpretative master code',[94] since the linguistic usage has to be traced back to the historical process.

In fact 'post-structuralist Marxism', i.e. Marxism which is responsive to structuralist and post-structuralist criticism, has devoted some attention to this problem and its conclusions appear to be more conducive for a historical understanding of the text. Tony Bennett has defined the concerns of Marxist literary theory thus:

> The development of a historical and materialist theory of the interactions between texts classified as literary, other ideological phenomena and broader social and political process and relationships, recognizing that the system of classification within which the 'literary' is produced are always culturally specific and that, therefore, their functioning and effects are a part of what needs to be studied.[95]

He adds a rider that such a theory cannot be adequately developed if predicated on the assumption that the relations between literary texts and the broader social processes can be determined, once and for all, by referring such texts to the conditions of production obtaining at the moment of their origin. On the contrary,

> the actual and variable functioning of texts in history can only be understood if account is taken of the ways in which such originary relations may be modified through the operation of subsequent determinations—institutional and discursive—which may retrospectively cancel out, modify or overdetermine those which marked the originating conditions of a text's production.[96]

On the basis of this consideration Bennett suggests that the proper object for Marxist literary theory consists not in the study of texts but in the study of 'reading formations'. By a reading formation he means 'a set of discursive and intertextual determinations which organize and animate the practice of reading, connecting texts and readers in specific relations to one another in constituting readers as reading subjects of particular types and texts as objects-to-be-read in particular ways'.[97] This understanding of course explicitly accepts context as the point of reference for the text, but this context is not an extratextual social context but a set of discursive and intertextual determinations, operating on material and institutional supports, which motivate a text not just externally but also internally. This insistence on intertextual and discursive determination of the meaning of texts argues for a method of analysis apparently so removed from the fundamental postulates of Marxism that it can hardly be considered a variant of Marxism at all. But Bennett points out that 'it is precisely because texts are material phenomena that their social and ideological articulations may be discursively reordered, and by social and material means since, of course, discursive processes are social and material processes produced within specifiable institutional conditions'.[98] Thus Bennett operates within recognizable Marxist categories. He only wishes to emphasize that a text must not be understood only with reference to its originating conditions of production, but should be viewed together with the manner in which it is discursively remoulded within an institutional framework, in order to appreciate the nature of its subsequent functioning.

I have found this approach helpful for an understanding of the Bengal *Purāṇas*. Instead of emphasizing the unproblematic superstructural character of literary production, this approach takes into account discursive practices without disregarding the materiality of text, context, and shared and evolving cultural presuppositions and their interrelationships. The Bengal *Purāṇas* are not the 'complex texts' of LaCapra; they are normative texts with an obvious pedagogical intention. It is therefore necessary to trace them to their authors, their audience and the discursive field, to appreciate both the manner of their codification as well as the modalities of their function in a communicative situation. Hence a brief statement on the brahmanical vision and the textual strategy of the Bengal *Purāṇas* will help to demonstrate how this method of analysis reveals the most significant and historically verifiable meaning of the *Purāṇas*.

The *brāhmaṇas*, especially in the peripheral areas, wanted to enter into a dialogue with the indigenous population through the composition and propagation of a set of texts, because the success of brahmanical hegemony depended on the acceptance of their normative prescriptions and the internalization of their cultural assumptions by the local people. They composed their texts with a view to invoking a particular response in their intended recipients. These socio-religious prescriptions consisted of a series of legitimations of local beliefs and practices already in vogue and the reiteration of the fundamental principles of brahmanism. These legitimations had to be worked out in such a way that they did not impair the recognition of the original model and yet privileged the *brāhmaṇas* with the authority to decide the degree of admissibility of the local usages. The brahmanical prescriptions are contained in the Bengal *Purāṇas*, composed and redacted over half a millennium or more, and propagated through mandatory expositions during the performance of the transformed indigenous *vratas*.

This context to a large extent determined the character and the textual strategy of the Bengal *Purāṇas*. In the first place, the need to accommodate diverse local customs had built into the *Purāṇas* fully valid multiple voices, voices other than exclusively those of their *brāhmaṇa* authors. I use the term voice in the Bakhtinian sense to include matters not just linguistic but also those relating to ideology and power in society, which attempt to situate the reader/listener in certain ways. 'Language is not a neutral medium that passes freely and easily into the private property of the speaker's intentions,' Bakhtin wrote, 'it is populated—overpopulated—with the intentions of others.'[99] The Bengal *Purāṇas* naturalize the speech of several others and in the process display inner tensions, collaborations and negotiations, which are more than mere authoritative statements, but are comparable to dialogues. The plurality of voices makes the *Purāṇas* truly polyphonic in character. However, in any text the voice of the narrator is also an essential presence, and the contending voices in the Bengal *Purāṇas* are harmonized by the governing attitude or the ideology of the *brāhmaṇas*. The Puranic texts were constituted through this complex process of negotiation. Once formulated, they became a part of the material context, and their subsequent discursive reordering within the institutional framework continued to redefine the brahmanical agenda in Bengal.

The formal and thematic features of the Puranic texts primarily derive from this process of formation of the brahmanical discourse in Bengal. The Bengal *Purāṇas* are highly persuasive. Even though they seldom engage in 'rational' argument, they do not issue commands without providing what they consider suitable justification. Justification is usually provided in the form of an anecdote describing an incident in the life of a mythical character. This illustrates the consequence of conforming to or transgressing a Puranic injunction; the threat of retribution and the lure of reward are delicately balanced. But the grounds of justification may vary from one narrative context to another and every slight shift in emphasis in the common and familiar plot presents a different message. Thus descriptive rhetoric is the principal mode of enunciation in the Bengal *Purāṇas*.

As a result, these texts are invariably prolix, hyperbolic, endlessly repetitive and in certain respects manifestly self-contradictory. They disproportionately exaggerate one possibility often only to contradict it later. This tension is sustained throughout. A particular *Purāṇa* may adopt an internally consistent sectarian position, but all the other *Purāṇas* are unlikely to subscribe to the same view. In several matters of detail, the *Purāṇas* implicitly differ with one another. The repetitions are apparently simple reminders, aimed at convincing a diverse audience. But often a statement is repeated with a minor, almost imperceptible, difference, so that the listener is lulled into believing that he is being told the same thing, while at the end the proposition may have changed substantially. This ceaseless reiteration of mutually exclusive statements is a narrative device which helps to create an impression of ambiguity. It allows interpretive space to the individual listener which unequivocally stated categorical positions do not permit.

It is not as if the *Purāṇas* do not make decisive statements; they always do. But the contrary statements are equally emphatic and self-assured. While no fixed value can be attached to each isolated statement in the *Purāṇas*, collectively they underscore the authority of the *brāhmaṇas*. Each statement is authentic in its ever-shifting relative context because it has been made by a *brāhmaṇa* and is included within a textual corpus which defines the social milieu within which it has normative significance. However, there are certain matters, such as the infallibility of the *Vedas*, the ritual prerogative of the *brāhmaṇas*, maintenance of the *varṇāśramadharma* and rejection of Buddhism, on which the *Purāṇas* display an absolute unanimity of opinion. It is this uniformity which saves the open-ended Puranic arrangement from dissolving into chaos. But in most other matters the *Purāṇas* offer their listeners a semblance of freedom through perpetual restatement of antitheses—popular customs and Vedic ordinance, indigenous goddesses and the brahmanical *śakti*, or local traditions and supra-local perspectives. Such duality, though deceptive, theoretically admits of several possibilities in a single situation. As O'Flaherty points out, 'the formal points of repetition, variation, contradiction, detail, and scale thus assume a dimension of content as well'. This textual strategy is particularly appropriate from the point of view of brahmanism for it diffuses the conflicts and reconciles the irreconcilable. Everything is constantly in flux; the conflicts are resolved in suspension rather than in solution.[100] But everything keeps coming back to the stable social order ensured by the institution of caste which limits individual options, to the dominant voice of the *brāhmaṇa* in which all oppositions are fused.

This dominant voice, however, is impersonal and unaffected by any one linguistic practice, because the *Purāṇas* were composed in a language to which the indigenous population had no access. By excluding the majority from access to one of the most potent symbols of brahmanical authority—literacy—*brāhmaṇas* succeeded in exercising much greater control. But if historical criticism consists of reading ancient tracts in the way in which they were supposed to have been understood, language usage does not help us recover the meaning of the Puranic texts as conveyed to their audience. The *Purāṇas* were written in Sanskrit, but purveyed in the vernacular for popular consumption. Therefore the exposition would have consisted of annotated commentary of the Puranic myths and legends by professional narrators, who presented the essential content and rhetoric rather than the exact words of the genre. Thus it is the internal arrangement of the *Purāṇas* more than the precise use of language that should concern the historian.

This view comes close to what Fredric Jameson has called the semantic approach to genre criticism.[101] Several genres can of course simultaneously coexist in a single discourse and therefore what is of interest to us is not the sensibility of a particular genre, but the totalizing world-view of a corpus of texts representing a coherent discourse. The Puranic texts of Bengal, despite sectarian discontinuities, form an indivisible corpus, and I explore the brahmanical world-view that they collectively portray, submerging the other minor differences. From the point of view of textual strategy it is as if 'a single text writ large', and what is at issue here is the unity or the identity of the corpus as a whole. Although LaCapra warns us that relation among texts in a corpus may involve uneven development and differing forms of repetition or displacement that may make simple models of intelligibility questionable,[102] it does not create much difficulty in the case of the Bengal *Purāṇas*. I have already mentioned that Puranic texts themselves reveal processes of exclusion or domination that tend to neutralize their more disconcerting or contestatory movements, such as sectarian tensions or attitude towards a body of rituals. It would have been more convincing if the synthesizing tendency of these texts could be brought out in a chronological sequence displaying a linear movement towards uniformity, but it is virtually impossible to set the Bengal *Purāṇas* (or, for that matter, any anonymous normative text of this kind) to such an order. Therefore generalizations on the entire corpus have to remain somewhat impressionistic.

This impression is strengthened by the absence of individual authors. R.C. Hazra and others established that many of these texts were written over a long stretch of time, often spanning centuries. They were strung together by group interests that justified a common denomination and authorship. Therefore the conclusion is inescapable that the *Purāṇas* were not written by individuals with a specific identity, but by an idealized collectivity—the *brāhmaṇa varṇa*. The Bengal *Purāṇas* have indeed been attributed to Kṛṣṇadvaipāyana Vedavyāsa, who is also supposed to have written the proto-Puranic *Mahābhārata* and all the *Mahāpurāṇas*. But obviously this was a generic name used for the convenience of classification. Michel Foucault has pointed out that when several authors of a number of texts are referred to by one name, it implies relationships of 'homogeneity, filiation, reciprocal explanation, authentication, or common utilization' among them.[103] He adds that in this sense the function of an author, however fictitious, is to characterize the existence, circulation, and operation of certain discourses within a society.[104] Thus if brahmanism found it reasonable to classify the authors of all these texts under a single name, it indicates a perception of the coherence of the Puranic discourse as an original underlying signification system, beyond the personal preference, intention, or idiosyncracy of an individual author. The significance of the anonymity of the early Indian texts was recognized by Velcheru Narayana Rao as early as 1983:

> Authorship in India does not signify the physical producer of the text, but rather authorizes the status of the text and a specific meaning that is derived from it. From this point of view, the author is a function of the text and a signifier of its received meaning. The author does not precede the text, as we think he does in our 'print-culture', but follows it. To put it differently, the author does not 'write' the text; rather, it is the text that 'writes' the author.[105]

In this sense, the Bengal *Purāṇas* took the name of Vyāsa as their author and thus imparted to themselves the necessary authority and a context-determined meaning.

Indeed, even within the realm of discourse, Foucault argues, a person can be the author of much more than a book—a discipline or a tradition for instance (he cites the examples of Marx and Freud)—within which new books and authors can proliferate. They clear the requisite space for the introduction of elements other than their own, which, nevertheless, remain within the discourse they initiated.[106] Then the subsequent elaborations and emendations may be understood with reference to the original text(s). It may appear at first sight that the usual anonymity of the brahmanical texts prevents us from even speculating about the possible initiator of the Puranic discourse. However, since it can be stated with a fair degree of certainty that the rules of composition of the Puranic texts were formulated pretty early and were commonly understood, it is not difficult to perceive why all subsequent contributions fed into the corpus without much friction. In fact there is such a symmetry even in the use of language in these texts that those Sanskritists who attempted to work out a comparative chronology of the redactions within each on the basis of linguistic peculiarities had to ultimately depend on extra-linguistic considerations such as the introduction of a new social custom or ritual, or intertextual references, as their guiding index. Even grammatical errors are uniformly distributed through the text in some of the Bengal *Purāṇas*.[107] But more than the distinctive use of language, it is the surprising uniformity in the major thrust of the contents which points to a shared understanding of the discourse.

Therefore the right question to ask from our point of view is not regarding the authenticity of the author or how an individual author is revealed in the texts, but where the discourse comes from, how it is circulated and who controls it. Undoubtedly it came from the *brāhmaṇas*. But they were a heterogeneous group, both socially and in sectarian persuasion. They had a closely guarded and complex hierarchy of status and ranking; they had personal loyalties to different gods and goddesses and their modes of worship were accordingly determined; not all of them pursued the same profession, nor were they expected to have the same intellectual ability or moral distinction. This diversity could put my argument about the coherence of Puranic discourse in jeopardy, but it does not, because the texts not only take infinite care to gloss over these differences but also make every conceivable effort to present *brāhmaṇas* as a single community. The *brāhmaṇa* to be revered and propitiated with gifts is never an individual but the representative of an entire social group, whatever be the internal differences. Puranic anxiety about the degenerate *brāhmaṇa* relates only to the future, the dreaded but hopefully remote *Kali* age. For the present they are one, or so the texts would have us believe. This common front is fostered by common interests. This is confirmed by the history of the *brāhmaṇas* in Bengal, as revealed in the other contemporary sources. When read in conjunction with these, it is impossible to overlook the Puranic attempt to foreground brahmanical interest. The many instances of self-contestation in the *Purāṇas* do indicate, among other things, collective authorship, but the brahmanical voices in them are diverse rather than discordant, because these are pulled together by the overriding motivation of self-interest.

Thus there was an intention to propagate the brahmanical values and establish brahmanical institutions which would guarantee the preservation of brahmanical interests. But were these the intentions of the authors of the *Purāṇas* or of the texts themselves? In the conventional understanding of the relationship between the author and the text, this question may appear absurd. But contemporary theories of literary criticism do make a distinction between the two. Indeed, Umberto Eco provides an ingenious answer to this question. He argues that the intention of the text plays an important role as a source of meaning which, while not being reducible to the pre-textual intention of the author, nonetheless operates as a constraint upon the free play of the intentions of the reader to make meaning of the text. Therefore Eco places the text between the 'empirical' and the 'model' author and the 'empirical' and the 'model' reader. The model author is not the empirical author who actually writes the text, but a textual strategy. The model reader is the one who reads the text as it is designed to be read and the empirical reader only makes conjectures about this designed reading. Placed between the two the text's intention is only revealed as the result of a conjecture on the part of the reader.[108]

But how can one prove that a conjecture about the intention of the text is appropriate or even tenable from among the potentially inexhaustible range of possible conjectures? Eco suggests that the only way is to 'check it upon the text as a coherent whole. . . . The internal textual coherence controls the otherwise uncontrollable drives of the reader.'[109] Thus between the model author and the model reader the empirical author's intention becomes largely redundant, because the finished text may differ from the author's original intention and in any case the author knows that he will be interpreted not according to his intentions but according to a complex strategy which involves the reader's competence in language—not just the grammatical rules, but the entire range of cultural conventions—as a social treasury. Eco has not completely abandoned the empirical author and has introduced the concept of the 'liminal' author who stands on the threshold between the intention of a given human being and the linguistic intention displayed by a textual strategy. On the threshold situation the liminal author is no longer an empirical person and not yet a mere text, but he obliges the words to set up a possible series of associations.[110] But Eco certainly prefers the intention of the text to that of both the author and the reader: 'Between the unattainable intention of the author and the arguable intention of the reader there is the transparent intention of the text, which disproves an untenable interpretation.'[111]

However, the intention of the text is transparent when it approximates the intended meaning of the author, as it is designed to be read. What is being referred to by meaning here is neither semantics or syntax of specific words or sentences, nor the subjective response of an individual reader to a text, but what the author means in what he says in the text. The fact that the author has a recognizable intention is derived from the reasonable supposition that any author must standardly be engaged in an intended act of communication in writing a text. Borrowing from J.L. Austin the concept of illocutionary force (what the author was doing in issuing a particular utterance, such as attacking or defending a particular line of argument, or criticizing or contributing to a particular tradition of discourse), Skinner has argued that the recovery of an author's illocutionary intentions is not merely a necessary condition of being able to interpret the meanings of his works, but is actually equivalent to a knowledge of the meanings. Taken in this specific sense, the author's intention is not altogether unattainable. Skinner suggests that to recover the illocutionary intention the reader should not focus on the text alone, but on the prevailing conventions governing the issues or themes with which the text is concerned, which in turn is conditioned by the author's mental world, and the world of his empirical beliefs.[112] The internal textual coherence of Eco is thus broadened to encompass the larger discourse. We are fortunate in possessing abundant evidence in texts other than those with which we are concerned about the empirical beliefs of the *brāhmaṇas* and it is not difficult to construct their mental world. The intentions of the Puranic texts of Bengal are transparent in that the illocutionary intentions of their authors have an unbroken continuity, and are therefore inescapable.

Thus the place of intention in the textual process is recognized, even though it may not be exactly the pre-textual intention of the author. The difference between the intention of the author and the text may appear too subtle for the historian (and the difference between the liminal author and the author's intention in the traditional sense of the term a mere quibbling with words), but theoretically it is possible to dissociate the two. Undoubtedly the author is not available to interpret his work, but the text remains. However, the strategy of the text embodies the intention of the model author. I have already done away with the notion of the empirical author for the Bengal *Purāṇas*; they were composed by the *brāhmaṇa varṇa*, by which I mean the collective identity of the community. Therefore we are effectively left with the textual strategy. But all the members of the community could not have actually written those texts.

Even if we assume for the sake of argument that the propagation of brahmanical interest was not the intention of those empirical authors, the texts themselves irrefutably point to it and repeat it with a tenacious regularity. This is the one coherent formulation that harnesses the many points of contestations, variations and displacements in these texts. Thus it would be nearly impossible for the model reader not to recognize it and make the right conjecture about it. The Bengal *Purāṇas* stand in the intersection between the long brahmanical tradition—the cultural repertoire of these texts—and the specific time and together they constitute their textual strategy. The meaning of the *Purāṇas* will have to be derived from the interaction of these two.

This is a perspective that both the authors and the listeners of these texts lacked. From my vantage point I see in the *Purāṇas* more than what their textual strategy could possibly contain. The *Purāṇas* consist of information which is purely provisional in nature. An attempt has been made to read in them an intention which, I believe, the texts intended. But I have also discovered in them a process which is my construction. I have picked up elements from the *Purāṇas* and arranged them in an order which is not necessarily the Puranic order and might have surprised their authors. The *Purāṇas* are, by their very nature, loosely organized and would have fallen apart but for the running thread of brahmanism. I have chosen to highlight this aspect, both its fixed and flexible structures in creative interplay with the indigenous elements, and, to borrow a phrase from Hayden White, 'emplotted'[113] all the other materials around it.

I have a certain advantage which the authors of the *Purāṇas* lacked, being both an observer of and a participant in the process that these texts had set in motion. I presume that I share with most Hindu Bengalis of my time the rules, sensibilities, and presuppositions of my culture. I may happen to know a little more about the Puranic texts than some others, but it is not this special knowledge but the 'tacit knowledge'[114] which I share with them that governed the choice of my plot structure. However much we may rationalize, such a choice is made by our cultural endowment, by a conflation of personal and public pasts. I have seen the brahmanization of Bengal primarily as a creative process—the creation of a regional tradition and a cultural identity. But this was gained at the cost of enforcing the oppressive institution of caste and all that follows from it. This regional tradition is my point of reference, the whole in relation to which the segments of this narrative have been arranged. But since the attempt is to trace the process rather than look at the product, I have laid much greater emphasis on the operational modalities of brahmanism in which the propagation and perpetuation of the *varṇāśramadharma*, symbolized by the figure of the *brāhmaṇa*, looms large. It was not the *Purāṇas* that saw any oppression in the system; that is my perception, as also the regional tradition which is the essential byproduct of the process.

V

It is difficult to trace the evolution of a process of interaction between various social groups spread over several centuries, particularly when the cultural matrix that governed the relationship of reciprocity, contestation and domination is not always sharply defined, and the primary evidence is limited to a single category of texts with an obvious bias. Therefore, all that I have attempted to do in this study is to follow the logic of cultural negotiation implicit in the Puranic records and on that basis construct a discernible pattern of the manner in which the negotiations were conducted. Indeed, the process led to a product—the establishment of the brahmanical social order, and a byproduct—the creation of a regional tradition.

The *Purāṇas* were composed with a view to revitalize the brahmanical social order which was seriously undermined during the early centuries of the Christian era. The *brāhmaṇas* attempted to meet this challenge by drawing people from the non-brahmanical fold into their sphere of influence. Thus an interaction between the brahmanical tradition and the many local traditions was initiated, which resulted in the creation of a composite, syncretic socio-religious system delineated in the *Purāṇas*. But the level of assimilation achieved in these *Purāṇas* must have proved inadequate to suit the needs of a particular region, for when, from the post-Gupta period, large-scale *brāhmaṇa* migrations started reaching areas peripheral to their influence, such as Bengal, a new category of regionally identifiable *Purāṇas* was composed, which offered a balance between the Puranic brahmanical tradition and the exclusively local traditions of a region.

The Bengal *Purāṇas* performed the delicate task of widening the scope of brahmanism to incorporate as many local cultural elements as could be accommodated and to induce as many local people to participate in this interactive process as was considered viable by the local *brāhmaṇa*s, without endangering their social supremacy. I have called the technique of accomplishing this task the Puranic process. The process involved repeated assertion of Vedic authority on the one hand and strong affirmation of local popular customs on the other. The Bengal *Purāṇas* attempted to make these two appear consistent.

I argue that the concept of great and little traditions, when viewed as elucidating a cultural continuum comprising ceaseless and multiple layers of negotiations between many strands of brahmanism and diverse local traditions, may serve as a workable taxonomic and heuristic device for an understanding of a fundamental civilizational process in India. Since we have only the brahmanical version of these negotiations, it may appear as if the *brāhmaṇas* could easily dictate terms. But in fact there are enough indications in both the Puranic texts and available ethnographic accounts to suggest that brahmanical prescriptions were frequently contested. Brahmanical acceptance of aspects of local cultures was also far from ungrudging. What was brahmanical in this assimilative synthesis was that *brāhmaṇas* assumed the initiative in the negotiations and that the cultural norms and objects created in the process had the stamp of brahmanical approval.

The *brāhmaṇas*, immigrants in Bengal, were themselves vulnerable. They were a heterogeneous group and had to depend on the generosity of the local people and the state for survival. Moreover, they had to contend with Buddhism which was already well entrenched in Bengal and enjoyed state patronage and local support. The *Purāṇas* therefore strove hard to gloss over the internal differentiation among the *brāhmaṇas*, projected Buddhism as brahmanism's external and deviant 'other', and urged kings and householders to make gifts and pay honorarium to *brāhmaṇas* for conducting sacrifices and other rituals on their behalf. Moreover the kings were instructed to follow the advice of the *brāhmaṇas*, exempt them from taxes, and above all, to grant them land and protect their property and privileges. This prescription appears to have had effect, for contemporary land-charters come remarkably close to the *Purāṇas* in endorsing the brahmanical world-view. Buddhism, under the influence of the *Tantras*, lost its distinct profile as an institutional religion in the eyes of the laity. While the Buddha was appropriated as an incarnation of Viṣṇu, lay followers were eventually subsumed within the expansive framework of brahmanism which emerged triumphant, at least in the ideological sphere, by the twelfth century.

In the Bengal *Purāṇas* we find adoption of the cult of the goddess to be the appropriate medium of assimilation of local cultural forms. The basic impulse behind the worship of the goddess is of non-Sanskritic, indigenous origin. She is usually a virgin and warrior deity, residing in inaccessible mountains and forests, and is propitiated with animal sacrifice. This goddess was embellished with brahmanical attributes. She was described as the repository of an abstract power or *śakti* that energized all beings. This justified her inclusion into the brahmanical pantheon without necessarily subverting her original identity or mode of worship. At the same time a special category called *mūlaprakṛti* or primordial nature was created, which made room for subsidiary or derived *prakṛtis*. Once the divisibility of *prakṛti* was established in principle, brahmanism could appropriate as many local goddesses as it perceived necessary as manifestations of the *mūlaprakṛti* with the help of a single theological justification. The Bengal *Purāṇas* carefully constructed a plausible genealogy of the goddess and attached her manifestations to the important male members of the brahmanical pantheon to ensure authenticity and a proper place for her in the divine hierarchy.

I submit that it is on the shared understanding of a variously represented common cult form that the earliest and still inarticulate foundation of Bengal's regional tradition was laid. In the absence of a central monitoring agency such as a hegemonic temple or an inclusive pilgrimage site, the cult of the regional goddesses, conceived and promoted by the Bengal *Purāṇas*, helped to create a common focus and integrate the highly stratified rural society of Bengal.

The *vrata*, a religious act of devotion and austerity undertaken for the fulfilment of specific desires, was the occasion for the dissemination of the brahmanical message. Brahmanism transformed the character of the indigenous *vrata*, drew upon its potential to arrange a gathering, widened its scope and inflated its number to make it as pervasive and frequent as possible. *Purāṇa* recitation was mandatory during these performances and this was the reason for such extraordinary emphasis on the *vrata* in the Bengal *Purāṇas*. Several *vratas* were observed in honour of specific goddesses, and the local legends connected with them were either restructured to make them fall in line with the archetypal brahmanical myth about the goddess, or were composed afresh. These *vratakathas* contained the quintessence of brahmanism which made the listeners familiar with the principal aspects of the *Purāṇas* in one sitting. Skilled professional narrators enjoyed the freedom and tacit brahmanical sanction to interpret the *Purāṇas* in accordance with the demands of a particular situation. Thus they could respond to local specificities and utilize the opportunity to make the brahmanical doctrines appear attractive and compatible with the local traditions.

The history of a process of negotiations that began with the arrival of the *brāhmaṇas* in Bengal and continued long after the completion of the composition of the Puranic texts does not lend itself easily to a tangible conclusion. I have attempted to unravel the intricacies of a dialogical process through which brahmanism in Bengal succeeded in creating a public realm where diverse local elements could converge on a common core through the mediation of a supra-local agency. Brahmanical culture, in creative interplay with the various local cultures, remoulded itself into a regional brahmanical culture, characterized by a range of common cultural denominators and a shared vocabulary of value later proved to be typical of Bengal. Hence, if there is any conclusion at all, it is that the Puranic synthesis in Bengal was a point of departure which generated cultural resources that enabled the little communities to transform themselves into a culturally identifiable regional community.

NOTES

1. Bibhuti Bhushan Bandyopadhyaya, *Ichāmatī*, in *Bibhūti Racanāvalī*, Vol. 3, Mitra O Ghosh Pvt. Ltd, Calcutta, 1388 BS, p. 87.
2. Anncharlott Eschmann, Hermann Kulke and Gaya Charan Tripathi (eds), 'Introduction', *The Cult of Jagannath and the Regional Tradition of Orissa*, Manohar, New Delhi, 1978, p. xiii.
3. *Ibid.*
4. Gregory Schopen, 'Archaeology and Protestant Presuppositions in the Study of Indian Buddhism', *History of Religions*, Vol. 31, No. 1, August 1991, pp. 1–23.
5. H.H. Wilson, *The Viṣṇu Purāṇa: A System of Hindu Mythology and Tradition* (with an introduction by R.C. Hazra), Punthi Pustak, Calcutta, 1961 (originally published in 1840).
6. 'Preface', *ibid.*, p. vi.
7. Wilson, *A Sketch of the Religious Sects of the Hindus*, Cosmo Publications, New Delhi, 1977 (originally published in 1861).
8. E.W. Hopkins, *The Religions of India*, Munshiram Manoharlal, Delhi, 1970 (originally published in 1855).
9. Wilson, 'Preface', *The Viṣṇu Purāṇa,* p. lvi.
10. M. Monier-Williams, *Hinduism*, Susil Gupta (India) Ltd, Calcutta, 1951 (originally published in 1877).
11. *Ibid.*, p. 60.
12. Monier-Williams, *Religious Thought and Life in India*, Oriental Books Reprint Corporation, New Delhi, 1974 (originally published in 1883).
13. *Ibid.*, p. 54.
14. A. Barth, *The Religions of India* (trans. Rev. J. Wood), The Chowkhamba Sanskrit Series Office, Varanasi, 1963 (originally published in 1881).
15. Wilkins, *Hindu Mythology: Vedic and Puranic*, Rupa and Co., Calcutta, 1979 (originally published in 1882).
16. F.E. Pargiter, *The Purāṇa Texts of the Dynasties of the Kali Age*, Deep Publications, Delhi, 1975 (originally published in 1913), 'Introduction', pp. v–xxxviii.

17. Ananda K. Coomaraswamy and Sister Nivedita, *Myths of the Hindus and Buddhists*, Dover Publications Inc., New York, 1967 (originally published in 1913).
18. R.G. Bhandarkar, *Vaiṣṇavism, Śaivism and Minor Religious Systems*, Indological Book House, Varanasi, 1965 (originally published in 1913).
19. Nicol Macnicol, *Indian Theism: From the Vedic to the Muhammadan Period*, Munshiram Manoharlal, Delhi, 1968 (originally published in 1915).
20. Macnicol writes that he had not had the advantage of consulting Bhandarkar's book while preparing his manuscript, *ibid.*, 'Preface', but his definition of theism itself is so amorphous (p. 9) that nearly everything could have been included under the title. In any case, it is inconceivable that the *Purāṇas* are left out of a discussion on Indian theism.
21. Hemchandra Raychaudhuri, *Materials for the Study of the Early History of the Vaishnava Sect*, Oriental Books Reprint Corporation, New Delhi, 1975 (originally published in 1920).
22. J.N. Farquhar, *An Outline of the Religious Literature of India*, Oxford University Press, London, 1920.
23. *Ibid.*, p. 136.
24. Sir Charles Eliot, *Hinduism and Buddhism: An Historical Sketch*, in three volumes, Routledge and Kegan Paul, London, 1921. Particularly, see the section on Hinduism in the second volume.
25. For instance, see Brian Brown, *The Wisdom of the Hindus*, Heritage Publishers, Delhi, 1973 (originally published in 1921), which contains selections from the *Ṛg Veda* to the writings of Swami Vivekananda, including the epics, the *Mahābhāṣya* of Patañjali and the compositions of the *bhakti* poets, but not from the *Purāṇa*s, or Lionel D. Barnett, *Hindu Gods and Heroes*, Ess Ess Publications, Delhi, 1977 (originally published in 1922), in which 'The Vedic Age' and 'The Age of the Brāhmaṇas' receive far greater attention than 'The Epics and Later'.
26. Haraprasad Shastri, 'The Maha-Puranas', *The Journal of the Bihar and Orissa Research Society*, Vol. 14, Part 3, September 1928, pp. 323–40.
27. V.R. Ramachandra Dikshitar, 'The Purāṇas: A Study', *Indian Historical Quarterly*, Vol. 8, No. 4, December 1932, pp. 747–67.
28. R.C. Hazra, *Studies in the Purāṇic Records on Hindu Rites and Customs*, Motilal Banarsidass, Delhi, 1975 (originally published in 1940).
29. Hazra, *Studies in the Upapurāṇas*, Vols I and II, Sanskrit College, Calcutta, 1958 and 1963.
30. R.C. Majumdar (ed.), *The History of Bengal*, Vol. I, University of Dacca, Dacca, 1963 (originally published in 1943).
31. Prabodh Chandra Bagchi, 'Religion', *ibid.*, pp. 394–428.
32. S.K. De, 'Sanskrit Literature', *ibid.*, pp. 290–373.
33. Niharranjan Ray, *Bāṅgālīr Itihāsa: Ādi Parva*, Pashchimbanga Nirak-

sharata Durikaran Samiti, Calcutta, 1980 (originally published in 1356 BS, 1949).
34. *Ibid.*, pp. 269–70, 316–22.
35. *Ibid.*, pp. 632–6, 648–63, 696–704.
36. *Ibid.*, pp. 622–3.
37. Majumdar, *History of Ancient Bengal*, G. Bharadwaj and Co. Calcutta, 1971, pp. 416–23.
38. *Ibid.*, pp. 486–90.
39. Rama Chatterjee, *Religion in Bengal during the Pāla and the Sena Times* (mainly on the basis of epigraphic and archaeological sources), Punthi Pustak, Calcutta, 1985.
40. P.G. Lalye, *Studies in Devī Bhāgavata*, Popular Prakashan, Bombay, 1973.
41. A.J. Rawal, *Indian Society, Religion and Mythology: A Study of the Brahma-Vaivartapurāṇa*, DK Publishers, Delhi, 1982.
42. Pushpendra Kumar, *Śakti Cult in Ancient India* (With special reference to the Purāṇic literature), Bharatiya Publishing House, Varanasi, 1974.
43. Cheever Mackenzie Brown, *God as Mother: A Feminine Theology in India* (An Historical and Theological Study of the *Brahmavaivarta Purāṇa*), Claude Stark and Company, Hartford, Vermont, 1974. In his excellent study of the theological visions of the goddess in the *Devībhāgavata Purāṇa*, Brown concedes that the text might have been written by one or a group of Bengali scholar(s) who migrated to Banaras and later to Ayodhya, and is on the whole a little more sensitive to the historical context than in his previous study of the *Brahmavaivarta-purāṇa*. C. Mackenzie Brown, *The Triumph of the Goddess: The Canonical Models and Theological Visions of the Devī-Bhāgavata Purāṇa*, Sri Satguru Publications (a division of Indian Book Centre), Delhi, 1992.
44. K.R. van Kooij, *Worship of the Goddess According to the Kālikāpurāṇa*, Part I (A Translation with an Introduction and Notes of Chapters 54–69), E.J. Brill, Leiden, 1972.
45. Eric Carlton, *Ideology and Social Order*, Verso, London, 1977, pp. 24–7.
46. Raymond Geuss, *The Idea of Critical Theory: Habermas and the Frankfurt School*, Cambridge University Press, Cambridge, 1981, p. 22.
47. This exact phrase has been used by Engels in his letter to Mehring 14 July 1893, K. Marx and F. Engels, *Selected Correspondence*, Moscow, 1965, p. 459, but throughout Marx's writings, the term ideology has been used in its critical and negative connotation, most notably in *Critique of Hegel's Philosophy of the State, German Ideology*, and *Grundrisse*, see Jorge Larrain, 'Ideology', in Tom Bottomore *et al.* (eds), *A Dictionary of Marxist Thought*, Basil Blackwell, Oxford, 1985, pp. 219–20.
48. Terry Eagleton, *Ideology: An Introduction*, Verso, London, 1991, pp. 14–15. For different approaches to the study of ideology, also see Jorge

Larrain, *The Concept of Ideology*, B.I. Publications, Bombay, 1980; John B. Thompson, *Studies in the Theory of Ideology*, Polity Press, Cambridge, 1984.

49. Clifford Geertz, 'Ideology as a Culture System', *The Interpretation of Cultures: Selected Essays*, Basic Books Inc., New York, 1973, p. 220.
50. Göran Therborn, *The Ideology of Power and the Power of Ideology*, Verso, London, 1980, p. 5, and *passim*; Alex Callinicos, *Marxism and Philosophy*, Clarendon Press, Oxford, 1983, p. 135; for a strong critique of the negative or prejorative meaning of ideology, also see Martin Seliger, *Ideology and Politics*, George Allen and Unwin, London, 1976, *passim*.
51. David Beetham, *The Legitimation of Power*, Macmillan Education Ltd, London, 1991, p. 101.
52. *Ibid*., pp. 104–7.
53. *Ibid*., p. 108.
54. Quintin Hoare and Geoffrey Noel Smith (ed. and trans.), *Selections from the Prison Notebooks of Antonio Gramsci*, International Publishers, New York, 1973.
55. For a lucid introduction to Gramsci's concept of cultural hegemony, see Roger Simon, *Gramsci's Political Thought: An Introduction*, Lawrence and Wishart, London, 1988.
56. Gwyn Williams, '*Egemonia* in the Thought of Antonio Gramsci: Some Notes on Interpretations', *Journal of the History of Ideas*, Vol. 21, No. 4, 1960, p. 587.
57. Joseph Femia, 'Hegemony and Consciousness in the Thought of Antonio Gramsci', *Political Studies*, Vol. 23, No. 1, 1975, p. 33. According to Femia, in Gramsci's formulation of hegemony, consent of subordinate groups is understood as essentially passive.
58. Walter L. Adamson, *Hegemony and Revolution: A Study of Antonio Gramsci's Political and Cultural Theory*, University of California Press, Berkeley, 1980, p. 174.
59. T.J. Jackson Lears, 'The Concept of Cultural Hegemony: Problems and Possibilities', *American Historical Review*, Vol. 90, No. 3, June 1985, p. 572.
60. Femia, 'Hegemony and Consciousness', p. 367.
61. *Ibid*., p. 38.
62. Perry Anderson, 'The Antinomies of Antonio Gramsci', *New Left Review*, No. 100, November 1976–January 1977, p. 76.
63. James C. Scott, *Weapons of the Weak: Everyday Forms of Peasant Resistance*, Oxford University Press, Delhi, 1990, p. 317.
64. Douglas Haynes and Gyan Prakash, 'Introduction: The Entanglement of Power and Resistance', in Douglas Haynes and Gyan Prakash (eds), *Contesting Power: Resistance and Everyday Social Relations in South Asia*, Oxford University Press, Delhi, 1991, p. 11.

65. Femia, 'Hegemony and Consciousness', pp. 29–48; Lears, 'The Concept of Cultural Hegemony', pp. 567–93; Adamson, *Hegemony and Revolution, passim.*
66. Since hegemony presumes the existence of a complex and highly stratified society, it is necessary to make a brief statement on the changing forms of social classes and their relationship with the state in early Bengal. Very little is known about the period preceding the establishment of Gupta rule towards the end of the fourth century AD, but available evidence indicates that north Bengal was for some time a part of the Mauryan empire and Bengal had most probably developed commercial ties with the Kuṣāṇa realm. Although agrarian settlements were the basis of the socio-economic structure of Bengal, traders and artisans had a formidable presence in society. The major cities of this period, Mahāsthāna, Koṭivarṣa, Tāmralipti, and Gaṅgānagara, were important trading or administrative centres.

    There is no dearth of information for the period between the fifth and twelfth centuries AD. Until about the seventh century traders and artisans retained their influence in society and politics. Representatives of their guilds, and others associated with commercial transactions, such as the chief scribe, were members of the municipal boards, who had to be notified of sale and purchase of land. It seems that they, along with highly placed state officials, the big landowners, the ritual specialists and those engaged in organizing and disseminating knowledge such as the Buddhist monks and the *brāhmaṇas,* were considered the elite. From the eighth century, with the establishment of the Pāla kingdom, the emphasis in economic activities gradually shifted from trade and business to agriculture. Consequently, as different categories of landowners from the extremely powerful *mahāsāmanta-mahāmāṇḍalikas* to the comparatively insignificant *mahattaras* and *kuṭumbins* came to occupy a pre-eminent position in society, the status of traders and artisans declined. Exchange of commodities and artisanal production continued, but primarily catered to the requirements of local markets. In the Bengal *Purāṇas* and *Smṛtis*, which began to be codified in this period, people engaged in these professions have been placed in the middle-ranking mixed castes among the *śūdras.*

    Under the Pālas, Bengal acquired for the first time a distinct political profile, which is reflected in the expansion of the state machinery. This included the representatives of the king and ordinary clerks, and the chief of the armed forces and anonymous foot-soldiers, with several intermediate positions between them. Most of the urban centres of this period, such as Karṇasuvarṇa, Vijayapura, and Rāmāvatī were administrative or military establishments. The various service classes such as barbers and washermen, sharecroppers and landless labourers, and even the lowliest *medāndhracaṇḍālas* have found mention in contemporary inscriptions and didactic literature. Thus we have a fairly accurate picture of the socio-economic structure of early medieval Bengal, stratified and hierarchized in both class and caste terms. Even though the social formation in which Gramsci visualized the operation of the concept of hegemony is not the one outlined above, it was complex enough to allow scope for a similar adjustment between the rulers and their ideologues for the purpose of exercising non-coercive control over the lower classes.

During the Gupta period traders and artisans received maximum patronage of the state. From the eighth century, with the decline in long-distance trade, the state came to be increasingly dependent on, and consequently closely identified with, the interests of the landowning *sāmantas*. The priestly and scholarly *brāhmaṇas*, who lived on professional fees and returns from tax-free land granted to them by the state and the landed aristocracy, predictably lent their support to their benefactors. The supremacy of the *brāhmaṇas* in society and their authority in affairs of state were unquestionably established by the seventh–eighth centuries. That it was the responsibility of society and the state to provide for the upkeep of the *brāhmaṇas* was also widely recognized. Their social position was further strengthened during the subsequent Sena-Varmaṇa period. In fact, these two royal dynasties founded their rule on a system of surplus expropriation which was sustained with the help of landed magnates and on a socio-political ideal which was legitimized by the *brāhmaṇa* intelligentsia. The nexus between the state, the big landowners, and the *brāhmaṇas* remained intact to the end of the twelfth century, thus offering the necessary condition for the exercise of hegemonic control over the other segments of society. For details, see Ray, *Bāṅgālīr Itihāsa*, pp. 218–66, 385–98.

67. Georges Duby, 'The Diffusion of Cultural Patterns in Feudal Society', *Past and Present*, No. 39, April 1968, p. 4.
68. Gramsci called all social relations and the organizations which embody them, other than the state, the civil society. Thus it is possible to conceive of civil society even in the pre-capitalist social formations. But the concept has got so inextricably enmeshed with the complex network of relations in capitalist societies that I have deliberately avoided the use of the term in the context of early medieval Bengal. However, this difference in detail does not abrogate the application of the concept of hegemony as a whole in the non-capitalist contexts.
69. Ainslie T. Embree, 'Brahmanical Ideology and Regional Identities', *Imagining India: Essays on Indian History*, Oxford University Press, Delhi, 1989, p. 10.
70. *Ibid*., pp. 12–18.
71. Nirmal Kumar Basu, *Hindu Samājer Gaḍan*, Visva-Bharati Granthalaya, Calcutta, 1356 BS, p. 51.
72. Ingalls, in a rather uncharacteristically simplistic description of the *brāh-*

maṇa tradition, makes this very significant point that 'there is a wide area where it is impossible to set a boundary between Brahman culture and the general culture of India', Daniel Ingalls, 'The Brahman Tradition', in Milton Singer (ed.), *Traditional India: Structure and Change*, Rawat Publications, Jaipur, 1975, p. 3.

73. See, for example, K.M. Shrimali, *Religion, Ideology and Society*, Presidential Address, Ancient India Section, Indian History Congress, 1988, distributed by Munshiram Manoharlal Publishers Pvt. Ltd, New Delhi, p. 30.
74. Shrimali has himself quoted Engels on this point, *ibid.*, p. 50, note 222.
75. Marc Bloch, for example, suggested that 'establishment of relations of cause and effect constitutes an instinctive need of our understanding', *The Historian's Craft*, Vintage Books, New York, 1953, p. 190, and E.H. Carr defined history as a selective system 'not only of cognitive, but of causal, orientations to reality', *What is History?* Penguin Books Ltd, Harmondsworth, 1965, p. 105. Both of them suggested a number of qualifications for determining the causal linkages but they maintained that this was an essential element in the process of the construction of history.
76. 'The cause of the event . . . means the thought in the mind of the person by whose agency the event came about: and this is not something other than the event, it is the inside of the event itself,' R.G. Collingwood, *The Idea of History*, Oxford University Press, Oxford, 1978, pp. 214–15. Carr similarly argues that the facts of history never come to us 'pure', because they are always refracted through the mind of the recorder, and therefore it is necessary for the historian to have an imaginative understanding of the minds of the people with whom he is dealing, *What is History?* pp. 22–4.
77. Quentin Skinner, 'Meaning and Understanding in the History of Ideas', *History and Theory*, Vol. 8, No. 1, 1969, pp. 39–40.
78. *Ibid.*, p. 49.
79. See *ibid.*, p. 48 also.
80. Joseph M. Kitagawa, 'Some Remarks on the Study of Sacred Texts', in Wendy D. O'Flaherty (ed.), *The Critical Study of Sacred Texts*, Berkeley Religious Studies Series, Berkeley, 1979, p. 234.
81. For a critique of post-modernist critical debate and its effects on history writing, see John E. Towes, 'Intellectual History After the Linguistic Turn: The Autonomy of Meaning and the Irreducibility of Experience', *The American Historical Review*, Vol. 92, No. 4, October 1987, pp. 879–907; and Gabrielle M. Spiegel, 'History, Historicism, and the Social Logic of the Text in the Middle Ages', *Speculum: A Journal of Medieval Studies*, Vol. 65, 1990, pp. 59–86. For a recent attempt to discover continuities between traditional and contemporary approaches to the study of history

and historical texts, see Ignacio Olabarri, ' "New" New History: *A Longue Duree* Structure', *History and Theory*, Vol. 34, No. 1, 1995, pp. 1–29.

82. Roland Barthes, 'The Death of the Author', in David Lodge (ed.), *Modern Criticism and Theory: A Reader*, Longman, London, 1988, p. 168.
83. *Ibid.*, p. 171.
84. *Ibid.*
85. Towes, 'Intellectual History', p. 886.
86. Spiegel, 'History, Historicism', p. 68.
87. For a discussion on the approaches to text in the writings of some of the 'semiotically oriented' historians, see Lloyd S. Krammer, 'Literature, Criticism and Historical Imagination: The Literary Challenge of Hayden White and Dominick LaCapra', in Lynn Hunt (ed.), *The New Cultural History*, University of California Press, Berkeley, 1989, pp. 97–128.
88. Dominick LaCapra, 'Rethinking Intellectual History and Reading Texts', in Dominick LaCapra and Steven L. Kaplan (eds), *Modern European Intellectual History: Reappraisals and New Perspectives*, Cornell University Press, Ithaca, 1982, pp. 58–9.
89. *Ibid.*, pp. 60–2.
90. *Ibid.*, p. 64.
91. J.R. de J. Jackson, *Historical Criticism and the Meaning of Texts*, Routledge, London and New York, 1989, p. 3, also see pp. 28–9.
92. Raymond Williams, *Marxism and Literature*, Oxford University Press, Oxford, 1977, pp. 37, 99, 165.
93. Fredric Jameson, *The Political Unconscious: Narrative as a Socially Symbolic Act*, Methuen and Co. Ltd, London, 1983, p. 81.
94. *Ibid.*, p. 10.
95. Tony Bennett, 'Texts in History: The Determinations of Readings and Their Texts', in Derek Attridge, Geoff Bennington, and Robert Young (eds), *Post-structuralism and the Question of History*, Cambridge University Press, Cambridge, 1987, pp. 68–9.
96. *Ibid.*, p. 69.
97. *Ibid.*, p. 70.
98. *Ibid.*, p. 75.
99. M.M. Bakhtin, *The Dialogic Imagination: Four Essays*, Caryl Emerson and Michael Holquist (trans.), University of Texas Press, Austin, 1981, p. 294.
100. Wendy Doniger O'Flaherty, *Asceticism and Eroticism in the Mythology of Śiva*, Oxford University Press, Delhi, 1975, pp. 316-18.
101. Jameson, *The Political Unconscious*, pp. 107–8.
102. LaCapra, 'Rethinking Intellectual History', p. 73.
103. Michel Foucault, 'What is an Author', *Language, Countermemory, Practice: Selected Essays and Interviews* (Donald F. Bouchard, ed.), Basil Blackwell, Oxford, 1977, p. 123.
104. *Ibid.*, p. 124.

105. Velcheru Narayana Rao, 'Texts without Authors and Authors without Texts', paper presented at the South Asia Conference, Madison, Wisconsin, 1983, cited in David Shulman, 'Toward a New Indian Poetics: Velcheru Narayana Rao and the Structure of Literary Revolutions', in David Shulman (ed.), *Syllables of Sky: Studies in South Indian Civilization*, Oxford University Press, Delhi, 1995, pp. 12–13.
106. Foucault, 'What is an Author', pp. 131–2.
107. See the detailed discussion on the grammatical irregularities in the *Devī Purāṇa*, Hazra, *Upapurāṇas*, Vol. II, pp. 94–143.
108. Umberto Eco, 'Overinterpreting Texts', in Umberto Eco *et al.*, *Interpretation and Overinterpretation*, Cambridge University Press, Cambridge, 1992, p. 65.
109. *Ibid.*, p. 65.
110. Eco, 'Between Author and Text', in *ibid.*, pp. 69–70.
111. *Ibid.*, p. 78.
112. Quentin Skinner, 'Motives, Intentions and Interpretation of Texts', in James Tully (ed.), *Meaning and Context: Quentin Skinner and his Critics*, Polity Press, Cambridge, 1988 (this essay was originally published in 1976), pp. 68–78. Recently Skinner has reiterated his position in 'On Meaning and Speech-acts', *ibid.*, pp. 260 ff.
113. Hayden White, 'The Historical Text as Literary Artifact', *Tropics of Discourse: Essays in Cultural Criticism*, Johns Hopkins University Press, Baltimore, 1978. By emplotment White means ' the encodation of the facts contained in the chronicle as components of specific kinds of plot structures' (p. 85). He argues that no given set of casually recorded historical events can in itself constitute a story: 'The events are made into a story by the suppression or subordination of certain of them and the highlighting of others, by characterization, motific repetition, variation of tone and point of view, alternative descriptive strategies, and the like—in short, all of the techniques that we would normally expect to find in the emplotment of a novel or a play' (p. 84).
114. For a discussion on the role of tacit knowledge in the social organization of knowledge for the reproduction and change of tradition, see Robert W. Heffner, *Hindu Javanese: Tengger Tradition and Islam*, Princeton University Press, Princeton, 1985, pp. 9–18, 267–70.

II

Texts and Traditions: The Bengal *Purāṇas*

I

In the older Vedic literature, the word *purāṇa* usually occurs in connection with *itihāsa* and originally it seems to have meant old narrative, without any special significance as to the character of the narrative.[1] By definition a *Purāṇa* is supposed to deal with five topics or *pañca-lakṣaṇa*: the creation of the universe, re-creation after destruction, genealogy, periods of time (with Manu as the primal ancestor), and the history of the solar and lunar dynasties. The *Purāṇas,* however, seldom adhere to this definition which suggests that if the definition was based on content the present *Purāṇas* must be thoroughly revised versions of either the originals or at least what they were ideally intended to be. The *Purāṇas* themselves state their number to be eighteen. Originally, like the epics, they were narrated by *sūtas* or bards. Thus in almost all the *Purāṇas* the *sūta* Lomaharṣaṇa or his son *souti* Ugraśravas appears as the narrator. However, according to the orthodox tradition as recorded in the *Atharva Veda* and *Bṛhadāraṇyaka Upaniṣad*, the *Purāṇas* were of divine origin.[2] Even the *Purāṇas* claim that the chief speaker gathered his information, through Vyāsa, from the creator himself; this has led to the speculation that originally there was a single *Purāṇa* from which the later ones were derived. Later the Puranic material was extensively revised by *brāhmaṇa* priests who continued to add matters of religious and social importance to the original core, so that the extant *Purāṇas* have practically turned into *Smṛti* codes.

The *Purāṇa* texts, as we have them now, were written at such divergent periods that it is difficult to fix their chronology with even an approximate degree of certainty. Although the word *purāṇa* occurs in the Vedic literature, their actual existence can be traced from the *Sūtra* period. Thus references to the *Purāṇas* in the *Dharma Sūtras* of Gautama and Āpastamba and in the *Mahābhārata* seem to indicate that they existed long before the Christian era.[3] R.C. Hazra has shown how different sections dealing with orthodox rites and customs in the manner of the *Smṛtis* were added on at widely varying periods.[4] Hazra's method may be described as a close comparative analysis of the Puranic material.[5]

This however is merely scratching the surface of the problem: in the great majority of the cases, the *Purāṇas* have not come down to us with only early incorporations; they have undergone continuous and substantial re-editions. This re-editing was done in three different ways: by adding fresh chapters, by substituting older ones with new, and by writing new works bearing old titles. But Hazra argues that all these practices had a common feature in that they came to have units belonging to different ages, and that fresh additions were not always fresh compositions but chapters and verses transferred from one to the other and from the *Smṛtis* to the *Purāṇas*.[6] He proves the truth of his assumption by comparing almost verse by verse the contents of the eighteen *Purāṇa*s and other *Smṛti* literature, and thus constructing a comparative chronology of the different sections of the *Purāṇas*.[7]

What necessitated this ceaseless revision? The *Purāṇas* themselves assert that in order to keep pace with social change such periodic revisions were required,[8] so that their importance as works of authority might not decrease. Thus the texts grew into encyclopaedic works by incorporating chapters not only on religious and social matters, but also on law, politics, poetics, grammar, medicine, music and sculpture.[9] If the *Purāṇas* were quoted as authority in Medhātithi's commentary on the *Manusmṛti* as early as the ninth century, and if by the medieval period they had acquired a status equal to that of the *Smṛtis*,[10] they obviously must be continuously revised to accommodate new social needs and incorporate matters which were traditionally considered to have been exclusively the province of the *Smṛti*s.

Hazra identified two main stages in the development of Puranic rites and customs. He argues that ancient India saw the rise of various religious movements which he classified as Vedic (*Śrauta* and *Smārta*), anti-Vedic (Buddhism, Jainism or Ājivikism), semi-Vedic (consisting primarily of Vaiṣṇavism, Śaivism and Brahmāism), and non-Vedic (Śāktism). The recognition of the authority of the *Vedas* and the superiority of the *brāhmaṇas* are the two essential constituents of the Vedic brahmanical religion. Hazra suggests that probably long before the time of Gautama Buddha there were protests against the brahmanical doctrines and with the rise and popularity of Buddhism, Jainism and Ājivikism these protests were institutionalized. Hazra adds that the original character of Vaiṣṇavism and Śaivism was also most probably non-brahmanical, as both the Pāñcarātras and the Pāśupatas were irreverent to the *varṇāśramadharma*. Besides, Vedic religion got into further trouble with the transfer of political authority from *kṣatriyas* to *śūdras* under the Nandas, Mauryas and probably the Āndhras.[11]

As a result the brahmanical social order was disrupted to such an extent that we perceive an obsessive fear of the Kali age in all the early *Purāṇas*. In that age people neglected the caste rules and the duties enjoined by the *Ṛg*, *Sām* and *Yajur Vedas*. The *brāhmaṇas* gave up the study of the *Vedas* and the performance of sacrifice and became wandering mendicants. They lost their social and ritual supremacy and people of all castes claimed equal status with them. The *kṣatriyas* and the *vaiśyas* were almost extinct and the prevailing caste was the *śūdra* who acquired political importance. Demoralization in the *Kali* age was particularly manifest in the conduct of women, who became wicked and self-willed, joined the Buddhist *saṅgha* in large numbers and disregarded the four stages of life (*caturāśrama*), one of the indispensable preconditions of the brahmanical way of living.[12]

Thus every aspect of the fabric of the ideal brahmanical social structure was undermined. Consequently, an attempt was made to re-establish the authority of the *Vedas*, the *varṇāśramadharma* and the moral order among women and lower castes. This attempt seems to have been made by two sections in two different ways: by orthodox *brāhmaṇas* who began to preach the performance of *gṛhya* rites through *smṛti* works and by the more numerous *Smārta*-Vaiṣṇavas and *Smārta*-Śaivas who introduced *Smṛti* materials into the *Mahābhārata* and *Purāṇas* for the propagation of their sectarian points of view against the heretical religions by upholding the brahmanical social order.[13]

Hazra locates the second stage in the development of Puranic rites and customs in the third to sixth centuries when Vedic religion was threatened by invaders from the north-west, identified by Hazra as Śakas, Yavanas, Bāhlīkas, and others. The early *Purāṇas* are eloquent about the evils brought about by these rulers.[14] From the brahmanical point of view the socio-political disruption created by the rule of such dynasties was somewhat remedied by the rise of the Guptas, but from about the beginning of the fifth century the Vaiṣṇavas and the Śaivas came under the influence of Tantrism. Hazra has shown how an analysis of the contents of the Pāñcarātra *Saṁhitās* and the Śaiva *Āgamas* decisively proves that the Tantric cult attained popularity at a very early period. The *Tantras* believed in equal opportunity of worship to all, including women and *śūdras,* and the ritual practices recommended by them were distinctly non-brahmanical in character. The spread of such ideas obviously affected the existing status of brahmanism in such an adverse manner that the authors of the *Purāṇas* could no longer remain satisfied with introducing only those *Smṛti* topics which came within the scope of the earlier *Smṛti Saṁhitās;* it was necessary to add chapters on popular religious practice such as *pūjā* (popular worship), *vrata* (vow), *homa* (sacrifice), *sandhyā* (daily rites), *utsarga* (gift), *tīrtha* (glorification of holy places), and *pratiṣṭhā* (consecration of images). These they tried to free from Tantric influence and infuse with Vedic rituals as far as practicable. The occurrence of these topics in the comparatively late *Purāṇas* and the way these *Purāṇas* denounce the scriptures that imbibed Tantric characteristics support this view.[15] However, the element of Vedic ritual in the *Purāṇas* diminished progressively with time and was increasingly replaced by popular material. In fact by the beginning of the ninth century some of these texts began to recognize even the Tantras as an authority on religious matters.[16]

This is how the Puranic tradition came into existence and eventually crystallized through a process of continuous revision. Tradition, however, is, as Heesterman puts it, 'the way society formulates and deals with the basic problems of human existence', and as these problems are insoluble, they are 'attacked, formulated and dealt with each time anew under a different aspect. Tradition therefore is and has to be bound up with the ever-shifting present. Hence the irritating flexibility and fluidity of tradition.'[17] Romila Thapar has also emphasized the aspect of 'contemporary requirements' as a determinant of tradition and consequently its renewability and the need to view it 'in its various phases'.[18] Even the eighteen *Purāṇas* must therefore have proved inadequate for brahmanical requirements at some point of time: another group of literature, belonging to the same genre but with a different emphasis, came into being. This was the *Upapurāṇas*, the formation of which, according to Hazra, should be placed approximately between AD 650 and 800.[19] This approximate date must not be taken to be the period of composition of the individual texts of the *Upapurāṇas*, for all of them could not have been written at the same time. Regarding their origin, the *Śiva-māhātmya Khaṇḍa* of the *Kūrma Purāṇa* records a tradition that the sages proclaimed the *Upapurāṇas* after listening to the eighteen *Purāṇas* from Vyāsa.[20] This tradition assigns to the *Upapurāṇas* a date following that of the *Purāṇas* and thus an inferior status. Indeed, the *Matsya Purāṇa* calls the *Upapurāṇas* mere sub-sections or supplements—*upabheda*—of the principal *Purāṇas*.[21] The *Upapurāṇas*, however, do not often look upon this characterization with the same respect as the principal or what were later called the *Mahāpurāṇas*, as a large number of the *Upapurāṇas* call themselves simply *Purāṇa* and do not try to attach themselves for the sake of authority to any of the principal *Purāṇas*.

The non-inclusion of the term *Upapurāṇa* in the *Amarakoṣa* which defines the *Purāṇa* in accordance with the *pañcalakṣaṇa*, and the mention of the titles of the eighteen *Purāṇas* in the *Viṣṇu* and *Mārkaṇḍeya Purāṇas* without any reference to the *Upapurāṇas*, shows that the group of eighteen *Purāṇas* had been formed before the *Upapurāṇas* came into existence.[22] After this group had been completed, there came into focus many sub-systems and offshoots of the Bhāgavata Pāñcarātra and Śaiva Pāśupata systems, either directly, or by identifying the local deities with one or the other of the prominent deities of the principal systems. In addition, there were also other independent systems such as Saura and Śākta, which began to rival those already established. These sub-systems also had their *Smārta* adherents who interpolated chapters in the *Purāṇas* already in vogue and in some cases wrote new and independent Puranic works in order to propagate their own views. But as the followers of the principal *Purāṇas* believed that there could be no *Purāṇa* beyond the eighteen, they were unwilling to assign to these new works a status equal to that of the *Mahāpurāṇas*. On the other hand, these new Puranic works had become too well known and popular to be completely ignored. The problem was resolved by maintaining the numerical rigidity of the eighteen 'original' *Purāṇas* and assigning to the *Upapurāṇas* an independent albeit subservient position.[23]

Following the tradition of the *Mahāpurāṇas,* orthodox opinion also tried to limit the number of *Upapurāṇas* to eighteen, but while in the enumeration of the *Purāṇas* there is almost complete agreement with regard to the titles, this is by no means the case with the *Upapurāṇas*. Hazra has compiled more than a hundred titles from the conflicting lists of *Purāṇas*, *Upapurāṇas* and other texts, most of which are no longer extant.[24]

One of the major differences between the *Mahāpurāṇas* and the *Upapurāṇas* is that the latter are regionally identifiable. It has been claimed that even some of the additions to the *Mahāpurāṇas* have a local tinge so that the *Brahma Purāṇa* may represent the Orissa version of the original work, just as the *Padma* may give that of Puṣkara, the *Agni* that of Gayā, the *Varāha* Mathurā, the *Vāmana* Thāneśvar, the *Kūrma* Vārānasī, and the *Matsya* that of the *brāhmaṇas* of the Narmadā.[25] In their entirety, however, none of these texts can be said to have been composed in these regions and although they partially reflect local interests, it is impossible to precisely locate their place of origin. The *Upapurāṇas*, on the other hand, are so overwhelmingly regional in their concerns, catering as they did to local requirements, that they can be identified with a particular locale with a fair degree of certainty. Thus Hazra points out that most of the available *Upapurāṇas* were written in the areas peripheral to the brahmanical sphere of influence. For example the *Viṣṇudharmottara* was composed in Kashmir,[26] the *Kālikā* in Assam,[27] and a great majority in Bengal. Another curious fact to which Hazra draws our attention is that while the *Mahāpurāṇas*, because of their status, have undergone innumerable modifications, the *Upapurāṇas* have remained comparatively free from later redactors. They are thus better preserved and among those extant there are some which are much older than many of the *Mahāpurāṇas*.[28]

While even the *Mahāpurāṇas* did not entirely adhere to the classical definition of the *pañcalakṣaṇa*, the *Upapurāṇas*, which were almost exclusively adapted to suit the requirements of local cults and the religious needs of sects other than those already assimilated in the *Mahāpurāṇas*, are never in consequence particularly concerned about these five topics. They especially neglect the genealogies of kings and sages, and even when they mention them, it is only to acquire a stamp of antiquity, and nothing is said about the dynasties of the *Kali* age. What the *Upapurāṇas* do discuss are the religion and social structure, particularly the assimilation of divergent values and practices through the reformulation of certain fundamental principles of brahmanism in the peripheral areas. They tell us about mythology, idol-worship, theism and pantheism, festivals and ceremonies, ethics and superstitions; in short, everything that constitutes the domain of religion in the widest possible sense.[29]

In deciding the date and provenance of these texts, I have accepted the suggestions of R.C. Hazra,[30] which are as follows:

Name	*Locale*	*Date*
Brahmavaivarta Purāṇa	unspecifiable, but so completely remodelled in Bengal, that it can be taken to represent unambiguously the specific regional context of Bengal[31]	tenth to sixteenth century[31]
Kriyāyogasāra (claims to belong to the *Padma Purāṇa*)[32]	Bengal[33]	not later than eleventh century[34]
Bṛhannāradīya Purāṇa	eastern Orissa or western Bengal (recognized by the early *Smṛti* writers of Bengal)[35]	750 to 900[36]
Devī Purāṇa	Bengal[37]	cannot be placed later than 850[38]
Kālikā Purāṇa	either in Assam or that part of Bengal which is adjacent to Assam[39]	tenth or the first half of the eleventh century[40]
Mahābhāgavata Purāṇa	eastern Bengal, close to Assam[41]	tenth or eleventh century, not later than twelfth century[42]
Devībhāgavata Purāṇa	Bengal[43]	eleventh or twelfth century[44]
Bṛhaddharma Purāṇa	Bengal[45]	latter half of the thirteenth century[46]

It may be observed that except the *Brahmavaivarta*, all the other *Purāṇas* were written between the eighth and thirteenth centuries, and most between the eleventh and twelfth, so that the Bengal *Purāṇas* may be broadly labelled as the product of the early medieval period. Indeed, by the late fifteenth century Puranic digests such as the *Purāṇa-sarvasva* were being compiled in Bengal[47] which shows that by then these *Purāṇas* had been accepted as normative texts and it was considered worthwhile to produce abridged compendia containing their essential message.

Numerous manuscripts of these *Purāṇas* are preserved in various collections all over the country and abroad. Sanskritists have prepared 'complete texts' from the extant manuscripts and all except the *Devī Purāṇa*, are available in more than one printed edition. I have used the Vaṅgavāsī Press (Calcutta) editions for this study for the following reasons.

Only the Vaṅgavāsī Press has published all the *Purāṇas* which have been identified as belonging to Bengal. For those *Purāṇas* which have several editions, the difference between the Vaṅgavāsī and the others is minor and, for my purpose, negligible. Besides, the texts of the Vaṅgavāsī editions are fuller in comparison with the others, except in the case of the *Devībhāgavata*. The chief editions of the *Devībhāgavata* are those published by the Saṁskṛta-pustakālaya (Benares), Veṅkaṭeśvara Press (Bombay), and Vaṅgavāsī Press. All have practically the same text, but the Saṁskṛta-pustakālaya edition contains a *Devībhāgavata-māhātmya* in five chapters, which extols the virtue of the text and the merits of reading it, not very different from what the text claims in bits and pieces throughout and more elaborately towards the end. The *Brahmavaivarta* was published by the Sarasvatī Press (Calcutta), Vaṅgavāsī Press, Veṅkaṭeśvara Press, and Anandāśrama Press (Poona), and the *Kriyāyogasāra* by the Vaṅgavāsī and Veṅkaṭeśvara. These editions are not substantially different from one another. The Veṅkaṭeśvara and the Vaṅgavāsī editions of the *Kālikā* contain 93 and 90 chapters respectively; in the Veṅkaṭeśvara some chapters of the Vaṅgavāsī are split into two, but the text in both the editions is more or less the same. The Gujarati Printing Press (Bombay) and the Vaṅgavāsī editions of the *Mahābhāgavata* have the same number of chapters, but the latter at times contains some additional verses. The *Bṛhaddharma* has been published by the Vaṅgavāsī Press and the Asiatic Society of Bengal (Calcutta). These two editions differ in readings on numerous occasions but, more importantly, the last seven chapters of the *Uttarakhaṇḍa*, contained in the Vaṅgavāsī edition, are missing in the latter. These chapters, however, must not be taken as spurious, for they occur in almost all the manuscripts of the text. The *Bṛhannāradīya* has also been published by the Vaṅgavāsī Press and the Asiatic Society of Bengal, but in the latter edition the verses have not always been correctly numbered. For the above reasons and for the sake of uniformity, I have relied on the Vaṅgavāsī editions. Recently, Navabhārata Publishers (Calcutta) have started reprinting the Vaṅgavāsī edition of some of these *Purāṇas*, re-edited by Śrījīva Nyāyatīrtha, which I have taken into account. But the re-editing only corrects the editorial lapses of the previous edition.

All the translations from the original texts are my own.

II

The *Purāṇas* were thus an instrument for the propagation of brahmanical ideals of social reconstruction and sectarian interests, a medium for the absorption of local cults and associated practices, and a vehicle for popular instruction on norms governing everyday existence. They combined scripture and the social codes of the *Smṛtis* in a manner acceptable to most people. In short the *Purāṇas* performed the delicate task of operating simultaneously at several levels, widening their scope to accommodate local elements as much as possible and involve as many people as permissible without compromising their principal objective of establishing the brahmanical social order. In the process at times they even ran the risk of appearing to be self-contradictory, without losing their essential unity. The technique of accomplishing this task may be described as the Puranic process. The cumulative effect of the composition of the *Purāṇas* and the popularization of Puranic religion was the construction of the somewhat imprecise category of what is popularly known today as Hinduism. The impressions of two English civil servants of the early twentieth century regarding what constitutes Hinduism will serve to illustrate the point. L.S.S. O'Malley, who edited the *Bengal District Gazetteer* in 1912, describes Hinduism thus:

> Considered purely as a religion . . . Hinduism may be described as a conglomerate of cults and creeds. The non-Aryan tribes who were admitted to the fold of Hinduism and the Hindus of Aryan descent reacted on one another, the former adopting the rites and customs of their conquerors, while the latter assimilated some of their less civilized cults and incorporated in their system the objects of popular devotion. The higher and the lower forms of religion still coexist side by side. At one end of the scale, therefore, is the cultured monotheist or the eclectic pantheist for whom no mysticism is too subtle. Pantheists actually form a small minority, and the great majority of Hindus are theists believing in one personal god, though they are at the same time polytheistic in their religious observances. At the bottom of the scale is a great multitude of people in a low state of religious development, some of whom have scarcely risen above mere fetishism.[48]

J.H. Hutton, who directed the Census of India in 1931, is more particular:

> If the view be accepted that the Hindu religion has its origin in pre-vedic times and that in its later form it is the result of the reaction by the religion of the

country to the intrusive beliefs of northern invaders, many features of Hinduism will become at once more comprehensible, while the very striking difference between the religion of the Rigveda and that of the Dharmashastras will seem natural . . . . This would explain Hinduism's amalgamation with and absorption of local cults and its excessive multiformity, and is, moreover, in entire accordance with the manner in which it still spreads at the present day, absorbing tribal religions by virtue of its social prestige, by identification of local gods with its own, by the experimental resort to Hindu priests, and by the social promotion of pagan chiefs who are provided with suitable mythological pedigrees. Into the early Hindu beliefs spread in this manner the religion of the Rigveda has been imposed and absorbed.[49]

Despite the explicit acceptance of the theory of Aryan invasion and the expression of such value judgements on high and low forms of religion that offend our understanding and sensibility, both men captured the essence of Puranic Hinduism with remarkable accuracy. Although neither of them actually uses the term *Purāṇa*, what they have in mind is evidently the Puranic religion, and in fact, in Hutton's description one can read *Purāṇa* for 'the Dharmashastras' without the slightest difficulty, particularly when both these categories of texts were the product of the same process and, in a sense, complementary to each other. Both O'Malley and Hutton view Puranic Hinduism as the result of continuous interaction between Vedic and indigenous forms of religion, ever enlarging its scope and authority. Hence what Hutton calls the 'multiformity' and O'Malley the 'scale' of Puranic Hinduism.

Puranic Hinduism is thus by its very nature and motivation assimilative rather than exclusive; it accommodates rather than rejects. Irawati Karve refers to this cultural process when she characterizes 'Indian society' as a 'culture by accretion'.[50] According to her, in this scheme of things, all phenomena are relative and the world of the humans as well as the gods share in this relativity. Even human values, including good and evil, have no absolute reality and have equal rights to prevail. This is the source and justification of the continuous and simultaneous existence of a multiplicity of behavioural patterns within society. This conception of the universe is, however, so relativistic that it would lead to anarchy—to a society in which there could be no agencies of control other than the individual's own. Yet, Karve points out, Indian society is governed by fairly strict rules of behaviour, the rules of the castes. She suggests that the coexistence of groups with different norms of behaviour and the structures governing the behaviour of coexisting caste groups are explained by the theory of *Brahman* and *karma* respectively.[51] *Brahman*, the Absolute, is above all attributes and thus all other categories belong to the world of partial truths; and *karma*, as the positive and negative worth of human action, is the regulating agency of such actions of the members of the caste groups. *Brahman*, as the origin of all beings, legitimates their right to exist while *karma* ensures that they exist within the societal framework of discipline and authority. Together they impart the requisite stability to the fluid structure of Puranic Hinduism and the society it presupposes.

All the *Purāṇas* acknowledge the centrality of *Brahman* and the caste-oriented social structure governed by *karma* as axiomatic in their assimilative synthesis. Within the framework of these given constants however, each *Purāṇa* has the manipulative space to choose a divine manifestation of the *Brahman* as the Absolute, depending on its sectarian leaning. Once this preliminary choice has been exercised, it can then gather around its chosen deity all the diverse elements it seeks to accommodate. At the philosophical level, a perfect example of the multiplicity of the Puranic ideation is evident in this passage from the *Brahmavaivarta*, which recognizes Kṛṣṇa as the supreme deity:

> The Lord has nine forms .... The six schools each assign to him a form, the Vaiṣṇavas and the *Vedas* one each, and the *Purāṇas* one also. In this way he has nine forms. The *Nyāya* and Śaṅkara call him indescribable; the *Vaiśeṣika* calls him eternal; the *Sāṁkhya* calls him the luminous everlasting god; the *Mīmāṁsā* calls him the form of all; the *Vedānta*, the cause of all; the *Pātañjala*, the infinite; the *Vedas*, the essence of truth; the *Purāṇas*, self-willed; and the devotees [visualize him as one] having an external form.[52]

Such adjustments in the realm of thought offered justification for accommodation at a more mundane level.

The interesting point about the characterization of the views of the various schools in this passage is that they are not merely imprecise, but are also unrelated to the specific philosophical positions of these different schools. Clearly therefore, these names have been thrown in, not to suggest that they have literally described Kṛṣṇa in this way, but to invoke figurative support for the recognition of Kṛṣṇa by the brahmanical authority. Brahmanical authority accepts Kṛṣṇa; therefore the entire tradition that it upholds must also accept him, no matter whether or not they actually do so. This is the principal mechanism of the Puranic process, and nowhere is it more visibly evident than in their handling of the *Vedas* as symbolic authority.

Brian K. Smith has identified two criteria as constitutive of Hinduism: (1) recognition of the authority of the *brāhmaṇa* class, and

(2) recognition of the authority of the *Vedas*.[53] He says that the *brāhmaṇas* are recognized as religious authorities because of their intimate and special relationship with the *Vedas*, the authoritative texts of Hinduism. The *brāhmaṇas* are the traditional bearers, purveyors, interpreters and protectors of the *Vedas*. The authority of the *brāhmaṇa* is dependent on the authority of the *Veda* and the *Veda* exists because of the traditional function the *brāhmaṇa* has assumed for its preservation. Thus Smith arrives at the following definition of Hinduism: '*Hinduism is the religion of those humans who create, perpetuate and transform traditions with legitimizing reference to the authority of the Veda.*'[54]

The importance of the *Vedas* in Hinduism arises out of what Heesterman calls the inescapable need for ultimate authority.[55] The great paradox of Hinduism is however that, although the religion is inextricably tied to the legitimizing authority of the *Vedas*, in post-Vedic times the subject matter of the *Vedas* was and is largely unknown to those who define themselves in relation to it, primarily because the lost their doctrinal and practical relevance to post-Vedic Hinduism. Thus the *Vedas* became notional authority and came to represent not the Vedic texts, but rather the totality of knowledge. And yet they are preserved in all their pristine sanctity. This paradox is resolved if we look upon the *Vedas* as the key to ultimate legitimation whereby even if they are unrelated to current ways of human life and society, one still has to come to terms with them. Smith has defined Hinduism as a process and not an essence. Consequently, it is not the essential content of the *Vedas* that is of defining import so much as the particular relationships Hindus establish with them.[56]

As for Giorgio Bonazzoli here too canon is either a body of works that are accepted as normative, or a complex of rules through which one can establish whether a work should be accepted as authentic and normative or not.[57] The *Vedas* provide the touchstone by which the *brāhmaṇas* decide which texts should be considered normative and authentic. In other words, the principal rule for determining canon in Hinduism is whether or not it is Vedic. The method through which later texts such as the *Smṛtis* and the *Purāṇas* are related to the symbolic authority of the *Vedas* has been characterized by Smith as 'strategies for orthodoxy'.[58] Smith has observed a variety of such strategies for constituting post-Vedic texts, doctrines and practices as Vedic: 'Reflection (this *is* the Veda); restatement (this is *based on* the Veda); reduction (this is the *simplified* Veda); reproduction (this *enlarges* the Veda); recapitulation (this is the *condensed essence* of the Veda); and even reversal (the Veda is *based on this*).'[59] Smith points out that by representing through deployment of these strategies, new texts, doctrines and practices as connected in some way or another to the *Vedas*, change is both legitimized and denied, and continuity is both affirmed and stretched.[60] It is immaterial whether the texts, doctrines and practices thus legitimized have in reality anything to do with the *Vedas*. Only the assertion of the *brāhmaṇas* counts.

This is a universal process in the living tradition of Hinduism and all post-Vedic texts raised to the status of normative and authentic have claimed connection with the *Vedas*, in one form or another. This method of seeking legitimation is particularly relevant for those texts which were composed with a view to introducing brahmanical socio-religious practices in the peripheral areas where the Vedic tradition had not sufficiently penetrated, such as the *Upapurāṇas* of Bengal, especially when, to begin with, they were combining the functions of both the *Purāṇas* and the *Smṛtis* in these areas. Thus it can be observed that all the techniques listed by Smith of establishing Puranic authority as derived from the *Vedas* were operative in the Bengal *Purāṇas*.[61] I will cite a selected few instances from among innumerable such examples.

In the *Devībhāgavata*, Nārāyaṇa, in response to Nārada's question on the sources of *dharma*, says that *Śruti* and *Smṛti* are the two eyes of the God and *Purāṇa* is his heart. None other than that which has been determined in these three is *dharma*.[62] Similarly, in enumerating the fruits of reading the *Rādhākavaca*, typical of the *Purāṇas*, the *Brahmavaivarta* declares that the result obtained from reading this *kavaca* is the same as that of studying the four *Vedas*.[63] Even if these instances cannot be described as exactly what Smith calls 'reflection' (this is the *Veda*), they certainly indicate an attempt to establish equivalence between the *Vedas* and the *Purāṇas*.

But the major thrust of the Bengal *Purāṇas* was to try and establish themselves as the 'restatement' (this is based on the *Veda*). Thus the *Brahmavaivarta* says, blessed are the four *Vedas* because everything is being done according to their prescription. All the *śāstras* are derived from the *Vedas*, and the *Purāṇas* also reside in them.[64] Instances of 'reduction' (this is the simplified *Veda*) are also numerous. For example, the *Devībhāgavata* states that in all the *manvantaras*, in every *Dvāpara* age, Vedavyāsa composes the *Purāṇas* in order to protect *dharma*. It is Viṣṇu, in the form of Vyāsa, who divides the one *Veda* into four units for the good of the universe. Knowing that in the *Kali* age the *brāhmaṇas* will be stupid and short-lived and thus unable to understand the

Vedas, he composes the holy *Purāṇa Saṁhitās* in each *manvantara*. In particular, women, *śūdras* and unworthy *brāhmaṇas* are debarred from listening to the *Vedas*. It is for their benefit that the *Purāṇas* have been written.[65] The same idea has been indirectly expressed in the *Bṛhannāradīya Purāṇa*.[66] Here the *sūta* says that there are two ways to salvation, *kriyāyoga* and *jñānayoga*. The long passage seems to indicate that only *yogīs*[67] can aspire to salvation through the practice of *jñānayoga* which involves, among other things, reading the *Upaniṣads* and repeated recitation of *praṇava* and the twelve-, eight- or five-lettered *mantras*,[68] presumably because this is difficult, while the common people (*mānava*) should follow the simpler procedure of *kriyāyoga* which demands fasting, listening to the *Purāṇas*, and worshipping Viṣṇu with flowers.[69] The implication is that Vedic scholarship, which is evidently superior, is for the select few and the *Purāṇas*, which are in consonance with the *Vedas* but much simpler, are for the masses.

The Bengal *Purāṇas* also claim that they are 'reproduction' (which enlarges the *Vedas*). Hence the *Devībhāgavata* declares that the half verse signifying the central thesis of the *Vedas* that the Devī had told the infant Viṣṇu lying on the banyan leaf during the great deluge, is the key to the *Devībhāgavata*. As an explanation of that key, Brahmā composed the *Bhāgavataśāstra* in myriads of verses. Vyāsa summarized it into the *Devībhāgavata Purāṇa* consisting of eighteen thousand verses distributed over twelve sections, for the enlightenment of his son Śuka.[70] But the easiest way of linking the Puranic corpus with the Vedic was to claim that the *Purāṇas* were the 'recapitulation' (the condensed essence) of the *Vedas*. Thus the *Bṛhannāradīya* begins with the statement that for the good of the universe Vedavyāsa has included the quintessence of the entire *Vedavedāṅgaśāstra* in the *Purāṇas*.[71] The *Devībhāgavata* ends with the same assertion and adds that the result of reading and listening to the *Devībhāgavata* is comparable to the fruits of reading the *Vedas*.[72] 'Reversal' (the *Veda* is based on this) is an attitude which was difficult for the Bengal *Purāṇas* to adopt, because they were operative in an area where the Vedic authority itself was not sufficiently well grounded and it would have been presumptuous to challenge it from the point of view of brahmanical interests which were uppermost in the *Purāṇas*. Nevertheless there are certain indirect suggestions, such as in the *Brahmavaivarta*, where Pārvatī tells Kṛṣṇa that she is known to him, but she does not know him, for who can know him? Not even the *Vedas* themselves, nor the Vedic scholar or interpreter,[73] which implies certain superiority over the *Vedas*. But the Bengal *Purāṇas* have permitted themselves to go only that far.

On the whole the message of the Bengal *Purāṇas* is that they are the confirming elaboration of the *Vedas*. They enshrine the essential wisdom of the *Vedas* but simplify, condense or enlarge it, depending on the needs of the common people, as perceived by the authors. The attempt was to forge a legitimating relationship with the *Vedas* in every possible way. The *brāhmaṇas* composed these *Purāṇas*, but, though necessary, this in itself was not sufficient to establish their status as normative texts, unless they also ensured the sanctifying support of the *Vedas*. The Bengal *Purāṇas* therefore subtly insist on continuity with the Vedic tradition. Innumerable statements such as 'it is a great secret even in the *Vedas* and the *Purāṇas*'[74] or 'the four *Vedas* and the *Purāṇas* assert that Mādhava is submissive to Rādhā',[75] are meant to confirm this continuity through endless repetition. Hazra cites an unidentified passage which captures the essence of this continuity in its fullest elaboration,

> That twice-born (Brāhmaṇa), who knows the four Vedas with the Aṅgas (supplementary sciences) and the Upaniṣads, should not be (regarded as) proficient unless he thoroughly knows the Purāṇas. He should reinforce the Vedas with the Itihāsa and the Purāṇa. The Vedas is [sic] afraid of him who is deficient in traditional knowledge (thinking) 'He will hurt me'.[76]

V.S. Agrawala interprets the crucial line *itihāsa-purāṇābhyāṁ vedaṁ samupabṛṁhayet* as 'the metaphysical truth of the Vedas is intended to be demonstrated in the Itihāsa-Purāṇa manner'.[77] The *Brahmavaivarta* closely follows this sentiment when it states, 'because of your ignorance you could not know him who has been ascertained in all the *Vedas*, *Purāṇas* and *itihāsa* as Sarveśa'.[78] The *Purāṇas* generally, and the Bengal *Purāṇas* in particular, have incorporated nearly everything that they considered relevant in the name of the *Vedas*, irrespective of the fact that often the matter had nothing to do with the *Vedas* or was even contradictory to them. The *Purāṇas* scrupulously maintained the cover of the *Vedas* not so much out of deference to them (which of course was given) as for their own survival. Thus when the *Brahmavaivarta* says that copulation during the day is prohibited in the *Vedas*,[79] it merely signifies that for some reason the *Brahmavaivarta* or more precisely the *brāhmaṇas* who were introducing brahmanism to Bengal through *Brahmavaivarta* and such other *Purāṇas,* consider this act to be improper (or at least wish this to be considered improper) and were merely calling on the *Vedas* to witness that they endorse this stricture. We have noted that the *Vedas* had lost practical and doctrinal relevance for post-Vedic Hinduism, and reformulations were necessary to match altered circumstances. This reformulation required the sanction of authority that could be passed off as legitimate. As Kosambi points out, the *Vedas* did not help in this, since 'their text was fixed by immutable routine', and no word or syllable could be changed. 'The *Smṛtis*, once written, could not be tampered with soon, or the conflict would mean loss of all authority. This meant raising new texts [the *Purāṇas*] to venerable antiquity in some plausible fashion which would allow revision of their contents.'[80]

This process has been characterized by Mackenzie Brown as shift from sound to image of the holy word. 'Earlier, the "*artha* tradition" was subservient to the "*śabda* tradition", the narrative history facilitating and ensuring the success of the mantra.' In the *Purāṇas*, narrative became 'the primary holy word, reincorporating the old mantric tradition under new terms. The saving story itself has taken on the character of mantric efficacy though not the mantric immutability.'[81] Once the emphasis was on meaning, it was no longer immutable, for meaning is always contextual and seldom, if ever, universal. Hence it can explain, absorb, recreate itself, and construct its own meaning, depending on the necessity. This flexibility of the *Purāṇas* helped brahmanism to penetrate peripheral areas such as Bengal, and write its own texts to suit its innovations. Thus R.C. Majumdar is mistaken in assuming a sharp distinction between the Vedic and Puranic traditions in Bengal when he claims that the former was 'replaced' by the latter.[82] Bengal was never a stronghold of Vedic religion, and if the *Vedas* in Majumdar's understanding stand for brahmanism, this was carried forward in the Bengal *Purāṇas* in their notional acknowledgement and glorification of the Vedic authority.

III

Invoking the authority of the *Vedas* for legitimation is common to all the *Purāṇas*, even if the tendency to emphasize the Vedic–Puranic continuum is somewhat stronger in the Bengal variants, because the need for such authentication was greater in their case. The Bengal *Purāṇas* were, however, unique in that they were consistent in their effort to assimilate local customs in the religious and cultural ethos and practices they attempted to introduce. We have already noticed that even some of the *Mahāpurāṇas* exhibit traces of regional interest,[83] but none so completely and systematically as the Bengal *Purāṇas* which even evolved general principles to justify such inclusions. It is the continuation of the same Puranic process of appropriating Vedic authority for Puranic innovations that they now extended to local customs, assimilating them by according them the sanction of brahmanical authority. The ideal gamut of Puranic Hinduism thus consists of the *Vedas* at one end of the continuum and the regional/popular at the other, with the *Purāṇas* mediating between these two poles. This process reached its culmination in the Bengal *Purāṇas*.

If the *Purāṇas* represent an attempt to extend brahmanical Hinduism into areas hitherto beyond its pale and to broaden its base of mass following, then assimilation of local customs in some form or other would appear inevitable. Indeed, in the epics, which are justly considered proto-Puranic, this tendency is already discernible. For example, the *Mahābhārata* says that the seven illustrious Citraśikhaṇḍin Ṛṣis unanimously proclaimed on Mount Meru an excellent *śāstra* which was made consistent with the four *Vedas* and was meant for the populace, that it consisted of one lakh verses and dealt with the best *lokadharma* (religious duties of the people).[84] What is called *lokadharma* in the *Mahābhārata* gets transformed into *ācāra* in the more explicit Bengal *Purāṇas*. *Ācāra* is a difficult term to translate. According to H.H. Wilson it means an established rule of conduct or custom or practice,[85] but in this context it also connotes specificity of region, a given time, and consonance with one's stage and order of life. Thus when the *Bṛhannāradīya Purāṇa* declares,

> One who dedicates himself to devotion to Hari without transgressing one's own *ācāra*, goes to the abode of Viṣṇu which is witnessed by the gods. O powerful sage, one who, while performing the duties declared by the *Vedas* and required by one's own order of life, engages himself in meditation on Hari, attains final beatitude. *Dharma* arises from *ācāra* and Acyuta is the lord of *dharma*. Being worshipped by one who is engaged in [the practice of] *ācāra* enjoined by one's stage of life, Hari gives everything. He who, though being a master of *Vedānta* together with the *aṅgas*, falls from his own *ācāra*, is known as *patita* (degraded), because he is outside [of *śrauta* and *smārta*] work. He who deviates from *ācāra* enjoined by his own order of life, is said to be *patita*, no matter whether he is given to devotion to Hari or engaged in meditation on him. O best of *brāhmaṇas*, neither the *Vedas*, nor devotion to Hari or Maheśvara can sanctify that confounded fool (*mūḍha*) who has fallen from *ācāra*. Neither visit to holy places, nor residence in sacred *tīrthas*, nor performance of various sacrifices saves one who has discarded *ācāra*. Heaven is attained by [the practice of] *ācāra*, happiness is attained by [the practice of] *ācāra*, and final release is attained by [the practice of] *ācāra*. What is not attained by [the practice of] *ācāra*?[86]

there is no uncertainty about its meaning. One must perform the duties prescribed by the *Vedas*, one must demonstrate unswerving allegiance to the Puranic high gods Hari or Maheśvara—because these are inescapable preconditions of *dharma*. But even these are rendered ineffective if one deviates from the prevailing custom, for 'in all sacred scriptures *ācāra* has the first consideration. *Dharma* arises from *ācāra*.'[87] Thus *ācāra* receives priority over all the other components of brahmanism. In these instances of course the term *ācāra* has been used in its widest possible sense which includes the duties of both *āśrama* and *varṇa*.

Yet *ācāra* also has specific implications. This is borne out by the use of such compounds as *vṛddhācāra*[88] [practice of old men] in the same text and the meaning gets even more specific when the text says, 'complete *ācāra* [is to be practised] in [one's] own village, half [of the same] on the way (during a journey), O best of sages, there is no rule in times of illness as well as in great distress'.[89] Finally, the *Purāṇa* sheds all ambiguity and asserts, 'all the *varṇas* should perform the practices of the village (*grāmācāra*) prevailing at the time, in consonance with the ways of the *Smṛtis*',[90] and again 'the practices of different countries/regions (*deśācāra*) should be followed by the people born in those particular countries. Otherwise one is known as *patita* and is excluded from all *dharma*.'[91] The *Bṛhannāradīya* further proclaims, 'correct statement is truth. Those who are committed to *dharma* will tell the truth which is not contrary to *dharma*. Therefore the statements wise men make after proper consideration of time and space (*deśakālādivijñānāt*), which are in conformity with their own *dharma*, are truth.'[92] Thus it does not hesitate to designate even truth context specific and hence conditional, such is the magnitude of importance placed on the local customs. The *Devībhāgavata* virtually equates *dharma* with *ācāra*. It says, 'the *dharma* of the village, of the caste, of the country and of the lineage has to be performed by all men. Under no circumstances can these be disregarded. Men of improper conduct (*durācāraḥ*) are condemned by the people.'[93]

Apart from *ācāra*, the other expression the authors of the Bengal *Purāṇas* frequently use is *laukika* (literally, popular). The *Bṛhaddharma* apportions *dharma* into two fundamental categories, *vaidika* and *laukika*.[94] At times they seem to be independent of and yet consistent with one another: 'adultery in women is prohibited in the *Vedas* and in popular custom',[95] and at other times they form a continuum: 'as milk cannot be separated from its whiteness . . . similarly there is no distinction between Rādhā and Mādhava in popular perception, in the *Vedas* and in the *Purāṇas*'.[96] Significantly, however, the *Brahmavaivarta* asserts that in case of a conflict between these two sources of *dharma*, popular custom must prevail. When the gods told Pārvatī, 'whatever is approved in the *Vedas* is *dharma* and anything to the contrary is the absence of *dharma*', Pārvatī replied, 'who can decide on the basis of the *Vedas* alone? Popular custom is more powerful than the *Vedas*. Hence who can renounce popular custom?'[97]

Indeed, these *Purāṇas* were written and revised over a long period of time and the contributions of multiple authors (presumably without absolute unanimity of opinion in every matter of detail), introduced confusing inconsistencies in them. Therefore, a stray statement should not be taken to represent the central argument of a *Purāṇa*. At the same time, upholding popular custom appears a dominant attitude in these texts, and since it runs as a continuous thread throughout the corpus of the Bengal *Purāṇas*, its importance in the Puranic scheme of things is inescapable. Besides, the *Vedas* constitute such an infallible symbol of sacred authority for the *Purāṇas* that if defied (by none other than Pārvatī) even once in favour of popular custom, this significant deviation should be given due weightage.

An example of how inconspicuously popular customs were incorporated into brahmanical proceedings will make our meaning clear. In connection with the preparation of the planting of the *Indradhvaja*, the *Devī Purāṇa* instructs that amidst the beating of drums, the music of prostitutes, the blowing of conch-shells and recitation of the *Vedas* by *brāhmaṇas* the pole should be taken to its hoisting place.[98] The songs of prostitutes must have been a popular custom that was retained. So long as the primary prerequisite of brahmanism—the recitation of the *Vedas* by *brāhmaṇas*—was fulfilled, it did not object to entertaining a prevailing social custom. On the contrary, the practice was conferred with the seal of brahmanical authority by declaring it a part of the ritual scheme. It did not upset the Puranic arrangement and at the same time it assured the local participants of continuity with existing usage, thus paving the way for an easier acceptance of the innovations the *Purāṇas* were attempting to introduce. This has indeed been the basic technique of the *Purāṇas* in their assimilative process. To select an instance at random, the *Devībhāgavata* decrees that after defecation a *brāhmaṇa* should cleanse himself with white coloured clay and the other *varṇas* with red, yellow and black coloured clay respectively, or whatever the practice in whichever country.[99] In the same context it later adds that in all matters one should act according to considerations of place, time, material and capability.[100] Purification of the body is an essential requirement. Provided that is performed, the *Purāṇas* are willing, even eager, to accommodate local constraints.

IV

In view of this explicitly stated Puranic need to acknowledge, and if possible, integrate regional specificities, we are confronted with an important question—the status of a normative text, such as the *Purāṇas*, in a given region. The question assumes greater significance if this happens to be a region where brahmanism came comparatively late. The question has been partly addressed, although inadvertently, in a major contemporary debate over the interpretation of the *Purāṇas*, in the journal *Purāṇa*. The crux of the discussion has been the possibility and significance of critical editions of *Smṛti* literature. Since a consensus exists on later human elaborations of the 'original' *Purāṇasaṁhitā* by Vyāsa, the issue was: if a Puranic text is edited along the lines laid down by V.S. Sukthankar for the critical edition of the *Mahābhārata*, will it violate the Puranic spirit? Madeleine Biardeau identified the problem as that of the application of methods of textual criticism to what is basically an oral tradition, only subsequently written down. She has pointed out that in India the spoken word is more revered than the written and more importantly, a further distinction is drawn between *Śruti* (revealed truth which is immutable) and *Smṛti* (remembered truth which is of human composition). She believes that the latter acquires normative value only through its acceptance by the *brāhmaṇas* of a particular region and it is this locus of authority at the local level which, Biardeau feels, Sukthankar has betrayed by trying to establish the earliest text and then treat it as authoritative by virtue of a supposed greater chronological proximity to Vyāsa. She claims that this method introduced the historical dimension into the realm of myth, where it cannot exist.[101] V.M. Bedekar defended Sukthankar's method against Biardeau's criticism on the grounds that once a tradition is committed to writing, it becomes liable to textual criticism, regardless of its origin and the text so constituted is simply a text which may or may not have been at sometime some place accepted as authoritative.[102] A.S. Gupta joined issue by attempting to find a compromise between the rigour of Sukthankar and the scepticism of Biardeau. He views the entire Puranic corpus as a whole, the individual *Purāṇas* representing its different parts. He believes that it is possible to characterize each of these parts according to its sectarian preference, and that it is then open to an editor to treat additions that do not accord with that bias as spurious and relegate them to the notes and appendices.[103]

The details of this debate are irrelevant here. Our concern is only an interesting by-product of this debate, namely the mechanism of the acceptability of such a text in a given region, particularly when such a region is not exposed to brahmanical influence for a long time. Biardeau has expressed her opinion unequivocally, 'any epic or purāṇic story is true if the local brahmins recognize it as part of their beliefs. These brahmins . . . warrant the authority of the local tradition because they are well-versed in the *śruti*. And if such a story is recognized by the brahmins, it is attributed to Vyāsa . . . regardless of whether it is mentioned in any of the classical text[s].'[104] Biardeau illustrates this with an experience she had with the Śrīvaiṣṇava pundits of the Simhacalam *pāṭhśālā* in Andhra. These pundits admitted to her that the local *Purāṇa*, relating the story of Narasiṁha and Prahlāda, was quite different from the *Skanda Purāṇa* version of the same story, though this was its avowed source. In spite of this difference the local *Purāṇa* was authoritative for them, since it expressed their belief and was therefore considered superior to any other local version. Biardeau believes that there is no contradiction here since the Śrīvaiṣṇava *brāhmaṇas* saw themselves as the source of the authoritativeness of the story without caring too much for the origin of the tradition in time or place.[105]

For my purpose this is an important point, the significance of which became lost in the debate. It should be noted, however, that both the critics of Biardeau concede her this point in passing. Bedekar, for example, does not deny that the traditional locus of authority was the local *brāhmaṇas* who expressed their 'subjective preference'[106] and Gupta does not dismiss the later revisions as mere corruptions, for he recognizes in them 'the desire on the part of the redactors to revise the text of the Purāṇas from time to time and keep them in line with the current religious and social ideas of their times'.[107] Thus, an inevitable condition of the *Purāṇas* seems to be to remain 'in line'. But in line with what? And who was to determine this?

Coburn rightly points out that the intention of the *Purāṇas* is to 'make the original Vedic truth available in a contemporarily relevant way'.[108] Whatever be the connotation of the term 'Vedic truth', I suggest that the contemporaneity relates both to time and place because it is absurd to assume homogeneity of tradition for so large and diverse a country as India, and that too in the early medieval period. How is this conformity with time and place ensured? For an answer to this it will be useful to recall Mackenzie Brown's discussion on the general role of the *Purāṇas* in Hindu culture.[109] He argues that for the Hindus, truth is something to be discovered by each generation. But it is merely a rediscovery, because truth was fully revealed in the past by the *Vedas*. The *Purāṇas* are primarily a means of rediscovering and reinterpreting truth. They are also an easier form of truth adapted to contemporary conditions: 'Implicit in this is the notion that mankind can accept only a modified form of truth. It is assumed that the revisions are made in complete harmony of the truth contained in the *śruti*. The Purāṇas represent then an interpretation or clarification of the *śruti*, revealing the eternal, immutable truth in a comprehensible form to all mankind in his changing, historical situation.'[110]

Since Gupta, Coburn, and Brown are concerned with the 'revisions' of the *Mahāpurāṇas*, their explanations naturally rest with changing needs of the 'time', although Brown is more inclusive in the sense that 'historical situation' takes into cognizance the specificities of both time and space. They however establish the principle behind the process through which new materials were incorporated in the *Purāṇas*. However, in the case of the *Upapurāṇas*, which were evidently composed with a view to transmitting brahmanical religion in the peripheral areas, the demands of place must have received precedence over the ever-changing needs of time. Otherwise it is difficult to explain the repeated insistence of the Bengal *Purāṇas* on the necessity to honour *deśācāra–lokācāra*. Most of these local customs must have been inconsistent with current brahmanical tradition. And yet the essential features of both of these had to be retained in some form for them to appear acceptable to both. Moreover, these customs, even within a region, are hardly expected to be uniform. Thus, which of the available choices is to be accepted and incorporated in the local *Purāṇas*, with suitable modifications, if need be?

In matters of such adjustments the judgement of the local *brāhmaṇas* was crucial. For instance, in the example cited by Biardeau, there was the brahmanical version of the Narasiṁha–Prahlāda story contained in the *Skanda Purāṇa* and many local variants. For the Śrīvaiṣṇava *brāhmaṇas*, however, the version of the local *Purāṇa* was considered superior to all others. Biardeau explains this in terms of the 'authoritativeness' of the local *brāhmaṇas*.[111] This is indeed true, but how in the first place did the version of the local *Purāṇa* come about, if it was neither an exact reproduction of the *Skanda Purāṇa*, nor in complete agreement with the many local variants? It is reasonable to speculate that the particular version adopted or constructed for the local *Sthala-purāṇa* was one which carried the fundamentals of brahmanism and at the same time appeared least disruptive to local traditions, in the assessment of the contemporary local *brāhmaṇas*. Brown suggests that the Puranic redactions reflect the 'reality as perceived and interpreted' by the redactors.[112] This reality of the redactors, or in the case of the Bengal *Purāṇas* the authors and redactors, consisted of mediating and striking a delicate balance between brahmanical authority and the local beliefs, customs and traditions. Thus a text could attain normative status in a given region only if it was approved, and in many instances written and rewritten, by the local *brāhmaṇas* and not by an impersonal brahmanical authority. The Bengal *Purāṇas* often repeat epic and Puranic stories, but this in itself was considered insufficient. These had to be retold with a minor or pronounced revision, depending on the necessity as perceived by the local *brāhmaṇas*. This is an integral part of the Puranic process and a particularly important one for the Bengal *Purāṇas*.

An example will serve to illustrate the foregoing discussion on the general aspects of this process. The following is an account of the circumstances leading to the introduction of Puranic religion in Kāmarūpa, as described in the *Kālikā Purāṇa*:

In the olden days, everyone started going to heaven after taking bath in the water of the river, drinking its water and worshipping the deities in the *mahāpīṭha* of Kāmarūpa. Yama, out of deference to Pārvatī, could not stop them, nor could he take them to his abode. Yama went to Vidhātā and complained that people in Kāmarūpa, after performing the ritual worship, are becoming attendants of Śiva and Kāmākhyā; he has no jurisdiction there. Brahmā, Yama and Viṣṇu went to Śiva and requested him to make an arrangement so that Yama retains his power over the people of Kāmarūpa. Śiva then asked Ugratārā and his Gaṇas to drive away the people from Kāmarūpa. When everybody, including the members of the four *varṇas* and even the *brāhmaṇas* started being thrown out, the sage Vasiṣṭha, residing at Sandhyācala, became extremely angry. When Ugratārā and the Gaṇas came to him he said, 'I am an ascetic and you want to evict me too? Therefore you, along with the Mātṛs, will be worshipped in the *vāma* way. Since your Pramathas are roaming around in a state of drunkenness like the Mlecchas, this Kāmarūpa *kṣetra* will be treated as Mleccha country. I am a sage versed in the *Vedas*. Mahādeva, like an inconsiderate Mleccha, tried to evict me. He should therefore stay here bedecked with ash and bones, loved by the Mlecchas. Let the Kāmarūpa *kṣetra* be infested with the Mlecchas. Till such time as Viṣṇu himself comes to this place, it will remain like this. The

Tantras which express the glory of Kāmarūpa will be rare.' Thus in the Kāmarūpa *pīṭha*—the abode of the gods—the gods became Mlecchas, Ugratārā became *vāmā* and Mahādeva came to be devoted to the Mlecchas. Within a moment Kāmarūpa became devoid of the *Vedas* and the four *varṇas*. Although after Viṣṇu came here, Kāmarūpa was released of its curse and began to deliver the fruits of worship again, gods and men remained oblivious of its former glory.[113]

The story admits two significant facts about Kāmarūpa: that it was devoid of the *Vedas* and the *brāhmaṇas*, and here the gods and the goddesses were worshipped in the left (*vāma*) way, prior to the penetration of brahmanical ideology. The story also reluctantly concedes that the process of brahmanization was not completely successful in the land of the Mlecchas, despite the cleansing presence of Viṣṇu. Indeed, the story is remarkably soft on the prevailing form of religion in Kāmarūpa, as it has no word of censure for a non-brahmanical mode of worship which made one defy death, and it is only through the obviously artificial device of a curse that the text creates an excuse to condemn the anti-Vedic religious practice of outcastes and finds a way of introducing Viṣṇu. This story is symptomatic of the message of the *Purāṇas*, particularly for Bengal.

Van Kooij suggests that the long exposition in the *Kālikā Purāṇa* on ceremonies and rites for the worship of the goddess in her various forms has no intrinsic unity and appears to describe multiple cults and practices current at the time of the final redaction of the text. However, it is possible to draw a distinction between two categories. One category closely corresponds to the general kind of worship, called common worship (*sāmānyapūjā*) in the text, as practised in large parts of India not only among the Śāktas but also among the Vaiṣṇavas and the Śaivas. The second category consists of more special rituals in which orgiastic rites play a major role and which were kept outside the brahmanical sphere for a long time.[114] Since this first category of common ritual covers by far the greater part of the fragment on Devī worship, Kooij takes this to be a clear indication of the author's concern to have the deities of Kāmarūpa propitiated by a cult form concordant with the contemporary brahmanical practice commonly accepted[115] in large parts of India and thus to draw the frontierland of Kāmarūpa into the Hindu fold.

For the second category, dealing with the religious forms of the heterodox communities, the author/redactor of the *Kālikā Purāṇa* is willing to allow much less room. This tradition is called the left method, or *vāmabhāva*, that is, unorthodox behaviour characterized by the use of intoxicating liquors and meat, and the stress laid on sexual intercourse.[116] It is centred on the ambivalent goddess Tripura-bhairavī, but significantly the *Kālikā Purāṇa* recommends this form of worship for brahmanical deities as well, when they assume their heterodox left shapes.[117] Although the *Kālikā Purāṇa* sanctions these forms of worship, it warns that a person practising them does not absolve himself from his debts to seers, gods, ancestors, men and demons. In other words, it does not release him from the obligation to carry out the five great sacrifices, which is the right method or *dakṣiṇabhāva*, i.e., the orthodox behaviour.[118] At the same time the text recognizes that orthodox behaviour may be an obstacle for an individual who wants to attain final emancipation through the *vāma* method.[119] Moreover, the results that can be obtained by the left worshipper, such as happiness, political power, radiating body, ability to seduce women, the freedom to move about like wind, and the power to control ghosts and wild animals[120] are so alluring that compared to these, absolving one's debts pales into insignificance. Thus it seems that the *Kālikā Purāṇa* does accept the *vāmabhāva* and actually instructs that some goddesses should be honoured with both forms of worship,[121] although, as Kooij rightly points out, it remains true to the general tendency of the *Purāṇas* to stimulate the performance of the brahmanical rituals and sacrifices, and attendance to the established forms of social behaviour.[122] Indeed, the text adds that those who worship through the left method do not fulfil the expectations of the other gods, while the right worshipper satisfies everybody. That is why the right method is the better of the two.[123]

Juxtaposed in this way the text of the *Kālikā Purāṇa*, as indeed the entire corpus of the Bengal *Purāṇas*, would appear hopelessly ambivalent. But seen in the context of the strength of local traditions, on the one hand, and the intentions of the purveyors of brahmanical religion, on the other, much of these inconsistencies are resolved. The brahmanical religion had to be introduced in eastern India, where strong local traditions had developed, as unobtrusively as possible and as much in keeping with the local customs as practicable. In other words, the strategy was necessarily assimilation rather than imposition. Thus while not a single *Mahāpurāṇa* ever dealt exhaustively or even principally with Śakti worship, although chapters on the praise and worship of the different forms of Devī are found in some of them, the foremost preoccupation of the Bengal *Purāṇas* is the goddess, primarily because the tradition of goddess worship and its associated customs were so firmly entrenched in that region.

There was no problem in principle with the goddess cult as such, because she was already integrated with the brahmanical religion. It was the near-indispensable corollary of goddess worship, the *Tantras*, which was problematic since it disregarded the infallibility of the *Vedas* and the authority of the *brāhmaṇas*. Hazra shows that until about the beginning of the ninth century Tantric elements were systematically purged from Puranic literature and it was only later that the *Purāṇas* started recognizing the *Tantras* as a result of 'the great spread of Tantricism among the people',[124] when it was no longer possible to ignore them. Even here the Bengal *Purāṇas* had to declare that only those *Tantras* could be accepted as authoritative that were not in conflict with the *Vedas*.[125] This obviously is a face-saving device, for the *Tantras* are, by their very nature, external to the Vedic tradition and all that it signifies. However, the authors of the Bengal *Purāṇas* had to arrive at an intermediate position where accommodation of local customs would not render the features of brahmanical religion unrecognizable, nor the assertion of brahmanical religion constitute such a threat to the local people that they would be persuaded to reject the entire package.

All theories of social change through cultural contact accept this process as the primary prerequisite of transmission of new ideas and order. Strasser and Randall have made a summary of the findings of those who have studied similar assimilative processes in a number of contexts:

> In the receiving system we will always find willingness to accept and to integrate innovations in varying degrees . . . . The acceptance or rejection of an innovation *may*, first, depend upon congruence conditions. An innovation is congruent if it shows some similarity to the existing cultural elements with which the public is confident. Secondly, the acceptance may depend upon the condition of compatibility that is met if the innovation fits into the new social context without incurring destructive consequences.[126]

It is precisely to satisfy the conditions of congruence and compatibility that the Bengal *Purāṇas* laid down separate provisions for separate groups of people. For instance, the *Kālikā Purāṇa* says that the *brāhmaṇa* should offer intoxicating liquor to the goddess only once, and that too through others, while it imposes no such restriction on *śūdras*.[127] The use of liquor was indispensable in *vāma* worship and had to be complied with by every member of society. But once this insuperable requirement is fulfilled, the text is willing to make exceptions for different social groups. Liquor plays no part in the brahmanical *dakṣiṇa* method of worship, recommended by the *Purāṇas* to be superior to the *vāma*, and therefore, for the *brāhmaṇa* outsider, the offering of liquor is merely the ritual acknowledgement of a local practice. But local *śūdras* were presumably used to this form of worship and hence allowed to continue with their custom without hasty attempts at peremptory reforms.[128] The consideration of minimum compatibility must have weighed heavily with these *Purāṇas*, for the *Kālikā Purāṇa*, despite its obvious preference for the brahmanical way of worship, suggests that when one goes to a *pīṭha* outside of one's region one should worship according to the advice of the local people; that one should follow the prevailing form of worship in a particular region, such as in Oḍra or in Pāñcāla.[129] In other words, the text concedes that so long as the locally prevailing form of worship is not brought in line with the brahmanical way, it is safer not to disturb the existing equilibrium.

V

I may add that this process of tacit adjustment with the local traditions through the mediation of some legitimating authority is in no way unique to the Bengal *Purāṇas*. This technique is indeed central to the complex process of reformulation and transmission of tradition throughout India in all periods. It is only when the *Purāṇas* themselves became firmly established as the source of brahmanical authority at a later date, that the *Vedas* were replaced by them as the effective symbol of mobilization, particularly at the village level. Two examples illustrate this point.

D.F. Pocock, in his study of beliefs and practices in a village in central Gujarat, has discussed a popular local text in vernacular (as contrasted with the high-profile texts such as the Bengal *Purāṇas*, which were written in Sanskrit and contributed to the creation of a regional great tradition) on 'The Most Glorious History of the Goddess'.[130] A typical book of this genre—thick, cheaply bound, printed in large characters and containing garish illustrations—it lays down the rules for animal sacrifice by the *brāhmaṇas*. In Pocock's translation the passage reads:

> Although many Brahmans are meat eaters they should not openly make flesh offerings. This prohibition derives from the first part of Kalika-purana. That we are to understand that this custom is directed to Kshatriya appears from that section called Sharadatilaka which says (here follow two lines of Sanskrit which the editor glosses in Gujarati). Pure Brahman who follow the ordinances should

make pure (*sātvik*) offerings for, when they have abandoned offerings associated with violence, these then become for other castes the highest.[131]

There is no such section as 'Sharadatilaka' in the *Kālikā Purāṇa*, but chapter 65 of the *Purāṇa* is entitled *Śāradātantra* which of course does not even mention the topic of sacrifice. The fact of the matter is that Gujaraṭ is a predominantly vegetarian area and the anxiety of the norm-setters to ensure that at least the *brāhmaṇas* do not violate this custom is understandable. What is interesting is that it invokes a spurious Puranic authority to enforce this prohibition.

The other example is directly related to Bengal and is a Bengali genre of local-level texts known as the *pāñcālī*, composed in simple verse usually in praise of a local deity. Cheaply produced thin books, these are read aloud before an audience on an appointed day of the week or month as a part of a ritual practised by women (*vrata-kathā*). The book that I discuss here is an intriguing variant of this genre.[132] Impressively printed and bound, it spreads over 285 pages which suggests that it was not meant to be recited in one sitting. Entitled *Śrī Śrī Padma Purāṇa vā Viṣaharir Pāñcālī*, it begins in typically Puranic Sanskrit with the *dhyāna* and eulogy of Manasā, Gaṇeśa, the Daśāvatāra and a number of goddesses. Then follows the central narrative in Bengali, a retelling of the Cānd Sadāgar–Lakhindar story of the popular *Manasāmaṅgala* of medieval Bengal, without innovation but suitably prefaced with stereotyped descriptions of the beginning of creation, the origin of the *Vedas* and time, the churning of the ocean, the sacrifice of Dakṣa, the burning of Madana and so on, episodes utterly irrelevant to the content of the story and not mentioned at all in the original *Manasāmaṅgala*. From the style of the composition and choice of topics and their arrangement, it is clear that the author of this text was claiming for his work the status of a *Purāṇa*. It indeed says as much: 'Says *dvija* Vaṁśīdāsa that one who listens to this [text] will be absolved of his sins, as it is stated in the Vālmīki *Purāṇa*.'[133]

In both these instances the point to note is that either a *Purāṇa* is quoted (whether or not the citation is authentic), or the style of the *Purāṇas* is simulated (however transparent the simulation may be) to acquire authority for a local custom or to elevate the status of a primarily regional deity in the divine hierarchy—a process already initiated by the *Purāṇas*. Besides, in both these instances the *Purāṇas* perform the same function for these local-level vernacular texts as the *Vedas* did for the *Purāṇas*. In orthodox Hinduism ultimate authority does stem from the *Vedas*, but in course of transmission, as the *Vedas* get further removed from the actual context, the symbol of authority gets transformed and, in the case of Bengal, it is largely appropriated by the epic-Puranic tradition, particularly in what may be termed the secondary elaboration of brahmanical authority at the grassroots level, for in the Bengal *Purāṇas* and in the vernacular rendering of the epics, the conditions of congruence and compatibility with regional requirements were already partially fulfilled, and their general acceptability paved the way for greater absorption in the future.

NOTES

1. M.A. Mehendale, 'The Purāṇas', in R.C. Majumdar (ed.), *The Classical Age*, Bharatiya Vidya Bhavan, Bombay, 1970, pp. 291–2.
2. *Ibid.*, pp. 296–7.
3. *Ibid.*, p. 294.
4. Hazra, *Purāṇic Records*, Chapters II to IV are devoted to working out the chronology of the *Mahāpurāṇas.*
5. For an example of how Hazra arrived at his dating of the Puranic corpus as a whole, see *ibid.*, pp. 5–6.
6. *Ibid.*, pp. 6–7.
7. In Appendix I Hazra has drawn up an exhaustive list of the numerous verses quoted by the *Nibandha* writers from the various *Purāṇas. Ibid.*, pp. 265–335.
8. *kālenāgrahaṇaṁ dṛṣṭvā purāṇasya tato nṛpa I*
   vyāsa-rūpam ahaṁ kṛtvā saṁhārāmi yuge yuge II
   This is what the fish says to Manu in *Matsya Purāṇa*, 53. 8–9, cited in *ibid.*, p. 6, note 38.
9. Hazra provides a glimpse of the assortment of topics dealt with in the *Purāṇas*:

   > glorification of one or more of the sectarian deities like Brahmā, Viṣṇu and Śiva, . . . numerous chapters on new myths and legends, and multifarious topics concerning religion and society, for instance, duties of the different castes and orders of life, sacraments, customs in general, eatables and non-eatables, duties of women, funeral rites and ceremonies, impurity on birth and death, sins, penances and expiations, purification of things, names and descriptions of hells, results of good and bad deeds, . . . pacification of unfavourable planets, donations of various types, dedication of wells, tanks and gardens, worship, devotional vows . . . places of pilgrimage, consecration of temples and images of gods, initiation, and various mystic rites and practices.

   R.C. Hazra, 'The Purāṇa', in S.K. De, U.N. Ghosal, A. D. Pusalkar and R.C. Hazra (eds), *The Cultural Heritage of India*, Vol. II, The Ramakrishna Mission Institute of Culture, Calcutta, 1969, pp. 246–7.

10. J. Duncan M. Derrett, 'The Purāṇas in Vyavahāra Portions of Medieval Smṛti Works', *Purāṇa*, Vol. 5, No.1, January 1963, p. 13.
11. Hazra, *Purāṇic Records*, pp. 193–205.
12. Despite obvious exaggerations in the dismal picture of the *Kali* age, portrayed by the *Purāṇas*, there must have been some substance in these descriptions, for Hazra points out that the *Jātakas* confirm that with the rise of Buddhism the Vedic sacrifice and the priestly class lost authority and with that the compulsion to follow caste demarcations, hereditary occupation, and the four stages of life. *Ibid*., pp. 210–11.
13. *Ibid*., pp. 206–14.
14. Although no inscriptional evidence exists to corroborate this supposition, the *Purāṇas*, particularly *Vāyu* (99, 387–412), *Brahmāṇḍa* (III. 74. 130–204), *Matsya* (273, 25–33), *Viṣṇu* (IV. 24. 18–25) and *Bhāgavata* (XII. 1. 38–41) are vehement in their condemnation of the misdeeds of these rulers, *ibid*., pp. 213–17. It can therefore be surmised that at least from the brahmanical point of view their rule was not perceived as conducive to the spread of Vedic religion and the social order that flowed from it.
15. *Ibid*., pp. 215–26.
16. *Ibid*., p. 260. Hazra points out that this tendency became so universal that by the medieval period the *Smṛti* writers, particularly of Bengal, such as Raghunandana, completely accepted the authority of the *Tantras* and drew profusely upon them on almost all matters concerning '*dharma*', *ibid*., p. 264. Hazra believes that the gradual recognition of the authority of the *Tantras* by the *Purāṇas*, and the latter's absorption of the Tantric elements enabled the *Tantras* to exercise a remarkable influence even on the *Smṛti-nibandhas*, *ibid*., p. 262. But Suresh Chandra Bandyopadhyaya feels that the Tantric influence on religious rites and social customs was so pervasive in Bengal by Raghunandana's time that he had to reluctantly accept its authority as an indispensable part of Bengal's religious life, and thus imbibed Tantric elements in his works directly from the *Tantras* themselves and not through the mediation of the *Purāṇas*. Suresh Chandra Bandyopadhyaya, *Smṛti Śāstre Bāṅgālī,* A. Mukherji and Co., Calcutta, 1961, pp. 198–9. Whatever be the process through which Tantric elements were assimilated, the point remains that the *Tantras* ultimately found their way even into the most conservative category of brahmanical texts, namely the *Smṛtis*.
17. J.C. Heesterman, 'India and the Inner Conflict of Tradition', *The Inner Conflict of Tradition*, The University of Chicago Press, Chicago, 1985, p. 10.
18. Romila Thapar, *Cultural Transaction and Early India: Tradition and Patronage*, Oxford University Press, Delhi, 1987, p. 8.
19. Hazra, *Upapurāṇas*, Vol. I, p. 15.
20. *Ibid*., p. 16.
21. *Ibid*., p. 17.

22. *Ibid.*, p. 23.
23. *Ibid.*, pp. 23–9.
24. *Ibid.*, pp. 2–13.
25. Mehendale, 'The Purāṇa', p. 296.
26. Hazra, *Upapurāṇas*, Vol. I, p. 214.
27. Hazra, *Upapurāṇas*, Vol. II, p. 232.
28. Hazra, *Upapurāṇas,* Vol. I, p. 27.
29. *Ibid.*, pp. 25–6.
30. Hazra has made a thorough textual analysis to arrive at his conclusions regarding the date and provenance of the individual *Purāṇas* and *Upapurāṇas* and no research of comparable scholarship has been subsequently attempted to contradict them. It has therefore become customary to accept his findings on these aspects of the *Purāṇas* as authoritative, in any discussion on the subject. For an example of his phenomenal textual scholarship, see his discussion on the provenance of the *Devī Purāṇa*, Hazra, *Upapurāṇas*, Vol. II, pp. 79–143.
31. Hazra, *Purāṇic Records,* p. 166. Hazra says that the *Brahmavaivarta* was first composed most probably in the eighth century, but from about the tenth century it began to be changed by 'the interfering hands' of the Bengal authors who recast it in its present form and content in the sixteenth century. In the chronological table of the Puranic chapters on Hindu rites and customs, Hazra assigns the sections on *Janmāṣṭamī* and *Ekādaśī vrata* to the eighth to the beginning of the fourteenth century and the rest from the tenth to the sixteenth century, pp. 187–8. In other words, the *Brahmavaivarta* has been so continuously revised that even Hazra, with his textual precision, could not go beyond pointing out the outer limits of the beginning of its composition to the end of the redactions.
32. Hazra, *Upapurāṇas*, Vol. I, p. 267.
33. *Ibid.*, p. 274.
34. *Ibid.*, p. 277.
35. *Ibid.*, pp. 344–5.
36. *Ibid.*, p. 344.
37. Hazra, *Upapurāṇas*, Vol. II, p. 79.
38. *Ibid.*, p. 73. However, he later adds that it is very probable that the *Devī Purāṇa*, as we have it now, comes down from the sixth century AD, most probably its latter half, p. 77. This of course does not contradict his final judgement that it cannot be later than AD 850.
39. *Ibid.*, p. 232. This *Purāṇa* exerted such an influence, particularly on the ritual pattern of goddess worship in Bengal, that even though it cannot be ascertained that it was definitely composed in Bengal, I take it into consideration for my study.
40. *Ibid.*, p. 245.
41. *Ibid.*, p. 277.
42. *Ibid.*, p. 282.

43. *Ibid*., p. 353.
44. *Ibid*., pp. 346–7.
45. *Ibid*., p. 455.
46. *Ibid*., p. 461.
47. R.C. Majumdar, *History of Medieval Bengal*, G. Bharadwaj and Co., Calcutta, 1974, p. 264. Majumdar refers to two other texts of the same nature, namely *Purāṇasāra* and *Purāṇārtha Prakāśaka*, p. 264.
48. L.S.S. O'Malley, *Popular Hinduism: The Religion of the Masses,* Cambridge at the University Press, 1935, reprinted by Johnson Reprint Corporation, New York, 1970, p. 2.
49. J.H. Hutton, *Caste in India: Its Nature, Function, and Origins*, Oxford University Press, Bombay, 1980 (originally published in 1946), p. 231.
50. Irawati Karve, *Hindu Society: An Interpretation*, Deshmukh Prakashan, Poona, 1968, p. 89.
51. *Ibid*., pp. 87-90.
52. *BvP*, IV. 129. 75–8.
53. Brian K. Smith, *Reflections on Resemblance, Ritual and Religion*, Oxford University Press, New York, 1989, p. 10.
54. *Ibid*., pp. 13–14.
55. J.C. Heesterman, 'Veda and Dharma', in Wendy Doniger O'Flaherty and J.D.M. Derrett (eds), *The Concept of Duty in South Asia*, Vikas Publishing House Pvt. Ltd, New Delhi, 1978, p. 84. Also see p. 93.
56. Smith, *Reflections on Resemblance*, p. 28.
57. Giorgio Bonazzoli, 'The Dynamic Canon of the Purāṇas', *Purāṇa*, Vol. 26, July 1979, pp. 127–8.
58. Smith, *Reflections on Resemblance*, p. 20.
59. *Ibid*., p. 29.
60. *Ibid*., p. 26.
61. For the opinions expressed on the relationship between the *Vedas* and the *Purāṇas* in general, from complete rejection to uncritical acceptance, see Ludo Rocher, *The Purāṇas* (A History of Indian Literature, Vol. II Part 3), Otto Harrassowitz, Wiesbaden, 1986, pp. 13–17, especially footnotes 1, 3–9.
62. *śrutismṛti ubhe netre purāṇaṁ hṛdayaṁ smṛtam I*
    etatruyokta eva syāddharmo nānyatra kūtracit II
    DbP, XI.1.21.
63. *pāṭhe caturṇāṁ vedānāṁ yatphalañca labhennaraḥ I*
    tatphalaṁ labhate nūnaṁ paṭhanāt kavacasya ca II
    BvP, II. 56.53.
64. *dhanyā vedāśca catvāraḥ karmmaiva yadvyavasthayā I*
    ... ...
    tasmācchāstrāṇi sarvāṇi purāṇāni ca santi vai II
    BvP, IV. 87. 60–1.

65. *manvantareṣu sarveṣu dvāpare dvāpare yuge I*
prāduḥkaroti dharmmārthī purāṇāni yathāvidhi II
dvāpare dvāpare viṣṇurvyāsarūpeṇa sarvvadā I
vedamekaṁ sa bahudhā kurute hitakāmyayā II
alpāyuṣo'lpabuddhīṁśca viprān jñātvā kalāvatha I
purāṇasaṁhitām puṇyāṁ kurute'sau yuge yuge II
strīśūdradvijavandhūnāṁ na vedaśravaṇaṁ matam I
teṣāmeva hitārthāya purāṇāni kṛtāni ca II DbP, I.3.18–21.

66. *BnP*, Chapter 31.

67. *jñānañca mokṣadaṁ prāhustajjñānaṁ yogināṁ bhavet I*
BnP, 31.31.

68. *praṇavañcopaniṣadaṁ dvādaśākṣarapañca ca I*
aṣṭākṣaraṁ mahāvākyamityādīnāñca yo japaḥ II
svādhyāyaśca samākhyāto yogasādhanamuttamam I
BnP, 31.90–1.

69. *upavāsādibhiścaiva purāṇaśravaṇādibhiḥ I*
puṣpādyaiḥ prārcanaṁ viṣṇoḥ kriyāyoga iti smṛtaḥ II
BnP, 31.44.

70. *ardhaślokātmakaṁ yattu devīvaktrāvjanirgatam I*
śrīmadbhāgavataṁ nāma vedasiddhāntabodhakam II
upadiṣṭaṁ viṣṇave yadvaṭapatranivāsine I
śatakoṭipravistīrṇaṁ tatkṛtaṁ brahmaṇā purā II
tatsāramekataḥ kṛtvā vyāsena śukahetave I
aṣṭādaśasahasrantu dvādaśaskandhasaṁyutam II
DbP, XII. 14.1–3.

71. *vedavedāṅga śāstrāṇāṁ sārabhūtaṁ munīśvaraḥ I*
jagaddhitārthaṁ tatsarvvaṁ purāṇeṣūktavān muniḥ II
BnP, 1.21.

72. *vedasāramidaṁ puṇyaṁ purāṇaṁ dvijasattamāḥ I*
vedāpaṭhasamaṁ pāṭhe śravaṇe ca tathaiva hi II
DbP, XII.14.25–6.

73. *kṛṣṇa jānāsi māṁ bhadra nāhaṁ tvāṁ jñātumīśvarī I*
ke vā jānanti vedajñā vedā vā vedakārakāḥ II
BvP, III.7.110.

74. *sudurlabhaṁ purāṇeṣu vedeṣu gopanīyakam I*
BvP, IV.96.4.

75. *vedāśca vaidikāḥ santaḥ purāṇāni vadantica I*
rādhāyā mādhavaḥ sādhyo bhagavāniti niṣphalam II
BvP, IV.126.63.

76. Hazra, 'The Purāṇas', p. 268.

77. V.S. Agrawala, 'Editorial', *Purāṇa*, Vol. 1, No. 2, 1960, p. 118.

78. *vedeṣu ca purāṇeṣu cetihāseṣu sarvataḥ I*
nirūpito yaḥ sarveśastaṁ na jānāsi mūḍhavat II
BvP, IV.25.67.

79. *divāmaithunadoṣañca vakti vedo viśeṣataḥ I*
BvP, IV.79.18.

80. D.D. Kosambi, *An Introduction to the Study of Indian History*, Popular Prakashan, Bombay, 1975, pp. 289–90.

81. C. Mackenzie Brown, 'Purāṇa as Scripture: From Sound to Image of the Holy Word in the Hindu Tradition', *History of Religions*, Vol. 26, No. 1, August 1986, p. 75.

82. Majumdar, *Ancient Bengal*, p. 508.

83. See p. 49.

84. Cited in Hazra, *Upapurāṇas*, Vol. II, pp. 162–3.

85. Horace Hayman Wilson, *Sanskrit-English Dictionary*, Nag Publishers, Delhi, enlarged edition 1979, p. 87.

86. *BnP*, 4.20–7.

87. *sarvāgamāṇāmācāraḥ prathamaḥ parikalpyate I*
ācāraprabhavo dharmo . . .
BnP, 14.210.

88. *BnP*, 24.45.

89. *svagrāme pūrṇamācāraṁ pathyarddhaṁ munisattamāḥ I*
āture niyamo nāsti mahāpadi tathaiva ca II
BnP, 25.16.

90. *yugadharmāḥ parigrāhyā varṇairetairyathocitam I*
grāmācārastathā grāhyaḥ smṛtimārgāvirodhataḥ II
BnP, 22.11.

91. *deśācārāḥ parigrāhyāstattaddeśīyajairnaraiḥ I*
anyathā patito jñeyaḥ sarvadharmabahiṣkṛtaḥ II
BnP, 22.17.

92. *yathārthakathanaṁ rājan satyamityabhidhīyate I*
dharmāvirodhato vācyaṁ taddhi dharmaparāyaṇaiḥ II
deśakālādivijñānāt svadharmasyāvirodhataḥ I
yadvacaḥ procyate sadbhistat satyamabhidhīyate II
BnP, 15.24–5.

93. *grāmadharmā jātidharmā deśadharmāḥ kulodbhavāḥ I*
parigrāhyā nṛbhiḥ sarve naiva tallaṅghayen mune II
durācāro hi puruṣo loke bhavati ninditaḥ I
DbP, XI.1.17–18.

94. *nacaiṣāmācareddharmaṁ vaidikaṁ laukikaṁ tathā I*
BP, III.4.15.

95. *lokācāreṣu vedeṣu na strī yāti parapriyam II*
BvP, IV.32.25.

96. *nāsti bhedo yathā devi dugdha-dhāvalyayoḥ sadā I*
. . .   .
loke vede purāṇe ca rādhā-mādhavayostathā II
BvP, IV.92.87–8.

97. *śrutau śruto yaḥ sa dharmo viparīto hyadharmakaḥ II*

pārvatyuvāca
kevalaṁ vedamāśritya kaḥ karoti vinirṇayam |
balavān laukiko vedāllokācārāñca kastyajet ||
BvP, III.7.49–50.

98. *paṭu paṭahaninādā veśyā śaṅghā dvijātayaḥ |*
maṅgalairvedaśabdaiśca tā neyā yatra ucchraet ||
DP, 12.26.

99. *gṛhītvā mṛttikāṁ kūlācchvetāṁ brāhmaṇasattamaḥ |*
raktāṁ pītāṁ tathā kṛṣṇāṁ gṛhṇīyuścānyavarṇakāḥ ||
athavā yā yatra deśe saiva grāhyā dvijottamaiḥ |
DbP, XI.2.18–19.

100. *deśakāladravyaśakti-svopapattīśca sarvaśaḥ ||*
DbP, XI.2.32.

101. Madeleine Biardeau, 'Some More Considerations About Textual Criticism', *Purāṇa*, Vol. 10, No. 2, July 1968, pp. 121–2.
102. V.M. Bedekar, 'Principles of Mahābhārata Textual Criticism: The Need for a Restatement', *Purāṇa*, Vol. 11, No. 2, July 1969, p. 219.
103. A.S. Gupta, 'A Problem of Purāṇic Text-Reconstruction', *Purāṇa*, Vol. 12, No. 2, July 1970, pp. 310–21.
104. Biardeau, 'Some More Considerations', p. 121.
105. *Ibid*., pp. 121–2.
106. Bedekar, 'Mahābhārata Textual Criticism', p. 221.
107. Gupta, 'Purāṇic Text-Reconstruction', pp. 306–7.
108. Thomas B. Coburn, *Devī-Māhātmya: The Crystallization of the Goddess Tradition*, Motilal Banarsidass, Delhi, 1984, p. 37.
109. Brown, *God as Mother*, pp. 18–19.
110. *Ibid*., p. 19.
111. Biardeau, 'Some More Considerations', p. 122.
112. Brown, *God as Mother*, p. 20.
113. *KP*, summary of 81.1–30.
114. Kooij, *Worship of the Goddess*, p. 6.
115. Kooij uses the expression 'usual', but this is an imprecise term and requires far too many qualifications to bring out its specific connotation. *Ibid*., p. 8.
116. *yatheṣṭamāṁsamadyādi bhojanārthaṁ mayā dhṛtaḥ |*
mahābhairavakāyo'haṁ tathā strīratisaṅgame ||
KP, 74.205.

117. Śiva is the best-known god with a heterodox nature and the *KP* actually narrates the incident where he was refused attendance at the great sacrifice of Dakṣa because he was a bearer of skulls (*kapālin*),
tato'haṁ na vṛtastena dakṣeṇa sumahātmanā |
kapālīti satī cāpi tajjāyeti ca no vṛtā ||
KP, 61.4.

Interestingly, this text also mentions the left shapes of most of the major brahmanical deities. For example, the left aspect of Brahmā is called Māyāmoha, Viṣṇu is Narasiṁha, Sarasvatī is Vāgbhairavī, Sūrya is Mārtaṇḍa-bhairava and Gaṇeśa is Agnivetāla, who should be worshipped in the *vāma* way. Even the Bāla-gopāla form of Viṣṇu has a left shape, encased in uterus, who eats fish and meat and is ever lustful of women. Goddess Caṇḍikā of course has many left forms, *KP*, 74.206–15. Indeed, the text says that from the left shape of Brahmā emanated the philosophical school of Cārvvāka,

vāmaḥ kāyo brahmaṇo'pi māṁsamadyādibhuktaye I
kṛto mahāmohanāmā cārvvākādipravarttakaḥ II
KP, 74.206–7,

which was known to be anti-brahmanical in its attitude and was opposed to all kinds of religious observance.

118. *ṛṣīn devān pitṝṁścaiva manuṣyān sutasañcayān I*
yojayet pañcabhiryajñairṛṇāni pariśodhayet II
vidhivat snānadānābhyāṁ kurvan yadvidhipūjanam I
kriyate sarahasyantu taddākṣiṇyamihocyate II
KP, 74.128–9.

yadpūjayedvāmabhāvairna tat syādṛṇaśodhanam I
pitṛdevanarādīnāṁ jāyate ca kadācana II
KP, 74.133.

119. *KP*, 74.135. Indeed, the text goes so far as to say that whether one performs the five sacrifices or not, in the worship of the *iṣṭadeva* one must follow the *vāma* method.
pañcayajñān na vā kuryād yadvā vāmyaprapūjane II
KP, 74.132.

120. *KP*, 74.136–8.

121. *KP*, 74.140.

122. Kooij, *Worship of the Goddess*, pp. 28–9.

123. *kintu yaḥ pūjako vāmaḥ so'nyāsāṁ paribarjjitaḥ I*
sarvāsāṁ pūjakaḥ syāttu dakṣiṇastena uttamaḥ II
KP, 74.144.

124. Hazra, *Purāṇic Records*, p. 260.

125. *vedāvirodhi cettantraṁ tat pramāṇaṁ na saṁśayaḥ I*
DbP, XI.1.25. In fact, the *vāma* worship of the *KP* is a variant of the Tantric mode of worship. Kooij points out that the method recommended in the *KP* agrees substantially with the methods of the *Kulacūḍāmaṇi* and *Kulārṇava Tantra, Worship of the Goddess*, pp. 29–30.

126. Hermann Strasser and Susan C. Randall, *An Introduction to Theories of Social Change*, Routledge and Kegan Paul, London, 1981, p. 77.

127. *sakṛttu dāpayedanyairmadirāṁ sādhako dvijaḥ I*

śūdrādayastu satataṁ dadurāsavamuttamam II

KP, 74.124.

128. One is reminded of the technique adopted by Vaiṣṇava preachers in the tribal areas of Bengal some centuries later. They apparently declared that the three cardinal tenets of Vaiṣṇavism were chicken curry, the lap of a young woman, and chanting of the name of Hari. (Personal communication, Hitesranjan Sanyal.)

129. *yadi deśāntarādyātaḥ pīṭhaṁ deśāntaraṁ prati I*
taddaiśikopadeśena tadā pūjāṁ samārabhet II
. . . .
yasmin deśe tu yaḥ pīṭha oḍrapāñcālakādiṣu I
taddeśajopadeśena pūjyaḥ pīṭhe suro naraiḥ II

KP, 64.34, 36.

130. D.F. Pocock, *Mind, Body and Wealth: A Study of Belief and Practice in an Indian Village*, Basil Blackwell, Oxford, 1973, pp. 77–9.

131. *Ibid*., p. 78.

132. *Śrī Śrī Padma Purāṇa vā Viṣaharir Pāñcālī*, written by Dvija Vaṁśīdāsa in *payāra* metre, collected and revised by Purna Chandra Chakrabarti, published by Ramnath Das for Tarachand Das and Sons, Calcutta, undated.

133. *Ibid*., p. 165.

III

Cultural Interaction and Religious Process

In the previous chapter I have attempted to demonstrate how the corpus of Puranic literature in Bengal evolved as a result of an interaction between the orthodox brahmanical authority and a conglomeration of local traditions. Since I consider this process to be of crucial importance for the creation of brahmanical hegemony, eventually leading to the formation of the regional culture of Bengal, it is necessary to make a critical evaluation of models which seek to capture this process in generalized terms. Over the last three decades, two anthropological models of cultural interaction have dominated the study of religious-cultural processes in India. These models of Sanskritization and great–little traditions, developed in the 1950s, have since been widely criticized as inadequate when applied to specific situations. Here I will argue that despite some very valid criticisms, these models, with necessary qualifications, can still elucidate a very significant aspect of the complex process of socio-religious transformation in India, and may actually provide a key to the understanding of the Puranic texts of early medieval Bengal.

I

M.N. Srinivas was not the first scholar to locate the essence of Indian identity in the synthesis of diverse cultural elements,[1] but the first to develop the argument systematically. In his *Religion and Society Among the Coorgs of South India*[2] he employs the term Sanskritization in at least two different ways without clearly distinguishing them. At the beginning he proposes it as a concept for the analysis of society, defining Sanskritization as essentially a mechanism of caste mobility:

The caste system is far from a rigid system in which the position of each component caste is fixed for all time. Movement has always been possible, and especially so in the middle regions of the hierarchy. A low caste was able, in a generation or two, to rise to a higher position in the hierarchy by adopting vegetarianism and teetotalism, and by Sanskritizing its ritual and pantheon. In short, it took over, as far as possible, the customs, rites, and beliefs of the Brahmins, and the adoption of the Brahmanic way of life by a low caste seems to have been frequent, though theoretically forbidden. This process has been called 'Sanskritization' in this book . . . .[3]

In addition to this usage there is another nuance to the term that emerges towards the end of the book where it begins to assume cultural as distinct from social overtones. Here Srinivas suggests that Sanskritization provides cultural links between disparate regions by means of the common bond of Sanskritic features of Hinduism:

Sanskritic Hinduism gives . . . certain common values to all Hindus, and the possession of common values knits people together into a community. The spread of Sanskritic rites, and the increasing Sanskritization of non-Sanskritic rites, tend to weld the hundreds of sub-castes, sects, and tribes all over India into a single community.[4]

Thus although in this initial formulation Srinivas seems to be a little uncertain about the precise connotation of the term Sanskritization, positing it as both a phenomenon facilitating social mobility and a process of cultural integration, presumably one promoting the other, the basic assumptions behind the formulation are clear. First, the Sanskritic tradition possesses enormous symbolic appeal, representing a norm of socio-cultural excellence worthy of emulation, and second, the Sanskritic tradition is not a monolithic entity but is involved in symbiotic interplay with many local traditions, so that Sanskritization is a very complex two-directional process, drawing from, as well as feeding into, non-Sanskritic culture.[5]

In his subsequent work, Srinivas has consistently emphasized the social aspect of Sanskritization. A few years after the publication of *Coorgs*, in a clarificatory note on Sanskritization, he wrote: 'The structural basis of Hindu society is caste, and it is not possible to understand Sanskritization without reference to the structural framework in which it occurs.'[6] In what appears to be his final statement on the subject so far, he has defined Sanskritization unequivocally in caste terms: 'Sanskritization is the process by which a "low" Hindu caste, or tribal or other group, changes its customs, ritual, ideology, and way of life in the direction of a high, and frequently, "twice-born" caste.'[7]

Since this statement Srinivas has stuck to this definition, even when he is admittedly discussing the integrative function of Sanskritization.[8] Initially formulated to conceptualize cultural interaction, Sanskritization has now come to be firmly identified with only a particular aspect of this vast and intricate process, that is, social mobility.[9]

The initial concern of Robert Redfield was to understand peasant community as an anthropologist.[10] He later developed methodological guidelines for the holistic study of traditional ways of life of the indigenous primary civilizations such as India and China, and their great literate traditions. In Redfield's first work of this kind, 'civilization' makes its appearance as the final stage of the kinds of integral entities into which humanity presents itself.[11] But he is still occupied with the distinctive, small, homogeneous and self-sufficient village community of peasants.[12]

It is in the next book[13] that Redfield explicitly comes to terms with 'civilization'. He writes that a peasant village is so incomplete a system that it cannot well be described as a social structure and that the anthropologist has to consider larger and more nearly complete systems such as the feudal society, the complex region, the national state.[14] Redfield illustrates this aspect of the anthropologist's enlarged area of investigation with the example of India. He observes that in the countryside each local community is connected with many others through caste and widespread networks of marriage that persist through generations. 'It is as if the characteristic social structure of the primitive self-contained community had been dissected out and its components spread about a wide area. Rural India is a primitive or a tribal society rearranged to fit a civilization.'[15]

Thus with the growth and spread of civilization social relations extend themselves out from the local community, lose much of their congruence and develop many kinds of impersonal and formal varieties of connections. As a result, Redfield tells us, in peasant societies we see a relatively stable and very roughly typical adjustment between local and national life, a developed larger social system in which there are two cultures within one culture, one social system composed of upper and lower halves. We may think of peasant culture as a small circle overlapping with much larger and less clearly defined areas of culture, or we may think of the peasant life as a lower circle unwinding into the upward spreading spirals of civilization.[16] Hence the culture of a peasant community cannot be autonomous. To maintain itself it requires continuous communication with the local community of thought originating outside of it, particularly in the intellectual output of the remote teachers, priests or philosophers whose thinking affects and perhaps is affected by the peasantry. The peasant village is witness to the long course of interaction between the community and centres of civilization. Peasant culture has an evident history and the history is not local; it is a history of the civilization of which the village culture is one local expression.[17]

This recognition of the coexistence of two cultures in peasant society led Redfield to the following formulation:

> In a civilization there is a great tradition of the reflective few, and there is a little tradition of the largely unreflective many. The great tradition is cultivated in schools and temples, the little tradition works itself out and keeps itself going in the lives of the unlettered in their village communities. The tradition of the philosopher, theologian, and literary man is a tradition consciously cultivated and handed down; that of the little people is for the most part taken for granted and not submitted to much scrutiny or considered refinement and improvement.[18]

Redfield adds that the two are interdependent. Great and little traditions have long affected each other and continue to do so. He suggests that great epics have arisen out of elements of traditional tale-telling by many people, and epics have returned again to the peasantry for modification and incorporation into local cultures. Thus great and little traditions can be viewed as two currents of thought and action, distinguishable, yet ever flowing into and out of each other;[19] similar and yet notably different. Redfield cites the examples of Mayan, Chinese, and Islamic civilizations in support of his formulation. But most of all, he emphasizes the case of India and its ancient and complex process of interaction, where great tradition slowly developed from primitive thought and practice, itself got divided and underwent much modification and restatement, influencing and being influenced by the thoughts and actions of millions of little people.[20]

In the last years of his career Redfield was increasingly concerned with the subject of civilization. Between 1951 and 1958 he wrote three essays which were to be the opening chapters for a book on civilization.[21] These essays contain his mature judgement on the subject. He thinks that the most important characteristic of a civilization is its unity and the unity of a civilization is its identity as defined by its substantial qualities. A civilization is thought of not as a congeries of perfectly heterogeneous elements, but rather as having a oneness of attributes—a prevailing set of views as to the nature of what is and ought to be. The attribution of substantial qualities of this inclusive nature asserts the unity, however imperfect, of a civilization.[22] Thus Redfield conceived of civilizations as a kind of construct or typical persisting arrangement of parts, both a social system in which the parts are kinds of people in characteristic relationships with one another, and a cultural system in which the parts making up the whole are ideas or products of ideas in characteristic relationships with one another.[23] The persistent quality of this arrangement constitutes the unity of a civilization and the nature of this arrangement imparts to a civilization its identity. Redfield contrasts his schematic concept of civilization with operational concepts, such as Sanskritization, which study the process of social transformation within a civilization. Borrowing from Milton Singer, Redfield describes these two kinds of constructs—the one a formulation of a very wide scheme within which fit many particulars and the other a concept directly guiding and instructing particular investigations—respectively as 'concepts of cogitation' and 'concepts of observation'.[24] He suggests that in approaching a civilization as a structure of tradition one has several choices of subject matter, for example, the content of thought, the kinds of specialists, media and institutions, the processes of modification and the works—textual or oral. But whichever one chooses, Redfield tells us, one is recognizing a large, overarching conception of a civilization as an arrangement for communication between components that are universal, reflective, and indoctrinating and components which are local, unreflective, and accepting. He however concedes that this is only the general nature of relationships between the levels or components of tradition. The real structure of tradition, in any civilization or part thereof, is an immensely intricate system of relationships and the categories of 'great' and 'little' enormously oversimplify it.[25] Throughout this analysis Redfield has consistently drawn on the example of Indian civilization in support of his generalizations.

Redfield's generalizations were based on secondary literature and intuitive understanding, not on field observations. He nevertheless succeeded in profoundly influencing a whole generation of anthropologists who have actually conducted field studies in India. They have on the whole upheld Redfield's theories in varying degrees,[26] but the anthropologist who seems to have explicitly accepted the pattern of cultural interaction outlined by Redfield for India is Milton Singer.

In 1955 Singer formulated several broad hypotheses concerning the relation of little and great traditions in Indian civilization. He wrote that because India was a primary or indigenous civilization which had been fashioned out of preexisting folk and regional cultures, its great tradition was culturally continuous with the little traditions of its diverse regions, villages, castes, and tribes; that this cultural continuity was both product and cause of a common cultural consciousness shared by most Indians and expressed in essential similarities of mental outlook and ethos; and that this common cultural consciousness has been formed with the help of certain processes and factors such as sacred books, sacred objects, and a special class of literati—the *brāhmaṇas*—and leading personalities who by their identification with the great tradition and with the masses mediate the one to the other.[27] Here Singer is obviously in complete agreement with Redfield.

In his reassessment of the applicability of the Redfield model to the Indian situation, Singer is more circumspect, but still essentially in agreement with Redfield's basic propositions.[28] Singer now expands the Redfield model to include Kroeber's formulation of civilization. For Kroeber, every human culture is a composite historical growth out of elements borrowed from other cultures. Most cultures succeed in re-working and organizing these elements into a distinctive overall pattern or style. Such total culture patterns are not arbitrary or sudden impositions; rather, they represent gradual drifts towards consistency and coherence of the sub-patterns in the different spheres of culture. Once crystallized, a total pattern gives a culture its distinctive character. In the case of self-conscious cultures, the total culture pattern may receive articulation in the form of a self-image and world-view formulated by the more articulate members of the culture.[29]

Kroeber's conception of a civilization as a coherent and historically derived assemblage of culture patterns is certainly congruent with Redfield's conception of civilization as a structure of communities of different scales of complexity and of different cultural levels held together by an essential unity. Thus Singer's diversification of the Redfield model does not lead to any real extension of the concept. Singer looks for the continuity of Indian civilization in some distinctive organizing values, and discovers the unity of the civilization in an organized coherence of social and cultural differences,[30] both implied in Redfield's analysis. His conclusion that the organizing principle may be found in the societal structure of networks and centres which at the same time act as a medium for the mutual communication of great and little traditions,[31] is an explication and not a modification of the Redfield model.

II

Srinivas's concept of Sanskritization has been widely used in Indian anthropology and critiques of this concept are more numerous than those of Redfield's. For example, it has been emphatically pointed out that Srinivas laid undue stress on the brahmanical model of Sanskritization while other models for emulation were available and frequently pursued. D.F. Pocock observed that the *kṣatriya* or royal model in Hindu society stood for considerable secular prestige and the process of emulation was mediated by the local dominant non-*brāhmaṇa* caste.[32] Milton Singer drew attention to four possible models of Sanskritization: 'Even the life-style of the merchant and peasant have been taken as models in localities where these groups are dominant.'[33] McCormack pointed out, perhaps with undue severity, that Sanskritization, by its implicit association with *brāhmaṇa* thought, could perpetually derail modern appreciation of the real organizing role of merchants in religious affairs in the past.[34] D.R. Chanana, who discussed the spread of Sanskritization in north-western India, found that Muslims enjoyed primary dominance and Sikhs exercised a secondary dominance in this region, while among the Hindus the trading castes were important and *brāhmaṇas* had neither wealth nor learning. Thus the very group which could have prompted Sanskritization was deeply influenced by Islam.[35]

Besides, as early as 1912 Athelstane Baines observed that the *brāhmaṇas* are perhaps the most heterogeneous collection of minute and independent subdivisions that ever bore a common designation.[36] Marriott and Cohn pointed out later that there are chains of specialists from the expert masters of authoritative texts down to semi-literate domestic priests, all classed as '*brāhmaṇa*' but generally belonging to several different *brāhmaṇa* castes.[37]

Micro-studies on trends of Sanskritization in predominantly tribal areas have also produced variable results. S.L. Kalia gives an example of the reverse process, tribalization occurring in Jaunsar-Bawar in Uttar Pradesh and in Bastar according to which high-caste Hindus temporarily resident among tribal people have taken over the latter's mores, rituals and beliefs, antithetical to their own.[38] Case studies of the Santals, who form a sizeable section of the tribal population of Bengal, have also shown resistance to Sanskritization. Martin Orans observed that the extent of Hindu absorption among the Santals was negligible.[39] Instead, M.K. Gautam noticed a trend toward Santalization, which involves revival of a golden past that provides internal unity through the creation of the Santal standard behaviour.[40] Orans attributes this tendency to the Santal commitment to tribal solidarity.[41] Sarita Bhowmick found evidence of the penetration of brahmanical ideas and style of life among the Santals of Western Midnapur (Bengal) but at the same time an equally important contra-process of absorption of local tribal traits by the brahmanical system which, she thinks, might have been designated as tribalization had there been a tribal Srinivas to chronicle it.[42]

A major intervention in the Sanskritization debate was made precisely on this point. Mckim Marriott, in his famous study of the village of Kishan Garhi, made an impressive documentation of the way in which Sanskritic and non-Sanskritic motifs intertwine at the popular level.[43] Noting that fifteen of the nineteen festivals in Kishan Garhi are known by one or more universal Sanskrit texts, he goes on to caution against ascribing undue significance to this fact. He argues that there are four festivals which have no evident Sanskritic rationale; those festivals which do, represent only a small selection out of the annual cycle of Sanskritic festivals; between the festivals of Kishan Garhi and those sanctioned by the Sanskritic tradition, connections are often loosened, confused or mistaken due to a multiplicity of competing meanings. Behind their Sanskritic names and rationales the festivals of Kishan Garhi contain much ritual that has no connection with the Sanskritic tradition.[44] Marriott thus concludes that it is not the upward process of Sanskritization through universalization of cultural contents but the downward process of parochialization that constitutes the creativity of little communities within Indian civilization.[45] While acknowledging the general applicability of the concept of Sanskritization, Marriott attaches another qualification. He observes that the process by which local and Sanskritic motifs are identified is so unsystematic that it renders the claim that Sanskritization fosters all-India solidarity rather vulnerable. He suggests that Sanskritization heightens the sphere of communication for each little community without necessarily widening it.[46]

In fact Sanskritization is an operational concept which arose out of a study of a specific situation and its validity requires to be proved in each case. So long as Sanskritization is restricted to denote only a generalized pattern of cultural exchange, it has usually been found efficacious, but as soon as scholars closed in on sociologically oriented tests of the behavioural meanings of Srinivas's concept, counter-examples began to turn up.[47] These examples have not in the main invalidated the existence or importance of Sanskritization but have rather made more precise the conditions and scope of its operation. Srinivas's restatement on Sanskritization[48] takes into account many of these criticisms, even as his original hypothesis has undergone only marginal modification.

III

Redfield's formulation of the great and little traditions has, on the whole, come under much less attack. It is pitched at a level of generalization where it is difficult to detect many situational variants. But Redfield's formulation has not remained completely unscathed, since, as Wadley remarks, it perhaps presented as many problems as it solved.[49]

The criticisms of Redfield's theory are different from those of Srinivas's. Instead of being case studies producing instances of individual aberrations to a general formulation, these are primarily concerned with the definition of tradition itself, questioning the validity of the idea of one great tradition as a normative category for India. Thus Robert Miller, in examining the process by which the Mahars as outcastes have been building a tradition of their own, challenges the assumed equivalence of an Indian great tradition as a single all-encompassing system of beliefs and patterns with the Hindu brahmanical tradition.[50] The literature and learning of the *brāhmaṇas* were not voluntarily extended to the Mahars, nor was any legitimate variant made directly available. Trapped within a system they had no part in shaping, the Mahar saw dimly that the *brāhmaṇa* was engaged in a gigantic cut-and-paste job, attempting to continually revise and propagate an orthodox version of the great tradition. Thus Miller:

> It is the directing of attention to a Great Tradition of this sort that obscures the issues. Traditions . . . are statements of a point of view concerning the world, the cultural system within which one operates, in short, a model of the culture as seen from a given point of view. To expect to find a Great Tradition in a civilization is to transfer one anthropological model, that of the relatively homogeneous, fully integrated, 'organismic' tribal culture, to the 'mechanical' world of multiple ethnic groups, regions, histories, articulated politically and literarily by those dominant in the culture. We have been, in truth, seeking not one Great Tradition, but many, all of which have been articulated by a dominant segment of the society to form a cultural system operative within India through millennia.[51]

In his quest for clues to multiple great traditions Miller cites Helen Lamb's explanation[52] of the prosperity of the Indian mercantile community over the ages in the face of persistent brahmanical injunctions. The Indian merchant's denial of *brāhmaṇa* supremacy in religious affairs through the adoption of non-brahmanical religions and the acceptance of new, non-Vedic deities in the form of Vaiṣṇavism suggests, according to Miller, another structuring of the cultural system. Miller also refers to F.G. Bailey's somewhat similar criticism[53] of Dumont and Pocock's assumption of the essential unity of Indian society, contained in the Hindu brahmanical system of ideas and values.[54] Miller is willing to concede that there is such a thing as Indian culture and that it has a structure. But he adds that the structure of Indian culture is composed of multiple traditions, each utilizing components (groups, centres, items, relationships) found throughout India. He insists that each tradition is of equal status on an all-India scale, and that our attention must be directed to the system which is dominant at any time, in any region or locality to assess which is the great tradition of the moment. He believes that such community-wide traditions as those of the Mahar are not variants of the system but entirely different and separate. This would suggest that shared components are not the indicators of participation in a single system or tradition. It is the perceived relationship between components, the organization of the meaning of these relationships and components which gives body to a tradition.[55]

Objections have also been raised with regard to the difficulty of specifying the content of Sanskritic tradition. J.F. Staal, a Sanskritist, for example, maintains that it is fallacious to equate the Sanskritic and the great cultural traditions.[56] He says that the oldest and apparently most pivotal forms of the great tradition are often of a type that may be described as non-Sanskritic, and whatever tradition one studies in the classical Sanskrit sources, almost always there are indications of popular cults, local usages and little traditions.[57] Many so-called non-Sanskritic forms have an all-India spread and the fact that the great tradition is considered an all-India phenomenon is merely because of lack of familiarity with what the great tradition consists of and because of the lack of geographical specifications in Indological research.[58]

Staal thus draws our attention to a central feature of the great tradition: it grew and continues to grow out of assimilation of little tradition materials. Therefore it is erroneous to conceive of a pristine great tradition, formally separable from the elements that perpetually feed it. Consider in this connection the comment of another Sanskritist, van Buitenen, that for the Indian, knowledge is not to be discovered but recovered. At its very origin the absolute truth stands revealed. It has been lost, but not irrecoverably. It is still available through ancient lifelines that stretch back to the original revelation. The present can be restored only when this original past has been recovered.[59] He then points to an important means that has always been employed to maintain contact with the primordial deposit of truth: 'Sanskrit is felt to be one of the lifelines, and Sanskritization in its literal sense, the rendering into Sanskrit, is one of the prime methods of restating a tradition in relation to a sacral past.'[60] It is a continuous process of restatement as the great tradition goes on accumulating material from various little traditions and then sanctifies them with reference to the *Vedas* by means of Sanskrit. And Sanskrit has usually been the exclusive province of the *brāhmaṇas*. Hence the great tradition, Sanskrit and brahmanical authority are inextricably intertwined and identifiable with each other as the ultimate symbol of true and ancient ideology and conduct.

Another emendation to the great–little traditions formulation has been suggested by Mandelbaum in terms of the functional division of Sanskritic and local pantheons.[61] He argues that the high Sanskritic gods are almost invariably found to be benevolent and keep the world in order and bestow supernatural merit, while the lesser gods grant specific boons pertaining to everyday existence but are inclined to be malevolent if displeased or defiled. The former, which he calls the transcendental complex, has long-term welfare as its religious aim, system maintenance as function, universal gods described in Sanskritic texts as form and priests as practitioners. The latter, which he calls the pragmatic complex, has personal or local exigencies as its religious form, individual welfare as function, local deities described in vernacular folklore as form and shamans as practitioners.[62] He says that the transcendental complex is usually associated with the great tradition and the pragmatic with the little tradition, but such terms can be misleading because both complexes are used practically everywhere in village India and there is no antagonism between the two usages and little or no friction between their respective practitioners. Both are observed at all levels of the social hierarchy and both contribute to the total religious practice of the village community.[63] Both the worlds have to be maintained and the local exigencies attended to; hence this specialization of functions and hierarchical arrangement in the supernatural and human worlds.[64]

It has even been suggested that the great–little traditions formulation is a set of sterile tautologies based on personal intuition. The anthropologists' objections of this kind have been summed up by Agehananda Bharati:

> [it] does not explain any phenomenon in the behaviour of people in the culture studied; that it at best gives a name to something which does not need a name

for any serious student of the situation; and that there is such an enormous overlap between ascriptive elements in the one or the other 'tradition', that it ceases to be operational at any important step.[65]

Even historians who profit from such anthropological formulations feel that the concept has now begun to exert a drag on the first impetus that it set in motion.[66]

None of these criticisms, except Miller's, negate the existence of the two-tier formula of the cultural pattern of Indian civilization. Miller's objection to the hegemony of the brahmanical tradition appears to be somewhat overstated. The others merely point to the inadequacies of the formulation, suggest modifications, but do not claim that it is fundamentally invalid. Thus Staal only cautions against the anthropological tendency to view the brahmanical tradition as a reified and given constant and van Buitenen explains the mechanism through which it assimilates and grows. Mandelbaum's functional categories merely imply that the ideas of great and little traditions are not mutually exclusive although perhaps differentially distributed within a village social hierarchy, from *brāhmaṇa* to untouchable. Even Bharati, who shares a certain scepticism about the operational utility of the concept, concedes that it provides a viable taxonomic and heuristic device.[67] The concepts of Sanskritization and great and little traditions, qualified and refined, have come to be recognized over the years as analytical tools of considerable value.

IV

Yet for the study of texts these concepts are anthropological and necessarily contextual and synchronic even as they propose to facilitate understanding of social change over a period of time. Here historical material is an invaluable supplement to anthropological field observation. But in historical enquiry the anthropological context is absent and one has to rely primarily on texts which are usually prescriptive and do not reflect a living reality. This is where Redfield's distinction between the system of cogitation and the system of observation becomes meaningful. Sanskritization is essentially a system of observation and therefore synchronic in scope. In a situation of immense multiplicity of cultures as in India, operational variants to such a formulation are bound to emerge. But taken as a system of cogitation, the concept of great–little traditions has a wider diachronic applicability. In the first place Redfield formulated this theory primarily as a means to understand the processes of evolution of cultural patterns through the interaction of literate and folk traditions and thus conceived of civilization as a 'historic structure'. Besides, this concept did not arise out of generalization from a specific example. Rather, it appears to be equally applicable to any society which possesses both an oral and a written corpus of canonical and other traditional themes. It moves from general to particular and therefore the question of operational variants is irrelevant. This combination of historical depth and universal applicability renders the concept suitable for the study of texts which, in Redfield's words, are both 'process and product' of a tradition.

The theory of Sanskritization is of limited use for the study of Sanskrit or great tradition texts for another reason. Sanskritization is concerned with the initiative of those who wish to raise themselves in social hierarchy. But the Sanskrit texts reveal the initiative of the *brāhmaṇas*, their preferences and choices, their perception of the need for assimilation of local traditions, i.e. the process of universalization. This process is best reflected in the *Purāṇas* which have been characterized as 'popular books . . . which provided a liaison between the learned classes and the masses'.[68] The *Purāṇas* accomplished this by first declaring the importance of *deśadharma* and *kuladharma*—local and family usages—and thus accepting in principle the need to respect these and then incorporating them into the brahmanical fold with necessary rationalization and legitimizing sanctions. The prime technique employed by the *Purāṇas* for this purpose was to identify the countless deities worshipped in various localities with the deities of comparable features in the Sanskritic tradition. The most prominent example of such identification is the innumerable local goddesses who coalesced with Devī as different manifestations of the same *śakti*. As the locale of brahmanical culture expanded, fresh shrines and sacred centres of pilgrimage were designated in the new areas. This process is elaborately exemplified in the Puranic texts.

This, indeed, has been the principal adaptive strategy of all great traditions which consciously exercised the option to integrate elements of little traditions in their effort to establish religio-cultural hegemony. Two examples from Islam and Christianity will serve to illustrate a common parallel process. von Grunebaum has studied the problem of the relation between Muslim civilization and the local cultures of the areas which in course of time have become technically Islamized.[69] He has shown that an integration of the two traditions has been most successful where correct identifications have been made. For this, the local tradition is tied in with, and accounted for, in terms of 'genuine' great tradition through an appropriate theological or philosophical explanation. In the absence of multiple gods in Islam, one of the most characteristic examples of this tendency is justification within the framework of orthodoxy of the cult of saints. The saint of the local culture is interpreted as the possessor of gnostic knowledge; he is closer to God than are his fellow-Muslims, and his miracles are ascribed to the grace of Allah. Even Koranic evidence is found to prove the existence of familiars of the Lord, and the theosophy of Ibn al-Arabic reconciles the saint of the little tradition with the prophet of the great tradition by arguing that all prophets are also saints but that the saintly aspect of each prophet is higher than the prophetic aspect. Besides, all prophets and saints are but manifestations of the spirit or reality of Mohammed.[70]

Terence Ranger has studied the remarkably successful attempt made by the Anglican church in the Masasi district of southern Tanzania in the 1920s and 1930s, led by Bishop Vincent Lucas, to Christianize African religious belief and practice.[71] Lucas, wanting to achieve within a short time the translation of faith of the new converts into conduct,'tinker-[ed] around with symbolic substitution'.[72] Lucas was fascinated by the possibility of leading African converts into an understanding of Christianity by an extension of the themes and symbols of their own religious belief. He found that anything that would show them that Christianity is the fulfilment for them of what had already been adumbrated in the immemorial customs of the past, would perhaps do more than anything to help the church become indigenous. Ranger has quoted extensively from Lucas to show how this act of identifying the traditional symbols and ritual sequences with Christian equivalents was actually implemented. The initiation ceremony, for example, is an extremely important rite for the Africans. In this the traditional use of flour was replaced by the holy water, the Cross took the place of the lupanda tree and the invocation of the saints of Christendom replaced the appealing to the great ones of the tribal past. Ashes in the initiation ceremony symbolized rejoicing over the passage of a child from childhood to manhood. Lucas suggested that ashes should mean the abandonment of the unworthy things of nature and the beginning once again of a new life of Grace, i.e. the burial service where the use of ashes is closely linked to the hope of resurrection.[73] If Christianity is understood here to represent great tradition and the African traditional religion as little tradition, then the process of absorption of little tradition elements is identical with the process outlined by von Grunebaum in the case of Islam or with the process embodied in the Bengal *Purāṇas*. In fact, wherever a great tradition has taken the initiative to universalize aspects of little traditions, it has inevitably adopted the mechanism of identification with suitable theological justifications as its strategy and the records of the modalities of this process are necessarily conserved in the textual repositories of the said great tradition. Since in India the great tradition is in many respects culturally continuous with little traditions, the Puranic manipulation of symbols appears more authentic and less superficial or enforced than in the Masasi example. Surely appropriate symbols will have to be available with the great tradition so that the transition looks smooth and convincing and is supported by a befitting theological rationale. Ranger points out that Lucas failed in his attempt to Christianize women's rites as there was no adequate theology of sexuality available with Christianity to allow for effective substitution of symbols.[74]

V

The tacit assumption so far has been that the brahmanical tradition constitutes the great tradition in Indian civilization. But is the brahmanical tradition a universal category with an all-India spread? Admittedly not. The point moreover is whether any generalization on normative codes of a civilization such as the Indian is possible. Part of the problem lies with nomenclature. Inherent in the great–little divide is the insinuation of the 'civilized' versus the 'primitive'. Even these could have been taken as purely descriptive categories had it not been for the fact that over a long period of time the two terms have come to acquire a value-laden significance. As pointed out by Charles Long, since the beginning of the modern period in the West the primitives have been understood as religious 'others'.

> These others are religious in two senses. In the first sense the primitives form one of the most important basis of data for a non-theological understanding of religion in the post-Enlightenment West. In the second sense, the primitives define a vague other whose significance lies not in their own worth and value but in the significance it offers to civilization when contrasted with it. The primitives operated as a negative structure of concreteness that allowed civilization to define itself as a superior structure to this ill-defined and inferior 'other'.[75]

It is to this value judgement that anthropologists like Miller implicitly object. The *brāhmaṇa* is not a homogeneous category nor is brahmanical tradition a fixed referent; but we cannot challenge the proposition that if in India's diverse cultural traditions there is one way of life and one medium of expression that can claim a semblance of pervasive influence these are brahmanism and Sanskrit. The brahmanical tradition has decidedly the widest horizontal spread which cuts across regional boundaries. It is a continuous, overarching tradition with an essential unity of content and purpose compared to the many localized traditions which, though rich in cultural content, are nevertheless varied and fragmented. In order to avoid the inherent value judgement, therefore, it is simpler to ascribe them a spatial denotation by linking the great tradition with the norms governing 'the large society' or *bṛhadāñcala* and the little traditions with 'small societies' or *kṣudrāñcala*, as has been implied by Ralph Nicholas[76] and Shashibhushan Dasgupta.[77] Suniti Kumar Chatterji's formulation of 'Indianism' as an alternative to Sanskritic Hinduism also touches this aspect of spatial spread.[78]

Moreover the brahmanical tradition is a culture by accretion. By definition an indigenous civilization is one whose great tradition evolves by a carrying forward of materials which are already present in the little traditions that it encompasses. Raghavan noticed three characteristics of the brahmanical tradition. First, it is not a destructive force; it constantly absorbs and conserves existing practices and customs. Second, it reduces a bewildering mass of cultural elements to some homogeneity and synthesis. And third, this incorporation and systematization by the great tradition result in refinement of the little tradition practices by conferring on them an esoteric significance.[79] Marriott is therefore correct in observing that it was wrong on the part of Srinivas to assume that Sanskritic culture spread 'at the expense of'[80] the little traditions. Instead, he found evidence of accretion and of transmutation in form without apparent replacement.[81] Even when replacement takes place with subsequent secondary transformation of its contents through rationalization, the brahmanical tradition recreates but never completely supplants the little tradition prototypes.

The brahmanical tradition is never a static entity but a dynamic reality with many intermediary layers. These cannot be separately identified because religious legitimation is a continuous process. But at a certain stage of its development the contents of the brahmanical tradition get crystallized into a complex set of meanings which are then codified into texts. Even these texts are elusive because they are subject to continuous revisions, but at a given point of time they embody the prevailing great tradition. Here the problem is that the Sanskrit normative texts of this kind in most cases suffer from regional anonymity. But the anthropologist wants to understand a text in relation to the culture and society in which it is found.[82] Thus the *Mahāpurāṇas*, which bear ample evidence of this cultural synthesis, cannot be interpreted in great and little tradition terms, except in a very general way, due to the absence of a specifiable context. This inconvenience does not apply to the Bengal *Purāṇas*. We have seen that when brahmanical tradition reached Bengal, it had already achieved a level of cultural assimilation which moved along a common pattern. In Bengal the brahmanical tradition met with a somewhat different situation. It confronted a congeries of little traditions with a common cult focus centring on the mother goddesses, in no way uniform, but with the potential of being harnessed into a collective identity through the theoretical assumptions of *Sāṁkhya*.[83] In other words, Bengal offered a regional cult which was distinctly different from those encountered by the brahmanical tradition so far.

Here 'regional cult' is used in the anthropological sense of the term: 'cults of the middle range—more far-reaching than any parochial cult of the little community, yet less inclusive in belief and membership than a world religion in its most universal form.'[84] This is not unique to Bengal but applies equally to any of the peripheral areas with a discernible identity, where brahmanism arrived comparatively later. Thus Eschmann, in her discussion on the process of Hinduization of tribal deities in Orissa, uses the great–little tradition paradigm in the context of 'one special regional tradition'.[85] Faced with such a situation the brahmanical tradition recognized that it required greater attention and more systematic treatment than what the generalized format of the *Mahāpurāṇas* could provide. Thus came into being the *Upapurāṇas*, which were 'more exclusively adapted to suit the purposes of local cults and the religious needs of different sects than the *Mahāpurāṇas*'.[86] They brought together dispersed elements but with an underlying commonality scattered over many little traditions and imparted to them a cohesive unity. From the point of view of anthropological understanding of texts one advantage with the *Upapurāṇas* is that since they have undergone much less revision, they preserve their historical context and sectarian character more truthfully than the *Mahāpurāṇas*.[87]

Thus Bengal presented the preconditions of a regional cult, but such conditions were transformed into an identifiable regional great tradition by the Bengal *Purāṇas*. This carried within its sweep many little tradition elements which were still to be recognized as part of an all-India tradition but were now certainly acknowledged as belonging to the Bengal brahmanical tradition. Henceforth the tradition developed by these texts became the point of reference for all subsequent amplifications within Bengal. The Bengal *Smṛtis*, which formulated and standardized the behavioural, ritual and legal codes for Bengal at a later period, drew heavily on these *Purāṇas*. The worship of the goddess Durgā, one of the major symbols that unites Bengal both as a community and a culture, ultimately derives from these texts. Even the vernacular *Maṅgalakāvya* literature of the medieval period is, in many respects, an extension of the same process, although these texts are much closer to the little traditions in emphasis and sympathy than the *Purāṇas* could either desire or afford. But the *Purāṇas* created the regional great tradition for a long time to come. When Bailey, who studied the changes taking place among the distiller castes in Orissa when they acquired land and raised their status, described the process for the Konds as 'social climbing by following standard Oriya behaviour',[88] he was actually referring to the regional great tradition of Orissa. In fact Corwin, in her essay on the cultural traditions of a small rural town of Mahishadal in the Midnapur district of West Bengal, conceived of the pattern of cultural interaction in terms of what she called 'the Bengali Great Tradition' and the local little tradition.[89] The resulting picture may be reduced to the two following diagrams.

A. INTERMEDIARY STAGES OF TRADITION

State
Region
Country
Village

Source: Robert Redfield.[90]

B. STRUCTURE OF HINDUISM

Establishment	Public Religion	
	Great tradition	Little tradition
Text	*Vedas*, etc.	Local *Purāṇas*, etc.
Performance	Vedic ritual	Local sacrifices, etc.
Social organization	Caste hierarchy	Sects and cults
Mythology	Pan-Indian deities	Regional deities

Source: A.K. Ramanujan.[91]

(In this construction of Ramanujan, little tradition actually stands for regional great tradition which also admits of caste hierarchy rather than a simple differentiation in terms of sects and cults.)

Although the theory of great–little traditions has dominated the anthropological understanding of Indian religions for the last three decades, it must be remembered that it was articulated in the 1950s, since when conceptual tools for the interpretation of religion in relation to society have advanced. In order to make a proper assessment of the applicability of the great–little traditions to the Puranic textual material, we should place it in the perspective of these newer concepts to see if they provide insights into the process of evolution of religious patterns.

Historians of religions with varying orientations, have mostly conformed to the two-tier formula of religious interaction, be it universal and folk, primitive and classical, universal and local, popular and institutional, great and little or traditional and rational. It was Nitalie Z. Davis who first challenged a model of European Christianity that distinguished folk religion from official religion and magic from religion.[92] She raised three issues that effectively defined the limits of the older dichotomies and set a new agenda for analysis of popular religion in general:

> First, . . . lay piety . . . could not be understood adequately when set off from so-called rational beliefs; second, such bifurcations inevitably failed to reveal the commonality among groups of laity and clergy in their recourse to various local practices and institutions; and third, the polarization of institutional and local levels of practice obscured the dynamics of change within the tradition as a whole.[93]

Influenced by the cultural anthropology of Clifford Geertz, Davis proposed to analyse how distinctions such as religion and magic were used in specific historical periods to create a whole that structured experience and reinforced the social order. The historian had to examine how the institutional contexts for popular religion shifted with economic, demographic, or political forces.

In 1982, Davis again suggested that ambiguous usage had obscured any analytical power that the term 'popular religion' might have had.[94] Davis seems to have felt, as Catherine Bell suggests, that the growing ambiguity of the term was due partly to an increasing distance from the historical conditions in which it first emerged as a corrective of earlier dichotomies. As a revisionist term, it was useful for suggesting the existence of social attitudes and practices that cut across the categories of previous analyses. Yet when removed from this historiographical context, popular religion degenerated into a trendy substitute for folk religion.[95] Given these difficulties, Davis suggested a focus on 'religious cultures'. 'Religious cultures' defined religious practice as those symbolic activities by which people made and remade the socio-cultural world in which they lived. Hence this approach saw religion as generating both cultural categories and social organization.[96] This approach would make the historian seek a notion of culture that would recognize how a society produces both differences and unities within its cultural categories and social organization.

It has been suggested that the question of fundamental unity or fundamental diversity in the religious spectrum is simply the result of the method of study. Textually based studies deal with the dissemination of universal values while ethnographic field studies are constantly confronted with heterogeneity. Thus historians may be prone by the nature of their work to inherit dichotomies basic to the literate elite who left their texts for posterity, while the anthropologist may be prone to absorbing the integrated world-view of a specific group. Hence the terminological choices directly reflect the various perspectives on culture and religion seen in every discipline.[97] This is obvious, but more important for us is to see if the emendations proposed by Davis call for a fundamental alteration of the great–little tradition categories. Her basic objections are that such bifurcations fail to reveal the commonality between laity and clergy and that such polarizations obscure the dynamics of change. After subsequent clarifications and innumerable reformulations, the original concepts have now come to represent a position that these two realms—great and little—do not confront each other at all, but are combined through several intermediary stages. In other words, these two poles are no longer posited as dichotomous but as a continuum with only a permeable membrane separating the two. And cultural categories and social organization of traditions are so integral to this formulation, as we have seen, that most of Davis's objections seem to have been taken care of through later modifications. Besides, such texts as the Bengal *Purāṇas* virtually obliterate the idea of rigid bipolarity against which Davis reacted. These texts are as much concerned with the dissemination of universal values as the universalization of parochial values and the frequency of recurrence of this process removes the pristine identity of great and little for all practical purposes.

Peter Burke, who has worked on popular culture in early modern Europe after the publication of Davis's first essay on popular religion, made use of Redfield's categories, albeit with reservation. Burke argues that Redfield's model is a useful point of departure but narrow because it omits upper class participation in popular culture, thus treating popular culture as a residual category; it is also too wide because it suggests that the little tradition was relatively homogeneous.[98] Burke restates Redfield's model for early modern Europe in the following way:

There were two cultural traditions in early modern Europe, but they did not correspond symmetrically to the two main social groups, the elite and the common people. The elite participated in the little tradition, but the common people did not participate in the great tradition. This asymmetry came about because the two traditions were transmitted in different ways. The great tradition was transmitted formally at grammar schools and at universities. It was a closed tradition in the sense that people who had not attended these institutions, which were not open to all, were excluded. In a quite literal sense, they did not speak the language. The little tradition, on the other hand, was transmitted informally. It was open to all, like the church, the tavern and the market place, where so many of the performances occurred.[99]

Redfield's model, as mentioned above, did not arise out of a study of a particular situation and is far too general. For each concrete study it has to be restated, as Burke has done. But the singular point to note is that Burke is conceding the existence of two divergent traditions even for Europe. Our problem is somewhat different. We have practically no material for the study of popular culture in early medieval Bengal and, what is worse, we have to reconstruct the popular belief system largely from elite cultural productions. Besides, in early medieval Bengal the very purpose of the composition of the Puranic texts—although the language was literally different—was dissemination of elite culture and appropriation of popular culture resulting in a reformulation where a modified popular culture prevailed in the belief system and the elite maintained its social supremacy.

Thus the making of great–little traditions can be seen as essentially a process of continuum construction. This presumes that the development or acculturation was taking place along some linearly conceived continuum. Such a simplification has great value, as Barrie Morrison points out, for it focuses on the process of acculturation and thus on the development of a coherent universal culture. Applied to smaller units it focuses on the degree of their autonomy from, or assimilation to, the universal culture.[100] But in effect the process is not so simple. The process of assimilation is so intricate and conditioned by so many considerations—social, cultural, political—any of which may take precedence over the other and thus dictate the particular nature of future development, that either of these traditions must appear fairly amorphous. Neither is the linearity as straight as this simplification may indicate. All that we can do, therefore, is to assign stations upon the continuum, to view the Puranic texts of Bengal, for example, as fluid though recognizable moments in an ever-unfurling process, so that they may be contextually and chronologically pinned down for historical analysis. The terms great tradition and little tradition were conceived of as heuristic devices, and if they are understood as just that and not as an inviolable doctrine, they have their uses.

NOTES

1. Nirmal Kumar Basu's *Hindu Samājer Gaḍan*, Visva-Bharati Granthalaya, Calcutta, 1356 BS (1949), is one of the most important of such examples. In the non-anthropological circle, S.K. Chatterji's 'The Indian Synthesis, and Racial and Cultural Intermixture in India', Presidential Address, All India Oriental Conference, Poona, 1953, also indicates the same process. Also see S.K. Chatterji, '*Kirāta-Jana-Kṛti*: The Indo-Mongoloids, their Contributions to the History and Culture of India', *Journal of the Royal Asiatic Society of Bengal, Letters*, Vol. 16, 1950, pp. 143–235.
2. M.N. Srinivas, *Religion and Society Among the Coorgs of South India*, Clarendon Press, Oxford, 1952, and Media Promoters and Publishers Pvt. Ltd, Bombay, 1978. I have used the Indian edition.
3. *Ibid.*, p. 30.
4. *Ibid.*, p. 209.
5. *Ibid.*, pp. 214, 221–2.
6. M.N. Srinivas, 'A Note on Sanskritization and Westernization', *The Far Eastern Quarterly*, Vol. 15, No. 4, August 1956, p. 482.
7. M.N. Srinivas, *Social Change in Modern India*, Orient Longman Limited, New Delhi, 1980 (first published in 1966), p. 6.
8. M.N. Srinivas, 'The Cohesive Role of Sanskritization', in Philip Mason (ed.), *India and Ceylon: Unity and Diversity, A Symposium*, Oxford University Press, London, 1967, pp. 67–8.
9. Many later contributions to the Sanskritization debate that this formulation generated have understood or interpreted this term in precisely this sense, for example Harold A. Gould, 'Sanskritization and Westernization: A Dynamic View', *Economic Weekly*, Vol. 13, No. 25, 24 June 1961, pp. 945–50, not to speak of the innumerable extensions and modifications of the concept, arising out of regional micro-studies, which will be discussed later. In fact much before Srinivas, Risley had described the same process for Bengal, which he called 'Brahmanising', in exclusively caste terms. H.H. Risley, *The Tribes and Castes of Bengal*, Vol. I, Firma Mukhopadhyay, Calcutta, 1981 (first published in 1891), pp. XV–XVIII.
10. See Robert Redfield, *The Folk Culture of Yucatan*, The University of Chicago Press, Chicago, 1941.

11. Robert Redfield, *Little Community: View Points for the Study of a Human Whole*, The University of Chicago Press, Chicago, 1955 (first delivered as a series of lectures at the University of Uppsala in 1953), p. 4.
12. *Ibid.*, p. 157.
13. Robert Redfield, *Peasant Society and Culture*, The University of Chicago Press, Chicago, 1956 (first delivered as lectures to Swarthmore College in March 1955 and parts of it had already appeared as 'The Social Organization of Tradition', *The Far Eastern Quarterly*, Vol. 15, No. 1, November 1955, pp. 13–22.)
14. *Ibid.*, p. 37.
15. *Ibid.*, pp. 56–7.
16. *Ibid.*, pp. 65–6.
17. *Ibid.*, pp. 68–9.
18. *Ibid.*, p. 70.
19. *Ibid.*, pp. 71–2.
20. *Ibid.*, pp. 75–86, 92–7.
21. Margaret Park Redfield (ed.), *Human Nature and the Study of Society: The Papers of Robert Redfield*, Vol. I, The University of Chicago Press, Chicago, 1962, pp. 364–414.
22. Redfield, 'Civilizations as Things Thought About', in *ibid.*, p. 373.
23. Redfield, 'Civilizations as Societal Structures? The Development of Community Studies', in *ibid.*, pp. 375–6.
24. Redfield, 'Civilizations as Cultural Structures?', in *ibid.*, p. 392.
25. *Ibid.*, pp. 392–5.
26. In fact those who lived and conducted fieldwork in India had observed this process, some with remarkable precision, long before Redfield's articulation of the theory. See, for example, J.H. Hutton, 'Hinduism in its Relation to Primitive Religions in India', in *Caste in India*, pp. 223–62.
27. Milton Singer, 'The Cultural Pattern of Indian Civilization', *The Far Eastern Quarterly*, Vol. 15, No. 1, November 1955, pp. 23–4.
28. Milton Singer, 'The Social Organization of Indian Civilization', in *When a Great Tradition Modernizes: An Anthropological Approach to Indian Civilization*, Vikas Publishing House Pvt. Ltd, New Delhi, 1972 (first published in *Diogenes*, 1964).
29. *Ibid.*, p. 252.
30. *Ibid.*, p. 251.
31. *Ibid.*, pp. 259, 268.
32. D.F. Pocock, 'The Movement of Castes', *Man*, Vol. 55, May 1955, pp. 71–2.
33. Singer, 'The Social Organization', p. 262.
34. William C. McCormack, 'Popular Religion in South India', in Giriraj Gupta (ed.), *Religion in Modern India*, Vikas Publishing House Pvt. Ltd, New Delhi, 1983, p. 107.

35. D.R. Chanana, 'Sanskritization, Westernization and India's North-West', *Economic Weekly*, Vol. 13, No. 9, 4 March 1961, pp. 409–14.
36. Sir Athelstane Baines, *Ethnography*, Strassburg, 1912, p. 26.
37. McKim Marriott and Bernard S. Cohn, 'Networks and Centers in the Integration of Indian Civilization', *Journal of Social Research* (Ranchi), Vol. I, No. 1, 1958, p. 5.
38. S.L. Kalia, 'Sanskritization and Tribalization', *Bulletin of the Tribal Research Institute* (Chindwara, MP), Vol. 2, No. 4, April 1959, pp. 49–54.
39. Martin Orans, *The Santal: A Tribe in Search of Great Tradition*, Wayne State University Press, Detroit, 1965, pp. 87–8.
40. Mohan K. Gautam, 'The Santalization of the Santals', in Kenneth David (ed.), *The New Wind: Changing Identities in South Asia*, Mouton Publishers, The Hague, 1977, p. 373.
41. Martin Orans, 'A Tribe in Search of a Great Tradition: The Emulation–Solidarity Conflict', *Man in India*, Vol. 39, No. 2, April–June 1959, p. 113.
42. Sarita Bhowmick, 'Brahmanisation in Border Bengal: A Case Study in Western Midnapur', *Man in India*, Vol. 64, No. 1, March 1984, pp. 35–56.
43. McKim Marriott, 'Little Communities in an Indigenous Civilization', in McKim Marriott (ed.), *Village India: Studies in the Little Community*, The University of Chicago Press, Chicago, 1955.
44. *Ibid.*, pp. 193–5.
45. *Ibid.*, p. 200.
46. *Ibid.*, pp. 217–18.
47. There are innumerable case studies testing the validity of this theory. It is not necessary for our purpose to catalogue the results of all of these. Nevertheless, it is profitable to note that it has also been suggested that even political considerations act as decisive determinants of the process of Sanskritization. For example, Epstein found a cultivator caste most interested in expressing its ritual status in local political terms of controlling rituals vis-a-vis a non-Sanskritic goddess, T. Scarlett Epstein, *Economic Development and Social Change in South India*, Manchester University Press, Manchester, 1962, pp. 132–5, 158–9, and Harper found from a study of a low caste's attempt to rise through Sanskritization that, without local economic and political power, such efforts produced no enhancement of the group's reputation and social ranking, Edward B. Harper, 'Social Consequences of an "Unsuccessful" Low Caste Movement', in James Silverberg (ed.), *Social Mobility in the Caste System in India*, Mouton, Paris, 1968, pp. 36–65. Social mobility in so emphatically hierarchized a society as in India is a multifaceted process and Srinivas outlined only one important aspect of its intricate mechanism.
48. Srinivas, *Social Change,* pp. 1–45.
49. Susan Snow Wadley, *Shakti: Power in the Conceptual Structure of*

Karimpur Religion, Department of Anthropology, The University of Chicago, Chicago, 1975, p. 7.

50. Robert J. Miller, 'Button, Button . . . Great Tradition, Little Tradition, Whose Tradition?, *Anthropological Quarterly*, Vol. 39, 1966. This equivalence is indeed taken for granted by Redfield, 'It is in India that the great (Sanskritic) tradition is in constant, various, and conspicuous interaction with the life of the local communities', *Peasant Society and Culture*, p. 92 and 'the relations of local tradition to widespread, reflective Brahmanical tradition in India . . . ', 'Civilizations as Cultural Structures', p. 394, as also by Milton Singer, the chief exponent of Redfield's theory, 'The Brahmanas are therefore the custodians par excellence of the great tradition of Indian society', 'Preface', in Milton Singer (ed.), *Traditional India: Structure and Change*, Rawat Publications, Jaipur, Indian reprint 1975 (first published in 1958), p. XII.
51. Miller, 'Button, Button . . . ', p. 27.
52. Helen B. Lamb, 'The Indian Merchant', in Milton Singer (ed.), *Traditional India*, pp. 27, 29–30. Scarcely do Lamb and Miller realize, though, that Vaiṣṇavism has always been a part of the brahmanical tradition (i.e. the tradition which accepts the social superiority of the *brāhmaṇas*) ever since it rose to eminence as an important sect.
53. F.G. Bailey, 'For a Sociology of India?', in L. Dumont and D. Pocock (eds), *Contributions to Indian Sociology*, Mouton and Co., Paris, No. 3, 1959, pp. 89–101.
54. L. Dumont and D. Pocock, 'For a Sociology of India', in L. Dumont and D. Pocock (eds), *Contributions to Indian Sociology*, Mouton and Co., Paris, No. 1, 1957, pp. 1–22.
55. Miller, 'Button, Button . . . ', pp. 40–1.
56. J.F. Staal, 'Sanskrit and Sanskritization', *The Journal of Asian Studies*, Vol. 12, No. 3, May 1963. Though this essay is ostensibly on Sanskritization, Staal is actually concerned with the formation of Indian traditions which directly belong to Redfield's domain.
57. *Ibid.*, pp. 266–8.
58. *Ibid.*, pp. 269–70.
59. J.A.B. van Buitenen, 'On the Archaism of the *Bhāgavata Purāṇa*', in Milton Singer (ed.), *Kṛṣṇa: Myths, Rites and Attitudes*, East-West Center, Honolulu, 1966, pp. 35–6.
60. *Ibid.*, p. 36. Sanskritization, however, is understood here primarily as a literary phenomenon, but this use of the term is not altogether unique. For example Coburn, *Devī-Māhātmya*, pp. 9–19, has used the term in precisely this sense.
61. David G. Mandelbaum, 'Introduction: Process and Structure in South Asian Religion', in Edward B. Harper (ed.), *Religion in South Asia*, University of Washington Press, Seattle, 1964. This division in fact originates from Harper's own study of certain village deities of Mysore. See

E.B. Harper, 'A Hindu Village Pantheon', *Southwestern Journal of Anthropology*, Vol. 15, 1959, pp. 227–34.

62. Mandelbaum, 'Introduction', p. 10.
63. *Ibid*., pp. 10–11.
64. *Ibid*., p. 11.
65. Swami Agehananda Bharati, *Great Tradition and Little Traditions: Indological Investigations in Cultural Anthropology*, Chowkhamba Sanskrit Series Office, Varanasi, 1978, pp. X–XI.
66. Wendy Doniger O'Flaherty, *Tales of Sex and Violence: Folklore, Sacrifice, and Danger in the Jaiminīya Brāhmaṇa*, Motilal Banarsidass, Delhi, 1987, p. 11.
67. Agehananda Bharati, 'Hinduism and Modernization', in Robert F. Spencer (ed.), *Religion and Change in Contemporary Asia*, Oxford University Press, Bombay, 1971, p. 71. Also Agehananda Bharati, 'Great Tradition and Little Traditions: An Anthropological Approach to the Study of Asian Cultures', in Th. Cummings (ed.), *Anthropology and Adult Education*, Center for Continuing Education, Boston, 1968.
68. V. Raghavan, 'Variety and Integration in the Pattern of Indian Culture', *The Far Eastern Quarterly*, Vol. 15, No. 4, August 1956, p. 500.
69. G.E. von Grunebaum, 'The Problem: Unity in Diversity', in Gustave E. von Grunebaum (ed.), *Unity and Diversity in Muslim Civilization*, The University of Chicago Press, Chicago, 1955.
70. *Ibid*., pp. 28–9.
71. Terence Ranger, 'Missionary Adaptation of African Religious Institutions: The Masasi Case', in T.O. Ranger and Isaria Kimambo (eds), *The Historical Study of African Religion*, Heinemann, London, 1972.
72. *Ibid*., p. 247. Ranger, however, points out that it was not merely Lucas's enthusiasm for substitution of symbols that made the adaptation policy a success, but various other factors contributed to it, such as the commitment of very many Africans whose interests and aspirations centred on the process. This indeed is the explanation in all such situations. A great tradition can only initiate the process of universalizing little tradition symbols, but its acceptance depends on at least minimal convergence of interests of the great tradition and the receiving group.
73. *Ibid*., pp. 229, 238–9. This of course is an extreme and an atypical example where Christianity attempted to establish itself through skilful manipulation rather than violent imposition. But even in such instances where the Christian authority systematically destroyed the traditional religions of the vanquished people, as in Mexico or in the Philippines, it is interesting to note how traces of traditional religions survived under a Christian garb and even valorized the Christian message which the missionaries had to eventually concede and accommodate. See Eva Alexandra Uchmany, 'Religious Changes in the Conquest of Mexico', and Rosario Mendoza Cortes, 'The Philippine Experience Under Spain: Christianization as

Social Change', in David N. Lorenzen (ed.), *Religious Change and Cultural Domination*, 30th International Congress of Human Sciences in Asia and North Africa, El Collegio De Mexico, Mexico, 1981, pp. 79–110, 111–20.

74. Ranger, 'Missionary Adaptation', p. 239.
75. Charles H. Long, 'Primitive/Civilized: The Locus of a Problem', *History of Religions*, Vol. 20, 1980–1, pp. 57–8.
76. Ralph W. Nicholas, 'Ritual Hierarchy and Social Relations in Rural Bengal', *Contributions to Indian Sociology*, New Series, No. 1, December 1967, p. 57.
77. Shashibhushan Dasgupta, *Bhārater Śakti Sādhanā O Śākta Sāhitya*, Sahitya Samsad, Calcutta, 1367 BS, p. 170.
78. Chatterji, 'The Indian Synthesis'.
79. Raghavan, 'Variety and Integration', p. 505.
80. Srinivas, *The Coorgs*, p. 209.
81. Marriott, 'Little Communities', p. 196.
82. Singer, 'Text and Context in the Study of Hinduism', in *When a Great Tradition Modernizes*, p. 50.
83. This reconstruction of the state of little traditions in Bengal during the composition of the *Purāṇas* is a little speculative, for there is no way of obtaining proper information on them. But to the extent that medieval vernacular literature and the anthropological accounts and census reports of a much later period allow us to form an opinion of the past, this conclusion appears to be reasonable. This is also partially corroborated by the excessive preoccupation of the Bengal *Purāṇas* with the goddess cult.
84. Richard P. Werbner, 'Introduction', in Richard P. Werbner (ed.), *Regional Cults*, A.S.A. Monograph no.16, Academic Press, London, 1977, p. IX.
85. A. Eschmann, 'Hinduization of Tribal Deities in Orissa: The Śākta and Śaiva Typology', in Eschmann, Kulke and Tripathi (eds), *The Cult of Jagannath,* p. 82.
86. Hazra, *Upapurāṇas*, Vol. I, pp. 25–6.
87. *Ibid.*, p. 27.
88. F.G. Bailey, *Tribe, Caste and Nation*, Manchester University Press, Manchester, 1960, p. 188, n.1.
89. Lauren Anita Corwin, 'Great Tradition, Little Tradition: The Cultural Traditions of a Bengal Town', *Contributions to Indian Sociology* (NS), Vol. 11, No. 1, 1977, p. 42.
90. Redfield, *Little Community,* p. 117. This is Redfield's diagram of Dr Starr's description of a Mexican villager as related not only to his village and its component sub-communities, but also to several communities outside of it at successive degress of remove from it. The villager has a sense of ingroup with respect to both country and region, but in lessening degree, p. 122.

91. A.K. Ramanujan (trans. and introduction), *Speaking of Śiva*, Penguin Books, Harmondsworth, 1985, p. 34.
92. Natalie Z. Davis, 'Some Tasks and Themes in the Study of Popular Religion', in Charles Trinkaus and Heiko A. Oberman (eds), *The Pursuit of Holiness in Late Medieval and Renaissance Religion*, E.J. Brill, Leiden, 1974, pp. 307–36.
93. Catherine Bell, 'Religion and Chinese Culture: Toward an Assessment of "Popular Religion" ', *History of Religions*, Vol. 29, No. 1, August 1989, pp. 37–8. This is an excellent summary of Davis's rather complicated arguments.
94. Natalie Z. Davis, 'From Popular Religion to Religious Cultures', in Steven Ozment (ed.), *Reformation Europe: A Guide to Research*, Center for Reformation Research, St Louis, 1982, pp. 321–43.
95. Bell, 'Religion and Chinese Culture', pp. 38–9.
96. *Ibid.*, p. 39.
97. *Ibid.*, p. 41.
98. Peter Burke, *Popular Culture in Early Modern Europe*, Temple Smith, London, 1978, pp. 23–4, 29.
99. *Ibid.*, p. 28.
100. Barrie M. Morrison, 'Sources, Methods and Concepts in Early Indian History', *Pacific Affairs*, Vol. 41, 1968, p. 81.

IV

The Diffusion of Brahmanism and the Transformation of Buddhism

The method by which brahmanism extended its influence in the peripheral regions followed a more or less common and predictable pattern, although the specific elements in the assimilative synthesis differed from one region to another, depending on the nature of the locally prevailing forms of culture and the judgement of the local *brāhmaṇas* on the manner of their appropriation. However, it took several centuries for brahmanism to overcome the initial resistance and gain a toehold in Bengal before the process of assimilation could formally begin with the codification of the *Purāṇas*. During this period, and even afterwards, brahmanism had to strive hard to first acquire and then maintain its social supremacy in Bengal. The history of brahmanical expansion in Bengal is recorded in several contemporary documents. While appropriating aspects of indigenous religious cultures, the Bengal *brāhmaṇas* had to contend with the presence of Buddhism that had enjoyed both state patronage and widespread popular support. However, the character of Buddhism in Bengal underwent such a radical transformation in course of time that it nearly lost its distinct profile, particularly in the eyes of the laity. State patronage also gradually but decisively shifted towards brahmanism, and the Buddhist popular support base was eventually subsumed within the expansive framework of brahmanical society. Therefore the significance of the establishment of *brāhmaṇa* ascendancy has to be understood against the backdrop of the twin processes of the diffusion of brahmanism and the transformation of Buddhism.

The Diffusion of Brahmanism

I

The *brāhmaṇas* hold centre-stage in this narrative and it is reasonable to begin with their coming to Bengal. A popular saying describes Bengal as a land where the Pāṇḍavas—the heroes of the epic *Mahābhārata*—had never set foot. Although the *Mahābhārata* itself contains ample evidence to the contrary,[1] this aphorism is lent substance by the fact that Bengal remained peripheral to the brahmanical scheme of things till about the early centuries of the Christian era. The early ethnographers and historians had noted that the 'Aryans' reached eastern India rather late and when they did arrive, they were resisted by the local people.[2] Such general statements of course presume a certain homogeneity of both the local and brahmanical cultures, as also a conscious design in the confrontation; they ignore the various stages of adjustment between the two cultural patterns. Nevertheless, they point to the essential truth that Bengal did not belong to the core area of brahmanical influence in the initial phase and its eventual induction into the brahmanical sphere involved a protracted process which was far from smooth.

The early brahmanical literature records the gradual expansion of brahmanism towards the east. The immediate surroundings of the Ṛg Vedic people were the Punjab and the northwest. The earliest undoubted reference to Magadha and Aṅga is found in the *Atharva Veda* in which these regions have been described as the land of the *vrātyas*. The famous story of Māthava, contained in the *Śatapatha Brāhmaṇa*, mentions the establishment of brahmanical settlements on the eastern bank of the river Sadānīrā. But up to this point, Bengal does not figure at all in the Vedic literature.[3] The first uncertain reference to Vaṅga appears in the *Aitareya Āraṇyaka* where it is assigned a place outside the Vedic realm. When Bengal begins to find mention in the Vedic literature, *brāhmaṇa* contempt for the land and its people is barely concealed. This attitude is exemplified in the *Aitareya Brāhmaṇa* story of the sage Viśvāmitra whose adoption of Sunaḥśepa was resented by his fifty sons. An angry Viśvāmitra cursed his sons that their descendants will inherit the easternmost margin of the earth and will be placed in the lowest rank of the *varṇa* order. They are said to be the progenitors of the Andhra, Puṇḍra, Śavara, Pulinda, and Mūtiba tribes, described as *dasyus*. In the *Mahābhārata* the people inhabiting the coastal regions of Bengal are called Mlecchas. According to the *Baudhāyana Dharmasūtra*, it was an offence to visit the lands of the Puṇḍras or Vaṅgas, and expiatory rites had to be performed if one transgressed this injunction. Evidently during the *Sūtra* period, Bengal was beginning to become known to brahmanism, but it was still forbidden territory.[4]

Some of this disdain for Bengal is also reflected in early Buddhist and Jaina literature. The *Ācāraṅga/Āyāraṅga Sutta* describes the harassment of Māhavīra and his disciples in the pathless Rāḍha country and makes disparaging comments about the food habits of the inhabitants of this region. The *Āryamañjuśrīmūlakalpa* says that the people of Gauḍa, Puṇḍra, Samataṭa and Harikela spoke in the *asura* language.

However, this antipathy did not last long; the distant northerners started to explore the tabooed east, which is implied in the stories of the conquests of Raghu, Karṇa and Bhīma. The *Rāmāyaṇa* says that the royal families of Matsya, Kāśī, and Kośala were marrying into Aṅga, Vaṅga and Magadha. Perhaps even more significant is the story contained in the *Vāyu* and the *Matsya Purāṇas* according to which the blind sage Dīrghatamas produced five sons through the wife of the *asura* king Bali. These were called Aṅga, Vaṅga, Kaliṅga, Puṇḍra, and Sumha, from which the names of the five *janapadas* are said to have been derived.[5]

Plainly Bengal was being recognized and slowly drawn into the brahmanical orbit. While during the period of the *Dharmasūtras* the eastern limit of Āryāvarta stretched up to Allahabad, in the *Mānava Dharmaśāstra* it stretches from the west to the east coast.[6] Interestingly, even in the Buddhist *Vinaya Piṭaka* the eastern frontier of Āryāvarta is set at Kajaṅgala near Rajmahal on the eastern fringe of Bihar, but the later Sanskrit *Vinaya* includes Puṇḍravardhana within its eastern boundary.[7] Benoychandra Sen has drawn our attention to the evolution of the concept of Āryāvarta, relevant to this context. He argues that though Manu used the term in an extended geographical sense, Madhyadeśa was for him the same region which in the *Vasiṣṭha* and the *Baudhāyana Dharmasūtras* is called Āryāvarta. Later writers such as Amara, the lexicographer, who belonged to the early Gupta period, and Rājaśekhara, who lived around AD 900, followed this distinction.[8] Thus the definition of the 'middle kingdom', the core area of brahmanism, remained more or less constant even when brahmanism, and along with it the eastern frontier of Āryāvarta, advanced. Manu refers to the Puṇḍras not just as an obscure tribe but as fallen *kṣatriyas*, and in the *Mahābhārata* the Vaṅgas and the Puṇḍras are described as true *kṣatriyas*. Surprisingly, the *Matsya* and the *Vāyu Purāṇas* not only call the Vaṅgas Sumhas and Puṇḍras *kṣatriyas,* but confer this exalted status on the Śavaras, Pulindas and Kirātas as well. That a small section of the population was even being recognized as *brāhmaṇas* is attested by reference to the existence of *brāhmaṇa* families in Bengal in the *Kāmasūtra* of Vātsyāyana.[9] Thus by the fourth century AD the brahmanical assimilation of Bengal had reached an identifiable stage of development. Not that the whole of Bengal was brought under brahmanical influence at the same time. It appears that brahmanism spread to Vaṅga through Puṇḍra, and Sumha was probably the last region to be brought within its pale.

Despite the abundance of material showing brahmanism's undisguised scorn for Bengal in the early historical period, D.C. Sircar remarks that some areas of 'Bengal already became strongholds of Aryan culture in the third and second centuries BC', on the strength of two stray inscriptions. According to Sircar, the earliest epigraphic record so far discovered in Bengal comes from Mahāsthān and is written in the Prākrit language and Brāhmī alphabet of about the third century BC. The other pre-Christian epigraph is the Silua (Noakhali district) image inscription, also in Prākrit and Brāhmī, which he assigns to the second century BC. Sircar argues that the 'popularity' of Prākrit, attested to by these two inscriptions, points to strong brahmanical influence in the northern and eastern parts of Bengal by this period.[10] This conclusion, based on such slender and uncertain evidence, is too weak to claim serious refutation, but the tendency to push Bengal's association with brahmanism as far back as possible has been displayed by several other scholars. Rama Chatterjee, for instance, is deeply mortified by the 'baseless reproaches' hurled at Bengal for its alleged non-brahmanical antecedents.[11] This anguish indicates the extent of internalization of brahmanical values and thus the ultimate triumph of brahmanism in Bengal.

As a matter of fact, the diffusion of brahmanical culture in Bengal is attested with a fair degree of certainty only from the Gupta period.[12] During the early Gupta period, even this link was tenuous. The earliest mention of Samataṭa in the Gupta epigraphs is found in the Allahabad Pillar Inscription of Samudragupta, and significantly it is grouped with Ḍavāka and Kāmarūpa as one of the border states, not directly administered by him.[13] When the Guptas began to exercise firm political control over Bengal, the *brāhmaṇas* did not enjoy the same privileges and place of honour as they did in other parts of contemporary north India. Chitrarekha Gupta shows that the *brāhmaṇas* of Bengal did not hold important administrative positions under the Gupta kings. Administrative divisions such as Koṭivarṣa were governed by prominent members of the professional groups such as merchants, and the

Kalaikuri and Jagadishpur copper-plates demonstrate that the *brāhmaṇas* had no special say even among the *kuṭumbins* and the *mahattaras* of the village community. Gupta records do not speak of any particular effort to establish brahmanical settlements in Bengal by Gupta kings. No special qualification of the *brāhmaṇa* donees has been mentioned in these inscriptions, and even their *gotra* names are conspicuous by their absence. Land was granted to *brāhmaṇas* for the performance of the *pañca-mahāyajñas*, which, Gupta believes, is a stereotyped expression and does not have much significance.[14] Nevertheless, it is from the Gupta period that we have definite information about *brāhmaṇas* and brahmanical institutions in Bengal. The Damodarpur and the Dhanaidaha copper-plates attest that a number of *brāhmaṇas* were settled with land and land was purchased for the worship of Kokāmukhasvāmī, Śvetavarāhasvāmī, Govindasvāmī and Nāmaliṅga, so that by the late fifth century north Bengal became a prominent centre of brahmanism.[15]

But it is really from the post-Gupta period that the influence of brahmanism began to increase at a rapid pace. It penetrated other parts of Bengal; *brāhmaṇas* assumed their position among the village *mahattaras* and were entrusted with administrative responsibilities. The seventh-century Nidhanpur inscription of Bhāskaravarmā says that two hundred and five *Vaidika brāhmaṇas* belonging to fifty-six *gotras* were settled in the Mayūraśālmala *agrahāra* (in Rangpur district) by Bhūtivarmā. The sixth-century Mallasārul inscription of Vijayasena and the seventh-century Vappaghoṣavāṭa inscription of Jayanāga record that *brāhmaṇas* were being established in the Rāḍha region of western Bengal. Similar information may be obtained for central and eastern Bengal as well. The records of Gopacandra and Dharmāditya show that *brāhmaṇas* were receiving land. The sixth-century Faridpur grant and the seventh-century Tippera grant of Lokanātha also testify to the donation of land to one Mahāsāmanta Pradoṣaśarmaṇ for the consecration of the Anantanārāyaṇa temple and settling two hundred and twenty-one *brāhmaṇas* versed in the four *Vedas*.[16] With the creation of large brahmanical settlements *brāhmaṇas* attempted to introduce their social codes among the local people, but without much success, as they themselves appear not to have been too particular in observing them. The Tippera record of Lokanātha shows that some *brāhmaṇas* had even married into *śūdra* families and changed profession.[17]

The process of brahmanization of Bengal gained further momentum with the establishment of the Pāla–Candra–Kāmboja kingdoms. *Brāh-*

maṇas received persistent royal support in the form of land, high administrative positions, and other social privileges. The first set of brahmanical texts of Bengal, such as the early Bengal *Purāṇas*, was also composed during this period, formulating the principles of social order and rules of religious performance. That those who adhered to the brahmanical form of worship far outnumbered the Buddhists in Bengal by the seventh century is attested by Yuan Chwang, and the *Āryamañjuśrīmūlakalpa* states that during the time of Gopāla, Bengal was inhabited by the *tīrthika brāhmaṇas* up to the sea.[18] The Badāla *praśasti* of Bhaṭṭa Gaurava Miśra provides positive evidence regarding appointment of successive generations of *brāhmaṇa* ministers by the Pāla rulers. The Kāmboja king Nayapāla of the Iḍḍā copper-plate donated land to the *brāhmaṇas* in the Varddhamāna-*bhukti* of western Bengal and the Rāmapāla copper-plate of Śrī-Candra informs us that he granted land to a *Śāntivārika* priest for the supervision of *Koṭihoma* ceremony. The Paścimbhāga copper-plates of Śri-Candra mention that he settled a colony called Candrapura in the Śrīhaṭṭa *maṇḍala* of Puṇḍravardhana-*bhukti* where he allotted land to six thousand *brāhmaṇas* of different categories.[19]

This process reached its culmination during the Sena–Varmaṇa period under active royal patronage. Such local dynasties as the Devas also contributed to this process. The Senas and the Varmaṇas came from the south, carrying with them a deep sense of commitment to brahmanical ideals and institutions. They consciously encouraged the propagation of brahmanical religion and the enforcement of *varṇāśramadharma*. This tendency is exemplified in three simultaneous developments: the composition of a large corpus of texts stating the essential brahmanical injunctions later elaborated in the medieval *Smṛtis*, an emphasis on the *gotra*, *pravara* and *Vaidika śākhās* of the *brāhmaṇa* beneficiaries of land grants (pointing to the importance placed on social classification), and the performance of Vedic and Puranic rites asserting the ultimate supremacy of the *brāhmaṇas*. These tendencies had their origin in the immediately preceding period, but they were given a purposeful direction by the Sena–Varmaṇa rulers.

Brahmanical ideals of social organization were systematically articulated for the first time in Bengal in the *Smṛti* texts of this period. Bhaṭṭa Bhavadeva, a minister of Harivarmaṇa, was the foremost thought-leader of his time, whose *Prāyaścitta-prakaraṇa* and *Karmānuṣṭhāna-paddhati* proved to be highly influential. The later *Smṛti* writers of Bengal have repeatedly quoted and discussed him and the process of standardization of the life-cycle rituals, which regulate the life of a Hindu Bengali, began with him. Jimūtavāhana, the famous author of *Vyavahāramātrikā*, *Dāyabhāga* and *Kālaviveka* also belonged to this period. Aniruddha Bhaṭṭa, the preceptor of Vallālasena, wrote *Hāralatā* and *Pitṛdayitā*. Vallālasena himself was the author of several *Smṛti* texts of which *Dānasāgara* and *Adbhutasāgara* have survived. But the most significant of them all was Halāyudha, the Mahādharmādhyakṣa of Lakṣmaṇasena. Among his works *Brāhmaṇasarvasva*, *Mīmāṁsāsarvasva*, *Vaiṣṇavasarvasva*, *Śaivasarvasva* and *Paṇḍitasarvasva* were considered to be the most authoritative by later writers such as Śūlapāṇi and Raghunandana. These texts discuss the caste hierarchy and caste inter-relationships, the rites of passage, rules governing inheritance and distribution of property, daily rites and expiations, permissible and prohibited items of food, auspicious and inauspicious actions, and, above all, the duties and prerogatives of the *brāhmaṇas*. Their decisions were definite and irrevocable. Together, these *Smṛiti* texts constituted the basis of the later *brāhmaṇa* domination of the lives of the Hindu population of Bengal.[20]

Royal gifts to the *brāhmaṇas* became more frequent and generous. The Sāmantasāra plate of Harivarmaṇa and the Belāva plate of Bhojavarmaṇa record donation of land to their *Śāntivārika* priests. The Barrackpur copper-plate of Vijayasena and the Naihāṭī copper-plate of Vallālasena mention grants of land to their priests for performing *Kanakatulāpuruṣa-mahādāna* and *Hemāśva-mahādāna* on behalf of the queen Vilāsadevī. The Tarpaṇadīghi and the Mādhāinagar copper-plates of Lakṣmaṇasena inform us that his priests received grants of land as fees for their supervision of *Hiraṇyāśvaratha-mahādāna* and the *Aindrīśānti* rituals respectively. Some of the later Sena inscriptions record grants of land to those *brāhmaṇas* who were professional narrators of brahmanical texts (*nīti-pāṭhaka*).[21] The Deopārā inscription of Vijayasena records that he lavished so much wealth on *brāhmaṇas* that the city-dwelling women had to teach the wives of the *brāhmaṇa* beneficiaries how to distinguish between pearls and cotton seeds, precious stones and seeds of pomegranate.[22] Presumably these are poetic exaggerations, but to the extent imagination approximates reality, such statements reflect the idealized intentions of the Sena state. The other most notable feature of these inscriptions is that they record in detail the genealogy, *gotra*, *pravara*, *vaidika śākhā* and *caraṇa* of the *brāhmaṇa* donees. The lists prepared by Puspa Niyogi[23] and Rama Chatterjee[24] reveal with what care and precision such information was documented.

In fact the inscriptions tend to suggest that Vedism, in all its ramifications, was actively patronized by the rulers of Bengal from the Pāla period onwards. The Badāla plates of Bhaṭṭa Gaurava Miśra say that Kedāra Miśra delighted the minds of gods and men by filling the circle of the quarters with the smoke of the sacrificial fire. The Iḍḍā copper-plate of the Kāmboja king Nayapāla describes his capital Priyaṅgu where heavy smoke from sacrificial fire, carrying *Śunāsīra* invoked for oblation, rose like clouds to the sky. The Bhuvaneśvara inscription of Bhaṭṭa Bhavadeva claims that the beauty of the village Siddhala in Rāḍha was augmented by the presence of *brāhmaṇas* who were proficient in various branches of the *Vedas* and that it was an ornament among hundred such villages. The Deopārā *praśasti* of Vijayasena contains the famous description of a hermitage in Rāḍha at the time of Sāmantasena where fragrance emanating from the sacrifices performed regularly by the hermits made the air free from impurity; the infant deer suckled the breasts of the ascetic mothers, and the parrots recited hymns from the *Vedas*.[25]

And yet Halāyudha, a contemporary of Lakṣmaṇasena and the foremost *Smṛti* writer of this period, said in justification of his composition of the *Brāhmaṇasarvasva* that the *brāhmaṇas* of Rāḍha and Varendra did not read the *Vedas*, and consequently were not acquainted with the rules of Vedic sacrifice. He wrote that in his time, proper knowledge of the *Vedas* was available only in Utkala and in the west. Before him, Aniruddha Bhaṭṭa also commented on the neglect of Vedic studies in Bengal.[26] However, Sanskrit learning was another matter. Not only epigraphic evidence, but the efflorescence of the Navyanyāya school of philosophy in the fifteenth–sixteenth century also suggests that Sanskritic studies must have had a long tradition in Bengal. But these two positions are not inconsistent with one another. Vedic studies and brahmanism were not synonymous in the period of our study and, as the Bengal experience shows, they were not even coextensive. The *Vedas* in the *Smārta*–Puranic phase of the evolution of brahmanism had outlived their necessity and had no functional value except as a source of symbolic authority. This authority was continuously espoused by the authors of the Bengal *Purāṇas* and *Smṛtis*, often completely inappropriately. That does not mean that these scholars were unfamiliar with the *Vedas*. On the contrary, there is ample evidence to suggest that at least some of them knew their *Vedas* and the later Vedic literature quite well.[28] Yet they misquoted and fabricated injunctions in the name of the *Vedas*—which suggests that they themselves hardly believed that the *Vedas* were infallible or immutable—in order to legitimize their Puranic and

Smṛti innovations. Propagation of pristine Vedism was not the agenda. The ritual prescriptions of Bhavadeva, Jīmūtavāhana and Halāyudha conform more to the Puranic socio-religious formulations than the Vedic sacrifices for the obvious reason that Vedism had become obsolete and therefore functionally redundant. The authoritative *Smṛtis* of the medieval period borrowed heavily from both the Bengal *Purāṇas* and this earlier group of *Smṛtis*, which points to a linear development rather than a disjunction in the formation of the brahmanical tradition in Bengal. Sanskrit scholarship was naturally kept alive and a distinct school of philosophical speculation also developed, but they had very little to do with the *Vedas* as such. My argument is that the role of the *Vedas* was minimal in the evolution of the syncretic religious system which grew out of an interaction between post-Vedic brahmanism and the local religious cultures of Bengal. Although brahmanism was the controlling agency (to the extent any involved party can retain control over the process of cultural exchange) in the creation of the distinctly regional profile of the composite Bengali culture, from the outset, the *Vedas* remained outside the purview of this process.

Rama Chatterjee, distressed by the supposed non-Vedic origin of Bengal brahmanism, herself indicates that there was a clear shift in emphasis in the epigraphs of the Senas, the most vigorous champions of orthodox brahmanism in Bengal, from Vedism to the 'ritualistic regulation of the Purāṇas', exemplified in their assertion of the importance of the Puranic *dāna* compared with the Vedic *yajña*.[29] Some of the *brāhmaṇa* donees mentioned in the Sena copper-plates had only partial knowledge of the *Vedas* or were completely ignorant of them. A good many of the Sena epigraphs are silent about the proficiency of the donees in any branch of Vedic knowledge and a few others only mention a branch or two. Therefore Chatterjee concludes that those *brāhmaṇas* who knew an entire branch of one of the four *Vedas* adopted the title of *Vaidika*, those who had partial knowledge of a branch of the *Vedas* were called *ekadeśādhyayī*, and those who were devoid of any scholarly attainment in the *Vedas* were simply described by their *gotra* and *pravara*.[30] Does this mean that the extravagant references to the Vedic sacrifice and ambience in the Bengal inscriptions are spurious? Perhaps not. They reveal brahmanism in its ideal construct. These are expressions of the ideology and the social orientation of the Senas in which the *Vedas* stood for brahmanism in its ultimate state of purity, and not necessarily an appreciation of their intrinsic worth. Quite inadvertently Rama Chatterjee betrays the connotation of the concept of Vedic culture in contemporary Bengal: 'In those days, a *Brāhmaṇa* was regarded as having attained proficiency in Vedic culture if he was adept in the studies of the Purāṇas and the Smṛtis.'[31] There is no reason why the references to the *Vedas* in the Bengal epigraphs should be taken literally.

II

The Bengal epigraphs provide us other significant information. We have seen that the first group of *brāhmaṇa* settlers in Bengal came from north India during the fifth–sixth centuries AD. Contemporary inscriptions show that they continued to migrate from Madhyadeśa to Bengal in even greater number from the eighth century onwards. They came from Kroḍañci, Tarkāri, Matsyāvāsa, Kuntīra, Candavāra, Hastipada, Muktāvāstu, and even as far as Lāṭa in Gujarat.[32] Puspa Niyogi infers from the appointment of these *brāhmaṇas* to important administrative positions by the Pāla rulers that those who came from outside enjoyed greater respect.[33] These fresh migrations indicate that the *brāhmaṇas* must have fulfilled some social requirement to justify their land grants and other honours and privileges. These facts and their implications contributed to the construction of the collective memory which found mythological expression in the late medieval *Kulajī* texts.

The *Kulajīs* are genealogical accounts of the *brāhmaṇa* families of Bengal of which *Mahāvaṁśāvalī* by Dhruvānanda Miśra, *Goṣṭhikathā* of Nulo Pañcānana, *Kularāma* by Vācaspati Miśra, *Kulapradīpa* of Dhanañjaya, *Vārendra Kulapañjikā*, *Kulārṇava*, the *Kārikās* of Hari Miśra and Eḍu Miśra and *Kulatattvārṇava* by Sarvānanda Miśra are well known. Most of these are early modern texts, although a few may go back to the fifteenth–sixteenth centuries.[34]

The stories that the *Kulajī* texts narrate are full of inconsistencies and they often contradict each other. But all these versions more or less converge on a common core which is as follows: A king of Bengal called Ādiśūra married Candramukhī, the daughter of the king of Kānyakubja. Candramukhī wanted to perform the *Cāndrāyaṇa vrata* and as the *brāhmaṇas* of Bengal were found deficient in their knowledge of the *Vedas*, Ādiśūra requested his father-in-law to send five *sāgnika brāhmaṇas* to conduct the ritual. Accordingly, five *brāhmaṇas* belonging to Śāṇḍilya, Kāśyapa, Vātsya, Bhāradvāja and Sāvarṇa *gotras* arrived in Gauḍa and eventually settled in different parts of Bengal. They married the daughters of the local Saptaśatī *brāhmaṇas* and in course of time fifty-nine sons were born to them. Kṣitiśūra gifted a village to each of these sons from which the fifty-nine *gāñīs* of the Rāḍhīya *brāhmaṇas* are traced. However, Dharaśūra observed that the moral standard of the Rāḍhīya *brāhmaṇas* was declining and consequently classified them into three categories—the primary and secondary Kulīnas and the Śrotriyas—in order of purity. The *Kulajīs* claim that later Vallālasena arrived at a similar classification for the same reason.[35] The *Kulajī* texts mention six different ceremonies for which the five Kānyakubja *brāhmaṇas* were requisitioned. Their accounts of the manner in which these *brāhmaṇas* were appointed also do not tally with each other. The date of this event is variously placed between Śaka 654 and 999, and they give three sets of names for the five *brāhmaṇas*.[36] However, there is no conflict with regard to the other details.

Several historians have found the Ādiśūra legend totally unacceptable. N.K. Dutt, for example, points out that while none of the names of the illustrious Pāla and Sena rulers seems to have been known to the authors of the *Kulajīs*, Ādiśūra is not mentioned in any of the contemporary epigraphic or literary records of Bengal. Nor is there any evidence to suggest that during the centuries between the coming of the five *brāhmaṇas* and the reign of Vallālasena the Bengal *brāhmaṇas* ever claimed descent from the Kānyakubja stock. Dutt therefore concluded that the story of Ādiśūra was 'fabricated out of disjointed materials' at a much later date.[37] R.C. Majumdar has also argued in his detailed study that the authenticity of the *Kulajī* texts is so questionable that they can hardly be accepted as evidence for the reconstruction of the social history of early Bengal.[38]

In spite of the disorderly and palpably contradictory nature of the evidence, there has been no dearth of attempts to try and establish Ādiśūra as a historical figure.[39] Apart from the early defence of the *Kulajī* texts by such scholars as Nagendranath Basu and Lalmohan Vidyanidhi,[40] and Rajendralal Mitra's somewhat clumsy attempt to arrive at a precise date (AD 937) for the migration of the Kānyakubja *brāhmaṇas*,[41] several historians have speculated on the possible identification of Ādiśūra with disparate historical characters. Pramode Lal Paul, who thought that the *Kulajīs* were factually incorrect 'propagandist' texts, nevertheless suggested that the Magadhan king Ādisiṁha of the Dudhpani Rock Inscription might have been Ādiśūra on the basis of similarity in names, proximity of time, and contiguity of kingdoms.[42] D.C. Sircar, conceding that the name of Ādiśūra does not figure in the Śūra royal dynasty of ancient Bengal, still argues that he is mentioned in the *Nyāyakaṇikā* of the Mithila scholar Vācaspati Miśra as a contemporary of the author. He composed his *Nyāyasūci* in AD 841. 'The historical Ādiśūra of eastern India thus seems to have ruled over Mithilā and the contiguous portion of North Bengal as a feudatory of the Pālas about the middle of the ninth century AD.'[43] Sukhamay Mukhopadhyaya appears to favour this reasoning, although he suggests that the period of the composition of *Nyāyasūci* should be taken as the latter half of the tenth century, in which case the date of Ādiśūra entirely agrees with the testimony of some of the *Kulajī* texts.[44]

The debate on the historicity of Ādiśūra is not strictly relevant to my problem. However, Kulinism, which is traced from this legend, exercised such an oppressive influence on the majority of the Hindu population of Bengal from the medieval period until about the beginning of the twentieth century and became a matter of such absurd pride for a small minority, that it deserves mention in a discussion on the social organization of the Bengal *brāhmaṇas*. At its worst, the non-Kulīna *brāhmaṇas* attempted to raise their status in the social hierarchy by giving their daughters in marriage to Kulīna men, however incompatible the match might have been, and there was no restriction on the number of wives they could take. Many began to live off these marriages. The vulgar cruelty of this system has been captured in all its ruthlessness by Sarat Chandra Chattopadhyaya in his novel *Bāmuner Meye*[45] and its effect on the womenfolk has been portrayed by Bibhuti Bhushan Bandyopadhyaya in his *Pather Pāñcālī*. The opening section of *Pather Pāñcālī*, called *Vallālī Bālāi* (the curse of Vallālasena), ends with the death of the poor, abandoned Kulīna widow Indir Ṭhākrun which, the author says, also marked the end of that era (*sekāla*) in the village of Niścindipur.[46] It is not without reason that Nimchand Datta, the protagonist of Dinabandhu Mitra's nineteenth-century farce *Sadhabār Ekādaśī*, who spoke unpleasant truths under the licence of drunkenness, told a Kulīna *kāyastha*, 'You are wicked, your father is wicked, your father's father is wicked, your seven generations of ancestors are wicked, your court of Ādiśūra is wicked.'[47] The imaginary Ādiśūra was unfortunately a social reality in Bengal.

Besides, even though the story was concocted for the purpose of legitimating social differentiation among the upper castes, it reflects with some accuracy the process of evolution of the social structure of Bengal. Niharranjan Ray therefore believes that although the testimony of the *Kulajīs* is not admissible as evidence, the intricate *varṇa* and *jāti* divisions of the Bengali society during the fifteenth to seventeenth centuries, and the *Smṛti* regulations which kept a close watch on this system, had a 'history'. Popular memory of that history led to the growth of this legend.[48]

Ronald Inden has identified four stages in the transformation of the Bengali Hindu community of the 'past' to 'the middle period' (AD 1450–1800). It began, he says, during the reign of the evil king Veṇa who forced men and women of the four *varṇas* to intermarry. This led to the creation of the occupational *jātis* which were classified by his virtuous son Pṛthu into *brāhmaṇas* and *śūdras*. Subsequently, king Ādiśūra recognized the immigrant ancestors of *brāhmaṇa* and *kāyastha* Kulīnas to be superior in rank to the indigenous *brāhmaṇas* and *śūdras* by virtue of their good conduct and Vedic scholarship. During the reign of the Sena kings, the ancestors of the *brāhmaṇas* and *kāyasthas* were divided into territorial *jātis* or subcastes and these in turn into ranked grades or clans, thereby initiating the dual organization scheme of medieval Bengali society. By the thirteenth–fourteenth centuries, Muslim conquest resulted in new and improper mixtures. Newly formed subcaste councils met this challenge by reorganizing the *brāhmaṇa* and *kāyastha* subcastes at the outset of the middle period.[49]

In this ordering, the first stage belongs to the Bengal *Purāṇas* which tell the story of Veṇa and Pṛthu which contains an echo of reality in that Bengal never had the two intervening *varṇas* of *kṣatriya* and *vaiśya*. The first group of immigrant *brāhmaṇas* classified the entire indigenous population into the broad category of *śūdras*, subdivided into pure and impure groups (*sat śūdra* and *asat śūdra*).[50] The Ādiśūra legend, justifying fresh *brāhmaṇa* migrations, was constructed much later but was foisted on a supposedly historical but actually mythical past. The developments attributed to the Sena period belong to that grey area where legend and history get intertwined and reinforce each other. The reorganization of the late medieval period is within the domain of both partially documented history and retrievable memory.

Thus the *Kulajīs* encapsulate the entire spectrum of developments, preserving history in legend. For instance, the *Kulajīs* connect the Senas with the spread of orthodox brahmanism in Bengal which is supported by reliable independent evidence. The *Kulajīs* do not claim that there were no *brāhmaṇas* in Bengal before the import of the five Kānyakubja *brāhmaṇas* by Ādiśūra. They clearly state that there were the seven hundred Saptaśatī *brāhmaṇas*, well versed in the *Dharmaśāstras*, who intermarried with the new migrants and thus created the complex social structure of the Bengal *brāhmaṇas*. The *Kulajīs* merely point to the tradition of the continuous inflow of *brāhmaṇas* from Madhyadeśa until at least the twelfth century, and the non-familiarity of the local *brāhmaṇas* with the Vedic tradition, in a convoluted mythological language. Although the Bengal epigraphs do not refer to the Kulīnas, they mention the *gāñī* differentiation, explained in the *Kulajī* texts. The inscriptions of the Deva dynasty plainly suggest that the Bengal *brāhmaṇas* increasingly came to be known by their *gāñī* identity, deriving their social status from their place of origin.[51] If only historians had not undertaken the futile task of trying to establish the actual historical antecedents of Ādiśūra, this debate would have been unnecessary.

Finally, the *Kulajī* texts draw our attention to the fact that the *brāhmaṇas* were not a homogeneous category, something that the Bengal *Purāṇas* tend to gloss over and would love to deny. The Rāḍhīya and Vārendra *brāhmaṇas*—subdivided into primary and secondary Kulīnas and *Bhaṅgas*, the Śrotriya and Vaidika *brāhmaṇas*, the Saptaśatī, Madhyaśreṇī, Gauḍīya, and Vaṅgaja *brāhmaṇas*, the Graha-vipra, Varṇa, and Agradānī *brāhmaṇas*, not to speak of the innumerable subcastes and clans, the *gotras*, *pravaras*, *caraṇas*, *śākhās*, *melas*, *gāñīs*, and the sectarian divisions—all belong to one overarching category. But they are graded into such an inflexible hierarchy that the members of the upper crust were not supposed to accept water from those at the bottom such as the Agradānī. Marriage restrictions were equally rigid. The Puranic attempt to cover up multiform heterogeneity of Bengal *brāhmaṇas* is clearly revealed in the obsessive fear of degenerate *brāhmaṇa* of the *Kali* age.[52]

III

The Bengal *Purāṇas* played a very crucial role in this process of brahmanization. It is important to note that although there were a number of *brāhmaṇa* settlements in Bengal by the end of the Gupta period, the process of codification of *Purāṇas* did not begin before about 800 or so. Evidently a period of gestation was required before the *Purāṇas* could be formally launched. Even though historians have persistently ignored the Puranic evidence, we shall see that in several spheres of life their prescriptions came so tantalizingly close to the actual state of affairs that it seems as if the state merely implemented what they recommended, and the rest of society simply fell in line.

The prime thrust of the *Purāṇas* was to create such an image of the *brāhmaṇas* that it would justify the many rights and privileges that the *Purāṇas* claim for them. They declared that the *brāhmaṇas* are gods on earth, entitled to unconditional veneration and all possible material comforts. Thus the *Brahmavaivarta Purāṇa*:

It is Nārāyaṇa himself who, out of pity for the living beings, appears as the *brāhmaṇa* in every age. Brahmā, Viṣṇu, Maheśa and all the other gods accept only those fruits, flowers and water which are offered by the *brāhmaṇas*. It is through the invocation of the *brāhmaṇas* that the gods receive worship on earth. There is no god greater than the *brāhmaṇa* because it is Hari himself who assumes the form of the brāhmaṇa. If the *brāhmaṇa* feels satisfied, Nārāyaṇa is pleased, and if Nārāyaṇa is pleased, all the gods are delighted. Just as there is no greater *tīrtha* than Gaṅgā, no greater god than Kṛṣṇa, no greater Vaiṣṇava than Śaṁkara, and none as patient as the earth; just as there is no greater *dharma* than truth, none so chaste and faithful as Pārvatī, none so invincible as fate and none so dear as the son; just as there is no greater enemy than illness, none so worthy of reverence as the teacher, none so helpful as the mother and none so friendly as the father; just as fasting on the day of *Ekādaśī* is the most commendable of all the *vratas* and knowledge is the best of all precious things, there is none greater than the *brāhmaṇa* in all the four stages of life. He is the best of all the preceptors. Brahmā said that the *Vedas* and the *Vedāṅgas* have unanimously resolved this.[53]

Not only are the *brāhmaṇas* as good as the gods, but they are in a sense more effective, for they are the directly observable gods on earth,[54] in whose body the gods reside.[55] The entire world and all the *dharmas* belong to them.[56] Therefore, whether scholarly or ignorant, they are always the best and no question should be raised about it. Even if they are of improper conduct and unclean habits (*anācārā*) they are still worthy of worship. Keśava himself, all the gods, ancestors and great sages, accept food in the house in which a *brāhmaṇa* has eaten. One who carries even a drop of water that has washed the feet of a *brāhmaṇa* is absolved of all sins. All the centres of pilgrimage that exist in this universe reside in the feet of a *brāhmaṇa*.[57] The earth remains stable as long as *brāhmaṇas* exist. Hence they should be propitiated for the protection of the universe.[58]

The *brāhmaṇas* should be propitiated with respectful devotion, because neither wise counsel nor *mantra*, *stava* or *kavaca*, indeed nothing can save the *śūdras* from adversity except devotion to the *brāhmaṇas*.[59] This devotion should be expressed primarily in the form of gifts (*dāna*). Ascetic practices in the *Kṛtayuga*, meditation in the *Tretā*, worship in the *Dvāpara* and making gifts in the *Kali* are the best of all acts. Therefore wise men should always make gifts in the *Kaliyuga* for the pleasure of Kamalāpati.[60] And of all the recipients of gifts, *brāhmaṇas* are the most deserving,[61] because gifts made to the gods and the *brāhmaṇas* produce similar results.[62] Between the two, the *brāhmaṇas* are even superior, for it is more beneficial to worship those gods who eat in person (*sākṣāt khādati*). Janārdana himself eats the offerings made to the gods who are the *brāhmaṇas*. Those who worship the *brāhmaṇas* need not worship any other god, for it is through them that all the other gods are worshipped. If offerings dedicated to the gods are not gifted to *brāhmaṇas*, these are reduced to ashes and worship itself is rendered fruitless. Even if a wise person does not offer anything to the gods but makes presents only to the *brāhmaṇas*, the gods eat those through the mouth of the *brāhmaṇas* and happily retire to heaven,[63] because the mouth of the *brāhmaṇa* is the principal mouth of the gods.[64] It is impossible to accuse the Puranic authors of undue modesty.

The list of articles to be gifted to *brāhmaṇas* is impressive and nearly exhaustive. It includes milk products, grain, fruits and water, copper (utensils?), clothes, dress and ornaments, jewellery and precious stones, gold and silver, land, house and wife, cows and bulls, and horses and elephants.[65] If one has the means, one must never be miserly in making these gifts.[66] Predictably, attractive rewards, such as eternal residence in Viṣṇuloka, Sūryaloka, Śvetadvīpa, etc., await those who donate generously to *brāhmaṇas*.[67]

Although no particular occasion is required to make gifts to *brāhmaṇas*, one must always pay them honorarium (*dakṣiṇā*) for conducting sacrifices and other rituals. The *Brahmavaivarta Purāṇa* narrates the following story about the origin of *dakṣiṇā*:

> Once, when the sacrifices performed by the gods did not yield the desired results, they approached Brahmā. Brahmā meditated on Nārāyaṇa who brought forth Dakṣiṇā, the goddess of wealth on earth (*marttyalakṣmī*), from the person of Mahālakṣmī, and gave her to Brahmā. Brahmā in turn handed her over to Yajña for the successful completion of action undertaken by honest men. Yajña married the extremely beautiful Dakṣiṇā and made love to her for hundred divine years, at the end of which she gave birth to Phala (literally fruit), the consequence of all actions. Those who are well versed in the *Vedas* know that Yajña and Dakṣiṇā along with their son Phala confer result on all duly completed action. The performer must bestow the honorarium (*dakṣiṇā*) immediately after the action has been carried out for it to bear fruit. If by mistake or out of ignorance he delays the payment of the honorarium by a second, he will have to pay double the amount, if it is delayed by a night, six times the amount, and so on. If it is not paid at all, the *yajamāna* is debarred from performing all religious duties. His ancestors do not accept oblations from him. He suffers from poverty and illness and finally ends up in hell. One who deceives a *brāhmaṇa* of his honorarium goes down like a vessel which is not secured by a rope.[68]

The grossly material aspect of the honorarium and the benefits that accrue to the conscientious *yajamāna* accords well with the tangible forms of Dakṣiṇā and Phala in this metaphorical story and drives home the message with unfailing directness.

However, gift of land is the greatest of all gifts. According to the *Bṛhannāradīya Purāṇa*, Viṣṇu, in his Vāmana incarnation, is said to have told the demon king Bali that no one in this world can describe the real greatness of making gifts of land. There has never been and will never be a gift as efficacious as donation of land. There is no doubt that one who donates land attains liberation. Even if one donates a small plot to a Śrotriya *brāhmaṇa*, who maintains a consecrated fire, he gains access to Brahmaloka for ever. One who makes gift of land acquires the merit of donating everything under the sun and achieves salvation at the end. Gift of land destroys sins of all kinds. Even if a sinner, steeped in every conceivable crime, donates a piece of land measuring ten cubits, all his sins immediately disappear. As a result, there is none so fortunate in the three worlds as the donor of land. I cannot express even in hundreds of years the merits of one who donates land to a *brāhmaṇa* without a means of livelihood. One who donates land with sugarcane, wheat, basil and areca-nut trees on it achieves the equivalence of Viṣṇu. One who donates a small plot of land to a poor *brāhmaṇa*, who is devoted to the worship of gods or is burdened with a large family, unites with Viṣṇu. One who donates a piece of land that produces an *āḍhaka* of paddy to a devout *brāhmaṇa*, acquires the merit of bathing in the river Gaṅgā for three days. One who donates a piece of land that produces a *droṇa* of paddy to a virtuous *brāhmaṇa*, acquires the merit of performing hundreds of *aśvamedha* sacrifices on the bank of the river Gaṅgā. One who donates a piece of land that produces a *khārī* of paddy to a poor *brāhmaṇa*, acquires the merit of performing hundreds of *aśvamedha* and *vājapeya* sacrifices on the bank of the river Gaṅgā. As a result, it is said that donation of land is the best and the greatest of all gifts (*atidāna*, *mahādāna*).[69]

This theme has been elaborated with endless variations in literally hundreds of passages in the Bengal *Purāṇas*. For example, the *Bṛhaddharma Purāṇa* says that the sages praise one as the consecrator of one thousand phallic icons of Śiva who settles (*sthāpayati*) poor *brāhmaṇa* cousins with land, and the propounders of *dharma* have declared that the donors of land reside in heaven for sixty thousand years.[70] The *Brahmavaivarta Purāṇa* says that one who donates twelve fingerlengths of land to a *brāhmaṇa* who performs the daily religious services in Bhārata, goes to the abode of Viṣṇu, and one who provides for the livelihood of a *brāhmaṇa* (*upajīvyaṁ*; the term usually employed is *vṛtti*, i.e. maintenance grant, and it refers to the return from land), acquires unlimited property and gains deliverance from four kinds of encumbrances.[71] The *Kriyāyogasāra* says that even if one donates a piece of land as small as that which is covered by the hide of a cow, he is absolved of all his sins and goes to the desired land, and one who donates villages to poor *brāhmaṇas*, stays happily in Viṣṇuloka for as many *manvantaras* as there are particles of dust and drops of water in that plot of land.[72]

However, the most striking representation of the consequence of making gifts of land to the *brāhmaṇas* can be found in the following ancient chronicle (*itihāsa*) contained in the *Bṛhannāradīya Purāṇa*:

> Once there was a poor *brāhmaṇa* called Bhadramati who was well versed in the *Vedas*, the *Purāṇas*, and the *Dharmaśāstras*. He had six wives and three hundred and thirty-four children, whom he could not feed. Seeking ways to overcome his wretched condition, Bhadramati decided that he must make a gift of land, since it leads to the attainment of all the desired objects. Accordingly, he arrived at the city of Kauśāmbī and requested a wealthy *brāhmaṇa* called Sughoṣa to grant him a piece of land measuring five cubits. Sughoṣa was delighted to be able to help and presented him with the land. Bhadramati, in his turn, donated this land to a poor Śrotriya who was devoted to Hari. As a result of this gift Sughoṣa and Bhadramati went to Viṣṇuloka and Brahmaloka respectively. Later, Bhadramati was reborn into a very affluent family with a memory of his former life. He enjoyed all the comforts on earth and made innumerable gifts of land to the poor *brāhmaṇas* which earned him salvation for ever.[73]

This story offers an ingenious solution to all earthly problems. Apparently Bhadramati had enough sense to realize that he could hardly expect to receive a grant of land sufficient for the upkeep of his three hundred and thirty-four children. Instead, he chose the more reasonable option of asking for such land as he, as an indigent *brāhmaṇa*, was justifiably entitled to obtain. Once in possession of land, however small, he could help himself with the merits of donating it, which, as the story illustrates, were enormous. It is perhaps not the most scrupulous method of acquiring religious merit, but this innocent subterfuge dramatically heightens the message the story seeks to deliver.

Once land was obtained for the *brāhmaṇas*, the *Purāṇas* attempted to ensure that it was made free of tax and that under no circumstances should the grant be resumed by the donor or allowed to be encroached on by others. The *Bṛhannāradīya* declares that one who collects taxes from a *brāhmaṇa* village suffers in hell so long as the moon and the stars exist. One who imposes additional taxes on such a village suffers in hell along with one thousand generations of ancestors for millions of *kalpas*. One who approves imposition of such taxes is degraded for committing the sin of brahmanicide.[74] Incidentally, it is also mentioned that no interest should be charged from the *brāhmaṇas*, but if necessary, loans should be advanced to them, for they are the directly observable gods and their blessing is the most precious thing on earth.[75] Worse still—because the descriptions are more detailed and gruesome—are the consequences of resuming or misappropriating land that belongs to a *brāhmaṇa*. One who does so, lives on putrid soil for one hundred million *kalpas* in hell and then on faeces for another sixty thousand years. One who cheats on the measurement of land remains immersed in boiling mud for hundred million generations in hell and is then reborn to be condemned as a leper for another hundred *yugas*.[76] Even if one steals the firewood or chaff (*tuṣa*) of a *brāhmaṇa*, he lives in hell for as long as the moon and the stars exist.[77]

Even though there is little documentary evidence to suggest that there was any real threat to the property of the *brāhmaṇa*, the *Purāṇas* naturally urged the state to protect it. In the brahmanical conception, monarchy was the most desirable form of government and a number of the Bengal *Purāṇas* contain chapters on the duties of the king (*rājanīti*, *rājadharma*) in some detail. The Bengal *Purāṇas* describe the king as Indra among the gods,[78] to whom all the subjects must declare their allegiance.[79] One of the primary duties of the king is devotion to the *brāhmaṇas* (*viprapūjā*) and willingness to serve them (*viprasevā*).[80] He should surround himself with those *brāhmaṇas* who are trained in the *Vedas*, the *Āgamas*, the *Purāṇas*, and in astrology, for, if abandoned by them, he becomes susceptible to calamities at every step.[81] Like a householder, he should follow the rules of good conduct which are prescribed in the *Āgamas*, *Purāṇas*, and *Saṁhitās*. He should cultivate the scriptures and must listen to the enumeration of the *Vedaśāstra* every day from the *brāhmaṇas*. A wise king follows what the *brāhmaṇas* recommend. Indeed, the king has been instructed to appoint those *brāhmaṇas* as his ministers who are polite, knowledgeable, and proficient in *dharma* and *artha*.[82]

The other essential duty of the king is to maintain the *varṇa* order. The *Bṛhaddharma Purāṇa* says that the idea of absolute equality among men is impossible to entertain and it can only lead to a profound disbalance in society. Therefore, in order to keep the four *varṇas* separate from one another and to frighten the impudent, the king should establish lawcourts.[83] He should appoint members of the four *varṇas* to their respective duties. If one forsakes one's *svadharma* (ancestral occupation and the code of conduct in consonance with one's *jāti* status) and embraces *paradharma* (the *dharma* of another *jāti* group), the king must punish him and put him back to his original status.[84] The king has been firmly and repeatedly advised to inflict severe punishment on those guilty of stealing others' property and violating others' wives, for it is the fear of punishment which keeps people subservient to the rule of the king.[85]

Having made the king commit himself to the ideals of brahmanism, the *Purāṇas* inevitably claim preferential treatment for *brāhmaṇas* from him. The king is told that there is nothing more meritorious for him than settling *brāhmaṇas* with land,[86] and that he should pay his priests and other *brāhmaṇas* gold, cows, and sesame as honorarium to the best of his ability, at the conclusion of the many sacrifices that he must regularly undertake to perform at an enormous expense.[87] Under no circumstances should the king resume the grant of a *brāhmaṇa*[88] or impose taxes on him, but it is his duty to collect taxes from the members of the other *varṇas*.[89] Finally, even if a *brāhmaṇa* commits an offence which in others would have deserved a death sentence, the king should not physically hurt him, but banish him from the kingdom or impose on him a lighter penalty.[90]

How do these normative prescriptions fit practice as reflected in the contemporary inscriptions? It seems that they matched each other perfectly well. We have noted that the Vedic authority as the ultimate symbol of legitimation was being invoked in most religious matters; the number of land grants to *brāhmaṇas* was steadily increasing; the ruling dynasties, even while professing formal allegiance to Buddhism, were encouraging performance of brahmanical rituals, such as *yajña* and *dāna*; the officiating priests were receiving such fabulous fees that their wives had to learn not to take pearls for cotton-seeds; and *brāhmaṇas* were being consistently appointed to ministerial positions.

But more than material favours, it is in endorsing the brahmanical world-view that the inscriptions come remarkably close to the *Purāṇas*. The overwhelming majority of contemporary inscriptions were land grants. Thus we have maximum information on the attitude of the donors in making and protecting gifts of land than on any other matter on which the *Purāṇas* happened to pronounce. Acquisition of religious merit for the donor and his lineage was the prime motive for making such grants, and since a place in heaven was assured as long as the land remained in the possession of a *brāhmaṇa* donee and his heirs, donors were anxious to protect it from possible transgression. A set of imprecatory statements, called the *dharmānuśaṁsinaḥ* verses, usually accompany these land charters, which were standardized into a formula by the Pāla period, and all the later rulers have included this in their proclamations with occasional and minor alteration. Here is a typical example:

There are verses in praise of Dharma in this matter:

Verse

9. He who receives a land grant and also he who bestows it, both attain merit and invariably go to Heaven.
10. The giver of land rejoices in Heaven for sixty thousand years and the transgressor (of a gift) as well as he who approves (of transgression) dwells in Hell for the same number of years.
11. He who takes away land given either by himself or by others, rots along with his forefathers as a worm in dirt [faeces].
12. Land has been given away by kings, Sagara and others; whosoever at any time owns the land, to him belongs at that time the fruit (of such grant).
13. The good deeds of others should not be effaced by people, considering that fortune as well as human life is as unsteady as a drop of water on a lotus petal, and also realising all that has been cited before.[91]

Since transgression of a land grant is an act of commission, the inscriptions place greater emphasis on the necessity to inhibit possible transgression through threat of dreadful consequences, rather than encourage preservation of grants through promise of rewards. As a result, we have greater variation in the threats and warnings issued to the transgressor, while for those who would respect a grant, the standard formula was considered sufficient. For example:

Whoever may himself appropriate this [land and other accessories] or cause it to be appropriated, shall see his sons and property perish before him and shall remain in Naraka for the period of a Kalpa.[92]

A man appropriating a cow, a piece of gold, or land even measuring half a finger, goes to hell, full of dangers.[93]

One who confiscates land is not purified, even if he excavates thousands of lakes and wells, performs hundreds of Aśvamedha sacrifices, and bestows crores of cows.[94]

The inscriptions, being records of actual grants, were understandably severe in their condemnation of those who might usurp donated land. The *Purāṇas*, on the other hand, merely encourage people to donate. They were more eager to hold out promises of material gain, periods of uninterrupted bliss in heaven, and finally salvation, for future donors. They also attempted to instil fear of inexorable destiny in the possible usurpers, but their natural inclination was to stimulate donation.

Despite varying emphases, however, what strikes the reader most is the outstanding similarity between the Puranic statements on donation of land and the inscriptions recording such donations, not merely in terms of ideas but also expressions. Juxtaposition of any cluster of *dharmānuśaṁsinaḥ* verses and a few Puranic passages on the subject will help illustrate this conspicuous resemblance. The following verses are from the Edilpur copper-plate of Keśavasena:

57 *. . . nṛpatibhirapaharaṇe naraka—*
58 *pātabhayāt pālane dharmmagauravāt pālanīyam ll Bhavanti cātra*
dharmmānuśaṁsinaḥ ślokāḥ l Āsphoṭayanti pitaro valgayanti
59 *pitāmahāḥ bhumidoo'smatkule jātaḥ sa nastrātā bhaviṣyati ll 25 Bhumiṁ*
yaḥ pratigṛhṇāti yaśca bhumiṁ prayacchati l Ubhau tau puṇyaka-
60 *rmmaṇau niyataṁ svargagāminau ll 26 Bahubhirvasudhādattā rājabhiḥ*
sagarādibhiḥ l Yasya yasya yadā bhumistasya tasya tadā phalam ll 27
Svada-
61 *ttāṁ paradattāṁ vā yo haret basundharām l Sa viṣṭhāyāṁ kṛmirbhutvā*
pitṛbhiḥ saha pacyate ll 28 Ṣaṣṭhi varṣasahasrāṇi svarge tiṣṭhati bhumi-
daḥ l
62 *Ākṣeptā cānumantā ca tānyeva narake vaset ll*
29 Sarvveṣāmeva dānānāmekajanmānugaṁ phalaṁ l
30 Iti kamaladalāmbubindulolāṁ śriya-
63 *manucintya manuṣyajīvitañca l Sakalamidamudāhṛtañca budhvā na hi*
puruṣaiḥ parakīrttayo vilopyāḥ ll 31[95]

Compare this statement with the following passages from the *Purāṇas*:

ṣaṣṭhi varṣasahasrāṇi svarge vasati bhumidaḥ ll
adātumanumantā vā tānyeva narake vaset l
. . . .
bhūdātā bhūgrahītā ca ubhau tau svargagāminau l[96]

svadattāṁ paradattāṁ vā yo haredvai basundharām l
tasya pāpaphalam vakṣey gadato me niśāmaya ll
sa koṭikulasaṁyuktaḥ prabhuñjan pūtimṛttikām l
yātanāsvāsu pacyante pratyekaṁ kalpakoṭiṣu ll
ṣaṣṭhivarṣasahasrāṇi jāyante viḍbhujaśca te ll[97]

Evidently, in this matter the inscriptions and *Purāṇas* imitate each other in letter and spirit. The similarity in imagery and stock phrases is inescapable. Even the hyperbole is typically Puranic in flavour. I am not suggesting that these land grants were inspired by the Puranic impetus alone. They were in vogue much before the Bengal *Purāṇas* began to be codified, and served a much wider purpose than help to accumulate religious merit for the individual donors. But this remarkable resemblance cannot be entirely coincidental and has to be traced to a common source of brahmanical conviction and the articulation of that conviction.

This is not surprising in view of the fact that the strong brahmanical ambience of eleventh- and twelfth-century Bengal fostered a large area of common interest between the temporal and the sacred authorities, and norms and practices reinforced each other. Lakṣmaṇasena admits as much:

> Having listened to (from scriptures) the principles regarding the bestowal of gifts and (proper) recipients (thereof), which had become extensive in number in course of ages, and also about the expectation of fruits in this matter (i.e. gifts), he [Lakṣmaṇasena] distributed such gifts as the sacred lore prescribed, sages enjoined and were praised in current practice.[98]

The only chink in this armour seems to have been a nagging doubt whether the *brāhmaṇas* would be able to justify the status and privileges that the *Purāṇas* claimed and society by and large extended to them. This doubt is expressed in the obsessive fear of the degenerate *brāhmaṇa*. In one voice the Bengal *Purāṇas* proclaim that in the *Kali* age the *brāhmaṇas* will be stupid and sensual; their feeble intellect will be inadequate for the comprehension of the *Vedas*; their avarice will induce them to act as priests of the lower order; they will be unable, even unwilling, to maintain the *varṇāśramadharma*, and will tend to succumb to heretical influence.[99]

Recent attempts to understand the social crisis of the third and fourth centuries in terms of the symptoms of the *Kali* age, as depicted in the epics and the early *Purāṇas*, have rendered it necessary to find a temporal location for this mythical period.[100] The suitability of adopting such an approach towards the Puranic conceptualization of time is perhaps questionable, but to the extent that texts which had been written and redacted over centuries can be temporally contextualized at all, there seems to be little doubt that by *Kali* age the Bengal *Purāṇas* were referring to the present. It is not merely that they encourage and justify donation of land and other material objects to the *brāhmaṇas* in terms of the convenient excuse that it is the best way to acquire religious merit in the *Kali* age, their description of a society divided primarily between the *brāhmaṇas* and the *śūdra*s, the bitter and repeated reference to the pre-eminence of the Buddhists, and above all the obsessive nature of their apprehension suggest an uncomfortable proximity with a time which they would love to consign to the future. If so, it is difficult to entertain respect for a class of men who come out as invariably mean, vile, unscrupulous and greedy.

These were the people that the Bengal *Purāṇas* presented as the gods on earth, as sentinels of the social order. But there is no reason to accept verbatim the palpably exaggerated accounts of the *Kali* age. The *brāhmaṇas* must have had among them men of intellect and integrity, who were instrumental in initiating the process of cultural assimilation that led to the slow and low-key Puranic transformation in Bengal. The Kulīnas, who were placed on top of the social hierarchy for supposedly possessing these qualities, eventually decayed, when the Bengali Hindu society plunged into its lowest depths in the late medieval period. The cleansing effort of the Gauḍīya *bhakti* movement was partly a reaction against the decrepit system. The Bengal *Purāṇas* cannot deny their role in this degeneration. The end of the final redaction of the Bengal *Purāṇas* coincides with the beginning of the composition of the *Kulajīs*. Uncritical acceptance of the superiority of the *brāhmaṇa varṇa*, advocated by the Bengal *Purāṇas* and reinforced in the later *Smṛtis*, reached its logical culmination in the social order documented and justified in the *Kulajī* texts.

The Transformation of Buddhism

I

Long before the coming of the *brāhmaṇas* Buddhism had struck roots in Bengal. Unlike the growth of brahmanism, which was slow and lacked clearly identifiable landmarks, a connected account of the history of Buddhism in Bengal has been presented by several scholars.[101] Therefore, I will merely provide an outline of the main contours of its development, until the time it came into interaction with brahmanical religion.

It is not definitely known when exactly Buddhism was introduced to Bengal. Early sources do not reveal any association of Bengal with Buddhism during the first few centuries of its existence. The *Divyāvadāna*, which extends the easternmost limit of the Buddhist Madhyadeśa to Puṇḍravardhana, however, indicates that Buddhism was firmly entrenched in this region during the reign of the Mauryan emperor Aśoka. The Chinese traveller Yuan Chwang also credits Aśoka with the erection of numerous *stūpas* in Puṇḍravardhana, but these literary traditions are not confirmed by corresponding archaeological evidence. Two votive inscriptions from Sāñcī mention the names of a few Bengalis who made donations for the construction of that monument and a Nāgārjunakoṇḍā inscription informs us that Sri Lankan monks preached Buddhism in Bengal during the second and third centuries AD. The discovery of Buddhist images from Candraketugaḍ lends substance to this statement. Thus Buddhism seems to have been fairly well known in at least some parts of Bengal in the pre-Gupta period.

According to I-tsing, Mahārāja Śrīgupta, founder of the Gupta dynasty, constructed a 'Chinese temple' and granted twenty-four villages for its upkeep at a place close to a sanctuary called Mi-li-kia-si-kia-po-no, believed to be somewhere in central West Bengal. Fa-hien found Buddhism flourishing at Tāmralipta, where he saw twenty-two monasteries with resident monks towards the end of Candragupta II's reign. The early sixth-century Guṇāighar inscription records that Mahārāja Vainyagupta had donated some land for the preservation of the *āśrama-vihāra* dedicated to Ārya-Avalokiteśvara and the worship of the icon of Buddha situated in it. The Kailāna inscription of Śrīdhāraṇarāta also states that his Mahāsāndhivigrahika Jayanātha granted land for the maintenance of the residents of a Buddhist *vihāra*. Thus Buddhism must have been well established in the eastern borders of Bengal by this time. Yuan Chwang, in approximately AD 639, saw twenty *vihāras* in Puṇḍravardhana, thirty in Samataṭa, and ten each in Karṇasuvarṇa and Tāmralipta, inhabited by thousands of monks despite the pronounced hostility of Śaśāṁka, the king of Gauḍa, to Buddhism. The description of Yuan Chwang seems to suggest that the majority of the Buddhists in Bengal followed the Hīnayāna way of religious practice. Another Chinese traveller, Tseng-chi, who came to Samataṭa in early seventh century, found Buddhism prospering under the active patronage of the then local ruling dynasty, which has been identified with the Khaḍgas. However, by now Buddhism was certainly on the decline in Tāmralipta. While Fa-hien saw twenty-two *vihāras* in Tāmralipta and Yuan Chwang ten, the number was still further reduced during the time of I-tsing. Niharranjan Ray infers that the situation must have been similar in other parts of Bengal as well, except in Samataṭa, where the influence of Mahāyāna Buddhism continued to increase until about the thirteenth century.

Buddhism in Bengal witnessed a distinct revival under the Pāla–Candra rulers, all Mahāyāna Buddhists, and it is through their vigorous support that Buddhism lived its last glorious period in Bengal between the eighth and the eleventh centuries. These kings established some of the most celebrated centres of Buddhist learning in eastern India where monks from Tibet and such other far-off places came to study regularly. It is in their writings that the state of Buddhism in Bengal of this period is best preserved. Dharmapāla founded the Vikramaśīlā, Odantapurī and Somapura *mahāvihāras* and he patronized Ācārya Haribhadra who composed his famous commentary on *Abhisamayālaṁkāra* in the Traikūṭaka *vihāra*. During the reign of Devapāla, Gomin Avighṇākara, a Buddhist from Bengal, went to Kaṅkanadeśa and constructed a big hall of worship in the Kṛṣṇagiri *mahāvihāra*. The Jagaddala *mahāvihāra* of Varendrī was founded by Rāmapāla. Besides these, we also get to know of Devīkoṭa, Paṇḍita, Sannagara, Phullahari, Paṭṭikera, Vikramapurī, Kanakastūpa and several other minor *vihāras* which then flourished in eastern Bihar and Bengal. Maintenance of these huge monastic establishments required large resources, and a considerable portion of which, it may be safely assumed, came from the royal exchequer. It is also during the latter part of Pāla rule that Buddhism in Bengal gradually began to change its character.[102]

II

The process of change probably began with a shift to Mahāyāna Buddhism from the early Pāla period itself. Even this Mahāyānism, which comprised *Sammatīyavāda*, *Sarvāstivāda*, and *Mahāsāṅghikavāda*, and the ideals of which are partly reflected in the *dhyāna* and *vandanā* sections of the royal epigraphs of this period, had little in common with the Buddhism that was practised in Bengal between the eighth and twelfth centuries. From an early period eastern India had established close political and trade links with regions in the foothills of the Himalayas, which were strengthened during the Pāla period. The resulting cultural interaction is supposed to have contributed to a very thorough spread of Tantrism in Bengal and adjoining areas. By the eighth–ninth centuries Mahāyāna Buddhism came under its influence and began to include *guhya sādhanā* (secret magical practices), *mantra*, *yantra*, *dhāraṇī* (monosyllabic words of mystical significance) and an elaborate pantheon mostly consisting of a large number of goddesses, which, according to the Buddhist tradition, were approved by Acārya Asaṅga. The abstruse philosophical doctrines of *Vijñānavāda* and *Mādhyamikavāda* were beyond the comprehension of the common Buddhists in any case; they now leaned more and more towards magical practice which emphasized the importance of *mantra* and *maṇḍala*, *dhāraṇī* and *vīja*. Mantrayāna was the first phase in the evolution of Mahāyānism.

The second phase is known as Vajrayāna. Nāgārjuna, who propounded the theory of *śūnya* or void, argued that sorrow, action, fruits of action, and material existence are all void. The knowledge of this void is *nirvāṇa*. The Vajrayānīs called this impersonal knowledge *nirātmā* or *nairātmā*. *Nirātmā* was imagined as a goddess and it was believed that when *bodhicitta* dissolves itself in the embrace of *nirātmā*, *mahāsukha* or great bliss results. The pleasurable concentration of the *citta* in sexual union is *bodhicitta* and this *bodhicitta* is *vajra*. Predictably, all the pratices of the Vajrayānīs were conduted in extreme secrecy. A variation of the Vajrayāna came to be known as Kālacakrayāna. It based its doctrines on the premise that *śūnyatā* (void) and *kālacakra* (wheel of time) are one and the same, and the objective of the practitioner is to stop the continuous motion of this wheel. Motion of time is reflected in the chain of actions which, in an individual, is the vibration of life. The Kālacakrayānīs argued that if the arteries of the body, the centres of the arteries, and the five vital winds are controlled through *yoga*, life forces cease to function, and with that time comes to a halt.

Another and possibly more widely practised form of the Vajrayāna was called Sahajayāna. Since Vajrayāna abounded in the iconic forms of the *mantras*, the places of worship had to be large enough to accommodate these images. But the Sahajayāna did not even recognize the existence of divinities, nor did it recommend the practice of rituals involving *mantras*, *mudrās*, and the other accessories. They were critical of the *brāhmaṇas* and the ritualist Buddhists alike and claimed that *bodhi* or ultimate knowledge was not realized even by the Buddha. Everybody has the right to attain Buddhahood and the state of *buddhatva* resides within the human body. They completely moved away from *sūnyatā* or *vijñāna*, and stressed the centrality of the material body and the practice of *kāyāsādhana*. The Sahajiyās believed that *sūnyatā* was *prakṛti* and *karuṇā* was *puruṣa,* and their union, that is the sexual union of men and women, creates the condition of bliss. All these *yānas* were based on yogīc practice. The three major arteries of the body were called *lalanā*, *rasanā* and *avadhūtī* and correspond to *iḍā*, *piṅgalā*, and *suṣumnā* of the brahmanical *Tantras*. The three *yānas* derived their basic principles from almost similar assumptions and the functional aspect of their worship did not differ much from one another except in minor ritualistic details. They were formulated and developed in Bengal and the history of the three *yānas* is the history of Bengal Buddhism during the Pāla–Candra period.[103]

Those who led this transformation of Mahāyāna Buddhism have been described in the contemporary Buddhist tradition as Siddhācāryas. It is doubtful whether all eighty-four of them were historical characters, but some did exist between the ninth and the twelfth centuries. The ideals of the Sahajayānī Siddhācāryas are reflected in the mystical verses of the *Dohākoṣa* and *Caryāgīti*, composed by them in a deliberately obscure proto-Bengali language known as *sandhyābhāṣā* or intentional speech. The special terminology in these verses to explain esoteric doctrine makes use of a number of analogies such as the image of the boat, rat and deer, the *vīṇā*, fermentation of wine and carding of cotton, and of course the analogy of sexual union, all charged with symbolic significance. For example, the boat is the *bodhicitta* which is semen virile (*śukra*). It is claimed that *śukra* can be carried up through the three principal arteries to the head by the practice of *yoga*. It then becomes the source of the supreme qualities to the *yogī*. When the *bodhicitta* proceeds upwards, there occurs an introversion of all the faculties of the senses and vital winds, and through further concentration the inflow of the illusion of the objective world can be stopped. In the analogies of union Ḍombi plays the most important part. She lives outside the city, dances on the lotus of sixty-four petals, and eats up the lotus stalk. When the *yogī* proceeds to marry her, existence and salvation, the mind and the vital winds act in perfect harmony. Ḍombi is explained as the *nirātmā* or *avadhūtī* (middle artery) purified. When *avadhūtī* is purified through the removal of illusion, the *śakti* or *nirātmā* ascends upwards and reaches the void where the lotus is located. The destruction of the lotus stalk implies that the way by which further influx of illusion may be possible is removed.[104] Evidently all these concepts were borrowed from the *Tantras*.

That these were not just abstract speculations but constituted the basis of actual worship is attested by the account of the Tibetan monk Tāranātha. In the chapters dealing with the Pāla kings he frequently mentions two Buddhist schools in particular—*Prajñāpāramitā* and *Tantra*. He says that during Rāsapāla's reign there lived a great *ācārya*, whose Tantric name was Līlāvajra, who delivered many sermons on the Tantrayāna. Rāsapāla was succeeded by Dharmapāla, who had built fifty centres for the study of *dharma*, thirty-five of which were devoted to *Prajñāpāramitā*. One of the centres had a large collection of treatises on *Tantra* which so shocked the resident monks from Sri Lanka that they declared these to have been composed by Māra, the evil one, and burnt them. During the reign of king Mahāpāla an *ācārya* named Piṭo introduced the Kālacakra-*tantra*. Another Buddhist *ācārya* of the Pāla period, Jetāri, was the author of a number of major Tantric texts. Yet another, *ācārya* Vāgīśvarakīrti, was famous for his many consorts and the preparation of an elixir which helped to regain one's youth. Tāranātha informs us that as a result of their activities, the teachings of the *guhya-samāja* and the *Tantras* were very widely spread.[105] Not all of what he says can be implicitly trusted, as some of the names of the Pāla rulers and their order of succession given by Tāranātha are incorrect, but his account seems to reflect the main thrust of Bengal Buddhism and the milieu in which it flourished during the Pāla period.

As a result of these Tantric developments, Mahāyāna Buddhism gradually began to lose its distinctive character. In a later chapter we will see that Tantrism, though based on some philosophical premises, is basically a set of techniques that can be appropriated by any form of religious practice. In such circumstances it becomes difficult to differentiate between the modes of worship of one religion and another. Shashibhushan Dasgupta has drawn our attention to the essential similarity between the Hindu and the Buddhist *Tantras*. He argues that Tantrism lays stress upon a fundamental postulate that truth resides within the body and the human body is the best medium through which truth is realized. This exclusive emphasis on the human body sets Tantrism apart from any other form of religion. Both the Hindu and the Buddhist *Tantras*, which share this assumption, have another feature in common—a belief in the theological principle of duality in non-duality. Both schools hold that the ultimate non-dual reality possesses two aspects, the negative and the positive, the static and the dynamic. These are represented in Hinduism by Śiva and Śakti and in Buddhism by *prajñā* and *upāya* or *śūnyatā* and *karuṇā*. Both schools believe that the metaphysical principles of these two aspects are manifested in the material world in the form of the male and the female. The ultimate goal of the practitioner is to achieve a perfect state of union beween the two and the realization of the non-dual nature of the self and non-self. Dasgupta points out that the difference between the Hindu and the Buddhist *Tantras* is superficial and one of tonal quality. Thus, while the Hindu *Tantras* draw on *Vedānta*, *Yoga*, *Sāṁkhya*, and *Nyāya* and *Vaiśeṣika*, the Buddhist *Tantras* pick up fragments of metaphysical thought and terms from the leading schools of Mahāyāna Buddhism. Since these are not intrinsic to either of the *Tantras*, they borrow indiscriminately without any knowledge of their context or original import.[106]

Agehananda Bharati argues in a similar vein that there has been so much of mutual borrowing of icons, *mantras*, *yantras*, indeed the entire apparatus of worship, that the Hindu and the Buddhist *Tantras* have become practically indistinguishable from one another. It is only in the realm of philosophical premises that certain specificities exist, which he has juxtaposed in the following manner:

Hindu Tantra				*Buddhist Tantra*
subject (*aham*) male	— — —	object (*idam*) female	homologized with	*śūnya* (void) *prajñā* (wisdom) *yum* (female)—inert, passive
Śiva wisdom inert, passive	—	Śakti power active		*karuṇā* (compassion) *upāya* (method) *yab* (male)—active[107]

This schema reveals that even in philosophical assumptions the differences between the two were negligible. The fact that the Hindu *Tantras* assign the static aspect to the male and the dynamic aspect to the female principle, and in the Buddhist *Tantras* the order is reversed, had little theoretical or operational significance. On the contrary, the similarities in concepts and procedures of worship, including the centrality of the *guru* or preceptor, whose guidance was considered indispensable for the attainment of salvation in both the systems,[108] obliterated the minor differences on the surface. Indeed, at times it becomes difficult to decide to which one of these a particular aspect of Tantric worship originally belonged. Kooij points out that the three supernatural powers of *pātāla*, *pādalepa* and *rasāyana*, mentioned in the *Kālikā*, a Bengal *Purāṇa*, seems to be typical of the Buddhist *Tantras*, although some of them appear in the Hindu texts as well.[109]

Another aspect of Mahāyāna Buddhism which came confusingly close to the Puranic religion in Bengal was its pantheon. There occurred an explosion of divinities in the Vajrayāna school of Bengal Buddhism which were supposed to be the iconic representations of the *mantras*. By far the most important material for the study of Buddhist iconography is provided by innumerable independent stone and metal images of deities as well as the ones sculpted on the walls of the *vihāras*, found throughout the Pāla dominion.[110] Besides, a number of texts contain detailed descriptions of the deities of the Vajrayāna pantheon, such as the *Sādhanamālā* and the *Niṣpannayogāvalī* by Abhayākara Gupta of the Vikramaśīlā monastery, who lived during the reign of Rāmapāla.

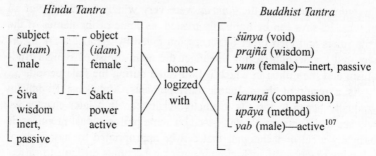

Many of the later developments are incorporated in the still-unpublished work entitled the *Dharmakoṣasaṁgraha*. There also exists another class of manuscripts containing miniature paintings of Buddhist gods and goddesses, which are often used for the purpose of comparison.[111]

These present such an amazing range of divinities, both on their own and in association with others, that it was nearly impossible to make any sense of the principle of their classification until N.K. Bhattasali reduced them to an elementary order. He says that Ādi Buddha and Ādi Prajñā may be taken as the universal father and universal mother in the Buddhist hierarchy of divinities. The five Dhyānī Buddhas were conceived to have emanated from them and were provided with their Śaktis. Thus we have the following pairs:

Vairocana	Vajradhātvīśvarī
Akṣobhya	Locanā
Ratna-sambhava	Māmakī
Amitābha	Pāṇḍarā
Amogha-siddhi	Tārā

The Dhyānī Buddhas are passive and remain engaged in deep meditation. However, each of them has an active counterpart, a Bodhisattva, who upholds creation in each successive age and then retires into his original source. The Bodhisattvas exercise their influence over the universe through the most exalted of all human beings called Mānuṣī Buddhas. Bhattasali has arranged these in the following table:

Dhyānī Buddhas	*Bodhisattvas*	*Mānuṣī Buddhas*
Vairocana	Sāmanta-bhadra	Krakucandra
Akṣobhya	Vajrapāṇi	Kanakamuni
Ratna-sambhava	Ratnapāṇi	Kaśyapa
Amitābha	Avalokiteśvara	Gautama
Amogha-siddhi	Viśvapāṇi	Maitreya

There are variations in name, even number, of Bodhisattvas. But, considering that unlike Puranic Hinduism they took shape in a comparatively short period of time, the really incredible variety is provided by the goddesses of the Buddhist pantheon. The more important ones among them have the rank of Bodhisattvas. They are as much emanations from the Dhyānī Buddhas as the male Bodhisattvas, and this oneness of origin led to the union of the male and female Bodhisattvas, although the union is not pronounced in all cases. A number of different and quite individualistic forms of the same goddess also adds to the confusion. Bhattasali has restored some order by arranging the goddesses into separate groups according to the parent Dhyānī Buddhas:

from Vairocana	White Tārā, Uṣṇīṣavijayā, Jāṅgulī Tārā, Mārīcī
from Akṣobhya	Nīlā Tārā or Ekajaṭā
from Ratna-sambhava	Yellow Tārā, Vasudhārā, Vajra Tārā
from Amitābha	Raktā Tārā or Kurukullā, Sitātapatrā, Bhṛkuṭi
from Amogha-siddhi	Green Tārā, Parṇaśavarī

Below this family of high-profile gods and goddesses, there exist three classes of divinities. First come the tutelary deities, who protect their devotees, such as Yamāntaka, Jambhala, Hevajra, Heruka, Mahāmāyā, Samvara, Kālacakra and the Pañcarakṣās. The next are a series of 'defenders of the faith' such as Kuvera, Yama, Hayagrīva and Mahākāla. Finally, there is a group of deified personages, foremost among whom are sixteen Mahāsthaviras, Nāgārjuna and Padmasambhava. The goddess Hāritī also seems to belong to this group.[112] In iconographic texts and sculptural representations these deities are often presented in association with several others, and given the variety of divinities, it is not difficult to imagine what a range of combinations this would allow. For example, the *Sādhanamālā* describes Lokeśvara, with Amitābha sitting on his head. Potalaka is placed below and Tārā behind him. Sudhanvā Kumāra is assigned a position to his right, Bhṛkuṭi to his west and Hayagrīva to his north.[113] All these were of course charged with tremendous symbolic significance and a slight change in the constellation would lead to a complete reorientation of meaning.

The common devotees were not expected to keep track of such complexities and what they saw on the surface was that a religion that had not admitted of the existence of godhead in its original conception, was now brimming with a profusion of divinities, not unlike the parallel stream of Puranic brahmanism. No wonder the two religions borrowed from and influenced each other, although Buddhist absorption of the brahmanical deities was more pronounced. It is perhaps ironic that many of the minor Vajrayāna divinities, called 'defenders of the faith' (Dharmapālas), were taken from the brahmanical pantheon.

Indeed, mutual borrowing must have been such a common, even open, practice that it did not surprise the votaries of the two religions then in the manner in which it strikes the historian of today. S.K.

Saraswati, for instance, believed that the sixty-three stone sculptures found on the lowest level of the Pāhārpur *stūpa* were taken from an earlier Hindu monument because a large number of them depict Hindu subjects. Frederick Asher, however, points out that it is very unlikely that the planners of a major monument would borrow wholesale the sculptures of an earlier neighbouring monument and place them indiscriminately in their new building. He argues that the depiction was deliberate and it was an acceptable and canonically prescribed practice to use Hindu images in this position. The contemporary text on Buddhist iconography, *Niṣpannayogāvalī*, describes *maṇḍalas* in which Hindu deities occupy the outer cirlce, corresponding to the lower level of a tiered monument.[114] Actually the controversy itself seems to be a little out of place, for this was not an isolated example. In the Nālandā *vihāra* Śiva, Viṣṇu, Pārvatī, Gaṇeśa and Manasā used to receive worship along with Buddhist gods and goddesses.[115]

The brahmanical deities eventually began to penetrate the inner circle of the Buddhist pantheon as well. The *Sādhanamālā* declared that Umā, Padmāvatī, and Vedamātā were undifferentiated forms of the goddess Tārā.[116] The Buddhist goddess Mahāmāyā, when worshipped in the Tantric way, could not possibly maintain a separate (Buddhist) identity from the Puranic Mahāmāyā. On the other hand, minor Buddhist deities found their way into the Puranic pantheon and either came to occupy an independent position or merged with an existing member having some common characteristics, enriching it with ritualistic or iconographic peculiarities.[117] Indeed, there are stray examples of rivalry, conflict and rejection, reflected in such images as Mārīcī trampling Śiva, Indra holding the umbrella for Aparājitā, and Avalokiteśvara riding on the shoulders of Viṣṇu.[118] But these could not impede the primary impulse behind those internal developments which brought the two religious systems so exceptionally close.

The committed Buddhist royal dynasties of the Pālas and the Candras also contributed to this process by simultaneously extending their patronage to brahmanism. Some of the Pāla rulers took *brāhmaṇa* wives and supported the *brāhmaṇas* and their temple-oriented mode of worship. Dharmapāla donated land for the Nārāyaṇa temple founded by his Mahāsāmantādhipati Nārāyaṇavarmā. Nārāyaṇapāla not merely claimed to have established one thousand temples but also made provisions for the daily worship of Śiva and the upkeep of the Pāśupata *ācāryas* attached to one of these. Rāmapāla founded a number of temples of Śiva, Sūrya, Skanda, and Gaṇapati in the city of Rāmāvatī. Citramatikā, the wife of Madanapāla, made him grant a piece of land to the *brāhmaṇa* Vaṭeśvara-śarmā as fee for reciting the *Mahābhārata* to her. In fact most of the Pāla land grants were made in favour of the *brāhmaṇas*. Vigrahapāla I used to attend the sacrifices organized by his minister Kedāramiśra and received the holy water. The *śrāddha* ceremony organized by Jayapāla at the death of his father, in which the *mahādāna* was received by a *brāhmaṇa* called Umāpati, seems to have been conducted in accordance with brahmanical prescription. When the news of his maternal uncle's death reached Rāmapāla, he gifted away his treasures to the *brāhmaṇas* and threw himself into the Gaṅgā. The Candra king Śrīcandradeva donated land to the *Śāntivārika* priest Śrīpītavāsaguptaśarmā who was reputed to have conducted *Koṭihoma*, and on another occasion to the *Śāntivārika* Vyāsagaṅgā-śarmā for conducting the *Adbhutaśānti* sacrifice. The ideology that prompted these royal gestures was undoubtedly brahmanical.[119]

III

Thus in the manifest aspects of religion, the difference between Buddhism and brahmanism was gradually disappearing. In popular understanding Buddhist and brahmanical icons came to perform similar functions. Even in the realm of underlying metaphysical premises, Tantrism brought the Buddhist and brahmanical ways of worship close. When both the religions began to receive royal patronage irrespective of the personal faith of the rulers, it carried the unmistakable message that the differences between them, if any, were marginal, and that both were entitled to be venerated in almost equal measure.

I hold this loss of distinctiveness in the eyes of the laity to be one of the most important reasons for the decline of Buddhism in Bengal. Conventional historiography, however, places highest emphasis on the withdrawal of royal patronage from among a number of factors such as a natural loss of vitality due to old age, brahmanical persecution, Muslim invasion, internal corruption, divisive effect of sectarianism, and insufficient cultivation of the laity, as explanations of the decline of Buddhism in India as well as Bengal.[120] Except perhaps the theory of old age, all the other factors must have had their fair share in the decline, and it is both unnecessary and ahistorical to try and create a hierarchy of causes in terms of their relative importance, as blanket explanations tend to view the decline as a steady linear development and do not always take into account situational specificities. That there was an undoubted shift in the pattern of royal patronage from the Pāla–Candra–Kāmvoja to the Sena–Varmaṇa period is obvious. In the long list of inscriptions belonging to the latter dynasties, there is not a single grant which was made in favour of a Buddhist institution. Indeed, the only reference to Buddhism in the Sena epigraphs appears in the Tarpaṇadīghi inscription of Lakṣmaṇasena where the eastern boundary of the land donated to a *brāhmaṇa* is said to be marked by a piece of land belonging to a Buddhist *vihāra*.[121] Susan Huntington points out that the peak of artistic productivity in Magadha under the Pālas occurred during the ninth–tenth centuries and was primarily in the service of the Buddhist religion, while the greatest period of Bengal was the eleventh–twelfth centuries which produced mostly brahmanical images, with Vaiṣṇava subjects outnumbering any other.[122] Thus a shift in patronage is evident from all available sources.

The accommodative attitude of the Pālas was completely subverted by the Senas who imposed the *Smārta-Paurāṇika* socio-religious order in Bengal with a single-minded fixity of purpose. This change in state policy must have largely contributed to the decline of Buddhism in Bengal, as noted by several scholars such as R.C. Majumdar.[123] Gayatri Sen-Majumdar almost involuntarily associates the fate of Buddhism in Bengal with the rise and fall of the Pāla dynasty.[124] Trevor Ling, on the other hand, has rather curiously suggested that the excessive popularity of Buddhism in Bengal provoked jealous reaction from the *brāhmaṇas* which led to the withdrawal of state patronage and consequently its downfall.[125] It seems that he has not noticed the contradiction inherent in this argument and therefore has made no attempt to explain what happened to Buddhism's large support base. Buddhism certainly had a popular following in Bengal, but Ling failed to observe that with the loss of its distinct identity, the popular support imperceptibly moved towards Puranic Hinduism which did not necessitate a radical readjustment in the daily lives of the lay followers, and that the change in state policy merely accelerated rather than initiated this eventually unstoppable process.

The other oft-cited reason for the decline is the nature of the Buddhist monastic establishments, inextricably linked with the transformation of the general character of Buddhism. B.N.S. Yadava has argued that the *Saṅgha* could never enter into a meaningful relationship with the laity, and as a result the social organization of Buddhists, both in terms of general structure and in the management of the family unit, remained loose and ineffectual. The evidence of Buston indicates that from the eighth century onwards monastic corruption became a marked feature of Buddhism, and the character of Vyasanākara, the Buddhist monk in the farce *Laṭakamelaka*, shows that by the twelfth century Buddhist monks and monasteries had come into disrepute, possibly due to the growth of Tantric practices.[126] Yadava's assessment of the state of monasteries in the early medieval period accords well with the description of Tāranātha. The right of admission of *śūdras* into the monasteries had once led to the rapid expansion of Buddhism but, as J.N. Bhattacharya puts it, the admission of 'fallen women' brought discredit to the faith, and when the monasteries became 'hot-beds of immorality', the system disintegrated.[127] Bhattacharya was obviously referring to Tantric practices and the way of life in the monasteries.

There was an essential difference between Puranic and Buddhist attitudes towards *Tantra*. The Bengal *Purāṇas*, for instance, consciously rationalized and absorbed some of the less disruptive elements of the *Tantras* and carefully purged the *vāma* or the left method from their rituals. Hence those who were inclined towards the left method either had to opt out of brahmanical society or conduct their rituals in secrecy. Buddhism, however, made no such distinction, and the Buddhist monasteries, which were pampered into huge establishments during the Pāla–Candra period and were therefore conspicuous, openly indulged in practices that the Bengal *Purāṇas* condemned. Tāranātha's account leaves us in no doubt that they began to attract public censure. The problem was that society expected the Tantric to conform to social rules if he chose to remain within its bounds.[128] But by definition the Tantric code of conduct runs contrary to social norms. The Sahajiyā Siddhācāryas declared themselves Kāpālins,[129] a Tantric sect which was unequivocally rejected by the *Purāṇas* precisely because it could not be accommodated even within their assimilative space. The uncritical acceptance of all forms of Tantric practice by the Buddhists created a disjunction between monk and common devotee, preacher and laity.

The *Saṅgha* was curiously placed in that it was neither outside society nor bound by it. The uneasy relationship between the *Saṅgha* and society has been imaginatively captured by Haraprasad Shastri in his *Bener Meye*, which he describes as a novel of the Sahajiyātantra, set in early eleventh-century Bengal. In a long passage Bhaṭṭa Bhavadeva, the minister of Harivarmaṇa, explains to the king why he feels that Buddhism has no future in Bengal:

So far the *bhikṣus* came from the society and became residents of the *Saṅgha*. Now the order has reversed. Now people are coming from the *Saṅgha* to the society, but the society is in no position to accept them. It is causing a good deal of disruption. As long as there was discipline in the *Saṅgha*, it did not allow sexual union and [people from all social groups such as] ***brāhmaṇa***, *kāyastha, bene, teli* have gone to the *Saṅgha* from the society. The society has nourished the *Saṅgha*. But what is happening now? Everyone is taking *śakti* in the *Saṅgha*. They say, there can be no worship without *śakti*. Whether or not it leads to spiritual upliftment, the practice is producing children. Towards the beginning, they were made to recite the *daśaśīla* and were included within the *Saṅgha*. But there are far too many of them now and there is no space left in the *Saṅgha*. Nor are new *vihāras* being constructed for them. Hence they are coming back to the society. But how can they be accommodated within the society? There is no place for them in our *varṇa*-oriented society. The Buddhist society does not admit of the four *varṇas* and they may be placed there. But what will be their occupation? Everybody must have to have an occupation. Hence a wise king gave them the title of *yugi* and asked them to weave coarse cloth. Therefore I was saying that the society no longer nourishes the *Saṅgha*. Such is the state of destruction.[130]

Despite the brahmanical bias of Bhaṭṭa Bhavadeva, and also perhaps the moral disapproval of Haraprasad Shastri, this seems to be a fairly accurate description of the state of the Buddhist monasteries in early medieval Bengal. As the larger Buddhist society and the *Saṅgha* ceased to reinforce each other, the system eventually fell apart.

So far I have argued that in doctrines, pantheon, rituals and even in iconography,[131] Buddhism had come so close to Puranic brahmanism that an effective distinction between the two was virtually lost in the eyes of the lay devotees. The Buddhist monastic organization did not help either. Still, the votaries of an institutional religion do not lose their essential religious identity and get automatically subsumed into another religion, unless they also conform to the social categories of the latter. In this, a lapse on the part of Buddhism proved to be of advantage to brahmanism. Having rejected the *varṇa* division as a principle of social organization, Buddhism did not pay attention to the necessity of creating an alternative social order, nor did it lay down a clearly defined set of social codes with which lay Buddhists could identify as marking them off as a separate group.[132] Whatever might have been the practice in an earlier period, the lay Buddhists of Pāla Bengal, for all practical purposes, followed the brahmanical rites of passage and other social injunctions. Tāranātha's history of Buddhism and the other Tibetan Buddhist texts indicate that there was hardly any difference between the Hindu and Buddhist laity in this respect.[133]

Haraprasad Shastri writes that it was difficult to ascertain the religious affiliation of such persons as Bihari Datta, the protagonist of his novel *Bener Meye*. They used to get the ten *saṁskāras* performed by the *brāhmaṇas*, and yet paid homage to the temple of Buddha. They took dust off the feet of the *brāhmaṇas* and bowed to Buddhist monks in respect. They made large donations to both communities.[134] But the story demanded that the social position of Bihari be determined once and for all. Therefore, a council of *brāhmaṇa* scholars was convened in the house of Vācaspati Miśra, presided over by Bhaṭṭa Bhavadeva. Bhavadeva decreed that the criterion for decision in such matters was the performance of the *saṁskāras* according to the instructions of the *Gṛhya Sūtras*. When Bihari declared that he followed them, he was recognized as a Hindu. But he had to be assigned to an appropriate place in the caste hierarchy. Some suggested that in view of his occupation (trade), he should be called a *vaiśya*. But at the end the injunction of 'the sacred texts' was upheld that in the *Kaliyuga* there remained only the first and the last *varṇas* (*kalāvādyaśca antyaśca*), and Bihari, along with all the members of his extended kin group, was proclaimed a *śūdra*.[155]

This fictional reconstruction of the process by which the caste of Bihari was fixed is entirely corroborated by the cumulative evidence of the *Smṛtis* and *Purāṇas* of Bengal. There is no reference to *kṣatriyas* or *vaiśyas* in the brahmanical texts and inscriptions, nor were the ruling dynasties or the merchant community of Bengal ever known to have claimed such status. The solitary evidence of *Rāmacarita* that the Pālas were *kṣatriyas*, or of *Vallāla Carita* that the *suvarṇavaṇiks* regarded themselves as *vaiśyas* is questionable.[136] In fact Bengal never had the traditional *varṇa* structure of orthodox brahmanism. The *brāhmaṇas*, who originally came from outside, divided the indigenous population into two broad categories, the *sat* and the *asat śūdras*. An intricate subdivision of mixed castes arranged them into a convenient hierarchy. Thus the lay Buddhists, who already accepted this social structure and followed the recommended rites of passage, could easily be formally absorbed in one or the other of the *śūdra jātis*, if the need arose.

The Pāla–Candra–Kāmvoja kings, who were Buddhists in personal faith but respectful towards brahmanism, also accepted this arrangement and assumed the traditional responsibility of the royal authority of maintaining the *varṇāśramadharma*. According to the Monghyr copper-plate inscription of Devapāla, Dharmapāla was engaged in putting the straying members of the different caste groups back to their respective duties in consonance with śāstric injunctions, and in the Āmgāchi copper-plate,

Vigrahapāla III has been described as the refuge of the four *varṇas*. King Śrīcandra noticed no inconsistency in his practice of making all the donations to his *brāhmaṇa* priests in the name of *Buddhabhaṭṭāraka* and stamping the deeds with the royal emblem of the *dharmacakra*.[137] The later Candra rulers Laḍahacandra and Govindacandra, who seem to have moved away from the family faith and made grants of land in favour of the brahmanical deities Vāsudeva and Śiva, continued to call themselves *Paramasaugata*.[138] The Kāmvoja king Nayapāladeva donated a village to *paṇḍita* Aśvatthaśarmā which was officially witnessed by his *brāhmaṇa* priests of different categories. It may be observed that many of the high officials of these ruling dynasties were *brāhmaṇas*.[139] However, in Bengal the *varṇa* order was not rigid in the Pāla–Candra period, primarily because the brahmanical *Smṛti* texts were yet to be composed. It was when the Senas, *brāhmaṇa* migrants from Karṇāṭa, systematically removed all traces of Buddhist influence from the state apparatus and aggressively promoted the cause of brahmanism, that the final redactions of some of the Bengal *Purāṇas* began to be made and the first group of Bengal *Smṛtis* was codified, and social life was circumscribed by the minutely defined rules and regulations of the brahmanical socio-religious order.

IV

The Bengal *Purāṇas* attempted to build a cultural system on a set of distinctions between the beliefs and practices that belonged to members of the brahmanical system and those that did not. However, brahmanism is a polytheistic religion with no hierarchically regulated monastic organization, nor a single revealed text of inviolable authenticity. Therefore it was all the more necessary to try and construct for itself an unambiguous self-identity which would mark it out from other religious communities. Out of this necessity were born the three fundamental points of reference: the infallibility of the *Vedas*, the social and ritual superiority of the *brāhmaṇas*, and preservation of the *varṇāśrama-dharma*, which, when crystallized, remained the cornerstone of brahmanism in all its subsequent developments.

But the self is often defined in relation to the non-self, 'the other'. There is then a relationship of opposition and exclusion. While social classification begins with the construction of a stable self, 'others' are conglomerations of entities, variously perceived as equal, inferior or simply outside the system. Since in the brahmanical conception all forms of otherness are manifestations of ignorance created by illusion, it did not entertain the notion of an equal other. A great many local cultures, some elements of which brahmanism absorbed and legitimized, were considered inferior, but they were eventually stripped of their otherness. The esoteric dissent groups on the fringe never really posed a threat, but Buddhism was an organized and well-entrenched religion in Bengal with which brahmanism had to compete for supremacy. It could not afford to ignore the fact that Buddhism was built on a conscious rejection of the cardinal principles of brahmanism. Hence the Bengal *Purāṇas* endeavoured to set up Buddhism as the external and deviant other, which is the most intense and powerful oppositional category in terms of social classification. Brahmanism, as we shall see, had assimilated the Buddha, in a manner of speaking, and was not averse to accepting lay Buddhists, provided they declared their allegiance to brahmanism. But it opposed and reviled the institutional identity of Buddhism with all its strength. Brahmanism has always grown through continuous accretion, and its ever-expanding fluid margin was not conducive to a sharp demarcation of the boundary between 'them' and 'us', except in opposition to Buddhism.

Accordingly, the Bengal *Purāṇas* took on themselves the task of defining the Buddhists as clearly as they attempted to define brahmanism. The *Bṛhannāradīya Purāṇa* states that the Buddhists are called *pāṣaṇḍas* (heretical, impious)[140] because they condemn the *Vedas*, and give up their traditional occupations and *varṇa* duties.[141] They are expelled from the path of the *Vedas* because they do not offer sacrifices to the gods and the ancestors.[142] Significantly, it is a wholly negative definition; 'they' are what 'we' are not. A set of other attributes follow, positive only in a derogatory sense: the Buddhists are wandering beggars, with dirty minds. They accept food cooked by others, live on bribes, and remain immersed in terrible sins.[143]

Questioning the authority of the *Vedas* was of course the primal sin, but judging by the evidence of the *Purāṇas*, they indulged in crimes which were worse. They instigated others to transgress the land of *brāhmaṇas*. The *Kriyāyogasāra* relates the story of the devout king Dharmabuddhi who allowed himself to be persuaded by the Buddhists to usurp a piece of land belonging to a *brāhmaṇa*. He was immediately forsaken by the goddess of fortune, lost his kingdom, and died a broken man. While reading out to Yama the balance-sheet of his actions on earth, Citragupta, Yama's ledger-keeper, said that this king had always remained virtuous, except once. That single instance of indiscretion, however, wipes out his entire stock of pious deeds, and he deserves to be consigned to hell.[144]

Understandably, Buddhists were projected as the symbol of evil in the Bengal *Purāṇas*. Visions of these red-robed, shaven-headed, mud-stained people foretell disaster.[145] It is inauspicious to see a Buddhist even in a dream. The fact that the other creatures who have been described as similarly inauspicious are asses, camels, monkeys, crows, owls, boars and snakes, is a measure of the extent of brahmanical antipathy towards the Buddhists.[146] The Bengal *Purāṇas* were therefore anxious to ensure that at least *brāhmaṇas* did not become Buddhists which, they feared, would happen in the degenerate *Kali* age.[147] Consequently, the *Purāṇas* strictly forbade *brāhmaṇas* from having any contact with Buddhists. Under no circumstances should a *brāhmaṇa* enter the house of a Buddhist, or even look at him. All those who did, either deliberately or by mistake, would be considered sinners, and the wilful sinner is beyond redemption.[148] Even kings were not immune to this rule. In the *Bṛhannāradīya Purāṇa* the powerful king Dharmakīrti was ruined through his association with the *pāṣaṇḍas*.[149] There are innumerable instances in the Bengal *Purāṇas* where persons engaged in performing brahmanical rituals have been instructed to take special care to stay away from Buddhists on these occasions.[150] The Buddhists were profane and their presence defiling.

These strictures do not appear surprising in view of what the *Devībhāgavata Purāṇa* narrates about the origin of the Buddhists:

> Once a prolonged drought for fifteen years caused a terrible famine on earth. People began to die of starvation. Then a number of *brāhmaṇas* got together and decided that only the sage Gautama could save them at this hour of peril. They approached Gautama in his hermitage and asked for his protection. Gautama meditated on the goddess Gāyatrī who blessed him with a vessel full of eatables and other necessities of life. With these Gautama fed the *brāhmaṇas* and supported them for twelve years like his children. Once the sage Nārada came to visit Gautama and told him that Indra himself praised Gautama for his consideration and magnanimity. This made the *brāhmaṇas* jealous and they conspired to defame him. When the famine passed away, they conjured through *māyā* an old dying cow. Gautama was engaged in performing a sacrifice when he saw that the cow was about to enter the sacred enclosure. He shouted to drive it away. The cow fell down and died. Then the ungrateful *brāhmaṇas* cried out, 'this sinner Gautama has killed a cow'. Gautama came to know about the conspiracy in due course and cursed the *brāhmaṇas* that they would be indifferent to the practice of proper conduct as prescribed in the *Vedas* and the *Smṛtis*. They would fail to perform the daily rituals, sacrifices and penances,

such as *Sandhyā*, *Agnihotra*, and *Cāndrāyaṇa*. They would be deprived of worshipping the most adorable Śiva and Bhagavatī. They would sell away their parents, brothers and sisters, sons and daughters, as well as the *Vedas*, the *tīrthas*, and *dharma*. They would be addicted to the ways of the Pāñcarātras, Kāpālikas, and Bauddhas. After a stint in hell, they would be reborn as Bauddhas, Jainas, Kāpālikas and Kaulas, wearing heretical signs (*taptamudrā*) on their bodies, and would eventually go back to hell.[151]

Perhaps nothing can be more abominable than the meanness of these wretched *brāhmaṇas* and they appropriately suffer the worst possible fate of being forsaken by the *Vedas* and embracing Buddhism. No wonder that those who originated in such reprehensible circumstances would conduct themselves with indignity in their incarnation as Buddhists. Brahmanism allows no space for even covert sympathy for those for whose fate only they themselves are to blame. It should also be noted that Buddhism provided a broad platform for brahmanism to denigrate all dissenting groups under the general rubric of the Buddhists, the prime target in Bengal.[152]

Differential access to opportunities are built into every hierarchically organized social system. But the amorphous structure of brahmanism and its apparently rigid but in effect flexible social code (due to its inner compulsion to accommodate spatio-temporal variables such as *deśācāra/lokācāra* and the constraints of the *yugas*) rendered it necessary to specify the terms of entitlement in practically every single situation. Neither caste status which was never permanently fixed for intermediate groups, nor adherence to *dharma* which remained imprecise in its connotation, could absolutely guarantee the promises the system held out to its members. And when membership itself was somewhat elastic and open-ended, the question of limits to entitlement became a matter of supreme import. Those who transgressed this limit ran the risk of being permanently debarred from the system which, in the context of Puranic Bengal, meant turning into a Buddhist. The following story from the *Devī Purāṇa* illustrates the extent of brahmanical hostility towards Buddhism, with the issue of entitlement at its core:

The demon Ghora was devoted to Viṣṇu and the brahmanical way of life. When he hoped to attain heaven, the gods sent the sage Nārada to corrupt him, so that Ghora was displaced from the path of *dharma*. Nārada told Ghora, 'You should learn to take pleasure in the enjoyment of property and women. Kingship and possession of young women are the fruits of worshipping the gods. Trilocana went to the pine forest to play around with (*prakrīḍāya)* the daughter of the sage and Viṣṇu keeps Lakṣmī close to his breast.' Ghora replied, 'What you said is not in accordance with *dharma.* Abstinence is auspicious and rewarding. Those who are intemperate and acquisitive of wealth end up in hell, while those who conquer their senses become respectful and humble. Sensuousness only feeds on itself.' When Nārada realised that Ghora was being guided by his conscience, he indulged in guile recommended by *dharma* (*dharmavyāja*) and said, 'Kingdom leads to acquisition of wealth. Enjoy your kingdom, your wife and other women. There is no harm in consuming meat and wine or indulging in copulation, if you feel so inclined. If a man enjoys one hundred women, he acquires a fortune; if he enjoys a thousand women, he is considered blessed; if he enjoys ten thousand women, he becomes as prosperous as the god of wealth; if he enjoys a hundred thousand women, he achieves equivalence with Kāmadeva; and if he enjoys ten million women, he achieves salvation. One who always revels in the company of teenage girls adorned with firm breasts, achieves immortality. Life, semen, vitality and power are all bestowed by women. It is through the grace of beautiful women that men rejoice and succeed in every venture. This is the way to fulfil one's obligation to *dharma*, *artha* and *kāma*. There lives a daughter of the mountain (*bhūdhara putrikā*) in the Vindhya hills who is eighteen years of age and is fit for your wealth and home. Go and take possession of her.' Being dissuaded by Nārada, Ghora lost respect for the *Vedas* and stopped worshipping the *brāhmaṇas*. Then Candramati, the virtuous wife of Ghora, became anxious about his well-being and told him, 'One should never lust for unknown or unwilling women. One who accepts food and drink, seat and bed, and mount and women without discretion, becomes diseased and falls prey to death. I am saying this for the safety of your kingdom and your own good.' Nārada felt that these wise words may bring Ghora back to his senses. Therefore, in order to delude Ghora, he began to chant the *bhairavā padamālā*. [Here follows a long Tantric formula which is quoted in full, and its history and method of application is explained in great detail.] As a result, Ghora, his ministers, priests, and the army came under its spell and deviated from the path of *dharma*. The queen Candramati became devoted to the *pāṣaṇḍas* and the *digamvaras* and began to abuse Śiva and Viṣṇu. She lost interest in preparing for the performance of sacrifices and lost respect for the Mātṛs, the *brāhmaṇas* and cows. Ghora and all his associates were brought to their ruin. Encouraged by Nārada, he proceeded to take the goddess of the Vindhyas by force and was killed in battle.[153]

Powerful demons often staked their claim to heaven, some attempting to occupy it by force, others using the more conventional and non-violent method of asceticism and good behaviour. Both invariably failed, because the brahmanical system does not permit it. In brahmanical cosmogony the relationship between gods and demons is a complex one. Although they exist in polar opposition, they are also in a sense complementary to one another. But permanent residence in heaven is a privilege exclusive to the gods; the demons are not entitled. This common theme has been very conveniently and effectively utilized to make several statements. Ghora entertained an impossible hope, and this initial act of transgression exposed him to the ultimate danger of excommunication and becoming a Buddhist. This seems to constitute the primary message of the story; the Buddhists are evil beyond redemption and are therefore irreversibly disqualified. This justifies the end of Ghora and helps to overcome the ethical problem of a virtuous person being misled into self-destruction. But he misled himself, and from there, his final delusion was but the next logical step. In the Bengal *Purāṇas* this inevitably assumes the form of conversion to Buddhism.

Buddhism must have been perceived as a formidable adversary in Bengal. The *Bṛhaddharma Purāṇa*, after providing a formulaic description of the *Kaliyuga*, adds:

The Vedic religion will be shrouded in *pāṣaṇḍa-dharma.* People will abandon the *Dharmaśāstras* and forget the name of Kṛṣṇa. As Kṛṣṇa will leave the earth, the Buddhists will [feel encouraged to] preach their faith with greater vigour. When [the practice of resolving] differences between the *Purāṇas* and the *darśaṇas* (. . . *purāṇe sarvasmin darśaṇeṣu ca sarvaśaḥ I vibhedeṣu* . . .) [will fall into disuse], Sarasvatī will wail in grief. To console her, Śiva and Viṣṇu will be born as *ācāryas* in a *brāhmaṇa* family. Sarasvatī will be married to Viṣṇu. Śiva will take to asceticism and become famous in the name of Śaṅkarācārya. He will compose many eulogies of gods and important treaties on philosophy. Together, they will refute the Buddhist doctrines with the help of *Nyāya* logic (*naiyāyikamatena*). The Buddhists will be forcibly burnt to death.[154]

If it needed the combined efforts of Śiva and Viṣṇu to defeat Buddhism, it must have proved to be a serious hindrance to the establishment of brahmanical hegemony in Bengal. The hagiographies of Śaṅkarācārya do include Bengal in the itineraries of his 'tours of victory' (*digvijaya*).[155] But that is incidental, for this fact, or legend, is not commonly known in Bengal. The Bengal *Purāṇas* were obviously invoking a pan-Indian idiom in support of their diatribe against Buddhism. Nor did they require the assistance of Śaṅkarācārya. Buddhism in Bengal decayed primarily due to its own internal contradictions.

The role of Viṣṇu in this process was much more insidious than that of Śiva. Instead of directly contributing to the eradication of Buddhism, Viṣṇu internalized the Buddha. The extent of the erosion of identity-markers between the two religions is exemplified by the most remarkable transformation of the Buddha. D.C. Sircar has referred to a Vajrayoginī tortoise-shell inscription of about the eleventh century, which begins with a joint adoration of the most worshipful Vāsudeva and the Buddha. Sircar suggests that this points to a rapprochement between the two deities.[156] Harunur Rashid reports that some comparatively late specimens of Buddha images found at Maināmati portray him as a *brāhmaṇa*, wearing the sacred thread.[157] These developments were bringing the Buddha increasingly closer to brahmanism. Niharranjan Ray believes that the Yogāsana and Lokeśvara Viṣṇu and the Dhyānī Śiva were modelled on the ideal prototype of the Dhyānī Buddha.[158] R.C. Hazra has suggested that the concept of the Buddha as an incarnation of Viṣṇu originated in the early seventh century, and must have received wide popular acceptance, so that by the early medieval period it came to be mentioned in such apparently secular literature as Kṣemendra's *Daśāvatāracarita* and the *Gītagovinda* of Jayadeva.[159]

Yet such recognition of the Buddha was not without its ambiguities. Wendy O'Flaherty has argued that the Buddha *avatāra* represents an attempt by orthodox brahmanism to discredit Buddhist doctrines. In many texts Viṣṇu first becomes the Buddha to delude demons by preaching a false system and making them heretics, and then becomes Kalkin to destroy the heretics in the *Kali* age. Thus the Buddha performed an important function in the cosmic design of brahmanism, but it was essentially a negative function. O'Flaherty points out that this strain is particularly evident in the early *Purāṇas*, beginning with the *Viṣṇu Purāṇa*, when revived brahmanism was fighting an intense battle for socio-religious supremacy with Buddhism. In the comparatively later *Purāṇas*, such as the *Varāha* and the *Matsya*, brahmanism displayed a more favourable attitude and the Buddha has been depicted as an embodiment of peace and beauty. Jayadeva, who was not constrained by the compulsion of the authors of the didactic texts, stated that Viṣṇu became the Buddha out of compassion for animals to end violent sacrifices. Historians have struggled to make sense of this double vision of the Buddha *avatāra* and have variously suggested that it was born out of an attempt to combat Buddhism by making brahmanism appear indistinguishable from Buddhism in the eyes of the Buddhist laity, on the one hand, and to render Buddhism harmless to the brahmanical orthodoxy by projecting the Buddha as one who misled the heretics to the advantage of the faithful, on the other.[160] Thus a set of complex motivations contributed to the creation of the image of the Buddha *avatāra* in the *Purāṇas*.

The process of assimilation of the Buddha as an incarnation of Viṣṇu may be said to have reached its culmination in the Bengal

Purāṇas. In their references to the Buddha *avatāra* they subsume the entire gamut of brahmanical attitudes discussed above, and move towards a more balanced synthesis. Viṣṇu's primary function as the Buddha was indeed to delude people and encourage them to embrace false beliefs.[161] Hence he is described as the founder of *Kalidharma* and *Śūdradharma,* which paved the way for the appearance of Kalkin. But in the same passage he is also described as one of pure disposition, devoid of anger and hatred.[162] He is said to be worthy of respect, for, being distressed by wanton killing of animals, he condemned the *Vedas*.[163] Finally, the Bengal *Purāṇas* offer homage to Viṣṇu who became incarnate as the Buddha in order to stop the slaughter of animals and to destroy wicked sacrifices.[164]

None of the *Mahāpurāṇas* has attempted to completely rationalize the cardinal sin of the Buddha's rejection of the *Vedas*, nor have they ever condemned the sacrifice in such unambiguous terms. Besides, the inclusion of this statement in the *Devībhāgavata Purāṇa* (which throughout its massive bulk, has consistently advocated animal sacrifice as the most appropriate ritual for the propitiation of the goddess) cannot be taken as the result of a casual oversight. It was a deliberately devised concession to the Buddha, who was absorbed within the brahmanical pantheon to the extent that the Puranic space permitted. Indeed, in the process the Buddha was completely decontextualized. In the *Devībhāgavata* story of the origin of the Buddhists, mentioned above, the Buddha is conspicuous by his absence. He had already gained brahmanical recognition by performing the necessary function of hastening the end of the epoch, and it was imperative to dissociate him from his evil followers, for, as we have seen, the Bengal *Purāṇas* retained their intense loathing for Buddhism and expressed it in no uncertain terms. A degree of ambiguity, however, remained. One wonders if it is a mere coincidence that the person circumstantially responsible for the creation of the Buddhists in the Puranic account is called Gautama. However, by the twelfth century, Buddhism had ceased to be a serious threat to brahmanism, and the appropriation of the Buddha symbolizes the final success of the brahmanical bid to outdo Buddhism in Bengal.

NOTES

1. The *Mahābhārata* betrays intimate knowledge of Bengal. It says that Bengal was divided into a number of states, of which nine are specifically mentioned. Karṇa is said to have vanquished the Sumhas, the Puṇḍras,

and the Vaṅgas, and Kṛṣṇa, who was particularly hostile to the 'false' Vāsudeva, the lord of the Puṇḍras, who supposedly united Vaṅga, Puṇḍra, and Kirāta into a powerful kingdom and made an alliance with Jarāsandha of Magadha, defeated both the Vaṅgas and the Pauṇḍras. Bhīma, in the course of his eastern campaign, subjugated all the local princes of Bengal, so that they were made to bring tribute to the court of Yudhiṣṭhira. Predictably, in the Bhārata war the Bengal kings are said to have taken the side of the Kurus. The text also refers to the Gaṅgā-sāgara-saṅgama, the Lauhitya and the Karatoyā rivers. See Majumdar, *Ancient Bengal*, pp. 27–8.

2. Edward Tuite Dalton, *Descriptive Ethnology of Bengal*, Indian Studies: Past and Present, Calcutta, 1973 (originally published in 1872), p. 317, and Nripendra Kumar Dutt, *The Aryanisation of India*, Firma K.L. Mukhopadhyay, Calcutta, 1970 (originally published in 1925), pp. 33–4.
3. Benoychandra Sen, *Some Historical Aspects of the Inscriptions of Bengal*, University of Calcutta, Calcutta, 1942, pp. 3–5.
4. Ray, *Bāṅgālīr Itihāsa*, p. 278.
5. *Ibid.*, pp. 278–9.
6. Sen, *Some Historical Aspects*, p. 16.
7. Dinesh Chandra Sircar, 'Spread of Aryanism in Bengal', *Journal of the Asiatic Society of Bengal, Letters*, Vol. 18, No. 2, 1952, p. 174.
8. Sen, *Some Historical Aspects,* pp. 16–17.
9. Ray, *Bāṅgālīr Itihāsa*, p. 280.
10. Sircar, 'Spread of Aryanism', p. 172.
11. Chatterjee, *Religion in Bengal*, pp. 35–79.
12. Bagchi, 'Religion', in Majumdar (ed.), *The History of Bengal*, pp. 394–7.
13. Shashi Bhushan Chaudhuri, *Ethnic Settlements in Ancient India: A Study on the Purāṇic Lists of the People of Bhāratavarṣa*, General Printers and Publishers Ltd, Calcutta, 1955, p. 165.
14. Chitrarekha Gupta, 'Early Brahmanic Settlements in Bengal—Pre Pāla Period', in B.N. Mukherjee, D.R. Das, S.S. Biswas and S.P. Singh (eds), *Sri Dinesacandrika: Studies in Indology*, Sundeep Prakashan, Delhi, 1983, pp. 215–16.
15. Ray, *Bāṅgālīr Itihāsa,* p. 281.
16. *Ibid.*, pp. 282–3.
17. Gupta, 'Early Brahmanic Settlements', pp. 221–2.
18. Ray, *Bāṅgālīr Itihāsa,* p. 297.
19. Chatterjee, *Religion in Bengal,* pp. 43–6, 60–1.
20. Ray, *Bāṅgālīr Itihāsa*, pp. 302–6.
21. Chatterjee, *Religion in Bengal*, pp. 49–55.
22. Ray, *Bāṅgālīr Itihāsa,* p. 307.
23. Puspa Niyogi, *Brahmanic Settlements in Different Subdivisions of Ancient Bengal*, Indian Studies: Past and Present, Calcutta, 1967, pp. 53–7.
24. Chatterjee, *Religion in Bengal,* pp. 62–5.

25. *Ibid.*, pp. 44, 46, 49–50.
26. Ray, *Bāṅgālīr Itihāsa,* p. 314.
27. The contribution of the Bengal school to the exposition of *Nyāya* and other branches of Indian philosophy was recognized by the most conservative and high-profile centres of brahmanical learning throughout north India for centuries to come. See, Dineshchandra Bhattacharya, *Bāṅgālīr Sārasvata Avadāna*, Vol. I (*Baṅge Navyanyāyacarccā*), Bangiya Sahitya Parisat, Calcutta, 1358 BS, particularly, pp. 36–60, 106–8, 249–59.
28. For example, the author(s) of the *Devībhāgavata Purāṇa* often refer to the four *Vedas*, the early *Dharmaśāstras* and quote extensively from several *Upaniṣads*, Hazra, *Upapurāṇas* Vol. II, pp. 359–60.
29. Chatterjee, *Religion in Bengal,* pp. 51–5.
30. *Ibid.*, pp. 66–7.
31. *Ibid.*, p. 41.
32. Ray, *Bāṅgālīr Itihāsa*, p. 312.
33. Niyogi, *Brahmanic Settlements,* p. 44.
34. Ray, *Bāṅgālīr Itihāsa,* pp. 272–3.
35. Mahimachandra Majumdar, *Gauḍe Brāhmaṇa*, Calcutta, 1900, pp. 37–8, 41–2, 52–61, 62–9.
36. Majumdar, *Ancient Bengal*, p. 472.
37. Nripendra Kumar Dutt, *Origin and Growth of Caste in India*, Vol. II (Castes in Bengal), Firma K.L. Mukhopadhyay, Calcutta, 1969, pp. 14–21.
38. Rameshchandra Majumdar, *Baṅgīya Kulaśāstra*, Bharati Book Stall, Calcutta, 1973, pp. 1–27.
39. R.C. Majumdar writes that when the corpus of the *Kulajī* texts were first brought to light by Nagendranath Basu towards the beginning of the twentieth century, a number of historians such as Akshayakumar Maitreya, Rakhaldas Bandyopadhyaya and Ramaprasad Chanda refused to accept them as historical evidence, while Haraprasad Shastri and Dineshchandra Sen found them admissible. The debate became so aggressive and personal that it is still fresh in his memory, *ibid.*, p. 1.
40. *Baṅger Jātīya Itihāsa* by Nagendranath Basu and *Samvandha Nirṇaya* by Lalmohan Vidyanidhi have been discussed in almost all the subsequent writings on the subject. Basu, for example, is of the opinion that when Jayanta became the ruler of Pañcagauḍa with the help of his son-in-law Jayāditya, mentioned in the *Rājataraṅgiṇī*, he assumed the title of Ādiśūra, *Ibid.*, p. 33.
41. Tarak Chandra Raychaudhuri and Bikash Raychaudhuri, *The Brāhmaṇas of Bengal: A Textual Study in Social History*, Anthropological Survey of India, Calcutta, 1981, pp. 16–17.
42. Pramode Lal Paul, 'Brāhmaṇa Immigrations in Bengal', *Proceedings of the Indian History Congress*, 1939, p. 576.
43. Sircar, 'Spread of Aryanism', p. 177.

44. Sukhamay Mukhopadhyaya, 'Bāṅglār Kulajīgrantha', Appendix to Majumdar, *Baṅgīya Kulaśāstra*, p. 134.
45. Sarat Chandra Chattopadhyaya, *Bāmuner Meye*, in *Śarat Racanā Samagra*, Ananda Publishers Pvt. Ltd, Calcutta 1392 BS, pp. 979–1013.
46. Bibhuti Bhushan Bandyopadhyaya, *Pather Pāñcālī*, in *Bibhūti Racanāvalī*, Vol. I, Mitra O Ghosh Pvt. Ltd, Calcutta, 1387 BS, p. 22.
47. Dinabandhu Mitra, *Sadhabār Ekādaśī*, in *Dinabandhu Racanāvalī*, Sahitya Samsad, Calcutta, 1967, p. 141.
48. Ray, *Bāṅgālīr Itihāsa*, p. 275.
49. Ronald B. Inden, *Marriage and Rank in Bengali Culture: A History of Caste and Clan in Middle Period Bengal*, Vikas Publishing House Pvt. Ltd, New Delhi, 1976, pp. 50–1.
50. *BP* III.13–14 narrates the following story about the origin of the *saṁkaravarṇas*. Once there was a king called Veṇa who was an atheist and cruel and oppressive by nature. As soon as he assumed the throne, he prohibited the pursuit of *dharma* in accordance with the norms of *varṇa*, *āśrama* and *kula*, and imposed restrictions on the performance of sacrifices and other prescribed rites. Then the *brāhmaṇas* approached Veṇa and told him that if the king forsook *dharma*, the subjects would also deviate from the path of right conduct. Veṇa was happy to hear this, and in his resolve to break all social codes, forced men and women of different *varṇas* to cohabit and produce children. When the situation became unbearable, the great sages assembled and killed the evil king with a menacing roar (*huṁkāra*). They churned the arms of Veṇa and created from these the righteous king Pṛthu who restored order by classifying the illegitimate children into a hierarchy of thirty-six mixed castes. Clearly this story was constructed to rationalize the brahmanical scheme of social organization, because there is nothing in it to account for Veṇa's violent and obsessive attempt to undermine the social order, except his natural perversity. It may perhaps contain a reflection of the state of society in Bengal prior to the establishment of the brahmanical order, seen from the brahmanical point of view. However, the classification itself is arbitrary, for there is no transparent reason why these mixed castes should be arranged into a ranked hierarchy of *uttama* (high), *madhyama* (middle) and *adhama* (low) *saṁkaras*, as the text recommends, *BP*, III.13.33–47. The hierarchy is explained in terms of order of relative purity and professed loyalty of these mixed castes to the brahmanical order, but it does not conform to any discernible pattern. Besides, compared to the thirty-six mentioned in the *BP*, the *BvP* (I.10.14–136) contains a list of at least seventy mixed castes, and their names and parentage do not necessarily tally with those in the *BP*. For example, according to the *BP*, III.13.34 Rājaputras were born of *kṣatriya* father and *vaiśya* mother, while in the *BvP*, I.10.111, the same combination is said to have produced the Kaivarttas. Thus it seems that the Bengal *Purāṇas* merely

stated the principle of admission of those outside the caste framework into the brahmanical order and left the actual working out of the occupational *jāti* groups and their relative positioning in the hierarchy to the Bengal *Smṛtis*.

51. Chatterjee, *Religion in Bengal*, p. 67.
52. Due to the Puranic attempt to project the *brāhmaṇas* as a homogeneous community, as well as for the sake of convenience, I refer to the *brāhmaṇas* as a single category throughout. But I have tried to remain conscious of differentiation and its implications.
53. *BvP*, I.11.12–20.
54. *sarvvadevāśrayo vipraḥ pratyakṣatridaśo vibhuḥ I*

    Ks, 21.5.
55. *brāhmaṇasya tanurjñeyā sarvvadevasamāśritā I*

    BnP, 14.141.
56. *brāhmaṇasya dharā sarvvā dharmmāśca nikhilā api I*

    BP, III.2.49.
57. *Ks*, 21.8, 10, 24–7.
58. *BP*, III.2.53–4.
59. *brāhmaṇe bhaktimāsādya śūdrastarati durgatim I*
    nopadeśaiśca mantraiśca na stavaiḥ kavacairapi II

    BP, III.4.25.
60. *Ks*, 20.3–4.
61. *brāhmaṇo dānapātraṁ hi nānyattasmāt paraṁ kvacit II*

    BP, III.15.45.
62. *brāhmaṇebhyoo'pi devebhyo dāne samaphalam labhet I*

    BvP, II.26.66.
63. *BvP*, IV.21.53–8, 62. *Ks*, 19.49.
64. *brāhmaṇānāṁ mukhaṁ rādhe devānāṁ mukhamukhyakam I*

    BvP, IV.124.24.
65. *BvP*, II.26.45, 47, 49, 51. *DP*, 28.6; 50(4).4; 50(4).40; 67.63.
66. *DbP*, III.26.15.
67. *BvP*, II.26.45–51.
68. *BvP*, II.42.36–63.
69. *BnP*, 11.120–35.
70. *BP*, I.14.20; III.15.31.
71. *BvP*, II.9.4; IV.76.52.
72. *Ks*, 20.144; 20.153–4.
73. *BnP*, 11.136–70.
74. *BnP*, 14.122–4.
75. *BP*, III.4.10.
76. *BnP*, 14.129–33. The more comprehensive description of the dreadful plight of one who misappropriates the grant of a *brāhmaṇa* in *BvP*, II.52.3–7 is a perfect example of sadistic fantasy.

77. *BnP*, 14.152.
78. *BP*, III.3.7–9.
79. *KP*, 84.86, unequivocally recommends corporal punishment for those who conspire against the king.
80. *BP*, III.3.54. *KP*, 84.17, 32.
81. *BP*, III.3.40.
82. *KP*, 85.3; 84.18, 29–30, 105.
83. *sāmyañca na syāt kasmiṁścit pravarttetādharottamam I*
cāturvarṇyavibhāgāya durbinītabhayāya ca II
daṇḍena niyataṁ loke dharmasthānañca rakṣyate I
BP, III.3.17–18.
84. *KP*, 85.6–7.
85. *BP*, III.3.11–16, 19, 25, 29. *KP*, 84.34–6, 49.
86. *brāhmaṇasthāpanādanyat karma rājño nacottamam II*
BP, III.3.35.
87. *KP*, 85.8–12, 65.
88. *śreyoo'rthī satataṁ rājā brahmavṛttiṁ na laṅghaet I*
BP, III.3.33.
89. *BP*, III.3.4.
90. *BP*, III.3.21, 23. *KP*, 84.86.
91. N.G. Majumdar (ed.), 'Rāmpal Copper-plate of Śrichandra', *Inscriptions of Bengal*, Vol. III, The Varendra Research Society, Rajshahi, 1929, p. 9.
92. Arthur Venis, 'Copper-plate Grant of Vaidyadeva, King of Kāmarūpa', verse 31, *Epigraphia Indica*, Vol. 2, 1894, p. 357.
93. R.D. Banerji, 'The Bangarh Grant of Mahi-pala I: The 9th Year', verse 15, *Epigraphia Indica*, Vol. 14, 1917–18, p. 328.
94. Majumdar (ed.), 'Rāmganj Copper-plate of Iśvaraghosha', *Inscriptions of Bengal*, Vol. III, p. 155.
95. S.K. Maity and R.R. Mukherjee (eds), 'Edilpur Copper-plate of Keśavasena', *Corpus of Bengal Inscriptions*, Firma K.L. Mukhopadhyay, Calcutta, 1967, p. 338. I chose this as an illustrative sample because it is one of the most elaborate examples of the *dharmānuśaṁsinaḥ* verses available among the land-charters of early medieval Bengal.
96. *BP*, III.15.31–2, 40.
97. *BnP*, 14.129–30.
98. Majumdar (ed.), 'Ānuliā Copper-plate of Lakshmaṇasena', verse 8, *Inscriptions of Bengal*, Vol. III, p. 89.
99. *BvP*, III.7.10–61. *DbP*, VI.11.41–54. *BP*, III.19.1–46. *Ks*, 25.18–33.
100. For a summary of the literature on the social crisis of the *Kaliyuga*, see D.N. Jha, 'Introduction', in D.N. Jha (ed.), *Feudal Formation in Early India*, Chanakya Publications, Delhi, 1987, pp. 7–9.
101. See Majumdar, *Ancient Bengal*, pp. 522–32; Ray, *Bāṅgālīr Itihāsa*, pp. 627–8, 637–42, 663–76; Chatterjee, *Religion in Bengal*, pp. 230–356;

Puspa Niyogi, *Buddhism in Ancient Bengal*, Jijnasa, Calcutta, 1980; Gayatri-Sen Majumdar, *Buddhism in Ancient Bengal*, Navana, Calcutta, 1983.

102. Ray, *Bāṅgālīr Itihāsa*, pp. 637–42, 665–8.
103. I have primarily depended on Niharranjan Ray for the above summary of the evolution of Mahāyāna Buddhism in Bengal, for his is easily the most lucid exposition of a set of rather complex ideas. *Ibid.*, pp. 669–74.
104. Prabodh Chandra Bagchi, 'Some Aspects of Buddhist Mysticism in the Caryāpadas', *Studies in the Tantras*, Part I, University of Calcutta, Calcutta, 1939, pp. 74–86, especially pp. 79–81, 84.
105. Trevor Ling, 'Buddhist Bengal, and After', in Debiprasad Chattopadhyaya (ed.), *History and Society: Essays in Honour of Professor Niharranjan Ray*, K.P. Bagchi and Co., Calcutta, 1978, pp. 318–19.
106. Shashibhushan Dasgupta, *An Introduction to Tantric Buddhism*, University of Calcutta, Calcutta, 1974, pp. 3–4.
107. Agehananda Bharati, *The Tantric Tradition*, B.I. Publications, Bombay, 1976, pp. 199–208.
108. N.N. Bhattacharyya, *History of the Tantric Religion: A Historical, Ritualistic and Philosophical Study*, Manohar, New Delhi, 1982, p. 230. The similarities are so obvious that those authors who are not concerned with the problem take them for granted and do not make any distinction between the two. See, B. Bhattacharyya, 'Scientific Background of the Buddhist Tantras', *Indian Historical Quarterly*, Vol. 32, 1956, pp. 290–6.
109. Kooij, *Worship of the Goddess*, pp. 24–5.
110. For varieties of Buddhist images from Pāla Bengal, see R.D. Banerji, *Eastern Indian School of Medieval Sculpture*, Manager of Publications, Delhi, 1933 (reprinted by Ramanand Vidya Bhawan, New Delhi, 1961); A.H. Dani, *Buddhist Sculpture in East Pakistan*, Karachi, 1959; Ramaprasad Chanda, *Medieval Indian Sculpture*, Indological Book House, Varanasi, 1972 (reprint), pp. 54–60; for treatment from stylistic point of view, B.N. Mukherjee, *East Indian Art Styles: A Study in Parallel Trends*, K.P. Bagchi and Co., Calcutta, 1980, pp. 4–13; for Tantric attributes and symbols of Vajrayāna divinities as reflected in the iconography of late Buddhism, K. Krishna Murthy, *Sculptures of Vajrayāna Buddhism*, Classics India Publications, Delhi, 1989, pp. 5–18.
111. Benoytosh Bhattacharya, *The Indian Buddhist Iconography: Mainly Based on Sādhanamālā and Cognate Tantric Texts of Rituals*, Firma K.L. Mukhopadhyay, Calcutta, 1968, pp. 1–5.
112. Nalini Kanta Bhattasali, *Iconography of the Buddhist and Brahmanical Sculptures in the Dacca Museum*, published by Rai S.N. Bhadra Bahadur, Honorary Secretary, Dacca Museum Committee, Dacca, 1929, pp. 16–22.
113. Benoy Kumar Sarkar, *The Folk-Element in Hindu Culture*, Oriental Books Reprint Corporation, New Delhi, 1972, pp. 178–80.

114. Frederick M. Asher, *The Art of Eastern India 300–800*, The University of Minnesota Press, Minneapolis, 1980, pp. 92–3.
115. Ray, *Bāṅgālīr Itihāsa*, p. 708.
116. *Ibid.*, p. 707.
117. H. Vedantasastri argues that Caṇḍīdāsa, the Vaiṣṇava poet of medieval Bengal, drew his inspiration from the Buddhist Sahajiyā school of thought, and was a worshipper of Vāśulī. The image of the deity found at Nānur, the birthplace of Caṇḍīdāsa, does not conform to the description of the Hindu Tantric goddesses. Hence he conjectures that Vāśulī was originally a Buddhist goddess who was later subsumed into the Tantric–Puranic pantheon. H. Vedantasastri, 'Buddhism in Bengal and its Decline', *The Journal of the Bihar Research Society*, Vol. 1 (Buddha Jayanti Special Issue), 1956, p. 70.
118. Ray, *Bāṅgālīr Itihāsa*, p. 706.
119. *Ibid.*, pp. 664–5. D.C. Sircar, in his introductory comments on the Belwā plates of Mahīpāla I, which records a grant of land made to the *brāhmaṇa* Jīvadhara-devaśarman by Mahīpāla I, on the occasion of a ceremonial bath in the Gaṅgā taken by him on the day of *viṣuva-saṁkrānti*, as enjoined by the brahmanical scriptures, wrote: 'The action of the Pāla king, who was a Buddhist as recorded in the document, no doubt points to the fact, often noted, that there was little difference between the lay followers of Buddhism and that of an ordinary brahmanical Hindu in the age of the Pālas, at least in Eastern India . . . the Buddhist laity was gradually nearing absorption into brahmanical society,' D.C. Sircar, 'Two Pāla Plates from Belwā', *Epigraphia Indica*, Vol. 29, 1951–2, p. 2.
120. R.C. Mitra, *The Decline of Buddhism in India*, Shantiniketan, 1954, *passim*.
121. Ray, *Bāṅgālīr Itihāsa,* pp. 308–9.
122. Susan L. Huntington, *The 'Pala-Sena' School of Sculpture*, E.J. Brill, Leiden, 1984, p. 155.
123. Majumdar, *Ancient Bengal*, p. 526.
124. Sen Majumdar, *Buddhism in Ancient Bengal*, pp. 40, 45, 47.
125. Ling, 'Buddhist Bengal', p. 321.
126. B.N.S. Yadava, *Society and Culture in Northern India in the Twelfth Century*, Central Book Depot, Allahabad, 1973, pp. 345–6.
127. Jogendra Nath Bhattacharya, *Hindu Castes and Sects: An Exposition of the Origin of the Hindu Caste System and the Bearing of the Sects Towards Each Other and Towards Other Religious Systems*, Editions Indian, Calcutta, 1973 (reprint), p. 527.
128. Malati J. Shendge, 'A Note on the Sociology of Buddhist Tantrism', *Man in India*, Vol. 49, No.1, March 1969, pp. 26–8.
129. David N. Lorenzen, *The Kāpālikas and the Kālāmukhas: Two Lost Śaivite Sects*, Thomson Press (India) Ltd, New Delhi, 1972, p. 69.

130. Haraprasad Shastri, *Bener Meye, Haraprasad Shastri Racanā-Saṁgraha*, Vol. I, Pashcimbanga Rajya Pustak Parshad, Calcutta, 1980, pp. 313–14.
131. Haraprasad Shastri in his *Bener Meye* describes the settlement of a new village called Devagrāma, next to the village Vikramamaṇipur which was abandoned by its Buddhist residents. The houses of Devagrāma were built with the materials taken from the dilapidated structures of Vikramamaṇipur. Thus the icon of Mañjuśrī came to be worshipped as Sarasvatī and the icon of Lokeśvara was accepted as the representation of Sūrya, *ibid.*, p. 277. This seems entirely likely, as there are enough historical examples of such substitution. Within the same religion, when a deity loses his former importance, his image may become identified with the deity currently in worship, with some similarity in features. When it happens across two institutional religions, it goes to show how close they have come to one another. *Bener Meye*, though a work of fiction, captures the tensions and adjustments between Buddhism and brahmanism, in fact the entire social milieu of eleventh-century Bengal, with remarkable sensitivity.
132. Padmanabh Jaini has cited this failure as one of the major causes of the eventual disappearance of Buddhism from India. He shows that in contrast, the Jaina clerics produced some fifty books on the proper conduct of a Jaina layperson, which gave him the sense of a unique religious identity and ensured the survival of Jainism. The reason why Jainism could not expand its popular base in the manner in which Buddhism did was also the reason why it managed to maintain its identity as a separate group, while Buddhism failed. Padmanabh S. Jaini, 'The Disappearance of Buddhism and the Survival of Jainism: A Study in Contrast', in A.K. Narain (ed.), *Studies in History of Buddhism*, B.R. Publishing Corporation, Delhi, 1980, p. 84.
133. Ray, *Bāṅgālīr Itihāsa,* p. 300.
134. Shastri, *Bener Meye*, pp. 221–2.
135. *Ibid.*, pp. 279–81.
136. Ray, *Bāṅgālīr Itihāsa*, p. 289.
137. *Ibid.*, pp. 299–300.
138. D.C. Sircar, *Epigraphic Discoveries in East Pakistan*, Sanskrit College, Calcutta, 1973, pp. 51–2.
139. Ray, *Bāṅgālīr Itihāsa,* p. 300.
140. Monier Monier-Williams, *A Sanskrit-English Dictionary*, Motilal Banarsidass, New Delhi, 1986, p. 624.
141. *bauddhāḥ pāṣaṇḍinaḥ proktā yato vai vedanindakāḥ* I

    ....

    yaḥ svakarma parityāgī pāṣaṇḍityucyate budhaiḥ I

    ....

    svavarṇadharmatyāgena pāṣaṇḍa procyate budhaiḥ II

    BnP, 14.70, 134; 22.9.

142. *utsannapitṛdevejyā vedamārgabahiṣkṛtāḥ* I
pāṣaṇḍā iti vikhyātā . . .
BnP, 14.186.

143. *aśaucayuktamatayaḥ parapakvānnabhojinaḥ* I
bhaviṣyānta durātmānaḥ śūdrāḥ pravrajitāstathā II
utkocajīvinastatra mahāpāparatāstathā I
bhaviṣyantyatha pāṣaṇḍāḥ kāpālā bhikṣavastathā II
BnP, 38.57–8.

144. *Ks*, 5.238–45.
145. *DP*, 13.24.
146. *DP*, 63.52.
147. *purvaṁ ye rākṣasā rājaṅste kalau brāhmaṇāḥ smṛtāḥ* I
pāṣaṇḍaniratā prāyo bhavanti janavañcakāḥ II
DbP, VI.11.42–3.

148. *BnP*, 14.69–71.
149. *BnP*, 21.51–6.
150. To cite a few illustrative examples:
DP, 27.18.
BnP, 17.20.
na pāṣaṇḍajanālāpaḥ kartavyo harivāsare I
paṣāṇḍālāpamātreṇa sarvadharmo vinaśyati II
Ks, 22.140.

151. *DbP*, summary of XII.9.
152. The Bengal *Purāṇas* refer to a number of such groups, but those who receive maximum attention and thus bear the brunt of their disapproval are the Buddhists, the Jains, the Kāpālikas and the Cārvvākas:
kāpālikāścīnamārgaratā valkaladhāriṇaḥ II
digamvarāstathā bauddhāścārvvākā evamādayaḥ I
DbP, XII.8.3–4.

153. *DP*, summary of chapters 8, 9, 13 and 20. The intervening chapters contain an exposition of the technical aspects of *padmālā vidyā*, a long philosophical discourse on *yoga*, and the details of the battle between Ghora and the goddess.
154. *BP*, III.19.12–26.
155. David N. Lorenzen, 'The Life of Śaṅkarācarya', in F. Reynolds and D. Capps (eds), *The Biographical Process*, Mouton, The Hague, 1975, p. 95.
156. D.C. Sircar, 'Decline of Buddhism in Bengal', *Studies in the Religious Life of Ancient and Medieval India*, Motilal Banarsidass, Delhi, 1971, pp. 186–7.
157. M. Harunur Rashid, 'The Early History of South East Bengal in the Light of Recent Archaeological Material', unpublished Ph.D. dissertation, University of Cambridge, December 1968, p. 187.

158. Ray, *Bāṅgālīr Itihāsa,* p. 707.
159. Hazra, *Purāṇic Records*, p. 41.
160. Wendy Doniger O'Flaherty, *The Origins of Evil in Hindu Mythology*, Motilal Banarsidass, Delhi, 1976, pp. 198–211; also see by O'Flaherty, 'The Image of the Heretic in the Gupta Purāṇas', in Bardwell L. Smith (ed.), *Essays on Gupta Culture*, Motilal Banarsidass, Delhi, 1983, pp. 107–27.
161. *tato lokabimohāya buddhastvaṁ hi bhaviṣyasi I*

    BP, II.11.72.
162. *śuddhasadbhāvabhāvāya śuddhabuddhatanūdbhava I*
    rāgadveṣavinirmmukta raktavāso namoo'stu te II
    aśvārūḍha mahāvāho kalidharmapravarttaka I
    digambaradharo deva śūdradharmapravarttaka II

    DP, 6.5–6.
163. *vedā vininditā yena vilokya paśughātanam I*
    sakṛpeṇa tvayā yena tasmai buddhāya te namaḥ II

    Ks, 5.423.
164. *duṣṭayajñavighātāya paśuhiṁsānivṛttaye I*
    bauddharūpaṁ dadhau yoo'sau tasmai devāya te namaḥ II

    DbP, X.5.13.

V

Appropriation as a Historical Process: The Cult of the Goddess

I

The central preoccupation of the Bengal *Purāṇas* is with the goddess cult. It was primarily through the appropriation and transformation of the local goddesses that the brahmanical attempt at achieving social dominance in Bengal was articulated.

Scholars dealing with the history of the goddess in India virtually unanimously proclaim that the basic impulse behind the worship of the goddess is non-brahmanical, non-Sanskritic, indigenous. Although contrary opinion is not altogether absent,[1] recent research is coming increasingly close to the conclusion that the Indian goddess dates to pre-Vedic times and has had an uneven but continuous history since, with its roots in the religious beliefs and practices of the autochthonous people.

The idea of the pre-Vedic origin of the goddess stems from the speculation that the people of the Indus Valley civilization worshipped a mother goddes. From the abundant semi-nude figurines found at the Indus Valley sites, Sir John Marshall concluded in his official report of the excavations that these were 'effigies of the great Mother Goddess or of one or other of her local manifestations'.[2] Since then emendations have been suggested to Marshall's original formulation, but the goddess has survived. For example, Mortimer Wheeler appears to be a little sceptical about 'the great Mother Goddess' and is more inclined to describe these figurines as related to 'a household cult than to a state religion',[3] but does not question the existence of the goddess. Recently Shubhangana Atre suggested that the main deity of the Harappans was 'a Great Goddess of animals and vegetations', while rejecting the idea of any male divinity. She has argued that both ideological manifestation and ritual organization of the Harappan religion were derived from the basic concept of 'the Archetypal Mother' who controlled the eternal cycle of biological regeneration.[4]

In the Vedic literature, however, the role of the goddess is in fact marginal. Although some scholars have affirmed the existence of a great goddess in the Vedic literature,[5] and others have tried to trace the development of some of the important goddesses of later Hinduism from the Vedic antecedents,[6] there is very little in the Vedic literature itself to show for it. David Kinsley, who made a survey of the goddesses in the Vedic literature, arrives at the following conclusions. First, none of the Vedic goddesses rivals the great male gods in these texts. Even Uṣas, the most popular goddess, is rather insignificant, and undoubtedly the male deities dominate the Vedic vision of the divine. Second, although there is evidence that some goddesses like Pṛthivī and Sarasvatī survive in the later Hindu tradition, and the idea of *śakti*, though not fully developed, is suggested in the various consorts of the male deities, especially in Indrāṇī, many of the Vedic goddesses simply disappear in the later Hindu tradition. Third, many of the most important goddesses of the later tradition, such as Pārvatī, Durgā, Kālī and Rādhā, are not found at all in Vedic literature. None of the Vedic goddesses is clearly associated with battle or blood sacrifice, both of which are important associations in the myths and cults of several later Hindu goddesses. Finally, there is no single great goddess in the Vedic literature, neither is there any evidence that the authors of the Vedic texts supposed that all the individual goddesses are manifestations of one great goddess. Kinsley thus argues that the great goddess, her various manifestations, and the elaborate mythological ritual structures around them, are late phenomena, the product of a carefully articulated theology that owes very little to the Vedic goddesses.[7]

Daniel Ingalls' foreword to Mackenzie Brown's study of the feminine theology in the *Brahmavaivarta Purāṇa* perhaps contains the best exposition of this point of view in a nutshell. Ingalls writes that the earliest literature of India tells us nothing of 'the Goddess' as the singular embodiment and the few references to the goddesses as we meet in ancient Sanskrit texts are decorative rather than essential. On the other hand, archaeologists have piled up evidence of goddess worship from the pre-Aryan sites of Harappa and Mohenjo Daro. But for a long period after the coming of the Aryans, from about 1500 BC to the early centuries of the Christian era, the evidence of her worship is indirect or uncertain.

It is after a silence of nearly two thousand years that the goddess slowly begins to surface in Sanskrit literature, both religious and secular. Ingalls says that what is strange about this Indian record is not so much the replacement of female by male hierophanies, a phenomenon that has occurred over most of the civilized world, as the fact that in India the goddess reappears. In Mediterranean culture, for example, her embodiments disappeared for good. In Christianity female hierophanies came back in the figures of Mary and the female saints, but there one cannot speak of a reappearance of the ancient goddess. Besides, the figure of the Virgin and its supporting theology are subordinate to those of her son and his father.

Ingalls' explanation of why the Indian record should have differed is the peculiarity of Indian culture which has shown a greater tolerance of religious diversity than Europe and the Middle East. Moreover, in India the political organization of religion was never as strong or as widely ramified as in the West. Ingalls thus suspects that within India's diversified culture the worship of the goddess never ceased. The two-thousand-year silence is due to the fact that all our texts from that period are either in Sanskrit or closely related languages, and the Aryan–Sanskrit culture was strongly oriented towards masculine goals. Those who worshipped goddesses are not likely in that period to have written at all; almost surely they did not write in Sanskrit. Therefore the earliest Sanskrit hymns to 'the Goddess', according to Ingalls' view, are the continuation of an old religion, not an innovation. They first appear at the conjunction of two historical processes. On the one hand, Sanskrit by the third century AD had become the nearly universal language of letters in India, and on the other, the pre-Aryan worship of the Indians had spread by that time very widely among the Aryans. As a result, from the third–fourth centuries, the religion of the Goddess became as much a part of the Hindu written record as the religion of God.[8]

This may be said to be the most reasonable explanation of the uneven history of the goddess[9] in early Indian written records, and almost all standard works on the subject repeat this view, though not always with such elegance and clarity. A look at some representative samples of this opinion will help to substantiate my point. R.G. Bhandarkar was the first to draw our attention to the fact that 'an aboriginal element' contributed to the formation of Rudra's consort in later times, in his landmark book on Vaiṣṇavism, Śaivism and minor religious systems.[10] Alain Danielou[11] and Sudhakar Chattopadhyaya[12] preface their discussion on the Śāktas with similar assertions. R.C. Hazra, in his introduction to the study of the *Śākta Upapurāṇas*, declares that 'in her present character she is pre-eminently a deity of non-Vedic origin', and devotes considerable space to establish this view.[13] Specialized monographs on the goddess cult may be exclusively concerned with this question and demonstrate the non-Vedic origin of the goddess with the help of the material background of her worship,[14] or accept her non-Vedic origin as a premise and proceed to illustrate how the Vedic and the non-Vedic interacted to transform the original monoethnical character of the goddess in the realm of ideas.[15] Essays on the evolution of individual goddesses have also confirmed this opinion. For example, D.D. Kosambi, looking into the antecedents of the goddesses at crossroads, refers to the Skanda-Tārakāsura episode in the *Śalya-parvan* of the *Mahābhārata* which mentions a hundred and ninety-two 'Mothers-companion' who came in aid of Skanda. Kosambi characterizes them as 'mother-goddesses in a group' and concludes that the fact that they spoke different languages clearly signifies that they were of 'varied tribal origin' and 'therefore undoubtedly pre-Aryan'.[16] Kosambi's goddesses were evidently non-Vedic, but Moti Chandra has argued on the basis of literary evidence that even Śrī, a brahmanical goddess *par excellence*, 'belonged to Pre-Aryan India' and was later on assimilated.[17] Indeed, the non-Vedic origin of the goddess has become so much of an axiom that discussions of other aspects of the deity such as iconography, or historical–philosophical exposition of the *Yoga*, also make passing references to it,[18] and it is included in textbooks as the standard opinion.[19]

Yet these female deities of the aboriginal tribes were not allowed an easy access into the Vedic pantheon. None of the names of the different forms of Durgā is ever mentioned in the Vedic *Saṁhitās* and the *Brāhmaṇas*. In the different texts of the *Yajurveda* as well as in its *Brāhmaṇas*, there are passages in which Ambikā has been mentioned as Rudra's sister and once even as his mother, but in these passages Ambikā, unlike other Śākta deities of the *Purāṇas* and the *Tantras*, is allowed a share of the sacrificial offerings. According to Hazra this shows that she could not have been derived from a mother-goddess of the non-Aryans.[20]

However, Umā has received a very different treatment. Several attributes of Umā, beginning with her name, her association with a mountain, and her *vāhana*, resonate with goddesses outside India, all of whom were mother-goddesses.[21] This Umā is neither mentioned in any of the Vedic *Saṁhitās* and *Brāhmaṇas* nor is she allowed any share in the sacrificial offerings. The earliest works mentioning Umā are the *Taittirīya-āraṇyaka* and *Kena-upaniṣad*. In the former work, Umā and

Ambikā are associated with Rudra, but now as his wife, while in the latter she is described as Haimavatī.[22] The *Taittirīya-āraṇyaka* also mentions Durgi (i.e. Durgā), but makes it clear that Umā and Durgi were different goddesses despite similarity in attributes. It is probable that originally this Durgi was, like Umā, a mountain goddess connected with the Himalayas, particularly when Durgā literally means lady of difficult terrain.[23] In the *Muṇḍakopaniṣad* Kālī and Karālī are mentioned as the names of two of the seven tongues of Agni.[24] These references indicate that towards the end of the Vedic period, some female deities of non-Vedic origin began to be associated with the Vedic gods in various ways, and that Umā was the first non-Aryan deity to be regarded as the wife of a Vedic god, though at this stage their relationship was not characterized by the *Sāṁkhya* or *Vedānta* concepts of *Puruṣa* and *Prakṛti* or *Brahma* and *Māyā*.

On the basis of this evidence B.P. Sinha concluded that in the later Vedic period there was 'a definite attempt of assimilating some pre-Aryan Mother-goddess forms'.[25] I suggest that by the end of the Vedic period, due to the coexistence of Vedic and non-Vedic forms of religion for a long time, an incipient interaction between the two must have begun and some non-Vedic goddesses inevitably found their way into the brahmanical written records. Yet the presence of these goddesses in the Vedic corpus was marginal, and they lacked the religious intensity witnessed in tribal worship and in the later Puranic literature. As Ingalls pointed out, the only evidence of a sense of female ultimacy in the Vedic literature is found in the great Atharvan hymn to Earth, but the Earth in that hymn, while both female and divine, is not anthropomorphic and is not clearly distinguished as a goddess.[26] Thus it is difficult to credit the later Vedic authors with the conscious motivation of attempting to *assimilate*. Rather, these were the first hesitant signs of the *association* of the names of some of the non-Vedic goddesses with Vedic deities at a very superficial level, even as this paved the way for more determined efforts at assimilation in the future.

The first unmistakable attempt to incorporate a non-Vedic goddess in all her essentials within the brahmanical fold was made in the *Mahābhārata* and the *Harivaṁśa*, supposedly a supplement to the *Mahābhārata*.[27] A striking feature of the hymns addressed primarily to Durgā in these texts is that they reveal a pattern of recurring motifs concerning the conception of the goddess, her basic attributes, her chief associations, and the nature of her worship. She is said to have several forms and names in which she is worshipped in different parts of India by the Śavaras, Varvaras, Pulindas and other tribes. The names, Kapālī and Bhadrakālī for instance, are significant in that early Vedic literature betrays no knowledge of them. She is a virgin deity, sporting on the mountains (the Vindhya or the Himalaya) and inaccessible forests and caves. She is followed by ghosts, associated with wild beasts such as tigers and lions, carries a bell and is adorned with peacock tails. She is described primarily as a war-goddess who is fond of battle and destroys demons—especially Mahiṣāsura, is endowed with varieties of weapons such as the *pāśa*, *dhanu, cakra* and *aṣṭaśūla* and protects her devotees. She is worshipped with meat and wine, and sacrifices are offered to her. Even human sacrifice is hinted at in the reference to *mahābali*.

This is a pre-eminently non-Vedic goddess, recognized for the first time in brahmanical literature. The process of assimilation had simultaneously begun, for she is described in the same texts as Svāhā and Svadhā, the mother of the *Vedas* as well as the end of the *Vedas*. This process was carried forward in some of the *Purāṇas*,[28] until the synthesis of her non-Vedic character and her brahmanical transfiguration reached its culmination in the *Devī-Māhātmya* section of the *Mārkaṇḍeya Purāṇa*[29] around the sixth century. In this text the non-Vedic features of the goddess are retained presumably for the sake of authenticity, but elaborated with the help of myths and epithets in a manner that subtly connects her with the Sanskritic tradition. Thomas Coburn has traced the earliest occurrence of virtually every epithet and myth attributed to the goddess in the *Devī-Māhātmya*, and it is amazing to see so many epithets drawn from the Vedic stock and so many myths shared with other figures of the epic pantheon.[30] It may be noted that this grafting operation was so smooth that there seems to be no contrivance, arbitrariness, or even insincerity in it, though it was born out of the compulsive Puranic need to accommodate non-brahmanical customs and practices. For example, the *Vāg Āmbhṛṇī Sūkta* of the *Ṛg Veda*[31] genuinely foreshadows the notion of *śakti* behind all divine and human actions. If the *Devī-Māhātmya* now wished to promulgate the idea that all the diverse goddesses were manifestations of that abstract notion called *śakti*, it did have its undeniable resonance in the most sacred Vedic literature. It is a different matter whether or not the *sūkta* was composed keeping this eventuality in mind. The *Devī-Māhātmya* created the goddess, in which form she is still conceived and worshipped. The later Mahapuranic accounts of the goddess are either repetitions or confirming elaborations of the model set by the *Devī-Māhātmya*. And this goddess is neither wholly non-Vedic nor entirely brahmanical; she is a product of interacting traditions. Indeed, the goddesses, in their individual identities, continued to be worshipped,[32] but the process of integration was accomplished in the *Devī-Māhātmya*. The Bengal *Purāṇas* took over at this point and proceeded to re-enact the process in a regional context.

II

Today Bengal is nearly synonymous with goddess worship. But can the same thing be said of the ancient period? Very little is known of Bengal's prehistory,[33] but popular memory has it that goddess worship originated in Bengal. Ramaprasad Chanda has quoted an anonymous Sanskrit verse which claims that the cult of the goddess was revealed in Gauḍa, popularized by the people of Mithilā, it prevails in some places of Maharashtra, and has dwindled in Gujarat.[34] It is important to examine the case behind such an assumption.

The area association of the goddess worship, as mapped by this verse, has a significant implication and Chanda draws our attention to it. He points out that 'with the questionable exception of Mithilā, all other countries (mentioned in the verse) belong to the Outer Indo-Aryan belt. Did Śāktism then originate among the Indo-Aryans of the Outer countries?'[35] By 'the Outer countries' Chanda presumably meant those areas where brahmanism arrived comparatively late. This suggestion becomes meaningful in the light of the discussion in the foregoing section where I tried to establish the non-Vedic origin of the goddess. As we have seen, Bengal remained outside the sphere of brahmanical influence for a long time, and large-scale *brāhmaṇa* migration to Bengal did not begin before the Gupta period. Thus it is possible to posit a correlation between Bengal's non-brahmanical antiquity and the existence of a goddess tradition. One can then argue that when brahmanism did eventually reach Bengal, the goddess tradition was so firmly established there that it demanded recognition by *brāhmaṇas*. The newcomers, who had to adjust with the prevailing tradition, adopted these goddesses with suitable modifications and transformed them into brahmanical divinities by means of a carefully constructed Śākta theology—precisely that phenomenon which I have called the Puranic process. But if one has to pursue this argument, a simple assertion made on the basis of an anonymous verse is insufficient, and connection between pre-brahmanical Bengal and the goddess tradition has to be convincingly demonstrated.

Moreover, there is a basic confusion in Chanda's proposition. On the one hand he traces the origin of Śāktism to the 'Indo-Aryans' of Bengal, and on the other points to the fact that Bengal was peripheral to the brahmanical scheme of things for a long time. There is indeed a connection between the two, namely the Bengal *brāhmaṇas* conformed to the existing tradition of goddess worship and moulded it through an elaboration of Śākta theology to suit their requirements. But he does not state so, because he seems to equate Śāktism with the tradition of goddess worship, two related but separate phenomena. If, however, he claims that Śāktism originated in Bengal, there is absolutely no evidence to suggest that the Bengal *brāhmaṇas* had ever taken any initiative in that direction prior to the composition of the *Devī-Māhātmya*, where the fundamental principles of Śāktism were worked out for the first time. It should also be remembered that Chanda does not indicate the date of composition of this verse, and it may well be a post-facto rationalization of the late medieval (or later) situation, when the knowledge of Bengal's association with the goddess tradition and even Śāktism had become fairly commonplace.

The claim made in the anonymous verse cited by Chanda may be exaggerated, but Bengal's overwhelming association with goddess worship is undeniable. Before the goddess tradition was transformed into Śāktism by the Bengal *Purāṇas* by the twelfth–thirteenth centuries, it did not exist as a well-defined religious system; yet the relative predominance of the goddesses in Bengal from a very early time is attested by all available sources. The list of religious festivals and fairs in Bengal, contained in the volumes of the village surveys during the Indian Census of 1961, is in itself sufficient to demonstrate the popularity of the goddess among the common people. A systematized list of names features twenty-two goddesses and eleven gods.[36] But even such a list is misleading, for the goddesses are mentioned in only their commonly identifiable names, while they are worshipped in an amazing variety of local nomenclatures in the interiors of villages which far outnumber any such diversity in the case of gods. Despite attempts to connect them with the goddesses of the brahmanical pantheon, many of them could not be accommodated at all, which suggests that they pre-date the brahmanical ordering process. This impression is confirmed by those who are personally familiar with the immense corpus of Bengal goddesses, such as Binoy Ghosh.[37]

The problem of tracing the antecedents of these local goddesses is that their worshippers seldom, if ever, left records of their faith. However, that the proliferation in the number of goddesses is not a recent phenomenon is amply attested by the numerous references to such deities in the *Maṅgalakāvyas* of medieval Bengal. Manik Ganguly's *Śrīdharmamaṅgala* alone furnishes a long list of such names of which Bāsulī, Jhakbuḍī, Nāneśvarī, Khepāi and Ghānṭudevī were clearly imperfectly integrated village goddesses.[38] The other varieties of vernacular literature of medieval Bengal, namely the biographies of Caitanya or the translations of the epics, do not have much scope to refer to the purely village goddesses, but they do mention regionally prominent goddesses such as Durgā or Rādhā. But the earliest vernacular text, *Caryācaryaviniścaya*, of the tenth–twelfth centuries AD, is replete with references to the goddess Nairātmā who is symbolically represented by Ḍombī, Caṇḍālī and Śavarī.[39]

While Bengal's continuous association with the non-brahmanical goddesses is thus attested by vernacular evidence as far back as it goes, it cannot take us beyond the beginning of the second millennium. In the absence of written records we may look into the ethnographic accounts of Bengal to gain insights into what might have been the archaic system of religious beliefs and practices in this region.

The following table of the religious practices of some of the major tribes and low castes of Bengal has been prepared on the basis of H.H. Risley's exhaustive survey of the subject. It should be remembered that even as Risley was collecting information in the late nineteenth century, many tribes had come under brahmanical influence. But some of their older practices were retained, and provide information.

Tribes/Castes	*Gods/Goddesses*	*Rituals and other details*
Bāgdi,[40] elements borrowed from orthodox Hinduism, animism and nature worship.	Śiva, Viṣṇu, Durgā, the śaktis, the Santali goddess Gosāin Erā and Barpahar, but the favourite and characteristic deity is Manasā.	Manasā is worshipped on the 5th and 20th of the four rainy months. Rams and he-goats are sacrificed, and rice, sweets, fruits and flowers are offered. On the last day of *Bhādra*, they carry in procession the effigy of the female saint Bhādu.

Bhuiyā,[41] somewhat advanced on the path of Hinduism.	Dāsum Pāṭ, Bāmoni Pāṭ, Koisar Pāṭ, and Borām. There exists some difference of opinion whether Borām is male or female. Ṭhākurāni Māi, the bloodthirsty tutelary god- dess, changed into Durgā.	Goats are offered to the Pāṭs in case of sickness, and goats and sheep to Ṭhākurānī Māi/Durgā. Ghosts are appeased by occasional offering of fowls. No *brāhmaṇa* priest officiates in their worship.
Bhūmij,[42] varied religious behaviour according to social position.	Well-to-do householders worship Kālī or Mahāmāyā. Common people worship the agricultural deities Jāhir-Buru and Kārākātā, village and mountain deities.	All the divinities are propitiated with sacrificial offerings of buffaloes, goats and fowls. Biṣaycaṇḍī and malignant ghosts of cannibalistic propensities are worshipped. Upper classes employ *brāhmaṇa* priests, while others make do with *lāyās* (priests) of their community.
Cāmār,[43] exhibit dislike for the *brāhmaṇas* and Hindu rituals; belong to the Śrī-Nārāyaṇī creed.	The 'Grantha' (sacred book) of the Śri-Nārāyaṇīs, the Devī (presumably Durgā, for she is worshipped on the 'Naumi' or Navamī), Śītalā and Jalkā Devī.	The annual festival of worshipping the 'Grantha' is accompanied by drinking spirits and smoking cannabis. The popular belief is, the 'Grantha' was unintelligible till Śītalā translated it for them. On the occasion of Naumi, shamanism is practised. Śītalā is worshipped in case of epidemic when swine is sacrificed. Risley thinks that Jalkā Devī is identical with Rakṣā Kālī.

Caṇḍāl,[44] profess Vaiṣṇavism but retain many animistic traits.	Earth goddess and Manasā.	On the thirteenth day of *Śrāvaṇa*, they perform boat worship. Gods and goddesses of the Hindu pantheon are paraded, but the central deity is Manasā. A kid, milk, fruits and sweetmeats are offered to her.
Ḍom,[45] mixture of animism and elements borrowed from neighbouring Hindu sects.	Lean towards Vaiṣṇavism—Rādhā–Kṛṣṇa. Ancestral deity Kalubir and goddess Bhādu. In central Bengal Kālī is the favourite goddess.	Sacrifice goats to Kalubir. On *Śrāvaṇiā Pūjā* a pig is sacrificed and its blood is caught in a cup. This cup, milk and three spirits are offered to Nārāyaṇa. No *brāhmaṇa* priest.
Kaivartta,[46] conform to Hindu observances and belong to the Vaiṣṇava sect.	The river goddess Gaṅgā, Śītalā and Caṇḍī.	Jālpālani festival begins on 1st of *Māgha* (literally laying by the net, the Kaivarttas being primarily fishermen). On the last day, Gaṅgā is worshipped with prayers recited by a *brāhmaṇa*, and a live kid is thrown into water. Goats are sacrificed in fulfilment of vows to Śītalā and Caṇḍī.
Kewaṭ,[47] moving towards orthodox Hindu pattern.	Bhagavatī is the special goddess. Kālī, the snake god Biṣahari, and ancestral deities.	Kālī is worshipped with sacrifice of goats, rice, milk and sweetmeats. Maithili *brāhmaṇas* officiate as priests.

Kochh-Rājbanśī,[48] in central Bengal profess Vaiṣṇavism; in north Bengal are influenced by Tantric ideas.	Kālī is the favourite goddess. Host of minor deities such as Manasā, Tistu Burī, Joginī, Hudum Deo, Balibhadra Ṭhākur, etc.	During a drought, two images of Hudum Deo are placed in the field and women strip themselves naked and dance round the images, singing obscene songs in the belief that it will cause rain. Seven months after childbirth they worship Shati (a variant of Ṣaṣṭhī). In north Bengal, a member of the caste officiates as priest.
Korā,[49] affect to be orthodox Hindus.	Kālī, Durgā, Manasā, Kṛṣṇa–Rādhā, Bhādu and Bhairab Ṭhākur. But Manasā, the snake-goddess, and Bhādu, the virgin daughter of the Pachete house, are more important.	Deities are worshipped with sacrifice of goats, fowls, and pigeons, and rice, sugar, and plantain are offered. Degraded *brāhmaṇas* act as their priests.
Muṇḍā,[50] retain most of their archaic beliefs and practices.	Siṅg-Boṅgā (sun—the high god), Marang Buru (mountain god), Garhāera (goddess of rivers), Deswali and Jāhir-Burhī (god and goddess of the village), and Chandor (moon, wife of Siṅg-Boṅgā, the sun).	The only ritual employed to propitiate these gods and goddesses is sacrifice of animals of various kinds—goats, cocks of all colour, buffaloes, bullocks and pigs. The moon is specially worshipped by women. Festivals are unrelated to their religion.

Orāon,[51] retain most of their archaic beliefs and practices.	Dharmesh—the supreme deity, Darhā—a spirit, and Sarna Burhī—lady of the grove.	Evil spirits are at the centre of their religion. If one is afflicted by them, an *ojhā* (shaman) decides what to sacrifice, which is usually a fowl and occasionally sheep and buffalo. Do not employ *brāhmaṇa* priests.
Sāntāl,[52] retain most of their archaic beliefs and practices.	Marang Buru (mountain—the high god), Moreko (fire), Jāir Erā (sister of Moreko—goddess of the sacred grove), Gosāin Erā (younger sister of Moreko), Pargana (master of witches), etc.	Sacrifice of animals, such as goat, sheep, cow, pig, etc. is the major aspect of the ritual. Even human sacrifice was performed as late as the 19th century. Harvest is the major festival that allows for a great deal of drunkenness and sexual licence, but other festivals centre round the worship of the deities.
Śavar,[53] have become thoroughly Hinduized.	Tend to worship the standard deities of Hinduism, but elder gods and goddesses, such as Thanapati, and Bānsuri, the bloodthirsty goddess, still receive worship.	Degraded *brāhmaṇas* officiate as priests, but the non-brahmanical deities are worshipped by the elders of the community with sacrifices of goats and fowls.

These examples have not been chosen to suit the convenience of argument. Rather, they constitute a fairly representative cross-section of the major tribes and low castes of Bengal today. Besides, this table reveals such a persistent pattern that a choice of other cases is also likely to yield similar results. Although the cases above present a wide spectrum from a relatively unadulterated set of archaic practices to a high degree of assimilation of great tradition norms, certain common factors are noticeable. The first is the overwhelming presence of the goddesses in their pantheons. Gods are by no means excluded and they occupy the highest position in the divine hierarchy of those tribes who have preserved their faith with greater authenticity, but the goddesses exist. Even when the high god is a male, he is more of a benign and honourable figurehead,[54] while the goddesses are active and directly concerned with the immediate necessities of their worshippers, agents of crisis and also deliverers, and therefore demand and receive greater attention. For instance, the highest object of worship for the Cāmārs, who profess the Śrī-Nārāyaṇī creed, is their sacred text. According to popular legend, this text was unintelligible to them until one Śītalā translated it. This Śītalā is not the local goddess of smallpox, though the similarity in name cannot be accidental, but an inspired female ascetic. The 'translated' text, as it stands today, is, however, a compilation from the *Purāṇas*, written in the Devanāgarī script by Sivanarayana of Ghazipur in 1735, and therefore could not be comprehensible to the Cāmārs. Thus it is only through the supposed mediation of Śītalā, whom they know and understand, that the text has become symbolically accessible. The goddess is a part of their familiar world and they can directly relate to her.

Another recurring feature of their religion is animal sacrifice to all the deities. Other aspects of religious behaviour and the degree of Hinduization may vary, but without exception animal sacrifice forms the major part of their ritual. Not only do the less Hinduized Sāntāls, Orāons, and Muṇḍās sacrifice animals to propitiate their deities, but even the Ḍoms, who worship Kṛṣṇa–Rādhā, offer the blood of a slain pig to Nārāyaṇa, and the Caṇḍāls, who profess Vaiṣṇavism, sacrifice kids to Mạnasā. This is undoubtedly a tribal custom, because brahmanism never sanctions animal sacrifice except to a few goddesses. Animal sacrifice is absolutely forbidden for the benign spouse goddesses of Sanskritic origin, such as Lakṣmī, though Nirmal Kumar Basu mentions that the members of the Juang tribe sacrifice roosters in her name.[55] This suggests that when a tribe or low caste moves towards brahmanical ways, it tends to accept the symbolic forms more easily than the actual practices. Thus the bloodthirsty Ṭhākurānī Māi of the Bhuiyās transforms into Durgā without causing inconvenience to the larger religious structure, because it does not entail a corresponding change in the other accessories of their rituals of worship.

Dalton refers to an interesting hierarchy of goddesses among the Birhors of Hazaribagh district. Devī stands at the head of their pantheon; Mahā Māyā is her daughter, Buriā Māi the granddaughter, and at the bottom of the scale is Dudhā Māi, Buriā's daughter.[56] Devī clearly represents the generic identity of the goddess and there is no problem about the tribal goddesses Buriā and Dudhā Māi being associated with her. But the fact that it has been possible for Mahā Māyā, one of the most complex of the brahmanical conceptions of the goddess, to peacefully coexist with the rest of them, is because the Birhors presumably adopted only the brahmanical name and treated her in exactly the same manner as any other tribal goddess, offering her the same sacrifices.

Thus the ethnographic data narrows the search for tribal association of the goddess from a general all-India phenomenon to the particular situation in Bengal. Indeed, so deep-seated and pervasive is this association in Bengal that even the low castes, who were included within the brahmanical social order through the Puranic and *Smṛti* restructuring, still adhere to tribal practices with regard to goddess worship, and the few superficial changes that arise out of their emulation of brahmanical ideals do not conceal their primary allegiance. This reinforces my hypothesis that the widespread popularity of the goddess cult in Bengal was due to her prolonged and ubiquitous tribal association on the one hand, and her delayed and restricted contact with brahmanical culture on the other. The ethnographic evidence, however, merely indicates the possibilities and the hypothesis can only be established if it is demonstrated that the goddesses co-opted and transfigured by brahmanism in Bengal recognizably conform to local tribal models, and that brahmanism in fact acknowledges Bengal's association with the goddess tradition before the process of brahmanization had begun.

III

The almost obsessive involvement of the Bengal *Purāṇas* with the goddess cult is in itself an indirect acknowledgement of the pre-eminence of the goddess tradition in Bengal prior to the composition of these texts, but they commit themselves to specific statements as well. The *Devī Purāṇa* declares that the Aṣṭavidyās, who assisted the Devī in the destruction of Subalāsura especially reside in Varendra and Rāḍha, as also in Kāmākhyā, Bhoṭṭadeśa, Jālandhara, in the Tūḍa, Hūṇa and Khasa countries, in the Kiṣkindhyā hills and the Himavat *pīṭha*, and such other places.[57] The text then goes on to elaborate the tribal associations of the goddess, and proclaims that she is worshipped by the coarse, fierce and naive Śaras, Varṣavaras (Śavaras, Varvaras?), and the Pulindas.[58] The *Kālikā Purāṇa* states that Kāmarūpa was a seat of goddess worship even when it was inhabited by the Kirātas, that is before Assam was brought within the sphere of brahmanical influence.[59]

For understandable reasons the Bengal *Purāṇas* never cared to provide a detailed description of the tribal characteristics of the goddess. If anything, they made every attempt to camouflage her tribal identity. But, partly in order to satisfy congruence conditions, and partly because the tribal associations of the goddess are virtually irrepressible, they had to retain some of these. The *Purāṇas*, therefore, adopted the technique of skilfully overlaying these elements with brahmanical attributes.

If we piece together the scattered information from the bewildering maze of Puranic accounts, the basic structure of the tribal goddess can be reconstructed as follows. She lives in the mountains and caves,[60] and protects her devotees from wild beasts[61] and ghosts[62] who surround her. She is associated with the sound of bells[63] and her distinctive mark is an ornament of peacock's tail.[64] Besides, she is a virgin[65] and a fierce warrior. No less than three long episodes of her encounter with Ghorāsura, Kṛṣṇadharmāsura, and the demon Ruru have been described in martial detail in the *Devī Purāṇa* alone.[66] She is also unequivocally eulogized as the only refuge of the gods in crisis.[67] This goddess is fond of blood, meat and wine,[68] and therefore animal sacrifice constitutes a major part of the ritual in her worship. A long chapter of two hundred and nine verses in the *Kālikā Purāṇa* lays down the rules and procedures of sacrifice. It says that birds of all kind, tortoise, fish, nine varieties of deer, buffalo, cow, sheep and goat, reptiles, tiger and lion, human beings and blood from one's own person should be offered to the goddess Caṇḍikā.[69] The methods and consequences of human sacrifice are specified in dreadful detail,[70] but the *brāhmaṇas* are debarred from offering human beings or wine to the goddess.[71] Finally, the *Devī Purāṇa* declares that these goddesses bestow success on the Pulindas, the Śavaras, and such other tribes in the socially disapproved *vāma* or left method of worship.[72]

This reconstruction of the clearly non-brahmanical goddess in the Bengal *Purāṇas* sounds remarkably similar to the goddess of the *Mahābhārata*, the *Harivaṁśa* and the later secular literature. Her association with tribes and inaccessible tracts, with ghosts and wild beasts, her role as a warrior and protector, and her fondness for meat and wine are self-explanatory. But even the repetition of such apparently insignificant details as the bell or the peacock's tail in both the instances cannot be a matter of coincidence and must reflect that these were actual accessories of the goddess as she was conceived by her original votaries. Moreover, the prohibition imposed on the *brāhmaṇas* to offer human sacrifice and wine incontrovertibly suggests that these were alien to the brahmanical ritual scheme and that brahmanism was willing to go a long way to accept the goddess within its fold, but the compromise was not altogether unconditional.

This goddess was then superimposed with brahmanical attributes. She was equated with the abstract energy—*śakti*—of which the diverse tribal and local goddesses were mere manifestations, and she was claimed to be the cause and moving force of all actions. This ensured and justified her inclusion in the brahmanical pantheon, without necessarily subverting her original identity. A representative example of the brahmanical conception of the goddess will illustrate the mechanism underlying this process of concatenation. When Brahmā expressed his inability to comprehend the immensity of the nature and functions of Bhagavatī Ādyāśakti, she volunteered to define herself:

> I am neither man, nor woman, nor eunuch at the time of the destruction of the world; these distinctions are only imagined. At the time of creation I am perception, prosperity, firmness, fame, remembrance, faith, intelligence, pity, shame, hunger, covetousness, patience, beauty, tranquillity, thirst, sleep, idleness, old age and youth, knowledge and ignorance, desire, longing, strength and weakness, serum, marrow, skin, vision, the various veins, and true and untrue speech. What is separate from me and what is not connected with me in this world? I am all-pervasive. In this creation I am the one and the many in various forms. I assume the names of all the gods and wield power as their *śakti*. I appear as Gaurī, Brāhmī, Raudrī, Vārāhī, Vaiṣṇavī, Śivā, Vāruṇī, Kauverī, Narasiṁhī, and Vāsavī. I enter into every substance and all actions. I execute while assigning to him [*Brahma/Puruṣa*] the role of the instrument. I am chillness in water, heat in fire, brightness in the sun, and coolness in the moon; and thus I manifest my authority. No living creature can even pulsate if I abandon them; forsaken by me, Śaṁkara cannot kill the demons. A weak person is described as one who is devoid of *śakti*, he is not said to be without Rudra or Viṣṇu. Thus *śakti* is the cause behind your creation. Gods such as Hari, Rudra, Indra, Agni, Candra, Sūrya, Yama, Viśvakarmā, Varuṇa and Pavana can perform their duties only when they are combined with their respective *śaktis*. When united with *śakti*, the earth remains stationary and can hold all the creatures. Śeṣa [the serpent], the tortoise, and the elephants of the quarters of the globe can act only with my assistance. I can drink all the water, suppress the fire and steady the wind if I please. I act as I wish.[73]

The point to notice in this long passage is that the goddess has been accorded absolute, unrestrained power; she is all-encompassing. As a result, she can be both strength and weakness, knowledge and ignorance. The advantage of such a conception of deity is that in her all contraries are fused, the boundaries of particular identities are obfuscated. She is rendered impersonal. Hence there is no anomaly in her remaining a tribal deity and also becoming a brahmanical deity. One does not negate the other. She is merely taken out of her exclusive association with her original devotees and universalized. This paves the way for her recognition by brahmanism and she is conferred with the ultimate seal of brahmanical credibility when Brahmā, in his eulogy of the goddess, quotes in full the *Vāg Āmbhṛṇī Sūkta* of the *Ṛg Veda*,[74] considered to be the earliest exposition of the idea of *śakti* in its embryonic form.

But legitimation is a tricky business. Mere assertion of omnipotence does not make the goddess acceptable, nor are past identities easily erased. It requires patient groundwork spread over a long period of time, careful evaluation of the factors to be added or subtracted, highlighted or underplayed, to obtain that delicate balance which does not impair recognition of the original model. And finally, it requires the construction of a plausible genealogy to ensure authenticity and due place in the hierarchy. Only then does a new entrant into the family of gods become admissible, that too by degrees. The right note is struck through a gradual process of trial and error. Therefore the passage cited above and many other similar passages in the Bengal *Purāṇas* are instances of overdetermination and are not to be taken literally. Statements going directly against the idea expressed in the above-mentioned passage are not hard to find in the same corpus of texts.[75] Therefore it is of no great consequence to the Puranic corpus as a whole whether the goddess or one or the other of the chief gods is assigned the supreme position in the hierarchy, as long as it does not upset the fundamental objective of the *Purāṇas*.

This may suggest that there was no sectarian rivalry in Puranic Hinduism. On the contrary, such rivalries were very real. But the written texts of the *Purāṇas* seldom emphasize this aspect. They tend instead to diffuse such differences by claiming that the divinities were equal with or derived from one another.[76] The *Purāṇas* could not afford to let sectarian loyalties supersede their principal objective, much less in a place like Bengal where Puranic Hinduism was trying to establish itself. Instead, they were interested in offering a choice, a wide range of options in which every believer could see his particular shade of opinion vindicated. As the *Purāṇas* were trying to broaden their base, they endeavoured to carry as many people with them as possible, provided they agreed to adhere to that one unwavering bedrock of Puranic priorities—the supremacy of brahmanism. The *Bṛhaddharma Purāṇa* declares that one should take refuge in gods according to one's own inclination, for all gods deliver the same results. One who pays tribute to a particular god and defames others, goes to hell.[77] Thus each of the important gods and goddesses in turn have been treated with similar generosity. This explains the disproportionate praise lavished on the goddess in the passage above. It sought to convince her votaries that brahmanism was conferring unreserved recognition on the goddess.

Thus the bald assertion of omnipotence only partially fulfilled the conditions of legitimation. The other details of the process of integration were still to be worked out, and predictably the Bengal *Purāṇas* devoted a lot of attention to this problem. A representative example indicates how this was accomplished. When the demon king Ruru was slain by the goddess, Indra and the other gods praised her thus:

We bow to the feet of Mahābhairavī whose ears are adorned with red gem-studded ear-rings, whose face is tarnished by frequent dreadful frowns, who is unconventionally dressed and has a violent temper, who holds *paraśu, vallakī, ḍamaru, khaṭṭāṅga*, and skull in her hands, who is three eyed and rides on a mount of ox.

We bow to the feet of the mother, who originated from that Pitāmaha who is seated on a large swan on top of a wide, unblemished, white lotus which is surrounded by humming bees, and who is served by the sages.

We bow to the feet of the mother, who originated from that Pramathanātha who is as bright as the autumnal moon, whose complexion resembles snow, conchshell, and the *kunda* flowers, who is aglow in his own lustre, who is seated on an ox, who holds the moon on his matted hair, and whose weapon is a trident.

We bow to the feet of the *śakti,* the destroyer of enemies, who has originated from Guha and has the gait of a peacock, who is pure complexioned, whose garment shines from the reflected lustre of the richly endowed small bells which adorn her feet and from the sharp weapons which she holds in her hands.

We bow to the feet of the success-bestowing Vaiṣṇavīśakti, whose complexion resembles a bouquet of *atasī* flowers, who holds mace, mallet, bow, conchshell, and discus, who rides on Garuḍa, and whose eyes are like full-bloomed lotuses.

We bow to the feet of the *śakti*, who originated from Kṛtānta, whose complexion is like deep collyrium and who has the face of a boar, who holds sword, club, and the noose of death in her hands, who has a thundering voice like the clouds of the doomsday and who rides on a mount of buffalo.

We bow to the feet of Indraśakti, whose complexion is like that of lightning, meteor, and pure gold, who is decorated with diverse ornaments and is seated on an elephant, whose weapon is thunder, who is worshipped by gods, and who bestows favour and enjoyment on her devotees.

We bow to the feet of Ugraśakti, the protectress, who resides in Śiva, whose splendour resembles hundreds of suns, who holds a garland of white skulls, who has frightful teeth and an attractive figure, whose eyes are reddish-brown like the sun of the doomsday, who is extremely fond of blood, meat, and fat, and who holds fierce weapons.

We bow to the feet of the *śakti*, the leader of men, who has sprung from the body of Pramathanātha, who has the face of an elephant, who, with her flapping fan-like ears, keeps the humming bees away, and with the fragrance of rut oozing out of her temples pleases the ten quarters, who is auspicious and removes all obstacles.[78]

The most striking feature of this passage is its sensual quality. The iridescent goddess is portrayed in multiple forms, and the visual effect accentuated by the sound of bells and humming bees and the exotic fragrance of rut. Why was this sensual representation necessary? In the first place we notice that the goddess embodies mutually exclusive attributes. She is fair and dark, beautiful and dreadful, she has the face of a boar and an elephant, she is fierce and gentle, generous and punishing. Her ornaments, weapons, and mounts also change accordingly. And she is addressed by different names. All are mothers and *śaktis*, but she is the Mahābhairavī, the Vaiṣṇavī, or the Indraśakti, as the context demands. Plainly, this cannot be the description of a single goddess. Indeed, the passage refers to the Mātṛs, the *śaktis* of the individual gods. In order to depart from the somewhat stylized and standardized image of the goddess created by brahmanism, and to distinguish between the various goddesses, these graphic details had to be provided. Puranic acknowledgement of the multiplicity of goddesses is a concession to the actual state of things, for the theological cover of the unifying principle of *śakti* was obviously invented later to facilitate assimilation of many independent non-brahmanical goddesses. Naturally, the idea of *śakti* is embedded in this passage as well, but the various *śaktis* are so dissimilar in their moods and appearances, preferences and functions, that it nearly admits that the concept of their fundamental indivisibility was an artificial (though convenient) and post-facto formulation. Besides, iconic representation of deities is a non-Vedic feature which found its way into Puranic Hinduism from the indigenous religious traditions. Thus, while an informed adept may take delight in such theoretical subtleties as the undifferentiated oneness of many, it is easier for an ordinary devotee to relate to a goddess who is familiar and accessible. Such passages therefore represent a historical process. They were authentic without giving away the brahmanical intention.

The other noticeable aspect of this passage is the manner in which the goddess has been associated with the prominent male figures of the brahmanical pantheon. She is stated to have emerged out of Śiva and Brahmā, and surprisingly even out of such relatively minor deities as Skanda and Yama. Since the gods are arranged in a hierarchy of power and importance, as their female counterparts she is also automatically subsumed into that hierarchy. She may embody that vast storehouse of unbound energy called *śakti*, she is at the same time trapped into multiple identities of a graded divine order. Moreover, if she is derived from these gods, she cannot be superior to them. Interestingly, as the Vaiṣṇavīśakti or the Indraśakti, she takes on the characteristics and the symbolic attributes of each of these deities. Similarly, when she is endowed with the features of Gaṇeśa, she is implicitly understood to have taken on the role of his *śakti*, even though Gaṇeśa is not specifically mentioned. Thus, although she is the driving force behind these gods, as their consorts she loses much of her individuality and is reduced to the status of clone of those who now appear to be her dominant partners. This presumably satisfies brahmanical conditions of acceptability. The introduction of an external element such as the goddess does not disrupt the existing structure of the brahmanical pantheon, and she seems to fall smoothly into her allotted slot in a prearranged order.

Finally, the passage represents a perfect fusion of the non-brahmanical reality and the brahmanical ideal in the depiction of the goddess. The fair, attractive, gentle and benevolent brahmanical goddess is placed by the side of the dark, deformed, capricious and bloodthirsty warrior. These two contrasting images became so inextricably intertwined and such descriptions had been so persistently repeated that they eventually blended into an inseparable composite figure. The deliberate juxtaposition of opposites lent both complexity and credibility to the goddess. The continuous dialectical progression from one point of contradiction to another created a divinity which encompassed a whole range of images, emotions, and loyalties. This legitimated the goddess in a manner that no rational explanation could hope to achieve.

IV

The tribal affiliation of the goddess is not the only reason why she was adopted in such a big way by the Bengal *Purāṇas*. Bengal has a long tradition of goddess worship, which did not acquire its present institutional form until about the seventeenth century. The history of Tantric practices in Bengal, however, goes back to a much earlier date. It was the impact of Tantrism that led to the transformation of Mahāyāna Buddhism into Vajrayāna, Sahajayāna and such other Tantric forms in Bengal and the neighbouring eastern Indian regions during the eighth to twelfth centuries. A very large number of the so-called Hindu *Tantras* were written in Bengal between the fourteenth and the sixteenth–seventeenth centuries.[79] This separation between the Buddhist and the Hindu *Tantras*, we have seen, is artificial. *Tantra* is primarily a set of techniques of worship, involving mechanisms of the body and the assumption that the body is the seat of divinity, in which philosophical doctrines occupy a marginal position.[80] When these techniques came in contact with popular Buddhism, the interaction gave rise to the Buddhist *Tantras*. The Hindu *Tantras* came into being in a similar fashion. Thus there is no fundamental difference between the two. A particular stream of Tantrism, expressed through the Buddhist *Dohākoṣa* and *Caryāgīti*, assumed the form of Vaiṣṇava Sahajiyā doctrines and practices which eventually metamorphosed into some of the Bāul sects of Bengal. So deep and pervasive is this influence that any religion that hopes to strike roots in Bengal has to come to terms with the *Tantras*.

But why should there be a continuous history of Tantric influence over Bengal for at least a millennium and a half? Shashibhushan Dasgupta has suggested a tentative explanation. He argues that there is a recognizable pattern in the regional distribution of Tantrism in what he calls greater India. The territories adjoining the Himalaya, beginning with Kashmir in the north to Nepal, Tibet, Bhutan, Bengal and Assam, may be described as the Tantric zone. As Tantric practices are popularly known as *Cīnācāra*, this extensive area may well be the Mahācīna of the *Tantras*. It should be observed that most of the older *Tantras* were composed in Kashmir. Although there is evidence that some were written in a few other places in India, the next phase of systematic codification of the *Tantras* took place in the Bengal–Assam region. In Nepal, Bhutan and Tibet these are still preserved.

Dasgupta further observes that the imagery of the *ṣaṭcakra* or the six nodal points within the body is an important constituent of the *Tantras*. The presiding goddesses of these points are Ḍākinī, Rākinī, Lākinī, Kākinī, Śākinī and Hākinī. Plainly, these are not Sanskritic names. On the other hand, Ḍāk is a Tibetan word meaning wise, the feminine form of which is Ḍākinī. Perhaps the original meaning of the term Ḍākinī was one who possesses secret knowledge. The Bengali word *Ḍāinī* contains a faint echo of this meaning. Maynāmatī, the mother of king Gopīcānd, of the Nātha literature of medieval Bengal was one such wise Ḍāinī. Thus it is not unreasonable to suppose that Ḍākinī was the name of a mystical Tibetan goddess. The names Lākinī and Hākinī do not figure among the innumerable goddesses of India, but they were prevalent in Bhutan. It is quite possible, therefore, that the local goddesses of the Tibet, Nepal, Bhutan region found their way into the *ṣaṭcakra* of the *Tantras*.

Mantra is another significant component of the *Tantras*. Among the *mantras*, the *vījamantras*, which usually consist of a single syllable such as *hrīṁ* or *klīṁ*, occupy the central position. Of these, *oṁ* is a common Vedic *mantra*. But the rest are non-Vedic, and it is doubtful whether they are at all derived from the Sanskrit language. Apart from the *vījamantras*, there is another set of slightly more elaborate ones which are apparently meaningless. Meaningless *mantras* are not the monopoly of the *Tantras*; they are found in the *Atharva Veda* as well; but this particular variety, widely used in Tantric worship, may well be the survival of a language once prevalent in the Tantric zone.[81]

These speculations of Dasgupta bring into relief the three crucial aspects of *Tantra* with which brahmanism in Bengal had to contend: a long and intimate association with Bengal, the centrality of the goddess, and a pronounced non-Vedic character. The mechanism devised in the Bengal *Purāṇas* to internalize the goddess tradition would have been adequate to appropriate Tantrism as well, had it not been for the fact that it was emphatically anti-Vedic in its basic premises. Tantrism offers the right of initiation to women and *śūdras*,[82] and neither accepts the infallibility of the *Vedas* nor the social supremacy of the *brāhmaṇas*. It is difficult to see how possibly to legitimize the *Tantras* without seriously compromising the brahmanical world-view.

Therefore, instead of attempting to internalize the whole of the *Tantras* in all their ramifications, the Bengal *Purāṇas* began cautiously by admitting that it is a different tradition.[83] For instance, the *Devībhāgavata* says that initiation is compulsory for the four *varṇas* and women, without which nobody earns the right to learn *Devīmantra*.[84] The *Bṛhaddharma* declares that *śūdras* are prohibited from listening to the *Vedas*, but can listen to the *Purāṇas* and study those *Āgamas* which are recommended by the *guru* (preceptor).[85] The *śūdras*' right to listen to the *Purāṇas* was a reluctant concession, for the text issues a stricture a few verses later that initiating such a person with *mantras* and reading the *Purāṇas* aloud to him are purely emergency measures for the *brāhmaṇas*.[86] Thus a *śūdra* is debarred from the *Vedas* and very nearly from the *Purāṇas* as well, although the Bengal *Purāṇas* are somewhat undecided on this point, because if they are completely denied access to the

Purāṇas, the very purpose of composition of these texts, transmission of brahmanical norms, would be defeated. However, if a *śūdra* is initiated in the Tantric mode of worship, his right to learn the sacred Tantric texts is unequivocally admitted. Similarly, when the *Devī Purāṇa* says that all women, children, old people, and *śūdras* must perform the *agnihoma* everyday,[87] and lays down the specifications of the ritual as involving the performance of *astravīja*, *pūrvavīja*, *śikhāvīja*, *kavaca-mantra*, *śaktinyāsa* of the menstruating Viśalākṣī with *yonimudrā*, the execution of several other *mudrās*, and placing the fire in the vagina with *jayamantra*,[88] it is referring to a Tantric ritual that guarantees the participation of all members of society, which brahmanism forbids. Clearly, these are instances of brahmanical recognition of two standards and preferences in two different religious systems.

The major thrust of the Bengal *Purāṇas* was however to establish that though different, the two traditions are not irreconcilable, that there are points of convergence between them. This tendency, however, is not confined to the Bengal *Purāṇas* alone. Several attempts have been made to demonstrate that the practise of Vedic as well as Tantric rituals is a necessary condition for spiritual emancipation. The *Kulārṇavatantra* claims that the *Tantras* are the essence of the *Vedas* which were churned out from the Vedic ocean by Śiva with the stick of his intuitive wisdom.[89] Bhāskararāya, in the *Setuvandha* section of the *Nityāṣoḍaśikārṇava* included in the *Vāmakeśvaratantra*, said that the sixty-four *Tantras* were comparable with the *Vedas*, because the *Tantras* were the residue of the *Upaniṣads*. In the *Niruttaratantra*, the *Tantras* have simply been described as the fifth *Veda*.[90] Often the *Vedas* are cited as an authority by the *Tantras*, and a number of Vedic stanzas are quoted—sometimes completely inappropriately—in a Tantric ritual context. The names of the four *Vedas* frequently figure in Tantric numerical symbolism. Thus the *Rudrayāmalatantra* connects them with four of their six internal *cakras*, allotting the highest position to the *Atharva Veda*.[91] The *Tantras* also offer an explanation why Tantric rituals should be practised at all if they are merely a continuation of the Vedic tradition. The *Mahānirvāṇatantra* declares that men in the *Kaliyuga* are weak and incapable of great effort; hence, in the *Tantras* the rites of passage have been shortened and simplified to suit their convenience.[92] Modern scholars of *Tantra*, who believe in the efficacy of the system, suggest similar justification.[93]

But the factual position is that there is no direct continuity from the *Vedas* to the *Tantras*.[94] Thus the persistent Tantric claim to Vedic connection is unfounded if understandable. A toehold in the Vedic tradition would give wider legitimacy. In the Bengal *Purāṇas*, however, it is brahmanism which is anxious to forge this linkage. Obviously Tantrism was so popular here that the *Purāṇas* had to make adjustments with it. Often this is explicitly stated. Satī, after displaying her Daśamahāvidyā forms to Śiva, says that of all her manifestations these are the best. They bestow success and preside over the performance of various kinds of black magic such as *māraṇa*, *uccāṭana*, *mohana* and *vaśīkaraṇa*, desired by the *sādhaka*. They should be kept concealed. The method of their worship by means of *mantra*, *homa, puraścaryā* and *kavaca*, will be revealed by Śiva and will be known as *Āgamaśāstra*.[95] Satī adds:

> Śaṁkara, the *Āgama* and the *Veda* are my two arms with which I sustain the whole universe consisting of stationary and moving objects. If, out of ignorance, one violates either of these two, he is sure to slip away from my hands. It is true that I cannot deliver him who worships [me], but disregards the *Vedas* and the *Āgamas*. Both the *Vedas* and the *Āgamas* lead to welfare. These are abstruse, very difficult to perform and comprehend even by the wise, and are limitless. Wise people should practise *dharma* by accepting these two as identical. An intelligent person must never distinguish between the two, even in a state of delusion.[96]

A similar opinion is expressed by the Devī in almost identical terms in the *Bṛhaddharma*, but with a significant variation. The goddess tells Śiva that he is the presiding deity of the *Āgamas* and Hari is the presiding deity of the *Vedas*. But Śiva was appointed first and Hari later. Even for those who worship in the Vaiṣṇava way, the *mantras* and the *Tantras* related to her are to be preserved with care. Therefore, one who is initiated in her *mantra*, makes no distinction between a Śākta and a Vaiṣṇava.[97] The Devī adds that she cannot deliver a person who violates either the *Āgamas* or the *Vedas* and takes refuge in only one of these, because this preference deforms her.[98]

These are rather transparent attempts at establishing equivalence between, in many respects, two mutually exclusive religious traditions. Appropriately, it is the goddess who usually initiates these moves, for the *Tantras* primarily pertain to her; she is incomplete without them. She even assigns chronological precedence to the *Tantras* over the *Vedas*. All these are predictable and fall in line with the Puranic method of exposition. What is interesting is the attempt to draw the Vaiṣṇavas into the orbit of Tantrism. Vaiṣṇavism in Bengal was indeed decisively influenced by the *Tantras* at a later date, a development to which these *Purāṇas* also contributed. But such statements should not be taken as intentionally presupposing a later development. Instead, as the Bengal *Purāṇas* sought to establish brahmanical hegemony in Bengal and not to foster sectarian interests, these statements should be read as attempts to muffle such rivalries by deploying the *Tantras* as a common bond. It was felt that if the goddess and the *Tantras*, both of which are external to Vedic brahmanism and therefore have no associative history, were projected as factors common to both sects, it might help to strengthen affiliation of the segments to the mainstream and smother the boundaries of their individual identities.

But, as we have seen, mere assertions do not serve any purpose. Integration should not merely be approved in principle, it must also be authenticated in practice. In other words, the acceptance of the *Tantras* must reflect in the performance of rituals. In this respect the task of the Bengal *Purāṇas* was easier compared to the case of the goddesses, because the *Tantras*, being essentially a set of rituals, could be accommodated into the brahmanical system without undue embarrassment. Brahmanism took advantage of this applied function of the *Tantras* and incorporated large chunks of their recommended practices in the ritual prescriptions of the *Purāṇas*, without providing any justification except in a very general way. Two examples of how the Tantric rituals were co-opted into the brahmanical framework will suffice. The sage Sumedhā instructed the king Suratha about the method of worship of the goddess:

> Collect the articles of worship according to the best of your ability and place them duly in their respective positions. Then perform *prāṇāyāma* and *bhūta-śuddhi.* Breathe life into the articles of worship with the *astramantra.* Mention the proper time of the year and perform *nyāsa* according to rules. Next, on an auspicious copper plate draw a hexagonal *yantra* and outside this figure an octagonal *yantra* with white sandal paste. Write the nine-lettered *vījamantra* [on it] and breathe the *yantra* into life according to Vedic procedure. Invoke the goddess in a metal figure with appropriate *mantras* and worship her according to the procedure laid down by the *Āgamas.* Then, merged in meditation, mutter silently the nine-lettered *mantras.*[99]

The goddess herself issued the following instructions regarding the performance of daily rituals by the householders:

> Getting up from the bed early in the morning, one should meditate on the bright lotus, of the colour of camphor, on his head. After this he should remember his *Śrīguru*, [who is] gracious, decorated with ornaments and united with his *śakti,* and should bow down to him. He should then meditate on the *Kuṇḍalinī* thus: I take refuge [in *Kuṇḍalinī*], of the nature of supreme consciousness, who is

manifest [as *caitanya*] while going up [to the *Brahmarandhra*] and who is the nature of nectar while returning back [in the *Suṣumnā* canal]. He should then meditate on the blissful form of mine within the [*Kuṇḍalinī*] fire [situated in the *Mūlādhāra*]. He should then perform his other morning duties. Then the best of the *brāhmaṇas* should, for my satisfaction, perform the *Agnihotra homa* and sitting on his *āsana* take a vow to do my worship. Next, he should perform *bhūtaśuddhi* and *mātṛkānyāsa* and execute *hṛllekhā mātṛkānyāsa*. In this, he is to place the letter *ha* in the *Mūlādhāra*, the letter *ra* in his heart, the vowel *ī* in the middle of his brow, and *hrīṁ* on top of his head. He should then perform the other *nyāsas* according to the *mantras* and should meditate on the great goddess in the lotus of his heart blown by *prāṇāyāma,* situated on the seats of the five *pretas.*[100]

After some more details of the rituals along the same lines, the devotee is told to recite the thousand names of the goddess, the *'ahaṁ rudrebhiḥ' sūkta*, the *Devī Atharvaśiromantra* and the *mantras* of the *Upaniṣads*.[101]

These examples are self-explanatory. The idea of a *yantra* being installed according to Vedic procedure is absurd. Similarly, invocation of the *Devīsūkta* of the *Ṛg Veda* in an explicitly Tantric ritual context is totally out of place. But the Bengal *Purāṇas* had every reason to resort to such forced juxtapositions. They introduced a set of norms which would eventually establish brahmanical supremacy while causing minimal disruption to existing socio-religious practices, and could scarcely afford to be too sensitive about doctrinal subtleties. If the adoption of the goddess was necessary, so was the method of her worship already in vogue. Brahmanism could have no qualms about this because the contents of the ritual were sanctified the moment the local *brāhmaṇas* had lent their approval to it. The practitioners of the *Tantra* could not care much whether it was being claimed to have been done according to Vedic procedure or not, so long as the *yantra* was actually installed with all its concomitant rites. Therefore, even if it appears somewhat incongruous at first glance that a *vidyā*, urging the goddess to destroy and kill with the exhortation *ghātaya ghātaya cāmuṇḍe kili kili vicce huṁ phaṭ*,[102] should be proclaimed by Brahmā as the best of its kind that facilitates action recommended by the *Vedas*,[103] this was the simplest and the most effective means available to brahmanism for reconciliation with the *Tantras* with self-respect. In matters of actual worship of the Devī, however, even the facade of brahmanical preference was dropped. The *Devī Purāṇa* categorically states that the goddess should be installed by those who know the meaning of the *śāstras* related to her, who are experienced in the *mātṛmaṇḍalas* and those who have worked hard at

Bhūtatantra, *Graha*, *Vyāla*, *Gāruḍa* and such other *Tantras*. It is inauspicious if she is installed by any other person.[104]

In spite of such open recognition accorded to the *Tantras*, the Bengal *Purāṇas* were uncomfortable with them. Thus the goddess herself was made to declare:

What is said in the *Śruti* and *Smṛti* is *dharma*; what is said in the other *śāstras* are merely semblance of *dharma*. The *Vedas* are derived from my omniscient and omnipotent self. Since I am not ignorant, the *Vedas* can never be invalidated. The *Smṛtis* have emanated from the meaning of the *Vedas*; therefore the *Smṛtis* composed by Manu etc., are authoritative. It has been suggested that there are other *śāstras*, keeping the *Tantras* in mind. Although matters relating to *dharma* are mentioned therein, these are not accepted by the practitioners of the *Vedas*. The authors of the other *śāstras* are ignorant, hence their utterances cannot be authoritative. Therefore one who aspires for final liberation must always resort to the *Vedas*.[105]

The goddess continues:

The extant *śāstras* which are contrary to the *Śrutis* and the *Smṛtis* are *tāmasa śāstras*. Śiva has composed the *Vāma*, *Kāpālaka*, *Kaulaka*, and *Bhairava Āgamas* for no other reason than to delude people. It is to deliver those *brāhmaṇas*, step by step, who were burnt by the curses of Dakṣa, Bhṛgu, and Dadhīci and were banished from the path of the *Vedas*, that Śaṁkara has written the Śaiva, Vaiṣṇava, Saura, Śākta and Gāṇapatya *Āgamas*.[106]

This is the position that brahmanism would have ideally liked to uphold, but the situation in Bengal compelled it to recognize the *Tantras*, which it did with evident reluctance. Since the adoption of the Tantric ritual form was practically unavoidable, the Bengal *Purāṇas* employed the familiar technique of being openly inconsistent, thus creating space for dissent either from the adherents of the *Vedas* or from the practitioners of the *Tantras*.

Yet there is an important difference between the goddess and the *Tantras*. When the goddess was made to proclaim that the *Vedas* were derived from her, her assimilation was complete. The same cannot be said about the *Tantras*. There were far too many points of friction between the two traditions to allow for such a complete take-over. The very complexity and multiformity of the goddess presented a number of possibilities of adjustment with brahmanism at different levels. Tantrism, in comparison, being primarily a set of rituals, was less flexible. This had its advantage in that large portions of Tantric rituals, particularly the *mantras*, could simply be included in brahmanical worship without much explanation. At the same time, a rigid frame of reference is not amenable to that variety of manipulative jugglery with which brahmanism usually appropriates external elements, such as the goddess. That is why brahmanism has always maintained a certain distance from Tantrism, granting it the status of a parallel tradition. Kullukabhaṭṭa, in his commentary on Manu, divides traditional knowledge into two categories—Vedic and Tantric.[107] So does the *Devībhāgavata* which differentiates between the Vedic and the Tantric in methods of external worship,[108] initiation,[109] *ācamana*,[110] and even in matters so trivial as the preparation of the holy ashes.[111] But the Bengal *Purāṇas* could not afford to leave the issue at that. They had to work out a strategy to resolve this dichotomy, and the strategy they eventually adopted proved to be fairly simple and open-ended. They declared:

> In the *Purāṇas* there are certain matters which, though derived from the *Tantras*, have been regarded as *dharma*, but one must not follow them [blindly]. If the *Tantra* does not go against the *Veda*, it should certainly be regarded as authoritative, but if it is directly opposed to *Śruti*, it can never be taken as an authority.[112]

And again:

> In some places of these works [the *Āgamas*] there are portions which do not go against the *Vedas*. By accepting them the *Vaidikas* do not incur sin. A *brāhmaṇa* is by no means entitled to do what is not supported by the *Vedas*; but one who is not privileged to study the *Vedas*, is qualified to perform such actions.[113]

The advantage of this formula was that the right to decide which aspects of the *Tantras* were in agreement with or opposed to the *Vedas* rested entirely with the local *brāhmaṇas*. And as the *Vedas* were not just immutable texts but a source of symbolic authority for the Bengal *Purāṇas*, the violation of that authority also became a matter of judgement for the *brāhmaṇas*. Thus nothing was firmly fixed and the whole question was conveniently open to interpretation. But there is a pattern in the manner in which interpretations have actually been offered. The Bengal *Purāṇas* have prescribed the use of Tantric *mantras* and *nyāsa* and have adopted the concept of the *ṣaṭcakra*. The *mantras* are usually meaningless sounds and the *ṣaṭcakra* is a harmless assumption. These could hardly undermine the sacredness of the *Vedas*, except in a puritanical sense. At the same time, the Bengal *Purāṇas* never recommended the practice of the *vāmācāra* aspect of the *Tantras*—as a matter of fact, they consistently opposed it—because *vāmācāra* emphatically disregards *varṇāśramadharma*, the fundamental premise of brahmanism.

The Bengal *Purāṇas* intended to be the vehicle of a popular and broad-based religion in Bengal. They relaxed some of the social codes of orthodox brahmanism. They allowed *śūdras* to listen to the *Purāṇas* and admitted the right of women to participate in mainstream religious activities, such as the performance of the *vratas*. For this purpose they imbibed elements of local cultures, and the influence of the *Tantras* helped them to reach out particularly to women and the lower *varṇas*, not merely by giving them wider acceptability, but also in terms of attitudes. But they were only willing to go so far.

A typical instance of Puranic worship of the goddess thus includes the following procedure:[114] veneration of the *guru*, activating the *kuṇḍalinī*, performance of the *Agnihotra homa*, execution of *bhūtaśuddhi* and *hṛllekhā mātṛkānyāsa*, meditation on the nature of the goddess, performance of her *japa* and handing over of the fruits of *japa* to her, ushering in of the goddess with *āsana*, *pādya*, *arghya*, and *ācamana*, offering of water for bath, clothes, ornaments, perfumes, flowers and other necessary articles with due devotion,[115] recitation of the *Devī Sūkta* and the *Upaniṣads*, ecstatic dancing and singing with heart filled with love, hair standing on end, tears of love flowing from the eyes and voice choked with emotion, feeding *brāhmaṇas*, virgins, children and the public, and finally taking leave of the deity by executing the *saṁhāra mudrā*.[116] This procedure is a combination of many elements. The Vedic component is present throughout; the preparatory rites are predominantly Tantric; the actual performance conforms to the Puranic innovation of popular worship (*pūjā*); and it ends in devotional ecstasy of an intensely personal kind (*bhakti*). *Bhakti* has no place in Vedic sacrificial religion, nor does it fit into Tantrism, for the *Tantras* assume that all men and women are gods and goddesses in their real selves. Thus *bhakti* was superimposed to hold together the many disparate segments in a common bond of emotion. The success of the Bengal *Purāṇas* was partially due to their capacity to bring contradictory, doctrinally exclusive, elements together and mesh them into a composite system, which never appeared implausible. Tantrism was one such element which the Bengal *Purāṇas* made extensive use of in their bid to internalize the goddess.

V

Apart from the compulsion of a pervasive local tradition, was there any other reason why the goddess was chosen as both instrument and symbol of assimilation? The question is worth addressing because the integrative role of the goddess has been noticed by a number of scholars in a variety of contexts other than Bengal. G.S. Ghurye, for example, has shown, on the basis of ancient texts and contemporary gazetteers, how the goddess combines 'the folk and the elite cultures' in the deep south, in Maharashtra, Gujarat, and Rajasthan.[117] His survey reveals that the goddesses served to integrate and maintain a balance between the brahmanical and the various local traditions through different types of symbolic compromises, particularly in the areas peripheral to the brahmanical sphere of influence. Thus it is reasonable to assume that even though the brahmanical adoption of the goddess in other parts of India was not as systematic as in Bengal, she was obviously a recognized medium of absorption of local cults throughout the country. Since the process was as widespread, it will be inappropriate to explain the phenomenon in terms of a set of context-specific external factors alone. It is now necessary to look into the internal development of brahmanism.

There was no place for the goddess in orthodox Vedism. But the assimilation of alien religious cults and practices requires the sanction of an internal authority. That sanction was curiously provided by the *Sāṁkhya* school of thought, one of the six major systems of Hindu philosophy. Shorn of its metaphysical subtleties, the *Sāṁkhya* explanation of the cosmic evolution is the following. *Sāṁkhya*, as we have it now,[118] admits of two principles, *prakṛti* or matter and *puruṣas* or souls. *Sāṁkhya* believes that before this world came into being, there existed a state of dissolution in which the *guṇa* compounds (the ultimate subtle entities) had disintegrated into a state of disunion and had by their mutual opposition produced an equilibrium, the *prakṛti*. Later on, disturbance arose in the *prakṛti* and as a result of that a process of unequal aggregation of the *guṇa*s in varying proportions took place which brought forth the creation of the manifold. The state of equilibrium is broken by the transcendental influence of the *puruṣas*. This influence means that there is inherent in the *prakṛti* a teleology that all its movements or modifications may serve the purpose of the *puruṣas*. Thus a return of this manifold world into the quiescent state of *prakṛti* takes place when the *puruṣas* collectively require that there should be a temporary cessation of all experience.[119]

Sāṁkhya therefore explains the creation of the universe in terms of an interplay between the *prakṛti* and the *puruṣas* without necessarily ascribing to either primacy in the creative process. Although the *prakṛti* is energized into action only when in contact with the *puruṣas*, just as iron moves while in proximity of a magnet,[120] the *puruṣas* are not agents of action (*kartā*) by themselves, but inert witnesses. To put it plainly, *prakṛti* and *puruṣas* are partners in the enterprise of creation. Not even a suggestion of the goddess is implied in this conception of the creation and dissolution of the universe, for *Sāṁkhya* denies the existence of god or any other exterior influence in matters of creation.[121]

Yet the term *prakṛti* is of feminine gender. Although, according to the rules of Sanskrit grammar, the gender of a particular word does not necessarily signify the gender of the object denoted by that word, in the *Sāṁkhya* formulation *prakṛti* has actually been conceived in feminine terms. *Prakṛti* has been variously depicted in the *Sāṁkhyakārikā* and the *Sāṁkhyasūtra* as a shy wife or a seductive dancing girl, who bewitches the *puruṣas* into the act of creation.[122] Thus, irrespective of whether *Sāṁkhya* had consciously intended it or not, in the subsequent philosophical discussions the separation and union between the *prakṛti* and the *puruṣas* have often been understood in the metaphor of the elemental man–woman relationship. Through this rather fortuitous development, the feminine principle as the material cause behind creation came to acquire its place in brahmanical thought. Attribution of divinity to this feminine principle was the next predictable step, and with the theistic transformation of *prakṛti*, brahmanism had created space for the goddess. It is difficult to ascertain with accuracy the chronological sequence of these developments, but as the *Purāṇas*, including the *Devī-Māhātmya* section of the *Mārkaṇḍeya Purāṇa*,[123] almost invariably draw upon the *Sāṁkhya* concept of *prakṛti* as the model for the supreme goddess, the identification must have taken place by the sixth century.

Because of their rambling style the *Purāṇas* sometimes comment on topics whose relevance is not immediately recognizable. The Bengal *Purāṇas* have also casually touched upon or even indulged in lengthy discourses on matters of philosophical import, often without apparent purpose. But the one philosophical question to which these texts keep coming back in all earnestness is the role of *prakṛti* in the cosmic cycle of creation and dissolution of the universe. For instance, the *Devībhāgavata* defines *prakṛti* thus:

> [The prefix] '*pra*' means exalted and [the affix] '*kṛti*' denotes creation. Thus the goddess who is excellent in creation is known as *prakṛti*. '*Pra*' signifies the exalted *sattva guṇa*, '*kṛ*' in the middle suggests *raja* [*guṇa*] and the word '*ti*' denotes *tama* [*guṇa*]. Thus one who is endowed with the three *guṇas* and energy, and is superior in the act of creation, is called *prakṛti*. The state preceding creation is denoted by '*pra*' and '*kṛti*' signifies creation. Thus the goddess who precedes creation is known as *prakṛti*.[124]

Despite the Puranic tendency to fiddle with philosophical ideas, there is seldom a significant intervention in the debate on the concerned subject. This definition is however treated with respect, in as much as it has been quoted along with a citation from Vācaspati Miśra's *Tattvakaumudī*, the authoritative commentary on *Sāṁkhyakārikā*, by *Bhāratīya Darśana Koṣa* in its discussion on the nature of *prakṛti*.[125]

But does this definition conform to the *Sāṁkhya* notion of *prakṛti*? The *Purāṇas* tend to pick out key words or concepts from the existing body of brahmanical literature and use them as instruments of legitimation. In the process they often distort their meaning by quoting them out of context, interpreting them in a manner which may have no connection with their original significance, or even fabricating an entirely new concept to pass on under the cover of an old established one. The Puranic treatment of the *Vedas* is a case in point.

In this instance, however, much of the original attributes of *prakṛti* are retained. She is described as one who is constituted of the three *guṇas* and is involved in the act of creation. This, indeed, is an explicit affirmation of the *Sāṁkhya* concept. But it also differs from the *Sāṁkhya* in its appreciation of the role of *prakṛti* in the act of creation. We have seen that the *Sāṁkhya* emphasizes the interdependence of *prakṛti* and *puruṣas* in the creative process. *Prakṛti* creates the universe, but being lifeless she cannot perceive her own creation; that is why she requires the *puruṣas*. And the *puruṣas*, though they represent consciousness, cannot perceive that which has not been created; that is why they require *prakṛti*. In other words, the *Sāṁkhya* accepts that both these elements are indispensable and equally involved in the enterprise of creation. If anything, it tends to endow consciousness with the creative impulse, particularly in view of the implied teleology inherent in the cyclical aggregation and dissolution of matter for the enjoyment of the *puruṣas*. In the *Devībhāgavata prakṛti* is unequivocally the sole creator. In this scheme of things, the *puruṣas* either do not figure at all, or, if they do, are divested of any share in the creative process. Let me quote another passage.

Once the sacred trinity of Puranic brahmanism, Brahmā, Viṣṇu, and Śiva, were in some confusion regarding how to go about the work of creation. They were flown into the presence of the *mūlaprakṛti* who, always in association with the *puruṣa*, creates this universe and shows it to *paramātmā*.[126] She smiled and they were immediately transformed into three young women.[127] They observed the entire universe, including themselves, reflected in her toe-nail,[128] and realized that she was the mother of the universe.[129] Viṣṇu then began to pray to her, saying:

Mother, I now comprehend that this whole universe rests on you. It rises from you and melts away in you. The creation of this universe shows your infinite power, which pervades all the regions. From *sat* [the two formless elements—sky and wind] and *asat* [the three manifest elements—fire, water and earth] you create the whole universe and show it to the *puruṣa,* the enjoyer, for his satisfaction. You become the twenty-three *tattvas* [*mahat*, etc., enumerated in the *Sāṁkhya* system] and appear to us like a mirage. Without you no object would be visible. You encompass the whole universe. That is why the wise declare that even the highest *puruṣa* can perform nothing without the aid of your power . . . . When Brahmā, Maheśvara, and I are born through your power and are not eternal, it is needless to say that the other gods are mere transient beings, created by you. It is only you, ancient *prakṛti*, the mother of the universe, who is eternal. Bhavāni, I now realize from my association with you that it is you who impart, out of mercy, the *brahmavidyā* to the ancient *puruṣa*; only then can he perceive his eternal nature. Otherwise, he will always remain under the delusion that he is the lord, he is the *puruṣa* without beginning, he is the universal soul, and will suffer from egoism.[130]

This passage clearly acknowledges that the Puranic conception of the goddess is derived from the *Sāṁkhya* explanation of the universe. But with a significant shift in emphasis, it assigns the entire initiative for creation to *prakṛti*. The *puruṣas*, or rather the *puruṣa* who is equated with the Vedantic *paramātmā*, exists, but he is completely marginalized. He is consciousness, but the function of consciousness is effectively transferred on to *prakṛti*. Thus the condition created by the *Sāṁkhya* was amended by the *Purāṇas* which brought about a qualitative change in the nature of *prakṛti*.

These amendments were of three kinds. First, *prakṛti* the supreme creator, was given the status of goddess. Second, a special category called *mūlaprakṛti* or primordial nature was created which made room for subsidiary or derived *prakṛtis*. And third, this *mūlaprakṛti* was invested with a creative energy or power called *śakti*. These innovations are alien to *Sāṁkhya*, but are not so removed from it as to render the ancestry of *prakṛti* unrecognizable. The goddess is still without a visible form and her only attribute, the power or energy, is an abstraction. The *Sāṁkhya* antecedents of the Puranic *mūlaprakṛti* are thus clearly intelligible, and up to this point these developments may be considered part of the evolutionary process of the brahmanical religion, the result of its internal dynamism rather than a response to external stimuli.

My aim is to ascertain the extent of brahmanical preparedness in terms of its own internal developments to accommodate the goddess. However, in the absence of an inviolable central canon, barring of course the notional status of the *Vedas*, Hinduism has always borrowed from indigenous non-brahmanical religious systems, as well as from 'foreign' sources. It has been argued that even the idea of a warrior goddess mounted on a lion began to develop in India partly under central Asian influence from the first or second century AD.[131] Hence, it is practically impossible to draw a firm line demarcating the exclusive domains of brahmanism and the external elements, if these may be so described. Such an effort also erroneously presupposes a fixed structure in brahmanism and a similar structure for all the diverse sources put together that contributed to the making of Puranic Hinduism. The point remains that the goddess proved to be the major vehicle for the brahmanical attempt to assimilate local cults throughout the country, and we must investigate whether brahmanism itself was predisposed towards the adoption of the goddess.

However, for the above-mentioned difficulties, such an inquiry cannot be pushed beyond a point, and any assessment of the brahmanical predisposition towards the goddess has to be somewhat impressionistic. We have seen that the *Sāṁkhya* conception of *prakṛti* contained the seed of her later transformation into the goddess, but it did not necessarily anticipate the goddess. The *mūlaprakṛti* was a Puranic formulation which was put to good use for the absorption of local goddesses *per se*, and particularly those of Bengal. Thus, however convincing the formulation may appear, the *mūlaprakṛti* was more of a theoretical justification contrived to suit the requirements of brahmanism, than the result of a spontaneous spurt of creative imagination or a natural extension of a philosophical query. It may, however, be said that due to the explicit allegiance to the *Sāṁkhya* antecedents of the *mūlaprakṛti* by the Bengal *Purāṇas* and the careful introspection that went into the formulation and elaboration of this concept, it sounds more internally consistent than some other similar explanatory devices of the *Purāṇas*.

The *mūlaprakṛti* was a very effective innovation. The *Sāṁkhya* does not admit of more than one *prakṛti*. Presumably in deference to that the *mūlaprakṛti* was conceived, theoretically one but (as the name suggests) the repository or sum-total of all the secondary *prakṛtis*. Once the divisibility of *prakṛti* was established in principle, it opened up endless possibilities, for now brahmanism could usurp as many goddesses as it perceived necessary in the name of the *mūlaprakṛti*, with the help of a single theological justification. It is a fairly simple mechanism as the following passage from the *Brahmavaivarta Purāṇa* indicates:

The *mūlaprakṛti*, who is *Viṣṇumāyā* and identical with *pūrṇabrahma*, is one, but at the time of creation splits herself into five forms. The presiding goddess of the soul of Śrīkṛṣṇa, the *paramātmā*, and the dearest to him among all women, is called Rādhā. Lakṣmī is the embodiment of wealth and the beloved of Nārāyaṇa. The presiding goddess of music is the venerable Sarasvatī. Sāvitrī, the mother of the *Vedas* and the beloved of Vidhi, is worshipped by all. Durgā is the beloved of Śaṁkara, whose son is Gaṇeśa.[132]

Then follows a long exposition of the character and attributes of these five goddesses[133] who are fully representative (*paripūrṇatamāḥ*) of the *mūlaprakṛti*,[134] and are described as *śaktisvarūpā*, *śaktirūpiṇī* and *brahmatejomayī śakti*.[135] The text then makes a general declaration that all the goddesses and all women in this universe are derived from *prakṛti* and arranges them in descending order of importance. Some are her parts, some are parts of the parts, and still others parts of the parts of the parts.[136] The principal parts (*pradhānāṁśarūpā*) are Gaṅgā, Tulasī, Manasā, Ṣaṣṭhī, Maṅgalacaṇḍikā, Kālī and Vasundharā.[137] The simple parts (*prakṛteśca kalā*) are either the wives of the minor gods, such as Svāhā the wife of Agni, Kṣamā the wife of Yama, Rati the wife of Kāma, or the wives of divinized human virtues and vices, such as Pratiṣṭhā the wife of Puṇya, Kīrti the wife of Sukarma, Dayā the wife of Moha, Mithyā the wife of Adharma, or the wives of the sages, such as Śatarūpā the wife of Manu, Arundhatī the wife of Vaśiṣṭha, Ahalyā the wife of Gautama.[138] Then some important epic and Puranic characters such as Kuntī, Gāndhārī, Draupadī, Devakī, Yaśodā, Mandodarī, Kauśalyā and Sītā are mentioned, who are also parts of *prakṛti*.[139] Finally, the text proclaims that the village goddesses who may exist in this Bhārata are all parts of *prakṛti*.[140]

Thus *mūlaprakṛti* is a metaphysical concept that easily assumes concrete forms. This quality of the *mūlaprakṛti* to move back and forth between abstract and concrete makes her an ideal medium of assimilation. As a symbol communicates a coherent greater whole by means of a part, the *mūlaprakṛti* ensures her presence in all her embodiments, while herself remaining an inscrutable abstract entity. The *paripūrṇatamā* representations are conveniently attached to the trinity as their consorts. They are also the *śaktis* of the respective gods. This gives them an additional *raison d'etre*, for they are not merely important in themselves but they also empower the gods to carry on with their assigned functions. In a reversal of roles they legitimize the existence of the gods.

The *pradhānāṁśarūpā* representations are symptomatic of the Puranic process. Here the regional goddesses of Bengal such as Manasā, Ṣaṣṭhī and Maṅgalacaṇḍikā are placed on a par with goddesses of much wider appeal like Gaṅgā, Tulasī and Kālī. Had these texts belonged to a different region, they would certainly have chosen goddesses of that region for similar treatment. Their placement in the hierarchy is also just right, for they are given neither unrealistic importance nor mere grudging recognition.

The simple parts of the *prakṛti*, represented by the wives of minor gods and sages and the epic-Puranic characters, are a formality, for they were never in active worship, except perhaps as obscure esoteric cults. But their inclusion serves a significant purpose. Though not in worship, they are revered and familiar figures. They therefore constitute that crucial step in the hierarchy which separates the high-profile goddesses from the purely local anonymous ones, the village goddesses. It does not matter if these village goddesses remain unnamed, for the *Purāṇas* have bestowed recognition on them in principle. They have created an uninterrupted chain from the lofty *mūlaprakṛti* to a petty guardian of a village with perhaps a cure for colic or prickly heat.

This was the simple but effective means by which brahmanism has sanctified and appropriated the entire gamut of non-brahmanical goddesses. It is not merely those goddesses who, due to their comparatively late entrance into the brahmanical pantheon, have managed to retain some of their characteristic features and can be traced to their origin, but even those with more 'authentic' brahmanical credentials have been so absorbed as manifestations of the *mūlaprakṛti*. Shashibhushan Dasgupta rightly conjectures that the fifty-one goddesses of the *śākta pīṭhas* and the ten forms of Daśamahāvidyā were perhaps originally independent local deities admitted into Puranic Hinduism through the myths of the dismemberment of Satī's body and Satī's visit to her natal family.[141] Indeed, Satī herself is a Puranic creation who, by virtue of her association with Śiva, had earned a credibility which could then be used for the purpose of secondary absorptions.

This is an open-ended process. If a local goddess, through a combination of factors, becomes sufficiently important to demand special recognition, she can be given a name and place in the hierarchy without the slightest difficulty. Judging by the popularity of Santoṣī Mā, the contribution of Indian cinema to the Hindu pantheon, a *Purāṇa* may soon be written glorifying her as 'a' principal aspect of the *mūlaprakṛti* and providing her with a suitable genealogy. This mechanism imparted to the goddess such a flexibility that it has, at times, assumed absurd proportions from the brahmanical point of view. For example, in the *Śūnyapurāṇa*, a vernacular text of medieval Bengal, the goddess Caṇḍikā is made to appear as Hāttā or Hāyābibi, a Muslim, to defend the *saddharmī* Buddhists against brahmanical oppression.[142] (Didn't she promise in the *Mārkaṇḍeya Purāṇa* to appear in defence of the weak in different identities, whenever such a need would arise?[143] After all, *śakti* exists everywhere, and can assume any form.)

IV

With the universalization of the goddess, brahmanism made itself accessible to followers of non-brahmanical religious systems. But what did it mean in operational terms? We have seen that brahmanism was attempting to establish socio-cultural hegemony in Bengal through the composition of these *Purāṇas*. But consensual relationship involves adjustment with subordinate groups. At what levels were these adjustments made and to what effect? The *Purāṇas* do not answer these questions as they represent primarily the brahmanical side of the story. Nor are there any contemporary accounts available revealing the reactions of the non-*brāhmaṇa* groups. Even so we could attempt to reconstruct the effects of this *brāhmaṇa*-initiated religious synthesis built around the goddess on the basis of anthropological evidence. We find therein both the multiplicity and the unitary function of the goddess cult, and the manner in which it simultaneously operates at several levels, while binding divergent castes, sects and other interest groups together.

Several anthropologists have observed a 'basic unity' in the worship of the goddess in great and little traditions. Since this unity is mostly on the surface, such observations are often superficial, though correct.[144] However, there are others who look into the complexity of relations that the goddess cult invokes and thus present this apparent unity in its full richness. Jacob Pandian has studied the beliefs and rituals associated with the mother goddesses of a Tamil village. He noticed that the goddess functions as an organizational system which helps to identify local religious specificities, and at the same time connects them with the philosophical abstractions of Hindu theodicy. Pandian argues that the symbol of the mother goddess embodies the historical/cultural experiences of a community—a group, village or region—and fuses order (exemplified in life, health and prosperity) and disorder (exemplified in disease, decay and death), thus providing believers with a particular religious perspective. The believer in the mother goddess organizes his experiences, including his knowledge of the existence of other deities and the multiplicity of rituals, using the symbol of the goddess as a conceptual category, and this enables him to make sense of his experiences of diverse domains. Such a symbol also mediates between the theory of retributive justice and the cycle of birth and rebirth which are founded on the principle of cosmic causation, and the traditional values and cultural themes of particular groups or regions which affirm life experiences, for the goddess inheres elements of both levels.[145]

Thus Pandian's findings point to an elemental duality in the conceptualization of the goddess, a conceptualization that encompasses and in a way sublimates the oppositions between pure and impure, remote and immediate, order and chaos. When these oppositions in the realm of ideas are translated into categories of social organization, they roughly correspond to the great and the little traditions, to the attitudes governing the actions of the upper and lower castes or those beyond the pale of the caste framework. Many anthropologists have shown how the presence of the goddess brings about tacit adjustments in the distribution of power and the division of social roles between these two spheres as well.

Edward Henry, working in a cluster of villages in eastern Uttar Pradesh, observes that the mother goddess cult varies in its mediation, functions, and even deities as one moves from the Sanskritic through the non-Sanskritic to shamanic contexts. In the Sanskritic context the ritual's goal is general welfare. In the non-Sanskritic context the approach is deferential, but worship has specific protective and acquisitive purposes. In the shamanic context the approach is domineering and commanding, and the objectives range from good to evil. In these villages, goddess worship plays a larger part in the devotions of the lower castes and untouchables than in the higher bloc of castes. But Henry shows how beliefs and practices regarding matters of crucial importance allow the non-Sanskritic traditions to attract even upper caste followers, whose adherence to the cult requires *brāhmaṇa* endorsement. The low-caste mediums have good rapport with the goddess because, like her, they are impure and autochthonous. When smallpox or cholera is imminent, the threat compels even upper caste men to worship the goddess, which requires support of and subordination to the untouchable mother goddess mediums. Henry refers to a report by Jack Planalp according to which the untouchable devotees of the goddess in the Senapur area became ritual influentials by mobilizing fear in the community that the goddess was coming to afflict those who did not worship her in a special way, and in so doing acquired a measure of power in the lives of their upper caste superiors.[146] Morris Opler[147] and Pauline Kolenda[148] have observed similar bargaining strength among the lower caste devotees who could be possessed by the spirit of the goddess. Spirit possession not only brings deference to the possessed but also licenses verbal (and occasionally physical) aggression against his social superiors. This dependence of the members of the higher castes on the low-caste spirit mediums contributes to the pride of the group as a whole.

The advantage of being a low-caste adherent of the goddess cult in the face of a disaster that threatens the whole community is obvious. It creates conditions for a temporary reversal of roles. The everyday social relations of a community are however more subtly and durably structured than those which call for a panic response to an emergency. That the goddess intervenes in a consensual tension balancing act even in such situations has been observed by Michael Moffatt in his extremely perceptive study of an untouchable community of Endavur village in south India. The village is divided into two parts—the *uur* and the Colony, inhabited by the upper castes and the untouchables respectively. The goddesses Mariyamman and Selliyamman are worshipped in common by all villagers. Since the upper castes have appropriated the cult of the goddess Mariyamman, the untouchables are entirely excluded from her worship and protection. Their predictable response is to replicate, ritual by ritual, among themselves the same cult, claiming that the Colony Mariyamman is the same as the goddess of the *uur*, or at least her 'younger sister'. What interests us, however, is the case of Selliyamman, in Moffatt's words 'the inclusive goddess'.

The untouchables of the Endavur village and the goddess Selliyamman are linked together by a complex set of metaphors of protection, summed up in the term *tai* or mother. Selliyamman is worshipped in an annual festival conducted by members of all the castes of Endavur, from the *brāhmaṇa* to the Chakkiliyan. It is mandatory that the festival to Selliyamman be conducted jointly; if the untouchables and the upper castes cannot agree on its timing and its finances, the festival cannot be held. The untouchables have two general roles in the festival. First, they are co-equal worshippers, and the necessity for them in her worship is acted out in an explicit ritual; Colony and *uur* play the roles of the groom's family and the bride's family respectively, in a marriage of the goddess to a form of Śiva. Second, the role of the untouchables in the worship of Selliyamman is consistent with their last-among-equals position as her worshippers; they are intermediaries on behalf of the higher castes as well as of the goddess herself. Moffatt argues that the marriage integrates the Colony and the *uur*, the two parts of the village that are most clearly separate in other ritual contexts, for the untouchables are essential actors in an essential act of marriage for the goddess. If they did not join with *uur* castes to form the two houses necessary for Selliyamman's marriage, her *śakti* could not be carried through the village, and her protection would not extend to the territory for the next year. Thus in the worship of Selliyamman, the untouchables are complementary; they complete a bipartite whole, one which is equally necessary for all in the village, one which is fundamentally incomplete without them.[149]

It is imperative to ensure co-ordination between the component parts of a village for it to function effectively as a socially integrated territorial unit. Even if the cult of Selliyamman was not available, the village organization, led by the upper castes, would surely have found another means of achieving this integration. But it so happens that it is achieved through the marriage festival of Selliyamman, in which the untouchables are, for once, co-equals of the upper castes, because they stand in a special relationship with the goddess. It may be mentioned that the Bengal *Purāṇas* consistently strove to promote the autumnal worship of Durgā,[150] a festival celebrating her annual visit to her parents to ensure the renewal of her protective care for her devotees for the year, which now helps to cement the community identity of the Hindu Bengalis through common participation. Reasonably therefore, the *Purāṇas* repeatedly emphasized the need for all to take part in the worship, irrespective of caste,[151] sect,[152] and gender[153] denominations. The *Purāṇas* also explicitly conceded her origin among the mountain-dwelling tribes[154] and recommend certain rituals, such as the *śavarotsava*,[155] in her worship which are symptomatic of non-*brāhmaṇa* celebrations.

The method employed for the integration of the different segments of a village may not produce the same results when applied to an entire region, characterized by a certain degree of linguistic and socio-cultural homogeneity and yet marked by the existence of relatively autonomous local traditions. Different regional traditions have worked out their own strategies to bring about a functional integration of their parts, which would acknowledge the cultural hegemony of the *brāhmaṇas* and also respect the varied local traditions. In an important survey of some of the major goddess temples of Orissa James Preston has demonstrated how the ritual patterns and social organization of these temples effect a compromise through resolution of oppositions between local tribal cults centring round the worship of the goddesses and Puranic Hinduism epitomized by the cult of Jagannātha. Let us consider the results of Preston's survey in some detail.

There are two distinct regions in Orissa. The western part of the state is a mountainous area occupied by large numbers of tribal people while the eastern coastal plains are mostly inhabited by Hindus. Preston found that the temples located near the eastern coast were characterized by dominant *brāhmaṇa* castes, vegetarian deities, absence of animal sacrifice and strong links to the Jagannātha cult at Puri. The temples near the inland mountainous region were distinguished by dominant non-*brāhmaṇa* priests, non-vegetarian deities, animal sacrifice and independence from ties to the Jagannātha complex. However, this duality is blunted by a middle zone with various types of compromise. Preston has chosen a temple each from the two extremes and two from the middle zone as his samples. Of these, the two from the middle zone are of interest to us.

The temple of Bhagavatī is located in a small town in the middle zone between coastal and interior Orissa. This temple has been considered an important centre of Orissan Tantrism from early times, but for hundreds of years it was under the control of the *Rājā* of Puri, the patron of Jagannātha, who attached several *brāhmaṇa* priests to the temple. But these *brāhmaṇas* never managed to undermine the importance of the fifty non-*brāhmaṇa* priests who continue to play a dominant role by virtue of their monopoly over the administration of the temple. The ten *brāhmaṇa* priests still play a minor role in the ceremonies, but the non- *brāhmaṇa* priests treat them as hired ceremonial assistants. Goats and buffaloes are offered to the goddess on various occasions throughout the year and her daily meals include fish from nearby Chilka lake. Despite the non-*brāhmaṇa* elements associated with the Bhagavatī temple, certain symbolic ties to the Puri complex remain. In the first place, the *bhoga* (ritual food offering) of Jagannātha is brought to Bhagavatī each week by a priest from the Puri temple. Besides, at the time of Durgā *pūjā*, a prominent priest is sent from Puri to preside over the animal sacrifices to Bhagavatī. Thus the Bhagavatī temple has worked out a balance between its non-*brāhmaṇa* origins and its subsequent linkage with the Jagannātha cult in favour of the former but acceptable to the latter.

The temple of Birajā is a large and famous pilgrimage shrine, also located in the middle zone. It was a popular centre of the Tantric cult between the eighth and the tenth centuries and is now the most influential focus of goddess worship in Orissa. Birajā incorporates various Orissan cults through an inclusive use of symbols. She unifies the five main sects of Orissan Hinduism by assimilating each of the major deities of these sects as one of her manifestations. Thus Birajā is Sūrya, Gaṇeśa, Durgā, Śiva and Jagannātha. On her crown are the snake, half moon, elephant image and *yoni-liṅga*. Also noteworthy is the fact that the Birajā temple has both a *triśūla* and a *cakra* at the top. Birajā is both vegetarian and non-vegetarian, reconciling Tantric and Vaiṣṇava elements. Over two hundred goats and a buffalo are offered to her through the year, but when a sacrifice takes place, the doors of the main shrine are closed. Also, the head and body of the sacrificed animal are distributed among lower castes; nothing is presented directly to the goddess. This symbolizes the Vaiṣṇavī aspect of Birajā. The priests at Birajā are mostly *brāhmaṇas*. The non-*brāhmaṇa* castes associated with the ceremonies here are not considered priests but temple servants. Since Birajā incorporates Jagannātha as part of herself, there is no need for a strong relationship with Puri. Indeed, Birajā is tied symbolically to north India rather than Puri, which acts in several ways to legitimize her independence and authority. This temple is believed to be located where the navel of Satī fell and this is symbolized by a deep well inside a small shrine within the temple compound. Legend connects this well with the Gaṅgā of Vārānasī. Thus, unlike the compromise seen at the Bhagavatī temple, based on the compartmentalized coexistence of *brāhmaṇa* and non-*brāhmaṇa* elements, sectarian tensions at the temple of Birajā have been resolved through a process of incorporation and universalization. At one level local sects are fused into the dominant symbol of Birajā, while at a higher level the deity is linked to the India-wide great tradition of Hinduism.[156]

The situation in Orissa closely parallels developments in Bengal in many respects, primarily due to the late arrival of brahmanism in both regions. But the points of departure are also equally conspicuous and significant. To begin with, Bengal never developed a sharply defined central cult focus as the Jagannātha of Orissa. It appropriated the goddess complex because an alternative cult focus was not available. But brahmanism in Bengal remained somewhat uncomfortable with her. As a compromise as it were, the Bengal *Purāṇas* probably decided to promote Durgā, who synthesized many contradictory aspects of the goddess in her person, such as the martial and the benign, the consort and the independent deity, thus projecting a middle-of-the-way position with wide margins on both sides to make room for the more unacceptable aspects of the goddess. At the same time, they consistently underplayed the fiercely energetic Kālī, who had a strong Tantric association and was in daily worship. Despite persistent Puranic effort, the annual worship of Durgā became popular in Bengal not earlier than the late medieval period, and even then it did not serve the functions that the Jagannātha performed for Orissa. Perhaps it is not possible for a cult to exercise that kind of influence without a strong temple base, its reputation as a centre of pilgrimage of subcontinental dimension, the repeated reminder of its continuous presence through daily worship, and its recognition as the supremely important religious symbol in an institutional sense among all other competing cults, as exemplified in the ritual distribution of Jagannātha's *bhoga* to the subcentres of worship in Orissa. Indeed, the autumnal worship of Durgā is more analogous to the marriage of Selliyamman than the pervasive influence of Jagannātha overshadowing all other religious activities.

Besides, by the time the central core of the Bengal *Purāṇas* was codified, state power passed into the hands of Muslims. In the absence of its support base, brahmanism in Bengal could not crystallize its gains in the manner in which it did in Orissa. That may be one of the reasons why the Bengal *brāhmaṇas* did not go in for that one decisive attempt to gather all the sprawling local goddesses around Durgā, and allowed them to gravitate towards the central goddess image in their own rhythm. Thus brahmanism in Bengal failed to create a Jagannātha, that ultimate symbol of brahmanical triumph, in relation to which the relative integration of the other cults may be measured.

Nevertheless Preston's survey raises a few issues which find their resonance in the Puranic reformulation of the goddess in Bengal as well as in the operational aspect of the cult as it has developed over the last millennium. Preston shows how the Jagannātha balances the brahmanical and the indigenous local traditions by attempting to fuse sectarian identities in the symbolic sphere, and more concretely, by accommodating non-brahmanical elements in the distribution of priestly functions. I have already cited two representative passages,[157] but there are any number of such references in the Bengal *Purāṇas* where the goddess has been made to straddle sectarian boundaries for similar reasons. Unfortunately, barring the ethnographic glossary of Risley, compiled just about one hundred years ago, no such survey has been conducted for the whole of Bengal. There are a few micro-studies which present empirical data on the pattern of interaction between regional goddess cults and rural society, characterized by the presence of an entire cross-section of caste groups from the *brāhmaṇas* to the untouchables, such as by R.M. Sarkar. Sarkar has done his fieldwork in western Bengal, in the two adjoining districts of Burdwan and Birbhum. His findings are startlingly similar to those of Preston with regard to the allocation of priestly functions in the worship of regional goddesses, with the obvious and significant difference that there is no central monitoring agency like the Jagannātha in Bengal. The tradition must have evolved on its own over the years, perhaps centuries.

Sarkar has conducted a detailed village-wise survey of the worship of the important regional goddesses of Bengal, such as Maṅgalacaṇḍī and Manasā, and has studied the nature of participation of different caste groups in the performance of their worship. His findings reveal a discernible pattern. For example, at the Lauberia village, a Bāuri family has in its possession a deity called Caṇḍī. During the annual festival held in her honour on the first day of *Māgha*, all the dominant castes of the village attend the ceremony and take active part in the proceedings. The *deyashi* (low-caste priest, a Bāuri in this case) performs the worship with the help of his fellow *deyashis*. He does not use Sanskrit *mantras*, nor does he follow any strict orthodox procedure. The *brāhmaṇa* priest, who takes his seat by the side of the altar, is requested to offer the sacred thread to the deity, in which he has the sole authority. He does so on behalf of the whole village. The *deyashi* then bows down and touches the feet of the *brāhmaṇa* priest.[158] But in Tantipara village, the *brāhmaṇa* priest is ceremonially engaged by the *deyashi*, a fisherman by caste, to perform the ritual of placing the *bari* (pot) before the idol of Manasā.[159] Similarly, the image of Cintāmani Manasā of Jayadeva-Kenduli village is carried from her village shrine through the famous Vaiṣṇava fair by a Bāgdi *deyashi*, accompanied by his caste men, for annual worship; but during the deity's two-day stay at the *gājan* festival at Tikarbeta village, organized principally by the higher castes, she is worshipped regularly by a *brāhmaṇa* priest in the presence of a gathering of all the villagers.[160]

Sarkar has presented much of his data in tabular form and I will quote two of these as illustrative examples of the division of duties and the extent of participation of the various caste groups in the worship of these goddesses.

NATURE OF CASTE PARTICIPATION DURING THE ANNUAL WORSHIP OF MAṄGALACAṆḌĪ AT KHAIRADIHI VILLAGE[161]

Caste Participation	Service Pattern	Village Affiliation
Brāhmaṇa	worship, Sanskritized aspects	Parasiya
Nāpit (barber)	bringing of the deity	Tantipara
Sūtradhara (carpenter)	holding of umbrella	Khairadihi
Bāgdi	cleaning of the shrine	Khairadihi
Ḍom	playing of drums	Khairadihi and neighbouring villages
Brāhmaṇa	bringing of clay horse from Goilaburi shrine	Paraśiya
Tantubāya (weaver)	showing of *maṅgalaghaṭ*	Khairadihi
Tantubāya	organization of worship	Khairadihi
Tantubāya	performance of *gāchberā*	Khairadihi
Kumbhakāra (potter)	supply of earthen vessels	Khairadihi
Nāpit	plucking of flowers	Khairadihi
All castes	supply of rice and vegetables	Khairadihi and neighbouring villages
Brāhmaṇa	preparation of prasāda	Parasiya and other villages
Vaiṣṇava	performance of *kīratan* (devotional songs)	Khairadihi and neighbouring villages

NATURE OF CASTE PARTICIPATION DURING THE ANNUAL WORSHIP OF AGAR MANASĀ AT METELA VILLAGE[162]

Caste Participation	Service Pattern	Village Affiliation
Goālā (milkman)	fixation of date for worship	Metela
Ḍom	sending of intimation to Agar	Metela
Ḍom	play music	Metela and neighbouring villages
Moirā (confectioner)	cleaning of the shrine	Metela
Sadgopa	carrying of Manasā to Metela	Agar
Grahācārya	supervision of the stages of worship	Metela
Brāhmaṇa	performance of *yajña*	Metela
Brāhmaṇa	animal sacrifice	Metela
Sadgopa	offering of ceremonial blessings of the deity	Agar
Goālā	receiving of blessings on behalf of the village	Metela
Brāhmaṇa	sprinkling of *śāntijal*	Metela
Karmakāra (blacksmith)	plucking of flowers	Metela
Sūtradhara (carpenter)	supply of wooden faggots for *yajña*	Metela
Bāgdi	supply of milk	Metela
Sadgopa	distribution of *prasāda*	Metela
Goālā	collection of subscription from the villagers	Metela

The two tables reveal an interesting overlap of caste duties among the villagers. For instance, at Khairadihi the Bāgdis clean the shrine of Maṅgalacaṇḍī while at Metela the Moirās perform the same function for Manasā, although Bāgdis also reside in this village. The Tantubāyas organize the worship at Khairadihi and the Grahācāryas do so at Metela. The *brāhmaṇas* prepare the *prasāda* at Khairadihi and the *prasāda* is distributed by the Sadgopas at Metela. Besides, at Metela, animal sacrifice is offered by the *brāhmaṇas*. This is curious, for usually in the *brāhmaṇa*-organized worship of deities with *brāhmaṇa* priests officiating at the ceremony, the actual sacrifice is carried out by a low caste, normally of blacksmiths, when such sacrifices are recommended. Milk is supplied by the Bāgdis at Metela, even though the Goālās (milkmen) of the village take active part in the ritual. Thus it is evident that though the respective duties of the socially identifiable groups of these villages are strictly assigned for these ceremonies, they do not necessarily correspond to the traditionally accepted occupational functions of the *jātis*. Moreover, since such discrepancies exist between two villages not far removed from one another, it seems that it is an internal arrangement worked out within each of these villages, which has come to acquire the authority of a tradition.

Beyond these details, what strikes us in this scenario is its underlying assumption. To generalize admittedly on the basis of a few samples, there exists a tacit agreement among all caste groups in Bengal that the worship of these regional goddesses is a shared responsibility of the entire community. The Bengal *Purāṇas* never laid this down in categorical terms, but they directly contributed to such an understanding. In the first place, the *Purāṇas* created the regional goddesses of Bengal. They picked up a handful from among a large inventory of indigenous local goddesses and consistently described them as principal parts of the *mūlaprakṛti*, thus bestowing on them a qualitatively higher status than their peers'. In theory of course every anonymous village goddess is derived from the *mūlaprakṛti*, but not all of them have been singled out for similar treatment. It is true that some of these goddesses with more-equal-than-others status have supra-regional affiliations—the ancestry of Manasā is traced from the snake sacrifice of Janamejaya described in the *Mahābhārata*[163] and Ṣaṣṭhī is said to be the wife of Skanda Kārttikeya[164]—but Maṅgalacaṇḍī can claim no such distinction. Thus a category of goddesses was created who were set apart for greater reverence.

In operational terms, this implied participation of even the *brāhmaṇas* in their worship, along with their original votaries. This produced at least one social space for the corporate existence of different castes in the highly stratified rural society of Bengal. In due course these goddesses grew out of their local boundaries and acquired a regional profile, thus widening the area of this common space. It should be mentioned that no instance of caste co-operation on such a large scale has ever been reported for the worship of the local gods of Bengal. They have usually remained identified with a particular caste group, and in case they are credited with the prevention or cure of a disease, higher castes do offer them worship but never officiate as priests in their rituals. Brahmanism ignored them and this prevented their entry into wider social networks. Indeed, they could not be refracted out of a convenient *mūlaprakṛti*, but some such rationalization could easily have been improvised if brahmanism had felt the need. It did not. It is not surprising therefore, that out of a fairly large collection of indigenous local gods, some of whom have extensive supra-local worshippers such as Jvarāsura, Dharma Ṭhākur and Dakṣiṇarāya, not one has ever been mentioned in the voluminous corpus of the Bengal *Purāṇas*. They simply had no place in the Puranic scheme of things.

The other noticeable aspect in this Puranic process of the creation of regional goddesses is the initiative of the local *brāhmaṇas*. I have already argued that in the absence of a central monastic organization, the judgement of the local *brāhmaṇas* proved decisive in the shaping of Hindu regional traditions.[165] But it is easier to create a deity on paper than to place her in the complex web of life and make her acceptable to every social group. Obviously it was not achieved in a day. The *brāhmaṇas* did not issue a command; they had neither state patronage in the medieval period, nor social sanction in the initial phase, to do so. Instead, they slowly and patiently moved towards a consensus. While the *brāhmaṇas* propagated the worship of the regional goddesses, they maintained the necessary social equilibrium by staying away from them as a group. The *brāhmaṇas* who act as priests for the lower castes are excluded from the ranks of the more respectable members of their community. Without institutional support of any kind, the *brāhmaṇas* had to carefully set themselves up as the undisputed authority in matters of social and religious codes. For this it was essential for them to participate in the system they were attempting to create but from a distance, with an apparent show of reluctance, almost as a concession. In this way, brahmanism would filter through, construct and legitimize the system, and yet the mystique of the symbol of authority would be established and maintained. By the sixteenth century, when the bulk of the *Smṛti* literature of Bengal was composed, brahmanism felt assured of this position, which also coincides with the end of the maximum time-stretch given by some scholars to the very final redactions of the Bengal *Purāṇas*.[166] The dynamics of the rural society of Bengal had by and large absorbed the basic tenets of brahmanism and had created the composite nature of the regional tradition of Bengal.

Notes

1. For a representative sample of such opinions, see A.P. Karmakar, *The Religions of India*, Vol. I (The Vrātya or Dravidian Systems), Mira Publishing House, Lonavla, 1950, pp. 116–18.
2. Sir John Marshall (ed.), *Mohenjo-Daro and the Indus Civilisation*, Indological Book House, Delhi, 1973 (originally published in 1931), pp. 50–1. Also Ernest Mackay, 'Figurines and Model Animals', in *ibid.*, p. 339.
3. Sir Mortimer Wheeler, *The Indus Civilization*, Cambridge University Press, Cambridge, 1968, pp. 91, 109.
4. Shubhangana Atre, *The Archetypal Mother: A Systemic Approach to Harappan Religion*, Ravish Publishers, Pune, 1987, pp. 191, 204.
5. J. Przyluski, 'The Great Goddess in India and Iran', *The Indian Historical Quarterly*, Vol. X, No. 3, September 1934, pp. 405–30 and Stella Kramrisch, 'The Indian Great Goddess', *History of Religions*, Vol. 14, No. 4, May 1975, pp. 235–65.
6. Sukumari Bhattacharji, *The Indian Theogony: A Comparative Study of Indian Mythology from the Vedas to the Purāṇas*, Firma KLM Private Limited, Calcutta, 1978, pp. 160–1.
7. David Kinsley, *Hindu Goddesses: Visions of the Divine Feminine in the Hindu Religious Tradition*, University of California Press, Berkeley, 1986, pp. 17–18.
8. Daniel H.H. Ingalls, 'Foreword', to Brown, *God as Mother*, pp. xiii–xv.
9. I use the term goddess in the singular but with a small 'g' intentionally, in contrast to Ingalls, because one can never be sure of the existence of a supreme Goddess in pre-Vedic India. Rather, it is more likely that there were many goddesses to one or the other of whom members of a tribe or a village or some other community offered absolute allegiance. Thus it is possible to speak of the Goddess of a particular community, but there were perhaps a number of them who might have shared many common characteristics and yet maintained separate identities. The concept of the *mūlaprakṛti* or the *ādyāśakti* from whom all the goddesses emanated as her manifestations was a later brahmanical construction to bring these diverse goddesses under a unifying umbrella. But it remained an idea, though a pervasive one, while these goddesses continued to *function* in their individual identities. Hence I have uniformly used a small 'g' throughout this chapter. If she appears in the plural, I refer to the collectivity of the goddesses, if in the singular, to the goddess tradition.
10. R.G. Bhandarkar, *Vaiṣṇavism, Śaivism and Minor Religious Systems*, in Narayan Bapuji Utgikar (ed.), *Collected Works of Sir R.G. Bhandarkar*, Vol. IV, Bhandarkar Oriental Research Institute, Poona, 1929, p. 205.
11. Danielou says that the goddess at first had no place in 'the Aryan Scriptures'. 'But the prehistoric cult of the mother goddess can be found there too, . . . latent, ready to spring forth. Some of the peoples who came to

be integrated into the Hindu fold had always worshipped the divine Mother.' Alain Danielou, *Hindu Polytheism*, Routledge and Kegan Paul, London, 1963, p. 256.

12. 'Thus in the Śākta cult of the present time we find the stamp of different ethnological groups.' Sudhakar Chattopadhyaya, *Evolution of Hindu Sects: Up to the Time of Śaṁkarācārya*, Munshiram Manoharlal, New Delhi, 1970, p. 151.
13. Hazra, *Upapurāṇas*, Vol. II, p. 16. Also see pp. 17–26.
14. N.N. Bhattacharyya, *Indian Mother Goddess*, Indian Studies: Past and Present, Calcutta, 1971. The 'Introduction' ends with, 'In fact, the Vedas are not the effective sources in which one may seek the origin of the idea of the Female Principle. It is to be sought elsewhere, obviously in the pre-Vedic tradition of India', (p.14) and the rest of the book is devoted to an exploration of the pre-Vedic origin of the goddess.
15. Coburn, *Devī-Māhātmya*, pp. 5–7.
16. D.D. Kosambi, 'At the Crossroad: A Study of Mother Goddess Cult Sites', *Myth and Reality: Studies in the Formation of Indian Culture*, Popular Prakashan, Bombay, 1962, p. 85.
17. Moti Chandra, 'Studies in the Cult of the Mother Goddess in Ancient India', *Bulletin of the Prince of Wales Museum of Western India*, No.12, 1973, p. 4. Moti Chandra makes this statement in the context of his more general argument that all goddesses created, transmuted or approved by brahmanism, are in one way or another derived from the religious beliefs and practices of the indigenous people of India, which is well taken. But the *Mahābhārata* story that he cites in support of his contention, according to which Śrī was unscrupulously lured away by Indra from the *asura* king Prahlāda, is insufficient evidence. This evidence can be accepted as conclusive only if it is proved that the *asuras* were the indigenous people. However, the *asuras*, though invariably opposed to the gods, were also consubstantial with them, and brahmanical mythology is perpetually beset with the problem of the 'good demon', which includes *asuras*, *daityas* and *rākṣasas*. See, for instance, Bruce Long, 'Life out of Death: A Structural Analysis of the Myth of the "Churning of the Ocean of Milk" ', in Bardwell L. Smith (ed.), *Hinduism: New Essays in the History of Religions*, E.J. Brill, Leiden, 1976, pp. 171–207, and O'Flaherty, *Origins of Evil*, pp. 94–138. Thus the *asuras* are an ambivalent and liminal category, often tricked into abandoning what they possessed or what they were legitimately entitled to obtain by the gods. The churning of the ocean myth, which relates how Śrī Lakṣmī emerged from the depths of the ocean and was bestowed on Viṣṇu, is a good example.
18. J.E. van Lohuizen-de Leeuw, 'Mother Goddesses in Ancient India', *Folia Indica*, Association of South Asian Archaeologists in Western Europe, Naples, 1990, p. 4, and Mircea Eliade, *Yoga: Immortality and Freedom*, Princeton University Press, Princeton, 1973, pp. 202, 360.

19. A.L. Basham, *The Wonder That Was India*, Fontana Books in association with Rupa and Co., Calcutta, 1975, p. 234.
20. Hazra, *Upapurāṇas*, Vol. II, pp. 21–2.
21. *Ibid.*, p. 23. Also see, Bratindranath Mukhopadhyaya, *Śaktir Rūp Bhārate O Madhya Asiāy*, Ananda Publishers Ltd, Calcutta, 1990, pp. 14–24.
22. Hazra, *Upapurāṇas*, Vol. II, p. 24.
23. Sukumar Sen, *The Great Goddess in Indic Tradition*, Papyrus, Calcutta, 1983, p. 22.
24. Hazra, *Upapurāṇas*, Vol. II, p. 24.
25. B.P. Sinha, 'Evolution of Śakti Worship in India', in D.C. Sircar (ed.), *The Śakti Cult and Tārā*, University of Calcutta, Calcutta, 1967, p. 50.
26. Ingalls, 'Foreword', to Brown, *God as Mother*, p. xiii.
27. In the *Mahābhārata* this attempt is reflected in the two eulogies to the goddess, contained in the *Virāṭa* and the *Bhīṣmaparvans* respectively. In the former Yudhiṣṭhira sang a hymn to Durgā and in the latter Arjuna sang in praise of Durgā for victory in the imminent war. In the critical edition of the *Mahābhārata*, edited by V.S. Sukthankar and others, both these hymns have been considered later interpolations and therefore relegated to the appendices, see Vol. 5: *The Virāṭaparvan*, Raghu Vira (ed.), Bhandarkar Oriental Research Institute, Poona, 1936, Appendices 1–4 (A–G) and Vol. 7: *The Bhīṣmaparvan*, S.K. Belvalkar (ed.), Bhandarkar Oriental Research Institute, Poona, 1947, Appendix 1.1. Moreover, in the *Virāṭaparvan* of the critical edition, seven different versions of the hymn are given, ranging in length from eight to eighty-seven lines, with some verses common to multiple versions. The *Bhīṣmaparvan* of the critical edition gives only a single version of the hymn, but there exist a number of variant readings. Similarly, in the *Harivaṁśa*, hymns to the goddess are scattered in book II (*Viṣṇuparvan*), Chapters 2–4 and 22 in Panchanan Tarkaratna (ed.), Vangabasi Press, Calcutta, 1312 BS, but many of these are considered interpolations in the critical edition of the text and included in the appendices, see P.L. Vaidya (ed.), 2 Vols, Bhandarkar Oriental Research Institute, Poona, 1969 and 1971. In order to avoid confusion I have refrained from citing individual verses.
28. For example, *Viṣṇu Purāṇa*, V.1; *Bhaviṣya Purāṇa*, IV.138; *Varāha Purāṇa*, chapters 21–8 and 90–6, etc., cited in Hazra, *Upapurāṇas*, Vol. II, p. 17, n. 60.
29. *Mārkaṇḍeya Purāṇa*, Chapters 81–93.
30. Coburn, *Devī-Māhātmya*, pp. 89–302. Tracy Pintchman, in her recent study of the evolution of the goddess tradition from the *Vedas* to the *Purāṇas*, has also shown how the great goddess developed over time as a result of the blending of brahmanical and non-brahmanical religious trends and divinities, even though the essential identity of the goddess as 'Great' was initially constructed in and by the brahmanical tradition, which provided the context for her definition. 'Many of the goddesses

and stories are not originally Vedic-Brahmanical, but the framework and the principles are both taken straight from the Vedas and the orthodox Brahmanical philosophical systems', *The Rise of the Goddess in the Hindu Tradition*, Sri Satguru Publications (a division of Indian Book Centre), Delhi, 1997, p. 16 and *passim*.

31. *Ṛg Veda*, 10.125.
32. The assimilation of the non-Vedic goddess into the brahmanical fold was achieved in the *Devī-Māhātmya*, and the later religious literature upheld it. But the secular literature was under no such obligation, and to the extent Sanskrit literary convention permits realism, they are expected to reflect objective condition as it existed. There are several references to the goddess, particularly in Sanskrit prose literature from the seventh century onwards, and they all confirm the terrible aspect of the goddess in which form she was worshipped by the tribals. For instance, Bāṇabhaṭṭa in his *Kādambarī* and *Harṣacarita* refers to the Śavara practice of animal and human sacrifice to the goddess. *Caṇḍī-śataka*, a text consisting of a series of independent stanzas also ascribed to Bāṇabhaṭṭa, is almost completely preoccupied with the theme of the victory of the goddess over the buffalo demon. Subandhu, a near contemporary of Bāṇa, in his *Vāsavadattā* mentions the bloodthirsty goddess Bhagavatī or Kātyāyanī of Kusumapura. But the most revealing information can be found in *Gauḍavaho*, a Prākrit *kāvya*, composed by Vākpati in the first half of the eighth century. A vivid picture of the atmosphere of the temple of Vindhyavāsinī is presented in which the destructive character of the goddess is emphasized. It refers to the daily human sacrifice before the goddess of the Śavaras, and the goddess herself is addressed as Śavarī in the text. Further light on her worship is shed by *Kathāsaritsāgara* of Somadeva, belonging to the eleventh century. One of its stories relates that one Jīmūtavāhana was captured by the robbers who led him in chains to a temple of Durgā in a Śavara village to sacrifice him as a victim before the goddess. Similar incidence of human sacrifice to the goddess Caṇḍikā is narrated in the story of Śrīdatta and Mṛgāṅkavatī. See A.K. Bhattacharya, 'A Nonaryan Aspect of the Devī', in Sircar (ed.), *The Śakti Cult*, pp. 58–9, J.N. Tiwari, *Goddess Cults in Ancient India*, Sundeep Prakashan, Delhi, 1985, pp. 66–7, Bhattacharyya, *Indian Mother Goddess*, p. 54. This shows that although integration was accomplished at the textual level, in actual practice the votaries of the goddess continued to worship her in their traditional forms for a long time and goddess worship was not brought within the mainstream of brahmanical religion until very late, after a good deal of compromise with heretical faiths such as Tantrism.
33. Majumdar, *Ancient Bengal*, pp. 21–5.
34. Ramaprasad Chanda, *The Indo-Aryan Races: A Study of the Origin of*

Indo-Aryan People and Institutions, Indian Studies: Past and Present, Calcutta, 1969 (originally published in 1916), p. 81.

35. *Ibid.*, p. 81. Chanda further argues that the concept of *śakti* very probably arose in a society where 'matriarchate or mother-kin' was prevalent, which makes his attempt to locate the origin of goddess worship among the Indo-Aryans of the outer countries even more vulnerable. In any case we assume that by mother-kin he meant matriliny and the importance of matrilateral kinship. Matriarchy, however, if meant as an antithesis of patriarchy, is a historical fallacy. See, for instance, Margaret Ehrenberg, *Women in Prehistory*, British Museum Publications, London, 1989; Joan Bamberger, 'The Myth of Matriarchy: Why Men Rule in Primitive Society', in M.Z. Rosaldo and L. Lamphere (eds), *Women, Culture and Society*, Stanford University Press, Stanford, California, 1974, pp. 263–80; Susan Pollock, 'Women in a Men's World: Images of Sumerian Women', in Joan M. Gero and Margaret W. Conkey (eds), *Engendering Archaeology: Women and Prehistory*, Basil Blackwell Ltd, Oxford, 1994, pp. 366–87. Yet a number of Marxist scholars of early Indian history, such as Debiprasad Chattopadhyaya (*Lokāyata: A Study in Ancient Indian Materialism*, People's Publishing House, New Delhi, 1978, originally published in 1959, pp. xx, 252–62), N.N. Bhattacharyya (*Indian Mother Goddess*, pp. 71–3) and D.D. Kosambi ('On the Origin of the Brahmin Gotra', *Journal of the Bombay Branch of the Royal Asiatic Society*, New Series, Vol. 26, 1951, pp. 70–1) have not only accepted the existence of matriarchy but also posited a direct correspondence between matriarchy and goddess worship in India. However, few scholars now adhere to the view that matriarchy was a historical stage that preceded patriarchy. See, for instance, Carolyn Fluehr-Lobban, 'A Marxist Reappraisal of the Matriarchate' and Rudiger Schott, 'Comments on Fluehr-Lobban', in *Current Anthropology*, Vol. 20, June 1979. When the very existence of matriarchy is doubtful, the theory that the goddess is an ideological expression of such a social organization becomes equally suspect. Besides, many scholars have argued that there is no logical equivalence in any society between exalted female objects of worship and a relatively high position for women. See, for instance, Marina Warner, *Alone of All Her Sex: The Myth and the Cult of the Virgin Mary*, Picador published by Pan Books, London, 1985, and Paula Webster, 'Matriarchy: A Vision of Power', in Rayna R. Reiter (ed.), *Toward an Anthropology of Women*, Monthly Review Press, New York and London, 1975. D.R. Ehrenfels, the strongest proponent of the existence of matriarchy in India (see *Mother-Right in India*, Oxford University Press, Hyderabad, 1941), discovered that in the pantheon of the matrilineal Khasis the creator deity is not conceived in exclusively feminine terms, but is a combination of 'He God creator' and 'She God perpetuator' (U.R. Ehrenfels [sic], 'The Double Sex Character of the Khasi Great Deity', in L.P. Vidyarthi (ed.), *Aspects of Religion in*

Indian Society, Kedar Nath Ram Nath, Meerut, undated, pp. 268–72). It is reasonable to argue that the recognition of the generative powers of women in prehistoric societies could have contributed to the conception of a deity that ran parallel to the mortal female in some of her attributes, but when the goddess was finally assimilated into the brahmanical pantheon and the concept of *śakti* was formulated in its fullest elaboration in the *Devī-Māhātmya*, social organization was undeniably patriarchal.

36. Ashok Mitra (ed.), *Paśchimbaṅger Pūjā-pārvan O Melā*, Vol. I, The Controller of Publications, Delhi, 1969, p. 0.10.
37. Binoy Ghosh, *Paśchimbaṅger Saṁskṛti*, Vol. 4, Prakash Bhavan, Calcutta, 1986, pp. 1–13, particularly p. 6.
38. Cited in Shashibhushan Dasgupta, *Bhārater Śakti-Sādhanā O Śākta Sāhitya*, Sahitya Samsad, Calcutta, 1367 BS, pp. 5–6. It should, however, be remembered that names in themselves are a very inadequate guide to the origin of a goddess. Some names are unmistakably non-Sanskritic, such as Jhakbuḍī, and there is no confusion about them. Problem arises with those Sanskritic names which sound so tantalizingly brahmanical and are yet not mentioned in the brahmanical texts. Sarvamaṅgalā, literally one who ensures the welfare of all, a fairly popular goddess of the city of Burdwan, could well have been the name of a brahmanical goddess, but she is not mentioned in any text. Who is she then? Bhīmā is an uncommon name, but she has a reliable Sanskritic ancestry. Is Bargabhīmā of Tamluk a transformation of the 'authentic' Bhīmā or a local goddess? Is Jayadurgā an extension of Durgā or is it merely a case of accidental similarity in names? (*ibid.*, pp. 6–7.) The difficulty is that it is not a straight choice between a tribal and a brahmanical goddess. The goddess, from her non-brahmanical origin to brahmanical adoption and later diversification, has undergone so many intermediate stages of development that the names have become practically unrecognizable.

Then there are the synthetic local goddesses. Since the predisposition in Bengal is towards goddess worship, when a new village is settled, it will almost invariably have a presiding goddess. The original settlers may bring their goddess along with them. If it is a *brāhmaṇa* family, the deity is likely to be brahmanical; if not, any other goddess of the original settlers. We have a strange coincidence where all villages of the Burdwan and Midnapur districts, which have Raṅkiṇī Devī as their presiding deity, are called Moula. She is originally said to have resided in a hill near Mohulia in Singbhum and Binoy Ghosh suggests that it is a case of diffusion where the founders of these villages carried not merely the name of the deity but also the name of the place (*Paśchimbaṅger Saṁskṛti*, Vol. 4, pp. 89–94). There is not much problem with such names.

But if this is not the case, then a goddess is created, through the concoction of a local myth or a dream; the possibilities are endless. The creation of such a deity is not necessarily the result of a cunning design but of a willing suspension of disbelief, and once, in a generation or two, she passes into the local folklore, she is firmly ensconced and another goddess is added to the ever-increasing family of goddesses. More often than not, such a goddess will be given a name with a Sanskritic flavour. These are very deceptive names and cannot be judged at their face value. Let me suggest an imaginary example. 'The Goddess' appears on her mount of swan in a dream to the local landlord and says, 'Institute my worship in the village. I will protect your people'. This is done, the icon replicates the dream image, and she is named Haṁseśvarī. Now, this name will have a misleading allusion to Sarasvatī while there may be no connection between the two, except that by some quirk of imagination on the part of the landlord she appeared on a mount of swan.

There are other kinds of complications too. Since in the *Devī-Māhātmya* the goddess is primarily Caṇḍī, this may be said to be the paradigmatic Sanskritic name for the goddess. Yet Dalton writes that Caṇḍī is the goddess of chase for the Orāons and she is always invoked preparatory to their starting on great hunting expeditions (E.T. Dalton, *Descriptive Ethnology of Bengal*, Indian Studies: Past and Present, Calcutta, 1973, originally published in 1872, p. 264.) Is the Caṇḍī of the *Devī-Māhātmya* taken from the Orāon hunting goddess? It seems unlikely, because at the time of the composition of this text the Orāons of eastern India possibly did not come in intimate contact with the brahmanical culture to be able to so decisively influence it. Is the Caṇḍī of the Orāons a case of adaptation of the Sanskritic goddess on their way to progressive brahmanization? That also appears to be a remote possibility, for Dalton says that any bit of rock, or stone, or excrescence on a rock, serves to represent the Orāon deity. If she was a borrowed goddess, some other Sanskritic features would also have been visible. Are they two entirely separate deities then? Bengal has a spate of Caṇḍīs—Olāi Caṇḍī, Nāṭāi Caṇḍī, Basan Caṇḍī, Nācan Caṇḍī and many more. The contexts in which they appear seem to suggest that there is no connection between them and the Caṇḍī of the *Devī-Māhātmya*, or, more precisely, they are not derived from the *Devī-Māhātmya*, although there is a connection. A major purpose of the Bengal *Purāṇas* was to establish that connection. The connection is made through Maṅgalacaṇḍī of the Bengal *Purāṇas*, but in this Purāṇic form she is nowhere worshipped in Bengal. Names are thus a very insufficient index. It is necessary to have the entire context—iconography, rituals, priests and other associations—to determine the origin of a particular goddess. Unfortunately, the vernacular literature in which they find mention does not supply such details except in a few cases. We are therefore left with no option but to deduce as much as we can from the names.

39. Atindra Majumdar, *Caryāpada*, Naya Prakash, Calcutta, 1981, pp. 119–84.
40. Risley, *The Tribes and Castes of Bengal*, Vol. I, pp. 41–2.
41. *Ibid.*, pp. 115–16.
42. *Ibid.*, pp. 124–5.
43. *Ibid.*, pp. 177–8.
44. *Ibid.*, pp. 187–8.
45. *Ibid.*, pp. 245–6.
46. *Ibid.*, pp. 380–1.
47. *Ibid.*, p. 457.
48. *Ibid.*, pp. 498–9.
49. *Ibid.*, p. 509.
50. Risley, *The Tribes and Castes of Bengal*, Vol. II, pp. 103–4.
51. *Ibid.*, pp. 143–7.
52. *Ibid.*, pp. 232–4.
53. *Ibid.*, p. 244.
54. For instance Siṅg-Boṅgā, who stands at the head of the Muṇḍā pantheon, is a beneficient but somewhat inactive deity, who is not concerned with human affairs, and leaves the details of the executive government of the world to other members of the pantheon in charge of particular departments of nature. Similarly Ṭhākur, the supreme deity of the Sāntāls, has long ceased to receive worship for the reason that he is by and large indifferent to the fate of mankind. *Ibid.*, pp. 103, 232.
55. Basu, *Hindu Samājer Gaḍan*, p. 37.
56. Dalton, *Descriptive Ethnology*, p. 231.
57. *veśyāsu gopavālāsu tuḍahūṇakhaseṣu ca* I
pīṭhe himavataścālpajālandhara-savaidiśe II
mahodare varendre ca rāḍhāyāṁ kośale pure I
bhoṭṭadeśe sakāmākhye kiṣkindhye ca nagottame II
malaye kolunāme ca kāñcyāñca hastināpure I
ujjayinyāñca tā vidyā viśeṣeṇa vyavasthitāḥ II
DP, 39.143–5.
58. *śaravarṣavaraiścāpi pulindaiścāpi pūjyase* I
vindhyavāsini vāsaughe amoghe ambike śubhe II
DP, 127.110–11.
Hazra suggests that the compound *śaravarṣavaraiścāpi* should possibly read *śavarair varvaraiś cāpi*. Hazra, *Upapurāṇas* Vol. II, p. 17, n. 62.
59. *madhyagaṁ kāmarūpasya kāmākhyā yatra nāyikā* I
. . . .
kirātairvalibhiḥ krūrairajñairapi ca vāsitaḥ II
KP, 38.95–6.
In fact, the hostility of the Kirātas towards the brahmanical gods, such as Nārāyaṇa, forms the central theme of the narrative of this chapter.
60. *hemakūṭe mahendre himādrau mahīdhāriṇi vindhyasahyālaye śrīgirau*

saṁsthite, and *śailaśṛṅgeṣu tuṅgeṣu nityaṁ vata kandaravāsini. DP*, 17.17 and 17.23. Chapter 38 of the same text is full of references to the association of the goddess with the mountains.

61. *mṛgendrairgṛhītaṁ gajendrairvibhinnaṁ... khagendrairviluptaṁ bhujaṅgaiśca daṣṭaṁ... vane cāpi mūḍhaṁ raṇe hīyamānaṁ... māteva saṁrakṣase putravannityaśaḥ. DP*, 17.26.

62. *dadyācca digvaliṁ śakra sarvadikṣu samanvitaḥ I*
bhūtavetālasaṁghasya mantreṇānena suvrata II
jaya tvaṁ kāli bhūteśi sarvabhūtasamāvṛte I
rakṣa māṁ nijabhūtebhyo baliṁ gṛhṇa śivapriye II
DP, 31.15–16.

The goddess is also described as *mṛgendradhvaje* in *DP*, 17.17, showing her intimate association with lion who serves the goddess as her mount.

63. *ghaṇṭāravodgītakarṇotsave*
DP, 17.23.

64. *picchadhvaje*
DP, 17.17.

65. *kanyā devyā svayaṁ proktā kanyārūpā tu śūlinī I*
yāvadakṣatayoniḥ syāt tāvaddevyā surārihā II
DP, 35.17–18.

Also *kanyārūpā mahābhāgā* in the same text, 7.39.

66. *DP*, chapters 14 to 20, 40 to 42, and 83 to 88.

67. *tvaṁ devī pararakṣā no brahmādīnāṁ bhayārṇave I*
DP, 42.2.

68. *rudhiramāṁsamadyapriye*
DP, 9.56.

69. *pakṣiṇaḥ kacchapā grāhā matsyā navavidhā mṛgāḥ I*
mahiṣo godhikā gāvaśchāgo ruruśca śūkaraḥ II
khaḍgaśca kṛṣṇasāraśca godhikā śarabho hariḥ I
śārddūlaśca naraścaiva svagātrarudhiraṁ tathā II
caṇḍikābhairavādīnāṁ balayaḥ parikīrttitāḥ II
KP, 67.3–5.

70. The following verses in *KP*, 67.19–20, 77–94, 106–8, 131–2, 141–3 discuss human sacrifice. The goddess is said to be satisfied for a thousand years with a single human sacrifice and for a hundred thousand years with three human sacrifices. The procedure for the preparation of human sacrifice is laid down in some detail. *Mantras* to be uttered on such occasions include: since death is inevitable, die and protect me along with my sons, ministers and friends. Those fit for sacrifice are classified. For example, a prince cannot be sacrificed, but the son of a defeated king can. A set of omens associated with the act of human sacrifice are also mentioned. If the severed head laughs, the enemy of the sacrificer is destroyed, but if it roars, the kingdom is harmed—and so on.

71. *siṁhaṁ vyāghraṁ narañcāpi svagātrarudhiraṁ tathā* I
na dadyād brāhmaṇo madyam mahādevyai kadācana II
and again,
avaśyaṁ vihitaṁ yatra madyaṁ tatra dvijaḥ punaḥ I
nārikelajalaṁ kāṁsye tāmre vā visrjenmadhu II
KP, 67.50, 67.120.

72. . . . *pulindaśavarādiṣu* I
lokāntareṇa mārgeṇa vāmācāreṇa siddhidā II
DP, 39.142.

73. *DbP*, III.6.7–25. Repetitions have been omitted in the translation.

74. *MbP*, 45.3–10.

75. Mārkaṇḍeya eulogized Viṣṇu in the following words:
sahasraśirasaṁ devaṁ nārāyaṇamanāmayam I
vāsudevamanādhāraṁ praṇato'smi janārddanam II
ameyamajaraṁ nityaṁ sadānandaikavigraham I
apratarkyamanirddeśyaṁ praṇato'smi janārddanam II
akṣaraṁ paramaṁ nityaṁ viśvākṣaṁ viśvasambhavam I
sarvvatattvamayaṁ śāntaṁ praṇato'smi janārddanam II
purāṇaṁ puruṣaṁ siddhaṁ sarvvajñānaikabhājanam I
parātparataraṁ rūpaṁ praṇato'smi janārddanam II
paraṁ jyotiḥ paraṁ dhāma pavitraṁ paramaṁ padam I
sarvvaikarūpaṁ paramaṁ praṇato'smi janārddanam II
taṁ sadānandacinmātraṁ parāṇāṁ paramaṁ param I
sarvvaṁ sanātanaṁ śreṣṭhaṁ praṇato'smi janārddanam II
saguṇaṁ nirguṇaṁ śāntaṁ māyātītaṁ sumāyinam I
svarūpaṁ vahurūpaṁ taṁ praṇato'smi janārddanam II
tatra tadbhagavān viśvaṁ srjatyavati hanti ca I
tamādidevamīśānaṁ praṇato'smi janārddanam II
BnP, 5.24–31.

The passage describes Viṣṇu as the supreme divinity. Unqualified and omnipotent, he is the cause of the cause, both formless and has multiple manifestations. This sounds like an echo of the passage above, with the goddess substituted by Viṣṇu. But there is an even more interesting passage where the goddess herself is addressing her *iṣṭadeva* Kṛṣṇa in identical terms, thus:
kṛṣṇa jānāsi māṁ bhadra nāhaṁ tvāṁ jñātumiśvarī I
ke vā jānanti vedajñā vedā vā vedakārakāḥ II
tvadaṁśāstvāṁ na jānanti kathaṁ jñāsyanti tvatkalāḥ I
tvañcāpi tattvaṁ jānāsi kimanye jñātumīśvarāḥ II
sūkṣmāt sūkṣmatamo'vyaktaḥ sthūlāt sthūlatamo mahān I
viśvastvaṁ viśvarūpaśca viśvavijaḥ sanātanaḥ II
kāryaṁ tvaṁ kāraṇaṁ tvañca kāraṇāñca kāraṇam I

tejaḥsvarūpo bhagavānnirākāro nirāśrayaḥ ॥
nirlipto nirguṇaḥ sākṣī svātmārāmaḥ parātparaḥ ।
prakṛtiśo virāḍvījaṁ virāḍrūpastvameva ca ॥
saguṇastvaṁ prākṛtikaḥ kalayāsṛṣṭihetave ।
prakṛtistvaṁ pumāṁstvñca ca vedānyo na kvacidbhavet ॥

BvP, III.7.110–15.

In a spirit of abject surrender, Pārvatī assigns to Kṛṣṇa the highest position in the divine hierarchy. Kṛṣṇa is not only the cause of this universe, but he is also both *puruṣa* and *prakṛti,* lord of *prakṛti* and beyond the perception of *prakṛti. Prakṛti* is merely a part of his part.

76. For example, *śakti* declares:

śivo brahmā tathā tvañca [viṣṇu] na bhinnā vai kadācana ।
manmayāḥ khalu yūyaṁ yat tasmādbhinnā na vo'pyaham ॥
abhinnānāñca bhedārthī nārakī paramo mataḥ ।

BP, II.11.96–7.

or Brahmā says:

yathā vayaṁ yathā viṣṇuryathā devo maheśvaraḥ ।
tathā saṁpūjanīyastu avicāreṇa bhāvitaḥ ॥

DP, 76.47.

Such statements are often put in the mouth of Brahmā, because he does not have a sectarian following. He is the neutral high god of Puranic Hinduism and therefore can safely articulate such sentiments without prejudice to the one or the other sects.

77. *yathāruci bhavet sarvā devatā phalataḥ samā ।*
bhajennākaṁ parāṁ nindan bhajate narakāya tat ॥

BP, III.6.97.

78. *DP*, 87.24–32.

79. All the major authors of the *Tantras* in Bengal, such as Parivrājakācārya, Sarvānanda, Kṛṣṇānanda Āgamavāgīśa, Brahmānanda Giri, Pūrṇānanda and Gauḍīya Śaṁkara lived and worked during this period. See S.C. Banerji, *Tantra in Bengal: A Study in its Origin, Development and Influence*, Naya Prakash, Calcutta, 1978, pp. 74–103.

80. Agehananda Bharati, in his exhaustive study of both the philosophical content and the method of worship of the *Tantras*, has observed that what distinguishes Tantric from other Hindu and Buddhist teachings is its systematic emphasis on the identity of the absolute (*paramārtha*) and the phenomenal (*vyavahāra*) world when filtered through the experience of *sādhanā*. Tantric literature does not belong to the philosophical genre and there is no intrinsic difference between Tantric and non-Tantric philosophy, as speculative eclecticism is pervasive. The difference is in the practical or the *sādhanā* aspect of Tantrism, Bharati, *The Tantric Tradition*, pp. 17–18. Indeed, the *Tantras* disapprove of philosophy as a means

to salvation. The *Kāmākhyātantra* says, as the thirsty deer comes back from a mirage unsatisfied, similarly those who seek salvation are let down by philosophy. One achieves release from bondage through the grace of the *guru*. He may then indulge in philosophical speculation in order to satisfy his curiosity, Upendra Kumar Das, *Śāstramūlak Bhāratīya Śakti-sādhanā*, Vol. I, Visva-Bharati, Shantiniketan and Calcutta, 1373 BS, p. 357.

81. Dasgupta, *Bhārater Śakti-Sādhanā*, pp. 12–13.

82. R.S. Sharma, 'Material Milieu of Tantricism', in R.S. Sharma (ed.), *Indian Society: Historical Probings: In Memory of D.D. Kosambi*, Peoples Publishing House, New Delhi, 1974, p. 175.

83. R.S. Sharma has argued that, 'Tantricism . . . was the ultimate product of the brahmanical colonization of the tribal area through the process of land grants . . . . The confrontation between the brāhmaṇa beneficiaries and the tribal people created social and economic problems which were partly solved through tantricism. On the one hand the new religion welcomed in its ranks women, śūdras and the incoming aborigines; on the other it recognized the existing social and feudal hierarchy. Therefore, it was acceptable to all sections of the people. It was a religious attempt at social reconciliation and integration . . . '. *Ibid.*, p. 189. Land grants did open up peripheral areas for penetration of brahmanical ideas, but Tantrism does not seem to have been a product of this process. At least in Bengal, Tantric practices almost certainly existed prior to the arrival of the *brāhmaṇas* and the resulting interaction left a greater imprint on brahmanism than the other way round. For example, after a detailed study of the linguistic peculiarities of the *DP*, R.C. Hazra has come to the conclusion that the language of this *Purāṇa* goes back to a much earlier period. This conclusion is supported by the Tantric *mantras* and *vidyās* recorded in it as well as in the striking similarity it has in some respects with the *Mahāvastu*. Undeniably, the Tantric *vidyās*, and more particularly the Tantric *mantras*, are not in every case new creations of the individual authors, but have long traditions behind them. Frequent reference to *Āgamas* and *Tantras* as authorities and the mention of a good number of them by name in the text show that a rich Tantric literature had developed before the composition of the *DP* and that this work derives its *vidyās* and *mantras* from these *Āgamas* and *Tantras*. Hazra, *Upapurāṇas*, Vol. II, p. 145. As a matter of fact, *DP* explicitly states with regard to a particular *mahāvidyā* called *Mantramālā* that Śiva compiled it from ten million works and gave it the name of *Mūlatantra*.

The Devī said,

kailāsapīṭhamadhyasthaṁ vīreśāṁ paramaṁ prabhum I
uktā ya ca mahāvidyā mūlatantre tvayā prabho I

koṭigranthāt samāhitya sarvakarmapravartakī ||

DP, 9.65.

Tantrism is a set of practices which assumes the shape of the vessel in which it is contained. Brahmanical recognition of Tantrism often led to substantial modification of many brahmanical rituals in Bengal; which then passed in the name of brahmanism and created the necessary condition for an easier acceptance of the syncretistic Puranic package, thus facilitating integration. It seems, therefore, that Sharma has put the cart before the horse in concluding that Tantrism was the result of 'the brahmanical colonization' of the tribal areas.

84. *adhunā śrotumicchāmi dīkṣālakṣaṇamuttamam |*
vinā yena na sidhyante devīmantreo'dhikāritā ||
brāhmaṇānāṁ kṣatriyāṇāṁ viśāṁ strīṇāṁ tathaiva ca |
DbP, XII, 7.2–3.

85. *vedaṁ na śṛṇuyācchūdrāḥ śṛṇuyācca purāṇakam |*
āgamaṁtu paṭhecchūdro guruṇā dīyate tu yat ||
BP, III, 4.19.

86. *śūdrebhyo mantradānañca purāṇaśrāvaṇaṁ tathā |*
āpaddharmaḥ samuddiṣṭo brāhmaṇasya ca nānyathā ||
BP, III.4.22.

87. *strībālavṛddhaśūdraistu hotavyaṁ pratyahaṁ yathā |*
DP, 121.5.

88. *DP*, chapter 126.
89. Cited in Teun Goudriaan, 'Introduction, History and Philosophy', in Sanjukta Gupta, Dirk Jan Hoens and Teun Goudriaan, *Hindu Tantrism*, E.J. Brill, Leiden/Koln, 1979, p. 15.
90. Cited in Das, *Śāstramūlak Bhāratīya Śaktisādhanā*, Vol. II, pp. 1015–17.
91. Cited in Goudriaan, 'Introduction, History and Philosophy', p. 16.
92. Cited in Das, *Śāstramūlak Bhāratīya Śaktisādhanā*, Vol. II, p. 1021.
93. Shibchandra Vidyarnaba Bhattacharya, *Tantratattva*, Navabharat Publishers, Calcutta, 1389 BS, pp. 46–50.
94. Teun Goudriaan, 'Hindu Tantric Literature in Sanskrit', in Teun Goudriaan and Sanjukta Gupta, *Hindu Tantric and Śākta Literature*, Otto Harrassowitz, Wiesbaden, 1981, p. 20.
95. *MbP*, 8.81–6.
96. *āgamaścaiva vedaśca dvau vāhu mama śaṁkara |*
tābhyameva dhṛtaṁ sarvvaṁ jagat sthāvara jaṅgamam ||
yastvetau laṅghaenmohāt kadācidapi mūḍhadhīḥ |
soo'dhaḥ pātati hastābhyām galito nātra saṁśayaḥ ||
yaścāgamaṁ vā vedaṁ vā samulaṅghyānyathā bhajet |
tamuddhartumaśaktāhaṁ satyameva maheśvaraḥ ||
dvāvevaśreyasāṁhetudurūhāvāti durghaṭau |
sudhībhirapidurjñeyaupārāpāravivarjitau ||

vivicyavānayoraikyaṁ matimān dharmamācaret I
kadācidapi mohena bhedayenna vicakṣaṇaḥ II
MbP, 8.87–91.

97. *āgamasya bhavān kartā vedakartā hariḥ svayam* II
ādāvāgamakarttṛtve bhavān vai viniyojitaḥ I
paścādvai vedakarttṛtve hariḥ samyaṅniyojitaḥ II
. . . . . .
tantramantrāstu me gopyā vaiṣṇavācāraśālibhiḥ II
tasmānmaddīkṣakāḥ śambho bhaveyuḥ śāktavaiṣṇavāḥ I
BP, II.6.138–9, 144–5.

98. *yaścāgamaṁ vā vedaṁ vā vilaṅghyānyatamaṁ bhajet* I
tasyāhaṁ vikalāṅgābhyāṁ samuddhartumaśaktikā II
BP, II.6.142.

99. *pūjādravyaṁ susaṁsthāpya yathāśaktyanusārataḥ* I
prāṇāyāmaṁ tataḥ kṛtvā bhūtaśuddhiṁ vidhāya ca II
kuryād prāṇapratiṣṭhāṁ tu sambhāraṁ prokṣya mantrataḥ I
kālajñānaṁ tataḥ kṛtvā nyāsaṁ kuryād yathāvidhi II
śubhe tāmramaye pātre candanena sitena ca I
ṣaṭkoṇaṁ vilikhed yantraṁ cāṣṭakoṇaṁ tato vahiḥ II
navākṣarasya mantrasya vījāni vilikhettataḥ I
kṛtvā yantrapratiṣṭhañca vedoktāṁ saṁvidhāya ca II
arccāṁ vā dhātavīṁ kuryād pūjāmantraiḥ śivoditaiḥ I
pūjanaṁ pṛthivīpāla bhagavatyāḥ prayatnataḥ II
kṛtvā vā vidhivat pūjāmāgamoktāṁ samāhitaḥ I
japennavākṣaraṁ mantraṁ satataṁ dhyānapūrvakam II
DbP, V.34.5–10.

100. *prātarutthāya śirasi saṁsmaret padmamujjvalam* I
karpūrābhaṁ smarettatra śrīguruṁ nijarūpiṇam II
suprasannaṁ lasadbhūṣābhūṣitaṁ śaktisaṁyutam I
namaskṛtya tato devīṁ kuṇḍalīṁ saṁsmared budhaḥ II
prakāśamānāṁ prathame prayāṇe, pratiprayāṇeo'pyamṛtāyamānām I
antaḥpadavyāmanusañcaranti-mānandarūpāmavalāṁ prapadye II
dhyātvaivaṁ tacchikhāmadhye saccidānandarūpiṇīm I
māṁ dhyāyedatha śaucādi-kriyāḥ sarvvāḥ samācaret II
agnihotraṁ tato hutvā matprītyarthaṁ dvijottamaḥ I
homānte svāsane sthitvā pūjāsaṁkalpamācaret II
bhūtaśuddhiṁ purā kṛtvā mātṛkānyāsameva ca I
hṛllekhāmātṛkānyāsaṁ nityameva samācaret II
mūlādhāre hakārañca hṛdaye ca rakārakam I
bhrūmadhye tadvadīkāraṁ hrīṁkāraṁ mastake nyaset II
tattanmantroditānanyān nyāsān sarvvān samācaret I
kalpayet svātmano dehe pīṭhaṁ dharmādibhiḥ punaḥ II

tato dhyāyenmahādevīṁ prāṇāyāmairvijṛmbhite I
hṛdambhoje mama sthāne pañcapretāsane budhaḥ II

DP, VII. 40.1–9.

101. *toṣayenmāṁ tvatkṛtena nāmnāṁ sāhasrakeṇa ca I*
kavacena ca sūktenāhaṁ rudrebhiriti prabho II
devyatharvvaśiromantrai hṛrlpekhopaniṣadbhavaiḥ I
mahāvidyāmahāmantraistoṣaenmāṁ muhurmuhuḥ II

DbP, VII. 40.21–2.

102. *DP*, 9.56.

103. *siddhāntavedakarmmaṇāmatharvvapadadīpanīm I*
anayā tu samā vidyā na bhūtā na bhaviṣyati II

DP, 9.64.

104. *devīśāstrārthatattvajñairmātṛmaṇḍalavedikaiḥ I*
bhūtatantragrahavālagāruḍeṣu kṛtaśramaiḥ I
pratiṣṭhāntu śivāntaistu yathāśaktyā tu dakṣayet II

DP, 32.43.

105. *DbP*, VII. 39.15–19.

106. *anyāni yāni śāstrāṇi lokeo'smin vividhāni ca I*
śrutismṛtiviruddhāni tāmasānyeva sarvvaśaḥ II
vāmaṁ kāpālakañcaiva kaulakaṁ bhairavāgamaḥ I
śiven mohanārthāya praṇīto nānyahetukaḥ II
dakṣaśāpādbhṛgoḥ śāpāddadhīcasya ca śāptaḥ I
dagdhā ye brāhmaṇavarā vedamārgavahiṣkṛtāḥ II
teṣāmuddharaṇārthāya sopānakramataḥ sadā I
śaivāśca vaiṣṇavāścaiva saurāḥ śāktāstathaiva ca II
gāṇapatyā āgamāśca praṇītāḥ śaṁkareṇa tu II

DbP, VII.39.26–30.

107. Cited in Bhattacharyya, *Tantric Religion*, p. 1.

108. *vāhyāpi dvividhā proktā vaidikī tāntrikī tathā I*

DbP, VII. 39.3.

109. *vaidikī vaidikaiḥ kāryā vedadīkṣāsamanvitaiḥ I*
tantroktadīkṣāvadbhistu tāntrikī saṁśritā bhavet II

DbP, VII. 39.4.

110. *śuddhaṁ smārtaṁ cācamanaṁ paurāṇaṁ vaidikaṁ tathā I*
tāntrikaṁ śrautamityāhuḥ ṣaḍvidhaṁ śrutinoditam II

DbP, XI. 3.1.

111. *tantroktavartmanā siddhaṁ bhasma tāntrikapūjakaiḥ I*
yatra kutrāpi dattaṁ cettadgrāhyam naiva vaidikaiḥ II

DbP, XI.12.11.

112. *purāṇeṣu kvaciccaiva tantradṛṣṭam yathātatham I*
dharmmaṁ vadanti taṁ dharmmaṁ gṛhnīyānna kathañcana II

vedāvirodhi cettantraṁ tat pramāṇaṁ na saṁśayaḥ I
pratyakṣaśrutiviruddhaṁ yattat pramāṇaṁ bhavenna ca II
DbP, XI.1.24–5.

113. *tatra vedāviruddhoo'ṁśoo'pyukta eva kvacit kvacit I*
vaidikaistadgrahe doṣo na bhavatyeva karhicit II
sarvvathā vedabhinnārthe nādhikārī dvijo bhavet I
vedādhikārahīnastu bhavettatrādhikāravān II
DbP, VII. 39.31–2.

114. *DbP*, VII.40.1–27.

115. *āsanāvāhane cārghyaṁ pādyādyācamanaṁ tathā I*
snānaṁ vāsodvayañcaiva bhūṣaṇāni ca sarvvaśaḥ II
gandhapuṣpaṁ yathāyogyaṁ dattvā devyai svabhaktitah II
DbP, VII.40.16–17.

116. *kṣamāpayejjagaddhātrīṁ premārdrahṛdayo naraḥ II*
pulakāṁkitasarvvāṅgairvvāṣparuddhākṣiniḥsvanaḥ I
nṛtyagītādighoṣeṇa toṣaenmāṁ muhurmuhuḥ II
. . . . . .
nityahomaṁ tataḥ kuryād brāhmaṇāṁśca suvāsinīḥ I
vaṭukān pāmarānanyān devībuddhyā tu bhojayet II
natvā punaḥ svahṛdaye vyutkrameṇa visarjjayet II
DbP, VII. 40.23–4, 26–7.

117. G.S. Ghurye, 'Devī: Female Principle Bridges the Gulf Between the Folk and the Elite', *Gods and Men*, Popular Book Depot, Bombay, 1962, pp. 238–63.

118. *Sāṁkhya* philosophy has a long and rather obscure history. From the *Sāṁkhya Kārikā* of Īśvarakṛṣṇa (*c.* AD 200) to the commentaries stretching up to the sixteenth century, it has undergone many changes, although these are more in the nature of details.

119. Surendranath Dasgupta, *A History of Indian Philosophy*, Vol. I, Motilal Banarsidass, Delhi, 1975, pp. 243–8.

120. This is the simile used by Ācārya Mādhava in his *Sarvadarśanasaṁgraha* to explain the relationship between the *prakṛti* and the *puruṣas*. Cited by Ramakant A. Sinari, *The Structure of Indian Thought*, Oxford University Press, Delhi, 1984, pp. 40–1.

121. Dasgupta, *A History of Indian Philosophy*, Vol. I, p. 258.

122. Umeshchandra Bhattacharya, *Bhāratadarśanasāra*, Visva Bharati, Calcutta, 1391 BS, pp. 138–9.

123. Coburn, *Devī-Māhātmya*, pp. 180–6.

124. *prakṛṣṭavācakaḥ praśca kṛtiśca sṛṣṭivācakaḥ I*
sṛṣṭau prakṛṣṭā yā devī prakṛtiḥ sā prakīrtitā II
guṇe sattve prakṛṣṭe ca praśabdo varttate śrutaḥ I
madhyame rajasi kṛśca tiśabdastamasi smṛtaḥ II
triguṇātmasvarūpā yā sā ca śaktisamanvitā I

pradhānā sṛṣṭikaraṇe prakṛtistena kathyate II
prathame varttate praśca kṛtiśca sṛṣṭivācakaḥ I
sṛṣṭerādau ca yā devī prakṛtiḥ sā prakīrtitā II
DbP, IX.1.5–8.

125. Srimohan Bhattacharya and Dinesh Chandra Bhattacharya (eds), *Bhārtīya Darśana Koṣa: Sāṁkhya and Pātañjala Darśana*, Vol. II, Sanskrit College, Calcutta, 1979, p. 44.
126. *mūlaprakṛtirevaiṣā sadā puruṣasaṁgatā* I
brahmāṇḍam darśayatyeṣā kṛtvā vai paramātmane II
DbP, III.3.60.
127. *DbP*, III.4.6.
128. *DbP,* III.4.14–20.
129. *DbP,* III.4.22.
130. *DbP,* III.4.30–2, 43–4.
131. Mukhopadhyay, *Śaktir Rūp*, pp. 14–24.
132. *mūlaprakṛtirekā sā pūrṇabrahmasvarūpiṇī* I
sṛṣṭau pañcavidhā sā ca viṣṇumāyā sanātanī II
prāṇādhiṣṭhātṛdevī yā kṛṣṇasya paramātmanaḥ I
sarvāsāṁ preyasī kāntā sā rādhā parikīrtitā II
nārāyaṇapriyā lakṣmīḥ sarvasampatsvarūpiṇī I
rāgādhiṣṭhātṛdevī yā sā ca pūjyā sarasvatī II
sāvitrī vedamātā ca pūjyarūpā vidheḥ priyā I
śaṁkarasya priyā durgā yasyāḥ putro gaṇeśvaraḥ II
BvP, I.30.17–20.
133. *BvP*, II.1.14–54.
134. *BvP*, II.1.56.
135. *BvP*, II.1.18, 33, 40.
136. *aṁśarūpā kalārūpā kalāṁśāṁśasamudbhavā* I
prakṛteḥ prativiśveṣu devī ca sarvajoṣitaḥ II
BvP, II.1.55.
137. *BvP*, II.1.57, 62, 68, 75, 82, 87, 93.
138. *BvP*, II.1.97–130.
139. *BvP*, II.1.131–7.
140. *vahvyaḥ santi kalāścaivaṁ prakṛtereva bhārate* I
yā yāśca grāmadevyastāḥ sarvāśca prakṛteh kalāḥ II
BvP, II.1.138.
141. Dasgupta, *Bhārater Śakti-Sādhanā*, p. 3.
142. Bhaktimadhab Chattopadhyaya (ed.), *Śūnyapurāṇa*, Firma K.L.M. Pvt. Ltd, Calcutta, 1977, pp. 160, 248.
143. *Mārkaṇḍeya Purāṇa*, 91.37–50.
144. For example see Ruth S. Freed and Stanley A. Freed, 'Two Mother Goddess Ceremonies of Delhi State in the Great and Little Tradition', *Southwestern Journal of Anthropology*, Vol. 18, 1962, pp. 246–77. The

two ceremonies studied are Durga Ashtami and Sili Sat (the Cold Seventh, related to the worship of Śītalā, the goddess of smallpox).

145. Jacob Pandian, 'The Sacred Symbol of the Mother Goddess in a Tamil Village: A Parochial Model of Hinduism', in Gupta (ed.), *Religion in Modern India*, pp. 198–214.

146. Edward O. Henry, 'The Mother Goddess Cult and Interaction Between Little and Great Religious Traditions', in *ibid.*, pp. 174–97.

147. Morris E. Opler, 'Spirit Possession in a Rural Area in Northern India', in William A. Lessa and Evon Z. Vogt (eds), *Reader in Comparative Religion: An Anthropological Approach*, Row, Peterson and Co., New York, 1958, pp. 553–66.

148. Pauline Mahar Kolenda, 'The Functional Relations of a Bhangi Cult', *The Anthropologist* (special volume), 2, 1968, p. 32.

149. Michael Moffatt, *An Untouchable Community in South India: Structure and Consensus*, Princeton University Press, Princeton, 1979, particularly chapter VI entitled 'Replication and Complementarity in Harijan Religion', pp. 219–89.

150. *śāradīya mahāpūjā yā devyāḥ prītidāyikā I*
vārṣikīti tvayā proktā yāṁ cakāra raghūttamaḥ II
MbP, 36.1.

śaratkāle mahāpūjā karttavyā mama sarvadā I
navarātravidhānena bhaktibhāvayutena ca II
DbP, III.24.20.

jaladānte āśvinemāsi mahiṣārinivarhiṇīm I
devīṁ sampūjayitvā tu aṣṭamī hyarddharātriṣu I
ye ghātayanti sadā bhaktyā te bhavanti mahāvalāḥ II
DP, 21.9.

kāle sarveṣu viśveṣu mahāpūjā ca pūjite I
bhavitā prativarṣe ca śāradīya sureśvarī II
BvP, I.6.60.

kathaṁ nu bhavatī bhūtā pitṛrūpā svadhārthinī I
śaratkāle tavārcā vā kathamākālikī śive II
BP, I.17.17.

durgātantreṇa mantreṇa kuryāddurgāmahotsavam I
mahānavamyāṁ śāradi balidānaṁ nṛpādayaḥ II
āśvinasya tu śuklasya bhaved yā aṣṭamī tithiḥ I
mahāṣṭamīti sā proktā devyāḥ prītikarī parā II
KP, 60.1–2.

to cite a few from among many such references.

151. *nādhipatyavicāro'sti na vā varṇavicāraṇā I*
tasyāṁ yasya matiḥ puṇyā tasyaiva sulabhā tu sā II
MbP, 43.86.

sarvatrabhārate loke sarva-varṇeṣu sarvathā I
bhajanīyā bhavānī tu sarveṣāmabhavattadā II

DbP, III.25.44.

sarvasvairapi me pūjā karttavyā tu dinadvayam I
brāhmaṇaḥ kṣatriyo vaiśyaḥ śūdro vā bhaktisaṁyutaḥ II

BP, I.22.30.

karttavyaṁ brāhmaṇādyaistu kṣatriyairbhūmipālakaiḥ I
godhanārthaṁ viśairvatsa śūdraiḥ putrasukhārthibhiḥ II

DP, 22.5.

once again, to cite only a few examples.

152. *tasmācchākto'tha śaivo vā sauro vā vaiṣṇavo'tha vā II*
avaśyaṁ pūjaeddevīṁ śāradīye mahotsave I

MbP, 48.14–15.

durgāsaṁkaṭahantrīti durgeti prathitā bhuvi II
vaiṣṇavānāñca śaivānāmupāsyeyañca nityaśaḥ I

DbP, IX.50.55–6.

153. Women are associated with the annual worship of Durgā, not only as devotees, but also as objects of co-worship. Certain Tantric rituals require worship of unmarried women, but the Bengal *Purāṇas* prescribe worship of married women too, along with the *kumārīs*. For example

devībhaktāṁśca pūjyeta kanyakāḥ pramadāni ca I
dvijān dīnānupāsannān annadānena prīṇayet II

DP, 22.19.

154. *DP*, 17.17, 127.110.

Durgā's association with forest- and mountain-dwelling tribes is not very specifically mentioned, but the Bengal *Purāṇas* are emphatic about this association for the goddesses *per se*, as I have discussed earlier. Brahmanism's attempt to project Durgā as the most acceptable of all the goddesses may explain why this association has been underplayed in her case, but as Durgā, the prime representative of the *mūlaprakṛti,* is also the repository of all the goddesses, the association extends to her as well, even if by implication.

155. *KP*, 61.17, 19–22.
156. James J. Preston, 'Goddess Temples in Orissa: An Anthropological Survey', in Gupta (ed.), *Religion in Modern India*, pp. 229–47.
157. *Supra*, pp. 181, 183–4; also n. 75.
158. R.M. Sarkar, *Regional Cults and Rural Traditions: An Interacting Pattern of Divinity and Humanity in Rural Bengal*, Inter-India Publications, New Delhi, 1985, pp. 182–3.
159. *Ibid.*, p. 305.
160. *Ibid.*, p. 316.
161. *Ibid.*, p. 285.

162. *Ibid.*, p. 291.
163. *BvP*, II.45–6. *DbP*, IX.47–8.
164. *BvP*, II.43.25–6. *DbP*, IX.46.25–6.
165. *Supra*, chapter II, pp. 64–6.
166. For example Mackenzie Brown is of the opinion that the extant *Brahmavaivarta Purāṇa* reached its final form during the fifteenth or sixteenth century, *God as Mother*, p. 29. R.C. Hazra also suggests that from about the tenth century the *Brahmavaivarta Purāṇa* began to be changed by the interfering hands of the Bengal authors who recast it into its present form and content in the sixteenth century, *Purāṇic Records*, p. 166.

VI

Vratas: The Transmission of Brahmanical Culture

I

That civilization, conceived as the product of a continuous interaction between great and little traditions requires a particularly efficient system of communication to function effectively is a truism. Brahmanism attempted to establish its social order in Bengal. A human social order is a cognitive order. 'The set of customs that comprise the constituent roles of a human social system consists of norms and rules—cognitive variables—that either prescribe or regulate behaviour. These norms and rules must be cognized by the members of the society if the social system is to be maintained.'[1]

Indeed, the early proponents of the two-tier theory of Indian society and culture had envisaged India as an intricate network of communication. According to Redfield, a civilization may be thought of as 'a persisting form of arrangements for the handing down of cultural substance (ideas and its products) within a great community . . . and as the characteristic processes for transmitting it.'[2] Singer is even more emphatic: 'The entire "social structure" of social networks of a civilization may function as transmissive channels for the communication of the different levels of tradition among the different communities connected by the networks.'[3] Cohn and Marriott concentrated on the integrative functions of the social and cultural networks creating a continuity of relationships and meanings from the purely local to an all-India level.[4] They especially noted the role of the cultural specialists who were 'expert managers of cultural media' and interceded between a more refined level of learning and the demands of the less learned local markets.[5] Later Marriott explained the change in Indian civilization from a rich old cultural mansion of many levels and varied styles to a more uniform structure with a few levels of standard design in terms of a change from an organization of networks and centres interrelating many territorial sub-cultures (articulated by cultural specialists or 'hinge groups') to the modern rather one-dimensional form of cultural transmission from a few metropolitan centres.[6] For a successful implementation of the brahmanical social order in Bengal institutional channels were required for the regular communication of the contents of the Bengal *Purāṇas*. I suggest that the performance of the *vrata* rite was the occasion for the dissemination of the brāhmanical message in early medieval Bengal.

Religious performance offers an ideal opportunity for communication in traditional societies. As Gumperz observes, the communicative advantages of religious performances are twofold. They differ from other types of social interaction in that they take place in a public location and are capable of simultaneously reaching a large number of diverse social nuclei. Second, by virtue of their religious character they are able to overcome many of the usual limitations of social differentiation. These features make them effective mass communication mediums.[7] We will see that the *vratas*, being congregational and caste and gender neutral in character, had fulfilled both these conditions. Thus the *vratas* provided the most appropriate occasion for the transmission of brahmanical culture.

II

Vrata is a vowed observance, a religious act of devotion and austerity, performed for the fulfilment of specific desires. The antiquity of the term goes back to the *Ṛg Veda* where it meant a variety of things generally related to command or law on the one hand and obedience or duty on the other.[8] During the time of the *Brāhmaṇas* the word had come to acquire two secondary meanings, an appropriate course of conduct and, more specifically, the sacrificer's staying at night near a *gārhapatya* fire, or fasting.[9] The *Śrautasūtras*, *Gṛhyasūtras*, and *Dharmasūtras* also refer to the *vrata* in this sense.

As expiations involved the observance of several strict rules of conduct, they have been described as *vratas* in Manu, Yājñavalkya, Saṁkha and other *Smṛtis*. In the *Mahābhārata* a *vrata* is a religious undertaking or a vow in which one has to observe certain restrictions about food or general behaviour.[10] In the *Purāṇas* the restrictive aspects of the *vrata* are emphasized. It is here called *tapas* because it causes hardship to the performer, and *niyama* because the performer has to restrain his sense organs while observing the *vrata*.[11] However, it is in the medieval *Smṛtis*, which devote long passages to the description of the *vratas*, that the Puranic conception has been fully elaborated. According to Raghunandana, for example, a *vrata* is a complex ritual which involves several items such as *snāna*, morning prayer, *saṁkalpa* (vow), *homa*, worship of the deity in whose honour the *vrata* is undertaken, *upavāsa* (fast), feeding *brāhmaṇas*, maidens and/or married women, *dakṣiṇā* (paying honorarium to the *brāhmaṇas*), and the observance of certain rules of conduct during the period of the *vrata*.[12]

It is precisely in this sense that *vrata* is understood in the Bengal *Purāṇas*. The description of a *vrata* is usually prefaced by the narration of a legend concerning its origin, and a few special regulations are thrown in depending on the context, but the format is by and large the same. The only additional condition the Bengal *Purāṇas* almost invariably impose is that the performers must listen to the recitation of the *Purāṇas*. The following is a summary of the description of a typical Puranic *vrata*:

After the creation of the universe, Viṣṇu created a *pāpapuruṣa* (sin incarnate). Those who served the *pāpapuruṣa* started going to hell. Once Viṣṇu went to the abode of Yama and saw the sinners suffering in hell. He took pity on them and made them observe the *Ekādaśī vrata*. As a result, all the sinners achieved salvation. Seeing that the *Ekādaśī* was the best of *vratas*, the *pāpapuruṣa* told Viṣṇu that if he was destroyed, everybody would be released from the cycle of repeated births and deaths, and Viṣṇu would have no one to play around with in this amusing universe. Therefore he should be assigned a place where he could remain concealed on the *Ekādaśī tithi* (eleventh day of the lunar fortnight). Viṣṇu asked him to take refuge in rice. Hence, it is absolutely forbidden to eat rice on the *Ekādaśī* day. Everybody, including the *brāhmaṇas*, the *kṣatriyas*, the *vaiśyas* and the *śūdras*, should perform the *Ekādaśī vrata*. The rite is as follows: On the tenth day (*daśamī*) the performer should have a bath in the morning and worship Viṣṇu. He should eat only once during the day and fish, meat, salt, honey, overeating, and sexual intercourse are prohibited on this day. In the evening he should go to the temple of Viṣṇu, ask for his protection for the performance of the *vrata* and spend the night there lying on a bed of *kuśa* grass. At night the performers must get together and keep awake along with all the members of their families and friends. The woman who keeps awake with her husband lives in the Viṣṇu temple for ever. Those who draw the symbols of Viṣṇu on the floor of the temple, those who hoist a flag or place an umbrella on the icon of Viṣṇu, and those who make floral designs before the icon are favoured by Viṣṇu. They enjoy all the comforts of life and finally go to the abode of Viṣṇu. Next morning the performer should take his bath and perform the daily rites. Then he should bathe the *śālagrāma* in *pañcāmṛta* (a concoction of milk, curd, clarified butter, honey and sugar), place the icon in front of him, adopt the resolution (*saṁkalpa*) and meditate on Viṣṇu thus: To Nārāyaṇa, who is seated on his golden throne with the beautiful Lakṣmī on his lap, I offer this worship. Please accept this water to wash your feet, this incense, this lamp full of clarified butter, these clothes with the sacred thread, this food and drink and betel leaf. The performer should thus generously offer presents to Viṣṇu every fourth part of the day and night. He should then go round the icon of Viṣṇu and chant his name. It is a sacrilege to talk to a *pāṣaṇḍa* (usually a Buddhist) on this day. If this rule is transgressed, all merits are immediately lost. Then the performer should sing and dance in front of Viṣṇu. Those who do not do so are born crippled and mute in their next lives. The performer must keep awake the whole night and listen to the *Purāṇas*. The *Rāmāyaṇa* and the *Mahābhārata*, the *Bhāgavata* as composed by Vyāsa, or any other Purāṇa should be read. On the next morning, the twelfth day (*dvādaśī*), the devoted performer should bathe Viṣṇu in milk, perform the five *mahāyajñas* and pay gifts and honorarium (*dakṣiṇā*) to the brāhmaṇa to the best of his capability. Then the performer should break his fast. Those who follow this ritual procedure achieve salvation.[13]

This is the standard procedure of the *vratas* that the Bengal *Purāṇas* recommend.

There exists another and less elaborate kind of a *vrata*, certainly much less 'religious', popularly described as *aśāstrīya* (not prescribed by the didactic brahmanical texts) or *meyelī* (belonging to women). The fairly simple procedure of an *aśāstrīya vrata* is as follows. It consists of *āharaṇa* or collection of commonly available and inexpensive articles of daily use for the observance of the rite, *ālpanā* or drawing of standard motifs on the floor, *chaḍā* or recitation of doggerel verses from memory which express the desire behind the performance of the rite, and *kathā* or listening to the story which establishes the justification of the rite. There is no place for the *brāhmaṇa* or sacred hymns in such observances. Unmarried and married women get together to observe the *vrata* for the fulfilment of rather mundane and unostentatious wishes such as a desirable husband or a happy and modestly prosperous life.[14]

A marked aspect of these *vratas* is the imitation of nature in their ritual practice, strongly reminiscent of sympathetic magic. For example, if the purpose of the *vrata* is to bring rain, the participants simply pour water from a jug. Symbolic patterns drawn on house floors are also supposedly imbued with magical qualities, and the presiding deities of these functions are usually personified nature.[15] These characteristics of the *aśāstrīya vrata*, coupled with the fact that they are never even mentioned in the Sanskritic texts, have led scholars to suggest that the *vrata* was originally a non-brahmanical ritual, practised exclusively by women, that was later adopted by Puranic Hinduism to suit a specific purpose.[16] Niharranjan Ray believes that it may not be possible to establish a correlation between the *vrata* and the *vrātyas* on the basis of conclusive evidence, but that is a reasonable assumption. He argues that the religion of the 'Ṛg-vedic Aryans' centred on sacrifice and those who lived beyond the pale of Aryanism, such as the people of the eastern regions, performed the indigenous *vratas* and possibly came to be known as *vrātyas*. Ray reminds us that the etymological meaning of the term *vrata* is to circumscribe, to draw a line in order to distinguish.[17]

Although Ray is somewhat speculative, the non-brahmanical origin of the *vrata* and its ubiquitous association with women is widely acknowledged. Some scholars even suggest that the non-brahmanical gods and goddesses were introduced into brahmanical households by young non-*brāhmaṇa* brides, presumably through their *vrata*-oriented mode of worship of these deities. Thus Ashutosh Bhattacharya points out that according to the vernacular *Maṅgalakāvyas* of medieval Bengal, the young brides Sanakā, Behulā and Khullanā worshipped Manasā and Caṇḍī, but the menfolk of the two families, Chānd Sadāgar and Dhanapati, were inimical to these indigenous local goddesses. Bhattacharya believes that the practice of victorious invaders marrying into local groups may explain the difference in attitude;[18] but brahmanism did not come to Bengal at the head of an invading army. However, if the preoccupation of the Bengal *Purāṇas* with the organization of the caste structure of Bengal and the carefully drawn up hierarchy of the innumerable *saṁkaravarṇas* in these texts are any indication, marriage between *brāhmaṇas* and local people must have been frequent. To that extent Bhattacharya has a point. Dinesh Chandra Sen also suggests that in *brāhmaṇa* households young brides were initiated into the *vrata* rites 'by the non-Aryan people with whom they came in contact and amongst whom the Aryan homes were built'.[19] Sen does not explain why women should be the carriers of this non-brahmanical practice and not men. Whatever be the explanation, if the cumulative evidence of the vernacular literature of medieval Bengal is not entirely dismissed, it seems likely that the non-brahmanical cults and their particular modes of worship were transmitted into the brahmanical homes primarily through the agency of women. It is necessary, therefore, to look closely into the crucial nexus of women–*vratas*–local goddesses.

III

The presiding goddess of a very popular non-brahmanical women's *vrata* of Bengal is Maṅgalacaṇḍī. Maṅgalacaṇḍī is not mentioned in any high-profile Sanskritic text from elsewhere but is rather prominent among the less important goddesses of the Bengal *Purāṇas*. A major *Maṅgalakāvya* was composed in sixteenth-century Bengal in her honour, and printed collections of *vratakathās* and *pāñcālīs* of Maṅgalacaṇḍī are produced even today. When these apparently disparate accounts of the goddess are matched, they reveal an intricate complex of interpenetration of traditions, of survivals and transformations, in the assimilative process spread over a millennium.

The *Devī Purāṇa* refers to a goddess called Maṅgalā who, it says, should be worshipped to ward off evil and attain happiness.[20] Shashibhushan Dasgupta believes that this Maṅgalā is the precursor of the later Maṅgalacaṇḍī. He cites a verse from the *Śabdakalpadruma* which mentions Maṅgalā along with Piṅgalā, Dhanyā, Bhrāmarī, Bhadrikā, Ulkā, Siddhi and Saṁkaṭā as the eight *yoginīs*.[21] Of these, Maṅgalā and Saṁkaṭā are worshipped through *vratas* by Bengali women.[22] But the Sanskritic texts neither recommend nor lay down procedures for the formal worship of these *yoginīs* in the brahmanical way. Dasgupta conjectures that they were non-brahmanical goddesses venerated by women. Therefore brahmanism was willing to accommodate them up to a point but was not prepared to accept them within the brahmanical pantheon as goddesses of independent status.[23]

It is possible that this Maṅgalā was later attached to the Caṇḍī of the *Devī-Māhātmya* section of the *Mārkaṇḍeya Purāṇa* which came to be recognized as the generic name for the high goddess of brahmanism by the Bengal *Purāṇas*, and was elevated to the status of a goddess. That Maṅgalacaṇḍī was a local goddess of non-brahmanical origin is indirectly acknowledged by the *Brahmavaivarta Purāṇa*. It says that Devakī worshipped Bhairavī, the presiding goddess (*grāmadevatā*) of Mathurā, and Ṣaṣṭhī and Maṅgalacaṇḍī on the occasion of the *upanayana* ceremony of Kṛṣṇa and Balarāma.[24] The non-brahmanical association of Maṅgalacaṇḍī is further reinforced by the offerings prescribed for her worship by the *Brahmavaivarta* and the *Devībhāgavata*. They declare that Śiva worshipped Maṅgalacaṇḍī with the sacrifice of sheep, goats, buffaloes, rhinoceros and birds of various kinds.[25] The *Kālikā Purāṇa*, however, categorically recommends human sacrifice and offering of wine to Maṅgalacaṇḍī.[26]

But the tribal connection of Maṅgalacaṇḍī is most unambiguously represented in the *Caṇḍīmaṅgalakāvya*, a long vernacular narrative poem of medieval Bengal. She is portrayed here as the tutelary deity of hunters (*vyādha*). The wild animals of the forest sought her protection against the prowess of Kālaketu, the hunter. She appeared before Kālaketu in the guise of a lizard (*godhikā*) and he became her devotee. Kālaketu later founded a city and, to redeem a promise, propagated the worship of Maṅgalacaṇḍī. Moreover, boar's meat, an absolutely forbidden item in brahmanical religion, is here described as an essential ingredient in the worship of Maṅgalacaṇḍī.[27]

Of all the accessories of the goddess described in the *Caṇḍīmaṅgala*, the lizard has an intriguing continuity in sculptural representations of the goddess in early medieval Bengal. A lizard is engraved on the pedestal of the majority of goddess icons discovered in Bengal.[28] The images of the goddess in association with a lizard are most commonly found in eastern India, especially in Bengal, and the *Rūpamaṇḍana* describes the lizard as the mount of Gaurī.[29] Indeed, the similarity between this iconic motif and the *Caṇḍīmaṅgala* story is so striking that J.N. Banerjee felt tempted to call these icons, collectively, representations of Caṇḍī.[30] It is possible that the connection actually had a historical basis. The *Kālikā Purāṇa* significantly remarks that the goddess is satisfied with the blood of the particular variety of lizard mentioned in the text, the *godhikā*.[31] It is alluring to see in the lizard a totem of a hunting tribe, but there is no evidence at our disposal for such a conclusion. What the cumulative evidence does suggest is that there must have been a substratum of reality for such a long-lasting association to develop. The *Caṇḍīmaṅgala*, in which the connection is most explicit, is a sixteenth-century work. Thus both sculptural representations and Puranic accounts predate it by several centuries.[32] It seems that authors and sculptors drew their material from a common pool of orally transmitted stories which had originated in a non-brahmanical tribal past.

Another clue also tends to confirm this connection. In an anonymous old Bengali verse, still popular, Caṇḍī is described as the daughter of a Hāḍi (Hāḍi-jhi Caṇḍī). The Hāḍi is a menial and scavenger caste of Bengal, occupying one of the lowest social ranks, and is regarded as the remnant of a Hinduized aboriginal tribe. They also have a tradition of sacrificing pigs and eating the flesh to appease the spirit of the dead.[33]

Ashutosh Bhattacharya conjectures that perhaps some daughter of a Hāḍi became known for her mystical powers and was considered a living goddess among the lower castes. Later, the generic name Caṇḍī got attached to this tradition and Hāḍi-jhi merged with Caṇḍī.[34]

We need not look, however, for fragments of elusive evidence to establish a connection between Maṅgalacaṇḍī and women. Both the *Brahmavaivarta* and the *Devībhāgavata* declare that Maṅgalacaṇḍī is the tutelary deity of women[35] who grants their wishes.[36] The *Brahmavaivarta* adds that women worship her with five kinds of offerings,[37] and that Maṅgalacaṇḍī herself, along with Ṣaṣṭhī, Manasā, Ahalyā, Mandodarī and a few others, is a manifested woman (*vāstavā strī*) who appears in every age as the best of them.[38] The *Rūpamaṇḍana* also proclaims that this image is worshipped inside the home[39] and presumably therefore by women. All these statements strengthen the surmise that Maṅgalacaṇḍī was a local deity of tribal origin, adopted by the womenfolk of brahmanical homes, perhaps as the presiding deity of their *vratas*, which they had learnt from the local people. This development compelled the authors of the *Purāṇas* to accept her and led to her eventual admission into the brahmanical pantheon.

Two more abiding traditions on the day and procedure of her worship link Maṅgalacaṇḍī with the *vratas*. The *Kālikā Purāṇa* says that Tuesday is her favourite,[40] and both the *Brahmavaivarta* and the *Devībhāgavata* prescribe that she should be worshipped on Tuesdays.[41] In the *Caṇḍīmaṅgala* the celestial nymphs asked Khullanā to perform the *vrata* of Maṅgalacaṇḍī on every Tuesday,[42] and all the printed manuals on women's *vratakathā* recommend that day for her worship.[43]

Similarly, there exists a uniformity about the ritual procedure. According to the *Brahmavaivarta* and the *Devībhāgavata*, Śiva is said to have worshipped Maṅgalacaṇḍī with *pādya, arghya, ācamanīya,* flowers and sandalwood paste, offerings of various kinds including slaughtered animals, song and dance, the chanting of the name of Kṛṣṇa, *dhyāna* in consonance with the *Mādhyandina śākhā*, and the *mūlamantra* consisting of *oṁ hrīṁ śrīṁ klīṁ sarvvapūjye devi maṅgalacaṇḍike hūṁ hūṁ phaṭ svāhā*.[44] This is very Puranic, clearly an artificial construction. But a stray reference in the *Kālikā Purāṇa* gives away this Puranic extravagance and reveals what was probably the original core of the worship. It says that she is pleased by *dūrvā* grass and grains of rice.[45] This sounds very much like the modest arrangement of a woman's *vrata*, and actually is so. In the *Caṇḍīmaṅgala*, the goddess Maṅgalacaṇḍī herself asked Khullanā to worship her with eight blades of *dūrvā* grass and eight grains of rice.[46] Ethnographic accounts confirm that these are the ingredients with which Maṅgalacaṇḍī is still worshipped in her *vrata*.[47] There is also an interesting continuity in the mode of representation of the goddess. The *Kālikā Purāṇa* declares that she should be worshipped in a *ghaṭa* (an earthen jug), or in a *paṭa* (pictorial representation of the goddess), or in a *pratimā* (icon of the goddess).[48] Raghunandana, the *Smṛti* writer of medieval Bengal, recommends precisely these forms of representation of Maṅgalacaṇḍī in his *Tithitattva*.[49]

That the inclusion of this presiding goddess of a woman's *vrata* into the brahmanical pantheon was an afterthought on the part of the authors of the Bengal *Purāṇas* is attested by the fact that they were evidently uncertain about her antecedents. A passage occurring in the *Brahmavaivarta* and the *Devībhāgavata Purāṇas* shows how a Puranic deity was fashioned almost as if by guess-work:

> 'You bestow delight and good fortune; you bestow bliss and auspiciousness (*maṅgala*)—that is why you are called Maṅgalacaṇḍikā. You are the most auspicious of all that is auspicious; you ensure welfare for the deserving. You are worshipped on Tuesdays (*maṅgalavāra*), desired by all. The king Maṅgala, born of the family of Manu, always worships you. You are the repository of all that is good in this universe. You are the bestower of auspicious salvation. You are the best of all . . . and you make one transcend the fruits of action. People worship you on every Tuesday and you bestow abundance of bliss on them.' Thus praising Maṅgalacaṇḍikā and worshipping her on Tuesday Śiva departed. The goddess Sarvamaṅgalā was first worshipped by Śiva, then by the planet Mars (*Maṅgala*), then by the king Maṅgala, and [she continues to be worshipped] on Tuesdays by the women of every household. Finally she was worshipped by all men desirous of their welfare.[50]

Thus all conceivable *maṅgalas* have been heaped on her and the original passage reads like an insensitively overdone example of alliteration. We have seen that the precursor of the Puranic Maṅgalacaṇḍī was in all likelihood known as Maṅgalā. Although the goddess Caṇḍī had already been described as *sarva-maṅgala-māṅgalye* in the *Mārkaṇḍeya Purāṇa*,[51] this had nothing to do with the local goddess Maṅgalā of non-brahmanical origin. Besides, proper names are often non-connotative, and the fact that auspiciousness (*maṅgala*) is a desirable quality in a goddess is an entirely coincidental occurrence in this case. Yet the Bengal *Purāṇas* accepted the literal meaning of the word *maṅgala* and proposed a simple equation between the name and the meaning in order to justify the Puranic reconstruction of this deity.

Either they were unaware of the popularity of the goddess Maṅgalā or they chose to ignore it.

The latter seems to be the more reasonable explanation, because the internal evidence of the *Purāṇas* indicates that the authors were familiar with popular stories associated with Maṅgalacaṇḍī, which came to acquire their poetical form much later in the various *Caṇḍīmaṅgalakāvyas* of medieval Bengal. The *Bṛhaddharma Purāṇa* contains a verse which says:

> You tricked Kālaketu by assuming the form of a lizard (*godhikā*) and granted him a boon. You are the auspicious Maṅgalacaṇḍī; you saved a merchant and his son from the king Śrīśālavāhana by devouring and throwing up an elephant, sitting on a lotus.[52]

These are, in a nutshell, the two stories narrated in the *Caṇḍīmaṅgala-kāvyas*. The vernacular poets of Bengal also knew of this verse. Indeed, Lālā Jayanārāyaṇa, a Bengali poet of the eighteenth century, has referred to the *Uttarakhaṇḍa* of the *Bṛhaddharma Purāṇa* where the verse is located, and has included a translation of this verse in his *Caṇḍikā-maṅgala-kāvya*.[53] In the Dacca University collection there is a Bengali manuscript of a *Caṇḍikā-khaṇḍa*, claiming to be a part of the *Devī Purāṇa*, which deals in sixteen chapters with these stories of Maṅgala-caṇḍī.[54] The vernacular *pāñcālīs* of Maṅgalacaṇḍī, which are read on the occasion of the observance of her *vrata*, also tell the same stories,[55] and there are allusions to them even in the doggerel verses (*chaḍā*) that young girls recite during the performance of a typical *kumārī vrata* in her honour. In one such *chaḍā* the goddess is asked, 'Mother, why are you so late today?' She replies that she had a lot of work including freeing the king from prison.[56] This, I suspect, is a corruption of the original or at any rate the popular story, where the merchant was freed from prison by the king through the grace of the goddess. Thus Maṅgala-caṇḍī is a unique example where the different layers of her story are traceable and correspond to and resonate with one another.

And yet the *Purāṇas* ignored these stories. In the chapters in the *Brahmavaivarta* and the *Devībhāgavata*, where they sought to establish the credentials of Maṅgalacaṇḍī with a suitable anecdote, the authors narrate the rather bald and ingenuous story of Śiva's battle with Tripurāsura whom he defeated with the help of the goddess Maṅgalacaṇḍī.[57] That they chose to succumb to such an unimaginative stereotype in preference to the more complex and exciting stories in circulation, is a clear reflection of the fact that they deliberately rejected the local popular goddess. But she was important enough for them to take note of her. Hence brahmanism constructed a synthetic archetypal story. That is why the rather transparent and laboured attempt was made to collect all the *maṅgalas* (auspiciousness) so that the popular Maṅgalā is substituted by the new Puranic Maṅgalacaṇḍī. The Bengal *Purāṇas* failed miserably in this attempt, but their primary purpose was served. Maṅgalacaṇḍī was raised to the rank of an approved brahmanical goddess.

The elevation was achieved by employing an old strategy, namely by demonstrating her identification with the goddess Caṇḍikā, the *mūlaprakṛti īśvarī* (goddess the primordial nature). Maṅgalacaṇḍī has been repeatedly described as the primary aspect of *prakṛti* and is said to have been born of her mouth.[58] She is Durgā *mūlaprakṛtirīśvarī* merely by a change of appearance.[59] Maṅgalacaṇḍī is then equated with the high-profile goddesses who had already been established in the upper echelons of the brahmanical hierarchy of divinities. Thus Lakṣmī, Sarasvatī, Durgā, Sāvitrī and Rādhikā pre-date Brahmā's creation of the universe. Those who emanate from them are their manifested selves, and Maṅgalacaṇḍī is one of them.[60] Similarly, Nārāyaṇa says that Rādhā assumes the forms of Sarasvatī, Sāvitrī, Gaṅgā, Lakṣmī, Durgā and Maṅgalacaṇḍikā; indeed, these forms are all-embracing.[61]

The identification is so complete that Maṅgalacaṇḍī has been assigned a *śākta-pīṭha*. In the *Bṛhaddharma Purāṇa* Durgā proclaims that she exists as Maṅgalacaṇḍī at the Maṅgakoṣṭhapīṭha in Ujjayinī.[62] R.C. Hazra points out that this Ujjayinī is the same as the ancient Ujānī, which comprises the modern villages of Kogrām, Maṅgalkoṭ (Sanskrit Maṅgakoṣṭhaka) and Arāl on the bank of the river Ajaya in Katwa subdivision in the Burdwan district of West Bengal.[63] Both the *Pīṭhanirṇaya* and the *Śivacarita*, two important treatises on the subject, mention Ujjayinī/Ujānī as a *mahāpīṭha*.[64] In the long list of the *śākta tīrthas* in the *Devībhāgavata*, Ujjayinī is referred to as Mahākāla, the seat of Śaṁkarī,[65] and in the *pīṭhamālā* section of Bhāratchandra's *Annadāmaṅgala*, composed in the eighteenth century, the goddess Maṅgalacaṇḍī is said to reside at Ujānī, served by a Bhairava.[66] It is important to remember that Dhanapati, the merchant protagonist of the second story of the *Caṇḍīmaṅgalakāvyas*, belonged to Ujānī.

At the end of this process, brahmanism succeeded in turning Maṅgalacaṇḍī into something of a Puranic celebrity. As a result, the vernacular *pāñcalīs* of Maṅgalacaṇḍī, which are the authentic carriers of her popular story, in an attempt to emulate the purposefulness and the method of enumeration of the *Purāṇas*, presumably for the sake of credibility, rather incongruously include a note on the procedure of her worship, complete with *sāmānyārghya*, *bhūtaśuddhi*, *prāṇāyāma* and *karaṅganyāsa*, and a *dhyāna*.[67] This *dhyāna* is an exact quote of the three verses of the *Kālikā Purāṇa*, describing Maṅgalacaṇḍī.[68] It also mentions the following *mantra*:

> *nārāyaṇyai vidmahe tvāṁ caṇḍikāyai tu dhīmahi* /
> *tanno lalitakānteti tataḥ paścāt pracodayāt* //

which it claims to be the *gāyatrī* of Maṅgalacaṇḍī, and is once again a straight lift from the *Kālikā Purāṇa*.[69] Thus Maṅgalacaṇḍī has been turned upside down. The history of this composite goddess is a good example of how brahmanism appropriated the indigenous *vratas* and their accessories.

IV

Another technique of appropriation was the fabrication of a relevant story in support of the Puranic claim that the *vrata* belonged to the brahmanical tradition. Such stories could barely disguise their non-brahmanical antecedents. The *Kukkuṭī vrata*, recommended by the *Bhaviṣya Purāṇa*, has one such accompanying story. Candramukhī, the queen of Nahuṣa, and Mallikā, the wife of his priest, once went to the banks of the river Sarayū and met a few *apsarās* who were engaged in performing a certain rite. They learnt on enquiry that the *apsarās* were observing a *vrata*, although they were actually worshipping Śiva and Durgā. They learnt the procedure of the *vrata* from the *apsarās* and began to practise it. However, Candramukhī soon forgot the procedure and discontinued it, while Mallikā carried on. In their next lives Mallikā was born a *kukkuṭī* (hen) with knowledge of the past and led a happy and prosperous life, while Candramukhī became a monkey and passed her days in great hardship. At last Mallikā once again taught the *vrata* to Candramukhī who performed it and was released of her adversity. The *vrata* was named after Mallikā in her *kukkuṭī* incarnation.[70] It seems that brahmanism was compelled to retain the name of the *vrata* by which it was popularly known, and then sought to cover it up with a suitable story. With all their ingenuity, however, the *brāhmaṇas* could not explain the connection between the worship of Śiva–Durgā and the performance of this *vrata*.

Let me cite a more complex but less obvious example from the

Bengal *Purāṇas*. These texts insist that *dhvajāropaṇa* or *dhvajādāna*—implanting or donating a flag in honour of a deity—is obligatory of all votaries of brahmanism and they narrate stories to illustrate the merits of this act. The following story from the *Devī Purāṇa* is a typical example. In the olden days there lived a poor Kaivartta, who earned his livelihood through fishing. One day he got up in the morning and went out to catch fish. On his way he came across a goddess temple in the middle of the Vindhya forest. His old fishing net had become scruffy and unusable. Hence he hung his net on a tree in front of the temple and went home. A few days later he came back to the temple and laughingly (*hasamānaḥ*) hung a piece of worn-out cloth on the same tree. After his death he became a *vidyādhara*, versed in all branches of knowledge. Then again, he donated a flag made of ornate white cloth in honour of the goddess and as a result became the king of all the *vidyādharas*.[71]

The tradition of worshipping flags on a post bearing different symbols such as *mīnadhvaja*, *indradhvaja*, *kapidhvaja*, etc. was prevalent in ancient India. The first-century BC Garuḍa pillar at Besnagar is a famous example. Niharranjan Ray points out that the fact that the worship of the *indradhvaja* was current in Bengal before the eleventh century is attested by Govardhana Ācārya. The worship of *śakradhvaja* is also mentioned in the *Kālaviveka* of Jimūtavāhana.[72] Ray argues that a bird or a beast used to be the mark of identification of a tribe and the worship of the flag bearing the representation of the sacred animal the distinctive religious practice of that tribe. No religious festival of the Santal, Munda, Khasi, Rajvamshi and the Garo tribes or lower castes of Bengal is complete without the worship of the *dhvajā*.[73]

The tribal association of *dhvajāpūjā* is corroborated by another typically local religious festival of central Bengal which is commonly known as *ind parab*. The leaves and branches of three sal trees are removed and their stems are scraped smooth and wrapped in cloth. These are then fixed to the ground and a basket, also wrapped in cloth, is placed on top of the middle one like an umbrella. A small pedestal is constructed at the foot of the trees on which articles of worship are arranged. On the twelfth day of the bright fortnight in the month of *Bhādra*, a *brāhmaṇa* priest performs a *homa* in front of the trees and rice, fruits, and sweets are offered. The priest proclaims that the central post, the *indradhvaja*, stands for Indra, the king of gods, and his *dhyānamantra* is chanted during the worship. The festival is patronized by landlords of the districts of Birbhum, Bankura, Burdwan and Midnapur of West Bengal.[74]

Gopendrakrishna Basu suggests that this festival is a carry-over of the tradition of tree worship among the tribal people of Bengal. He says the festival originally belonged to the Santals of this region who are known to be particularly respectful to the sal tree. It was appropriated and brahmanized by its patron landlords, who often came from outside the region and were champions of Puranic Hinduism. Basu argues that if *ind* was derived from the Puranic worship of *indradhvaja*, it would have had a far wider religious appeal. Instead, it is localized in the tribal belts of central Bengal. Besides, the local landlords organize several other religious festivals in which tribesmen do not participate at all, while thousands of Santals take active part in the *ind parab*. They sing and dance in the worship ground (*indkuḍi*) and offer parched rice and curd to the trees. Moreover, carrying the sal trees from the forest and immersing them at the end of the worship are a Santal privilege, which reminds us of the similar exclusive right of the Śavaras of Orissa with regard to the twelve-yearly renewal (*navakalevara*) of the icons of the Jagannātha trinity at Puri and their original involvement with Jagannātha worship.[75]

Totem worship and tribal veneration of trees seems to have combined to give rise to the Puranic *Dhvajāropaṇa vrata*. The *Devī Purāṇa* story, mentioned above, is an imperfectly concealed Puranic attempt at assimilating this practice in its original form. The Kaivarttas are a large and important fishing caste of Bengal and the characteristic religious festival of this community is *jālapālani* or laying by of the net.[76] Despite the impressive presence of the Vindhya forest, the story unmistakably refers to Bengal. It is difficult to determine at what point of time brahmanism took over this tribal custom, but the *Devī Purāṇa* story implicitly admits that a crude prototype of the brahmanical *Dhvajāropaṇa vrata* did exist. Therefore, the Bengal *Purāṇas* constructed another story in which the two versions are juxtaposed to underscore the superiority of the brahmanical method. The following is the story that the *sūta* narrates in the *Bṛhannāradīya Purāṇa*:

In the *Satyayuga* there lived a very powerful and virtuous king called Sumati. He had all the qualities of an ideal king and was devoted to the worship of Hari. The name of his queen was Satyamati. Satyamati used to dance in the Viṣṇu temple and the king had decorated the temple with beautiful flags. One day the sage Vibhāṇḍaka came to see the king and asked him, 'There are several ways of worshipping Viṣṇu which are pleasing to him. Why do you implant flags in honour of him even now, and why does your chaste wife dance before him everyday?' The king replied, 'In my previous life I was a wayward *śūdra* of the name of Mātuli. I used to harm others and steal articles of worship. Thus I lost all my friends and property and went to live in a forest. One day I saw a dilapidated Viṣṇu temple in the forest and made it my home. I repaired the temple, cleaned it up, and lived there for twenty years, pursuing the occupation of a hunter. Then a woman called Kokilinī arrived there. She came from the Vindhyadeśa and was the daughter of a hunter. After the death of her husband she was abandoned by her friends and came to this forest in a state of great distress. The two of us started living in that Viṣṇu temple like man and wife. One night, in a fit of drunkenness, we tied a piece of cloth to the end of a stick and started waving it while dancing within the temple. We died that instant. The fierce messengers of Yama arrived with their noose and Madhusūdana also sent his messengers to take us away. A quarrel ensued between them. The messengers of Yama claimed that we were sinners, but the messengers of Viṣṇu pointed out that we were absolved of our sins because we served the Viṣṇu temple. My wife danced in it, and I donated a flag at the end of my life. They took us to the abode of Viṣṇu where we lived in great comfort and later I have become the king of this earth. I was unaware of the consequence of what I was doing, and yet I have been so rewarded. Now I am serving the god with utmost devotion for my ultimate welfare.[77]

The distinction the story makes between the actions of the king and those of the *śūdra* is that the latter lacked conscious motivation. The story seeks to convey the message that brahmanism is recommending the practice of a ritual already in vogue, but it is more effective in the brahmanical way because it is deliberate and refined. In the process the ritual was stripped of its spontaneity and was thoroughly institutionalized, as the procedure prescribed in the same text reveals:

On the twelfth day of the bright fortnight in the month of *Kārttika* the observer of the *Dhvajāropaṇa vrata* should get up in the morning, bathe, perform his daily rites, and worship Viṣṇu. He should perform the *nāndīmukhaśrāddha* and *svastivācana* with the help of four *brāhmaṇas*. He should then purify the two flagstaffs with *gāyatrī mantra* and worship Sūrya, Garuḍa and Candra on them. Next he should worship Vidhātā on the flagstaffs with turmeric, rice, and flowers. He should then prepare a *sthaṇḍila* of the measurement of a cow's hide and perform *homa* hundred and eight times according to his *gṛhya* affiliation with sweetened milk and clarified butter. He should first make an offering to Viṣṇu in the *Puruṣasūkta mantra* and then eight offerings to Garuḍa. Next, he should perform *homa* five times with the *mantra: sāmī dhenu, svāhā,* and simultaneously mutter the *Śāntisūkta* and the *mantra* of Sūrya. He should keep awake at night in front of Hari. Next morning he should perform the daily rites and bring the flags to the Viṣṇu temple, accompanied by auspicious music, dancing, and recitation of *sūktas*. He should then place them gently either on top of the temple or on two sides of the door, and worship Hari with flowers, incense, lamps, parched rice and other items of food. Once the flag is placed, the performer should go round the temple behind a *brāhmaṇa* and read this prayer. [The prayer is a long and philosophical exposition of the nature of Hari who is the unchanging, indestructible and subtle *nirguṇa Brahman*.] Then he should bow to Viṣṇu, pay fees and present clothes to the priest, and worship and feed the *brāhmaṇas*. Finally, concentrating on Nārāyaṇa, along with friends and members of the family, the performer should break his fast.[78]

Evidently this *vrata*, like so many others recommended in the Bengal *Purāṇas*, could not be performed by common people, and was possibly never observed exactly in this form except by a handful of rich householders. The procedures prescribed for the same *vrata* in the Puranic texts are not always uniform. For example, the *Devībhāgavata* separately prescribes Vedic and Tantric methods for the performance of the *Navarātra vrata*.[80] Such passages are therefore declarations of brahmanical intention and are not meant to be taken literally. But in the process a local practice was appropriated and authenticated.

Although the *vratas* are discussed in great detail in some of the *Mahāpurāṇas*, they seem to occupy a special position in Bengal. This is attested by the importance attached to them in the Bengal *Smṛtis*, composed towards the end of the Puranic and the immediately post-Puranic period. The *Karmānuṣṭhāna-paddhati* and *Prāyaścitta-prakaraṇa* of Bhaṭṭa Bhavadeva, *Kālaviveka* of Jimūtavāhana, *Vratakālaviveka* of Śūlapāṇi, *Vratatattva* and *Kṛtyatattva* of Raghunandana and *Varṣakriyākaumudī* of Govindānanda are some of the more influential *Smṛti* texts which devote a good deal of space to the *vratas*.[81] It is doubtful whether the exclusively Puranic *vratas* were ever popularly observed, but the *Smṛti* recognition of the *vratas* gave them the required sanction. However, once its importance was established in principle, brahmanism always made room for simplified versions, emergency measures, and even exemptions, for a fee.

Plainly the Puranic *vrata* was an artificial device. The *Purāṇas* garnished the substratum of a non-brahmanical rite with Vedic and Tantric elements, many of which were impracticable and therefore redundant. But they insisted on four mandatory aspects essential from the brahmanical point of view: performance by all members of the community including women and *śūdras*, celebration of a *vrata* involving an entire neighbourhood if not the whole village, the *brāhmaṇa* conduct of the ritual for gifts in return, and reading out of the *Purāṇas* to the performers. That even brahmanism considered many of the additional rites imposed on the simple structure of the indigenous *vrata* superfluous is suggested by a statement in the *Mahābhārata*. It declares that the Vedic rites and the rites recommended by Manu are too elaborate to perform in the *Kaliyuga*, and is prescribing a simpler option which is the essence of the *Purāṇas*, namely one should not eat on *Ekādaśī* day. The text adds that there is no higher self-regulation than fasting and even poor people can secure the rewards of sacrifice by resorting to it.[82] Hemādri quotes two verses on *Arka vrata* from the *Bhaviṣya Purāṇa* stating that if a man observes *nakta* on the sixth and seventh days in each fortnight for a year, he obtains the merit secured by those who perform the Vedic sacrifices called *sattras*.[83]

Thus there were several advantages to *vratas* as the vehicle for propagation of the *Purāṇas*. They were easy to perform and yet effective. The name of the ritual itself proved to be of advantage. The term *vrata* occurs in Vedic literature, but in a different context. The Puranic *vrata* was a brahmanical innovation which had very little to do with the Vedic. And yet the term *vrata* was retained for the ritual in order to maintain continuity with the legitimizing authority of the *Vedas*. The authors of the *Purāṇas* thus invented a tradition which was related to both orthodox brahmanism and indigenous local traditions in one way or another. Eric Hobsbawm[84] suggests that invented tradition normally attempts to establish continuity with a suitable historic past and is usually a response to novel situations that takes the form of reference to old situations.[85] Brahmanism went on inventing traditions in its assimilative effort; the *vrata* is a particularly germane example. The term *vrata* was borrowed from the Vedic literature but it was invested with a new meaning, and the *kathā* element was picked up from the indigenous rite but the simple folk-tales were replaced by the Puranic myths and legends. Thus in the Puranic *vratakathā* an illusion of convergence was created, even as the contents were subverted. However, this innovation paved the way for the participation of local people in the brahmanical *vrata* and ensured the ritual prerogative of *brāhmaṇas* as mediating agents.

V

If brahmanical adoption of the indigenous *vrata* was meant to earn the trust of the local population, to create a platform for the dissemination of the *Purāṇas*, and to provide for a steady income to the *brāhmaṇas*, it is natural that attempts would be made to ensure the widest possible participation. Therefore the *Purāṇas* issued blanket sanctions to men and women of the four *varṇas* regarding the performance of the *vratas*. Indeed, the *vrata* and *tīrtha* are the only two brahmanical religious practices in which right of participation is extended to all, irrespective of caste or gender. In the Bengal *Purāṇas*, this sanction is either categorically stated or taken for granted. Here are a few representative examples.

Of all the *vratas* recommended in the Bengal *Purāṇas*, the *Ekādaśī* is most frequently mentioned, and the texts make it a point to assert that its performance is obligatory for men and women of all the four *varṇas*. Thus the *Brahmavaivarta*[86] and the *Bṛhannāradīya Purāṇas*[87] issue the standard injunction that the *Ekādaśī vrata* is eternal and should be observed by people of all the four *varṇas* including women; the *Kriyāyogasāra*[88] adds 'others' to this already exhaustive list in case any group is inadvertently left out. (Significantly, *Vratārka* quotes from Hemādri a passage of the *Devī Purāṇa* which says that even the Mlecchas were authorized to perform the *vratas*, if they had faith in them.[89]) The *Devī Purāṇa* for the *Nandā vrata*[90] and the *Bṛhannāradīya* for the *Pūrṇimā vrata*[91] repeat the same formula. Often the *Purāṇas*, while making a reluctant concession to lower castes and women, set a limit to the privilege granted. But no such restriction is imposed on the performance of *vratas*.

The *Purāṇas* do not stop at approval of women's participation. They are specific in their instruction that the performance of *vratas* is compulsory for them. We have seen that the indigenous *vrata* was an exclusively woman's rite. The *Purāṇas* indirectly acknowledge this when they declare that even though the *vratas* may be observed by all, they are particularly for women.[92] The Bengal *Purāṇas* never tire of repeating this sentiment, if not in so many words. The *Devībhāgavata* furnishes a long list of *vratas*, consisting of *Anantatṛtīyā, Rasakalyāṇinī, Ārdrānandakara, Śukravāra, Kṛṣṇacaturdaśī, Bhaumavāra* and *Pradoṣa*, which should be observed by both men and women,[93] but even when a *vrata* is prescribed for all, a special condition is attached to the woman performer. For example, the *Bṛhaddharma Purāṇa* states that the *Ekādaśī vrata* should be performed by men of the four *varṇas* and four *āśramas* and by women. However, married women should keep a fast and may drink water only at night.[94] Similarly, the *Devī Purāṇa* declares that the *Nakṣatra vrata* should be observed by all, but women must not give it up under any circumstances.[95]

This preference for women is particularly noticeable in the *Umā–Maheśvara vrata* prescribed for married couples, though its benefits accrue only to the wives. Such wives never suffer the loss of their dear ones. They enjoy the company of sons and grandsons in this life and attain the abode of Umā–Maheśvara at the end. There, after a life of comfort, they are reborn into good families, and being attractive, get married to those who deserve them. They are loved and respected. They never suffer mental agony or crippling diseases. They are blessed with worthy sons who survive them. They enjoy these earthly pleasures and at a ripe old age go to heaven before their husbands.[96] Even the *pāñcālīs* do not promise more to the faithful performer.

Apart from these, a good number of *vratas* are set aside for women, such as the *Gaurī vrata* recommended in the *Brahmavaivarta Purāṇa*.[97] Indeed, many are performed for procuring a desirable husband or to beget a son. Thus in the *Brahmavaivarta* Śiva advised Pārvatī to perform the *Puṇyaka vrata* to have a son and the text supplies a convincing list of illustrious women such as Śatarūpā the wife of Manu, Arundhatī the wife of Vaśiṣṭha, Aditi the wife of Kaśyapa, and Śacī the wife of Indra, who performed this *vrata* and gave birth to sons of great distinction.[98]

But this concession granted to women and *śūdras* created an anomaly. The basic structure of the Puranic *vrata* was borrowed from indigenous traditions. Therefore it had to be embellished with the accessories of brahmanical religious practice in order to appear authentic. Thus the simple procedure of *pūjā* was overlain with the preparatory *sāmānyakāṇḍa*, consisting of *bhūtaśuddhi, mātṛkānyāsa* and so on, followed by *homa* and *dhyāna* in *Vedamantra*. The *Brahmavaivarta* prescribes a *vrata* called *Patisaubhāgyavarddhana* in which the performer is asked to worship the *śālagrāma* and meditate on Kṛṣṇa by uttering a *mantra* mentioned in the *Sāma Veda*.[99] The *Devībhāgavata* instructs the observer of the *Navarātra vrata* to perform *homa* one-tenth times the number of *japa*.[100] The *Bṛhannāradīya Purāṇa* provides detailed specifications of *homa* in connection with the performance of the *Pūrṇimā vrata*. The performer of this *vrata* is required to prepare a *sthaṇḍila* consisting of four corners and place fire on it in accordance with his/her *gṛhya* rites. He/She should perform the *homa* with a preparation of milk and rice (*caru*), sesamum and clarified butter in the *Puruṣasūkta mantra*. He/She should carefully perform the *homa* once, twice, or three times, to destroy his/her sins. After completing the *prāyaścitta* and *homa*, the performer should chant the *Śāntisūkta*.[101]

These *vratas* are also meant for women and *śūdras*, but brahmanism does not permit them the performance of *homa* with Vedic *mantras*. Nor are they allowed to worship *śālagrāma*. Though, theoretically, the three upper *varṇas* were entitled to perform the *homa*, some *brāhmaṇas* held the view that pure *kṣatriyas* and *vaiśyas* do not exist in the *Kaliyuga*.[102] Thus even the two intermediary *varṇas* were effectively barred from observing these. Opinion was divided on whether a woman could get the *homa* performed by another. Kane points out that *Vyavahāra-mayūkha*, following Parāśara, holds that a *śūdra* can get the *homa* in adoption performed through a *brāhmaṇa*, and that the same rule applies to women. *Nirṇayasindhu* supports *Vyavahāramayūkha* but Nīlakaṇṭha, the author of the *Vyavahāramayūkha*, presents a different opinion in his *Prāyaścittamayūkha*.[103] Thus it is unclear whether women and *śūdras* had the legal mandate to get a *homa* performed even through others for the purpose of the *vrata*, and in the three instances cited, the *Purāṇas* unambiguously confer the right to perform *homa* with Vedic *mantras* to the observers of these *vratas*. Clearly this is in direct opposition to the entire body of brahmanical literature on the permissible degree of participation of women and the lower castes in the rituals. It is absurd to presume that the authors of these *Purāṇas* were unaware of this restriction, nor does it seem likely that *brāhmaṇas* were willing to give up a fundamental prerogative. Therefore it is reasonable to assume that the Vedic elements introduced into the Puranic *vratas* were largely decorative. At any rate, the right of women and *śūdras* to perform *homa* with Vedic *mantras* could never have been operative; they would not know the procedure. But even the theoretical concession was a very major compromise and goes to show the eagerness of the Bengal *brāhmaṇas* to accommodate a local practice.

However, this right of worship granted to women was not altogether unconditional and tended to take away more than it gave. The inner apartments of the traditional households (*antaḥpura*) in India form a social domain, separable and understandable in its own terms. This domain is not defined by separate gender-specific activities alone. Rather, a woman's domain is defined and interpreted in relation to society at large by the cultural dimension of social action. A number of anthropologists who have worked on women's rituals in India confirm this. Lina Fruzzetti, for instance, points out in her study of the actions and meaning of marriage as they relate to women in Bengali society that in women's rituals there exists a certain consistency of action and intent, a link between ideas and life, between what women do and what they say. The rituals form and express the relation between the world of daily action and the concept and ideas concerning women on their own and in the wider society.[104] Thus the representations of gods and goddesses in their rituals differ from those in Sanskritic rites. Sometimes no object stands for the gods; on other occasions divinities are represented by a pot of rice (Lakṣmī), a grinding stone (Ṣaṣṭhī), or other items of daily use sacred to the gods.[105] These rituals carry symbolic meanings which can be understood through the performances as well as through the exegeses given exclusively by women.

Similarly, Suzanne Hanchett, in her study of the symbolic significance of women's folk festivals in Karnataka (very similar to the *vrata* ritual of Bengal) observed that though the festivals assume patrilineality and virilocality as a backdrop, they parade so many females and cross-sex ties across the stage that a strong bilateral emphasis is impossible to ignore. In most of the stories recounted on such occasions, women occupy the central position—a daughter seeks the protection of her mother, or a brother is delivered from a crisis by the ingenuity of his resourceful sister, and so on. In balancing patrilineal and other types of kinship links, these festivals repeat and reinforce the importance attributed to women in local genealogies. Like genealogies, family festivals counteract a tendency towards a male-centred view natural in patrilineal and virilocal systems. Women are key creative and destructive figures in nearly all these festivals and their relationships are central to the concept of family that emerges in these festivals.[106] Though confined to the interiors of the household, these ritual cycles create their own networks through which women socialize and make contact with relatives in nearby villages.[107]

In other words, the rituals exclusive to women reveal a woman's universe largely independent of male intervention. They embody the daily existence of a woman and strengthen her uncertain worth in the family. The ingredients necessary for a *meyelī vrata* are the ordinary, inexpensive articles of daily use such as leaves and fruits of easily available plants, *dūrvā* grass and sandalwood paste, aniconic representations of deities made of mud or ground rice (*piṭuli*), and auspicious marks of a married woman such as vermilion, conch-shell bangle, and betel leaves and nuts. Women are the chief actors of the stories they tell; in a wish-fulfilling reversal of the acknowledged code, they save their menfolk from disaster. *Vrata* is one occasion in which women meet and mutually reinforce their roles in a male-dominated world.

But the Puranic *vrata* attempted to destroy this exclusive social domain of women. They opened it up for men, which effectively took away the woman's initiative in the management of the *vrata*, and they introduced a *brāhmaṇa* priest which wrecked the uniquely feminine character of the ritual. Worst of all, they very nearly denied them the right to perform the *vratas*. Brahmanism had always been averse to participation of women in religious ceremonies on their own, and Manu categorically stated that there is no separate *yajña, vrata*, or *upavāsa* for women; those who serve their husbands attain heaven.[108] Although *vrata* had a different connotation in Manu, the Bengal *Purāṇas* did use the same term, and they could hardly disregard the injunction issued by this paradigmatic *Smṛti* text. Thus, to circumvent this injunction, the *Bṛhaddharma Purāṇa* first repeats the verse from Manu,[109] and then adds that no *vrata* or fast is recommended for married women; whatever they do in accordance with the instructions of their husbands is considered the best of *vratas*.[110] This is an ambivalent statement and is open to a variety of interpretations. For example, it is possible to argue that the verse allows women to perform the *vratas* with the permission of their husbands. This is precisely what the *Smṛtis* of medieval Bengal recommended in their attempt to bring about a compromise between the *Smṛti* denial and the Puranic acceptance of the woman's right to perform the *vratas*.[111] They did not directly transgress the older *Smṛtis* but attached a condition. As both the Bengal *Purāṇas* and the Bengal *Smṛtis* insist that women must perform the *vratas*, perhaps the required permission would not have been difficult to obtain, and therefore, this condition looks rather innocuous. But actually it fundamentally altered the character of the indigenous *vrata*. The performance of the *vrata* becoming dependent on the discretion of men, the social space enjoyed by women was further reduced. They first quietly took away and then graciously gave back to women what used to be their exclusive privilege.

This discussion is of course largely theoretical, for the *Purāṇas* did allow women to participate in the *vratas*, and the *meyelī vratas* also continued to be performed in a slightly modified form along with the Puranic *vratas*. But then the didactic texts are concerned with the formulation of general principles and their implications cannot be ignored in an undertaking which attempts to get to the actual state of things through the idealized proclamations of these texts.

VI

Brahmanism transformed the character of the indigenous *vrata* and what was merely a woman's rite became a community festival. The idea was to create at least one religious occasion acceptable to the *brāhmaṇas* and the local population in which every member of the community could actively participate. Individual worship is the predominant mode of Hindu religious practice, but *vrata* by definition is congregational. Abanindranath Thakur points out that when one person performs a religious act for the fulfilment of his desire, it is not a *vrata* in the true sense. A *vrata* must involve a group of people with a common end in view. Individual desires must have a collective basis.[112] Brahmanism drew upon the potential of the indigenous *vrata* to arrange a gathering, and widened its scope and inflated its number to make it as pervasive and as frequent as possible. Kane has prepared a list of *vratas* prescribed by brahmanism that covers two hundred and ten printed pages and go up to an impracticable number of nearly one thousand.[113]

This extraordinary emphasis on the *vrata* may be explained by the fact that it was considered the simplest and most effective means of dissemination of brahmanical religion. The *vratas* offered an occasion for the public exposition of the contents of the *Purāṇas*, which could reach out to the lowest strata of society. We have seen that women and *śūdras* had no access to the *Vedas*. This injunction was absolute and inviolable. Indeed, they were debarred from taking part in any form of brahmanical worship. The *Bṛhannāradīya Purāṇa*, for instance, proclaims:

> One who bows down to a Śivaliṅga or an icon of Viṣṇu worshipped by a *śūdra* is not absolved of his sin even after thousands of expiations. One who bows down to a Śivaliṅga or an icon of Hari touched by a *śūdra* suffers in hell as long as the moon and the stars exist. One who bows down to a Śivaliṅga worshipped by a *pāṣaṇḍa* turns into a *pāṣaṇḍa* himself, even if he is well versed in the *Vedas* and all the other *śāstras*. One who bows down to a Śivaliṅga worshipped by an Ābhīra goes to hell. One who bows down to a Śivaliṅga or an icon of Viṣṇu worshipped by a woman stays in the *Raurava* hell until the end of the creation, along with all his ancestors.[114]

Puranic prohibition regarding the *Vedas* was equally categorical and unrelenting. The *Bṛahannāradīya* states that one who reads the *Vedas* in the presence of a woman or a *śūdra* suffers in hell for a thousand crore *kalpas*.[115] Similarly, the *Devī Purāṇa* declares that if a *brāhmaṇa* pronounces the *Vedas* before a Caṇḍāla or a *śūdra* becomes a *śūdra*. The text even forbids one to recite the *Vedas* after accepting rice from a *śūdra*.[116]

But women and *śūdras* were entitled to listen to the *Purāṇas*. Indeed, many of the *Purāṇas* claim this concession to be their *raison d'etre*. Thus the *Devībhāgavata* states that knowing that *brāhmaṇas* would be stupid and short-lived in the *Kali* age (and hence unable to comprehend the *Vedas*), Viṣṇu as Vedavyāsa reveals the *Purāṇasaṁhitās* in every *yuga*. Particularly women, *śūdras*, and inferior *brāhmaṇas* are not allowed to listen to the *Vedas*. It is for their benefit that the *Purāṇas* are composed.[117] This became such a common precept of brahmanism that the other *Purāṇas* simply mention it as a matter of fact without providing any justification.[118]

The entitlement of women to listen to the *Purāṇas*, however, is often specifically stated. For example, the *Brahmavaivarta* says that if an ill-fated woman listens to this *Purāṇa*, she will find a desirable husband, and barren women, women who can bear only one child, and women who deliver still-born babies, will give birth to immortal sons.[119] However, brahmanism seems to have been a little uncertain whether women and *śūdras* were allowed to read the *Purāṇas* on their own, or whether these were to be read out to them. The *Devībhāgavata* unequivocally states that women and *śūdras* must never read this *Purāṇa* even by mistake; they should always listen to it from a *brāhmaṇa*.[120] The *Kālikā Purāṇa* is equally emphatic.[121] But the *Devī Purāṇa* separately mentions the results which can be obtained from reading *and* listening to the eulogy of the goddess by women and *śūdras*, among others, contained in the text.[122] In any case the question had no operative significance, for women and *śūdras* could not possibly read the Sanskrit *Purāṇas* in the original.

But there is no ambiguity about the Puranic recommendation that the *brāhmaṇas* should read aloud the *Purāṇas* to members of the other *varṇas* and to women. Indeed, the Bengal *Purāṇas* strove hard to make this an institutional practice. The *Bṛhaddharma Purāṇa* declares that it is the duty of the *brāhmaṇa* to read the *Caṇḍīsaptaśatī* included in the *Mārkaṇḍeya Purāṇa*, and the *Śrīmadbhagavadgītā*.[123] This instruction refers to private reading, which the *brāhmaṇas* were supposed to keep up as a part of their professional requirement. But the Bengal *Purāṇas* also consistently encouraged the practice of the reading out of *Purāṇas* to an audience. The *Bṛhannāradīya* proclaims:

> There is no doubt that one who always reads the *Purāṇas* with devotion, for his own sake or for others, is Hari himself . . . The narrator of the *Purāṇasaṁhitās* is Hari in person. Those who respect him, earn the merit of bathing in the Gaṅgā everyday. The desire to listen to the *Purāṇa* and devotion to its reader yield results comparable to bathing in the Gaṅgā and at Prayāga respectively. There is no doubt that one who rescues people, immersed in the ocean that is this earthly existence, through religious instruction from the *Purāṇas*, is Hari himself.[124]

The same sentiment has been repeated at every conceivable opportunity. For example, the text says that one who is engaged in the transmission of knowledge is served by Brahmā, and the reader of the *Purāṇas* is eulogized by the sages.[125] Similarly, the practice of listening to the *Purāṇas*, fasting, and worshipping Viṣṇu with flowers, has been described as the essence of *kriyāyoga*.[126] Such instances can be multiplied.

The Bengal *Purāṇas* have also laid down in great detail exactly how and where these texts should be read. The *Devī Purāṇa* declares that the *Purāṇas* should be read in the *pīṭhasthānas*, meeting places, temples, holy mansions, river banks, gardens, and assemblies full of people, which are embellished with incense, garlands, and sandalwood paste.[127] The text adds that the *Purāṇa* should be placed on a decorated pedestal. The narrator should dress in attire fit for a teacher and apply perfume to his palms. The audience should worship and meditate on Śiva and sit in a gradually descending order according to age, silently and with folded hands. Both narrator and audience must pronounce the *Devīmantra* at the beginning and conclusion. The narrator should make the audience perform purificatory rites and give them a flower each with which the text should be worshipped. One who arranges such public reading of the *Purāṇa* for the good of all and for his own salvation, enjoys the material comforts of life and attains peace at the end.[128]

The *Purāṇas* made every effort to make the listening as attractive as possible. The *Devībhāgavata* states that if the greatest sinner, devoid of *Vedadharma* and the *ācāras*, listens to this excellent *Purāṇa* even by deceit, he will enjoy all the comforts in this life and will attain the station assigned to *yogīs* after his death.[129] Apart from material comforts, the other allurements, such as scholarship and fame, promised by the *Purāṇas* as a reward for listening to them,[130] were unlikely to entice the common people, and the pleasures of heaven are at best a distant and unverifiable possibility. Therefore the *Purāṇas* also offered to take care of mundane problems. The *Devī Purāṇa* says that those who read the eulogy of the goddess therein are protected from evil stars, ghosts and demons, snakes, poisonous insects, disease and the guilt of murder.[131] The *Brahmavaivarta* says that those holy persons who listen to this *Purāṇa* never suffer from blindness, leprosy, poverty, dreaded diseases, or grief,[132] and the *Bṛhannāradīya* says that they are safe from fire and theft.[133] Even Gaṅgā, the last resort for the salvation of sinners, has been advised by Viṣṇu to relieve her burden of accumulated sins by listening to the *Purāṇas*.[134] Finally, brahmanism stamped the act of listening to the *Purāṇas* with its ultimate word of recognition. The *Brahmavaivarta* claims that its merit is greater than the performance of sacrifice, visit to the *tīrthas*, participation in the *vratas,* practice of penance, circumambulation of the world, and even reading the four *Vedas.*[135]

Thus there was a consistent attempt to create a tradition of public reading of the *Purāṇas.* As it required a ritual occasion to make it a regular practice, brahmanism chose the *vrata* as the appropriate occasion. The *Purāṇas* should be listened to as often as possible, but it was made obligatory for the *vratas.* The *Kriyāyogasāra* instructs that for the *Ekādaśī vrata* the Vaiṣṇavas should keep awake at night and read the *Purāṇas.* The *Rāmāyaṇa*, the *Bhāgavata*, the *Bhārata* as composed by Vyāsa, and the other *Purāṇas* should be read on such an occasion. Those who read the *Purāṇas* and those who listen to them on the day of Hari (*Ekādaśī*) earn the merit of donating Kapilā on each word of it.[136] The text also specifies that the performer should keep awake along with his parents, brothers, sons and wife, and friends.[137] Thus the occasion provided a captive audience for the exposition of the *Purāṇas.* The same instruction has been repeated for the *vratas* at *Janmāṣṭamī*,[138] *Dvādaśī*,[139] *Pūrṇimā*,[140] and *Ekādaśī.*[141] Although listening to the *Purāṇas* at night is prescribed as the general rule, the performers have been advised to do so at any other time of the day in connection with the *Navarātra vrata*[142] as well as the *Dvādaśī vrata.*[143] It has even been suggested that if one does not perform the *vrata*, but merely listens to the account of it in the *Purāṇas*, he obtains the desired results, as in the case of *Durgā,*[144] *Haripañcaka,*[145] and *Māsopavāsa vratas.*[146] The *Devībhāgavata* instructs the performer of the *Navarātra vrata* to invite nine, five, three, or at least one *brāhmaṇa* for the purpose of reading out the *Purāṇa.*[147]

VII

The advantage of persistently repeating the *Purāṇas* to those performers of the *vratas* who were evidently willing to take on trust the rewards promised by the *Purāṇas*, is obvious from the brahmanical point of view, but an example will help to bring out the implications better. On the fourteenth day of the dark lunar half in the month of *Jyaiṣṭha*, women, whose husbands are still alive, perform even now in Bengal a *vrata* called the *Sāvitrī.* The story of Sāvitrī, which originally appeared in the *Mahābhārata,* is as follows. Sāvitrī chose to marry Satyavān who was destined to die within a year of his marriage. On the appointed day, Satyavān went to the forest to gather fruit and firewood and Sāvitrī accompanied him. After a while Satyavān fell ill under a tree and died. When Yama came to take Satyavān's soul away, Sāvitrī followed him, and a lengthy conversation ensued in which Sāvitrī raised many moral questions. Finally Yama relented and Satyavān was brought back to life.[148] This became the source of a very popular Puranic *vrata*, later adopted by the *Smṛti* digests of the medieval period. Kane points out that the *Matsya*, the *Skanda*, and the *Viṣṇudharmottara Purāṇas* all describe the *Sāvitrī vrata* in great detail. The *Bhaviṣya Purāṇa* account of the story is cited in the *Kṛtyaratnākara*. Hemādri mentions a *vrata* called *Brahma–Sāvitrī* from the *Bhaviṣyottara Purāṇa*, which contains the story of Sāvitrī as in the *Matsya Purāṇa*, and also a *Vaṭasāvitrī vrata* from the *Skanda Purāṇa*. The latter is called the *Mahāsāvitrī vrata* by the *Vratakālaviveka*.[149]

It is curious that the same *vrata* is known by various names in the brahmanical texts. Another noticeable feature of the *vrata* is the complete absence of unanimity on when it should be performed. Hemādri says that the *Brahma-Sāvitrī vrata* should be performed for three days from the thirteenth to the full moon of *Bhādrapada*, while the *Vaṭasāvitrī vrata* should be observed on the full moon of *Jyaiṣṭha*. The *Nirṇayasindhu* recommends the *pūrṇimā* of *Bhādrapada*, but the *Nirṇayāmṛta*, following the *Bhaviṣya Purāṇa*, holds that the *vrata* should be performed on *amāvasyā*; the *Kṛtyatattva* prescribes the dark fourteenth after the full moon of *Jyaiṣṭha* and the *Rājamārtaṇḍa* the fourteenth of the bright half of *Jyaiṣṭha*.[150]

These discrepancies are rather unusual, for the brahmanical texts have always attempted to present a standard version of rituals. Even if they allowed for a slight variation in name or procedure, they are generally firm on dates. Therefore there has to be an explanation for this divergence. Women performing magical rites to ensure the long life of their husbands must have been common. Since this is a universal desire, these rites were also likely to have been performed in different parts of the country, generating a good deal of regional diversity. Brahmanism superimposed the relevant story of Sāvitrī, portraying the ideal wife who can ward off the death of her husband, on these rituals, but did not tamper much with the other specificities. From the names of the *vratas* it may appear that they have all emanated from a core brahmanical *Sāvitrī vrata*. But it is entirely possible that all these *vratas* independently existed in different names, but with a shared objective, much before the brahmanical adoption of them under the common denominator of Sāvitrī. This hypothesis is supported by the fact that the *Agni Purāṇa* briefly describes a *vrata* which is essentially the same as the modern *Vaṭasāvitrī vrata* without mentioning the name.[151]

Another feature that deserves notice is the centrality of the banyan tree (*vaṭa*) in ritual procedures. The banyan is not even mentioned in the *Mahābhārata* story, but the *Purāṇas* refer to it and in the *Smṛti* digests it is as essential to the ceremony as Sāvitrī herself. The procedure of this *vrata*, as set out in the *Vratārka* and other medieval works, is as follows: The woman should take a vow that she will perform this *vrata* for securing health and long life for her husband and sons. She should then sprinkle water at the root of the banyan tree, surround it with cotton threads and worship. Next, she should offer worship to Sāvitrī mentally or in an image, and pray to her for freedom from widowhood in this and subsequent lives. Finally she should worship Yama and Nārada and present gifts to the *brāhmaṇas*.[152] Sujit Chaudhuri, in his analysis of the *Sāvitrī vrata*, has described the preparation for the ritual as practised by women in eastern Bengal. A small pedestal of mud is constructed in the courtyard of the house. Four branches of a banyan tree are posted on the four corners of the pedestal. A red cotton thread is wrapped seven times around the posts and banyan leaves are hung from them, so that the pedestal becomes the symbolic replica of a forest. The figures of Sāvitrī and Satyavān are drawn on two banyan leaves with vermilion and ground rice paste and are placed on two sides of the pedestal. The figure of Yama is drawn in the middle of it with charcoal.[153]

Thus the Sāvitrī story of the *Mahābhārata* forms the backdrop to the *vrata*, and the banyan is the object of particular attention in both the *Smṛti*–Puranic and the indigenous versions of the *vrata*. But the absence of the banyan in the *Mahābhārata* episode has led scholars to look for the possible origin of the *vrata* in non-brahmanical sources. For example, Albert Henry Allen has referred to a ceremony concerning the banyan in Buddhist sources, which he thinks might conceivably have been something similar to the Sāvitrī rite. According to the story, there lived in Uruvelā a girl named Sujātā. On reaching maturity she made a prayer to a certain banyan tree that if she got a husband of rank equal to hers and her first-born was a son, she would make a yearly offering to the tree. Her prayer was granted.[154] Allen suggests that the banyan's striking powers of self-perpetuation might have been at the root of the *vrata*.[155] B.A. Gupte has speculated that the Sāvitrī story is derived from a nature myth,[156] while Chaudhuri has discovered in the *vrata* traces of a fertility rite, reminiscent of the pre-eminent role of women in primitive agriculture.[157] Whatever be the precise origin of the *vrata*, it seems likely that there existed an indigenous women's rite expressing the natural desire for progeny and a long-lived spouse, and involving veneration of the ubiquitous banyan tree of the Indian village, presumably because of its regenerative quality. As the Sāvitrī story presents the most dramatic realization of this desire, the *Purāṇas* foisted it on the indigenous rite. The story naturally had a great appeal for women and it persisted, while the ritual was left substantially untouched except for embellishment in the form of the customary *dhyāna-mantra* and *aṅgapūjā*. In the process the significance of the banyan was completely lost (possibly it came to be believed that Satyavān fell ill and died under a banyan tree, which explains its presence), but it retained its importance in the ritual.

This is the history of many a Puranic *vrata* and the *Sāvitrī vrata* is no exception. What makes it unique in the Bengal context, however, is the subversion of the *Mahābhārata* story. The *Brahmavaivarta Purāṇa* has described the *Sāvitrī vrata* at great length, over twelve chapters.[158] The procedure recommended is much the usual: Sāvitrī should be worshipped with sixteen *upacāras* at the end of which the performer should present gifts to *brāhmaṇas*.[159] In fact the procedure is much simpler than several other Puranic *vratas*, and the absence of the banyan robs it of its only distinction. The remaining eleven chapters narrate the story of Sāvitrī, which is the *kathā* section of the *vrata*. Up to the point where Sāvitrī meets Yama, the *Brahmavaivarta* account closely follows the *Mahābhārata*. But while in the *Mahābhārata* the spirited Sāvitrī indulged in lengthy moralizings and Yama for the most part was a silent listener, in the *Brahmavaivarta* the roles were reversed. Here Sāvitrī humbly asked a set of questions which Yama answered.

Sāvitrī's questions related to the nature of *karma*, its origin, auspicious and inauspicious acts and their consequences, and the means by which one can transcend the fruits of action. Yama said in reply that actions which are recommended in the *Vedas* are auspicious and actions contrary to them are inauspicious.[160] Gods, demons, *gandharvas, rākṣasas*, and human beings are all governed by their actions and enjoy the fruits of actions committed in previous lives. Living beings go to heaven because of their auspicious deeds or to hell for inauspicious ones, and when the fruits of their actions are neutralized, they attain salvation.[161] Those who donate land, gold and silver, house and wife, cows, clothes and food to *brāhmaṇas* live in the celestial abodes.[162] Those who perform the *Janmāṣṭamī, Śivarātri, Rāmanavamī* and *Ekādaśī vratas*, those who worship the goddess during the autumn, as well as Mahālakṣmī, Indra, Sūrya,

Sāvitrī and Sarasvatī, and those who bathe in all the *tīrthas*, go to heaven and are reborn as rich, wise and powerful.[163] Those who laugh at the devotees of Kṛṣṇa, those women who torment their husbands with harsh words, those who steal the gold of the gods and the *brāhmaṇas*, those *śūdras* who violate *brāhmaṇa* women and those *brāhmaṇas* who take *śūdra* wives, are consigned to hell and suffer many afflictions.[164] There is no way of transcending the fruits of action other than service of Hari. The four *Vedas*, all the *Dharmasaṁhitās, Purāṇas, Itihāsa, Pañcarātra* and such other texts have designated that the service of Hari is the best, the most auspicious and desired. It drives away birth and death, disease and old age, loss and bereavement. It bestows success and releases one from the fear of hell. The service of Kṛṣṇa generates devotion and destroys the tree which is action.[165] Yama was satisfied by Sāvitrī's thirst for knowledge and brought Satyavān back to life.

This is the summary of what Yama elaborated with infinite examples in nearly eigh: hundred verses, and the discourse has been grafted so neatly onto the original story that it seems to grow naturally out of its internal requirement and not to be a purposely created artificial adjunct. This improvisation on the *Mahābhārata* story was necessary, for it contains the quintessence of brahmanism and makes listeners familiar with the principal aspects of the *Purāṇas* in one sitting. Besides, the exposition of Yama is made with such persuasive skill, the heavens are so inviting and the hells so repelling, it has been driven home with such a determined persistence, and it has an air of such assured finality, that it is bound to create an impact on its audience. The *Sāvitrī vrata* is a typical example of how the *Purāṇas* appropriated an indigenous rite with the help of a leading story, how inconspicuously they introduced brahmanical themes into the proceedings, and how an occasion was created for the propagation of these themes.

VIII

This material became doubly effective as an instrument of communication when handled by professional narrators or *kathakas*. Khagendranath Mitra points out that while *pāṭha* literally means the reading of a scripture, usually an epic or *Purāṇa, kathakatā* is a discourse on them, and that while *kathā* should be translated as speech, it is also used in the sense of descriptive narrative.[166] This derivative sense has its origin in the practice, prevalent in most parts of India, of the public, institutionalized exposition of popular religious texts. The Bengal *Purāṇas* obviously used the terms *pāṭha* and *kathā* in this sense, for if a set of texts, admittedly composed for the benefit of the lower castes and women, are simply read out to them in the original without suitable clarificatory annotations, they will convey no meaning and serve no purpose.

Besides, that the reader and commentator had separate functions has been underscored in a Bengal *Purāṇa* itself. According to the *Bṛhaddharma Purāṇa*,[167] Vālmīki wished to retire after composing the *Rāmāyaṇa* and refused to be persuaded by Brahmā to write the *Mahābhārata* and the thirty-six *Purāṇas*. However, he agreed to pass on the eternal seed of poetry (*kāvyavījam sanātanam*) to Vedavyāsa.[168] This annoyed other sages who considered themselves equally capable of composing these texts. Finally, it was decided through the mediation of Vālmīki that Vyāsa would compose the verses, but some of the sages would be writers (*lekhaka*), some narrators (*vaktā*) and some others would determine and expound the meaning of these verses (*artha nirūpaka, artha kāraka*).[169] By the grace of Vyāsa even they would become poets (*kavi*) entitled to original composition.[170] The *Purāṇas* are one category of didactic Sanskritic texts which have not attracted detailed annotations from later scholars, partly because they permit the introduction of the required explanation in the text itself or in the course of exposition by commentators (*vyākhyātṛ*). There are references to the existence of *vyākhyāna saṁgrahas* (a kind of ready reckoner) in the *Purāṇas*,[171] which suggest that formal exposition of the *Purāṇas* was a recognized profession, complete with its system of training, rules and manuals.

Professional narrators were trained by masters and possessed considerable histrionic skills. They employed a variety of strategies—dramatizing the stories, enlivening the proceedings with apposite anecdotes, witticisms, play of words, and above all simplifying the scriptural complexities without losing their seriousness,[172] so that these performances became attractive as they purveyed the essentials of the *Purāṇas*. The rules of these performances were standardized almost into a ritual procedure, as is evident in references in the *Purāṇas* themselves, and in other normative texts. The *Niyata-kāla-kāṇḍa* of the *Kṛtyakalpataru*, for instance, contains a section called *Purāṇa-śravaṇa-vidhi*.[173] It is primarily due to these performances that the vast illiterate masses of India were initiated into the brahmanical view of proper conduct at a time when the modern means of communication and mechanical aids for the dissemination of information were not available.[174]

These performances must have become regular fairly early, for the

Purāṇas claim that they were recited to large congregations of people gathered at sacrificial sessions by a class of narrators called the *sūta-paurāṇikas* whose original ancestor emerged from the sacrificial pit of Brahmā.[175] According to the *Harṣacarita*, the *Purāṇas* were recited in the native village of Bāṇabhaṭṭa after the mid-day meal by the *pustakavācaka* Sudṛṣṭi.[176] V. Raghavan mentions that there is epigraphic evidence to suggest that in north India arrangements were made for popular recital of the epics and the *Purāṇas*. But it was particularly in the south that the Pallava, Cōḷa and Pāṇḍya rulers systematically attempted to disseminate religious education amongst the people by extending their patronage to such performances. Raghavan cites a long list of inscriptions to show how provisions were made for the reading and exposition of the epics, *Purāṇas*, and even some difficult philosophical texts. Endowments in the form of land were given to reciters, stages were assigned for their discourse in temples, and special privileges were conferred on them.[177] Such performances were also organized by some sectarian monastic establishments. William McCormack points out that each year in the month of *Śrāvaṇa* the Vīraśaiva *maṭhas* arrange for a public exposition of their *Purāṇas* (which consist of stories of the miracles of saints and deities, authored by 'modern Vīraśaiva saints'), and the performances are paid for from their funds. He says that the specialized skill is not in reading the *Purāṇas*, which an assistant often does, but rather in explaining the significance by means of *vacanas* from the authoritative Vīraśaiva books, in a mixed dialect of colloquial forms and forms approved by literary convention.[178] The Vīraśaiva example shows that not merely the dominant voice of brahmanism, but even some of the dissent groups made use of this highly effective channel of mass communication.

However, most forms of oral exegesis tended to advocate preservation of the brahmanical social order rather than non-conformity. In a detailed study of the *Harikathā*, prevalent in Maharashtra, Y.B. Damle observed that it has always argued for the maintenance of a stable social structure. Even when some of the *kathākāras* perceived the need for change, they preferred gradual reform to a radical break with the established order. The emphasis was on accommodation and adjustment.[179] Linda Hesse observed a similar tendency with regard to the public exposition of the *Rāmcaritmānas* of Tulsidas, a strong cultural influence in north India. She argues that there is an inherent tension between *bhakti* and orthodoxy in the original text of Tulsidas, arising out of a dichotomy between protest against religious formalism and priestly domination on the one hand and allegiance to the brahmanical social order on the other. But in the interpretation of the text by the narrators, an attempt was made to sublimate this tension as *bhakti* changed from counter-culture to a devotional religion. This tilt made *bhakti* more consistent with orthodoxy, thus deemphasizing social equality of women and untouchables.[180]

This is not to suggest that the narrators always blindly propagated the brahmanical dictates. Gautam Bhadra points out that although they primarily upheld the socio-cultural values of the elite, there was ample scope within the framework for accommodating elements that emerged out of the lives of the common people. Especially, they always responded to the local specificities.[181] Damle has reported a particular variety of *Harikathā*, described by him as 'Nationalist *Harikathā*', which attempted to highlight the misrule of the British in order to spread discontent among the audience and provoke them into suitable action by means of such traditional themes as Kṛṣṇa and Kaṁsa or Bhīma and Jarāsandha.[182] Evidently the narrators had considerable freedom and the skilled ones would put it to good use. As the *Purāṇas* in Bengal attempted to make the brahmanical doctrines appear consistent with the many strongly developed but non-canonized local traditions, and in the process created several ambiguities, the narrators enjoyed the liberty and tacit brahmanical sanction to interpret texts in accordance with the requirements of a specific situation, so long as they did not transgress the basic premises of the *Purāṇas*. To that extent *kathakatā* in Bengal was an extension of the Puranic enterprise.

In the absence of definitive evidence it is difficult to know when the tradition of *kathakatā* began to take root in Bengal. The many references to the public exposition of the *Purāṇas* in the *Purāṇas*, and their recommendation to invite as many as nine *brāhmaṇas* for this purpose,[183] suggest that the tradition was fairly well developed by the early medieval period. When the Gauḍīya Vaiṣṇava movement swept across Bengal in the sixteenth century, it adopted an almost identical technique for the dissemination of their message. The *līlākīrtana*, the prime instrument of communication of the Gauḍīya Vaiṣṇavas, made use of such explanatory devices as *kathā*, *ākhar* and *tuk*, which are very similar to the more conventional methods of *kathakatā*.[184] Official documents testify that *kathakatā* was popular in late eighteenth-century Bengal and the arrival of the wandering *kathakas* created great excitement among rural people.[185] Bankimchandra Chattopadhyaya, the nineteenth-century novelist and thinker, held the perverse taste of the new generation of

Bengalis and the spread of English education through formal schools responsible for causing a breach between the educated and the illiterate and the consequent decline of *kathakatā* in his time.[186] Thus the process initiated by the *Purāṇas* at the turn of the millennium remained alive for nearly a thousand years and acted as the crucial intermediary between the brahmanical great tradition and peasant society.

IX

Whatever the rewards in the afterlife of observing the *vrata* and listening to the *Purāṇas*, it required effort to induce the common people to perform these acts, for they had to pay for them in this life. The payment of gifts to priests and narrators was voluntary and depended on the generation of the right motive.[187] The *Purāṇas* sought to create this motivation by employing the familiar and useful technique of rhetorical communication.

The essential difference between instructional/informational and persuasive/rhetorical communication is that the former stresses learning and the latter yielding. The process of persuasion consists of introducing some information which prompts the receiver to reappraise his perception of his environment, and through that reappraise his needs and the ways to meet them. If the goal is a reappraisal of needs, one tactic is to encourage a new social need, another is to make an old need salient, and yet another is to present a new way to satisfy an old need. If the goal is to bring about a new social organization, this may be accomplished by undermining the receiver's confidence in existing social relationships and offering new ones that reward him for desired opinions and behaviour. Rhetorical communication often attempts to attain its goal by exploiting the human tendency to conform to the dominant attitudes, beliefs and behaviours.[188]

Indeed, the brahmanical tradition has always made use of the rhetorical technique to ensure consensus of opinion and action. All brahmanical didactic discourse made a serious effort to show that the point of view it was espousing was precisely the value system of the entire community. There was no scope for disagreement or a contrary opinion, for the attempt was to depict inevitable conclusions that must arise from contemplation of the truest principles of Hinduism. This was practicable in a society where individual responsibility for one's own status was strongly emphasized even as individualism was not only deprecated but rendered difficult by predominant influences of family, community and caste. Within this milieu one type of speech particularly flourished, that is the explication of meanings in a manner intended to lead to unanimous agreement or at least to an acceptable consensus. It followed that such discourse was often trite and platitudinous, and its tone moralistic and dogmatic.[189] Yama's long exposition to Sāvitrī is an excellent example.

But rhetoric has its problems. Rhetorical communication has to delicately balance between threat and reward to bring divergent opinion round to its own point of view, and an excessive use of the former may become counter-productive.[190] The Bengal *Purāṇas* therefore underplayed the possibility of punishment in case of non-conformity, keeping it as a distant threat, while attempting to motivate action through temptation of rewards. This is in keeping with what Madeleine Biardeau calls the centrality of desire in the Hindu scheme of things. Knowledge leads to desire, which culminates in the inclination to act. Fear is an underlying motive, but it is also the negative side of desire. It can be said that a man acts with the desire to obtain something beneficial or to avoid something harmful. Possession of both the knowledge of the rites leading to the acquisition of the desired object and the prevention of the occurrence of the undesirable, and the monopoly of performance of those rites make the *brāhmaṇas* the indispensable agents of the prosperity of this world.[191] Subservience to the *brāhmaṇas* was therefore a new way of satisfying an old and universal need. The *Purāṇas* never tire of repeating this formula at the conclusion of every *vrata*.

Rhetorical communication is also limited in its persuasive capacity. It has been repeatedly demonstrated that by far the most common effect of rhetorical communication is to reinforce pre-existing interests, attitudes and behaviour of the audience and that the least common effect is to convert the latter to an altogether new set of attitudes and behaviour.[192] Rhetorical communication seeks to overcome this difficulty by advocating behavioural adjustment through reorientation rather than reversal of existing attitudes. Adjustment can be effected by emphasizing not change or a completely new fact but an existing feature of the environment, and reminding listeners that their needs would be served if they adjusted their ways, or by bringing to their attention a new way of patterning their relationships to the environment.[193] The Bengal *Purāṇas* adopted both alternatives. They brought to the receivers' attention a new way of rearranging their relationships to the social environment. A new pattern of behaviour would serve their needs better than the existing pattern and people were taught to change the emphases they placed on different values. For example, the observer of the *vrata* was made to believe that he was performing the same functions as before, yielding the same results, but it was more effective when in the brahmanical way. The *Dhvajāropaṇa vrata* is a case in point. If this belief was successfully implanted, other behavioural adjustments—such as to the brahmanical social hierarchy—would necessarily follow.

A third problem with rhetorical communication is that attitudinal changes tend to decline over time. To make its impact as enduring as possible, five techniques can be employed.[194] The Bengal *Purāṇas* made use of all five. The performance of a *vrata* requires conscious effort which keeps the observer 'aware' of the fact that he has acquired a new attitude. Stories accompanying a *vrata* are often 'vivid and memorable'. Allurements of reward and threats of punishment ritually reiterated at the conclusion of every *vrata* are directly related to the 'self-interest' of the observer. Accounts of the *vratas* usually contain a section which narrates the circumstances in which the *vrata* was first performed and how the performer was rewarded. This is 'information' intended to serve as 'evidence'. The oft-repeated injunction that the observer must never speak to a Buddhist during the performance of a *vrata* is 'inoculation' against counter-persuasion. Besides, several other tested techniques such as endless repetition, emphatic assertion, and frequent appeal to authority have also been employed by the Bengal *Purāṇas.* The sudden mushrooming of the *vratas* in the *Purāṇas* was a ploy to expose the common people to brahmanical rhetoric as often as possible.

Yet, if the process of transmission was dependent on oral communication, why write texts? Jack Goody suggests that writing may affect the procedures and con.ent of the knowledge of individuals in society, even though they are unable to read, let alone write. Non-literate peoples or cultures may acquire, be influenced by, indeed be dominated by, forms of knowledge developed through literacy. It is possible therefore for the literati to communicate the products of writing to others by oral means.[195] Oral communication makes for a directness of relationship between symbol and referent, and as a result the totality of symbol–referent relationships is more immediately experienced by the individual and is thus more deeply socialized.[196] Also, the actual impact of a literate culture is relatively shallow when compared with an oral one, for the abstractness of written texts and the compartmentalization of knowledge that they foster disregard individual experience and immediate personal context.[197] Oral communication of written texts therefore combines the advantages of both cultures. Writing in itself is not the decisive factor but, as Ruth Finnegan puts it, who the texts are read out to, by whom and how, are of crucial social significance.[198] The most significant advantage of this arrangement from the brahmanical point of view was that the author—or in the case of the anonymous *Purāṇas* the *brāhmaṇa varṇa*—retained absolute control over the material.[199]

When oral communication of the contents of written texts became a regular practice, these texts came to be notionally available to even those who could not have direct access to them. They acquired a referential base for the whole society with the result that the actor was eventually presented with a single field of vision in which the written and the oral tended to become homologous. This was by no means unique, for Brian Stock and S.J. Tambiah have observed the adoption of a similar method of communication by Christianity and Buddhism in medieval Europe and Thailand respectively.[200] What strikes us is that brahmanism succeeded in spite of the absence of an institutional support base such as the church or the monastery.

Above all there is the magic of the written word. Whenever a literate culture, with written texts as its repository of knowledge, comes in contact with an oral culture, it assumes an aura of authority before which the oral is inevitably vulnerable. When brahmanism appropriated parts of local cultures with suitable modifications, these froze and acquired an authenticity which the fluid oral traditions could not match. Thus brahmanism became the custodian of the very local traditions which it usurped. Besides, the power of exact recall of a written text gave brahmanical reformulations the status of a standard version over the many disparate local versions. When it further modified the contents of the texts on the basis of feedbacks—the many redactions to the Bengal *Purāṇas*—it had already established itself as the deciding authority in matters of tradition, which it then used as a justification of its continued superiority.

One question still remains: if these texts were meant to be transmitted orally (and keeping in mind the audience, almost certainly in the vernacular), why were they written in Sanskrit? The Jainas and Buddhists preferred to adopt the languages (Pāli and Prākrit) spoken and understood by common people, but the *Purāṇas* were written in Sanskrit.

Emerging primarily as protest movements against *brāhmaṇa* dominance, Buddhism and Jainism dissociated themselves from the official brahmanical medium of codification. For the same reason brahmanism could not possibly write its texts in Pāli and Prākrit in Bengal, as these languages had come to be too closely identified with the heterodox religions. Besides, brahmanism had to contend for religious ascendancy in Bengal with Buddhism. Predictably therefore the Bengal *Purāṇas* systematically opposed everything that Buddhism stood for, and the *Bṛhaddharma*, while preparing a list of the symptoms of the degenerate *Kaliyuga*, says in utter contempt that the jealous *śūdras* will compose texts in Prākrit and imagining them to be *śāstras*, will propagate *dharma*.[201]

Another disadvantage of Prākrit was that, long before the composition of the Bengal *Purāṇas*, it was beginning to break into regional languages.[202] Then why were the texts not written in the regional language in which they were meant to be transmitted? The obvious reason is the legitimating status of Sanskrit. Suniti Kumar Chatterji has defined the *Purāṇas* as a 'repository of the floating mass of popular literature in all departments of life, expressed in terms of the Sanskrit language'.[203] He points out that many texts which have a Puranic character do not qualify as *Purāṇas* simply because there was no attempt at any time to render them into Sanskrit and include them within one of the canonical *Purāṇas*.[204] Since the contents of the *Purāṇas* were very often drawn from various local cultures and then put to use for the maintenance of the brahmanical social order, the only way they could remain the exclusive preserve of the *brāhmaṇas* was through their reification into Sanskrit. It is precisely for this reason that brahmanism could not afford to write its texts in the regional language of Bengal and had to rely on the supra-regional character of Sanskrit. Sanskrit gave the texts the necessary distance from the immediate context and made them a part of the world of common discourse.

Finally, there was the awe-inspiring quality of Sanskrit, the language of the gods (*devabhāṣā*). Even if the gods did not appear in person to provide substance to this claim, it was certainly the language of gods on earth, the *brāhmaṇas*. The *Bṛhaddharma Purāṇa* says, when the members of the three lower *varṇas* bow to *brāhmaṇas*, the latter should bless them in Sanskrit.[205] It seems that in issuing this instruction the authors were motivated to make use of the sacredness of the Sanskrit language. The act will of course defy the elementary rules of communication, for the good words will be lost on the recipients, but it will still have served its purpose in eliciting the desired response of awe-struck respect for the *brāhmaṇas*.

However, if this was the stature of Sanskrit and the social position of the *brāhmaṇas*, it is expected that they would try to impose Sanskrit at least in matters pertaining to religion and would themselves remain impervious to the influence of the local language. It is well known that the medium of exchange between two speech communities is determined by the culturally dominant group.[206]

Clearly, this rule is not valid for all situations. In early medieval Bengal the cultural dominance of the *brāhmaṇas* was unquestionable and yet the local people did not learn Sanskrit; in fact they were prevented from doing so because the *brāhmaṇas* took care to restrict the cultivation of Sanskrit to themselves. Instead, the *brāhmaṇas* learnt the local language and even allowed it to corrupt the purity of Sanskrit. Some of the Bengal *Purāṇas* abound in instances of incorrect grammatical forms due to the influence of Bengali.[207] This is because cultural domination is not the only factor which dictates the nature of bilingual communication. When a culturally dominant group happens to be a small minority, a migrant group and substantially dependent on the charity of the majority, it will have to establish interlingual communication with the regional language on an unequal linguistic exchange or non-reciprocal intelligibility basis in favour of the regional language. But to safeguard the prestige of the language of the dominant group, it may be necessary to exclude the local population from learning it. This is precisely what brahmanism did in Bengal. Sanskrit remained the charmed language, the unattainable key to the storehouse of brahmanical wisdom, reified in the *Purāṇas* and such other texts, while everyday affairs including religious matters except for the utterance of *mantras* were conducted in the local language. This norm, set by the early centuries of this millennium, remained valid until the *brāhmaṇas* partially lost their overwhelming socio-cultural advantage in Bengal under colonial conditions.

Thus the Sanskrit texts became the symbol of distant authority and narrators purveyed their essence in the vernacular, interpreting and improvising in accordance with the purely local needs, but always remaining within the permissible limits of the brahmanical world-view. This process generated an enormous sub-regional variation in religious practice under the umbrella of brahmanism, a consistent characteristic of the South Asian religions. This became such a fixed pattern that the intensified efforts at the spread of literacy and the beginning of the production of printed literature in the vernacular on aspects of popular religion from the late nineteenth century did not substantially alter this situation, as Susan Wadley's study of 'the festivals of the twelve months' (annual calendar of *vratas*) in north India shows.[208] Counter-examples are not altogether absent. Ralph Nicholas on the goddess Śītalā and printed texts of her myth in Bengal observes that while the several publishers printing ostensibly different versions of her myth would suggest a diversifying effect on the mythology, an examination of these so-called variant versions shows a 'common core' which he calls 'standardization'.[209] But the common core is not the issue here. The multiple manuscripts of the various *Maṅgalakāvyas* also often reveal a common core and so do the Puranic stories. Nicholas, however, significantly observes that standardization through the printed medium prevents further mythological development.[210] This is entirely likely, but is not attributable to the spread of literacy, nor to the effect of the printing press. It is the decline in the tradition of *kathakatā* which has destroyed autonomy and creativity in the religion of rural Bengal.

Brahmanism in Bengal did not aim at total conversion of the local population which would result in a sharp, decisive break with the former traditions, belief systems and behaviour patterns, as happens with proselytization. Rather, it attempted to slowly draw the indigenous non-brahmanical communities of Bengal within the brahmanical social order. The Puranic treatment of the *vrata* is a perfect example of this process. Paradoxical as it may seem at first sight, through the composition of the Sanskrit *Purāṇas* brahmanism succeeded in achieving what it attempted. Through the introduction, not of literacy, but of literate form of knowledge, brahmanism ensured conformity.

X

I suggest that the Puranic *vratas* did not take over the indigenous *vratas* which continued to be performed by women in the seclusion of the inner apartments of the households. Brahmanism created a new community festival to be organized by the relatively well-to-do in the village. Its parallel structure with the local rite paved the way for its acceptance; the original rite itself remained largely unaffected by the brahmanical innovation. Popular instruction presented as entertainment by way of *kathakatā*, feeding of the poor and such other community activities, encouraged the participation of the whole village or at least the caste or kin group of the neighbourhood. That served the purpose of brahmanism. It had no particular interest in undermining the women's rites already in vogue. Their domains were different. At the same time it created practically the only brahmanical ritual which granted equal right of participation to women and the lowest social groups. Brahmanism must have anticipated that once drawn into this process, the Puranic stories would be ploughed back in some form even in the *kathā* section of the exclusively women's *vratas*. Oral transmission of the written text is one of the most potent means for the dissemination of a message and Blackburn and Ramanujan show how intricately they reinforce each other in an unending cycle of ever-increasing spread.[211] There are oblique references to the *Purāṇas* in some of the *meyelī vratakathās* now available in printed form, and once they had penetrated the *antaḥpura* they had really engulfed the whole rural society.

NOTES

1. Melford Spiro, 'Culture and Personality', in David L. Sills (ed.), *International Encyclopaedia of Social Sciences*, Vol. III, The Macmillan Company and the Free Press, USA, 1968, p. 560.
2. Redfield, 'Civilizations as Cultural Structures?' pp. 392–3.
3. Singer, 'The Social Organization of Indian Civilization', p. 256.
4. Marriott and Cohn, 'Networks and Centres in the Integration of Indian Civilization', pp. 1–9.
5. *Ibid.*, p. 6.
6. McKim Marriott, 'Changing Channels of Cultural Transmission in Indian Civilization', *Journal of Social Research*, Vol. 4, 1961, pp. 13–25.
7. John J. Gumperz, 'Religion and Social Communication in Village North India', in Edward B. Harper (ed.), *Religion in South Asia*, University of Washington Press, Seattle, 1964, p. 94.
8. P. V. Kane, *History of Dharmaśāstra*, Vol. V, Part I, Bhandarkar Oriental Research Institute, Poona, 1974 (second edition), p. 5.
9. *Ibid.*, p. 25.
10. *Ibid.*, pp. 26–7.
11. *Ibid.*, p. 28.
12. *Ibid.*, pp. 29–31.
13. *Ks*, summary of chapter 22.
14. S.R. Das, 'A Study of the Vrata Rites of Bengal', *Man in India*, Vol. 32, No. 3, 1952, p. 216.
15. *Ibid.*, p. 217.
16. See Ray, *Bāṅgālir Itihāsa,* pp. 613–16; Hazra, *Upapurāṇas,* Vol. II, pp. 380–1; Ashutosh Bhattacharya, *Bāṅglā Maṅgalakāvyer Itihāsa*, A. Mukherji and Company Pvt. Ltd, Calcutta, 1975 (sixth edition), p. 112; Abanindranath Thakur, *Bāṅglār Vrata*, Visva-Bharati, Calcutta, 1350 BS, pp. 1–2; Dineshchandra Sen, *The Folk Literature of Bengal*, B.R. Publishing Corporation, Delhi, 1985 (reprint), pp. 246–8; Shahanara Hussain, *The Social Life of Women in Early Medieval Bengal*, Asiatic Society of Bangladesh, Dhaka, 1985, p. 85; Das, 'Vrata Rites of Bengal', pp. 222–42; Pallab Sengupta, *Pūjā Pārvaṇer Utsakathā*, Pustak Bipani, Calcutta, 1984, pp. 39–55. In fact there exists a rare unanimity of opinion among all those who have written on this subject.

17. Ray, *Bāṅgālīr Itihāsa,* p. 613.
18. Bhattacharya, *Bāṅglā Maṅgalakāvyer Itihāsa*, pp. 451–2.
19. Sen, *The Folk Literature of Bengal*, pp. 247–8.
20. *māghādyairmaṅgalāṁ saukhyāṁ jyaiṣṭhādyairbrahmajāṁ yajet /*
iṣādyaiḥ kālikādyāstu yaṣṭavyā vidhinā mune //
DP, 45.19.

maṅgalā maṅgalaṁ dhatte vidhinā pūjitā mune /
utpātakṣobhanirghāta-vikṛtīnāṁ śamāya ca //
DP, 50.9.

21. *maṅgalā piṅgalā dhanyā bhrāmarī bhadrikā tathā /*
ulkā siddhiḥ saṁkaṭā ca yoginyo'ṣṭāḥ prakīrtitāḥ //
Cited in Dasgupta, *Bhārater Śakti-Sādhanā,* p. 175.
22. 'Saṁkaṭā Maṅgalacaṇḍī Vrata', in Gopalchandra Bhattacharya (ed.), *Bāromāser Meyeder Vratakathā*, Nirmal Book Agency, Calcutta, undated, pp. 200–3.
23. Dasgupta, *Bhārater Śakti-Sādhanā,* p. 175.
24. *bhairavīṁ pūjayāmāsa mathurāgrāmadevatām /*
upācāraiḥ ṣoḍaśabhiḥ ṣaṣṭhīṁ maṅgalacaṇḍikām //
BvP, IV.100.12.
25. *chāgairmeṣaiśca mahiṣairgaṇḍairmāyātibhirvaraiḥ //*
BvP, II. 44.17.

chāgairmeṣaiśca mahiṣairgavayaiḥ pakṣibhistathā //
DbP, IX.47.17.

26. *pāneṣu madirā śastā naro baliṣu pārthiva /*
KP, 80.51.
27. Bhattacharya, *Bāṅglā Maṅgalakāvyer Itihāsa*, pp. 438, 459–61.
28. Ray, *Bāṅgālīr Itihāsa,* p. 658.
29. *godhāsanā bhavedgauri līlayā haṁsavāhanā /*
siṁhārūḍhā bhaveddurgā mātarassvasvavāhanā //
Cited in T.A. Gopinatha Rao, *Elements of Hindu Iconography*, Vol. I, Part 2, Motilal Banarsidass, Delhi, 1968 (Appendix C), p. 113.
30. Jitendra Nath Banerjea, *Development of Hindu Iconography*, Munshiram Manoharlal Publishers Pvt. Ltd, New Delhi, 1974 (third edition), p. 502.
31. *godhikānāṁ gorudhirairvārṣikīṁ tṛptimāpnuāt //*
KP, 67.9.
32. According to Hazra, the present *Kālikā Purāṇa* is a work of the tenth or the first half of the eleventh century. Hazra, *Upapurāṇas*, Vol. II, p. 245.
33. Risley, *The Tribes and Castes of Bengal*, Vol. I, pp. 314–16.
34. Bhattacharya, *Bāṅglā Maṅgalakāvyer Itihāsa*, p. 438.
35. *kṛpārūpātipratyakṣā yoṣitāmiṣṭadevatā //*
BvP, II.44.6 and *DbP,* IX.47.6.

The phrase reminds us of a similar usage by Raghunandana, the *Smṛti* writer of medieval Bengal, who characterized the religious customs traditionally practised by women but not sanctioned in the sacred texts, such as the *vrata*, as *yoṣit vyavahāra siddhā* and accorded them the seal of brahmanical approval; cited in Thakur, *Bāṅglār Vrata*, p. 12.

36. *parituṣṭā sarvavāñchāpradātrī sarvayoṣitām* ||

BvP, II.1.86 and *DbP*, IX.1.86.

37. *pañcopacārairbhaktyā ca yoṣidbhiḥ paripūjitā* ||

BvP, II.1.84.

38. *BvP*, II.16.64–72.

39. *akṣasūtraṁ tathā padmam abhayaṁ ca varaṁ tathā* |
godhāsanāśritā mūrti gṛhe pūjyā śriye sadā ||
Cited in Gopinatha Rao, *Elements of Hindu Iconography*, Vol. I, Part 2 (Appendix C), p. 120.

40. *lohitāṅgasya divasaḥ priyo'syāḥ parikīrttitaḥ* ||

KP, 80.57.

41. *pratimaṅgalavāreṣu prativiśveṣu pūjitā* |

BvP, II.1.84 and *DbP*, IX.1.85.

prati maṅgalavāre ca pūjye ca maṅgalaprade ||

BvP, II.44.34.

pūjye maṅgalavāre ca maṅgalābhīṣṭadevate |

DbP, IX.47.29.

42. *pūjive caṇḍikā prati maṅgalavāsare* |
vipad-sāgare caṇḍī hava karṇadhāre ||
Sukumar Sen (ed.), *Caṇḍīmaṅgala (Kavikaṁkaṇa Mukunda viracita)*, Sahitya Akademi, New Delhi, 1975, p. 143.

43. Bhattacharya (ed.), *Bāromāser Meyeder Vratakathā*, p. 33, and Suhasini Devi, *Meyelī Vratakathā*, Pustak Bipani, Calcutta, 1392 BS, pp. 6–9. These are just two representative examples, picked up at random.

44. *BvP*, II.44.15–20 and *DbP*, IX.47.15–20.

45. *dūrvvāṅkuraiḥ samāyuktamakṣataṁ prītidaṁ param* ||

KP, 80.60.

46. *aṣṭataṇḍula dūrvā nite nite niyā* |
pūjiha maṅgalavāre jaya jaya diyā ||
Sen (ed.), *Caṇḍimaṅgala*, p. 144.

47. Tarak Chandra Ray Chaudhuri and Sarat Chandra Mitra, 'On the Cult of the Goddess Mangala Chandi in Eastern Bengal', *The Journal of the Anthropological Society of Bombay*, Vol. 13, 1927, p. 104.

48. *paṭeṣu pratimāyāṁ vā ghaṭe maṅgalacaṇḍikām* ||

KP, 80.63.

49. Cited in Bhattacharya, *Bāṅglā Maṅgalakāvyer Itihāsa*, p. 457. In the *Caṇḍīmaṅgala* also Khullanā worshipped her in a *ghaṭa*, *ibid*., p. 451.

50. *harṣamaṅgaladakṣe ca harṣamaṅgaladāyike /*
śubhe maṅgaladakṣe ca śubhe maṅgalacaṇḍike //
maṅgale maṅgalārhe ca sarvvamaṅgalamaṅgale /
satāṁ maṅgalade devi sarvveṣāṁ maṅgalālaye //
pūjye maṅgalavāre ca maṅgalābhīṣṭadevate /
pūjye maṅgalavaṁśasya manuvaṁśasya santatam //
maṅgalādhiṣṭhātṛdevi maṅgalānāñca maṅgale /
saṁsāramaṅgalādhāre mokṣamaṅgaladāyini //
sāre ca maṅgalādhāre pāre ca sarvvakarmmaṇām /
prati maṅgalavāre ca pūjye maṅga-sukhaprade //
stotreṇānena śambhuśca stutvā maṅgalacaṇḍikām /
pratimaṅgalavāre ca pūjām dattvā gataḥ śivaḥ //
prathame pūjitā devī śivena sarvvamaṅgalā /
dvitīye pūjitā sā ca maṅgalena graheṇa ca //
tṛtīye pūjitā bhadrā maṅgalena nṛpeṇa ca /
caturthe maṅgale vāre sundarībhiḥ prapūjitā //
pañcame maṅgalākāṅkṣi-narairmaṅgalacaṇḍikā /

DbP, IX.47.27–35.

BvP II.44.30–8 is similar except verse 36, which is an addition.

51. *Mārkaṇḍeya Purāṇa*, 91.9.

52. *tvaṁ kālaketuvaradā cchalagodhikāsi*
ya tvaṁ śubhā bhavasi maṅgalacaṇḍikākhyā /
śrīśālavāhananṛpād vaṇijaḥ sasūno
rakṣeo'mvuje karicayaṁ grasatī vamantī //

BP, III.16.45.

53. *bṛhaddharmapurāṇer uttarakhaṇḍete /*
likhā mahāmāyā-prati viṣṇura stavete //
. . . .
bhāratabhūmete caṇḍī līlā prakāśiyā /
kālaketu uddhārive godhikā haiyā //
maṅgalacaṇḍikā nāma kariyā prakāśa /
samvaraṇe karivara karivena grāsa //
vaṇiksutake pheli ghora saṁkaṭete /
uddhāra karive nṛpa-śālavāhana hate //
Cited in Hazra, *Upapurāṇas*, Vol. II, pp. 458–9.

54. *Ibid*., p. 189.

55. Krishnachandra Gupta (ed.), *Śrī Śrī Maṅgalacaṇḍīr Pāñcālī*, General Library and Printers, Calcutta, 1391 BS.

56. *kena mā tomār āj eta velā?*
hāste, khelte, pāṭer dolāy dulte,
nirdhanīke dhan dite, aputrakke putra dite,

kānāke cakṣudān karte, khoḍāke kāmadeva karte,
rājāke kārāgāre khālās karte,
tāi āj āmār eta velā /

Personal communication, Rupamanjari Sen.

57. *BvP*, II.44 and *DbP*, IX.47.1–37.
58. *pradhānāṁśasvarūpā yā devī maṅgalacaṇḍikā* /
prakṛtermukhasambhūtā sarvamaṅgalā sadā //
BvP, II.1.82 and *DbP*, IX.1.83–4.
59. *tasya pūjyābhīṣṭadevī tena maṅgalacaṇḍikā* //
mūrttibhedena sā durgā mūlaprakṛtirīśvarī /
BvP, II.44.5–6 and *DbP*, IX.47.5–6.
60. *lakṣmī sarasvatī durgā sāvitrī rādhikādikam* /
sṛṣṭisūtrasvarūpañcāpyādyaṁ srasṭuranirmitam //
etāsāmamśarūpaṁ yat strīrūpaṁ vāstavaṁ smṛtam /
tat praśaṁsya yaśorūpaṁ sarvamaṅgalakāraṇam //
. . . .
ṣaṣṭhī maṅgalacaṇḍī ca mūrttiśca dharmakāminī //
BvP, II.16.65–6, 70.
61. *namaḥ sarasvatīrūpe namaḥ sāvitri śaṁkari* /
gaṅgāpadmāvatīrūpe ṣaṣṭhī maṅgalacaṇḍike //
manase tulasīrūpe namo lakṣmīsvarūpiṇi /
namo durge bhagavati namaste sarvvarūpiṇi //
DbP, IX.50.48–9.
62. *ujjayinyāṁ tathā puryyāṁ pīṭham maṅgakoṣṭhakam* /
śubhā maṅgalacaṇḍyākhyā yatrāhaṁ varadāyinī //
BP, I.14.14.
63. Hazra, *Upapurāṇas,* Vol. II, pp. 48–9, footnote 125.
64. D.C. Sircar, 'The Śākta Pīṭhas', *The Journal of the Royal Asiatic Society of Bengal, Letters*, Vol. 14, 1948, distributed in book form by Motilal Banarsidass, Delhi, pp. 35, 41.
65. *DbP*, VII.38.23. In the translation Mahākāla has been rendered as Ujjayinī, as some other names are also similarly transformed. Since the text is edited by no less a scholar than Pt. Panchanan Tarkaratna, I assume that there must be a tradition which connects Mahākāla with Ujjayinī.
66. *ujānite kafoṇi maṅgalacaṇḍī devī* /
bhairava kapilāmvara śubha yāre sevi //

Annadāmaṅgala, in *Rāmprasāda Bhāratachandra Rachanāsamagra*, Reflect Publications, Calcutta, 1986, p. 260; *pīṭhamālā* section, verse 22.

67. Gupta (ed.), *Śrī Śrī Maṅgalacaṇḍīr Pāñcālī*, p. 2.
68. *yaiṣā lalitakāntākhyā devī maṅgalacaṇḍikā* /
varadābhayahastā sā dvibhujā gauradehikā //
raktapadmāsanasthā ca mukuṭojjvalamaṇḍitā /

raktakauśeyavasanā smitavaktrā śubhānanā II
navayauvanasampannā cārvvaṅgī lalitaprabhā I

KP, 80.52–4.

69. *KP*, 80.56. The original *gāyatrī:*

tat saviturvareṇyaṁ
bhargo devasya dhīmahi
dhiyo yo naḥ pracodayāt

is a verse from a hymn of the *Ṛg Veda* (III.62.10) addressed to the solar god Savitṛ. This is whispered in the ear of the initiate by the officiating *brāhmaṇa* during the *upanayana* (investiture of the sacred thread) ceremony and is considered 'the most holy passage of the most holy text' (Basham, *The Wonder That Was India*, p. 163). Although the contexts are entirely different, the similarity in words does indeed entitle the verse from the *Kālikā Purāṇa* to be called 'the *gāyatrī*' of Maṅgalacaṇḍī. She thus gets connected with the Vedic corpus through the echo of the most sacred *mantra* of brahmanism.

70. Das, 'Vrata Rites of Bengal', p. 237.
71. *DP*, 34.12–16.
72. Ray, *Bāṅgālīr Itihāsa,* p. 611.
73. *Ibid.*
74. Gopendrakrishna Basu, 'Indpūjā', *Bāṅglār Laukika Devatā*, Dey's Publishing, Calcutta, 1976, pp. 112–13.
75. *Ibid.*, pp. 114–15.
76. Risley, *The Tribes and Castes of Bengal*, Vol. I, pp. 375, 380.
77. *BnP*, summary of 18.52–127.
78. *BnP*, summary of 18.10–44.
79. *DbP*, III.26.9–37.
80. *DbP*, V.34.3–16.
81. Bandyopadhyaya, *Smṛtiśāstre Bāṅgālī*, p. 95, and Das, 'Vrata Rites of Bengal', p. 214.
82. Kane, *History of Dharmaśāstra*, Vol. V, Part I, p. 44.
83. *Ibid.*
84. Eric Hobsbawm, 'Introduction: Inventing Traditions', in Eric Hobsbawm and Terence Ranger (eds), *The Invention of Tradition*, Cambridge University Press, Cambridge, 1983, p. 1.
85. *Ibid.*, pp. 1–2.
86. *karttavyañca caturṇāñca varṇānāṁ nityameva ca I*
yatīnāṁ vaiṣṇavānāñca brāhmaṇānāṁ viśeṣataḥ II

BvP, IV.26.22.

87. *brāhmaṇakṣatriyaviśāṁ śūdrāṇāñcaiva yoṣitām I*
mokṣadaṁ kurvatāṁ bhaktyā viṣṇoḥ priyataraṁ dvijāḥ II

BnP, 21.2.

88. *brahmakṣatriyaviṭśūdrairanyaiścāpi dvijottama /*
sarvvairekādaśī kāryyā caturvvargaphalapradā //
Ks, 22.54.

89. Kane, *History of Dharmaśāstra*, Vol. V, Part I, p. 54.

90. *DP*, 99.1.

91. *BnP*, 17.2.

92. *ānantarya-vrataṁ brūhi . . . /*
hitāya sarvabhūtānāṁ lalanānāṁ viśeṣataḥ //
Bhaviṣya Purāṇa, IV.29.1–2. Cited in Hazra, *Upapurāṇas*, Vol. II, p. 381.

93. *adhunā kathayiṣyāmi vratāni tava suvrata /*
nārībhiśca naraiścaiva karttavyāni prayatnataḥ //
vratamanantatṛtīyākhyāṁ rasakalyāṇinīvratam /
ārdrānandakaraṁ nāmnā tṛtīyāyāṁ vratañca yat //
śukravāravratañcaiva tathā kṛṣṇacaturddaśī /
bhaumavāravratañcaiva pradoṣavratameva ca //
DbP, VII.38.36–8.

94. *sarvve varṇāśramā yāśca striyaścaikādaśīparāḥ /*
. . . .
sadhavānāntu nārīṇāṁ rātrau peyaṁ jalaṁ matam //
BP, III.10.5–6

95. *āpatsvapi na bhedantu striyaiḥ kāryyaṁ yaducyatām /*
DP, 101.27.

96. *DP*, 79.4, 13–17.

97. *sarvaṁ vratavidhānañca matto vatsa niśāmaya /*
khyātaṁ gaurīvrataṁ nāma mārge māsi kṛtaṁ striyā //
BvP, IV.27.122.

98. *BvP*, III.3.3 and III.5.17–24.

99. *ghaṭe maṇau śālagrāme jale vā pūjayed vratī /*
. . . .
dhyānañca sāmavedoktaṁ nivodha kaṭhayāmi te /
BvP, IV.16.79–80.

100. *homaṁ daśāṁśataḥ kuryyāddaśāṁśena ca tarpaṇam /*
DbP, V.34.11.

101. *devasya purataḥ kuryyāt sthaṇḍilaṁ caturasrakam /*
aratnimātraṁ tatrāgniṁ sthāpayedgṛhyamārgataḥ //
ājyabhāgāntaparyyantaṁ kṛtvā puruṣasūktataḥ /
caruṇā ca tilaiścāpi ghṛtena juhuyāt tathā //
ekavāraṁ dvivāraṁ vā trivāraṁ vāpi śaktitaḥ /
homaṁ kuryyāt prayatnena sarvvapāpanivṛttaye //
prāyaścittādikaṁ sarvvaṁ svagṛhyoktavidhānataḥ /
samāpya homaṁ vidhivacchāntisūktaṁ japedvudhaḥ //
BnP, 17.10–13.

102. Kane, *History of Dharmaśāstra*, Vol. V, Part I, p. 32.
103. *Ibid*., p. 52.
104. Lina M. Fruzzetti, *The Gift of a Virgin: Women, Marriage, and Ritual in a Bengali Society*, Rutgers University Press, New Brunswick, New Jersey, 1982, p. 122.
105. *Ibid*., p. 65.
106. Suzanne Hanchett, *Coloured Rice: Symbolic Structure in Hindu Family Festivals*, Hindustan Publishing Corporation, Delhi, 1988, p. 278.
107. James J. Preston, *Cult of the Goddess: Social and Religious Change in a Hindu Temple*, Vikas Publishing House Pvt. Ltd, New Delhi, 1980, p. 14.
108. *nāsti strīṇāṁ pṛthag yajño na vratam nāpyupoṣaṇam l*
patiṁ śuśrūṣate yena tena svarge mahīyate ll
Cited in Das, 'Vrata Rites of Bengal', p. 213.
109. *BP*, III.8.3.
110. *sadhavānāṁ hi nārīṇāṁ nopavāsādikaṁvratam l*
patyājñayā caredyat tu bhūtānāṁ tadvrataṁparam ll
BP, III.8.7.
111. Bạndyopadhyaya, *Smṛtiśāstre Bāṅgālī*, p. 98.
112. Thakur, *Bāṅglār Vrata*, p. 8.
113. Kane, *History of Dharmaśāstra*, Vol. V, Part I, pp. 253–462.
114. *yaḥ śūdreṇārccitaṁ liṅgaṁ viṣṇuṁ vā praṇamennaraḥ l*
na tasya niṣkṛtiścāsti prāyaścittāyutairapi ll
namedyaḥ śūdrasaṁspṛṣṭaṁ liṅgaṁ vā harimeva vā l
sa sarvvayātanābhogī yāvadācandratārakam ll
pāṣaṇḍapūjitaṁ liṅgaṁ natvā pāṣaṇḍatāṁ vrajet l
rājan vedavido vāpi sarvvaśāstrārthavid yadi ll
ābhīrapūjitaṁ liṅgaṁ natvā narakamaśnute ll
yoṣidbhiḥ pūjitaṁ liṅgaṁ viṣṇuṁ vāpi namettu yaḥ l
sa koṭikulasaṁyukta ākalpaṁ raurave vaset ll
BnP, 14.54–8.
115. *strīśūdrāṇāṁ samīpe tu vedādhyayanakṛnnaraḥ l*
kalpakoṭisahasreṣu prāpnoti narakān kramāt ll
BnP, 14.144.
116. *śūdrasya annamaśitvā vedaṁ yadi udīrate l*
ucchiṣṭabhojī varṇānāṁ narake parṣyupāsate ll
caṇḍāla-caṇḍakarmme ca vṛṣalīpatisannidhau l
yadi udīrate vedaṁ tadā vipro'pi tatsamaḥ ll
DP, 96.7–8.
117. *alpāyuṣo'lpabuddhīṁśca viprān jñātvā kalāvatha l*
purāṇasaṁhitāṁ puṇyāṁ kuruteo'sau yuge yuge ll
strīśūdradvijavandhūnāṁ na vedaśravaṇaṁ matam l
teṣāmeva hitārthāya purāṇāni kṛtāni ca ll
DbP, I.3.20–1.

118. *vedaṁ na śṛṇuyācchūdraḥ śṛṇuyācca purāṇakam* /

BP, III.4.19.

119. *śṛṇoti durbhagā cettu saubhāgyaṁ svāmino labhet* //
mṛtavatsā kākavandhyā mahāvandhyā ca pāpinī /
purāṇaśravaṇāllabhe putrañca cirajīvinam //

BvP, IV.133.46–7.

120. *strī śūdro na paṭhedetat kadāpi ca vimohitaḥ* /
śṛṇuād dvijavaktrāttu nityameveti ca sthitiḥ //

DbP, XII.14.24.

121. *mohādvā kāmataḥ śūdraḥ purāṇaṁ saṁhitāṁ smṛtim* /
paṭhannarakamāpnoti pitṛbhiḥ saha pāpakṛt //
śūdrebhyo vihitaṁ yattu yaśca mantra udāhṛtaḥ /
tadvipravacanādgrāhyaṁ dvayaṁ śūdraiḥ sadaiva hi //

KP, 88.48–9.

122. *DP*, 6.39–46.

123. *mārkaṇḍeya purāṇasthaṁ caṇḍīsaptaśatīstavam* /
gītaśāstram bhāratīyaṁ vipraḥ sarvvāśramaḥ paṭhet //

BP, III.7.2.

124. *yo vadet satataṁbhaktyā purāṇāni dvijottamāḥ* /
ātmārthaṁ vā parārthaṁ vā sa harirnātra saṁśayaḥ //
. . . .
purāṇasaṁhitāvaktā harirityabhidhīyate /
tadbhaktiṁ kurvvatāṁ nṛṇāṁ gaṅgāsnānaṁ dine dine //
purāṇaśravaṇe bhaktirgaṅgāsnānopamā smṛtā /
tadvaktari ca yā bhaktiḥ sā prayāgopamā smṛtā //
purāṇairdharmakathanairyaḥ samuddharate janam /
saṁsārasāgare magnaṁ sa harirnātra saṁśayaḥ //

BnP, 6.51, 53–5.

125. *vidyādānarato yāti pūjyamāno'vjasūnunā* /
purāṇapāṭhako yāti stūyamāno munīśvaraiḥ //

BnP, 29.37.

126. *upavāsādibhiścaiva purāṇaśravaṇādibhiḥ* /
puṣpādyaiḥ prārcanaṁ viṣṇoḥ kriyāyoga iti smṛtaḥ //

BnP, 31.44.

127. *pīṭhasthānāni goṣṭhañca devī-devagṛhāṇi ca* /
vicitrāṇi ca puṇyāni saudhāni suśubhāni ca //
nadītīradrumodyāna-viviktajanasaṁsadi /
kīrttayeccopalipteṣu dhūpagandhasragādibhiḥ //

DP, 1.58–9.

128. *DP*, 128.5–23.

129. *pāpīyānapi vedadharmarahitaḥ svācārahīnāśayo,*
vyājenāpi śṛṇoti yaḥ paramidaṁ śrīmatpurāṇottamam /

bhuktvā bhogakalāpamatra vipulaṁ dehāvasāneo'calaṁ,
yogiprāpyamavāpnuyādbhagavatīnāmāṁkitaṁ sundaram //
DbP, I.3.40.

130. *aspaṣṭakīrttiḥ suyaśā mūrkho bhavati paṇḍitaḥ* //
BvP, IV.133.48.

131. *DP*, 6.39–44.

132. *āndhyaṁ kuṣṭhañca dāridryaṁ rogaṁ śokañca dāruṇam* /
purāṇaśravaṇādeva naiva jānāti puṇyavān //
BvP, IV.133.50.

133. *na cāgnirvādhate tatra na caurādibhayaṁ tathā* //
BnP, 38.141.

134. *harernāmāni yatraiva purāṇāni bhavanti hi* /
tatra gatvā sāvadhānamābhiḥ sārddhañca śroṣyasi //
purāṇaśravaṇāccaiva harernāmānukīrtanāt /
bhasmībhūtāni pāpāni bhaviṣyanti kṣaṇena ca //
BvP, IV.129.54–5.

135. *yajñānāmapi tīrthānāṁ vratānāṁ tapasāṁ tathā* /
bhuvaḥ pradakṣiṇasyāpi phalaṁ nāsya samānakam /
caturṇāmapi vedānāṁ pāṭhādapi varaṁ phalam //
BvP, IV.133.44.

136. *kurvanti jāgaraṁ viṣṇorvedādhyayanamuttamam* /
purāṇapaṭhanaṁ vāpi kartavyaṁ niśi vaiṣṇavaiḥ //
rāmāyaṇaṁ bhāgavataṁ bhārataṃ vyāsabhāṣitam /
anyāni ca purāṇāni pāṭhyāni harivāsare //
ye paṭhanti purāṇāni ye śṛṇvanti harerddine /
pratyakṣare labhante te kāpilādānajaṁ phalaṁ //
Ks, 22.148–50.

137. *samātṛkaḥ sabhāryyaśca sabhrātā sapitā budhaḥ* /
saputraśca samitraśca kurute jāgaraṁ hareḥ //
Ks, 22.104.

138. *BvP*, IV.8.46.
139. *BnP*, 16.80.
140. *BnP*, 17.20.
141. *BnP*, 21.17.
142. *DbP*, V.34.12.
143. *BnP*, 16.92, 16.102.
144. *śravaṇādapi prāpnoti sarvvakāmasukhāni ca* /
DP, 33.109.

145. *BnP*, 19.30.
146. *BnP*, 20.33.
147. *nava pañca trayaścaiko devyāḥ pāṭhe dvijāḥ smṛtā* //
DbP, III.26.16.

148. Vishnu S. Sukthankar (ed.), *Mahābhārata* (*The Āraṇyakaparvan*, Part 2), Bhandarkar Oriental Research Institute, Poona, 1942, *Parva* III, Chapters 277–83, pp. 960–89.
149. Kane, *History of Dharmaśāstra*, Vol. V, Part I, p. 92.
150. *Ibid*., pp. 92–3.
151. *Ibid*.
152. *Ibid*., p. 93.
153. Sujit Chaudhuri, 'Sāvitrī–Satyavān: Kiṁvadantīr Punarvicār', in *Prācīn Bhārate Mātrprādhānya: Kiṁvadantīr Punarvicār*, Papyrus, Calcutta, 1990, p. 2.
154. Albert Henry Allen, 'The *Vaṭa-sāvitrī-vrata*, According to Hemādri and the *Vratārka*', *Journal of the American Oriental Society*, Vol. 21, July–December 1900, p. 63.
155. *Ibid*., p. 58.
156. B.A. Gupte, 'The Symbolism of the *Sāvitrīvrata*', *The Indian Antiquary*, Vol. 35, 1906, pp. 116–19.
157. Chaudhuri, 'Sāvitrī–Satyavān', pp. 1–38.
158. *BvP*, II.23–34.
159. *BvP*, II.23.42–74.
160. *BvP*, II.25.7.
161. *BvP*, II.26.16, 18–19.
162. *BvP*, II.26.45–51.
163. *BvP*, II.27.73, 75, 80, 82–4, 86–8, 94, 96–9, 101–2, 118.
164. *BvP*, II.30.25–6, 50, 84, 202–3.
165. *BvP*, II.31.1, II.32.9–12.
166. Khagendranath Mitra, 'Diffusion of Socio-religious Culture in North India', in Haridas Bhattacharyya (ed.), *The Cultural Heritage of India*, Vol. IV, The Ramakrishna Mission Institute of Culture, Calcutta, 1956, p. 520.
167. *BP*, I.27–9.
168. *BP*, I.27.11.
169. *BP*, I.29.23, 26.
170. *BP*, I.29.28.
171. Giorgio Bonazzoli, 'Composition, Transmission and Recitation of Purāṇas', *Purāṇa*, Vol. 25, No. 2, July 1983, p. 275.
172. Jogesh Chandra Ray Vidyanidhi, *Paurāṇik Upākhyāna*, Calcutta, 1361 BS, pp. 87–8, and Philip Lutgendorf, 'Rāma's Story in Shiva's City: Public Arenas and Private Patronage', in Sandria B. Freitag (ed.), *Culture and Power in Banaras: Community, Performance and Environment 1800–1980*, Oxford University Press, Delhi, 1990, pp. 34–6.
173. Yadava, *Society and Culture in Northern India,* p. 422, note 141.
174. Even now, when sophisticated means of communication are in use, direct communication through word of mouth remains the most effective source of dissemination of information in village India. A recent study assesses the actual and potential contribution of mass communication media

(printed works, radio, television, etc.) to the process of development in India. The conclusion is that 'locally based' (locally conceived in response to particular local needs) rather than centralised strategies for communication show the most promise of success. Both the surveys and the observational studies conducted by them indicate that in most respects mass communications are far less important sources of information and influence than interpersonal communication. When people were asked how they first learned about various improved agricultural techniques, in all cases interpersonal sources were more frequently mentioned than media sources, even in Kerala, where literacy is common. The authors feel that the centrality of word-of-mouth communication in the information economy of the Indian villages and the relative marginality of mass communication through mechanical means for most people is readily apparent. Paul Hartmann, B.R. Patil, and Anita Dighe, *The Mass Media and Village Life: An Indian Study*, Sage Publications, New Delhi, 1989, pp. 259–60, 266–7.

175. *BvP*, I.10.134–5.
176. Abhay Kant Chaudhary, *Early Medieval Village in North Eastern India (A.D. 600–1200)*, Punthi Pustak, Calcutta, 1971, p. 248.
177. V. Raghavan, 'Methods of Popular Instruction in South India', in Singer (ed.), *Traditional India,* p. 131.
178. William McCormack, 'The Forms of Communication in Vīraśaiva Religion', in *ibid*., p. 123.
179. Y.B. Damle, 'Harikathā—A Study in Communication', *Bulletin of the Deccan College Research Institute*, Vol. 20, Part I, October 1960 (S.K. De Felicitation Volume), p. 105.
180. Linda Hesse, 'The Poet and the People', cited in Sandria B. Freitag, 'Performance and Patronage', in Freitag (ed.), *Culture and Power in Banaras,* p. 26.
181. Gautam Bhadra, 'The Mentality of Subalternity: *Kāntanāmā* or *Rājadharma*', in Ranajit Guha (ed.), *Subaltern Studies VI: Writings on South Asian History and Society*, Oxford University Press, Delhi, 1989, p. 63.
182. Damle, 'Harikathā', p. 68.
183. See note 147.
184. Hitesranjan Sanyal, *Bāṅglā Kīrtaner Itihāsa*, K.P. Bagchi and Co., Calcutta, 1989, pp. 196–8.
185. Bhadra, 'The Mentality of Subalternity', p. 62.
186. Bankimchandra Chattopadhyaya, 'Lokaśikṣā', *Baṅkim Racanāvalī*, Vol. II, Sahitya Samsad, Calcutta, 1376 BS, pp. 376–7.
187. R.S. Sharma, 'Communication and Social Cohesion', *Perspectives in Social and Economic History of Early India*, Munshiram Manoharlal Publishers Pvt. Ltd, New Delhi, 1983, p. 80.
188. Wilbur Schramm, 'The Nature of Communication Between Humans', in Wilbur Schramm and Donald F. Roberts (eds), *The Process and Effects*

of Mass Communication, University of Illinois Press, Urbana, 1971, pp. 43–7.

189. Robert T. Oliver, *Communication and Culture in Ancient India and China*, Syracuse University Press, New York, 1971, pp. 27–30.
190. Morris Janowitz, 'The Study of Mass Communication', in Sills (ed.), *International Encyclopaedia of Social Sciences*, Vol. III, p. 50.
191. Madeleine Biardeau, *Hinduism: The Anthropology of a Civilization*, Oxford University Press, Delhi, 1989, pp. 70–3.
192. Joseph T. Clapper, 'Mass Communication: Effects', Sills (ed.), *International Encyclopaedia of Social Sciences*, Vol. III, p. 82.
193. W. Phillips Davison, 'On the Effects of Mass Communication', in Lewis Anthony Dexter and David Manning White (eds), *People, Society, and Mass Communications*, The Free Press, New York, 1964, pp. 81–2.
194. James C. McCroskey, *An Introduction to Rhetorical Communication*, Prentice-Hall Inc., Englewood Cliffs, New Jersey, 1978, pp. 37–8.
195. Jack Goody, 'Oral Composition and Oral Transmission: The Case of the Vedas', *The Interface Between the Written and the Oral*, Cambridge University Press, Cambridge, 1987, pp. 110, 114.
196. J. Goody and I. Watt, 'The Consequences of Literacy', in Pier Paolo Giglioli (ed.), *Language and Social Context*, Penguin Books Ltd, Harmondsworth, 1980, p. 313.
197. *Ibid.*, p. 343.
198. Ruth Finnegan, 'Transmission in Oral and Written Traditions: Some General Comments', *Literacy and Orality: Studies in the Technology of Communication*, Basil Blackwell, Oxford, 1988, p. 172.
199. K.G. Ghurye has observed that the *brāhmaṇa* attempt to retain monopoly of codified knowledge was intrinsic to the preservation of learned tradition in India. He recounts a rather telling story of how Vāsudeva Sārvabhauma, the founder of the *Navyanyāya* school at Navadvīpa, went to Mithilā for further studies under Pauṣadhara Miśra. This teacher had in his possession the only manuscript of the foremost work on logic, the *Cintāmaṇi* by Gaṅgeśa. He imposed a condition on his students that they were not to copy the book, so that Mithilā may maintain its monopoly. However, Sārvabhauma memorized the text and started a new school at Navadvīpa which eventually outrivalled Mithilā as a centre of learning. K.G. Ghurye, *Preservation of Learned Tradition in India*, Popular Book Depot, Bombay, 1950, pp. 24–5.
200. Brian Stock, *The Implications of Literacy: Written Language and Models of Interpretation in the Eleventh and Twelfth Centuries*, Princeton University Press, Princeton, 1983, p. 3; S.J. Tambiah, *Buddhism and Spirit Cults in North-east Thailand*, London, 1970, pp. 372–3.
201. *śāstraṁ prākṛtabhāṣābhiḥ kalpayitvā hyaśāstrataḥ I*
dharmabhāvān vadiṣyanti śūdrā matsaracetasaḥ II
BP, III.19.14.

202. D.D. Kosambi, 'Social and Economic Aspects of the Bhagavad-Gītā', *Myth and Reality: Studies in the Formation of Indian Culture*, Popular Prakashan, Bombay, 1962, p. 18.
203. Suniti Kumar Chatterji, 'Purāṇa Apocrypha: A "Manipur Purāṇa"', *Select Writings*, Vol. I, Vikas Publishing House Pvt. Ltd, New Delhi, 1976, p. 127.
204. *Ibid.*, p. 128.
205. *brāhmaṇaṁ sammukhaṁ dṛṣṭvā praṇameyustataḥ pare* /

 . . . .

 brāhmaṇaḥ saṁskṛtoktyā tu vācaṁ dadyāt sukhānvitaḥ //

 BP III.1.25–6.
206. See, for instance, Hans Wolff, 'Intelligibility and Inter-Ethnic Attitudes', in Dell Hymes (ed.), *Language in Culture and Society: A Reader in Linguistics and Anthropology*, Allied Publishers Pvt. Ltd, Bombay, 1964, pp. 440–5; A. Tabouret-Keller, 'Sociological Factors of Language Maintenance and Language Shift: A Methodological Approach Based on European and African Examples', in Joshua A. Fishma *et al.* (eds), *Language Problems of Developing Nations,* John Wiley and Sons Inc., New York, 1968, pp. 107–18; J.R. Rayfield, *The Language of a Bilingual Community*, Mouton, The Hague, 1970; Wallace E. Lambert, 'A Social Psychology of Bilingualism', in W.H. Whitely and Daryll Ford (eds), *Language Use and Social Change*, Oxford University Press, London, 1971, pp. 95–110.
207. Hazra has listed nineteen kinds of such mistakes for the *Devī Purāṇa* alone, *Upapurāṇas*, Vol. II, pp. 85–90.
208. Susan S. Wadley, 'Popular Hinduism and Mass Literature in North India: A Preliminary Analysis', in Gupta (ed.), *Religion in Modern India*, pp. 81–104.
209. Ralph W. Nicholas, 'Sitala and the Art of Printing: The Transmission and Propagation of the Myth of the Goddess of Small Pox in Rural West Bengal', in Mahadev L. Apte (ed.), *Mass Culture Language and Arts in India*, Popular Prakashan, Bombay, 1978, pp. 152–80.
210. *Ibid.*, p. 178.
211. Stuart H. Blackburn and A.K. Ramanujan, 'Introduction', in Stuart H. Blackburn and A.K. Ramanujan (eds), *Another Harmony: New Essays on the Folklore of India*, University of California Press, Berkeley, 1986, p. 5.

VII

****

The Making of the Regional Tradition of Bengal

I

Social science interest in the formation of regional identities in South Asia is of comparatively recent origin.[1] Predictably there is no consensus on the definition of a region. After examining forty such definitions from a variety of contexts, Beajeau-Garnier, for example, was able to detect only one point of unanimity among them: A region is 'a spatial unit distinct from the space that surrounds it.'[2] This fundamental and rather obvious constituent of a region is of little use here, as we are concerned with the process of how the socially bounded space designated Bengal (roughly corresponding to the present West Bengal and Bangladesh) came to acquire its identity—the distinctive characteristics that mark it off as a cultural unit at a certain level of generalization.

Unlike culture, which at least has a material basis and other identifiable characteristics, identity, the culmination of a long historical process, is primarily a mental construct, a consciousness of participating in a culture which endows a group of people with a sense of belonging to a community over and above the differences of caste, class, gender, occupation and other variables that tend to undermine this common bond. This consciousness is elusive and unquantifiable because the recognition of a common culture is often implicit. If identity is the self-description of a person or a group which outlines defining characteristics, this description is seldom articulated. It may be intensely felt but is difficult to spell out. Identity formation therefore is the product of social imagination.

The processual aspect of identity formation needs to be emphasized, as our problem is the brahmanical initiative in reorganizing the social structure and religious mores of the indigenous people of Bengal through the codification of the Bengal *Purāṇas* during the early medieval period, which may be considered the first systematic attempt to create a cultural tradition transcending local boundaries. The emergence of the regional identity of Bengal was the eventual outcome of this process, neither consciously contemplated nor instantaneously created by brahmanism. Besides, several other factors like Islam and colonial rule decisively contributed to the shaping of this tradition. However, it is the Puranic formulation, elaborated, ratified and institutionalized by the medieval *Smṛtis*, which still governs the lives and sensibilities of the majority of the Hindu Bengalis in varying degrees. It was as a result of this brahmanical initiative, supported by the regional political structure during the Pāla–Sena period, that the crucial ingredients which went into the making of Bengal's cultural identity came together for the first time.

As early as 1967 Niharranjan Ray had laid down the major characteristics of 'medievalism' in Indian history, which he traced from the seventh century. These included, among others, regionalization of ruling dynasties, script, language and literature, and schools of art. In short, he considered the formation of regional patterns an essential feature of the historical developments in India from, what is now called, the early medieval period.[3] This period, often characterized as one of crisis and transition, has been viewed by several scholars as representing a major breakdown of the early historical social order, brought about by such external agencies as recurrent nomadic invasions or decline in foreign trade, leading to an increased reliance on agriculture, growth of self-sufficient rural units, decay in artisanal production, money economy and urban centres, and the complete subjection of *śūdra* peasantry, within an overall frame of weak state authority and *brāhmaṇa* dominance.[4] In a recent article B.D. Chattopadhyaya has argued that the changes occurring in the early medieval period will have to be understood in the context of larger historical/societal processes operative throughout early India, and even later. These processes were, according to him, expansion of state society through local state formation, peasantization of tribes and formation of castes, and cult appropriation and integration.[5] In other words, he suggests that the phenomenon of early medieval India, one of the most visible features of which is the emergence of regional societies, should be seen in terms of an internal dynamics at the regional and local levels. These processes, he argues, contributed to the constitution of a cultural matrix which was subcontinental and yet not epicentric.

It is important to consider Chattopadhyaya's exposition of the process of the emergence of historical regions in early medieval India in some detail, because this study of the Puranic process in the same period, despite its understandable emphasis on cult appropriation and integration and the formation of Bengal's typical socio-religious order, closely parallels his general formulation in several ways. Even though Chattopadhyaya gives primacy to the role of regional state formation as the key factor in the crystallization of the other trends which were simultaneously at work, he also tacitly acknowledges the compelling centrality of the *brāhmaṇas* in this process, including that of the state formation itself. To begin with, state formation between the third–fourth and the sixth centuries, Chattopadhyaya argues, decided once and for all that monarchy would remain the norm of polity for centuries to come and finally vindicated the brahmanical ideology which equates the absence of kingship with anarchy. The significance of this resolution was not limited to the political sphere as there was no necessary opposition between heterodoxy and monarchy. 'What it signified more importantly was the ultimate affirmation of the Brahmanical view of the *varṇa* order in the political context. This was the most comprehensive framework of social stratification available, and its expansion in the *varṇasaṁkara* was capable of both horizontal and vertical spread. Since the framework was pliable, it left the working out of actual social details to their temporal–spatial contexts.'[6]

The nexus between brahmanical ideology, adapted to the specificities of a particular region, and the regional state, invariably monarchical in its form of governance, was so firmly established by the early medieval period that it would be impossible to conceive of the success of the one without the other. The Bengal *Purāṇas*, ostensibly religious texts, offer chapters on 'politics' (*rājanīti*, *rājadharma*) which instruct the king to conduct the affairs of the state in accordance with brahmanical precepts. He must follow the wise counsel of the *brāhmaṇas*, grant them land in perpetuity, should not impose taxes on them, and administer lighter punishment on the erring *brāhmaṇas*. But most important of all, the king's primary responsibility was to maintain the *varṇa* hierarchy and to ensure that no one strayed from the path of *svadharma*. That these Puranic injunctions were accepted without qualification—often literally but certainly in essence—by the rulers of early medieval Bengal has been discussed in detail in Chapter 4. Even the Buddhist Pālas proclaimed themselves the refuge of the four *varṇas*, because this was perceived to be the only viable social order, on the preservation of which the stability of the state depended.[7] Chattopadhyaya rightly points out that it was the regional state which brought a measure of cohesion among local elements of culture by providing them a focus and mediating in the assimilation of supra-local ideas, symbols and rituals. But he concedes that this political initiative was largely influenced by and frequently revolved around the *brāhmaṇas*:

> Common modes of royal legitimation and interrelated phenomena such as the practice of landgrants, the creation of *agrahāras*, the emergence of major cult centres and temple complexes, social stratification subscribing to the *varṇa* order . . . all these were manifestations of the manner in which local level states mediated in the absorption of ideas and practices which had been taking shape as a wider temporal and ideological process.[8]

The brahmanical attempt at social reorganization in the peripheral areas through *varṇasaṁkara*, presided over by the state, was ubiquitous, but as the occupational status of diverse social groups were far more important in determining the social structure of a given region than the theoretical classification of the *varṇa* hierarchy, such categories fail to explain the composition of regional societies from the post-Gupta period. Chattopadhyaya therefore suggests that it is necessary to look at the actual names by which the various cultivating and other specialized occupational groups were mentioned in the contemporary sources, and the manner in which they were drawn into the caste network and arranged into a convenient hierarchy.[9]

In the Bengal *Purāṇas*, which state the principle of admission of outsiders into the caste framework, the number of the *saṁkaravarṇas* vary between thirty-six and seventy, indicating that it was an open-ended process. Many of these, particularly the major occupational groups such as the carpenters, blacksmiths, weavers, potters and leather workers were in common with most of the other regions of north India, except those who made their living from the typical products of a particular region such as the *śaṁkhika* (conchshell cutter) and the *vārajīvī* (betel-vine grower) or those belonging to the comparatively insignificant lowest social stratum such as the *haḍḍi* (hāḍi) and the *kartāra* (kāorā), as in the case of Bengal. What lends a region its characteristic flavour, however, is the relative positioning of mixed castes within the hierarchy. For example, the Bengal *Purāṇas* assigned the *karaṇas* (forerunners of the *kāyasthas*) and the *ambaṣṭhavaidyas* a status superior to all the other occupational groups, while the *suvarṇavaṇiks* and the *gaṇakas* placed amongst the lowest in the caste hierarchy. The *Purāṇas* provide explanations of these seemingly arbitrary preferences which may point to stages in the incorporation of the indigenous population into the brahmanical social order, but the fact that the classification presented by the Bengal *Purāṇas* corresponds to the present caste structure of Bengal (not only in the general scheme but also in many specific details) goes to show that the distinctive elements by which the regional society of Bengal is identified today had come into being by the end of the early medieval period.[10]

The state virtually implemented the Puranic recommendations by conferring on these caste groups the official seal of recognition. There are instances where the king granted land to some of these groups, mentioned by their caste names in the inscriptions, to provide service to a newly established temple.[11] Indeed, in this process of regionalization, the ritual authority of the *brāhmaṇas* and the temporal authority of the state worked in tandem, and at times it becomes difficult to differentiate between the domains of these two interrelated structures of power.

Chattopadhyaya has argued elsewhere that the brahmanical legal texts conceived of *dharma* as social norms (obviously approved by brahmanism) which ensured smooth functioning of society by regulating the conduct of the members of its constituent groups. With the decline of *dharma*, the king was entrusted with the responsibility of enforcing these norms (*daṇḍa*) by taking cognizance of the different *dharmas* (norms of each individual caste group), in order to maintain the brahmanical social order. In this sense, *dharma* encompassed *daṇḍa*. And yet, as the need for the state arose as a result of a conflict caused by the erosion of *dharma*, it was superseded by *daṇḍa*.[12] Mutual recognition of this interdependence between *dharma* and *daṇḍa* became particularly noticeable in the socio-political processes in early medieval India, with the assertion of the brahmanical ideology in the political sphere. The Bengal *Purāṇas* narrate the legend of the deviant king Veṇa who disrupted the social fabric by forcing indiscriminate cohabitation between males and females of different *varṇas* and the righteous king Pṛthu who restored order by sorting out the progenies born of promiscuity into thirty-six endogamous *saṁkaravarṇas*, sanctioned by the *brāhmaṇas*.[13] The legend illustrates the importance of *daṇḍa* for the preservation of *dharma* and reveals how a convergence between the two creates the necessary condition for the innovation of a social order characteristic of a particular region.

The formation of Bengal's regional tradition through brahmanical appropriation of local cults is one of the major themes of this study. Puranic Hinduism grew out of a long and complex interaction between Vedism and the diverse, localized indigenous religious systems. From the early medieval period, however, the *brāhmaṇas* began to take over, transform and directly control many of the local cults and cult centres, particularly in the peripheral areas. Consequently, these deities began to find mention in the contemporary Sanskritic sources and some of these developed in course of time into major cult figures. Chattopadhyaya remarks: 'Cult assimilation does not necessarily imply harmonious syncretism, but it does imply the formation of a structure which combines heterogeneous beliefs and rituals into a whole even while making (or transforming) specific elements as dominant.'[14]

I have endeavoured to trace the process by which the Bengal *Purāṇas* creatively transformed a set of heterogeneous beliefs and rituals, converging on a common motif, into an interlocking whole, and the method of selection by which some of the specific elements came to acquire a position of dominance, both with regard to the evolution of the goddess tradition per se and the career of such individual goddesses who were shot into regional prominence by the *Purāṇas* as Maṅgalacaṇḍī.[15] The goddess cult thus became the vehicle of a wider process of integration and eventually a recognized symbol of the region. In Bengal this was achieved with the consent of the state power, but not with such active support as was received by Jagannātha, for instance, in Orissa. This was primarily because Bengal did not develop an overwhelming cult focus around a single deity or a temple-based centre of pilgrimage as in the case of Orissa. Although both Durgā and some of the *Śākta pīṭhas* are repeatedly mentioned in the Bengal *Purāṇas*, they began to acquire their present status only in the late medieval period. The goddess cult in Bengal therefore remained a generic though pervasive tradition with many sub-regional and sectarian varieties connected by the common thread of brahmanism, which collectively came to represent one of the most important signifiers of Bengal's regional culture.

II

Apart from these subcontinental trends contributing to the growth of regional societies, there are other factors, partly deriving from these trends, which more immediately and closely identify a region. Empirically rich studies of the process of regional formation in India are still rare and it may be worthwhile to look into one of the very recent examples in some detail. (Indeed, I have deliberately adopted a comparative perspective in this chapter in order to bring into relief the specificities of the cultural developments in Bengal in the backdrop of the process of regional formation as a whole at the pan-Indian level.) Deryck Lodrick, speaking of Rajasthan, distinguishes between the 'denoted' or 'instituted' region which is imposed on a particular geographical area by observers from the outside for the purpose of organizing information, and the 'experienced' region which has an internal perspective and represents 'a people's shared reaction to their particular segment of space, or specific features associated with that space, that leads to an awareness of its distinctiveness'.[16] In other words, by 'experienced' region Lodrick means what I have called the subjective understanding of a cultural unit by the inhabitants of an area.

Lodrick locates the distinctiveness of Rajasthan, as recognized by its people, in the specificities of caste, former landholders, dialect, history, physical environment and economic patterns.[17] Of these he tends to accord primacy to history, which includes Rajasthan's isolation from the sphere of dominance of any of the political and cultural cores of India, the formalization of its political boundary established under Akbar at the end of the sixteenth century, and most importantly the Rajput factor and the former princely states as 'the most persistent, the most readily defined, and in many ways the most significant' regional entity of Rajasthan. To these he adds the development of the literary language Rajasthani as the underlying cohesive force—'the standard of a regional culture'—through which its speakers gained access into the history, traditions, and myths of the region.[18]

Historically, Bengal was always peripheral to the Gangetic valley mainland, the seat of the important empires of northern India, throughout the ancient period, except for the brief interlude in the fifth and early sixth centuries when it came under Gupta rule, and its administrative control was established in north Bengal with the creation of Puṇḍravardhanabhukti.[19] *Brāhmaṇa* settlements in different parts of Bengal from the Gupta period onwards ended its cultural isolation, although the Bengal *brāhmaṇas* quickly evolved their own norms, including an internal sub-classification of social groups typical of Bengal, and such seemingly minor but significant departures from the established codes of brahmanical conduct as the licence to eat fish with scales on them,[20] which made them partially unacceptable to the 'cleaner' *brāhmaṇas* of the north. But politically it remained internally fragmented and independent of external domination. With the establishment of the Pāla kingdom, which included substantial parts of modern Bihar, the process of regional state formation in Bengal had already begun. During the medieval period also, Bengal maintained its distance from the centre—except in the sixteenth century when, following Akbar's conquest of Bengal (subsequently consolidated under his three successors in the seventeenth century), the *subah* of Bengal was set up in 1586. The Mughal *subah* of Bengal more or less conforms to the undivided Bengal of the pre-independence period[21] which effectively formalized political boundary. This period has been described by Jadunath Sarkar as one when 'the outer world came to Bengal and Bengal went out of herself to the outer world' with the growth of Bengal's vast sea-borne trade with the European East India Companies and the organization of the Gauḍīya Vaiṣṇava sect which made pilgrimage to Puri and Vṛndāvana mandatory for its members.[22]

Thus, up to the beginning of the seventeenth century, Bengal's connection with the rest of India was sporadic and tenuous, and runs parallel with developments in Rajasthan in several respects. Soon after, Bengal, along with Bihar and Orissa, passed into the political control of the English East India Company and by 1810 the administrative unit of the Bengal Presidency stretched up to Delhi and beyond the Sikh frontier. The size of the Presidency was subsequently reduced in 1833 and further in 1874, but it still remained as large as the combined Mughal *subahs* of Bengal, Bihar and Orissa. Such a clustering might have drowned Bengal's socio-cultural and political individuality, but it seems to have become established much earlier, as the reaction to Lord Curzon's decision in 1905 to unite Assam and Chittagong with fifteen districts of eastern Bengal to form a new province suggests.[23] The nationalist sentiment underlying the strong protest movement, which viewed this ostensibly administrative measure as a deliberate attempt to undermine Bengal's identity as an indissoluble unit, was partly the outcome of a new awareness brought about by the colonial experience, but the consciousness of a community must already have developed though it remained dormant until it resurfaced under what was perceived as an attack on its essential indivisibility. Eventually the partition had to be revoked in 1911.

It is really from the mid-eighteenth century that the political histories of Bengal and Rajasthan began to traverse entirely different trajectories and the reason for this does not lie merely in the circumstance of the British occupation of Bengal, but in the socio-political formations traceable to the early medieval period. Unlike Bengal, most of which came under Muslim rule in the thirteenth century, the political space of Rajasthan was divided between various Rajput ruling families, and although it was brought under British control in the aftermath of the Maratha wars, this arrangement was never formally disturbed by the British. Thus the Rajput tradition, with its claim of descent from ancient *kṣatriya* dynasties legitimized by the genealogies prepared and transmitted by the wandering bards, individual clan loyalties and clan exogamy, segmented polities and internecine conflicts, the role of bureaucratic lineages in state administration, and the virtues of valour and honour of a warrior ruling aristocracy, came to represent the ethos of Rajasthan. The highly selective popular memory chose the Mewar tradition of opposition to the Mughals as standard Rajput history, and just as Rajasthan came to be identified as a desert land ignoring its physical and climatic diversities, the Rajputs, who are a small minority (5.6 per cent according to the 1931 Census of India) in the total population of Rajasthan, became one of the major symbols of its regional culture.[24]

Bengal, on the other hand, despite its relative political autonomy from the centre till the late sixteenth century, never developed a comparable structure of indigenous ruling aristocracy, although attempts have been made to discover the counterparts of such hereditary chieftains as the Śiśodiā and the Rāṭhor clans of Rajasthan in the Bāro Bhuiyāns (the twelve influential zamindars) of Bengal,[25] who briefly rose to prominence during the interval between the setting Afghan kingship and the rising Mughal power in Bengal. Jadunath Sarkar has dismissed this suggestion as 'absurd', stating that they were nearly all of them 'upstarts', who, during their own time or a generation earlier, acquired some portions of the dissolving Karrani kingdom of Bengal and set up their zamindaris in the inaccessible regions of the sea-coast in Khulna and Baqarganj and the still remoter jungles of north Mymensingh and Sylhet.[26] In describing the Bāro Bhuiyāns as 'usurpers', 'bloated zamindars', 'masterless Rajas', and 'mushroom captains of plundering bands', Sarkar was reacting to 'a false provincial patriotism' of the modern Bengali writers, whose attempt to portray the Bhuiyāns as local heroes fighting a war of independence against 'foreign invaders' and the comparison with the Rajput chiefs he found factually incorrect and preposterous.[27]

However, historical accuracy is not the issue here. Such a claim was also an assertion of regional tradition in support of the nascent tide of nationalism against colonial rule, and if it had stayed, it would have become as inalienable a part of Bengal's regional tradition as any valid observation on aspects of Bengal's history. But this is not the kind of regional identity I have in mind, not a forged identity in response to a contemporary aspiration, but a popular awareness developed inexorably but imperceptibly over the centuries through a process of natural selection of intrinsic and fundamental elements in regional culture, recognized by people all over the region. The nationalist claims were a different discourse. Thus the political factor did not contribute directly to the formation of Bengali identity, except that the regional state acted as a catalyst in the coming together of these elements.

III

An important criterion for the formation of regional identity is the development of the literary language of a region. Adherence to a particular language by a group of people is unmistakably a cultural statement, and it is in language that 'perceived cultural space and instituted political space coincide'.[28] But loyalty to a language may be so overwhelming that it can disregard instituted boundaries of any kind, as the emergence of linguistic nationalities in nineteenth-century Europe suggests. However, as V. Narayana Rao has observed in a recent article on the relative status of Sanskrit and Telugu in medieval Andhra,

> there is no evidence of language serving as symbol of 'national' identity before the nineteenth century. There were Telugu-speaking people, Telugu land, and even love of one's own language—but no Telugu people whose identity was formed by the 'mother-tongue'. Indeed, there is no such word as mother-tongue in medieval Telugu. The modern *mātṛbhāṣā* is a loan translation from English.[29]

It is suggestive that an exact equivalent of the expression mother-tongue (now *mātṛbhāṣā* in Bengali as well) cannot be found in medieval Bengali either. Thus the notion that linguistic consciousness was the determining constituent of regional identity even in pre-modern India seems to be exaggerated, if not entirely the result of an anachronistic transposition. Even so the evolution of a literary language and a corpus of literature particular to a region must have contributed to a heightened awareness of cultural homogeneity among the people of that region. Therefore, the process of the growth of Bengali language and literature from the early medieval period and its implications for the formation of the identity of Bengal should be examined in some detail.

It is suggested that the essential elements of Bengal's regional identity had already begun to crystallize in the early medieval period through brahmanical initiative and mediation. This hypothesis may appear somewhat vulnerable, because the Bengal *Purāṇas* were written in Sanskrit and the *brāhmaṇas* continued to emphasize the indispensability of Sanskrit by writing all their didactic texts in that language throughout the medieval period even when literary Bengali, fairly standardized, had become a vehicle for the expression of complex ideas. The earliest vernacular texts in Bengal were composed by the Buddhist Sahajiyās, and the spurt in the Bengali literary production from the fifteenth century was partly due to the initial interest and patronage of the independent Muslim Sultans of Bengal. Despite these contrary indications, however, the brahmanical contribution to the development of Bengali language and literature cannot be denied.

Till the middle of the first millennium BC the people of Bengal were not Aryan speakers. Suniti Kumar Chatterji has shown that linguistic evidence as well as tradition and history go to prove that the Aryan language came to Bengal as an overflow from Bihar. During the fourth–third centuries BC Bengal began to develop commercial ties with Magadha, and the influence of Jainism and Buddhism started to spread among the people of north, central and west Bengal. With the induction of parts of Bengal within the Gupta empire around AD 400, and the beginning of large-scale brahmanical settlement, this cultural and linguistic influence became stronger. The evidence of Yuan Chwang shows that by the seventh century the Aryan language had been adopted all over Bengal. During the period between the eighth and the eleventh centuries all the Magadhan languages were in a fluid state and each local form solved more or less independently its own particular needs. Towards the beginning of the twelfth century, with the decline of the Pālas, Bengal broke away from Magadha and composition in proto-Bengali had begun. By the fifteenth century the Bengali group of dialects came to be united by a common literary language based on West Bengali.[30]

Thus the Bengali language is a derivative of Sanskrit which passed through several stages of evolution before assuming its present form. There is nothing uniquely brahmanical in this process. Rather, the Bengal *brāhmaṇas* wrote their texts in Sanskrit and took exemplary care to keep its cultivation confined within the *brāhmaṇa varṇa*. We have seen why such caution had to be exercised to maintain the distinctiveness of Sanskrit as a legitimizing authority, particularly in the peripheral regions such as Bengal.[31] Instead, the *brāhmaṇas* learnt the contemporary dialects of Bengal and wrote their texts in a language that considerably overlapped with the vernacular, not only in terms of loan-words but also in grammatical forms and usages peculiar to the region. Sarvānanda's *Ṭīkā-sarvasva*, a commentary on the *Amarakoṣa* written in Bengal in about the middle of the twelfth century, contains a glossary of over three hundred words which belong to the 'Old Bengali' period.[32] The inclusion of these words in a text such as this indicates the recognition of the closeness between the two languages which both the physical proximity of the *brāhmaṇas* with the indigenous speakers of local language(s) and bilingualism rendered inevitable. The *Caryā-carya-viniścaya*, containing the oldest specimen of literary Bengali written sometime in the twelfth century, reveals a strong influence of Śaurasenī Apabhraṁśa and occasionally Sanskrit. The manuscript of the text, discovered by Haraprasad Shastri in Nepal, carries a supplement in which the poems are first given in Prākrit, and then a Sanskrit commentary follows, which quotes from similar Prākritic literature, both in Old Bengali and Western Apabhraṁśa. *Prākṛta Paiṅgala*, an anthology of the floating mass of popular poetry current among the people of north India during 900–1400, also contains a few verses in proto-Bengali along with others in Western Apabhraṁśa and even in regular literary Prākrit.[33]

These examples show the near-inseparable linkage of the dialects closer to Sanskrit with the emergent Bengali literature in its transitional phase. But the best example is perhaps provided by the *Gītagovinda* of Jayadeva, professedly in Sanskrit, but, as Chatterji points out, in style and execution, and in metre, 'more like vernacular than anything else'.[34] This has led scholars such as Pischel and B.C. Mazumdar to suggest that it was originally composed in some Prākritic speech such as Old Bengali, and Chatterji speculates that perhaps some contemporaneous *brāhmaṇas* 'touched these poems up a bit, and garbed them in the dignity of Sanskrit'. He implies that the close similarity between Old Bengali and Sanskrit rendered this transposition relatively simple.[35]

The really significant contribution of brahmanism, however, to the development of Bengali literature came from the first important Sanskrit texts to be composed in Bengal, the Bengal *Purāṇas*. These *Purāṇas* were written in 'highly incorrect Sanskrit', comparable with the Buddhist hybrid Sanskrit found in the *Mahāvastu, Lalita-vistara* and such other texts of east Indian origin, and they contain many words and expressions which were clearly based on popular Bengali usage. R.C. Hazra has prepared a list of nineteen kinds of conspicuous examples from the *Devī Purāṇa* alone where the influence of Bengali has corrupted the purity of Sanskrit. He mentions that these are merely illustrative samples.[36] On the other hand, from the early Middle Bengali period itself (AD 1300–1500), literary Bengali came to be dominated by Sanskrit, the most noticeable features of which were a great proliferation of the *tatsama* words which rendered the old *tadbhava* forms obsolete or restricted, and an excessive use of conventional similes approved by the rules of Sanskrit figures of speech.[37]

Mutual borrowing between the parent language and the evolving derived language, particularly a pronounced dependence of the latter in its formative phase on the parent language, is not uncommon. But more than these surface exchanges, it is the style, mood, and substance of medieval Bengali literature that is most heavily indebted to the Sanskrit compositions of early medieval Bengal. Language is not merely a series of abstract and impersonal signs but an aggregate of associations that these signs collectively evoke. These associations took shape within the large corpus of Sanskritic literary productions in Bengal, both didactic and creative, which provided thematic direction and literary conventions to the Bengali literature characteristic of its own.

Medieval Bengali literature may be divided into two clearly identifiable categories; one distinguished by its indebtedness to Sanskrit and the other by its independence from the influence of Sanskrit. The first group includes translations of the epics and parts of some of the major *Purāṇas* such as the *Bhāgavata*, the *Maṅgalakāvyas*, and the *bhakti* literature inspired by the Gauḍīya Vaiṣṇava movement such as the *padāvalīs* and the biographies of Śrī Caitanyadeva. Popular songs about the Pāla kings, Nāth literature like the songs of Maynāmatī-Gopīcandra and *Gorakṣavijaya*, stories concerning the worship of Dharma, and several varieties of fairy-tales, folklore and ballads belong to the second group. The majority of the works in the second group were conceived of and transmitted orally, some of which were subsequently committed to writing, and some others are still in the process of being collected and published.[38] Therefore it is virtually impossible to decide on their chronology. However, it may be reasonably assumed that some of these date back to the early medieval period, if not earlier, and remained in circulation throughout the medieval period.[39] They were particularly popular in eastern Bengal where the impact of brahmanism was relatively weak. The texts belonging to the first group are easier to date, several manuscripts of each being extant and giving clues to the approximate period of their composition. Although considerable difference of opinion exists even on their dating, the range of possibilities is limited to the period between the late fifteenth and the mid-eighteenth centuries.[40] A few in this category of course go back to an even earlier period.

It is difficult to draw a firm line between the folk and the literary in medieval Bengal, especially with regard to a particular genre of literature called the *Maṅgalakāvyas*. Muhammad Abdul Khalek defines the folk literature of Bengal (*loka-sāhitya*) as oral composition by illiterate and anonymous village poets which has the plain, worldly existence of the common people as its subject; he goes on to cite all the examples from the *Maṅgalakāvyas*.[41] At one level this characterization is valid, because in the citations the gods and goddesses are depicted as removed from their brahmanical ambience and are placed in a daily routine and familial relationships which are recognizably human and typical of rural Bengal. At the same time, the *Maṅgalakāvyas*, being textual accounts of the exploits of divinities, do not strictly conform to some of the basic attributes of folk literature as defined by Khalek. Therefore thematic differentiation may prove more fruitful.

Dineshchandra Sen has observed that the substantive characteristics of the medieval Bengali literature inspired by brahmanism are fatalism, dependence on divine intervention in periods of crisis, and an uncritical acceptance of the superiority of the *brāhmaṇas*; in contrast the folk literature displays a rugged earthiness in which divinities are conspicuous by their absence and the human protagonists are responsible for their own actions.[42] Even when they seek divine assistance, on the occasion of the performance of the indigenous *vratas* for example, their attitude is positive, and they ask for fulfilment of simple material needs in this life rather than compensation in the next.[43]

The *Maṅgalakāvyas* are a curious set of texts, for they combine the elements of both. One reason for this unusual combination is that these *kāvyas* were probably composed in two phases. The core stories, made up of folk elements, were in circulation from at least the thirteenth century (some suggest even the ninth), and from the late fifteenth century onwards a number of talented poets started to recast them into the brahmanical mould.[44] They did not alter the original story much, as these were obviously well known by then, but superimposed brahmanical elements on them. The result is a queer blend of two dissimilar, if not conflicting, attitudes to life in which Śrīmanta, the resourceful merchant, makes no attempt to save his life except by reciting the *cautiśā* of Caṇḍī in the execution ground; Kālaketu, the hunter, loses faith in his strong arms and takes refuge in the name of Caṇḍī; and Lāusen, the warrior-hero, derives all his powers from unconditional devotion to Dharma

Ṭhākur. By the middle of the eighteenth century, with Bhāratacandra's *Annadāmaṅgala*, this genre of narrative poetry had unmistakably accepted the Sanskritic–brahmanical values and literary conventions as its model and also reached its culmination.[45]

I have already explained how the Bengal *Purāṇas* conferred recognition on Maṅgalacaṇḍī, the popular presiding goddess of a women's *vrata*, by providing her with a suitable myth and devising an elaborate ritual procedure consisting of brahmanical, Tantric, and folk elements for her worship.[46] Maṅgalacaṇḍī thus notionally came to represent a synthesis of local goddesses by virtue of the brahmanical approval and in the process was raised to the status of a regional deity. When the popular stories about Maṅgalacaṇḍī were committed to writing, the vernacular poets of the *Caṇḍīmaṅgalakāvyas* took no notice of the thin and hackneyed Puranic myth, but laced them with some of the essentials of brahmanical values, so that Maṅgalacaṇḍī became an unobtrusive vehicle for the dissemination of these values throughout Bengal and acquired a uniquely regional character. The later *pāñcālīs* and *vratakathās* of Maṅgalacaṇḍī, now available in their printed form, reproduce the abridged version of the *Maṅgalakāvya* stories with a smattering of Puranic *mantras* and an emphasis on *bhakti*. These developments further obscured the distinction between the elite and the popular, the folk and the literary, and Maṅgalacaṇḍī eventually became the common inheritance of nearly all sections of the Hindu Bengalis.[47]

It is virtually impossible to try and establish a chronology of such overlapping developments, simultaneously operative at many levels. For example, was Maṅgalacaṇḍī a goddess of distinctly personal profile in pre-Puranic Bengal, merely ratified by brahmanism, or were there many local goddesses of similar characteristics which coalesced into the synthesized figure of Maṅgalacaṇḍī through brahmanical mediation? If so, was the name Maṅgalacaṇḍī, a very Sanskritic name with no Sanskritic antecedent, already in existence, or was it the creation of the Bengal *Purāṇas* which the authors of the *Caṇḍīmaṅgalakāvyas* borrowed as a convenient medium? These questions cannot be answered with certainty. What is known for sure is that the authors of the Bengal *Purāṇas* were familiar with folk material about Maṅgalacaṇḍī which they chose to ignore, and that the various *Caṇḍīmaṅgalakāvyas* reflect an awareness of the brahmanical world-view which they appropriated without acknowledging the source.[48] Through this complex interaction a deity with an elaborate baggage came into its own, and eventually became one of the widely recognized symbols of Bengal.

The contribution of the vernacular literature in the making of this tradition is obvious, and as a result the decisive share of the Bengal *Purāṇas* in this process is often minimized. In fact, the *Maṅgalakāvyas*, despite basic and pronounced differences, also have a lot in common with the Bengal *Purāṇas*. Many historians of Bengali literature, such as Sukumar Sen, have pointed out that the anthologies of Sanskrit court poetry, compiled in early medieval Bengal, presage several significant themes and motifs of later vernacular literature. Descriptions of uneventful rural life, the ostentation of the rich and the miseries of the poor, the typical items of food and dress in the verses of *Saduktikarṇāmṛta* or *Subhāṣitaratnakoṣa* frequently anticipate similar descriptions in medieval Bengali literature.[49] Yet the Bengal *Purāṇas* treat the same subjects with far greater elaboration and, shorn of literary frills, are much closer to the realistic and homely depiction of rural Bengal in the *Maṅgalakāvyas* than the cryptic and ornate verses in any of these anthologies. Perhaps the identity of the Bengal *Purāṇas* as primarily religious literature dissuades scholars from looking into them for such information.

One direct outcome of the translation of Sanskrit epics and the *Mahāpurāṇas* into Bengali was large-scale borrowing of *tatsama* words which, after an initial uncertainty and a few examples of misapplication such as discordant *sandhis*, entered the mainstream and immensely enriched the vernacular language.[50] But a more far-reaching consequence of this access into Sanskrit literature was the dissemination of the brahmanical *bhakti* ideal. There is a greater accent on *bhakti* in the Bengali transcreations of the epics than in the originals, and Gauḍīya Vaiṣṇavism, which had largely moulded Bengal's cultural consciousness in the sixteenth–seventeenth centuries,[51] was thoroughly influenced by this ideal.

However, while Bengal Vaiṣṇavism drew its inspiration from Kṛṣṇa's divine play in Vṛndāvana as depicted in the *Viṣṇu* and the *Bhāgavata Purāṇas*, both of which were translated in parts into Bengali during the medieval period, Rādhā, the chief playmate in the love-games of Kṛṣṇa, was largely an innovation of Bengal.[52] The early Vaiṣṇavite *Mahāpurāṇas*, and the *Harivaṁśa* do not even mention Rādhā, but as the paradigmatic ideal devotee she occupies the key position in both the philosophical formulations of Gauḍīya Vaiṣṇavism as well as the large corpus of vernacular literature that grew around the movement.

Rādhā made her appearance as a fully developed deity in the Bengal *Purāṇas*, particularly in the *Brahmavaivarta Purāṇa*, where her singular devotion to Kṛṣṇa and her irrepressible vivacity, which encouraged an endless cycle of anxious separation, proud rejection and joyous reunion, established her as the dominant partner in the relationship. Such is her authority over Kṛṣṇa that Cheever Mackenzie Brown has described Rādhā of the *Brahmavaivarta Purāṇa* as an embodiment of a 'feminine theology'.[53] But even in the other Bengal *Purāṇas*, wherever Kṛṣṇa's Vṛndāvana-*līlā* is mentioned, Rādhā is overwhelmingly present.[54] Jayadeva, in the (twelfth century) *Gītagovinda*, created an archetype of adulterous love with an explicit erotic connotation between Kṛṣṇa and Rādhā[55] which was accepted as the model for all subsequent Vaiṣṇava *padāvalī* literature of Bengal, often taken literally by creative artists and metaphorically by theologians. Indeed, in the *Brahmavaivarta Purāṇa* Kṛṣṇa and Rādhā are correctly and conveniently married, but in a number of episodes portraying their complex and involved relationship, the *Purāṇa* is tantalizingly close to the mood of the *Gītagovinda* and the medieval vernacular poems. In fact the love-songs of Rādhā and Kṛṣṇa are the staple of Bengali devotional music, far outnumbering the other popular theme of Umā's annual visit to her natal family. Abdul Kadir has quoted extensively from popular folk-songs to show how the origin and development of the different varieties of folk music of Bengal, such as *Fakirī-gān, Murshīdī-gān* and *Ghāṭu-gān* would have been inconceivable without internalization of the stories of the love-games of Rādhā and Kṛṣṇa.[56] The setting shifts effortlessly from Vṛndāvana to the soft soil of rural Bengal and the songs express the eternal longing of ordinary men and women for an experience of that passionate and elusive union idealized in the relationship between this divine couple. Many of these songs were actually a product of Islamic syncretism in Bengal which sought to approximate spiritual truth through the idiom of the love between Rādhā and Kṛṣṇa.

Thus many strands converged in the making of this socio-religious and literary complex—the indigenous tradition of the prevalence of numerous goddesses, the brahmanical transformation of the goddess into *śakti*, the Tantric emphasis on *kāyāsādhana*, the folk substratum of celebration of the man–woman relationship, and the mysticism of the Sahajiyās and other similar sects. What was a creation of the Bengal *Purāṇas* found its natural extension in the subsequent religious developments in Bengal, and its adaptation by vernacular literature and several branches of performing arts turned Kṛṣṇa–Rādhā and all the associations they invoke into a unique cultural expression characteristic of Bengal. Such examples can be multiplied, but those mentioned above should be sufficient to allow one to assess the extent of indebtedness of Bengali language and literature, that ultimate and most manifest token of any regional identity, to brahmanism and Sanskrit.

IV

Another and more tangible object around which regional identities in India began to crystallize from the early medieval period, is the cult centre around an impressive temple. The best example of this process is the temple of Jagannātha at Puri.

Hermann Kulke has shown that the resolve of Anantavarman Coḍagaṅga, who was a Śaiva all his life, to build a temple for Jagannātha at Puri around the middle of the twelfth century was a political decision. By the eleventh century Vaiṣṇavism had begun to exercise considerable influence in Orissa. Keenly aware of this religious trend, Anantavarman decided to erect a temple for Puruṣottama and take advantage of a rising movement. Thus, from the beginning, the religious complex at Puri was conceived as a legitimating agency for the rulers of Orissa. Eventually, king Anaṅgabhīma III adopted the god Puruṣottama at Puri as the official state deity in 1230, dedicated the Orissan empire to Jagannātha, and proclaimed himself the 'deputy' (*rāutta*) of the god.[57]

As the temple gained in importance as a centre of pilgrimage both within Orissa and throughout north India, its legitimizing authority increased in scope and intensity. By the late sixteenth century the temple records began to describe Jagannātha as 'the overlord of the kingdom of Orissa', and no ruler of Orissa, Oriya or not, could hope to establish hegemonic control over the territory of Orissa without at least notionally acknowledging this supra-temporal seat of power. Except Sultan Sulaiman of Bengal, who during his brief occupation of Cuttack in the later sixteenth century had destroyed the image of Jagannātha and desecrated the temple, all the other invaders of Orissa, including the Mughals, Marathas, and English East India Company, sought legitimation for their rule by attempting to gain control over the temple.[58] When the kingdom disappeared, 'Jagannātha began to symbolize a growing secular force, the language centred Oriya nationalism in its formative phase'.[59] This undisputed regional pre-eminence of Jagannātha is due primarily to its physical location in a monumental temple which received sustained state patronage for a considerable period.

Bengal did not have any such temple, and in fact never developed the culture of temple building as a part of state policy. In the seventh and eighth centuries the rulers of various regional dynasties such as the Pratihāras, the Rāṣṭrakūṭas, the Pāṇḍyas and the Pallavas, started establishing centralized state cults, which found expression in the performance of a new ceremony called the great-gift or *mahādāna*. It consisted of the king's honouring his patron deity by installing its image in a monumental and elaborately carved temple. The temple stood for the cosmic order, of which the gift-giving king was the earthly representative. *Brāhmaṇas* became integrated into the ritual life of the Hindu courts and officiated at the great-gift and other ceremonies. These ideas began to penetrate the courts of Bengal from the tenth century onwards. Donation in land became purely a royal prerogative which *brāhmaṇas* received for performing courtly rituals.[60]

Richard Eaton writes that like the other Hindu kings of their time, the Senas also projected their vision of the cosmos and their own place in it through the medium of architecture, particularly the monumental royal temple, and goes on to cite one or two examples, such as the Pradyumneśvara temple, which, from the fragments of remains, he surmises 'must have been a magnificent edifice'.[61]

It is true that there are references to a number of temples in Bengal inscriptions from the Gupta period onwards, and excavations have unearthed the ruins of several, some of which were large and impressive.[62] Even the *Rāmacarita* mentions that opulent temples were in worship in different parts of Varendrī and credits Rāmapāla with the construction of three rows of temples dedicated to Śiva in his newly founded capital Rāmāvatī.[63] Thus obviously there was no dearth of temples in early Bengal, but none of these were built on the assumptions on which the Jagannātha temple was predicated from the beginning, nor did they compare with the Jagannātha temple in dimension or significance. It is possible that the Senas had internalized the political culture of the other contemporary ruling dynasties; they did patronize the *mahādāna*, presided over by the *brāhmaṇas*. But the fact remains that they did not construct a grand temple which would legitimize their rule and make their subjects identify themselves with the temple as the pre-eminent cultural symbol of the region. From the available evidence it seems that the temples of early Bengal were local centres of worship which eventually decayed due to lack of patronage or were destroyed by Muslim invaders.

Bengal did witness a temple-building spree from the late fifteenth century which reached its culmination in the late eighteenth and the nineteenth centuries. But the phenomenon of the mushrooming of modest brick and terracotta temples of late medieval Bengal has been explained in terms of a large scale socio-economic transformation resulting in the upward mobility of several depressed social groups.[64] Due to the wider social relevance of the temple in traditional society, temple-building was considered an important form of social service. The temple was therefore a visible symbol of the wealth and status of its founder as well as a means of spreading and consolidating his influence in local society. When local deities, once worshipped in thatched huts in villages, gained brahmanical recognition and crystallized into established cult forms that incorporated the services of *brāhmaṇas*, their images began to be housed in temples which copied their original settings, leading to the evolution of the vernacular idiom in temple architecture in medieval Bengal. It has been rightly suggested by Hitesranjan Sanyal that the distribution of a distinctive style of temple terracotta throughout undivided Bengal can be taken as an indication of its territorial boundary.[65] A large majority of these temples housed the Puranic deities, adopted and further popularized by Gauḍīya Vaiṣṇavism. However, the similarity in their architectural and decorative patterns should be considered as an affirmation of rather than a determining factor in the formation of the identity of Bengal, the fundamental elements of which had already come into existence.

In the absence of an over-arching temple, integrating diverse local elements into a common bond of loyalty, a cult centre (insignificant to begin with but gradually gaining in importance over a period of time) can perform the same social function. Victor Turner refers to pilgrimages and the organization of pilgrimage centres in complex large-scale societies and 'historical religions', such as Hinduism, as examples of inclusive cults, and localized religious activities focused on local shrines (themselves parts of bounded social fields) as examples of exclusive cults.[66] It is the inclusive cult centre which has the potential to develop a large catchment and eventually transform itself into a major pilgrimage site, that can submerge parochial affiliations of small communities and impart to them a sense of belonging to a wider network, encompassing what has been termed a cult region.[67] Unlike the monumental temple, instituted and supported by the regional kingdom from above, such cult centres become inclusive through a historical process, as people themselves define and organize their cult regions over time.

Cult regions may develop in a variety of ways, and we have a fascinating account of the evolution of the cult of Viṭhobā at Paṇḍharpur in western Maharashtra from the sixth century to the present day.[68]

Paṇḍharpur is an inclusive cult centre *par excellence*. It presents the story of the successive layers of transformation of a local deity in a peripheral area, through brahmanical mediation to begin with but later reclaimed by the lower castes, until its final incarnation as Viṭhobā, in which form it straddled many differences to emerge as a common cultural inheritance of the Maharashtrians. Paṇḍharpur attracts pilgrims from nearly all over Maharashtra, but scarcely from outside, which is the hallmark of an inclusive cult region.

The parallels Paṇḍharpur offers to developments in Bengal are obvious, but the departures are no less conspicuous. While the importance of Viṭhobā rests primarily on its being at the centre of a pilgrimage site, Bengal never produced a centre of pilgrimage of comparable regional dimension. Gaṅgāsāgara (the confluence of Gaṅgā and the Bay of Bengal) is perhaps the only major pilgrimage site of Bengal of at least early medieval antiquity, and it has been systematically promoted in the Bengal *Purāṇas*.[69] But there is no firm evidence to suggest that it took off as a significant centre of religious congregation before the early nineteenth century. Besides, the site remains deserted throughout the year except on the day of *Pauṣa-saṁkrānti* in the month of January, when a fair is organized in honour of Kapila, the reputed founder of *Sāṁkhya* philosophy. But neither the river Gaṅgā nor the sage Kapila invoke typically Bengali associations, and the pilgrims who come from all over the country, and particularly from neighbouring Bihar, far outnumber the Bengali participants.[70] The popularity of the Śākta *pīṭhas*, a few of which are mentioned in the Bengal *Purāṇas*,[71] though not necessarily corresponding to the ones now in worship, is also a late medieval phenomenon and is not unique to Bengal. The success of the Gauḍīya Vaiṣṇava movement had thrown up some sacred sites in the sixteenth-seventeenth centuries, such as Navadvīpa, the birthplace of Śrī Caitanyadeva. But its religious appeal, which remained largely confined to southwestern Bengal, declined over the years. Moreover, both the Śākta *pīṭhas* and the Vaiṣṇava sites retained their essentially sectarian character. The *bhakti* movement itself, despite its professed egalitarian ideals, was initiated by a *brāhmaṇa* in Bengal. The subsequent theological debates were conducted partly in Sanskrit, and even though it was fairly broad-based and encouraged the development of vernacular literature, *bhakti* in Bengal never assumed the aspects of an overwhelmingly low-caste protest movement, as happened at Paṇḍharpur. Thus Bengal cannot be described as a cult region in terms of a universally recognized pilgrimage site.

Bengal does qualify, however, to be considered as a cult region.

Indeed, it is on the shared understanding of a variously represented common cult form that the earliest and still inarticulate foundation of Bengal's regional tradition was laid. In the absence of a central monitoring agency such as the temple of Jagannātha or an inclusive pilgrimage site such as Paṇḍharpur, the cult of the regional goddesses, conceived and promoted by the Bengal *Purāṇas*, helped to create a common focus and integrate the highly stratified rural society of Bengal. The annual worship of Durgā, also repeatedly mentioned in the Bengal *Purāṇas*[72] but not popularized before the late medieval period, now functions as the supreme signifier of Bengali religious culture to the 'outsider'. Here we have traced the evolution of Maṅgalacaṇḍī in preference to Durgā in order to highlight the processes by which the local goddesses were universalized within the cultural space of an 'experienced region', and to show how the newly acquired syncretic identity of these goddesses in turn helped reinforce the regional identity of Bengal. I have referred to anthropological surveys which reveal that there exists an unstated agreement among the various caste groups of rural Bengal that the worship of these regional goddesses is a shared responsibility of the entire village community.[73] The religious culture of Bengal is embedded in this system of social practice. The practice is kept going by a busy sacred calendar which, in my opinion, has contributed more to the construction of the internal perspective than the spectacular annual worship of Durgā. There are minor subregional variations in the procedures of worship or in the nature of caste participation, but a common orientation towards the regional goddesses makes Bengal a cult region, though almost by default. Those local goddesses who, due to the absence of brahmanical recognition, could not make the regional grade, continue to be an integral feature of the religious culture of Bengal, but their exclusive character barred them from providing an active input into the growth of Bengal's regional consciousness.

This scenario is not unique to Bengal, but nowhere else did a set of texts play such a crucial role in the cultural transformation of a region. Brahmanism in Bengal, through the codification and transmission of the *Purāṇas*, succeeded in creating a public realm in which diverse local elements could converge on a common core through the mediation of a supra-local agency. This common core had set the terms for a larger community consciousness. By community I mean a process of social interaction which gives rise to a more extensive attitude and practice of interdependence among its constituents. Community is often viewed as a structure of institutions capable of objective definition. But I have used the term in the sense of an internal perception of a cultural identity, a common way of thinking and behaving. According to this approach community is an aggregative device in which the commonality is not necessarily a uniformity. 'It is a commonality of *forms* (ways of behaving) whose content (meanings) may vary considerably among its members. The triumph of community is to so contain this variety that its inherent discordance does not subvert the apparent coherence which is expressed by its boundaries.'[74] Thus, although the members of a community may recognize important differences among themselves and the meanings they attach to cultural symbols may also vary, they nevertheless share the symbols. Symbols are by definition multivalent and part of their meaning is subjective. But the common form of the symbol helps to aggregate the various meanings assigned to it, just as the symbolic repertoire of a community aggregates the individual and group differences that exist within the community. The process of aggregation so transforms the differences into an appearance of similarity that people tend to invest the community with ideological integrity.[75] This integrity derives from the self-definition of the community as the bearers of the same culture.[76] Hence, culture rather than structure is the point of departure in my understanding of community.

In Bengal, brahmanism performed the role of combining the small parochial communities with the dominant symbol of the regional goddess which became one of the enduring features of its regional tradition. Brahmanical culture, in creative interplay with the diverse local cultures of Bengal, transformed itself into a regional brahmanical culture, characterized by a range of common cultural denominators and a shared vocabulary of value, later proved to be typical of Bengal. In the process, brahmanism helped local cultures transcend their purely local boundaries, encouraged them to participate in and eventually develop a sense of belonging to a larger cultural system. The system was flexible enough to continue to accommodate new elements, and yet sufficiently firm to soften discordance and maintain a commonality of forms. In other words, brahmanism was instrumental in creating a wider cultural community by extending the frontiers of recognition of local cultures.

This does not mean that the boundaries of the local cultures were completely obliterated. The process of cultural transaction created an altered conception of cultural space in which the region became another unit of identification. In the hierarchy of cultural units, the region stands half-way between the pan-Indian level, represented by brahmanism and described by Hitesranjan Sanyal as *mārga* (literally the path and by implication classical) culture, and the local level, represented by ethnic groups and described by Sanyal as *jana* (literally people and by implication indigenous) culture.[77] The interaction between these two levels resulted in the inauguration of a cultural growth through elaboration and modification at both levels which helped the local society to overcome the limitations inherent in it and allowed the new cultural pattern to assume a broader significance.

> New idioms emerged in the process of cultural growth. These idioms . . . may be local in origin but they cut across the boundaries of localized ethnic group identities and spread over a larger territory with common cultural characteristics and aspirations, that is to say, *des* [*deśa*] (in the traditional sense of the term, as against its modern meaning of nation state) . . . The growth of the intermediate level of culture is an effective force in consolidating the concept of *des* as a cultural phenomenon, as also in defining the boundaries of the physical space covered by a *des*.[78]

Indeed, this was a period when neither the national identity of India nor the provincial identity of Bengal as politico-administrative units had developed. These nomenclatures are being applied only in retrospect. However, from the cultural imbroglio caused by the intervention of brahmanism in the existing order of fragmented little communities, an inchoate idea of a cultural territory larger than the purely local and consequently the first imperfect awareness of a cultural community wider than those of the parochial ethnic groups had begun to emerge. The Puranic testimony points in that direction and the vernacular literature of the medieval period confirms it. Surely the indigenous local cultures, involved in this process of cultural transformation, did not give up all their internal differences and become one homogeneous cultural community. Not all of them comprehended the implications of the transformative process in exactly the same way, nor did they relate to the ideological underpinnings of the process or the cultural objects created in the process with equal intensity. Needless to say, there were instances of imperfect integration and dissent. But to the extent that the large majority of them accepted the newly emerging cultural symbols in one way or another, a different order of cultural identity was established.

V

We revert to the central problematic of this chapter: what is the minimal level of consensus on cultural characteristics required for a cluster of local cultures to be aware of and be recognized as a regional culture, unique by itself and different from others? The cultural affinity among the members of a particular local culture must be much stronger than among the members of a regional culture, and certain aspects of the brahmanical culture are to some extent shared by almost all regional cultures of India. Between these two then, how does one demarcate the boundary of the intermediate level, conveniently and somewhat imprecisely described as the regional culture? There can be no one answer to these questions, as regions acquire their distinct personalities over a period of time, each having its own history, and the articulation of regional consciousness surfaces in situations of real or perceived threats, which are unique in each individual instance. But it is possible to indicate a general pattern through which the cultural unity of a region comes about, marking it off from the rest.

For a long time South Asia has been viewed as a single cultural area. This 'holistic approach' is now at a discount and the so-called 'middle-run history' is increasingly receiving greater attention from historians and social anthropologists alike. In a sharp critique of cultural holism in the anthropology of South Asia, John Leavitt has recently argued that such an approach seeks to explain the variety of data available from different parts of India in terms of a relatively small and simple set of underlying cultural or ideological pattern. While Redfield's model of great and little traditions 'freezes' and 'perpetuates' the view of the nineteenth-century British observers that the Indian culture consists of 'an ideal–typical real pan-Indian civilization' and a number of 'survivals' from an earlier, locally represented semi-civilized stages, Louis Dumont replaces this 'dualism' with a 'monism' which claims that the two traditions are no more different than a general idea and the local working out of that idea. All particularities are therefore reduced to just a variation of a broader pattern, a mere epiphenomena, which radically underestimates the reality and importance of regional and historical specificity in South Asia. There exist a number of factors, Leavitt says, which prove refractory to holistic analysis, such as annual seasonal and calendrical cycles of regional rituals, the social patterning within which these rituals take place, the regionally distinctive divinities and the people's background knowledge of the divinities who are a part of the myths and songs invoked in these rituals. He cites Kumaon as an example of such a culturally specific region.[79]

There is much in this argument with which I agree. Most importantly, Leavitt seems to suggest that of all the characteristic features by which a region is often identified, such as geographical specificity (which is not adequate in itself and is only a precondition for the formation of a regional tradition), or political division (the outlines of which have remained unstable for most areas later recognized as regions), it is the distinctive religious culture in the widest possible sense of the term, apart from language, that most appropriately defines regional tradition in India.

However, the problem of how to demarcate the boundary of a regional culture still remains unresolved. For instance, Kumaon may well constitute a cultural region by virtue of its possessing a common calendar of annual seasonal rituals and a distinctive pantheon. But it is very likely that a greater homogeneity of socio-religious pattern will be discovered if we further localize the unit of investigation. Conversely, if we enlarge the unit of investigation to include let us say Garhwal, the cultural diversity this would admit may not disqualify the combined regions from being considered a single cultural unit at a higher level of generalization. In other words, the principle by which the unit itself may be isolated for the purpose of generalization has not been laid down by Leavitt. This is perhaps due to the fact that it is virtually impossible to do so. Each individual or group carries multiple identities at the same time which find expression in their appropriate realm in different situations. Regional identity is only one among many such overlapping identities, and even within it the linguistic or the cultural factor may receive priority depending on which one offers access to opportunities or is perceived as threatened at a particular point of time.[80] Thus the question of cultural identity can never be satisfactorily settled. Suffice it to say that the consciousness of distinction among the participants of a common religious culture is an important constituent in the formation of the identity of a region, and in Bengal this consciousness contributed as much to the crystallization of its regional identity as the consciousness of a common language which began to take over as the prime index of regional identity from the medieval period.

We may therefore turn to a more fundamental objection of Leavitt, namely that of the role of brahmanism as the determining factor in the process of identity formation for most regions in India. Leavitt's objection seems to stem from his not altogether inaccurate observation that the anthropology of South Asia has, by and large, tended to privilege the brahmanical model at the cost of locally prevailing forms of religious and social practices, disregarding the fact that the process of multidirectional interaction between the two has been simultaneously operative at many levels and has produced unique cultural systems which are not just variations of an all-encompassing brahmanical mould. Indeed, he argues that anthropology has a lot to learn from 'a poor cousin', folkloristics, and refers to an earlier work of Dumont on the dragon ritual of Tarascon in southern France in which he followed 'a processual model'—characteristic of modern folklore studies—to show how pre-Christian beliefs and symbols, such as the protective dragon of particularized local legends and associated values, can exist with transformed significance within a Christian universe. Leavitt cites the works of the folklorist Nicole Belmont to assert that conceptualization of the complex relationship between high and folk materials is possible only when Christianity is not treated as a static entity but the relationship is viewed as a continuing historical process of Christianization, which then offers 'an alternative both to simple binary divisions and to chaos, while still not reducing local variation to expression of a pan-Christian essence'. Leavitt suggests that this approach is particularly helpful for analysing complex civilizations, which are made up of 'partially coherent patterns . . . on many levels', so that instead of eliminating or dissolving some of the data, a relationship, involving specific differences between the many types of data that have been grouped under the labels of great and little traditions, may be established.[81]

While there can be no disagreement with this general proposition, Leavitt seems to ignore the heuristic aspect of the 'labels' great and little traditions discussed in Chapter 3. However, we face a curious paradox here. If it is the adoption of a processual model that Leavitt advocates for the study of the formation of cultural regions, this is precisely what history attempts to do and I have followed this model as far as my sources permitted. But in studying the evolution of societies, the historian, due to the very nature of his discipline, misses out on the elements that combine to form the social group he studies and the relationships which provide the group's synchronic unity. It is this sense of here and now that recreates the dynamics of real life in all its singularity which I have borrowed from the anthropological findings to compensate for the inadequacy inherent in history and to fill up the gaps in the restricted series of causal relationships I was compelled to construct due to the fragmentary nature of my (and all historical) documents. The paradox is that early anthropological explorations in South Asia, confronted with the enormity and multiformity of this 'indigenous civilization', fell back on generalizations typical of history, in order to construct recognizable patterns from this vast assortment of cultural forms and make sense of what they thought was the basic character of the Indian civilization.

This accounts for the holistic vision that Leavitt disapproves, but it is perhaps unfair to accuse Redfield, Dumont and others of neglecting historical specificities in their studies of the process of 'Hinduization', for anthropology is constrained to analyse changing relationships within a temporally static framework. They therefore necessarily looked at the end result of the process of cultural interaction involving a wide range of attitudes from acceptance to rejection and came up with brahmanical assimilation of local cultures as the major axis around which regional variations, different degrees and rhythms of assimilation as well as the simultaneous occurrence of what Leavitt calls folklorization could be worked out, as has been successfully demonstrated by a number of micro-studies which came after them. In fact, Redfield went against the grain of his discipline to emphasize the processual element in the making of the end product(s) which helped me to integrate textual evidence of the past with the anthropological insight about the present, to combine the process with the product. The process itself is so intricate and admits of such infinite variations that no broad perspective study which aspires to arrive at pan-Indian generalizations (useful in their own way) can hope to accommodate all the discontinuities and contrarieties in time and space.

It is a natural disadvantage of history that it lacks the contemporary perception of events, institutions, norms and values, except in reified documentary form. For early medieval Bengal this problem is accentuated by the fact that most of these documents are either official in nature or of anonymous brahmanical authorship. Thus we have only partial representation of a one-dimensional version of the past at our disposal. In any study of the process of social interaction, this is a very serious drawback. Undeniably our understanding of the process would have been fuller if we had access to the knowledge of how the indigenous population of Bengal experienced and interpreted the cultural infiltration of brahmanism or indeed what their cultural world was like prior to the arrival of the *brāhmaṇas*. Only then would we be in any position to assess the extent of brahmanical presence and its role in shaping the regional tradition of Bengal.

In a landmark monograph, described by the author as 'an essay in "ethno-history",' Nathan Watchel has discussed the consequences of the Spanish conquest of Peru in the sixteenth century from the point of view of the colonized Indians on the basis of a number of contemporary 'authentic native sources'.[82] The conquest unleashed a process of 'acculturation', by which the author means cultural interaction between 'societies of unequal strength, the one dominant and the other dominated',[83] which resulted in 'destruction' of the indigenous society. Some of the traditional institutions and customs survived, but the old structure of interrelated elements governed by an internal logic disintegrated. This is particularly evident in the field of religion where the state cult lapsed with the execution of the Inca chief Atahuallpa, and serious campaigns were organized to 'root out idolatry' of the Indians and replace it with Christianity. The Indians responded to this situation in a variety of ways. Even though 'nominally' converted to Christianity, most of them continued to believe in and practise their traditional cults in secret, at times concealing them beneath a veneer of Christianity or viewing the Western cultural imports according to the old logic.

The Christianization of Peru appears to offer a certain parallel to the process of brahmanization in early medieval Bengal. However, a close look at the final outcome of the Spanish conquest of Peru reveals that the similarity between the two processes is only a superficial one. 'Authentic native sources' do not exist to allow us a window into the contemporary indigenous response to brahmanization of Bengal. Also, the *brāhmaṇas* did not invade and conquer Bengal, nor was brahmanism such an alien entity to the local population as Christianity was to Indians. Thus there was no 'event' in the diffusion of brahmanism in Bengal, and such terms as 'victor', 'vanquished' and 'trauma' do not apply in this case. More importantly, with the Spanish conquest of Peru the links between different parts of the traditional social system were so suddenly and irreversibly snapped, and a new 'total system' was so ruthlessly and unilaterally imposed in its place that there was no scope for the 'two systems of values, one all-conquering and oppressive, the other conquered and transformed'[84] to come to terms with each other. Besides, 'no new ideology intervened to give any meaning, for Indians, to the domination imposed by Spain'.[85] This 'disjunction' inspired the majority of the Indians to a fierce determination to resist the Spanish and revive their old traditions. But the resistance ultimately failed because there was no supporting structure to sustain it.

Even though we have no definite knowledge of the social system of the indigenous local cultures of pre-brahmanical Bengal or their initial response to the brahmanical penetration, we can safely assert that despite unequivocal Sena patronage for brahmanism, it could not afford to completely destabilize the existing social system, and its cultural domination was not established or maintained only by coercion. Nor did the votaries of local religions in Bengal, unlike the native Indians, have had to suffer the symbolic violence of witnessing 'their gods die a new death every day'.[86] Instead, brahmanism attempted to co-opt the indigenous population and its goddesses over a period of time and construct an ideology which would give meaning to the reconstituted socio-cultural sphere for the new admitees. In other words, the brahmanization of Bengal was a gradual and continuous process of restructuration without any violent and traumatic act of destructuration preceding it. In the case of the Spanish conquest of Peru, the advantage of having the native point of view was that Watchel could lay bare the strategies of the Indians to cope with the imposition of an alien religion, including their desperate attempt to keep alive the traditional religious cults by camouflaging them under the garb of Christianity, which was clamped on them with a brutal unconcern for the mental universe of the natives. This must have led to a kind of acculturation which was actually a means of escaping what was officially inescapable. Acculturation, thus conceived, should be studied primarily from the native Indian perspective. Judging by the evidence of the local *Purāṇas*, however, the process of acculturation, which, in the context of Bengal, takes on an altogether different connotation, was initiated by the culturally superior *brāhmaṇas* themselves. Thus it seems that for Bengal the brahmanical texts provide the vantage point from which the process of cultural assimilation can be better understood and the absence of 'native sources' is not such a severe handicap as it may appear at first sight.

In fact, the term acculturation is somewhat inappropriate as a description of the Puranic process in Bengal as it carries the historical charge of unquestioned supremacy of a dominant group and presumes a wide cultural gap between the dominant and the dominated. Instead, the process in the context of early medieval Bengal should be seen as negotiation of meanings between brahmanism and the local cultures. By the post-Gupta period, the absorption of indigenous religious forms hitherto unacceptable to brahmanism was well under way through the codification of the *Mahāpurāṇas*, and *brāhmaṇas* were by no means unfamiliar with the local cultures of Bengal. What the Bengal *Purāṇas* narrate is the brahmanical version of the ceaseless negotiations with the indigenous local cultures. Thus the Christianization of Peru is not an apposite analogy to the Bengal situation. Rather, the process by which saints were canonized in the Counter-Reformation Church as the result of negotiations between the peripheral regions in which the cult of a local hero grew up and Rome where the ecclesiastical authority decided whether to accept or reject it[87] is germane, except that in the absence of a central brahmanical authority the process of negotiations, often implicit and muted, must have been rendered infinitely more complex in Bengal and such other regions of India where regional traditions began to take shape through brahmanical intervention.

This does not mean that brahmanism in Bengal had the unquestioned authority enjoyed by Rome to accept or reject local religious forms at its will. It certainly began with an initial advantage, derived from its prestige of being a supra-local/regional institution of great antiquity, with exclusive access into the only pan-Indian language, and possessing superior organizational strength, enhanced by state patronage. But such authority as brahmanism eventually mastered in Bengal was acquired and maintained through complex and intense negotiations which made it give up a good deal of what it cherished as some of its fundamental tenets in order to retain the prerogative of being able to decide what and how much to give up. These negotiations generated the social space which enabled the *brāhmaṇas* to preserve their ritual supremacy and gave them a near-decisive say in the making of the popular religious culture that characterizes the regional tradition of Bengal today, for the majority of the Bengali Hindus subscribe to it in some form or the other, but it was not dictated by the *brāhmaṇas* from above. It may perhaps be argued that the regional tradition of Bengal is not brahmanical in its essential content; yet its creation is inconceivable without the active mediation of brahmanism. The key to the resolution of this apparent paradox lies in the nature of the negotiation itself.

Social scientists are becoming increasingly sensitive to the fact that the categories elite and popular religion and the distinction between the two were created by the clerics which the historians of late medieval and early modern Europe often uncritically adopted. It is true that the folkloric culture, on which popular religion was based, had been transformed and worked over by the church.

> The Church not only prohibited, regulated, and purged collective behaviour . . . of all that was contrary to legitimate belief but also persuaded adherents to condemn their own practices. In this way, the Catholic Reformation was, perhaps above all, the gradual enforcing over an entire society of a clerical definition of what was permissible or not.[88]

But culture is conditioned by daily practices which cannot be entirely dictated by one section of a community, however strong their moral and institutional authority may be, for the interplay between a standard model and everyday experience is always dual. That is why historians such as Dave Harker and Carlo Ginzburg emphatically reject the notion that culture is a given something that is fed to people and they merely passively absorb. Instead, it is being argued that culture is what people create by breaking down the received message and reassembling it for their own purpose. It is a process of appropriation which involves both mediation and struggle.[89] This process of appropriation has been described by Roger Chartier as 'consumption' which is also a form of creation that cannot be limited to the intention of the original producer. He therefore argues that popular culture is a kind of relation with cultural objects 'such as legitimate ideas and attitudes', and the task of the historian is to identify and distinguish 'not cultural sets defined as "popular" but rather the specific ways in which such cultural sets are appropriated'.[90]

When *brāhmaṇas* began to move into Bengal in large numbers from the Gupta period onwards and were settled with land in different parts of the region, they carried with them an inventory of dos and don'ts with regard to what they conceived as 'legitimate' religion. These were considerably modified in the light of their experience of the locally prevailing religious forms (though the twin a priori assumptions of brahmanism were never compromised), and they sanctioned practices which in another context would certainly have figured in their list of don'ts. Thus, though it is hazardous to attempt to construct a chronology of cultural developments, it appears that the process of appropriation in Bengal was formally initiated by the *brāhmaṇas* themselves with the beginning of the codification of the Bengal *Purāṇas*. At the same time they introduced a set of new ideas and practices, by example to begin with and later in more articulate forms, which the indigenous cultures interpreted in their own way and began to imbibe in varying degrees. The process of direct transmission of the already reconstituted brahmanical message through *vratakathā* and such other means created conditions for cultural exchange of a different order, for it now had to take into account both specific local requirements as well as immediate audience response, and this opened up possibilities of further appropriation on both sides.

The brahmanization of Bengal, if it may be so described, has been a continuous creative process, which in its ever-increasing sweep, seems to have engulfed most of the indigenous local cultures by the time the last redactions to the *Purāṇas* were made, and succeeded in forging a common religious cultural tradition, flexible enough to accommodate sub-regional variations and indifference to the emerging consensus on the dominant cultural mode among some social groups, and strong enough to take dissent in its stride. Some of these elements of dissent were eventually subsumed within the cultural mainstream. Even the folk-tales which traditionally mock at the symbols of power such as the *brāhmaṇas*, often end up reinforcing what they are supposed to subvert,[91] indicating the pervasiveness of the process of appropriation and counter-appropriation on which the ideological hegemony of brahmanism was based. Besides, distinctive patterns of dissent are as much a part of the regional tradition as the dominant discourse, for it determines to a large extent the nature of dissent.

This tradition, like all living traditions, continued to undergo transformations even after its distinctive contours became recognizable. The accounts of the post-Puranic developments are contained in the vernacular literature of medieval Bengal, particularly in the *Maṅgalakāvyas* and the *pāñcālīs*, where the local divinities and associated religious practices, released from the constraint of Sanskrit, asserted themselves with much greater vigour. Many of these divinities were already appropriated by the *Purāṇas* and were thus universalized, and for some of the local-level texts, such as the *pāñcālīs*, the *Purāṇas* began to function as a source of legitimation,[92] thus completing the circle of mutual appropriation. The Gauḍīya Vaiṣṇava movement, with its emphasis on Rādhā and the tacit recognition it conferred on the secret religious practices of the esoteric groups condemned by the mainstream,[93] actually pushed the process along and provided it with a well-defined organizational base for the first time. This, in a nutshell, is the history of the evolution of the Hindu religious culture of Bengal, and the tradition it embodies defies the categories of both elite and popular, for it is neither exclusively brahmanical nor purely indigenous in content or form.

This is where I would like to join issue with Leavitt and suggest modifications to his critique of the essentialist pan-Indian brahmanical model which, he believes, is seriously contested by the particularity of regional traditions. While it is obvious that each regional tradition must be endowed with unique cultural characteristics to distinguish it from other similar traditions, I argue that the common factor of the brahmanical presence in different degrees in each of these does not necessarily undermine their uniqueness. Indeed, I would go further and assert that it was as a result of the brahmanical intervention, especially in the peripheral areas, that clusters of fragmented but interrelated indigenous local cultures could converge on a common forum and acquire a wider identity which both included and transcended the local specificities. In other words, it is not so much in content as in agency that we can acknowledge the role of brahmanism in the making of regional traditions. It is important to bear in mind that whatever brahmanism authorizes, either explicitly through texts or implicitly through participation in ritual cycles at the local or regional levels, becomes part of its amorphous and ever-expanding structure, and therefore one will be well advised not to underestimate 'the brahmanical factor' as a catalyst in the composition of most regional traditions.

In this I do not see much scope for Leavitt to disagree with me on methodological grounds, for I place as much emphasis on the process as he does, except that we approach the process from the two ends of the time scale and that our respective disciplines make me rely more on the didactic brahmanical texts and him on the lived experience for an understanding of the dynamics of the traditions, which may account for the difference in our perspectives. The incapacity or unwillingness of many scholars to recognize the apparently unlimited flexibility of brahmanical doctrines and practices, even at the cost of being flagrantly self-contradictory, also results in their failure to appreciate the nature and extent of brahmanical contribution to the shaping of regional traditions in India. This contribution had naturally differed from one regional context to another. In one case it may have assumed the form of the codification of a set of texts, in another the establishment of a hegemonic temple, and in yet another the evolution of an inclusive cult centre that acted as the agent of transformation. Accordingly, the process of regional formations has moved along different historical trajectories in different parts of India. In Maharashtra, for instance, the contribution of brahmanism seems to have been less and in Rajasthan even more so than in Orissa or Bengal. But the crucial involvement of brahmanism in the process, in whatever form, is undeniable, and the formation of regional traditions has been the unintended consequence of this process.

VI

A sense of unease remains because of the complete absence of information on the functional role of the *Purāṇas* in the everyday life of the medieval Bengali society and even later. Was the authority of the *Purāṇas* actually invoked to settle caste disputes or differences of opinion on other religious matters in the villages? We do not know, but it seems most unlikely. There exists an institution known as the Muktimaṇḍapa Paṇḍita Sabhā of *brāhmaṇas* associated with the Jagannātha temple at Puri, which has a library of manuscripts. The Muktimaṇḍapa is a high stone pavilion lying to the south of the main temple of Jagannātha and is said to have been built along with it for deliberations on temple matters by the priests, *sannyāsīs*, and other *brāhmaṇas*, although the Sabhā was formally instituted in 1904 by one Mahāmahopādhyāya Sadashiva Mishra. 'Cases' concerning transgression of caste rules and such other controversial issues of wider religious significance are brought up regularly before the Sabhā for judgement, by individuals or groups, from the remote corners of Orissa. The Sabhā's verdict, based on authoritative Sanskrit texts and their interpretations by the *paṇḍitas* (the written judgements cite the texts and often quote relevant verses in the original), are presumably considered final.[94] The legitimacy of the Sabhā is obviously derived from the institutional status of the temple itself. In the absence of any such institution in Bengal the *brāhmaṇas* never acquired a platform which could act as the final court of appeal for the Hindu Bengalis. The *samājapatis* (elderly *brāhmaṇas* of a village community) had the customary privilege to settle local disputes, but there is little evidence to suggest that they actually consulted these normative texts to arrive at their decisions.

It is difficult to overlook the correspondence that exists between the socio-religious culture prescribed in the *Purāṇas* and the directly observable ground reality with regard to both the social structure and the religious norms of modern Bengal, and therefore, in retrospect, one can reasonably assume that these texts had played an active part in their formation. The fact that multiple copies of the *Purāṇas* in manuscript form have been discovered from all over Bengal would also suggest that these texts were not altogether unfamiliar to a wide cross-section of the Bengal *brāhmaṇas*.[95] And yet it seems that the Puranic *texts* as such had a marginal presence in the everyday life of rural Bengal. The answer to this riddle may be found in the nature of the *Purāṇas* as well as in their role in the making of the regional tradition of Bengal. The *Purāṇas* had no legal status like the *Smṛtis*, nor did they deal in any detail with the caste regulations or with life-cycle rituals which govern the life of a Hindu Bengali. The general recommendations they made regarding the formation of caste groups and their respective rights and duties, or *vratas* and rites of passage, or matters of regional religious import such as the annual worship of Durgā, were later incorporated into the Bengal *Smṛtis*,[96] which came to be regarded as the authoritative texts on these issues. What the *Purāṇas* did in Bengal was to lay down the principle of negotiation between the *brāhmaṇas* and the indigenous communities and initiated the process of mutual appropriation of the cultural objects which were thrown up in course of these negotiations. Once the frame of reference was firmly established and the process was set in motion, it became relatively autonomous of the text of the *Purāṇas*, which by the fifteenth–sixteenth centuries became more or less fixed, and acquired a dynamism of its own. The process continued but the actual contents of the *Purāṇas* lost some of their operational significance. However, cultural syncretism of the variety that characterizes the regional tradition of Bengal owes its origin and direction to the *Purāṇas*.[97]

Charuchandra Datta, a distinguished member of the Indian Civil Service and the eldest son of the Dewan of Nripendranarayana, the Mahārājā of Coochbehar (a small state in northwest Bengal), published his memoirs in 1937. He recounts that once in his youth (it must have been towards the late 1890s) he was invited by the priests of the temple of Bāṇeśvara (Śiva), situated on the outskirts of the city of Coochbehar, to partake of the *prasāda* on the occasion of *Śivarātri*. He was pleasantly surprised to discover that the fare included mutton and curried pigeon. Contentment induced him to delve into antiquity (*pratna carcā*). He enquired from the priests how animals could be sacrificed to Śiva and was informed that the pigeons were strangled and the goat was clubbed to death. Not a drop of blood was shed. He writes:

> The problem was resolved. However, even though blood was not spilt here, in Darjeeling, in front of Mahākālabābā (Śiva), the sacrificial animal is slaughtered in the traditional way. All these people are Hindus, whether the *paṇḍitjīs* (orthodox *brāhmaṇa* scholars) accept this fact or not . . . . Somehow I feel that these instances very clearly indicate that the culture, or the absence of it, of the Bengalis is constituted of scraps picked up from different sources. It is not received as an inheritance from the ancient sages alone . . . . Is there any reason to suppose that the Gambhīrā dance, the *bhāsān* of Manasā, the songs in honour of Biṣahari or the worship of Madanakāma of Coochbehar are derived from the *Śrutis*?
>
> In this connection let me narrate another old story. In Coochbehar, the golden icon of Madanamohana (Viṣṇu) playing the flute was placed in a temple, flanked by two other temples dedicated to the goddesses Kālī and Tārā on both sides. All the three temples were located within the same edifice. Goats were sacrificed daily before the goddesses. Once a year Madanamohana had to face a trial for the offence of consuming the sacrificial meat by association (*parokṣe*). Bāṇeśvara, who was brought by a palanquin, used to declare him guilty, impose a fine of one rupee and go back after collecting the money. I have not been able to detect any connection between this custom and the *Śruti-Smṛti*.[98]

It is true that the *Śruti–Smṛtis* have nothing to do with this custom, but the same cannot be said about the Bengal *Purāṇas*. It is not that any of the *Purāṇas* had actually recommended this practice, but the brahmanism which worked out this ingenious method of adjustment between the conflicting beliefs and practices of innumerable religious cults and sects—brahmanical, brahmanized, and non-brahmanical—and presided over this delicate balance for centuries, owes its existence to these texts. This is precisely what the Bengal *Purāṇas* did; they created the precondition for the evolution of a regional tradition which the Hindu Bengalis identify as their own.

NOTES

1. For example, see, Robert I. Crane (ed.), *Regions and Regionalism in South Asian Studies: An Exploratory Study*, Duke University, Durham, 1967, particularly the essays by Bernard S. Cohn, 'Regions Subjective and Objective: Their Relation to the Study of Modern Indian History and Society', pp. 5–37, Barun De; 'A Historical Perspective on Theories of Regionalization in India', pp. 48–88; and Richard G. Fox (ed.), *Realm and Region in Traditional India*, Vikas Publishing House Pvt. Ltd, New Delhi, 1977, particularly Richard G. Fox, 'Introduction', pp. IX–XXV.
2. Cited in Deryck O. Lodrick, 'Rajasthan as a Region: Myth or Reality', in Karine Schomer, Joan L. Erdman, Deryck O. Lodrick and Lloyd I. Rudolph (eds), *The Idea of Rajasthan: Explorations in Regional Identity*, Vol. I: *Constructions*, Manohar (American Institute of Indian Studies), New Delhi, 1994, p. 2.
3. Niharranjan Ray, 'The Medieval Factor in Indian History', *Proceedings of the Indian History Congress*, Patiala, 1967, pp. 1–30.
4. R.S. Sharma, in his *Indian Feudalism: c. 300–1200*, University of Calcutta, Calcutta, 1965, first systematically expounded this process. This thesis has been later substantiated with either empirical evidence or theoretical justification by several scholars, including Sharma himself. For example, see Yadava, *Society and Culture in Northern India*; D.N. Jha (ed.), *Feudal Social Formation in Early India*, Chanakya Publications, Delhi, 1987; R.S. Sharma, 'Problem of Transition from Ancient to Medieval in Indian History', *Indian Historical Review*, Vol. 1, No. 1, 1974, pp. 1–9, and 'How Feudal was Indian Feudalism', in Harbans Mukhia and T.J. Byres (eds), *Feudalism and Non-European Societies*, Frank Cass, London, 1985, pp. 19–43. In a recent article on transition to 'medieval' in Indian history, Sharma takes cognizance of the emergence of regions as a characteristic feature of this period, but he continues to adhere to the feudalism thesis in explaining this transition, including that of the formation of regions, R.S. Sharma, 'Antiquity to the Middle Ages in India', *Social Science Probings*, Vol. 5, Nos. 1–4, March–December 1988 (published in January 1992), pp. 20–37.

5. B.D. Chattopadhyaya, 'Introduction: The Making of Early Medieval India', *The Making of Early Medieval India*, Oxford University Press, Delhi, 1994, p. 16.
6. *Ibid.*, p. 19.
7. *Supra*, Chapter IV, p. 147.
8. Chattopadhyaya, 'Introduction', p. 35.
9. *Ibid.*, p. 25.
10. *Supra*, Chapter IV, p. 121 and note 50 (pp. 157–8).
11. Chattopadhyaya, 'Introduction', p. 26.
12. B.D. Chattopadhyaya, ' "Autonomous Spaces" and the Authority of the State: The Contradiction and its Resolution in Theory and Practice in Early India', in Bernhard Kölver (ed.), *Recht, Staat und Verwaltung im Klassischen Indien* (The State, the Law, and Administration in Classical India), Munich, 1997.
13. *Supra*, Chapter IV, pp. 157–8.
14. Chattopadhyaya, 'Introduction', p. 30.
15. *Supra*, Chapter VI, pp. 239–45.
16. Lodrick, 'Rajasthan as a Region', p. 4.
17. *Ibid.*, p. 27.
18. *Ibid.*, pp. 12, 22, 29, 32.
19. Majumdar, *Ancient Bengal*, pp. 39–40. However, I agree with Chattopadhyaya that affiliation with a larger political structure does not necessarily impede the process of regional state formation: 'It is sharp fissions within communities and regions and the emergence of a complex of relations of domination and subordination which characterize a regional state society; this is irrespective of whether the polities representing such societies remained autonomous or semi-autonomous from, or became parts of, large state structures', Chattopadhyaya, 'Introduction', p. 21.
20. *BP*, III.5.46. This is an illustrative example of many such rules prescribed by the Bengal *Purāṇas* regarding food habits, personal hygiene, etc., without any justification except the blanket concession to local customs, the wide prevalence of which had set Bengal apart even from the adjoining regions. These conventions became such an integral part of the daily routine of a Bengali Hindu that many of these are still followed simply as a matter of habit.
21. Irfan Habib, *An Atlas of the Mughal Empire*, Oxford University Press, Delhi, 1982, 'Bengal Political 1595', map no. 11A, and notes on the map, pp. 42–6.
22. Jadunath Sarkar, 'Transformation of Bengal Under Mughal Rule', in Jadunath Sarkar (ed.), *The History of Bengal: Muslim Period, 1200–1757*, Janaki Prakashan, Patna, 1977 (reprint), pp. 216–22. For the opening up of Bengal as a result of new trading opportunities, also see Tapan Raychaudhuri, *Bengal Under Akbar and Jahangir: An Introductory Study in Social History*, Munshiram Manoharlal, Delhi, 1969, pp. 206–9, and for

Caitanyadeva's attempt to establish Bengal's cultural contact with the outside world, see Sanyal, *Bāṅglā Kīrtaner Itihāsa*, pp. 3–8.

23. Vincent Smith, *The Oxford History of India*, third edition, edited by Percival Spear, Clarendon Press, Oxford, 1967, pp. 758–9.
24. Lodrick, 'Rajasthan as a Region', pp. 10, 13–15, 18, 29–30.
25. This became one of the favourite themes of popular Bengali theatre in the late nineteenth and early twentieth centuries and a number of plays were written and enacted on the heroic patriotism of the Bāro Bhuiyāns. Most of these were sensational, pedagogic, and not of very high literary quality. But even Kshirodprasad Vidyavinod, a leading playwright, in his *Pratāpāditya* (1903), actually compared him with Rana Pratap Singh of Mewar. In this play Kshirodprasad's nationalism, expressed in provincial terms, is evident in his synonymous use of Jessore, where Pratāpāditya's zamindari was located, and '*Vaṅgabhūmi*', and in such statements as 'Bengal does not belong to the Hindus or the Muslims, but to the Bengalis'. He made emperor Akbar pronounce, 'The Bengalis have become united. The Bengalis have become one people (*jāti*). The revolt of Bengal is not an insignificant insurgence of the Bhuiyāns, but a great national uprising of the seven crores of Bengalis' (5/IC), Prabhatkumar Bhattacharya, *Bāṅglā Nāṭake Svādeśikatār Prabhāv*, Sahityasri, Calcutta, 1385 BS, pp. 550–3. It is futile to look for historical authenticity in the articulation of nationalist sentiment under adverse circumstances. Even when such comparisons were not explicitly made, the Bengalis drew inspiration from Rajput opposition to the Mughals in their struggle against colonial rule, as reflected in the plays of Girish Chandra Ghosh, Jyotirindranath Thakur and Dvijendralal Ray and in such novels as *Rājput Jīvansandhyā* by Ramesh Chandra Datta.

   Another common theme of some of these plays was the resistance offered to the ruthless Portuguese pirates whose plundering raids had struck terror among the inhabitants of coastal Bengal during the sixteenth–seventeenth centuries. This was similarly projected as an instance of the martial fervour and nationalist spirit of Bengalis. Such sentiments were not confined to popular plays and novels. Satyendranath Datta, an important poet among the later contemporaries of Rabindranath Thakur, in a famous poem significantly titled 'Āmrā' (We, i.e. the Bengalis), produced a long list of mostly fictitious or exaggerated glorious achievements of the Bengalis. He claimed that 'we' have resisted the incursions of the Mughals on the one hand and the Maghs (a generic name for seafaring buccaneers of European and East Asian origin) on the other, and the emperor of Delhi had to retreat in the face of the prowess of Chānd Rāi and Pratāpāditya—*Kāvyasañcayan*, M.C. Sarkar and Sons Pvt. Ltd, Calcutta, 1372 BS, p. 28. This impression is reinforced in Dineshchandra Sen's monumental history of Bengal, first published in 1935, where he depicted the Bāro Bhuiyāns, particularly Pratāpāditya, as fearless champions of Bengal's independence who fought against the Mughals and tamed the Magh-Portuguese pirates. Although he has faithfully recorded Pratāpāditya's many acts of mindless cruelty, Sen's admiration for his bravery ('*vīravikrama*') and irrepressible urge for freedom ('*svādhīnatār sei ciraposita icchā*') is barely concealed, Dineshchandra Sen, *Bṛhat Vaṅga*, Vol. II, Dey's Publishing, Calcutta, 1993 (reprint), pp. 786–808. It is important to note that a good deal of the material in Sen's account or Satish Chandra Mitra's *Jashohar O Khulnār Itihāsa*, Vol. II, Dasgupta and Co., Calcutta, 1963, where Pratāpāditya has received similar adulation, was collected from orally circulated local legends, some of which have since been committed to writing. It is natural that the activities of these powerful and influential zamindars would pass into local folklore with all the necessary embellishments, but they had just missed the status of being the common property of Bengal's regional heritage. This is not because much of what has been attributed to them is untrue, but that mysterious process of elimination and condensation of available material by which social memory is constituted did not allow them the space which these modern creative writers and chroniclers desired them to occupy for an entirely different purpose.

26. Sarkar, 'Transformation of Bengal Under Mughal Rule', p. 225.
27. *Ibid*., p. 225.
28. Lodrick, 'Rajasthan as a Region', p. 31.
29. Velcheru Narayana Rao, 'Coconut and Honey: Sanskrit and Telugu in Medieval Andhra', *Social Scientist,* Vol. 23, Nos. 10–12 (269–71), October–December 1995, p. 25.
30. Suniti Kumar Chatterji, *The Origin and Development of the Bengali Language*, Vol. I, Rupa and Co., Calcutta, 1985 (reprint), pp. 72–81, 97–8.
31. *Supra*, Chapter VI, pp. 270–2.
32. Chatterji, *The Origin and Development*, Vol. I, p. 109.
33. *Ibid*., pp. 123–4.
34. *Ibid*., p. 125.
35. *Ibid*., p. 126.
36. Hazra, *Upapurāṇas*, Vol. II, pp. 79, 86–90.
37. Chatterji, *The Origin and Development*, Vol. I, p. 132 and Sen, *Bṛhat Vaṅga*, Vol. II, p. 963.
38. Some of this folk literature was collected mainly through the individual initiative of such scholars as Dineshchandra Sen, Panchanan Mandal and others, and was published by the Calcutta University, Visva-Bharati, etc., during the first half of the twentieth century. Now a systematic effort is being made by the Bangla Academy, Dhaka, to collect and publish this, and the series already runs into some fifty volumes.
39. Dineshchandra Sen described this body of literature as belonging to the pre-Sanskritic period. But such free-floating mass of oral literature, which

was being continuously reworked by anonymous village poets, cannot be chronologically segmented into clearly identifiable periods. Therefore what he obviously meant was—and this is evident from his subsequent discussion—literature unaffected by the influence of Sanskrit, *Bṛhat Vaṅga*, Vol. II, p. 966.

40. Practically all historians of medieval Bengali literature have come up with their conclusions on the date of the original texts, because these too have often been partly reworked while being copied, and the available manuscripts of each of these texts collected from different parts of Bengal do not always tally with each other in details, thus creating further confusion. Sukhamay Mukhopadhyaya has carefully considered the arguments in favour of the dates suggested by various scholars and offered his own conclusions which, as a non-specialist, I found most convincing, *Madhyayuger Bāṅglā Sāhityer Tathya O Kālakram*, G. Bharadwaj and Co., Calcutta, 1974. In any case precise dates are immaterial for our purpose as most scholars seem to agree that the bulk of this literature was composed between the late fifteenth and mid-eighteenth centuries.
41. Muhammad Abdul Khalek, *Madhyayuger Bāṅglā Kāvye Lokupādān*, Bangla Academy, Dhaka, 1985, pp. 612–18.
42. Sen, *Bṛhat Vaṅga*, Vol. II, pp. 963–6, 972.
43. Wakil Ahmad, 'Bāṅglā Lok-Purāṇa O Aitihya Cetanā', in Shamsujjaman Khan (ed.), *Bāṅglādeśer Lokaitihya*, Bangla Academy, Dhaka, 1985, p. 454.
44. Shivaprasad Haldar, *Paurāṇik Saṁskṛti O Baṅgasāhitya*, Firma KLM Pvt. Ltd, Calcutta, 1983, p. 10; Bhattacharya, *Bāṅglā Maṅgalakāvyer Itihāsa*, p. 67; Sen, *Bṛhat Vaṅga*, Vol. II, pp. 970, 974.
45. Sen, *Bṛhat Vaṅga*, Vol. II, pp. 974–5.
46. *Supra*, Chapter VI, pp. 239–44.
47. *Supra*, Chapter VI, p. 245.
48. Dineshchandra Sen points out that Mukundarām, the most accomplished of all the poets of the various *Caṇḍīmaṅgalakāvyas*, could not ignore the prevalent story according to which Khullanā was married in the full bloom of her youth, but expressed his disapproval by making Janārdan *ghaṭak* (professional match-maker) sharply reproach her father Lakṣapati for not conforming to the brahmanical prescription of *gauridāna* (giving one's daughter in marriage at the auspicious age of eight years), *Bṛhat Vaṅga*, Vol. II, p. 974.
49. Sukumar Sen, *Bāṅglā Sāhityer Itihāsa*, Vol. I, Ananda Publishers Ltd, Calcutta, 1991, pp. 27–31; *Prācīn Bāṅglā O Bāṅgālī*, Visva-Bharati Granthanvibhaga, Calcutta, 1972 (reprint), pp. 63–5.
50. Chatterji, *The Origin and Development,* Vol. I, p. 132; Sen, *Bṛhat Vaṅga*, Vol. II, p. 982.
51. Hitesranjan Sanyal attributes the unprecedented socio-cultural efflorescence in Bengal during this period to the rise and growth of Gauḍīya

Vaiṣṇavism. He believes that eighty-five per cent of Bengali Hindus were followers of this movement and the Bengali people as a whole are successors to their cultural legacy, *Bāṅglā Kīrtaner Itihāsa*, p. 15 and *passim*. Tapan Raychaudhuri, on the other hand, argues that Vaiṣṇavism never became the creed of the majority of Bengalis. The invocations to the divinities which appear in the Bengali *pāñcālīs* of the sixteenth–seventeenth centuries suggest to him that most of the shrines were dedicated to Tantric or local deities, *Bengal Under Akbar and Jahangir,* p. 135. I am inclined to accept Sanyal's view because even though the Vaiṣṇava Sahajiyās followed the Tantric way in the ritual aspect of their worship, they should be formally included within Gauḍīya Vaiṣṇavism in an institutional sense. It is due to this essential syncretism of the movement that it succeeded in drawing members from so many disparate religious sects, and imparted to them a sense of collective identity. For detailed discussion on this issue, see Kunal Chakrabarti, '*Kīrtan* and Social Organization in Medieval Bengal', *The Indian Economic and Social History Review*, Vol. 28, No. 4, 1991, pp. 456–8.

52. The origin of Rādhā is a much debated issue. Brahmanism would tend to support the theory that Rādhā is a Puranic formulation, but there is no reference to her in the early Vaiṣṇavite *Mahāpurāṇas*, although attempts have been made to discover her in a favoured cowherd girl who was desired or worshipped (*ārādhitā*), or in an arrogant *gopī* (*dṛptā*) in the *Bhāgavata Purāṇa*. Some scholars have traced the origin of Rādhā from her closest analogue in the south, Pinnai. At the same time there are enough stray references to Rādhā in the secular literature of north India between the second and the twelfth centuries, scattered in Hāla's *Gāthāsaptaśatī*, Vākpati's *Gauḍavaho*, Bhaṭṭa Nārāyaṇa's *Veṇīsaṁhāra*, Ānandavardhana's *Dhvanyāloka*, Abhinavagupta's *Dhvanyālokalocana*, Rājaśekhara's *Kāvyamīmāṁsā*, Bhoja's *Sarasvatīkaṇṭhābharaṇa*, Kṣemendra's *Daśāvatāracarita*, Vidyākara's *Subhāṣitaratnakoṣa*, Śrīdharadāsa's *Saduktikarṇāmṛta*, Bilhaṇa's *Vikramāṅkadevacarita*, Hemacandra's *Siddhahemaśabdānuśāsana,* Śrīharṣa's *Naiṣadhīyacarita* and Govardhana's *Āryasaptaśatī*, not to speak of Jayadeva's *Gītagovinda*, and in some of the western Indian inscriptions, to suggest that there might have been an independent parallel tradition, a folk-tale or a legend about a courtly or folk heroine, who was later co-opted by the brahmanical religious leaders. It has been suggested that in the mythology Kṛṣṇa has always been associated with a great goddess who eventually came to assume the form of Rādhā, although she is not universally accepted as his prime consort by all Kṛṣṇa-worshipping sects. Bengali and Hindi poets of medieval India have variously conceived Rādhā as the supreme goddess to the heroine of secular, courtly love. For the antecedents and the evolution of the concept and image of Rādhā, see Asoke Kumar Majumdar, 'A Note on the Development of Rādhā Cult', *Annals of the*

Bhandarkar Oriental Research Institute, Vol. 36, Parts 3-4, 1955, pp. 231–57; Barbara Stoler Miller, 'Rādhā: Consort of Kṛṣṇa's Springtime Passion', in Barbara Stoler Miller (ed. and trans.), *Love Song of the Dark Lord: Jayadeva's Gītagovinda*, Columbia University Press, New York, 1977, pp. 26–37; Shashibhushan Dasgupta, *Śrīrādhār Kramavikāś: Darśane O Sāhitye*, A. Mukherji and Co. Pvt. Ltd, Calcutta, 1381 BS (reprint), pp. 103–92; Charlotte Vaudeville, 'Krishna Gopāla, Rādhā, and the Great Goddess', Karine Schomer, 'Where Have All the Rādhās Gone? New Images of Women in Modern Hindi Poetry', Dennis Hudson, 'Pinnai, Krishna's Cowherd Wife', in John Stratton Hawley and Donna Marie Wulff (eds), *The Divine Consort: Rādhā and the Goddesses of India*, Motilal Banarsidass, Delhi, 1984, pp. 1–12, 89–115, 238–61.

Despite this diversity of opinion on her origin and on the significance of multiple conceptions of Rādhā, I would still insist that in Bengal she was primarily a Puranic innovation, for nowhere else do we find an extended treatment of her in such theological and emotional intensity before the Bengal *Purāṇas*, except perhaps in the contemporaneous Jayadeva. However, while in Jayadeva one particular dimension of Rādhā has been emphasized, the Bengal *Purāṇas* foreshadow the many Rādhās of subsequent centuries. It is indeed possible that *Śrīkṛṣṇa Kīrtana* of Caṇḍīdāsa, a vernacular text of medieval Bengal where Rādhā figures prominently as the unmarried playmate of Kṛṣṇa, was composed before the final redactions to the *Brahmavaivarta Purāṇa* were made. But assuming that this chronological sequence is correct, it does not make much of a difference to my argument as both texts were the product of the same cultural milieu. And in any case, the Bengal *Purāṇas* certainly pre-date the Gauḍīya Vaiṣṇava movement in which theorization about Rādhā reached its most subtle and elaborate culmination. Thus it is futile to look for a pristine 'origin'of Rādhā in any particular tradition or to categorize her in a particular mould. Recently Sumanta Banerjee has emphatically argued that Rādhā was originally a folk heroine later appropriated by brahmanism. This approach ignores the complexity in the relationship between folk and elite in medieval Bengal, symbolized by the multiformity of Rādhā. The problem with any such strongly argued position is that it tends to look for one Rādhā embodied in a particular category of source in obvious but unstated preference to others, and in Sumanta Banerjee's case it is accentuated by his reliance on such unsupported assumptions as 'the Abhiras established their control in Bengal' around the ninth century, *Appropriation of a Folk-Heroine: Rādhā in Medieval Bengali Vaishnavite Culture*, Indian Institute of Advanced Study, Shimla, 1993, p. 10 and *passim*. Rādhā, the common inheritance of the Bengalis, draws most on the Bengal *Purāṇas*—themselves the product of an assimilative process. Yet evidently she is made up of several other elements, derived from diverse, even mutually exclusive, sources, and the Gauḍīya Vaiṣṇava movement which contributed most to the popularization of Rādhā, found the prototype of their Rādhā in the Rādhā of the Bengal *Purāṇas*.

53. Brown, *God as Mother*, 1974.
54. See, for example, *MbP*, Chapters 49, 53; *DbP*, IX.50.
55. Jayadeva does not explicitly state that Rādhā is married to another man, but she is definitely older than Kṛṣṇa and is entrusted with the responsibility of seeing the child Kṛṣṇa home. However, Lee Siegel believes that in the *Gītagovinda* 'Rādhā is clearly a *parakīyā nāyikā*—her love-making with Kṛṣṇa is in defiance of Nanda, Kṛṣṇa's foster-father, who as a representative of authority exemplifies the social order', *Sacred and Profane Dimensions of Love in Indian Traditions as Exemplified in the Gitagovinda of Jayadeva*, Oxford University Press, Delhi, 1978, p. 119. Thus one can observe three stages in the evolution of this relationship. In the Bengal *Purāṇas* all the elements of an illicit liaison are present, even though, somewhat incongruously, they are married to each other. In the *Gītagovinda* the pair is unmarried and their explicitly sensual relationship is socially disapproved of in more ways than one. But Rādhā is not married to anyone else as she is in the medieval *padāvalī* literature of Bengal and in such key theological texts of Gauḍīya Vaiṣṇavism as *Caitanya Caritāmṛta* of Kṛṣṇadās Kavirāj. Later the question of the ambiguous status of Rādhā as *svakīyā/parakīyā nāyikā* generated much debate among the Bengal Vaiṣṇavas, as the Goswamis of Vṛndāvana took conflicting positions on this issue.
56. Abdul Kadir, 'Bāṅglār Pallīsaṅgīte Līlāvāda', *Bāṅglār Lokāyata Sāhitya*, Bangla Academy, Dhaka, 1985, pp. 16–41.
57. H. Kulke, 'Early Patronage of the Jagannātha Cult', in Eschmann, Kulke, Tripathi (eds), *The Cult of Jagannāth*, pp. 139–55.
58. Akbar censured his general Rājā Mānsingh for being disrespectful to Rāmacandra, the rājā of Khurda, who had revived the Jagannātha temple after its temporary eclipse under the Afghan rulers of Bengal. Indeed, Akbar humoured Rāmacandra in order to secure an ally against the powerful Sultanate of Golkonda, but the claim of Rāmacandra to be recognized as the lawful zamindar of the Cuttack–Puri region and its neighbourhood was based on his reputation as 'the renewer of the national cult of the Oriyas'. The subsequent history of Mughal rule in Orissa is one of continuous struggle for domination over the cult; the Mughal Subahdar returned the image of Jagannātha to the temple of Puri in 1735.

    In 1751 Orissa came under the administration of Raghuji Bhonsla, the Maratha king of Nagpur. The Marathas were suspicious of the high position held by the rājās of Khurda by virtue of their close connection with the Jagannātha cult. Therefore when Sheo Bhatt Sathe, the first Hindu governor of the Marathas in Orissa, took charge in 1759, the first few things he did were dismantle the Khurda territory, dispossess rājā Bīrakeśarī Dev of the Puruṣottama Kṣetra, and assume direct administration of the Jagannātha temple. Once in control of the temple, the Marathas extended unqualified support to it and strictly adhered to the existing customs. W. Laurie had observed as early as 1850 that even though Maratha rule was marked by 'rapacity and violence', this 'veneration' for the temple 'must have covered a multitude of [their] sins' in the eyes of the people of Orissa.

In 1765 the English East India Company secured the Dewani right of Orissa from Shah Alam. Next year the Company approached the Maratha king Januji Bhonsla with the proposal that he would cede the province of Orissa to the Company for an annual tribute. Negotiation continued for several years, but failed because the two parties could not agree on their share of responsibility in the management of the Jagannātha temple. Thus the importance of the temple was appreciated by the British from the very beginning and it was not without reason that W.W. Hunter remarked several decades later that 'the possession of the god had always given the dominion of Orissa'. Eventually, when the Company declared war against the Marathas in 1803, it made every effort to ensure that the temple was treated with utmost respect. Prabhat Mukherjee shows how anxious the British were to 'conciliate' and win the support of the local population by taking 'every precaution to preserve the respect due to the Pagoda and to the religious prejudices of the Brahmins and the pilgrims'. It was only after the temple priests agreed to place the Jagannātha temple under British administration that the Company's troops entered Puri without resistance.

For details, see H. Kulke, 'The Struggle Between the Rājās of Khurda and the Muslim Subahdars of Cuttack for Dominance of the Jagannātha Temple', ' "Juggernaut" under British Supremacy and the Resurgence of the Khurda Rājās as "Rājās of Puri" ', in *ibid.*, pp. 321–9, 337–8, 345–8; Prabhat K. Mukherjee, *History of the Jagannātha Temple*, Firma KLM, Calcutta, 1977, pp. 17–18, 30.

59. G.N. Dash, 'Jagannātha and Oriya Nationalism', in Eschmann, Kulke, Tripathi (eds), *The Cult of Jagannāth,* p. 362.
60. Richard M. Eaton, *The Rise of Islam and the Bengal Frontier, 1204–1760*, Oxford University Press, Delhi, 1994, pp. 14–15.
61. *Ibid.*, pp. 16–17.
62. Majumdar, *Ancient Bengal*, pp. 510–11, 603–4, 612–21.
63. *Rāmacarita*, III.10, 30, 33–4, 39–41.
64. During the Mughal period, such temples were usually built by powerful individuals, often located in or around the provincial capitals, or by the upper-caste landholders. However, in the latter half of the eighteenth century, Bengal experienced a phenomenal increase in its overseas trade and consequently a rise in demand for the industrial products of Bengal.

This enlarged the scope for alternative job opportunities of the lower occupational groups such as the Telis, Kalus, Nāpits, Tāmbulīs and Śuṇḍis, who now began to produce and trade in cotton textiles, silk, sugar, salt and iron, and brass and bell-metal ware. The new economic opportunities helped a large section of these *jāti* groups to become prosperous and their desire for social recognition found expression in the acquisition of landed property and construction of temples. Temple building became a part of a broad-based social movement, as attested by the fact that more than eighty per cent of the existing temples of Bengal were built during the second half of the eighteenth and in the nineteenth centuries. For details, see George Michell, 'Historical Background', in George Michell (ed.), *Brick Temples of Bengal: From the Archives of David McCutchion*, Princeton University Press, Princeton, 1983, pp. 3–10; Hitesranjan Sanyal, 'Temple Promotion and Social Mobility in Bengal', *Social Mobility in Bengal*, Papyrus, Calcutta, 1981, pp. 65–81.

65. Hitesranjan Sanyal, 'The Nature of Peasant Culture of India: A Study of the Pat Painting and Clay Sculpture of Bengal', *Folk* (Copenhagen), Vol. 26, 1984, p. 168.

66. Victor Turner, 'Pilgrimages as Social Processes', *Dramas, Fields, and Metaphors: Symbolic Action in Human Society,* Cornell University Press, Ithaca and London, 1974, pp. 185–6.

67. Werbner, 'Introduction', in Werbner (ed.), *Regional Cults*, pp. IX–XII. Werbner disagrees with Turner on a few minor matters, but those are irrelevant for our purpose.

68. Paṇḍharpur was initially a tiny hamlet on the trade route between the agricultural settlements of the eastern plains and the creek-ports on the west coast. In AD 516 the village was donated to a *brāhmaṇa* called Jayadvṛtha. Every tribal group that joined the expanding settlement was given a *jāti* name and was assimilated within the *śūdra varṇa.* Those from the neighbourhood who were not assimilated often raided the new villages, lifting their cattle. In the fight, if a villager died in a special feat of bravery, a commemorative stone was erected in his honour. From an inscription dated AD 757, it seems that the hero who possibly died at Paṇḍharpur was called Biṭṭaga. He soon became the object of a cult.

Meanwhile, integration of tribal godheads into the brahmanical pantheon continued through the construction of justificatory myths. One recounts that Kṛṣṇa had come down to Paṇḍharpur from Dvārakā with a huge herd of cattle to look for his wife Rukminī who had taken refuge in a nearby forest. He met her here and decided to stay on. This myth may be an echo of the popular memory, unsupported by documentary evidence, that the first *brāhmaṇa* settlers in this area had come from Dvārakā. The Puranic phase in the history of Viṭhobā began with the transformation of Biṭṭaga into Viṭhṭhala and his identification with Kṛṣṇa in the ninth century. A regular statue with characteristic iconographic features was erected in place of the old hero-stone. By the middle of the twelfth century the fame of Kṛṣṇa–Viṭhṭhala had spread so wide that a Hoyasāla king had built temples dedicated to the god.

With the arrival of the ascetic Puṇḍalik at Paṇḍharpur towards the late twelfth century, the Puranic phase was replaced by *bhakti*. A Marathi and a proto-Vārkarī, Puṇḍalik's mystical experiences centred on Viṭhṭhala and he transformed the elaborate Sanskritic–Puranic mode of worship through *brāhmaṇa* priests into an interiorized adoration, prescinding caste distinction. The *śūdra jātis*, organized by the *brāhmaṇas*, had now come of age, and the very success of brahmanization had in a way precipitated this new development at Paṇḍharpur. A new myth was devised according to which Hari (rather than Kṛṣṇa), while in Vaikuṇṭha (rather than in Dvārakā), had learnt about Puṇḍalik and came down to see him. Impressed by his devotion he stayed back in the form of Viṭhobā. This time, it was his wife who came later, looking for him. Puṇḍalik left no written work behind, but his memory was kept alive by his disciples, the great poet-saints Nāmdeva and Jñānadeva. The names of a number of eminent saints from the lower *jāti* groups and the outcastes came to be associated with the religious complex and Marathi was accepted as the sacred language for ritual purposes, as the influence of the non-*brāhmaṇa* Vārkarī-panth continued to grow. Temples were built and rebuilt and eventually Paṇḍharpur established itself as the most important pilgrimage site in Maharashtra. The complex was officially thrown open to the outcastes in 1958, thus closing the circle in the evolution of the cult of Viṭhobā at Paṇḍharpur. For details, see G.A. Delewury, *The Cult of Viṭhobā*, Deccan College Postgraduate Research Institute, Poona, 1960, particularly pp. 193–203.

69. See, for example, *MbP*, 73.37; 75.28; *DP*, 66.10; *Ks*, 4.112; *BvP*, III. 30.215; *BP*, I.6.34.
70. Tarundev Bhattacharyya, *Ganga Sagar Mela*, Government of West Bengal, Calcutta, 1976.
71. See, for example, *DbP*, VII.30.65; *KP*, 18.42–5.
72. *MbP*, 36.71–2, 45.33–42, 48.15; *DbP*, III.24.19–20; *DP*, Chapter 22, 59.16; *BvP*, I.6.60; *KP*, 60.1–44.
73. *Supra*, Chapter V, pp. 209–12.
74. Anthony P. Cohen, *The Symbolic Construction of Community*, Ellis Horwood Limited, Chichester, 1985, p. 20.
75. *Ibid*., p. 21.
76. Here it is not the question of the self-definition of the Bengalis as a community, which is currently articulated in terms of language rather than religion. The issue is the beginning of a historical process which created the conditions for evolution of a community consciousness among those whose descendants have been described by themselves as 'Ben-

galis', and thus made *any* self-definition (because it is subject to continuous revision) possible at a later date.

77. Sanyal, 'The Nature of Peasant Culture in India', pp. 148–73.
78. *Ibid*., p. 168.
79. John Leavitt, 'Cultural Holism in the Anthropology of South Asia: The Challenge of Regional Traditions', *Contributions to Indian Sociology*, Vol. 26, No. 1, January–June 1992, pp. 3–33.
80. To continue with the hypothetical case suggested earlier, it is possible that a Kumaoni may wish to distance himself from a Garhwali if he feels that his Kumaoni identity is in danger of being submerged by the assertion of cultural superiority of Garhwal (for whatever reasons—political, economic, social), and may yet readily agree to join hands with the Garhwali to emphasize their common identity as *pāhāḍīs* in order to distinguish both from the plains people who surround them.
81. Leavitt, 'Cultural Holism', pp. 33–44.
82. Nathan Watchel, *The Vision of the Vanquished: The Spanish Conquest of Peru Through Indian Eyes*, The Harvester Press, Sussex, 1977. See particularly pp. 1–32, 140–65, 201–13.
83. *Ibid*., p. 4.
84. *Ibid*., p. 160.
85. *Ibid*., p. 165.
86. *Ibid*., p. 205.
87. Peter Burke, *Historical Anthropology of Early Modern Italy*, Cambridge, 1987, pp. 48–62.
88. Roger Chartier, 'Culture as Appropriation: Popular Cultural Uses in Early Modern France', in Steven L. Kaplan (ed.), *Understanding Popular Culture: Europe from the Middle Ages to the Nineteenth Century*, Mouton Publishers, Berlin, 1984, p. 232.
89. See John Gillis's report of the 'Discussion' on Peter Burke's 'The "Discovery" of Popular Culture', in Raphael Samuel (ed.), *People's History and Socialist Theory* (History Workshop Series), Routledge and Kegan Paul, London, 1981, pp. 224–5.
90. Chartier, 'Culture as Appropriation', pp. 229–36. We may recall however the observation of Georges Duby that it is far easier for the historian to approach the ideologies of the dominant order, 'because only these groups had the means to construct cultural objects sufficiently permanent for the historian today to be able to analyse what remains of them'. This is not to deny the existence of 'popular ideologies', by which Duby implies the manner of appropriation of the cultural objects by those social groups who are 'deprived of direct access to cultural tools which would have enabled them to translate into some durable form their world view', and he merely wishes to draw attention to the inherent bias in the 'documents' 'to correct the errors of perspective which it is likely to cause'. Duby adds that such ideologies can only be 'guessed at', if ruling classes for

some reason took notice of them, Georges Duby, 'Ideologies in Social History', in Jacques Le Goff and Pierre Nora (eds), *Constructing the Past: Essays in Historical Methodology*, Cambridge University Press, Cambridge, 1985, p. 156. We are fortunate in being able to deal with a corpus of texts, representing the dominant ideology, which nevertheless takes notice of the cultural objects (including the texts themselves as well as the cultural sets these helped to create) in a web of multiple relationships, partly because their *brāhmaṇa* authors, though belonging to the dominant order, were not necessarily of 'the ruling class'. Thus, even though rendered 'vague, partial and deformed by the intervening party', this made 'guessing' easier.

91. For a discussion on how the folk-tales reinforce the dominant ideology, see Kunal Chakrabarti, 'Brahmanical Hegemony and the "Revolt" of the Oppressed Social Groups: Notes on Two Readings', forthcoming.
92. *Supra*, Chapter II, pp. 71–2.
93. Sanyal, *Bāṅglā Kīrtaner Itihāsa*, pp. 119–38. For a discussion on how the cultural syncretism of this movement contributed to the growth of Bengali identity, see Hitesranjan Sanyal, 'Trends of Change in Bhakti Movement in Bengal (Sixteenth and Seventeenth Centuries)', in D.N. Jha (ed.), *Society and Ideology in India: Essays in Honour of Prof. R.S. Sharma*, Munshiram Manoharlal Publishers Pvt. Ltd, New Delhi, 1996, pp. 183–212.
94. Chandrika Panigrahi, 'Muktimandap Sabha of Brahmans, Puri', in Nirmal Kumar Bose (ed.), *Data on Caste: Orissa*, Anthropological Survey of India, Memoir No. 7, Calcutta, 1960, pp. 179–92. Panigrahi has quoted in full the texts of both the 'petitions' and the 'decisions' of nine representative cases brought up before the *Sabhā* in the late 1950s.
95. R.C. Hazra has prepared a catalogue of all the available manuscripts of each of the *Purāṇas* discussed here. See Hazra, *Upapurāṇas*, Vol. I, pp. 267–8, note 1; pp. 310, note 113; and Vol. II, pp. 35–6, note 105; pp. 194–5, note 421; pp. 259–60, note 598; pp. 284–5, note 650; pp. 306–7, note 80. It is important to note that of all the manuscripts of the *Mahābhāgavata Purāṇa* preserved in the Dacca University, three were discovered in Sylhet and the rest in other parts of eastern Bengal, where the impact of brahmanism was relatively weak. Since the *Brahmavaivarta Purāṇa* is not considered an *Upapurāṇa*, Hazra has not discussed it in his *Studies in the Upapurāṇas*.
96. For instance, see Hazra, *Purāṇic Records*, p. 128; Hazra, *Upapurāṇas*, Vol. II, pp. 2–9.
97. The contention that the *Purāṇas* above all signify a process which, in the ultimate analysis, even overshadows their contents, is the focus of a recent collection of essays on the subject, Wendy Doniger (ed.), *Purāṇa Perennis: Reciprocity and Transformation in Hindu and Jaina Texts*, State University of New York Press, Albany, 1993. See particularly the 'Intro-

duction' (pp. VII–XII) which makes use of the Redfield model but claims that because of the continuities and overlaps the distinction between 'Great' and 'Little Tradition' is getting increasingly obliterated and suggests that perhaps it would be better to say that 'each is within the other'.

98. Charuchandra Datta, *Purāno Kathā*, Vol. I, Visva-Bharati, Calcutta, 1962 (originally published in 1343 BS), pp. 22–3.

Bibliography

I. PRIMARY SOURCES

A. *Bengal* Purāṇas

Brahmavaivartapurāṇam. Panchanan Tarkaratna (ed. and trans. into Bengali), Vangavasi Press, Calcutta, 1332 BS.

Bṛhaddharmapurāṇam. Panchanan Tarkaratna (ed. and trans. into Bengali), Vangavasi Press, Calcutta, 1314 BS.

Bṛhannāradīyapurāṇam, Panchanan Tarkaratna (ed. and trans. into Bengali), Vangavasi Press, Calcutta, 1316 BS.

Devībhāgavatam. Panchanan Tarkaratna and Srijib Nyayatirtha (eds and trans. into Bengali), Navabharat Publishers, Calcutta, 1388 BS.

Devīpurāṇam. Panchanan Tarkaratna and Srijib Nyayatirtha (eds and trans. into Bengali), Navabharat Publishers, Calcutta, 1384 BS.

Kālikāpurāṇam. Panchanan Tarkaratna and Srijib Nyayatirtha (eds and trans. into Bengali), Navabharat Publishers, Calcutta, 1384 BS.

Kriyāyogasāraḥ. Tarakanta Devasharmma (ed. and trans. into Bengali), Vangavasi Press, Calcutta, 1320 BS.

Śrīmahābhāgavatam. Panchanan Tarkaratna (ed. and trans. into Bengali), Vangavasi Press, Calcutta, 1321 BS.

B. *Inscriptions*

Banerji, R.D. 'The Bangarh Grant of Mahi-pala I: The 9th year', *Epigraphia Indica*, Vol. XIV, 1917–18.

Maity, S.K. and R.R. Mukherjee (eds), *Corpus of Bengal Inscriptions*, Firma K.L. Mukhopadhyay, Calcutta, 1967.

Majumdar, N.G. (ed.), *Inscriptions of Bengal*, Vol. III, The Varendra Research Society, Rajshahi, 1929.

Sircar, D.C. 'Two Pāla Plates from Belwa', *Epigraphia Indica*, Vol. XXIX, 1951–2.

Venis, Arthur, 'Copper-plate Grant of Vaidyadeva, King of Kāmarūpa', *Epigraphia Indica*, Vol. II, 1894.

C. *Other Sanskrit Texts*

The Harivaṁśa. P.L. Vaidya (ed.), 2 Vols, Bhandarkar Oriental Research Institute, Poona, 1969 and 1971. Panchanan Tarkaratna (ed.), Vangavasi Press, Calcutta, 1312 BS.

The Hymns of Ṛg Veda. Ralph T. H. Griffith (trans.), Vol. II, The Chowkhamba Sanskrit Series Office, Varanasi, 1971. *Ṛg Veda*, Part VII, Vishva Bandhu (ed.), Vishveshvaranand Vedic Research Institute, Hoshiarpur, 1965.

Love Song of the Dark Lord: Jayadeva's Gītagovinda. Barbara Stoler Miller (ed. and trans.), Columbia University Press, New York, 1977.

The Mahābhārata. Critically edited by Vishnu S. Sukthankar, Bhandarkar Oriental Research Institute, Poona, Vol. 4: *The Āraṇyakaparvan* (Pt. II), V. S. Sukthankar (ed.), 1942; Vol. 5: *The Virāṭaparvan*, Raghu Vira (ed.), 1936; Vol. 7: *The Viṣmaparvan,* S.K. Velvalkar (ed.), 1947.

Mārkaṇḍeyapurāṇam. Panchanan Tarkaratna and Srijib Nyayatirtha (ed. and trans. into Bengali), Navabharat Publishers, Calcutta, 1390 BS.

Rāmacarita (Gauḍakavi-Sandhyākaranandi-viracita). Radhagovinda Basak (ed. and trans.), General Printers and Publishers Ltd, Calcutta, 1953.

D. *Bengali Texts*

Annadāmaṅgala: Rāmprasāda Bhāratchandra Racanāsaṁgraha. Reflect Publications, Calcutta, 1986.

Caṇḍīmaṅgala (*Kavikaṁkaṇa Mukunda Viracita*). Sukumar Sen (ed.), Sahitya Akademi, New Delhi, 1975.

Śrī Śrī Maṅgalacaṇḍīr Pāñcālī. Krishnachandra Gupta (ed.), General Library and Printers, Calcutta, 1391 BS.

Śrī Śrī Padma Purāṇa vā Viṣaharir Pāñcālī by Dvija Vaṁśīdāsa. Collected and revised by Purna Chandra Chakrabarti, published by Ramnath Das for Tarachand Das and Sons, Calcutta, undated.

Śūnyapurāṇa. Bhaktimadhab Chattopadhyaya (ed.), Firma KLM Pvt. Ltd, Calcutta, 1977.

II. SECONDARY SOURCES

Adamson, Walter L., *Hegemony and Revolution: A Study of Antonio Gramsci's Political and Cultural Theory*, University of California Press, Berkeley, 1980.

Agrawala, V.S., 'Editorial', *Purāṇa*, Vol. 1, No. 2, 1960.

Ahmad, Wakil, 'Bāṅglā Lok-purāṇa O Aitihya Cetanā', in Samsujjaman Khan (ed.), *Bāṅglā Deśer Lokaitihya*, Bangla Academy, Dhaka, 1985.

Allen, Albert Henry, 'The Vaṭa-Sāvitrī-vrata, According to Hemādri and the

Vratārka', *Journal of the American Oriental Society*, Vol. 21, July–December 1900.

Anderson, Perry, 'The Antinomies of Antonio Gramsci', *New Left Review*, No. 100, November 1976–January 1977.

Asher, Frederick M., *The Art of Eastern India 300–800*, University of Minnesota Press, Minneapolis, 1980.

Atre, Shubhangana, *The Archetypal Mother: A Systemic Approach to Harappan Religion*, Ravish Publishers, Pune, 1987.

Babb, Lawrence A., *The Divine Hierarchy: Popular Hinduism in Central India*, Columbia University Press, New York and London, 1975.

Bachofen, J.J., *Myth, Religion and Mother Right*, Princeton University Press, Princeton, 1967 (reprint).

Bagchi, Prabodh Chandra, 'Some Aspects of Buddhist Mysticism in the Caryāpadas', *Studies in the Tantras*, Part I, University of Calcutta, 1939.

———, 'Religion', in R.C. Majumdar (ed.), *The History of Bengal*, Vol. I, University of Dacca, Dacca, 1963 (reprint).

Bailey, F.G., 'For a Sociology of India?', *Contributions to Indian Sociology*, No. 3, 1959.

———, *Tribe, Caste and Nation*, Manchester University Press, Manchester, 1960.

Baines, Sir Athelstane, *Ethnography*, Strassburg, 1912.

Bakhtin, M.M., *The Dialogic Imagination: Four Essays*, Caryl Emerson and Michael Holquist (trans.), University of Texas Press, Austin, 1981.

Bamberger, Joan, 'The Myth of Matriarchy: Why Men Rule in Primitive Society', in M.Z. Rosaldo and L. Lamphere (eds), *Women, Culture and Society*, Stanford University Press, Stanford, California, 1974.

Bandyopadhyaya, Bibhuti Bhushan, *Pather Pāñcālī*, in *Bibhūti Racanāvalī*, Vol. I, Mitra O Ghosh Pvt. Ltd, Calcutta, 1387 BS.

———, *Ichāmatī*, in *Bibhūti Racanāvalī*, Vol. III, Mitra O Ghosh Pvt. Ltd, Calcutta, 1388 BS.

Bandyopadhyaya, Suresh Chandra, *Smṛti Śāstre Bāṅgālī*, A. Mukherji and Co., Calcutta, 1961.

Banerjea, Jitendra Nath, *Development of Hindu Iconography*, Munshiram Manoharlal Publishers Pvt. Ltd, New Delhi, 1974 (third edition).

Banerjee, Sumanta, *Appropriation of a Folk-Heroine: Rādhā in Medieval Bengali Vaishnavite Culture*, Indian Institute of Advanced Study, Shimla, 1993.

Banerji, Mangovind, 'Aryan Attitude to Female Deities', *The Journal of the Bihar and Orissa Research Society*, Vol. 25, 1939.

Banerji, R.D., *Eastern Indian School of Medieval Sculpture*, Ramanand Vidya Bhawan, New Delhi, 1961 (reprint).

Banerji, S.C., *Tantra in Bengal: A Study in its Origin, Development and Influence*, Naya Prakash, Calcutta, 1978.

Barnett, Lionel D., *Hindu Gods and Heroes*, Ess Ess Publications, Delhi, 1977 (reprint).

Barth, A., *The Religions of India* (trans. Rev. J. Wood), Chowkhamba Sanskrit Series Office, Varanasi, 1963 (reprint).

Barthes, Roland, 'The Death of the Author', in David Lodge (ed.), *Modern Criticism and Theory: A Reader*, Longman, London, 1988.

Basham, A.L., *The Wonder That Was India*, Fontana Books in association with Rupa and Co., Calcutta, 1975.

Basu, Gopendrakrishna, *Bāṅglār Laukika Devatā*, Dey's Publishing, Calcutta, 1976.

Basu, Nirmal Kumar, *Hindu Samājer Gaḍan*, Visva-Bharati Granthalaya, Calcutta, 1356 BS.

Beauvoir, Simone de, *The Second Sex*, Penguin Books, Harmondsworth, 1975.

Bedekar, V.M., 'Principles of Mahābhārata Textual Criticism: The Need for a Restatement', *Purāṇa*, Vol. 11, No. 2, July 1969.

Beetham, David. *The Legitimation of Power*, Macmillan Education Ltd, London, 1991.

Bell, Catherine, 'Religion and Chinese Culture: Toward an Assessment of "Popular Religion"', *History of Religions*, Vol. 29, No. 1, August 1989.

Bennett, Tony, 'Texts in History: The Determinations of Readings and Their Texts', in Derek Attridge, Geoff Bennington and Robert Young (eds), *Post-Structuralism and the Question of History*, Cambridge University Press, Cambridge, 1987.

Bhadra, Gautam, 'The Mentality of Subalternity: *Kāntanāmā* or *Rājadharma*', in Ranajit Guha (ed.), *Subaltern Studies VI: Writings on South Asian History and Society*, Oxford University Press, Delhi, 1989.

Bhandarkar, R.G., *Vaiṣṇavism, Śaivism and Minor Religious Systems*, Indological Book House, Varanasi, 1965 (reprint).

Bharati, Agehananda, 'Great Tradition and Little Traditions: An Anthropological Approach to the Study of Asian Cultures', in Th. Cummings (ed.), *Anthropology and Adult Education*, Center for Continuing Education, Boston, 1968.

———, 'Hinduism and Modernization', in Robert F. Spencer (ed.), *Religion and Change in Contemporary Asia*, Oxford University Press, Bombay, 1971.

———, *The Tantric Tradition*, B.I. Publications, Bombay, 1976.

———, *Great Tradition and Little Traditions: Indological Investigations in Cultural Anthropology*, Chowkhamba Sanskrit Series Office, Varanasi, 1978.

Bhattacharji, Sukumari, *The Indian Theogony: A Comparative Study of Indian Mythology from the Vedas to the Purāṇas*, Firma KLM Pvt. Ltd, Calcutta, 1978.

Bhattacharya, Ashutosh, *Bāṅglā Maṅgalakāvyer Itihāsa*, A. Mukherji and Co. Pvt. Ltd, Calcutta, 1975 (sixth edition).

Bhattacharya, A.K., 'A Nonaryan Aspect of the Devi', in D.C. Sircar (ed.), *The Śakti Cult and Tārā*, University of Calcutta, Calcutta, 1967.

Bhattacharya, Benoytosh, *The Indian Buddhist Iconography: Mainly Based on Sādhanamālā and Cognate Tantric Texts of Rituals*, Firma K.L. Mukhopadhyay, Calcutta, 1968.

Bhattacharya, Dineshchandra, *Bāṅgālīr Sārasvata Avadāna*, Vol. I (*Baṅge Navyanyāyacarccā*), Bangiya Sahitya Parishat, Calcutta, 1358 BS.

Bhattacharya, Gopalchandra, *Bāromāser Meyeder Vratakathā*, Nirmal Book Agency, Calcutta, undated.

Bhattacharya, Jogendra Nath, *Hindu Castes and Sects: An Exposition of the Origin of the Hindu Caste System and the Bearing of the Sects Towards Each Other and Towards Other Religious Systems*, Editions India, Calcutta, 1973 (reprint).

Bhattacharya, Prabhatkumar, *Bāṅglā Nāṭake Svādeśikatār Prabhāv*, Sahityasri, Calcutta, 1385 BS.

Bhattacharya, Shibchandra Vidyarnaba, *Tantratattva*, Navabharat Publishers, Calcutta, 1389 BS.

Bhattacharya, Srimohan and Dineshchandra Bhattacharya (eds), *Bhāratīya Darśana Koṣa: Sāṁkhya and Pātañjala Darśana*, Vol. II, Sanskrit College, Calcutta, 1979.

Bhattacharya, Umeshchandra, *Bhāratadarśanasāra*, Visva-Bharati, Calcutta, 1391 BS.

Bhattacharyya, B., 'Scientific Background of the Buddhist Tantras', *Indian Historical Quarterly*, Vol. 32, 1956.

Bhattacharyya, N.N., *Indian Mother Goddess*, Indian Studies: Past and Present, Calcutta, 1971.

———, *Bhāratīya Dharmer Itihāsa*, General Printers, Calcutta, 1977.

———, *History of the Tantric Religion: A Historical, Ritualistic and Philosophical Study*, Manohar, New Delhi, 1982.

Bhattacharyya, Tarundev, *Ganga Sagar Mela*, Government of West Bengal, Calcutta, 1976.

Bhattasali, Nalini Kanta, *Iconography of the Buddhist and Brahmanical Sculptures in the Dacca Museum*, published by Rai S.N. Bhadra Bahadur, Honorary Secretary, Dacca Museum Committee, Dacca, 1929.

Bhowmick, Sarita, 'Brahmanisation in Border Bengal: A Case Study in Western Midnapur', *Man in India*, Vol. 64, No. 1, March 1984.

Biardeau, Madeleine, 'Some More Considerations About Textual Criticism', *Purāṇa*, Vol. 10, No. 2, July 1968.

———, *Hinduism: The Anthropology of a Civilization*, Oxford University Press, Delhi, 1989.

Blackburn, Stuart H. and A.K. Ramanujan, 'Introduction', in Stuart H. Blackburn and A.K. Ramanujan (eds), *Another Harmony: New Essays on the Folklore of India*, University of California Press, Berkeley, 1986.

Bloch, Marc, *The Historian's Craft*, Vintage Books, New York, 1953.

Bonazzoli, Giorgio, 'The Dynamic Canon of the Purāṇas', *Purāṇa*, Vol. 21, No. 2, July 1979.

———, 'Composition, Transmission and Recitation of the Purāṇas', Purāṇa, Vol. 25, No. 2, July 1983.

Briffault, Robert, *The Mothers*, Antheneum, New York, 1977 (reprint).

Brown, Brian, *The Wisdom of the Hindus*, Heritage Publishers, Delhi, 1973 (reprint).

Brown, C. Mackenzie, *God as Mother: A Feminine Theology in India* (An Historical and Theological Study of the Brahmavaivarta Purāṇa), Claude Stark and Co., Hertford, Vermont, 1974.

———, 'Purāṇa as Scripture: From Sound to Image of the Holy Word in the Hindu Tradition', *History of Religions*, Vol. 26, No. 1, August 1986.

———, *The Triumph of the Goddess: The Canonical Models and Theological Visions of the Devī-Bhāgavata Purāṇa*, Sri Satguru Publications (a division of Indian Books Centre), Delhi, 1992.

Brown, J.A.C., *Techniques of Persuasion: From Propaganda to Brainwashing*, Penguin Books Ltd, Harmondsworth, 1977.

Buitenen, J.A.B. van, 'On the Archaism of the *Bhāgavata Purāṇa*', in Milton Singer (ed.), Kṛṣṇa: Myths, Rites and Attitudes, East-West Center, Honolulu, 1966.

Burke, Peter, *Popular Culture in Early Modern Europe*, Temple Smith, London, 1978.

———, *Historical Anthropology of Early Modern Italy*, Cambridge, 1987.

———, *History and Social Theory*, Polity Press, Oxford, 1992.

Callinicos, Alex, *Marxism and Philosophy*, Clarendon Press, Oxford, 1983.

Carlton, Eric, *Ideology and Social Order*, Verso, London, 1977.

Carr, E.H., *What is History*?, Penguin Books Ltd, Harmondsworth, 1965.

Chakrabarti, Kunal, '*Kīrtan* and Social Organisation in Medieval Bengal', *Indian Economic and Social History Review*, Vol. 28, No. 4, 1991.

———, 'Brahmanical Hegemony and the "Revolt" of the Oppressed Social Groups: Notes on Two Readings', forthcoming.

Chanana, D.R., 'Sanskritization, Westernization and India's North-West', *Economic Weekly*, Vol. 13, No. 9, 4 March 1961.

Chanda, Ramaprasad, *The Indo-Aryan Races: A Study of the Origin of Indo-Aryan People and Institutions*, Indian Studies: Past and Present, Calcutta, 1969 (reprint).

———, *Medieval Indian Sculpture*, Indological Book House, Varanasi, 1972 (reprint).

Chandra Moti, 'Studies in the Cult of the Mother Goddess in Ancient India', *Bulletin of the Prince of Wales Museum of Western India*, No. 12, 1973.

Chartier, Roger, 'Culture as Appropriation: Popular Cultural Uses in Early Modern France', in Steven L. Kaplan (ed.), *Understanding Popular Culture: Europe from the Middle Ages to the Nineteenth Century*, Mouton Publishers, Berlin, 1984.

Chatterjee, Rama, *Religion in Bengal During the Pāla and the Sena Times*, Punthi Pustak, Calcutta, 1985.

Chatterji, S.K., '*Kirāta-Jana-Kṛti*: The Indo-Mongoloids, Their Contributions to the History and Culture of India', *Journal of the Royal Asiatic Society of Bengal, Letters*, Vol. 16, 1950.

———, 'The Indian Synthesis, and Racial and Cultural Intermixture in India', *Presidential Address*, All India Oriental Conference, Poona, 1953.

———, 'Purāṇa Apocrypha: A "Manipur Purāṇa" ', *Select Writings*, Vol. I, Vikas Publishing House Pvt. Ltd, New Delhi, 1976.

———, *The Origin and Development of the Bengali Language*, Vol. I, Rupa and Co., Calcutta, 1985 (reprint).

Chattopadhyaya, Bankimchandra, 'Lokaśikṣā', *Baṅkim Racanāvalī*, Vol. II, Sahitya Samsad, Calcutta, 1376 BS.

Chattopadhyaya, B.D., 'Introduction: The Making of Early Medieval India', *The Making of Early Medieval India*, Oxford University Press, Delhi, 1994.

———, ' "Autonomous Spaces" and the Authority of the State: The Contradiction and its Resolution in Theory and Practice in Early India', in Bernhard Kölver (ed.), *Recht, Staat und Verwaltung in Klassischien Indien* (The State, the Law, and Administration in Classical India), Munich, 1997.

Chattopadhyaya, Debiprasad, *Lokāyata: A Study in Ancient Indian Materialism*, People's Publishing House, New Delhi, 1978.

Chattopadhyaya, Sarat Chandra, *Bāmuner Meye,* in *Śarat Racanā Samagra*, Ananda Publishers Pvt. Ltd, Calcutta, 1392 BS.

Chattopadhyaya, Sudhakar, *Evolution of Hindu Sects: Up to the Time of Śaṁkarācārya*, Munshiram Manoharlal, New Delhi, 1970.

Chaudhari, Abhay Kant, *Early Medieval Village in North Eastern India (A.D. 600–1200)*, Punthi Pustak, Calcutta, 1971.

Chaudhuri, Shashi Bhushan, *Ethnic Settlements in Ancient India: A Study on the Puranic Lists of the People of Bhāratavarṣa*, General Printers and Publishers Ltd, Calcutta, 1955.

Chaudhuri, Sujit, 'Sāvitrī-Satyavān: Kiṁvadantīr Punarvicār', *Prācīn Bhārate Mātṛprādhānya: Kiṁvadantīr Punarvicār*, Papyrus, Calcutta, 1990.

Childe, Gordon, *Social Evolution*, Collins—The Fontana Library, London, 1963.

Chrétien, Jean-Pierre, 'Confronting the Unequal Exchange of the Oral and the Written', in Bogumil Jewsiewicki and David Newbury (eds), *African Historiographies: What History for Which Africa*?, Sage Publications, Beverly Hills, 1986.

Coburn, Thomas B., *Devī-Māhātmya: The Crystallization of the Goddess Tradition*, Motilal Banarsidass, Delhi, 1984.

Cohen, Anthony P., *The Symbolic Construction of Community*, Ellis Horwood Ltd, Chichester, 1985.

Cohn, Bernard S., 'Regions Subjective and Objective: Their Relation to the Study of Modern Indian History and Society', in Robert I. Crane (ed.),

Regions and Regionalism in South Asian Studies: An Exploratory Study, Duke University, Durham, 1967.

Collingwood, R.G., *The Idea of History*, Oxford University Press, Oxford, 1978.

Coomaraswamy, Ananda K. and Sister Nivedita, *Myths of the Hindus and Buddhists*, Dover Publications Inc., New York, 1967 (reprint).

Cortes, Rosario Mendoza, 'The Philippine Experience Under Spain: Christianization as Social Change', in David N. Lorenzen (ed.), *Religious Change and Cultural Domination*, El Collegio De Mexico, Mexico, 1981.

Corwin, Lauren Anita, 'Great Tradition, Little Tradition: The Cultural Traditions of a Bengal Town', *Contributions to Indian Sociology*, Vol. 11, No. 1, 1977.

Crooke, William, *The Popular Religion and Folklore of Northern India*, Vol. I, Munshiram Manoharlal, New Delhi, 1978 (reprint).

Dalton, Edward Tuite, *Descriptive Ethnology of Bengal*, Indian Studies: Past and Present, Calcutta, 1973 (reprint).

Damle, Y.B., 'Harikathā—A Study in Communication', *Bulletin of the Deccan College Research Institute*, Vol. 20, Part 1, October 1960 (S.K. De Felicitation Volume).

Dani, A.H., *Buddhist Sculpture in East Pakistan*, Karachi, 1959.

Danielou, Alain, *Hindu Polytheism*, Routledge and Kegan Paul, London, 1963.

Das, S.R., 'A Study of the Vrata Rites of Bengal', *Man in India*, Vol. 32, No. 3, 1952.

Das, Upendra Kumar, *Śāstramūlak Bhāratīya Śaktisādhanā*, Vols I and II, Visva-Bharati, Shantiniketan and Calcutta, 1373 BS.

Dasgupta, Shashibhushan, *Bhārater Śakti-Sādhanā O Śākta Sāhitya*, Sahitya Samsad, Calcutta, 1367 BS.

———, *Śrīrādhār Kramavikāś: Darśane O Sāhitye*, A. Mukherji and Co. Pvt. Ltd, Calcutta, 1381 BS (reprint).

———, *An Introduction to Tantric Buddhism*, University of Calcutta, Calcutta, 1974.

Dasgupta, Surendranath, *A History of Indian Philosophy*, Vol. I, Motilal Banarsidass, Delhi, 1975 (reprint).

Dash, G.N., 'Jagannātha and Oriya Nationalism', in A. Eschmann, H. Kulke and G.C. Tripathi (eds), *The Cult of Jagannath and the Regional Tradition of Orissa*, Manohar, New Delhi, 1978.

Datta, Charuchandra, *Purāno Kathā*, Vol. I, Visva-Bharati, Calcutta, 1962 (reprint).

Datta, Satyendranath, 'Āmrā', *Kāvyasañcayan*, M.C. Sarkar and Sons Pvt. Ltd, Calcutta, 1372 BS.

Davis, Natalie Z., 'Some Tasks and Themes in the Study of Popular Religion', in Charles Trinkaus and Heiko A. Oberman (eds), *The Pursuit of Holiness in Late Medieval and Renaissance Religion*, E.J. Brill, Leiden, 1974.

———, 'From Popular Religion to Religious Cultures', in Steven Ozment (ed.),

Reformation Europe: A Guide to Research, Center for Reformation Research, St Louis, 1982.

Davison, W. Phillips, 'On the Effects of Mass Communication', in Lewis Anthony Dexter and David Manning White (eds), *People, Society, and Mass Communications*, The Free Press, New York, 1964.

De, Barun, 'A Historical Perspective on Theories of Regionalization in India', in Robert I. Crane (ed.), *Regions and Regionalism in South Asian Studies: An Exploratory Study*, Duke University, Durham, 1967.

De, S.K., 'Sanskrit Literature', in R.C. Majumdar (ed.), *The History of Bengal*, Vol. I, University of Dacca, Dacca, 1963 (reprint).

Delewury, G.A., *The Cult of Viṭhobā*, Deccan College Postgraduate Research Institute, Poona, 1960.

Derrett, J. Duncan M., 'The Purāṇas in Vyavahāra Portions of Medieval Smṛti Works', *Purāṇa*, Vol. 5, No. 1, January 1963.

Devi, Suhasini, *Meyelī Vratakathā*, Pustak Bipani, Calcutta, 1392 BS.

Dikshitar, V.R. Ramachandra, 'The Purāṇas: A Study', *Indian Historical Quarterly*, Vol. 8, No. 4, December 1932.

Dobrowolski, Kazimierz, 'Peasant Traditional Culture', in Teodor Shanin (ed.), *Peasants and Peasant Societies*, Penguin Books Ltd, Harmondsworth, 1975.

Doniger, Wendy (ed.), *Purāṇa Perennis: Reciprocity and Transformation in Hindu and Jaina Texts*, State University of New York Press, Albany, 1993.

Duby, Georges, 'The Diffusion of Cultural Patterns in Feudal Society', *Past and Present*, No. 39, April 1968.

———, 'Ideologies in Social History', in Jacques Le Goff and Pierre Nora (eds), *Constructing the Past: Essays in Historical Methodology*, Cambridge University Press, Cambridge, 1985.

Dumont, L. and D. Pocock, 'For a Sociology of India', *Contributions to Indian Sociology*, No. 1, 1957.

Dutt, Nripendra Kumar, *Origin and Growth of Caste in India*, Vol. II *(Castes in Bengal)*, Firma K.L. Mukhopadhyay, Calcutta, 1969.

———, *The Aryanisation of India*, Firma K.L. Mukhopadhyay, Calcutta, 1970 (reprint).

Eagleton, Terry, *Ideology: An Introduction*, Verso, London, 1991.

Eaton, Richard M., *The Rise of Islam and the Bengal Frontier, 1204–1760*, Oxford University Press, Delhi, 1994.

Eco, Umberto, 'Overinterpreting Texts' and 'Between Author and Text', in Umberto Eco *et al.*, *Interpretation and Overinterpretation*, Cambridge University Press, Cambridge, 1992.

Ehrenberg, Margaret, *Women in Prehistory*, British Museum Publications, London, 1989.

Ehrenfeles, D.R., *Mother-Right in India*, Oxford University Press, Hyderabad, 1941.

———, 'The Double Sex Character of the Khasi Great Deity', in L.P. Vidyarthi (ed.), *Aspects of Religion in Indian Society*, Kedar Nath Ram Nath, Meerut, undated.

Eliade, Mircea, *Yoga: Immortality and Freedom*, Princeton University Press, Princeton, 1973.

Eliot, Sir Charles, *Hinduism and Buddhism: An Historical Sketch* (3 vols), Routledge and Kegan Paul, London, 1921.

Embree, Ainslie T., 'Brahmanical Ideology and Regional Identities', *Imagining India: Essays on Indian History*, Oxford University Press, Delhi, 1989.

Engels, F., *The Origin of the Family, Private Property and the State*, Foreign Language Publishing House, Moscow, 1948 (reprint).

Epstein, T. Scarlett, *Economic Development and Social Change in South India*, Manchester University Press, Manchester, 1962.

Eschmann, A., 'Hinduization of Tribal Deities in Orissa: The Śākta and Śaiva Typology', in A. Eschmann, H. Kulke and G.C. Tripathi (eds), *The Cult of Jagannath and the Regional Tradition of Orissa*, Manohar, New Delhi, 1978.

Farquhar, J.N., *An Outline of the Religious Literature of India*, Oxford University Press, London, 1920.

Femia, Joseph, 'Hegemony and Consciousness in the Thought of Antonio Gramsci', *Political Studies*, Vol. 23, No. 1, 1975.

Finnegan, Ruth, 'Transmission in Oral and Written Traditions: Some General Comments', *Literacy and Orality: Studies in the Technology of Communication*, Basil Blackwell, Oxford, 1988.

Fleuhr-Lobban, Carolyn, 'A Marxist Reappraisal of the Matriarchate', *Current Anthropology*, Vol. 20, June 1979.

Foucault, Michel, 'What is an Author', in Donald F. Bouchard (ed.), *Language, Countermemory, Practice: Selected Essays and Interviews*, Basil Blackwell, Oxford, 1977.

Fox, Richard G., 'Introduction', in Richard G. Fox (ed.), *Realm and Region in Traditional India*, Vikas Publishing House Pvt. Ltd, New Delhi, 1977.

Freed, Ruth S. and Stanley A. Freed, 'Two Mother Goddess Ceremonies of Delhi State in the Great and Little Traditions', *Southwestern Journal of Anthropology*, Vol. 18, 1962.

Freitag, Sandria B., 'Performance and Patronage', in Sandria B. Freitag (ed.), *Culture and Power in Banaras: Community, Performance and Environment 1800–1980*, Oxford University Press, Delhi, 1990.

Fruzetti, Lina M., *The Gift of a Virgin: Women, Marriage, and Ritual in a Bengali Society*, Rutgers University Press, New Brunswick, New Jersey, 1982.

Gatwood, Lynn E., *Devī and the Spouse Goddess: Women, Sexuality and Marriage in India*, Manohar, New Delhi, 1985.

Gautam, Mohan K., 'The Santalization of the Santals', in Kenneth David (ed.),

The New Wind: Changing Identities in South Asia, Mouton Publishers, The Hague, 1977.

Geertz, Clifford, 'Ideology as a Culture System', *The Interpretation of Cultures: Selected Essays*, Basic Books Inc., New York, 1973.

Geuss, Raymond, *The Idea of Critical Theory: Habermas and the Frankfurt School*, Cambridge University Press, Cambridge, 1981.

Ghosh, Binoy, *Paśchimbaṅger Saṁskṛti*, Vol. IV, Prakash Bhavan, Calcutta, 1986.

Ghurye, G.S., 'Devi: Female Principle Bridges the Gulf Between the Folk and the Elite', *Gods and Men*, Popular Book Depot, Bombay, 1962.

Ghurye, K.G., *Preservation of Learned Tradition in India*, Popular Book Depot, Bombay, 1950.

Gillis, John, 'Discussion' on Peter Burke's 'The "Discovery" of Popular Culture', in Raphael Samuel (ed.), *People's History and Socialist Theory* (History Workshop Series), Routledge and Kegan Paul, London, 1981.

Goody, Jack, 'Oral Composition and Oral Transmission: The Case of the Vedas', *The Interface Between the Written and the Oral*, Cambridge University Press, Cambridge, 1987.

———, *The Logic of Writing and the Organization of Society*, Cambridge University Press, Cambridge, 1988.

Goody, J. and I. Watt, 'The Consequence of Literacy', in Pier Paolo Giglioli (ed.), *Language and Social Context*, Penguin Books Ltd, Harmondsworth, 1980.

Goudriaan, Teun, 'Introduction, History and Philosophy', in Sanjukta Gupta, Dirk Jan Hoens and Teun Goudriaan (eds), *Hindu Tantrism*, E.J. Brill, Leiden/Koln, 1979.

———, 'Hindu Tantric Literature in Sanskrit', in Teun Goudriaan and Sanjukta Gupta, *Hindu Tantric and Śākta Literature*, Otto Harrassowitz, Wiesbaden, 1981.

Gough, Kathleen, 'Implications of Literacy in Traditional China and India', in Jack Goody (ed.), *Literacy in Traditional Societies*, Cambridge University Press, Cambridge, 1968.

Gould, Harold A., 'Sanskritization and Westernization: A Dynamic View', *Economic Weekly*, Vol. 13, No. 25, 24 June 1961.

Grunebaum, G.E. von, 'The Problem: Unity in Diversity', in Gustave E. von Grunebaum (ed.), *Unity and Diversity in Muslim Civilization*, The University of Chicago Press, Chicago, 1955.

Gumperz, John J., 'Religion and Social Communication in Village North India', in Edward B. Harper (ed.), *Religion in South Asia*, University of Washington Press, Seattle, 1964.

Gupta, A.S., 'A Problem of Purāṇic Text-Reconstruction', *Purāṇa*, Vol. 12, No. 2, July 1970.

Gupta, Chitrarekha, 'Early Brahmanic Settlements in Bengal—Pre-Pāla Period', in B.N. Mukherjee, D.R. Das, S.S. Biswas and S.P. Singh (eds), *Śrī Dīneśacandrikā: Studies in Indology*, Sundeep Prakashan, Delhi, 1983.

Gupte, B.A., 'The Symbolism of the Sāvitrīvrata', *Indian Antiquary*, Vol. 35, 1906.

Habib, Irfan, *An Atlas of the Mughal Empire*, Oxford University Press, Delhi, 1982.

Haldar, Shivaprasad, *Paurāṇik Saṁskṛti O Baṅgasāhitya*, Firma KLM Pvt. Ltd, Calcutta, 1983.

Hanchett, Suzanne, *Coloured Rice: Symbolic Structure in Hindu Family Festivals*, Hindustan Publishing Corporation, Delhi, 1988.

Harper, E.B., 'A Hindu Village Pantheon', *Southwestern Journal of Anthropology*, Vol. 15, 1959.

———, 'Social Consequences of an "Unsuccessful" Low Caste Movement', in James Silverberg (ed.), *Social Mobility in the Caste System in India*, Mouton, Paris, 1968.

Hartman, Paul, B.R. Patil and Anita Dighe, *The Mass Media and Village Life: An Indian Study*, Sage Publications, New Delhi, 1989.

Haynes, Douglas and Gyan Prakash, 'Introduction: The Entanglement of Power and Resistance', in Douglas Haynes and Gyan Prakash (eds), *Contesting Power: Resistance and Everyday Social Relations in South Asia*, Oxford University Press, Delhi, 1991.

Hazra, R.C., *Studies in the Purāṇic Records on Hindu Rites and Customs*, Motilal Banarsidass, Delhi, 1975 (reprint).

———, *Studies in the Upapurāṇas*, Vols I and II, Sanskrit College, Calcutta, 1958 and 1963.

———, 'The Purāṇa', in S.K. De, U.N. Ghoshal, A.D. Pusalkar and R.C. Hazra (eds), *The Cultural Heritage of India*, Vol. II, Ramakrishna Mission Institute of Culture, Calcutta, 1969.

Heesterman, J.C., 'Veda and Dharma', in Wendy Doniger O'Flaherty and J.D.M. Derrett (eds), *The Concept of Duty in South Asia*, Vikas Publishing House Pvt. Ltd, New Delhi, 1978.

———, 'India and the Inner Conflict of Tradition', *The Inner Conflict of Tradition*, The University of Chicago Press, Chicago, 1985.

Heffner, Robert W., *Hindu Javanese: Tengger Tradition and Islam*, Princeton University Press, Princeton, 1985.

Henry, Edward O., 'The Mother Goddess Cult and Interaction Between Little and Great Religious Traditions', in Giriraj Gupta (ed.), *Religion in Modern India*, Vikas Publishing House Pvt. Ltd, New Delhi, 1983.

Hoare, Quintin and Geoffrey Noel Smith (eds and trans.), *Selections from the Prison Notebooks of Antonio Gramsci*, International Publishers, New York, 1973.

Hobsbawm, Eric, 'Introduction: Inventing Traditions', in Eric Hobsbawm and Terence Ranger (eds), *The Invention of Tradition*, Cambridge University Press, Cambridge, 1983.

Hopkins, E.W., *The Religions of India*, Munshiram Manoharlal, Delhi, 1970 (reprint).

Hudson, Dennis, 'Piṉṉai, Krishna's Cowherd Wife', in John Stratton Hawley and Donna Marie Wulff (eds), *The Divine Consort: Rādhā and the Goddesses of India*, Motilal Banarsidass, Delhi, 1984.

Huntington, Susan L., *The 'Pāla–Sena' School of Sculpture*, E.J. Brill, Leiden, 1984.

Hussain, Shahanara, *The Social Life of Women in Early Medieval Bengal*, Asiatic Society of Bangladesh, Dhaka, 1985.

Hutton, J.H., *Caste in India: Its Nature, Function, and Origins*, Oxford University Press, Bombay, 1980 (reprint).

Inden, Ronald B., *Marriage and Rank in Bengali Culture: A History of Caste and Clan in Middle Period Bengal*, Vikas Publishing House Pvt. Ltd, New Delhi, 1976.

Ingalls, Daniel, 'The Brahman Tradition', in Milton Singer (ed.), *Traditional India: Structure and Change*, Rawat Publications, Jaipur, 1975.

———, 'Foreword', to C. Mackenzie Brown, *God as Mother: A Feminine Theology in India* (An Historical and Theological Study of the Brahmavaivarta Purāṇa), Claude Stark and Co., Hartford, Vermont, 1974.

Jackson, J.R. de J., *Historical Criticism and the Meaning of Texts*, Routledge, London and New York, 1989.

Jaini, Padmanabh S., 'The Disappearance of Buddhism and the Survival of Jainism: A Study in Contrast', in A.K. Narain (ed.), *Studies in History of Buddhism*, B.R. Publishing Corporation, Delhi, 1980.

Jameson, Fredric, *The Political Unconscious: Narrative as a Socially Symbolic Act*, Methuen and Co. Ltd, London, 1983.

Janowitz, Morris, 'The Study of Mass Communication', in David L. Sills (ed.), *International Encyclopaedia of Social Sciences*, Vol. III, The Macmillan Company and the Free Press, USA, 1968.

Jha, D.N., 'Introduction', in D.N. Jha (ed.), *Feudal Social Formation in Early India*, Chanakya Publications, Delhi, 1987.

Kadir, Abdul., 'Bāṅglār Pallīsaṅgīte Līlāvāda', *Bāṅglār Lokāyata Sāhitya*, Bangla Academy, Dhaka, 1985.

Kalia, S.L., 'Sanskritisation and Tribalisation', *Bulletin of the Tribal Research Institute* (Chindwara, MP), Vol. 2, No. 4, April 1959.

Kane, P.V., *History of Dharmaśāstra*, Bhandarkar Oriental Research Institute, Poona, 1974 (second edition).

Karmakar, A.P., *The Religions of India*, Vol. I (*The Vrātya or Dravidian Systems*), Mira Publishing House, Lonavla, 1950.

Karve, Irawati, *Hindu Society: An Interpretation*, Deshmukh Prakashan, Poona, 1968.

Khalek, Muhammad Abdul, *Madhyayuger Bāṅglā Kāvye Lokupādān*, Bangla Academy, Dhaka, 1985.

Kinsley, David, *Hindu Goddesses: Visions of the Divine Feminine in the Hindu Religious Tradition*, University of California Press, Berkeley, 1986.

Kitagawa, Joseph M., 'Some Remarks on the Study of Sacred Texts', in Wendy D. O'Flaherty (ed.), *The Critical Study of Sacred Texts*, Berkeley Religious Studies Series, Berkeley, 1979.

Klapper, Joseph T., 'Mass Communication: Effects', in David L. Sills (ed.), *International Encyclopaedia of Social Sciences*, Vol. III, The Macmillan Company and the Free Press, USA, 1968.

Kolenda, Pauline Mahar, 'The Functional Relations of a Bhangi Cult', *The Anthropologist* (special volume) 2, 1968.

Kooij, K.R. van, *Worship of the Goddess According to the Kālikāpurāṇa*, Part I (A Translation with an Introduction and Notes of Chapters 54–69), E.J. Brill, Leiden, 1972.

Kosambi, D.D., 'On the Origin of the Brahmin Gotra', *Journal of the Bombay Branch of the Royal Asiatic Society* (New Series), Vol. 26, 1951.

———, 'At the Crossroad: A Study of Mother Goddess Cult Sites', *Myth and Reality: Studies in the Formation of Indian Culture*, Popular Prakashan, Bombay, 1962.

———, 'Social and Economic Aspects of the Bhagavad-Gītā', *Myth and Reality: Studies in the Formation of Indian Culture*, Popular Prakashan, Bombay, 1962.

———, *An Introduction to the Study of Indian History*, Popular Prakashan, Bombay, 1975 (reprint).

Krammer, Lloyd S., 'Literature, Criticism, and Historical Imagination: The Literary Challenge of Hayden White and Dominick LaCapra', in Lynn Hunt (ed.), *The New Cultural History*, University of California Press, Berkeley, 1989.

Kramrisch, Stella, 'The Indian Great Goddess', *History of Religions*, Vol. 14, No. 4, May 1975.

Kulke, H., 'Early Patronage of the Jagannātha Cult', in A. Eschmann, H. Kulke and G.C. Tripathi (eds), *The Cult of Jagannath and the Regional Tradition of Orissa*, Manohar, New Delhi, 1978.

———, 'The Struggle Between the Rājās of Khurda and the Muslim Subahdārs of Cuttack for Dominance of the Jagannātha Temple', in A. Eschmann, H. Kulke and G.C. Tripathi (eds), *The Cult of Jagannath and the Regional Tradition of Orissa*, Manohar, New Delhi, 1978.

———, '"Juggernaut" Under British Supremacy and the Resurgence of the Khurda Rājās as "Rājās of Puri"', in A. Eschmann, H. Kulke and G.C. Tripathi (eds), *The Cult of Jagannath and the Regional Tradition of Orissa*, Manohar, New Delhi, 1978.

Kumar, Pushpendra, *Śakti Cult in Ancient India* (with special reference to the Purāṇic literature), Bharatiya Publishing House, Varanasi, 1974.

LaCapra, Dominick, 'Rethinking Intellectual History and Reading Texts', in Dominick LaCapra and Steven L. Caplan (eds), *Modern European Intel-*

lectual History: Reappraisals and New Perspectives, Cornell University Press, Ithaca, 1982.

Lalye, P.G., *Studies in Devī Bhāgavata*, Popular Prakashan, Bombay, 1973.

Lamb, Helen B., 'The Indian Merchant', in Milton Singer (ed.), *Traditional India: Structure and Change*, Rawat Publications, Jaipur, 1975.

Larrain, Jorge, *The Concept of Ideology*, B.I. Publications, Bombay, 1980.

———, 'Ideology', in Tom Bottomore *et al.* (eds), *A Dictionary of Marxist Thought*, Basil Blackwell, Oxford, 1985.

Lears, T.J. Jackson, 'The Concept of Cultural Hegemony: Problems and Possibilities', *American Historical Review*, Vol. 90, No. 3, June 1985.

Leavitt, John, 'Cultural Holism in the Anthropology of South Asia: The Challenge of Regional Traditions', *Contributions to Indian Sociology*, Vol. 26, No. 1, January–June 1992.

Leeuw, J.E. van Lohuizen-de, 'Mother Goddesses in Ancient India', *Folia Indica*, Association of South Asian Archaeologists in Western Europe, Naples, 1990.

Ling, Trevor, 'Buddhist Bengal, and After', in Debiprasad Chattopadhyaya (ed.), *History and Society: Essays in Honour of Professor Niharranjan Ray*, K.P. Bagchi and Co., Calcutta, 1978.

Lodrick, Deryck O., 'Rajasthan as a Region: Myth or Reality', in Karine Schomer, Joan L. Erdman, Deryck O Lodrick and Lloyd I. Rudolph (eds), *The Idea of Rajasthan: Explorations in Regional Identity,* Vol. I: *Constructions*, Manohar (American Institute of Indian Studies), New Delhi, 1994.

Long, Charles H., 'Primitive/Civilized: The Locus of a Problem', *History of Religions*, Vol. 20, 1980–1.

Long, J. Bruce, 'Life Out of Death: A Structural Analysis of the Myth of the "Churning of the Ocean of Milk" ', in Bardwell L. Smith (ed.), *Hinduism: New Essays in the History of Religions*, E.J. Brill, Leiden, 1976.

Lorenzen, David N., *The Kāpālikas and the Kālāmukhas: Two Lost Śaivite Sects*, Thomson Press (India) Ltd, New Delhi, 1972.

———, 'The Life of Śaṅkarācārya', in F. Reynolds and D. Capps (eds), *The Biographical Process*, Mouton, The Hague, 1975.

Lutgendorf, Philip, 'Rāma's Story in Śiva's City: Public Arenas and Private Patronage', in Sandria B. Freitag (ed.), *Culture and Power in Banaras: Community, Performance and Environment 1800–1980*, Oxford University Press, Delhi, 1990.

Mackay, Ernest, 'Figurines and Model Animals', in Sir John Marshall (ed.), *Mohenjo-Daro and the Indus Civilization*, Indological Book House, Delhi, 1973 (reprint).

Macnicol, Nicol, *Indian Theism: From the Vedic to the Muhammadan Period*, Munshiram Manoharlal, Delhi, 1968 (reprint).

Majumdar, Asoke Kumar, 'A Note on the Development of Rādhā Cult', *Annals of the Bhandarkar Oriental Research Institute*, Vol. 36, Parts III–IV, 1955.

Majumdar, Atindra, *Caryāpada*, Naya Prakash, Calcutta, 1981.

Majumdar, Mahimachandra, *Gauḍe Brāhmaṇa*, Calcutta, 1900.

Majumdar, R.C., *History of Ancient Bengal*, G. Bharadwaj and Co., Calcutta, 1971.

———, *History of Medieval Bengal*, G. Bharadwaj and Co., Calcutta, 1974.

———, (ed.), *The History of Bengal*, Vol. I, University of Dacca, Dacca, 1963 (reprint).

———, *Baṅgīya Kulaśāstra*, Bharati Book Stall, Calcutta, 1973.

Mandelbaum, David G., 'Introduction: Process and Structure in South Asian Religion', in Edward B. Harper (ed.), *Religion in South Asia*, University of Washington Press, Seattle, 1964.

Marriott, McKim, 'Little Communities in an Indigenous Civilization', in McKim Marriott (ed.), *Village India: Studies in the Little Community*, The University of Chicago Press, Chicago, 1955.

———, 'Changing Channels of Cultural Transmission in Indian Civilization', *Journal of Social Research* (Ranchi), Vol. 4, 1961.

Marriott, McKim and Bernard S. Cohn, 'Networks and Centers in the Integration of Indian Civilization', *Journal of Social Research* (Ranchi), Vol. 1, No. 1, 1958.

Marshall, Sir John (ed.), *Mohenjo-Daro and the Indus Civilization*, Indological Book House, Delhi, 1973 (reprint).

McCormack, William, 'The Forms of Communication in Vīraśaiva Religion', in Milton Singer (ed.), *Traditional India: Structure and Change*, Rawat Publications, Jaipur, 1975.

———, 'Popular Religion in South India', in Giriraj Gupta (ed.), *Religion in Modern India*, Vikas Publishing House Pvt. Ltd, New Delhi, 1983.

McCroskey, James C., *An Introduction to Rhetorical Communication*, Prentice-Hall Inc., Englewood Cliffs, New Jersey, 1978.

Mehendale, M.A., 'The Purāṇas', in R.C. Majumdar (ed.), *The Classical Age (The History and Culture of the Indian People*, Vol. III), Bharatiya Vidya Bhavan, Bombay, 1973.

Michell, George, 'Historical Background', in George Michell (ed.), *Brick Temples of Bengal: From the Archives of David McCutchion*, Princeton University Press, Princeton, 1983.

Miller, Barbara Stoler, 'Rādhā: Consort of Kṛṣṇa's Springtime Passion', Barbara Stoler Miller (ed. and trans.), *Love Song of the Dark Lord: Jayadeva's Gītagovinda*, Columbia University Press, New York, 1977.

Miller, Robert J., 'Button, Button . . . Great Tradition, Little Tradition, Whose Tradition', *Anthropological Quarterly*, Vol. 39, 1966.

Mitra, Ashok (ed.), *Paśchimbaṅger Pūjā-pārvan O Melā*, Vol. I, Controller of Publications, Delhi, 1969.

Mitra, Dinabandhu, *Sadhabār Ekādaśī*, in *Dīnabandhu Racanāvali*, Sahitya Samsad, Calcutta, 1967.

Mitra, Khagendranath, 'Diffusion of Socio-religious Culture in North India', in

Haridas Bhattacharyya (ed.), *The Cultural Heritage of India*, Vol. IV, Ramakrishna Mission Institute of Culture, Calcutta, 1956.

Mitra, R.C., *The Decline of Buddhism in India*, Shantiniketan, 1954.

Mitra, Satish Chandra, *Jashohar O Khulnār Itihāsa*, Vol. II, Dasgupta and Co., Calcutta, 1963.

Moffatt, Michael, *An Untouchable Community of South India: Structure and Consensus*, Princeton University Press, Princeton, 1979.

Monier-Williams, M., *Hinduism*, Susil Gupta (India) Ltd, Calcutta, 1951 (reprint).

———, *Religious Thought and Life in India*, Oriental Books Reprint Corporation, New Delhi, 1974 (reprint).

———, *A Sanskrit-English Dictionary*, Motilal Banarsidass, New Delhi, 1986 (reprint).

Morgan, Lewis Henry, *Ancient Society*, Eleanor Burke Leacock (ed.), Peter Smith, Gloucester, 1974 (reprint).

Morrison, Barrie M., 'Sources, Methods and Concepts in Early Indian History', *Pacific Affairs*, Vol. 41, 1968.

Mukherjee, B.N., *East Indian Art Styles: A Study in Parallel Trends*, K.P. Bagchi and Co., Calcutta, 1980.

———, *Śaktir Rūp Bhārate O Madhya Asiy*, Ananda Publishers Ltd, Calcutta, 1990.

Mukherjee, Prabhat K., *History of the Jagannātha Temple*, Firma KLM, Calcutta, 1977.

Mukhopadhyaya, Sukhamoy., 'Bāṅglār Kulajīgrantha', in R.C. Majumdar, *Baṅgīya Kulaśāstra*, Bharati Book Stall, Calcutta, 1973.

———, *Madhyayuger Bāṅglā Sāhityer Tathya O Kālakram*, G. Bharadwaj and Co., Calcutta, 1974.

Murthy, K. Krishna, *Sculptures of Vajrayāna Buddhism*, Classics India Publications, Delhi, 1989.

Nicholas, Ralph W., 'Ritual Hierarchy and Social Relations in Rural Bengal', *Contributions to Indian Sociology* (New Series), No. 1, December 1967.

———, 'Sitala and the Art of Printing: The Transmission and Propagation of the Myth of the Goddess of Small Pox in Rural West Bengal', in Mahadev L. Apte (ed.), *Mass Culture Language and Arts in India*, Popular Prakashan, Bombay, 1978.

Niyogi, Puspa, *Brahmanic Settlements in Different Subdivisions of Ancient Bengal*, Indian Studies: Past and Present, Calcutta, 1967.

———, *Buddhism in Ancient Bengal*, Jijnasa, Calcutta, 1980.

O'Flaherty, Wendy Doniger, *Asceticism and Eroticism in the Mythology of Śiva*, Oxford University Press, Delhi, 1975.

———, *The Origins of Evil in Hindu Mythology*, Motilal Banarsidass, Delhi, 1976.

———, 'The Image of the Heretic in the Gupta Purāṇas', in Bardwell L. Smith (ed.), *Essays on Gupta Culture*, Motilal Banarsidass, Delhi, 1983.

———, *Tales of Sex and Violence: Folklore, Sacrifice, and Danger in the* Jaiminīya Brāhmaṇa, Motilal Banarsidass, Delhi, 1987.

Olabarri, Ignacio, '"New" New History: A *Longue Duree* Structure', *History and Theory*, Vol. 34, No. 1, 1995.

Oliver, Robert T., *Communication and Culture in Ancient India and China*, Syracuse University Press, New York, 1971.

O'Malley, L.S.S., *Popular Hinduism: The Religion of the Masses*, Johnson Reprint Corporation, New York, 1970 (reprint).

Opler, Morris E., 'Spirit Possession in a Rural Area in Northern India', in William A. Lessa and Evon Z. Vogt (eds), *Reader in Comparative Religion: An Anthropological Approach*, Row, Peterson and Co., New York, 1958.

Oppert, Gustav, *On the Original Inhabitants of Bhāratavarṣa or India*, Archibald Constable and Co., Westminster, 1893.

Orans, Martin, 'A Tribe in Search of a Great Tradition: The Emulation–Solidarity Conflict', *Man in India*, Vol. 39, No. 2, April–June 1959.

———, *The Santal: A Tribe in Search of Great Tradition*, Wayne State University Press, Detroit, 1965.

Packard, Vance, *The Hidden Persuaders*, Penguin Books Ltd, Harmondsworth, 1975.

Pandian, Jacob, 'The Sacred Symbol of the Mother Goddess in a Tamil Village: A Parochial Model of Hinduism', in Giriraj Gupta (ed.), *Religion in Modern India*, Vikas Publishing House Pvt. Ltd, New Delhi, 1983.

Panigrahi, Chandrika, 'Muktimandap Sabha of Brahmans, Puri', in Nirmal Kumar Bose (ed.), *Data on Caste: Orissa*, Anthropological Survey of India, Memoir No. 7, Calcutta, 1960.

Pargiter, F.E., *The Purāṇa Texts of the Dynasties of the Kali Age*, Deep Publications, Delhi, 1975 (reprint).

Parsons, Talcott, 'An Approach to the Sociology of Knowledge', in James E. Curtis and John W. Petras (eds), *The Sociology of Knowledge: A Reader*, Gerald Duckworth and Co. Ltd, London, 1982.

Paul, Pramode Lal, 'Brāhmaṇa Immigrations in Bengal', *Proceedings of the Indian History Congress*, 1939.

Pocock, D.F., 'The Movement of Castes', *Man*, Vol. 55, May 1955.

———, *Mind, Body and Wealth: A Study of Belief and Practice in an Indian Village*, Basil Blackwell, Oxford, 1973.

Pollock, Susan, 'Women in a Men's World: Images of Sumerian Women', in Joan M. Gero and Margaret W. Conkey (eds), *Engendering Archaeology: Women and Prehistory*, Basil Blackwell Ltd, Oxford, 1994.

Preston, James J., *Cult of the Goddess: Social and Religious Change in a Hindu Temple*, Vikas Publishing House Pvt. Ltd, New Delhi, 1980.

———, 'Conclusion: New Perspectives on Mother Worship', in James J. Preston (ed.), *Mother Worship: Themes and Variations*, The University of North Carolina Press, Chapel Hill, 1982.

———, 'Goddess Temples in Orissa: An Anthropological Survey', in Giriraj Gupta (ed.), *Religion in Modern India*, Vikas Publishing House Pvt. Ltd, New Delhi, 1983.

Przyluski, J., 'The Great Goddess in India and Iran', *The Indian Historical Quarterly*, Vol. 10, No.3, September 1934.

Raghavan, V., 'Variety and Integration in the Pattern of Indian Culture', *The Far Eastern Quarterly*, Vol. 15, No. 4, August 1956.

———, 'Methods of Popular Instruction in South India', in Milton Singer (ed.), *Traditional India: Structure and Change*, Rawat Publications, Jaipur, 1975.

Ramanujan, A.K., *Speaking of Śiva*, Penguin Books, Harmondsworth, 1985.

Ranger, Terence, 'Missionary Adaptation of African Religious Institutions: The Masasi Case', in T.O. Ranger and Isaria Kimambo (eds), *The Historical Study of African Religion*, Heinemann, London, 1972.

Rao, T.A. Gopinatha, *Elements of Hindu Iconography*, Vol. I, Part II, Motilal Banarsidass, Delhi, 1968.

Rao, Velcheru Narayana, 'Texts Without Authors and Authors Without Texts', paper presented at the South Asia Conference, Madison, Wisconsin, 1983.

———, 'Coconut and Honey: Sanskrit and Telugu in Medieval Andhra', *Social Scientist*, Vol. 23, Nos. 10–12 (269–71), October–December 1995.

Rashid, M. Harunur, 'The Early History of South East Bengal in the Light of Recent Archaeological Material', unpublished Ph.D. dissertation, University of Cambridge, December 1968.'

Rawal, A.J., *Indian Society, Religion and Mythology: A Study in the Brahma-Vaivartapurāṇa*, D.K. Publications, Delhi, 1982.

Ray, Niharranjan, 'The Medieval Factor in Indian History', *Proceedings of the Indian History Congress*, Patiala, 1967.

———, *Bāṅgālīr Itihāsa: Ādi Parva*, Vols I and II, Pashchimbanga Niraksharata Durikaran Samiti, Calcutta, 1980 (second edition).

Raychaudhuri, Hemchandra, *Materials for the Study of the Early History of the Vaishnava Sect*, Oriental Books Reprint Corporation, New Delhi, 1975 (reprint).

Raychaudhuri, Tapan, *Bengal Under Akbar and Jahangir: An Introductory Study in Social History*, Munshiram Manoharlal, Delhi, 1969.

Raychaudhuri, Tarak Chandra and Bikash Raychaudhuri, *The Brāhmaṇas of Bengal: A Textual Study in Social History*, Anthropological Survey of India, Calcutta, 1981.

Raychaudhuri, Tarak Chandra and Sarat Chandra Mitra, 'On the Cult of the Goddess Mangala Chandi in Eastern Bengal', *The Journal of the Anthropological Society of Bombay*, Vol. 13, 1927.

Ray Vidyanidhi, Jogesh Chandra, *Paurāṇik Upākhyāna*, Calcutta, 1361 BS.

Redfield, Robert, *The Folk Culture at Yucatan*, The University of Chicago Press, Chicago, 1941.

———, *Little Community: View Points for the Study of a Human Whole*, The University of Chicago Press, Chicago, 1955.

———, *Peasant Society and Culture*, The University of Chicago Press, Chicago, 1956.

Redfield, Margaret Park (ed.), *Human Nature and the Study of Society: The Papers of Robert Redfield*, Vol. I, The University of Chicago Press, Chicago, 1962.

Risley, H.H., *The Tribes and Castes of Bengal*, Vols I and II, Firma Mukhopadhyay, Calcutta, 1981 (reprint).

Rocher, Ludo, *The Purāṇas (A History of Indian Literature*, Vol. II. 3), Otto Harrassowitz, Wiesbaden, 1986.

Sanyal, Hitesranjan, 'Temple Promotion and Social Mobility in Bengal', *Social Mobility in Bengal*, Papyrus, Calcutta, 1981.

———, 'The Nature of Peasant Culture of India: A Study of the Pat Painting and Clay Sculpture of Bengal', *Folk* (Copenhagen), Vol. 26, 1984.

———, *Bāṅglā Kīrtaner Itihāsa*, K.P. Bagchi and Co., Calcutta, 1989.

———, 'Trends of Change in Bhakti Movement in Bengal (Sixteenth and Seventeenth Centuries)', in D.N. Jha (ed.), *Society and Ideology in India: Essays in Honour of Prof. R.S. Sharma*, Munshiram Manoharlal Publishers Pvt. Ltd, New Delhi, 1996.

Sarkar, Benoy Kumar, *The Folk Element in Hindu Culture*, Oriental Books Reprint Corporation, New Delhi, 1972 (reprint).

Sarkar, Jadunath, 'Transformation of Bengal Under Mughal Rule', in Jadunath Sarkar (ed.) *The History of Bengal: Muslim Period, 1200–1757*, Janaki Prakashan, Patna, 1977 (reprint).

Sarkar, R.M., *Regional Cults and Rural Traditions: Interacting Pattern of Divinity and Humanity of Rural Bengal*, Inter-India Publications, New Delhi, 1985.

Schomer, Karine, 'Where Have All the Rādhās Gone? New Images of Women in Modern Hindi Poetry', in John Stratton Hawley and Donna Marie Wulff (eds), *The Divine Consort: Rādhā and the Goddesses of India*, Motilal Banarsidass, Delhi, 1984.

Schopen, Gregory, 'Archaeology and Protestant Presuppositions in the Study of Indian Buddhism', *History of Religions*, Vol. 31, No. 1, August 1991.

Schott, Rudiger, 'Comments on Fluehr-Lobban', *Current Anthropology*, Vol. 20, June 1979.

Schramm, Wilbur, 'The Nature of Communication Between Humans', in Wilbur Schramm and Donald F. Roberts (eds), *The Process and Effects in Mass Communication*, University of Illinois Press, Urbana, 1971.

Scott, James C., *Weapons of the Weak: Everyday Forms of Peasant Resistance*, Oxford University Press, Delhi, 1990.

Seliger, Martin, *Ideology and Politics*, George Allen and Unwin, London, 1976.

Sen, Benoychandra, *Some Historical Aspects of the Inscriptions of Bengal*, University of Calcutta, Calcutta, 1942.

Sen, Dineshchandra., *The Folk Literature of Bengal*, B.R. Publishing Corporation, Delhi, 1985 (reprint).

———, *Bṛhat Vaṅga*, Vols I and II, Dey's Publishing, Calcutta, 1993 (reprint).

Sen, Sukumar, *Prācīn Bāṅglā O Bāṅgālī*, Visva-Bharati Granthanvibhaga, Calcutta, 1972 (reprint).

———, *The Great Goddess in Indic Tradition*, Papyrus, Calcutta, 1983.

———, *Bāṅglā Sāhityer Itihāsa*, Vol. I, Ananda Publishers Ltd, Calcutta, 1991.

Sengupta, Pallab, *Pūjā Pārvaṇer Utsakathā*, Pustak Bipani, Calcutta, 1984.

Sen Majumdar, Gayatri, *Būddhism in Ancient Bengal*, Navana, Calcutta, 1983.

Sharma, R.S., *Indian Feudalism: c.* 300–1200, University of Calcutta, Calcutta, 1965.

———, 'Problem of Transition from Ancient to Medieval in Indian History', *Indian Historical Review*, Vol. I, No. 1, 1974.

———, 'Material Milieu of Tantricism', in R.S. Sharma (ed.), *Indian Society: Historical Probings* (In Memory of D.D. Kosambi), People's Publishing House, New Delhi, 1974.

———, 'Communication and Social Cohesion', *Perspectives in Social and Economic History of Early India*, Munshiram Manoharlal, New Delhi, 1983.

———, 'How Feudal was Indian Feudalism', in Harbans Mukhia and T.J. Byres (eds), *Feudalism and Non-European Societies*, Frank Cass, London, 1985.

———, 'Antiquity to the Middle Ages in India', *Social Science Probings*, Vol. 5, Nos. 1–4, March–December 1988.

Shastri, Haraprasad, 'The Mahāpurāṇas', *The Journal of the Bihar and Orissa Research Society*, Vol. 14, Part 3, September 1928.

———, *Bener Meye,* in *Haraprasād Shastrī Racanā Saṁgraha*, Vol. I, Pashchimbanga Rajya Pustak Parshad, Calcutta, 1980.

Shendge, Malati J., 'A Note on the Sociology of Buddhist Tantrism', *Man in India*, Vol. 49, No. 1, March 1969.

Shrimali, K.M., 'Religion, Ideology and Society', *Presidential Address*, Ancient India Section, Indian History Congress, 1988, distributed by Munshiram Manoharlal Publishers Pvt. Ltd, New Delhi.

Shulman, David, 'Toward a New Indian Poetics: Velcheru Narayana Rao and the Structure of Literary Revolutions', in David Shulman (ed.), *Syllables of Sky: Studies in South Indian Civilizations*, Oxford University Press, Delhi, 1995.

Siegel, Lee, *Sacred and Profane Dimensions of Love in Indian Traditions as Exemplified in the* Gītagovinda *of Jayadeva*, Oxford University Press, Delhi, 1978.

Simon, Roger, *Gramsci's Political Thought: An Introduction*, Lawrence and Wishart, London, 1988.

Sinari, Ramakant A., *The Structure of Indian Thought*, Oxford University Press, Delhi, 1984.

Singer, Milton, 'The Cultural Pattern of Indian Civilization', *The Far Eastern Quarterly*, Vol. 15, No. 1, November 1955.

———, 'The Social Organization of Indian Civilization', *When a Great Tradition Modernizes: An Anthropological Approach to Indian Civilization*, Vikas Publishing House Pvt. Ltd, New Delhi, 1972.

Sinha, B.P., 'Evolution of Śakti Worship in India', in D.C. Sircar (ed.), *The Śakti Cult and Tārā*, University of Calcutta, Calcutta, 1967.

Sircar, D.C., 'The Śākta Pīṭhas', *The Journal of the Royal Asiatic Society of Bengal, Letters*, Vol. 14, 1948, distributed in book form by Motilal Banarsidass, Delhi.

———, 'Decline of Buddhism in Bengal', *Studies in the Religious Life of Ancient and Medieval India*, Motilal Banarsidass, Delhi, 1971.

———, *Epigraphic Discoveries in East Pakistan*, Sanskrit College, Calcutta, 1973.

———, 'Spread of Aryanism in Bengal', *The Journal of the Royal Asiatic Society of Bengal, Letters*, Vol. 18, No. 2, 1952.

Skinner, Quentin, 'Meaning and Understanding in the History of Ideas', *History and Theory*, Vol. 8, No. 1, 1969.

———, 'Motives, Intentions and Interpretation of Texts' and 'On Meaning and Speech-acts', in James Tully (ed.), *Meaning and Context: Quentin Skinner and His Critics*, Polity Press, Cambridge, 1988.

Smith, Brian K., *Reflections on Resemblance, Ritual and Religion*, Oxford University Press, New York, 1989.

Smith, Vincent, *The Oxford History of India*, Third edition, edited by Percival Spear, Clarendon Press, Oxford, 1967.

Spiegel, Gabrielle M., 'History, Historicism, and the Social Logic of the Text in the Middle Ages', *Speculum: A Journal of Medieval Studies*, Vol. 65, 1990.

Spiro, Melford, 'Culture and Personality', in David L. Sills (ed.), *International Encyclopaedia of Social Sciences*, Vol. III, The Macmillan Company and the Free Press, USA, 1968.

Srinivas, M.N., 'A Note on Sanskritization and Westernization', *The Far Eastern Quarterly*, Vol. 15, No. 4, August 1956.

———, 'The Cohesive Role of Sanskritization', in Philip Mason (ed.), *India and Ceylon: Unity and Diversity, A Symposium*, Oxford University Press, London, 1967.

———, *Religion and Society among the Coorgs of South India*, Media Promoters and Publishers Pvt. Ltd, Bombay, 1978 (reprint).

———, *Social Change in Modern India*, Orient Longman, New Delhi, 1980.

Staal, J.F., 'Sanskrit and Sanskritization', *The Journal of Asian Studies*, Vol. 12, No. 3, May 1963.

Stein, Burton, 'Devī Shrines and Folk Hinduism in Medieval Tamilnad', in Edwin Gerow and Margery D. Lang (eds), *Studies in the Language and*

Culture of South Asia, University of Washington, Seattle and London, 1973.

Stock, Brian, *The Implications of Literacy: Written Language and Models of Interpretation in the Eleventh and Twelfth Centuries*, Princeton University Press, Princeton, 1983.

Strasser, Hermann and Susan C. Randall, *An Introduction to Theories of Social Change*, Routledge and Kegan Paul, London, 1981.

Thakur, Abanindranath, *Bāṅglār Vrata*, Visva-Bharati, Calcutta, 1350 BS.

Thapar, Romila, *Cultural Transaction and Early India: Tradition and Patronage*, Oxford University Press, Delhi, 1987.

Therborn, Goran, *The Ideology of Power and the Power of Ideology*, Verso, London, 1980.

Thompson, John B., *Studies in the Theory of Ideology*, Polity Press, Cambridge, 1984.

Tiwari, J.N., *Goddess Cults and Ancient India*, Sundeep Prakashan, Delhi, 1985.

Towes, John E., 'Intellectual History After the Linguistic Turn: The Autonomy of Meaning and the Irreducibility of Experience', *The American Historical Review*, Vol. 92, No. 4, October 1987.

Turner, Victor, 'Pilgrimages as Social Processes', *Dramas, Fields, and Metaphors: Symbolic Action in Human Society*, Cornell University Press, Ithaca and London, 1974.

Uchmany, Eva Alexandra, 'Religious Changes in the Conquest of Mexico', in David N. Lorenzen (ed.), *Religious Change and Cultural Domination*, El Collegio De Mexico, Mexico, 1981.

Vaudeville, Charlotte, 'Krishna Gopāla, Rādhā, and the Great Goddess', in John Stratton Hawley and Donna Marie Wulff (eds), *The Divine Consort: Rādhā and the Goddesses of India*, Motilal Banarsidass, Delhi, 1984.

Vedantasastri, H., 'Buddhism in Bengal and its Decline', *The Journal of the Bihar Research Society*, Vol. I (Buddha Jayanti Special Issue), 1956.

Waardenburg, Jacques, 'The Language of Religion, and the Study of Religions as Sign Systems', in Lauri Honko (ed.), *Science of Religion: Studies in Methodology*, Mouton Publishers, The Hague, 1979.

Wadley, Susan Snow, *Shakti: Power in the Conceptual Structure of Karimpur Religion*, Department of Anthropology, The University of Chicago Press, Chicago, 1975.

———, 'Popular Hinduism and Mass Literature in North India: A Preliminary Analysis', in Giriraj Gupta (ed.), *Religion in Modern India*, Vikas Publishing House Pvt. Ltd, New Delhi, 1983.

Warner, Marina, *Alone of All Her Sex: The Myth and the Cult of the Virgin Mary*, Picador, published by Pan Books, Cavaye Place, London, 1985.

Watchel, Nathan, *The Vision of the Vanquished: The Spanish Conquest of Peru Through Indian Eyes*, The Harvester Press, Sussex, 1977.

Webster, Paula, 'Matriarchy: A Vision of Power', in Rayna R. Reiter (ed.),

Toward an Anthropology of Women, Monthly Review Press, New York and London, 1975.

Werbner, Richard P., 'Introduction', in Richard P. Werbner (ed.), *Regional Cults*, A.S.A. Monograph no. 16, Academic Press, London, 1977.

Wheeler, Sir Mortimer, *The Indus Civilization*, Cambridge University Press, Cambridge, 1968.

White, Hayden, 'The Historical Text as Literary Artifact', *Tropics of Discourse: Essays in Cultural Criticism*, The Johns Hopkins University Press, Baltimore, 1978.

Whitehead, Henry, *The Village Gods of South India*, Sumit Publications, Delhi, 1976 (reprint).

Wilkins, W.J., *Hindu Mythology: Vedic and Puranic*, Rupa and Co., Calcutta, 1979 (reprint).

Williams, Gwyn, '*Egemonia* in the Thought of Antonio Gramsci: Some Notes on Interpretations', *Journal of the History of Ideas*, Vol. 21, No. 4, 1960.

Williams, Raymond, *Marxism and Literature*, Oxford University Press, Oxford, 1977.

Wilson, H.H., *A Sketch of the Religious Sects of the Hindus*, Cosmo Publications, New Delhi, 1977 (reprint).

———, *The Viṣṇu Purāṇa: A System of Hindu Mythology and Tradition* (with an introduction by R.C. Hazra), Punthi Pustak, Calcutta, 1961 (reprint).

———, *Sanskrit-English Dictionary*, Nag Publishers, Delhi, enlarged edition, 1979.

Wolff, Hans, 'Intelligibility and Inter-Ethnic Attitudes', in Dell Hymes (ed.), *Language in Culture and Society: A Reader in Linguistics and Anthropology*, Allied Publishers Pvt. Ltd, Bombay, 1964.

Yadava, B.N.S., *Society and Culture in Northern India in the Twelfth Century*, Central Book Depot, Allahabad, 1973.

Index

ācāra, 60–1, 65
Ādiśūra, 118–22
Agni Purāṇa, 49, 260
Agrawala, V.S., 58, 76
Allen, Albert Henry, 261, 284
Aṅga, 110–11
anthropological models of great–little traditions and Sanskritization, relevance for study of Puranic texts, 92–5, 97–8, 100, 102
see also great–little traditions; Sanskritization
Āryāvarta, 111
Asher, Frederick, 141, 161

Bailey, F.G., 90, 98, 105, 107
Bakhtin, M.M., 24, 42
Banerjea, J.N., 240, 275
Barthes, Roland, 19–20, 42
Basu, Nirmal Kumar, 17, 40, 102, 178, 221
Bedekar, V.M., 63–4, 78
Bengal *Purāṇas*
accommodation of local beliefs and practices by, 23–5, 32–3, 59–63, 65–70
admission of outsiders into caste framework by, 291–2
attributed to Vyāsa, 27
the *brāhmaṇa* in, 122–6
brahmanical vision of, 23–6, 28, 30–3
and Buddhism, 148–50, 152–4
for the common people, 58
and the development of Bengali literature, 299
editions of, 51
final redactions, 213
and the goddess cult, 165, 172, 179–80, 185, 205, 207–8, 211–12
on the king, 127–28, 290
and local *brāhmaṇas*, 32
match with contemporary inscriptions, 128–31
neglect of, 6–7, 36–7
negotiation in, 24–6, 32–3
period of composition of, 26
public exposition of, 256–9
and *Tantra*, 144, 187–94
textual strategy of, 23–6, 30–1
and the *Vedas*, 56–9
widened the scope of brahmanism, 32
Bennett, Tony, 22–3, 42
Bhadra, Gautam, 266, 285
Bhāgavata Purāṇa, 303
bhakti, 4–5, 132, 194, 300, 302–3, 308
Bhandarkar, R.G., 167, 214
Bharati, Agehananda, 91–2, 106, 137, 160
Bhattacharya, Ashutosh, 238, 241, 275
Bhattacharya, J.N., 144, 161
Bhattasali, N.K., 139–40, 160
Bhaviṣya Purāṇa, 216, 245, 250, 260
Biardeau, Madeleine, 63–5, 78, 268, 286
Blackburn, Stuart H., 274, 287
Bonazzoli, Giorgio, 55, 75
Brahma Purāṇa, 49
Brāhmaṇa
'authoritativeness' of local *brāhmaṇas*, 63–6
heterogeneous, 122

and Hinduism, 54–5
image in the Bengal *Purāṇas*, 122–3
migration into Bengal, 118, 121
recipients of gifts, 123–6
and the *Vedas*, 55
brahmanical expansion in Bengal
epics on, 111
in the Gupta period, 112–13
Kāmasūtra on, 112
Mahāsthān and Silua image inscriptions on, 112
in the Pāla–Candra–Kāmboja kingdoms, 113–14, 116, 141–2
in the post-Gupta period, 113
and the propagation of Vedism, 115–18
Purāṇas on, 111
in the Sena–Varmana period, 114–17, 147
Sūtras on, 110–11
Vedic texts on, 110
Brahmavaivarta Purāṇa, 7–8, 50–1, 54, 56–8, 62, 75–8, 123–5, 157–9, 200, 224, 230–1, 233, 239, 241–3, 251–2, 257–9, 262, 275–6, 278–80, 282–5, 303–4
bṛhadañcala, 96
Bṛhaddharma Purāṇa, 7, 50–1, 61, 125, 127, 152, 157–9, 163–4, 182, 187, 189, 224, 226–7, 231, 239, 244, 251, 255, 257, 264, 271, 277–8, 280–2, 284, 286
Bṛhannāradīya Purāṇa, 50–1, 57, 60–1, 76–7, 125–6, 148–9, 158–9, 162–3, 247, 251–2, 256, 258, 279–82
Brown, C. Mackenzie, 8, 37, 59, 65–6, 77–8, 166, 214, 304, 331
Buddhism in Bengal
in the Gupta period, 133
in the Pāla–Candra period, 133–4
in the post-Gupta period, 133
in the pre-Gupta period, 132–3
see also Mahāyāna Buddhism from the Pala period
Buitenen, J.A.B. van, 90–2, 105

Chanda, Ramaprasad, 171–2, 217–18
Chandra, Moti, 168, 215
Chartier, Roger, 318, 335
Chatterjee, Rama, 7, 37, 112, 115, 117–18, 155–6
Chatterji, S.K., 96, 102, 107, 271, 287, 298–9, 327–8
Chattopadhyaya, B.D., 289–93, 325
Chattopadhyaya, Sudhakar, 167, 215
Chaudhuri, Sujit, 261, 284
Coburn, Thomas B., 64–5, 78, 170, 216
communication, 234–5
oral and involving literacy, 269–70, 272–3
and religious performance, 235
rhetorical communication, 267–9
and Sanskrit, 270–3
see also Finnegan; Goody; narrators of *Purāṇas;* Stock; Tambiah; *vrata*
Corwin, Lauren Anita, 98, 107

dakṣiṇabhāva, 68–9
Damle, Y.B., 265, 285
Danielou, Alain, 167, 214–15
Dasgupta, Shashibhushan, 96, 107, 137, 160, 187, 201, 225, 230, 239, 275
Davis, Natalie Z., 99–100, 108
Devī Māhātmya, 170–2, 196, 216–17, 219–20, 229, 239
Devī Purāṇa, 50–1, 62, 78, 163–4, 179–80, 188, 191, 221–4, 226, 228, 232, 239, 243, 246–7, 251, 256–8, 275, 279–83, 299
Devībhāgavata Purāṇa, 7, 50–1, 56–7, 61–2, 75–9, 149, 154, 158, 163–4, 193, 196–7, 226–32,

241–4, 249, 251–2, 256–9, 262, 275–80, 282–3
disdain for Bengal
in brahmanical literature, 110–11
in early Buddhist and Jaina literature, 111
Dumont, Louis, 90, 105, 312, 314–15
Durgā, 166, 168–9, 173–4, 176, 178, 200, 205–8, 232, 244–5, 293, 309, 322
Dutt, N.K., 119, 156

Eaton, Richard M., 306, 322
Eco, Umberto, 29–30, 43
Embree, Ainslie T., 15–16, 40
Eschmann, A., 35, 97, 107

Finnegan, Ruth, 269, 286
Foucault, Michel, 27, 42–3
Fruzzetti, Lina, 253, 281

Gauḍa, 111, 118, 133, 171
Gauḍīya Vaiṣṇavism, 132, 300, 303, 307–8, 320
Geertz, Clifford, 10, 38, 99
Ghosh, Binoy, 172, 219
Ghurye, G.S., 195, 229
Gītagovinda, 153, 304, 331
goddess
accorded absolute power, 181
in the Bengal *Purāṇas*, 165, 172, 179–80, 185, 205, 207–8, 211–12
as Hāttā or Hāyābibi, 202
integrative role outside Bengal, 195, 199
in the *Mahābhārata*, 169
non-Vedic origin of, 15–16, 33, 165, 168, 171
in pre-brahmanized Bengal, 171
in the Purāṇas, 170, 216
and the Puranic concept of *mūlaprakṛti*, 197–201, 212–13
nature of caste participation in worship, 209–12
product of interacting traditions, 170, 185
and the *Sāṁkhya* concept of *prakṛti*, 196–9
and the structure of the tribal goddess, 180
superimposed with brahmanical attributes, 15–16, 33, 181, 185
and Tantrism, 187, 192, 194
temples of, 205–8
tradition transformed into Śāktism by Bengal *Purāṇas*, 172, 183–5
uneven history in early Indian written records, 167
in Vedic literature, 166, 168–9
widespread popularity in Bengal, 177, 179
Goody, Jack, 269, 286
great–little traditions
Bharati on, 91–2, 106
Burke on, 100–1, 108
Mandelbaum on, 91–2, 105–6
Miller on, 89–90, 92, 105
Redfield on, 84–5, 92–3, 103
Singer on, 85–6, 103
Staal on, 90, 92, 105
Grunebaum, G.E. von, 93–4, 106
Gupta, A.S., 63–5, 78
Gupta, Chitralekha, 112–13, 155
Gupte, B.A., 261, 284

Hanchett, Suzanne, 254, 281
Heesterman, J.C., 47, 55, 73, 75
hegemony
critics of Gramsci on, 13–14, 38
Gramsci on, 11–13, 38
relevance of the concept for early Bengal, 14–15, 17, 39–40
Henry, Edward O., 203, 231
Hīnayāna, 133
Hesse, Linda, 265, 285

Hinduism
  authority of the *brāhmaṇa* class in, 54–5
  authority of the *Vedas* in, 55–6
  Smith on, 54–6, 75
historiography on Indian religions and the *Purāṇas*, 3–6, 35–6
Huntington, Susan L., 143, 161
Hutton, J.H., 52–3, 75

ideology, 8–10, 12–17, 37–8, 40
Inden, Ronald, 121, 157
'Indianism', 96
Ingalls, Daniel H.H., 166–7, 169, 214
itihāsa, 44, 58, 126

Jackson, J.R., 21, 42
Jagannātha, 2, 35, 206–8, 247, 293, 305–6, 309, 321–2
Jameson, Fredric, 21–2, 26, 42
Jimūtavāhana, 115, 117, 217, 246, 249

Kadir, Abdul, 304, 331
Kālī, 166, 169, 174–6, 200–1, 208, 323
Kālikā Purāṇa, 8, 49–51, 66–71, 78–80, 138, 159, 179–80, 221–3, 231, 240–2, 245, 257, 275–6, 279, 282
Kaliyuga
  bhāhmaṇas in, 28, 46, 56, 122, 131, 149, 256
  and the Buddha, 153
  kṣatriyas in, 46, 123
  and gift-making, 123
  neglect of the *Vedas* in, 46
  śūdras in, 46, 253
  vaiśyas in, 46
  women in, 46
Kane, P.V., 253, 256, 260, 281, 284
Karve, Irawati, 53, 75
kathā, 237, 250, 262–4, 266, 273
kathaka, 263, 266
kathakatā, 263, 266–7, 273
Kinsley, David, 166, 214
Khalek, Muhammad Abdul, 301, 328
Kirāta, 112, 179–80
Kitagawa, Joseph M., 19, 41
Kolenda, Pauline M., 204, 231
Kooij, K.R. van, 8, 37, 68, 78–9, 138, 160
Kosambi, D.D., 59, 77, 168, 215
Kriyāyogasāra, 50–1, 126, 148, 158, 163–4, 251, 259, 280, 283
kṣudrāñcala, 96
Kulajī texts, 118–22, 132
Kulīna, 119–22, 132
Kulke, Hermann, 305, 331
Kumar, Pushpendra, 8, 37
Kūrma Purāṇa, 48–9

LaCapra, Dominick, 21, 23, 26, 42
Leavitt, John, 312–5, 320–1, 335
Lalye, P.G., 7, 37
Lamb, Helen, 89, 105
Ling, Trevor, 143, 161
Lodrick, Deryck O., 294, 324–7
Lomaharṣaṇa, 44
Long, Charles, 95, 107

Madhyadeśa, 111, 118, 121
Magadha, 110–11, 143
Mahābhāgavata Purāṇa, 50–1
Mahābhārata, 27, 46, 60, 63, 110–11, 142, 154, 168–9, 180, 212, 215–16, 235, 237, 250, 259, 261–3
Mahāyāna Buddhism from the Pāla period
  declined, 142–4, 152, 154
  divinities of, 138–41
  lost its distinctive character, 137–8, 140–2, 145, 152–3
  and the spread of Tantrism, 134, 136–8, 144
Majumdar, R.C., 6–7, 36–7, 59, 79, 119, 143, 156, 161
Manasā, 1, 141, 173, 175–6, 178,

200–1, 209, 211–12, 238, 241, 323
Maṅgalā, 239, 242–4
Maṅgalacaṇḍī, 1, 209–10, 212, 220, 239–45, 293, 302, 309
Maṅgalakāvya literature, 98, 173, 238–9, 273, 300–3, 320
Mārkaṇḍeya Purāṇa, 48, 170, 196, 216, 239, 242, 257
Matsya Purāṇa, 48–9, 111, 153, 260
Mleccha, 67, 110
Moffat, Michael, 231
mūlaprakṛti
as an ideal medium of assimilation, 199–201
see also *prakṛti*

narrators, of *Purāṇas*, 263–6
Nicholas, Ralph W., 272–3, 287
Niyogi, Puspa, 115, 118, 155–6, 160

O'Flaherty, Wendy Doniger, 25, 42, 106, 153, 164
O'Malley, L.S.S., 52–3, 75
Opler, Morris E., 204, 231

Padma Purāṇa, 49
pāñcālis, 71, 243, 302
Pandian, Jacob, 202–3, 231
pāṣaṇḍa, 148–9, 151–2, 237, 256
Pocock, D.F., 70, 80, 87, 103
prakṛti
and *mūlaprakṛti*, 198–201
the Puranic conception of, 196–8
the *Sāṁkhya* concept of, 195–6, 199
Preston, James, 205–6, 208–9, 232
Pulinda, 110–11, 179–80
Puṇḍra, 110–12
purāṇa, 44–5
Purāṇas
assimilate local traditions, 93
chronology of, 45, 72
divine origin of, 44
extensively revised over time, 44–5, 47
fear of the *Kali* age in, 46
for the masses, 57, 93, 256–7
narrated by *sūtas*, 44
number of, 44, 48
pañcalakṣaṇa of, 44
replaced the *Vedas* as the source of brahmanical authority, 70–2
and the *Vedas*, 55, 57
Puranic process, 32, 52, 54, 60, 66, 81, 171, 213, 290, 317

Rādhā, 166, 173, 175–6, 178–9, 200, 244, 303–4, 320, 329–31
Raghavan, V., 106–7, 265, 285
Raghunandana, 115, 242, 249
Ramanujan, A.K., 98, 108, 274, 287
Rāmāyaṇa, 111, 237, 259, 264
Randall, Susan C., 69, 79
Ranger, Terence, 94–5, 106–7
Rao, Velcheru Narayana, 27, 43, 297, 327
Rashid, Harunur, 153, 163
Rawal, A.J., 7, 37
region, 288, 312
regional formation
and brahmanism, 313–15, 320–1
and cult centres, 303–8
and the development of a literary language, 294, 297–305
and a distinctive religious culture, 313
and the importance of political history, 294–7
see also Leavitt; regional identity of Bengal
regional identity of Bengal
and the Bengal *Purāṇas*, 289, 292, 302–4, 309, 322–4
and brahmanical initiative, 289, 298
and brahmanism, 293, 309–11, 318–19

by the end of the early medieval period, 292, 298
and the growth of Bengali language and literature, 297–305
and Gauḍīya Vaiṣṇavism, 303
and the goddess cult, 293, 309–10
and negotiations between local cultures and brahmanism, 317–18
supported by regional political structure, 289, 293
and temple architecture, 307
regional societies in early medieval India, subcontinental trends; see Chattopadhyaya, B.D.
regional traditions
neglected by Indologists and social anthropologists, 1
significant work on a regional tradition, 1–2
Risley, H.H., 173, 208, 221

Śāktism
fundamental principles worked out in *Devī Māhātmya*, 172
goddess tradition transformed into Śāktism by Bengal *Purāṇas*, 172, 183–5
and *mūlaprakṛti*, 198, 200–1
sāmānyapūjā, 67
Samataṭa, 111–12, 133
Sāṁkhya
prakṛti and *puruṣa* in, 195–6, 199
and the Puranic conception of the goddess, 196–9
system of Hindu philosophy, 195
Śankarācārya, 152
Sanskrit
and Bengali language and literature, 298–300, 303
its legitimating status, 271
as preserve of *brāhmaṇas*, 271
Sanskritization, 81–3, 87–8, 90, 92, 96, 102–5, 107
Santoṣi Mā, 210
Sanyal, Hitesranjan, 307, 310, 311, 333, 335–6
Sarasvatī, 166, 200, 244, 263
Sarkar, Jadunath, 295–6, 325, 327
Sarkar, R.M., 209, 232
Ṣaṣṭhī, 176, 200, 201, 212, 239, 241, 254
Śavara, 110–11, 179–80
Sāvitrī, 244, 259–63, 268
Schopen, Gregory, 2, 35
Sen, Benoychandra, 111, 155
Sen, Dineshchandra, 238, 275, 301, 327–8
Sen, Sukumar, 303, 328
Sen-Majumdar, Gayatri, 143, 161
Shastri, Haraprasad, 6, 36, 144–5, 162, 299
Sinha, B.P., 169, 216
Sircar, D.C., 112, 119, 152, 155–6, 162–3
Skanda Purāṇa, 64–6, 260
Skinner, Quentin, 18–19, 30, 41, 43
Smith, Brian K., 54–6, 75
Smṛtis, 4, 44–7, 52, 59, 61, 63, 114–18, 120, 132, 179, 213, 235–6, 242, 249, 255, 260–1, 289, 322–3
Spiegel, Gabrielle M., 20, 41–2
Stock, Brian, 270, 286
Strasser, Hermann, 69, 79
Sukthankar, V.S., 63, 284
Sumha, 111–12
sūta, 44, 57, 247, 265

Tambiah, S.J., 270, 286
Tantrism
and the Bengal *Purāṇas*, 144, 187–94
centrality of the goddess in, 187, 194
claims connection with the *Vedas*, 188
and equal opportunity of worship to all, 47

and Mahāyāna Buddhism, 137–8, 186
non-Vedic character of, 187
regional distribution of, 186–7
separation between Buddhist and Hindu Tantrism, 137–8, 186
Tāranatha, 136–7, 144–5
'text'
historians' traditional understanding of, 18–19, 41
recent interpretations of, 19–23, 29–30, 41–3
relevance of debate for understanding the Bengal *Purāṇas*, 24–8, 30–1, 43
see also Bakhtin, Barthes, Bennett, Eco, Foucault, Jackson, Jameson, Kitagawa, LaCapra, O'Flaherty, Rao, Skinner, Spiegel, White, Williams
Thapar, Romila, 47, 73
Turner, Victor, 307, 333

Ugraśravas, 44
Umā, 168–9, 252
Universalization and parochialization, 88
Upapurāṇas
date of, 2, 47–50
number of, 48
pañcalakṣaṇa in, 49
provenance of, 49–50
and redactions, 49
regionally identifiable, 49
see also Bengal *Purāṇas*

vāma/*vāmabhāva*, 67–70, 180
Vāmana Purāṇa, 49
Vaṅga, 110–12, 155
Vaṅgavāsī Press, 51
Varāha Purāṇa, 49, 153
varṇāśramadharma, 25, 31, 46, 131, 146–7
Vāyu Purāṇa, 111
Vedas
and the *brāhmaṇa* class, 55
and Hinduism, 55–6
Viṣṇu Purāṇa, 3, 48, 153, 303
Viṣṇudharmottara Purāṇa, 49, 260
Viṭhobā, 307–9, 333–4
vrata
appropriated by brahmanism, 34, 245, 247–50, 255, 262–3
aśāstrīya, 237–8
in the Bengal *Purāṇas*, 236–7, 242, 246–9, 251–2, 255
caste neutral, 235, 249, 251–2
congregational, 34, 235, 249, 256
and goddesses, 34, 239
and listening to the *Purāṇas*, 34, 236–7, 249, 259
in literature pre-dating the Bengal *Purāṇas*, 235–6, 250
medium of mass communication, 235
meyelī, 237, 254–5, 274
non-brahmanical origin, 34, 238
occasion for transmission of brahmanical culture, 15–16, 34, 235, 250, 259, 263, 268–9
in post-*Purāṇa* literature, 249
procedure of, 237
transformation of, 255–6
Vedic elements in, 252–3
and *vrātyas*, 238
and women, 239, 241–3, 251–5
Vyāsa, 27, 48, 56–7, 63–4, 237, 257, 259, 264

Wadley, Susan Snow, 89, 104, 272, 287
Watchel, Nathan, 315, 335
White, Hayden, 31, 43
Williams, Raymond, 21, 42

Yadava, B.N.S., 143–4, 161
Yuan Chwang, 114, 132–3, 298